W9-BKW-014

DNS and BIND

DNS and BIND

DNS and BIND

Fourth Edition

Paul Albitz and Cricket Liu

O'REILLY®

Beijing · Cambridge · Farnham · Köln · Paris · Sebastopol · Taipei · Tokyo

DNS and BIND, Fourth Edition
by Paul Albitz and Cricket Liu

Copyright © 2001, 1998, 1997, 1992 O'Reilly & Associates, Inc. All rights reserved.
Printed in the United States of America.

Published by O'Reilly & Associates, Inc., 101 Morris Street, Sebastopol, CA 95472.

Editors: Mike Loukides and Debra Cameron

Production Editor: Emily Quill

Cover Designer: Edie Freedman

Printing History:

October 1992:	First Edition.
January 1997:	Second Edition.
September 1998:	Third Edition.
April 2001:	Fourth Edition.

Nutshell Handbook, the Nutshell Handbook logo, and the O'Reilly logo are registered trademarks of O'Reilly & Associates, Inc. Many of the designations used by manufacturers and sellers to distinguish their products are claimed as trademarks. Where those designations appear in this book, and O'Reilly & Associates, Inc. was aware of a trademark claim, the designations have been printed in caps or initial caps. The association between the image of grasshoppers and the topic of DNS and BIND is a trademark of O'Reilly & Associates, Inc.

While every precaution has been taken in the preparation of this book, the publisher assumes no responsibility for errors or omissions, or for damages resulting from the use of the information contained herein.

ISBN: 0-596-00158-4

Table of Contents

Preface

You may not know much about the Domain Name System—yet—but whenever you use the Internet, you use DNS. Every time you send electronic mail or surf the World Wide Web, you rely on the Domain Name System.

You see, while you, as a human being, prefer to remember the *names* of computers, computers like to address each other by number. On an internet, that number is 32 bits long, or between zero and four billion or so.* That's easy for a computer to remember because computers have lots of memory ideal for storing numbers, but it isn't nearly as easy for us humans. Pick 10 phone numbers out of the phone book at random and then try to remember them. Not easy? Now flip to the front of the phone book and attach random area codes to the phone numbers. That's about how difficult it would be to remember 10 arbitrary internet addresses.

This is part of the reason we need the Domain Name System. DNS handles mapping between host names, which we humans find convenient, and between internet addresses, which computers deal with. In fact, DNS is the standard mechanism on the Internet for advertising and accessing all kinds of information about hosts, not just addresses. And DNS is used by virtually all internetworking software, including electronic mail, remote terminal programs such as Telnet, file transfer programs such as FTP, and web browsers such as Netscape Navigator and Microsoft Internet Explorer.

Another important feature of DNS is that it makes host information available all over the Internet. Keeping information about hosts in a formatted file on a single computer only helps users on that computer. DNS provides a means of retrieving information remotely from anywhere on the network.

---

* And, with IP Version 6, it's a whopping 128 bits long, or between zero and a decimal number with 39 digits.

More than that, DNS lets you distribute the management of host information among many sites and organizations. You don't need to submit your data to some central site or periodically retrieve copies of the "master" database. You simply make sure your section, called a *zone*, is up to date on your *name servers*. Your name servers make your zone's data available to all the other name servers on the network.

Because the database is distributed, the system also needs the ability to locate the data you're looking for by searching a number of possible locations. The Domain Name System gives name servers the intelligence to navigate through the database and find data in any zone.

Of course, DNS does have a few problems. For example, the system allows more than one name server to store data about a zone, for redundancy's sake. But inconsistencies can crop up between copies of the zone data.

But the *worst* problem with DNS is that despite its widespread use on the Internet, there's really very little documentation about managing and maintaining it. Most administrators on the Internet make do with the documentation their vendors see fit to provide and with whatever they can glean from following the Internet mailing lists and Usenet newsgroups on the subject.

This lack of documentation means that the understanding of an enormously important internet service—one of the linchpins of today's Internet—is either handed down from administrator to administrator like a closely guarded family recipe, or relearned repeatedly by isolated programmers and engineers. New administrators of zones suffer through the same mistakes made by countless others.

Our aim with this book is to help remedy this situation. We realize that not all of you have the time or the desire to become DNS experts. Most of you, after all, have plenty to do besides managing your zones and name servers: system administration, network engineering, or software development. It takes an awfully big institution to devote a whole person to DNS. We'll try to give you enough information to let you do what you need to do, whether that's running a small zone or managing a multinational monstrosity, tending a single name server or shepherding a hundred of them. Read as much as you need to know now, and come back later if you need to learn more.

DNS is a big topic—big enough to require two authors, anyway—and we've tried to present it as sensibly and understandably as possible. The first two chapters give you a good theoretical overview and enough practical information to get by, and later chapters fill in the nitty-gritty details. We provide a roadmap up front to suggest a path through the book appropriate for your job or interest.

When we talk about actual DNS software, we'll concentrate almost exclusively on BIND, the Berkeley Internet Name Domain software, which is the most popular implementation of the DNS specs (and the one we know best). We've tried to distill our experience in managing and maintaining zones with BIND into this book. (One of our zones, incidentally, was once one of the largest on the Internet, but that was a long time ago.) Where possible, we've included the real programs we use in administration, many of them rewritten into Perl for speed and efficiency.

We hope this book will help you get acquainted with DNS and BIND if you're just starting out, refine your understanding if you're already familiar with them, and provide valuable insight and experience even if you know 'em like the back of your hand.

Versions

The fourth edition of this book deals with the new 9.1.0 and 8.2.3 versions of BIND as well as the older 4.9 versions. While 9.1.0 and 8.2.3 are the most recent versions as of this writing, they haven't made their way into many vendors' versions of Unix yet, partly because both versions have only recently been released and many vendors are wary of using such new software. We also occasionally mention other versions of BIND, especially 4.8.3, because many vendors continue to ship code based on this older software as part of their Unix products. Whenever a feature is available only in the 4.9, 8.2.3, or 9.1.0 version, or when there is a difference in the behavior of the versions, we try to point out which version does what.

We use *nslookup*, a name server utility program, very frequently in our examples. The version we use is the one shipped with the 8.2.3 BIND code. Older versions of *nslookup* provide much, but not quite all, of the functionality in the 8.2.3 *nslookup.** We've used commands common to most *nslookup*s in most of our examples; when this was not possible, we tried to note it.

What's New in the Fourth Edition?

Besides updating the book to cover the most recent versions of BIND, we've added a fair amount of new material to the fourth edition:

- More extensive coverage of dynamic update and NOTIFY, including signed dynamic updates and BIND 9's new *update-policy* mechanism, in Chapter 10
- Incremental zone transfer, also in Chapter 10

---

* This is also true of the version of *nslookup* shipped with BIND 9. See Chapter 12, *nslookup and dig*, for details.

- Forward zones, which support conditional forwarding, in Chapter 10

- IPv6 forward and reverse mapping using the new A6 and DNAME records, as well as bitstring labels, at the end of Chapter 10

- Transaction signatures, also known as TSIG, a new mechanism for authenticating transactions, in Chapter 11

- An expanded section on securing name servers, in Chapter 11

- An expanded section on dealing with Internet firewalls, in Chapter 11

- Coverage of the DNS Security Extensions, or DNSSEC, a new mechanism for digitally signing zone data, also in Chapter 11

- A section on accommodating Windows 2000 clients, servers, and Domain Controllers with BIND, in Chapter 16

Organization

This book is organized to more or less follow the evolution of a zone and its administrator. Chapters 1 and 2 discuss Domain Name System theory. Chapters 3 through 6 help you decide whether or not to set up your own zones, then describe how to go about it should you choose to. The middle of the book, Chapters 7 through 11, describe how to maintain your zones, configure hosts to use your name servers, plan for the growth of your zones, create subdomains, and secure your name servers. Finally, Chapters 12 through 16 deal with troubleshooting tools, common problems, and the lost art of programming with the resolver library routines.

Here's a more detailed, chapter-by-chapter breakdown:

Chapter 1, *Background*, provides a little historical perspective and discusses the problems that motivated the development of DNS, and then presents an overview of DNS theory.

Chapter 2, *How Does DNS Work?*, goes over DNS theory in more detail, including the organization of the DNS namespace, domains, zones, and name servers. We also introduce important concepts like name resolution and caching.

Chapter 3, *Where Do I Start?*, covers how to get the BIND software if you don't already have it, what to do with it once you've got it, how to figure out what your domain name should be, and how to contact the organization that can delegate your zone to you.

Chapter 4, *Setting Up BIND*, details how to set up your first two BIND name servers, including creating your name server database, starting up your name servers, and checking their operation.

Chapter 5, *DNS and Electronic Mail*, deals with DNS's MX record, which allows administrators to specify alternate hosts to handle a given destination's mail. This chapter covers mail routing strategies for a wide variety of networks and hosts, including networks with Internet firewalls and hosts without direct Internet connectivity.

Chapter 6, *Configuring Hosts*, explains how to configure a BIND resolver. We also include notes on the idiosyncrasies of many major Unix vendors' resolver implementations, as well as the Windows 95, NT, and 2000 resolvers.

Chapter 7, *Maintaining BIND*, describes the periodic maintenance that administrators need to perform to keep their zones running smoothly, such as checking name server health and authority.

Chapter 8, *Growing Your Domain*, covers how to plan for the growth and evolution of your zones, including how to get big and how to plan for moves and outages.

Chapter 9, *Parenting*, explores the joys of becoming a parent zone. We explain when to become a parent (create subdomains), what to call your children, how to create them (!), and how to watch over them.

Chapter 10, *Advanced Features*, goes over some less-often-used name server configuration options that can help you tune your name server's operation and ease administration.

Chapter 11, *Security,* describes how to secure your name server and how to configure your name servers to deal with Internet firewalls, and also describes two new security enhancements to DNS: the DNS Security Extensions and Transaction Signatures.

Chapter 12, *nslookup and dig*, shows the ins and outs of the most popular tools for doing DNS debugging, including techniques for digging obscure information out of remote name servers.

Chapter 13, *Reading BIND Debugging Output*, is the Rosetta Stone of BIND's debugging information. This chapter will help you make sense of the cryptic debugging information that BIND emits, which in turn will help you understand your name server better.

Chapter 14, *Troubleshooting DNS and BIND*, covers many common DNS and BIND problems and their solutions, and describes a number of less common, harder-to-diagnose scenarios.

Chapter 15, *Programming with the Resolver and Name Server Library Routines*, demonstrates how to use BIND's resolver routines to query name servers and retrieve data from within a C program or a Perl script. We include a useful (we hope!) program to check the health and authority of your name servers.

Chapter 16, *Miscellaneous*, ties up all the loose ends. We cover DNS wildcards, hosts and networks with intermittent Internet connectivity via dialup, network name encoding, experimental record types, and Windows 2000.

Appendix A, *DNS Message Format and Resource Records*, contains a byte-by-byte breakdown of the formats used in DNS queries and responses, as well as a comprehensive list of the currently defined resource record types.

Appendix B, *BIND Compatibility Matrix*, contains a matrix showing the most important features of the most popular BIND releases.

Appendix C, *Compiling and Installing BIND on Linux*, contains step-by-step instructions on how to compile the 8.2.3 version of BIND on Linux.

Appendix D, *Top-Level Domains*, lists the current top-level domains in the Internet's domain name space.

Appendix E, *BIND Name Server and Resolver Configuration*, summarizes the syntax and semantics of each of the parameters available for configuring name servers and resolvers.

Audience

This book is intended primarily for system and network administrators who manage zones and one or more name servers, but it also includes material for network engineers, postmasters, and others. Not all of the book's chapters will be equally interesting to a diverse audience, though, and you don't want to wade through 16 chapters to find the information pertinent to your job. We hope the following roadmap will help you plot your way through the book.

System administrators setting up their first zones should read Chapters 1 and 2 for DNS theory, Chapter 3 for information on getting started and selecting a good domain name, and Chapters 4 and 5 to learn how to set up a zone for the first time. Chapter 6 explains how to configure hosts to use the new name servers. Later, you should read Chapter 7, which explains how to "flesh out" your implementation by setting up additional name servers and adding additional zone data. Chapters 12, 13, and 14 describe troubleshooting tools and techniques.

Experienced administrators will benefit from reading Chapter 6 to learn how to configure DNS resolvers on different hosts, and Chapter 7 for information on maintaining your zones. Chapter 8 contains instructions on planning for a zone's growth and evolution, which should be especially valuable to administrators of large zones. Chapter 9 explains parenting—creating subdomains—which is de rigueur reading for those considering the big move. Chapter 10 covers many new and advanced features of the BIND 8.2.3 and 9.1.0 name servers. Chapter 11 goes over securing name servers, which may be of particular interest to experienced administrators. Chapters 12 through 14 describe tools and techniques for troubleshooting, which even advanced administrators may find worth reading.

System administrators on networks without full Internet connectivity should read Chapter 5 to learn how to configure mail on such networks, and Chapter 11 to learn how to set up an independent DNS infrastructure.

Programmers can read Chapters 1 and 2 for DNS theory, then Chapter 15 for detailed coverage of how to program with the BIND resolver library routines.

Network administrators not directly responsible for any zones should still read Chapters 1 and 2 for DNS theory, Chapter 12 to learn how to use *nslookup* and *dig*, and Chapter 14 for troubleshooting tactics.

Postmasters should read Chapters 1 and 2 for DNS theory, then Chapter 5 to find out how DNS and electronic mail coexist. Chapter 12, which describes *nslookup* and *dig*, will help postmasters extract mail routing information from the domain name space.

Interested users can read Chapters 1 and 2 for DNS theory, and then whatever else you like!

Note that we assume you're familiar with basic Unix system administration, TCP/IP networking, and programming using simple shell scripts and Perl. We don't assume you have any other specialized knowledge, though. When we introduce a new term or concept, we'll do our best to define or explain it. Whenever possible, we'll use analogies from Unix (and from the real world) to help you understand.

Obtaining the Example Programs

The example programs in this book are available electronically via FTP from the following URLs:

ftp://ftp.uu.net/published/oreilly/nutshell/dnsbind/dns.tar.Z
ftp://ftp.oreilly.com/published/oreilly/nutshell/dnsbind/dns.tar.Z

In either case, extract the files from the archive by typing:

```
% zcat dns.tar.Z | tar xf -
```

System V systems require the following *tar* command instead:

```
% zcat dns.tar.Z | tar xof -
```

If *zcat* is not available on your system, use separate *uncompress* and *tar* commands.

If you can't get the examples directly over the Internet but can send and receive email, you can use *ftpmail* to get them. For help using *ftpmail*, send an email to *ftpmail@online.oreilly.com* with no subject and the single word "help" in the body of the message.

Contacting O'Reilly

You can address comments and questions about this book to the publisher:

O'Reilly & Associates, Inc.
101 Morris Street
Sebastopol, CA 95472
(800) 998-9938 (in the United States or Canada)
(707) 829-0515 (international/local)
(707) 829-0104 (fax)

O'Reilly has a web page for this book, which lists errata and any additional information. You can access this page at:

http://www.oreilly.com/catalog/dns4

To comment or ask technical questions about this book, send email to:

bookquestions@oreilly.com

For more information about books, conferences, software, Resource Centers, and the O'Reilly Network, see the O'Reilly web site at:

http://www.oreilly.com

Conventions Used in This Book

We use the following font and format conventions for Unix commands, utilities, and system calls:

- Excerpts from scripts or configuration files are shown in a constant-width font:

```
if test -x /usr/sbin/named -a -f /etc/named.conf
then
     /usr/sbin/named
fi
```

- Sample interactive sessions, showing command-line input and corresponding output, are shown in a constant-width font, with user-supplied input in bold:

```
% cat /var/run/named.pid
78
```

- If the command must be typed by the superuser (root), we use the sharp or pound sign (#):

```
# /usr/sbin/named
```

- Replaceable items in code are printed in constant-width italics.

- Domain names, filenames, functions, commands, Unix manpages, and programming elements taken from the code snippets are printed in italics when they appear within a paragraph.

Quotations

The Lewis Carroll quotations that begin each chapter are from the Millennium Fulcrum Edition 2.9 of the Project Gutenberg electronic text of *Alice's Adventures in Wonderland* and Edition 1.7 of *Through the Looking-Glass*. Quotations in Chapters 1, 2, 5, 6, 8, and 14 come from *Alice's Adventures in Wonderland*, and those in Chapters 3, 4, 7, 9, 10, 11, 12, 13, 15, and 16 come from *Through the Looking-Glass*.

Acknowledgments

The authors would like to thank Ken Stone, Jerry McCollom, Peter Jeffe, Hal Stern, Christopher Durham, Bill Wisner, Dave Curry, Jeff Okamoto, Brad Knowles, K. Robert Elz, and Paul Vixie for their invaluable contributions to this book. We'd also like to thank our reviewers, Eric Pearce, Jack Repenning, Andrew Cherenson, Dan Trinkle, Bill LeFebvre, and John Sechrest for their criticism and suggestions. Without their help, this book would not be what it is (it'd be much shorter!).

For the second edition, the authors add their thanks to their sterling review team: Dave Barr, Nigel Campbell, Bill LeFebvre, Mike Milligan, and Dan Trinkle.

For the third edition, the authors salute their technical review Dream Team: Bob Halley, Barry Margolin, and Paul Vixie.

For the fourth edition, the authors owe a debt of gratitude to Kevin Dunlap, Edward Lewis, and Brian Wellington, their crack review squad.

Cricket would particularly like to thank his former manager, Rick Nordensten, the very model of a modern HP manager, on whose watch the first version of this book was written; his neighbors, who bore his occasional crabbiness for many months; and of course his wife, Paige, for her unflagging support and for putting up with his tap-tap-tapping during her nap-nap-napping. For the second edition, Cricket would like to add a thank you to his former managers, Regina Kershner and Paul Klouda, for their support of Cricket's work with the Internet. For the third edition, Cricket acknowledges a debt of gratitude to his partner, Matt Larson, for his co-development of the Acme Razor. For the fourth edition, Cricket thanks his loyal, furry fans, Dakota and Annie, for kisses and companionship, and wonderful Walter B., for popping his head into the office and checking on Dad now and again. Paul would like to thank his wife, Katherine, for her patience, for many review sessions, and for proving that she could make a quilt in her spare time more quickly than her spouse could write his half of a book.

We would also like to thank the folks at O'Reilly & Associates for their hard work and patience. Credit is especially due our editors, Mike Loukides (first through third editions) and Debra Cameron (fourth edition), as well as countless others who worked on the various editions: Nancy Kotary, Ellie Fountain Maden, Robert Romano, Steven Abrams, Kismet McDonough-Chan, Seth Maislin, Ellie Cutler, Mike Sierra, Lenny Muellner, Chris Reilley, Emily Quill, Anne-Marie Vaduva, and Brenda Miller. Thanks besides to Jerry Peek for all sorts of miscellaneous help and to Tim O'Reilly for inspiring us to put it all in print.

And thanks, Edie, for the cricket on the cover!

In this chapter:
- A (Very) Brief History of the Internet
- On the Internet and internets
- The Domain Name System in a Nutshell
- The History of BIND
- Must I Use DNS?

1

Background

The White Rabbit put on his spectacles. "Where shall I begin, please your Majesty?" he asked.

"Begin at the beginning," the King said, very gravely, "and go on till you come to the end: then stop."

It's important to know a little ARPAnet history to understand the Domain Name System. DNS was developed to address particular problems on the ARPAnet, and the Internet—a descendant of the ARPAnet—remains its main user.

If you've been using the Internet for years, you can probably skip this chapter. If you haven't, we hope it'll give you enough background to understand what motivated the development of DNS.

A (Very) Brief History of the Internet

In the late 1960s, the U.S. Department of Defense's Advanced Research Projects Agency, ARPA (later DARPA), began funding the ARPAnet, an experimental wide area computer network that connected important research organizations in the United States. The original goal of the ARPAnet was to allow government contractors to share expensive or scarce computing resources. From the beginning, however, users of the ARPAnet also used the network for collaboration. This collaboration ranged from sharing files and software and exchanging electronic mail—now commonplace—to joint development and research using shared remote computers.

The TCP/IP (Transmission Control Protocol/Internet Protocol) protocol suite was developed in the early 1980s and quickly became the standard host-networking protocol on the ARPAnet. The inclusion of the protocol suite in the University of

California at Berkeley's popular BSD Unix operating system was instrumental in democratizing internetworking. BSD Unix was virtually free to universities. This meant that internetworking—and ARPAnet connectivity—was suddenly available cheaply to many more organizations than were previously attached to the ARPA-net. Many computers being connected to the ARPAnet were connected to local area networks (LANs), too, and very shortly the other computers on the LANs were communicating via the ARPAnet as well.

The network grew from a handful of hosts to tens of thousands of hosts. The original ARPAnet became the backbone of a confederation of local and regional networks based on TCP/IP, called the *Internet*.

In 1988, however, DARPA decided the experiment was over. The Department of Defense began dismantling the ARPAnet. Another network, funded by the National Science Foundation and called the NSFNET, replaced the ARPAnet as the backbone of the Internet.

Even more recently, in the spring of 1995, the Internet made a transition from using the publicly funded NSFNET as a backbone to using multiple commercial backbones, run by long-distance carriers like MCI and Sprint, and long-time commercial internetworking players like PSINet and UUNET.

Today, the Internet connects millions of hosts around the world. In fact, a significant proportion of the non-PC computers in the world are connected to the Internet. Some of the new commercial backbones can carry a volume of many gigabits per second, tens of thousands of times the bandwidth of the original ARPAnet. Tens of millions of people use the network for communication and collaboration daily.

On the Internet and internets

A word on "the Internet" and "internets" in general is in order. In print, the difference between the two seems slight: one is always capitalized, one isn't. The distinction in meaning, however, *is* significant. The Internet, with a capital "I," refers to the network that began its life as the ARPAnet and continues today as, roughly, the confederation of all TCP/IP networks directly or indirectly connected to commercial U.S. backbones. Seen close up, it's actually quite a few different networks—commercial TCP/IP backbones, corporate and U.S. government TCP/IP networks, and TCP/IP networks in other countries—interconnected by routers and high-speed digital circuits.

A lowercase internet, on the other hand, is simply any network made up of multiple smaller networks using the same internetworking protocols. An internet (little "i") isn't necessarily connected to the Internet (big "I"), nor does it necessarily use TCP/IP as its internetworking protocol. There are isolated corporate internets, and there are Xerox XNS-based internets and DECnet-based internets.

The relatively new term "intranet" is really just a marketing term for a TCP/IP-based "little i" internet, used to emphasize the use of technologies developed and introduced on the Internet within a company's internal corporate network. On the other hand, an "extranet" is a TCP/IP-based internet that connects partner companies to each other, or a company to its distributors, suppliers, and customers.

The History of the Domain Name System

Through the 1970s, the ARPAnet was a small, friendly community of a few hundred hosts. A single file, *HOSTS.TXT*, contained all the information you needed to know about those hosts: it held name-to-address mappings for every host connected to the ARPAnet. The familiar Unix host table, */etc/hosts*, was derived from *HOSTS.TXT* (mostly by deleting fields that Unix didn't use).

HOSTS.TXT was maintained by SRI's *Network Information Center* (dubbed "the NIC") and distributed from a single host, SRI-NIC.* ARPAnet administrators typically emailed their changes to the NIC, and periodically FTPed to SRI-NIC and grabbed the current *HOSTS.TXT*. Their changes were compiled into a new *HOSTS.TXT* once or twice a week. As the ARPAnet grew, however, this scheme became unworkable. The size of *HOSTS.TXT* grew in proportion to the growth in the number of ARPAnet hosts. Moreover, the traffic generated by the update process increased even faster: every additional host meant not only another line in *HOSTS.TXT*, but potentially another host updating from SRI-NIC.

And when the ARPAnet moved to the TCP/IP protocols, the population of the network exploded. Now there was a host of problems with *HOSTS.TXT*:

Traffic and load
> The toll on SRI-NIC, in terms of the network traffic and processor load involved in distributing the file, was becoming unbearable.

Name collisions
> No two hosts in *HOSTS.TXT* could have the same name. However, while the NIC could assign addresses in a way that guaranteed their uniqueness, it had no authority over host names. There was nothing to prevent someone from adding a host with conflicting name and breaking the whole scheme. Someone adding a host with the same name as a major mail hub, for example, could disrupt mail service to much of the ARPAnet.

Consistency
> Maintaining consistency of the file across an expanding network became harder and harder. By the time a new *HOSTS.TXT* reached the farthest shores

---

* SRI is the former Stanford Research Institute in Menlo Park, California. SRI conducts research into many different areas, including computer networking.

of the enlarged ARPAnet, a host across the network had changed addresses, or a new host had sprung up that users wanted to reach.

The essential problem was that the *HOSTS.TXT* mechanism didn't scale well. Ironically, the success of the ARPAnet as an experiment led to the failure and obsolescence of *HOSTS.TXT*.

The ARPAnet's governing bodies chartered an investigation into a successor for *HOSTS.TXT*. Their goal was to create a system that solved the problems inherent in a unified host table system. The new system should allow local administration of data, yet still make that data globally available. The decentralization of administration would eliminate the single-host bottleneck and relieve the traffic problem. And local management would make the task of keeping data up to date much easier. The new system should use a hierarchical namespace to name hosts, thus ensuring the uniqueness of names.

Paul Mockapetris, then of USC's Information Sciences Institute, was responsible for designing the architecture of the new system. In 1984, he released RFCs 882 and 883, which described the Domain Name System. These RFCs were superseded by RFCs 1034 and 1035, the current specifications of the Domain Name System.* RFCs 1034 and 1035 have now been augmented by many other RFCs, describing potential DNS security problems, implementation problems, administrative gotchas, mechanisms for dynamically updating name servers and securing zone data, and more.

The Domain Name System in a Nutshell

The Domain Name System is a *distributed* database. This allows local control of the segments of the overall database, yet the data in each segment is available across the entire network through a client-server scheme. Robustness and adequate performance are achieved through replication and caching.

Programs called *name servers* constitute the server half of DNS's client-server mechanism. Name servers contain information about some segments of the database and make it available to clients, called *resolvers*. Resolvers are often just library routines that create queries and send them across a network to a name server.

The structure of the DNS database is very similar to the structure of the Unix filesystem, as shown in Figure 1-1. The whole database (or filesystem) is pictured as an inverted tree, with the root node at the top. Each node in the tree has a text label, which identifies the node relative to its parent. This is roughly analogous to a "relative pathname" in a filesystem, like *bin*. One label—the null label, or ""—is

---

* RFCs are Request for Comments documents, part of the relatively informal procedure for introducing new technology on the Internet. RFCs are usually freely distributed and contain fairly technical descriptions of the technology, often intended for implementors.

reserved for the root node. In text, the root node is written as a single dot (.). In the Unix filesystem, the root is written as a slash (/).

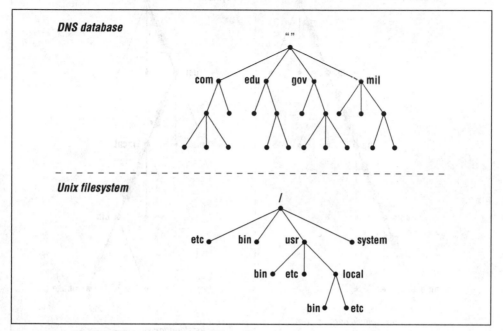

Figure 1-1. The DNS database versus a Unix filesystem

Each node is also the root of a new subtree of the overall tree. Each of these subtrees represents a partition of the overall database—a "directory" in the Unix filesystem, or a *domain* in the Domain Name System. Each domain or directory can be further divided into additional partitions, called *subdomains* in DNS, like a filesystem's "subdirectories." Subdomains, like subdirectories, are drawn as children of their parent domains.

Like every directory, every domain has a unique name. A domain's *domain name* identifies its position in the database, much as a directory's "absolute pathname" specifies its place in the filesystem. In DNS, the domain name is the sequence of labels from the node at the root of the domain to the root of the whole tree, with dots separating the labels. In the Unix filesystem, a directory's absolute pathname is the list of relative names read from root to leaf (the opposite direction to DNS, as shown in Figure 1-2), using a slash to separate the names.

In DNS, each domain can be broken into a number of subdomains, and responsibility for those subdomains can be doled out to different organizations. For example, Network Solutions runs the *edu* (educational) domain, but delegates responsibility for the *berkeley.edu* subdomain to U.C. Berkeley (Figure 1-3). This is something like remotely mounting a filesystem: certain directories in a filesystem

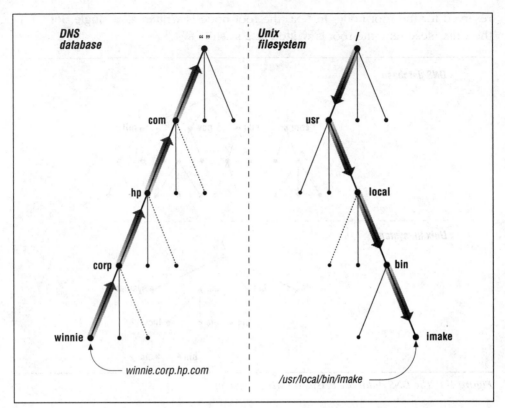

Figure 1-2. Reading names in DNS versus in a Unix filesystem

may actually be filesystems on other hosts, mounted from a remote host. The administrator on host *winken*, for example (again, Figure 1-3), is responsible for the filesystem that appears on the local host as the directory */usr/nfs/winken*.

Delegating authority for *berkeley.edu* to U.C. Berkeley creates a new *zone*, an autonomously administered piece of the namespace. The zone *berkeley.edu* is now independent from *edu* and contains all domain names that end in *berkeley.edu*. The zone *edu*, on the other hand, contains only domain names that end in *edu* but aren't in delegated zones like *berkeley.edu*. *berkeley.edu* may be further divided into subdomains like *cs.berkeley.edu*, and some of these subdomains may themselves be separate zones if the *berkeley.edu* administrators delegate responsibility for them to other organizations. If *cs.berkeley.edu* is a separate zone, the *berkeley.edu* zone doesn't contain domain names that end in *cs.berkeley.edu* (Figure 1-4).

Domain names are used as indexes into the DNS database. You might think of data in DNS as "attached" to a domain name. In a filesystem, directories contain files and subdirectories. Likewise, domains can contain both hosts and subdomains. A

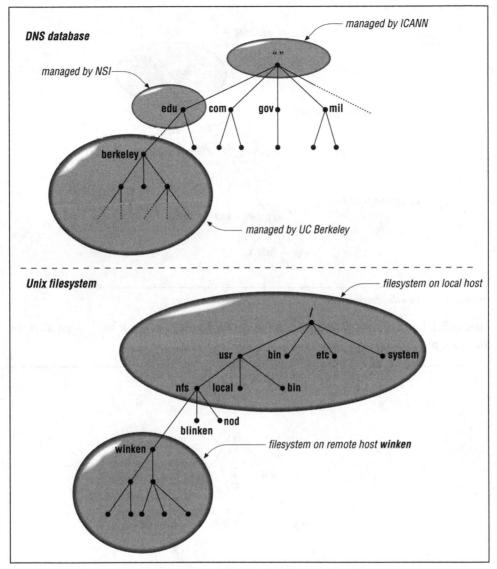

Figure 1-3. Remote management of subdomains and filesystems

domain contains those hosts and subdomains whose domain names are within the domain.

Each host on a network has a domain name, which points to information about the host (see Figure 1-5). This information may include the IP address, information about mail routing, etc. Hosts may also have one or more *domain name aliases*, which are simply pointers from one domain name (the alias) to another

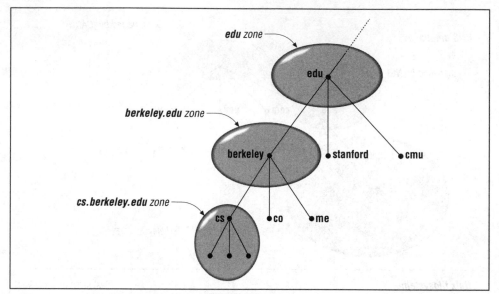

Figure 1-4. The edu, berkeley.edu, and cs.berkeley.edu zones

(the official or *canonical* domain name). In the figure, *mailhub.nv...* is an alias for the canonical name *rincon.ba.ca....*

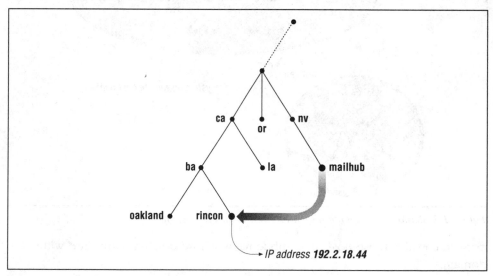

Figure 1-5. An alias in DNS pointing to a canonical name

Why all the complicated structure? To solve the problems that *HOSTS.TXT* had. For example, making domain names hierarchical eliminates the pitfall of name collisions. Each domain has a unique domain name, so the organization that runs the domain is free to name hosts and subdomains within its domain. Whatever name is chosen for a host or subdomain, it won't conflict with other domain names because it ends in the organization's unique domain name. For example, the organization that runs *hic.com* can name a host *puella* (as shown in Figure 1-6), since it knows that the host's domain name will end in *hic.com*, a unique domain name.

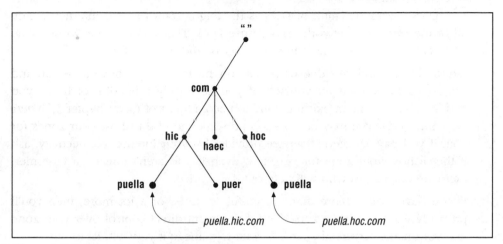

Figure 1-6. Solving the name collision problem

The History of BIND

The first implementation of the Domain Name System was called JEEVES, written by Paul Mockapetris himself. A later implementation was BIND, an acronym for *Berkeley Internet Name Domain*, which was written for Berkeley's 4.3 BSD Unix operating system by Kevin Dunlap. BIND is now maintained by the Internet Software Consortium.[*]

BIND is the implementation we'll concentrate on in this book and is by far the most popular implementation of DNS today. It has been ported to most flavors of Unix and is shipped as a standard part of most vendors' Unix offerings. BIND has even been ported to Microsoft's Windows NT.

Must I Use DNS?

Despite the usefulness of the Domain Name System, there are still some situations in which it doesn't pay to use it. There are other name resolution mechanisms besides DNS, some of which may be a standard part of your operating system. Sometimes the overhead involved in managing zones and their name servers

---

[*] For more information on the Internet Software Consortium and its work on BIND, see *http://www.isc.org/ bind.html.*

outweighs the benefits. On the other hand, there are circumstances in which you have no other choice but to set up and manage name servers. Here are some guidelines to help you make that decision:

If you're connected to the Internet . . .

. . . DNS is a must. Think of DNS as the lingua franca of the Internet: nearly all of the Internet's network services use DNS. That includes the World Wide Web, electronic mail, remote terminal access, and file transfer.

On the other hand, this doesn't necessarily mean that you have to set up and run zones *by* yourself *for* yourself. If you have only a handful of hosts, you may be able to find an existing zone to become part of (see Chapter 3, *Where Do I Start?*). Or you may be able to find someone else to host your zones for you. If you pay an Internet service provider for your Internet connectivity, ask if they'll host your zone for you, too. Even if you aren't already a customer, there are companies who will help out, for a price.

If you have a little more than a handful of hosts, or a lot more, then you'll probably want your own zone. And if you want direct control over your zone and your name servers, then you'll want to manage it yourself. Read on!

If you have your own TCP/IP–based internet . . .

. . . you probably want DNS. By an internet, we don't mean just a single Ethernet of workstations using TCP/IP (see the next section for that); we mean a fairly complex "network of networks." Maybe you have a forest of Apple-talk nets and a handful of Apollo token rings.

If your internet is basically homogeneous and your hosts don't need DNS (say you have a big DECnet or OSI internet), then you may be able to do without it. But if you've got a variety of hosts, and especially if some of those run some variety of Unix, you'll want DNS. It'll simplify the distribution of host information and rid you of any kludgy host table distribution schemes you may have cooked up.

If you have your own local area network or site network . . .

. . . and that network isn't connected to a larger network, you can probably get away without using DNS. You might consider using Microsoft's Windows Internet Name Service (WINS), host tables, or Sun's Network Information Service (NIS) product.

But if you need distributed administration or have trouble maintaining the consistency of data on your network, DNS may be for you. And if your network is likely to be connected to another network soon, like your corporate internet or the Internet itself, you'd be wise to set up your zones now.

2

How Does DNS Work?

> *"... and what is the use of a book,"* thought Alice,
> *"without pictures or conversations?"*

The Domain Name System is basically a database of host information. Admittedly, you get a lot with that: funny dotted names, networked name servers, a shadowy "namespace." But keep in mind that, in the end, the service DNS provides is information about internet hosts.

We've already covered some important aspects of DNS, including its client-server architecture and the structure of the DNS database. However, we haven't gone into much detail, and we haven't explained the nuts and bolts of DNS's operation.

In this chapter, we explain and illustrate the mechanisms that make DNS work. We also introduce the terms you'll need to know to read the rest of the book (and to converse intelligently with your fellow zone administrators).

First, though, let's take a more detailed look at concepts introduced in the previous chapter. We'll try to add enough detail to spice it up a little.

The Domain Name Space

DNS's distributed database is indexed by domain names. Each domain name is essentially just a path in a large inverted tree, called the *domain name space*. The tree's hierarchical structure, shown in Figure 2-1, is similar to the structure of the Unix filesystem. The tree has a single root at the top.* In the Unix filesystem, this is called the root directory, represented by a slash (/). DNS simply calls it "the root." Like a filesystem, DNS's tree can branch any number of ways at each intersection

---

* Clearly this is a computer scientist's tree, not a botanist's.

point, or *node*. The depth of the tree is limited to 127 levels (a limit you're not likely to reach).

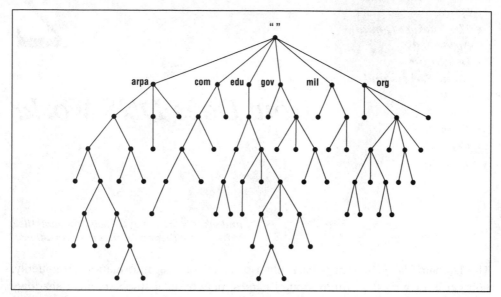

Figure 2-1. The structure of the DNS namespace

Domain Names

Each node in the tree has a text label (without dots) that can be up to 63 characters long. A null (zero-length) label is reserved for the root. The full *domain name* of any node in the tree is the sequence of labels on the path from that node to the root. Domain names are always read from the node toward the root ("up" the tree), with dots separating the names in the path.

If the root node's label actually appears in a node's domain name, the name looks as though it ends in a dot, as in "www.oreilly.com.". (It actually ends with a dot— the separator—and the root's null label.) When the root node's label appears by itself, it is written as a single dot (.) for convenience. Consequently, some software interprets a trailing dot in a domain name to indicate that the domain name is *absolute*. An absolute domain name is written relative to the root and unambiguously specifies a node's location in the hierarchy. An absolute domain name is also referred to as a *fully qualified domain name*, often abbreviated *FQDN*. Names without trailing dots are sometimes interpreted as relative to some domain name other than the root, just as directory names without a leading slash are often interpreted as relative to the current directory.

DNS requires that sibling nodes—nodes that are children of the same parent— have different labels. This restriction guarantees that a domain name uniquely identifies a single node in the tree. The restriction isn't really a limitation, because the labels need to be unique only among the children, not among all the nodes in the tree. The same restriction applies to the Unix filesystem: you can't give two sibling directories or two files in the same directory the same name. Just as you can't have two *hobbes.pa.ca.us* nodes in the namespace, you also can't have two */usr/bin* directories (Figure 2-2). You can, however, have both a *hobbes.pa.ca.us* and a *hobbes.lg.ca.us* node, as you can have both a */bin* directory and a */usr/bin* directory.

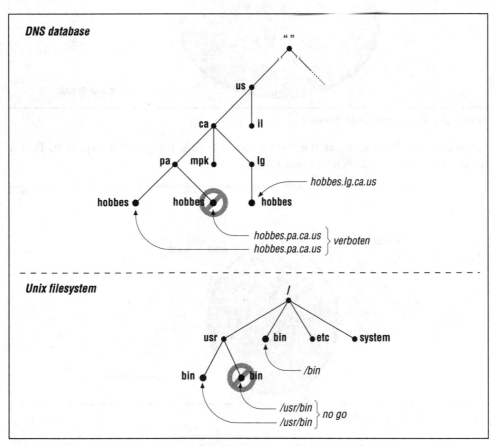

Figure 2-2. Ensuring uniqueness in domain names and in Unix pathnames

Domains

A *domain* is simply a subtree of the domain name space. The domain name of a domain is the same as the domain name of the node at the very top of the domain. So for example, the top of the *purdue.edu* domain is a node named *purdue.edu*, as shown in Figure 2-3.

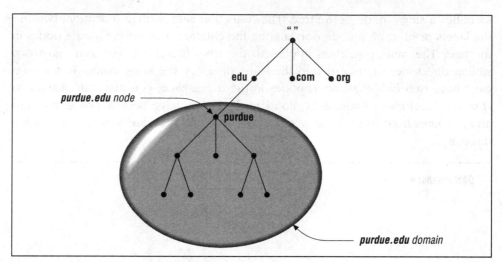

Figure 2-3. The purdue.edu domain

Likewise, in a filesystem, at the top of the */usr* directory, you'd expect to find a node called */usr*, as shown in Figure 2-4.

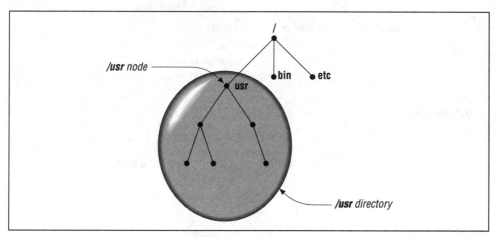

Figure 2-4. The /usr directory

Any domain name in the subtree is considered a part of the domain. Because a domain name can be in many subtrees, it can also be in many domains. For example, the domain name *pa.ca.us* is part of the *ca.us* domain and also part of the *us* domain, as shown in Figure 2-5.

So in the abstract, a domain is just a subtree of the domain name space. But if a domain is simply made up of domain names and other domains, where are all the hosts? Domains are groups of hosts, right?

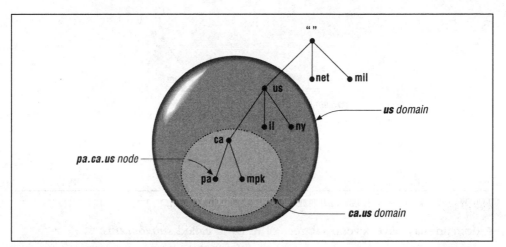

Figure 2-5. A node in multiple domains

The hosts are there, represented by domain names. Remember, domain names are just indexes into the DNS database. The "hosts" are the domain names that point to information about individual hosts. And a domain contains all the hosts whose domain names are within the domain. The hosts are related *logically*, often by geography or organizational affiliation, and not necessarily by network or address or hardware type. You might have 10 different hosts, each on a different network and perhaps even in a different country, all in the same domain.*

Domain names at the leaves of the tree generally represent individual hosts and may point to network addresses, hardware information, and mail routing information. Domain names in the interior of the tree can name a host *and* can point to information about the domain. Interior domain names aren't restricted to one or the other. They can represent both the domain they correspond to and a particular host on the network. For example, *hp.com* is both the name of the Hewlett-Packard Company's domain and the domain name of the hosts that run HP's main web server.

The type of information retrieved when you use a domain name depends on the context in which you use it. Sending mail to someone at *hp.com* returns mail routing information, while telneting to the domain name looks up the host information (in Figure 2-6, for example, *hp.com*'s IP address).

---

* One note of caution: don't confuse domains in the Domain Name System with domains in Sun's Network Information Service (NIS). Though an NIS domain also refers to a group of hosts, and both types of domains have similarly structured names, the concepts are quite different. NIS uses hierarchical names, but the hierarchy ends there: hosts in the same NIS domain share certain data about hosts and users, but they can't navigate the NIS namespace to find data in other NIS domains. NT domains, which provide account management and security services, also don't have any relationship to DNS domains.

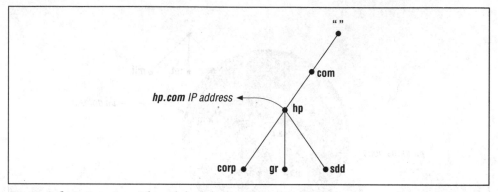

Figure 2-6. An interior node with both host and structural data

A domain may have several subtrees of its own, called *subdomains.**

A simple way of deciding whether a domain is a subdomain of another domain is to compare their domain names. A subdomain's domain name ends with the domain name of its parent domain. For example, the domain *la.tyrell.com* must be a subdomain of *tyrell.com* because *la.tyrell.com* ends with *tyrell.com*. Similarly, it's a subdomain of *com*, as is *tyrell.com*.

Besides being referred to in relative terms, as subdomains of other domains, domains are often referred to by *level*. On mailing lists and in Usenet newsgroups, you may see the terms *top-level domain* or *second-level domain* bandied about. These terms simply refer to a domain's position in the domain name space:

- A top-level domain is a child of the root.

- A first-level domain is a child of the root (i.e., a top-level domain).

- A second-level domain is a child of a first-level domain, and so on.

Resource Records

The data associated with domain names is contained in *resource records*, or RRs. Records are divided into classes, each of which pertains to a type of network or software. Currently, there are classes for internets (any TCP/IP-based internet), networks based on the Chaosnet protocols, and networks that use Hesiod software. (Chaosnet is an old network of largely historic significance.)

The internet class is by far the most popular. (We're not really sure if anyone still uses the Chaosnet class, and use of the Hesiod class is confined mostly to MIT.) In this book, we concentrate on the internet class.

---

* The terms *domain* and *subdomain* are often used interchangeably, or nearly so, in DNS and BIND documentation. Here, we use subdomain only as a relative term: a domain is a subdomain of another domain if the root of the subdomain is within the domain.

Within a class, records also come in several types, which correspond to the different varieties of data that may be stored in the domain name space. Different classes define different record types, though some types are common to more than one class. For example, almost every class defines an *address* type. Each record type in a given class defines a particular record syntax, which all resource records of that class and type must adhere to. (For details on internet resource record types and their syntaxes, see Appendix A, *DNS Message Format and Resource Records.*)

If this information seems sketchy, don't worry—we'll cover the records in the internet class in more detail later. The common records are described in Chapter 4, *Setting Up BIND*, and a more comprehensive list is included as part of Appendix A.

The Internet Domain Name Space

So far, we've talked about the theoretical structure of the domain name space and what kind of data is stored in it, and we've even hinted at the types of names you might find in it with our (sometimes fictional) examples. But this won't help you decode the domain names you see on a daily basis on the Internet.

The Domain Name System doesn't impose many rules on the labels in domain names, and doesn't attach any *particular* meaning to the labels at a particular level. When you manage a part of the domain name space, you can decide on your own semantics for your domain names. Heck, you could name your subdomains A through Z and no one would stop you (though they might strongly recommend against it).

The existing Internet domain name space, however, has some self-imposed structure to it. Especially in the upper-level domains, domain names follow certain traditions (not rules, really, as they can be and have been broken). These traditions help domain names from appearing totally chaotic. Understanding these traditions is an enormous asset if you're trying to decipher a domain name.

Top-Level Domains

The original top-level domains divided the Internet domain name space organizationally into seven domains:

com
>   Commercial organizations, such as Hewlett-Packard (*hp.com*), Sun Microsystems (*sun.com*), and IBM (*ibm.com*).

edu
>   Educational organizations, such as U.C. Berkeley (*berkeley.edu*) and Purdue University (*purdue.edu*).

gov

> Government organizations, such as NASA (*nasa.gov*) and the National Science Foundation (*nsf.gov*).

mil

> Military organizations, such as the U.S. Army (*army.mil*) and Navy (*navy.mil*).

net

> Formerly, organizations providing network infrastructure, such as NSFNET (*nsf.net*) and UUNET (*uu.net*). Since 1996, however, *net*, like *com*, has been open to any commercial organization.

org

> Formerly, noncommercial organizations, such as the Electronic Frontier Foundation (*eff.org*). Like *net*, however, restrictions on *org* were removed in 1996.

int

> International organizations, such as NATO (*nato.int*).

Another top-level domain called *arpa* was originally used during the ARPAnet's transition from host tables to DNS. All ARPAnet hosts originally had domain names under *arpa*, so they were easy to find. Later, they moved into various subdomains of the organizational top-level domains. However, the *arpa* domain remains in use in a way you'll read about later.

You may notice a certain nationalistic prejudice in the examples: all are primarily U.S. organizations. That's easier to understand—and forgive—when you remember that the Internet began as the ARPAnet, a U.S.-funded research project. No one anticipated the success of the ARPAnet, or that it would eventually become as international as the Internet is today.

Today, these original domains are called *generic top-level domains*, or gTLDs. In early 2001, we will have a few more of these, including *name, biz, info*, and *pro*, to accommodate the rapid expansion of the Internet and the need for more domain name "space." The organization responsible for management of the Internet's domain name system, the Internet Corporation for Assigned Names and Numbers (ICANN) OK'd adding these new gTLDs, along with the decidedly nongeneric *aero*, *coop*, and *museum*, in late 2000. For information on ICANN's work and the new TLDs, see *http://www.icann.org*.

To accommodate the increasing internationalization of the Internet, the original implementers of the Internet namespace compromised. Instead of insisting that all top-level domains describe organizational affiliation, they decided to allow geographical designations, too. New top-level domains were reserved (but not necessarily created) to correspond to individual countries. Their domain names followed an existing international standard called ISO 3166.* ISO 3166 establishes official, two-letter abbreviations for every country in the world. We've included the current list of top-level domains as Appendix D, *Top-Level Domains*.

Further Down

Within these top-level domains, the traditions and the extent to which they are followed vary. Some of the ISO 3166 top-level domains closely follow the U.S.'s original organizational scheme. For example, Australia's top-level domain, *au*, has subdomains such as *edu.au* and *com.au*. Some other ISO 3166 top-level domains follow the *uk* domain's lead and have organizationally oriented subdomains such as *co.uk* for corporations and *ac.uk* for the academic community. In most cases, however, even these geographically oriented top-level domains are divided up organizationally.

That's not true of the *us* top-level domain, however. The *us* domain has 50 subdomains that correspond to—guess what?—the 50 states.† Each is named according to the standard two-letter abbreviation for the state, the same abbreviation standardized by the U.S. Postal Service. Within each state's domain, the organization is still largely geographical: most subdomains correspond to individual cities. Beneath the cities, the subdomains usually correspond to individual hosts.

Reading Domain Names

Now that you know what most top-level domains represent and how their namespaces are structured, you'll probably find it much easier to make sense of most domain names. Let's dissect a few for practice:

lithium.cchem.berkeley.edu
> You've got a head start on this one, as we've already told you that *berkeley.edu* is U.C. Berkeley's domain. (Even if you didn't already know that, though, you could have inferred that the name probably belongs to a U.S. university because it's in the top-level *edu* domain.) *cchem* is the College of Chemistry's subdomain of *berkeley.edu*. Finally, *lithium* is the name of a particular host in the domain—and probably one of about a hundred or so, if they've got one for every element.

---

* Except for Great Britain. According to ISO 3166 and Internet tradition, Great Britain's top-level domain name should be *gb*. Instead, most organizations in Great Britain and Northern Ireland (i.e., the United Kingdom) use the top-level domain name *uk*. They drive on the wrong side of the road, too.

† Actually, there are a few more subdomains under *us*: one for Washington, D.C., one for Guam, and so on.

winnie.corp.hp.com

> This example is a bit harder, but not much. The *hp.com* domain in all likelihood belongs to the Hewlett-Packard Company (in fact, we mentioned this earlier, too). Their *corp* subdomain is undoubtedly their corporate headquarters. And *winnie* is probably just some silly name someone thought up for a host.

fernwood.mpk.ca.us

> Here you'll need to use your understanding of the *us* domain. *ca.us* is obviously California's domain, but *mpk* is anybody's guess. In this case, it would be hard to know that it's Menlo Park's domain unless you knew your San Francisco Bay Area geography. (And no, it's not the same Menlo Park that Edison lived in—that one's in New Jersey.)

daphne.ch.apollo.hp.com

> We've included this example just so you don't start thinking that all domain names have four labels. *apollo.hp.com* is the former Apollo Computer's subdomain of the *hp.com* domain. (When HP acquired Apollo, it also acquired Apollo's Internet domain, *apollo.com*, which later became *apollo.hp.com*.) *ch.apollo.hp.com* is Apollo's Chelmsford, Massachusetts, site. And *daphne* is a host in Chelmsford.

Delegation

Remember that one of the main goals of the design of the Domain Name System was to decentralize administration? This is achieved through *delegation*. Delegating domains is a lot like delegating tasks at work. A manager may break up a large project into smaller tasks and delegate responsibility for each of these tasks to different employees.

Likewise, an organization administering a domain can divide it into subdomains. Each of those subdomains can be *delegated* to other organizations. This means that an organization becomes responsible for maintaining all the data in that subdomain. It can freely change the data, and even divide up its subdomain into more subdomains and delegate those. The parent domain retains only pointers to sources of the subdomain's data so that it can refer queriers there. The domain *stanford.edu*, for example, is delegated to the folks at Stanford who run the university's networks, as shown in Figure 2-7.

Not all organizations delegate away their whole domain, just as not all managers delegate all their work. A domain may have several delegated subdomains and also contain hosts that don't belong in the subdomains. For example, the Acme Corporation (which supplies a certain coyote with most of his gadgets) has a division in Rockaway and its headquarters in Kalamazoo, so it might have a *rockaway. acme.com* subdomain and a *kalamazoo.acme.com* subdomain. However, the few

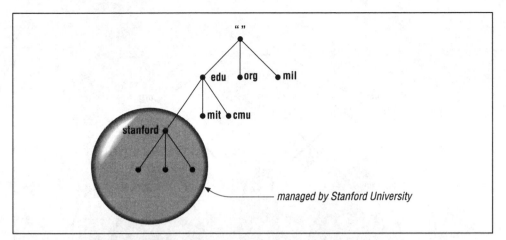

Figure 2-7. stanford.edu is delegated to Stanford University

hosts in the Acme sales offices scattered throughout the U.S. would fit better under *acme.com* than under either subdomain.

We'll explain how to create and delegate subdomains later. For now, it's only important to understand that the term *delegation* refers to assigning responsibility for a subdomain to another organization.

Name Servers and Zones

The programs that store information about the domain name space are called *name servers*. Name servers generally have complete information about some part of the domain name space (a *zone*), which they load from a file or from another name server. The name server is then said to have *authority* for that zone. Name servers can be authoritative for multiple zones, too.

The difference between a zone and a domain is important, but subtle. All top-level domains, and many domains at the second level and lower, such as *berkeley.edu* and *hp.com*, are broken into smaller, more manageable units by delegation. These units are called zones. The *edu* domain, shown in Figure 2-8, is divided into many zones, including the *berkeley.edu* zone, the *purdue.edu* zone, and the *nwu.edu* zone. At the top of the domain, there's also an *edu* zone. It's natural that the folks who run *edu* would break up the *edu* domain: otherwise, they'd have to manage the *berkeley.edu* subdomain themselves. It makes much more sense to delegate *berkeley.edu* to Berkeley. What's left for the folks who run *edu?* The *edu* zone, which would contain mostly delegation information for subdomains of *edu*.

The *berkeley.edu* subdomain is, in turn, broken up into multiple zones by delegation, as shown in Figure 2-9. There are delegated subdomains called *cc, cs, ce, me*, and more. Each of these subdomains is delegated to a set of name servers, some

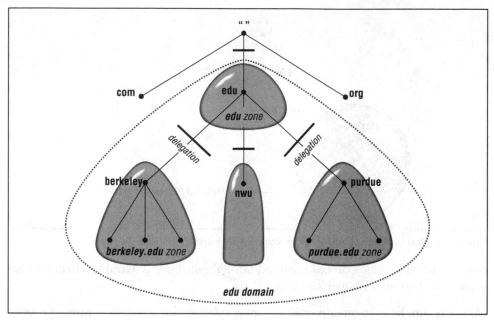

Figure 2-8. The edu domain broken into zones

of which are also authoritative for *berkeley.edu*. However, the zones are still separate, and may have a totally different group of authoritative name servers.

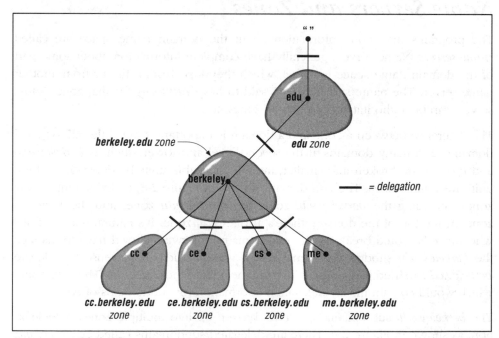

Figure 2-9. The berkeley.edu domain broken into zones

A zone and a domain may share the same domain name but contain different nodes. In particular, the zone doesn't contain any nodes in delegated subdomains. For example, the top-level domain *ca* (for Canada) has subdomains called *ab.ca*, *on.ca*, and *qc.ca*, for the provinces Alberta, Ontario, and Quebec. Authority for the *ab.ca*, *on.ca*, and *qc.ca* subdomains may be delegated to name servers in each of the provinces. The domain *ca* contains all the data in *ca* plus all the data in *ab.ca*, *on.ca*, and *qc.ca*. But the zone *ca* contains only the data in *ca* (see Figure 2-10), which is probably mostly pointers to the delegated subdomains. And *ab.ca*, *on.ca*, and *qc.ca* are separate zones from the *ca* zone.

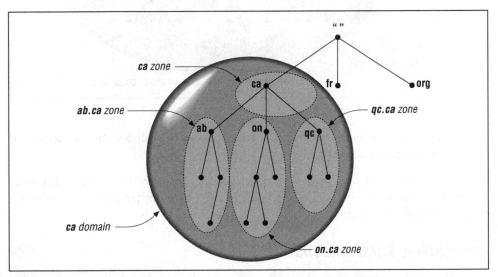

Figure 2-10. The domain ca . . .

If a subdomain of the domain isn't delegated away, however, the zone contains the domain names and data in the subdomain. So the *bc.ca* and *sk.ca* (British Columbia and Saskatchewan) subdomains of the *ca* domain may exist, but might not be delegated. (Perhaps the provincial authorities in B.C. and Saskatchewan aren't yet ready to manage their own zones, but the authorities running the top-level *ca* zone want to preserve the consistency of the namespace and implement subdomains for all of the Canadian provinces right away.) In this case, the zone *ca* has a ragged bottom edge, containing *bc.ca* and *sk.ca* but not the other *ca* sub-domains, as shown in Figure 2-11.

Now it's clear why name servers load zones instead of domains: a domain might contain more information than the name server needs.[*] A domain could contain

---

[*] Imagine if a root name server loaded the root domain instead of the root zone: it would be loading the entire namespace!

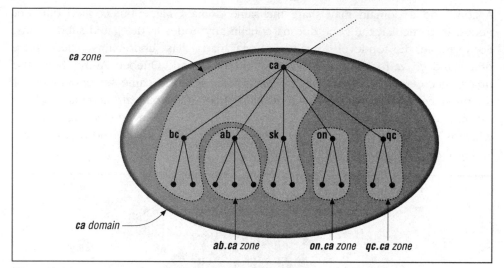

Figure 2-11. . . . versus the zone ca

data delegated to other name servers. Since a zone is bounded by delegation, it never includes delegated data.

If you're just starting out, however, your domain probably won't have any subdomains. In this case, since there's no delegation going on, your domain and your zone contain the same data.

Delegating Subdomains

Even though you may not need to delegate parts of your domain just yet, it's helpful to understand a little more about how the process of delegating a subdomain works. Delegation, in the abstract, involves assigning responsibility for some part of your domain to another organization. What really happens, however, is the assignment of authority for your subdomains to different name servers. (Note that we said "name servers," not just "name server.")

Your zone's data, instead of containing information in the subdomain you've delegated, includes pointers to the name servers that are authoritative for that subdomain. Now if one of your name servers is asked for data in the subdomain, it can reply with a list of the right name servers to talk to.

Types of Name Servers

The DNS specs define two types of name servers: primary masters and secondary masters. A *primary master* name server for a zone reads the data for the zone from a file on its host. A *secondary master* name server for a zone gets the zone data from another name server that is authoritative for the zone, called its *master server*.

Quite often, the master name server is the zone's primary master, but that's not required: a secondary master can load zone data from another secondary. When a secondary starts up, it contacts its master server and, if necessary, pulls the zone data over. This is referred to as a *zone transfer.* Nowadays, the preferred term for a secondary master name server is a *slave,* though many people (and much software, including Microsoft's DNS Manager) still use the old term.

Both the primary master and slave name servers for a zone are authoritative for that zone. Despite the somewhat disparaging name, slaves aren't second-class name servers. DNS provides these two types of name servers to make administration easier. Once you've created the data for your zone and set up a primary master name server, you don't need to fool with copying that data from host to host to create new name servers for the zone. You simply set up slave name servers that load their data from the primary master for the zone. Once they're set up, the slaves transfer new zone data when necessary.

Slave name servers are important because it's a good idea to set up more than one name server for any given zone. You'll want more than one for redundancy, to spread the load around, and to ensure that all the hosts in the zone have a name server close by. Using slave name servers makes this administratively workable.

Calling a *particular* name server a primary master name server or a slave name server is a little imprecise, though. We mentioned earlier that a name server can be authoritative for more than one zone. Similarly, a name server can be a primary master for one zone and a slave for another. Most name servers, however, are either primary for most of the zones they load or slave for most of the zones they load. So if we call a particular name server a primary or a slave, we mean that it's the primary master or a slave for *most* of the zones it's authoritative for.

Zone Data Files

The files from which primary master name servers load their zone data are called, simply enough, zone data files. We often refer to them as data files or database files. Slave name servers can also load their zone data from data files. Slaves are usually configured to back up the zone data they transfer from a master name server to data files. If the slave is later killed and restarted, it will read the backup data files first, then check to see whether its zone data is current. This both obviates the need to transfer the zone data if it hasn't changed and provides a source of the data if the master is down.

The data files contain resource records that describe the zone. The resource records describe all the hosts in the zone and mark any delegation of subdomains. BIND also allows special directives to include the contents of other data files in a zone data file, much like the *#include* statement in C programming.

Resolvers

Resolvers are the clients that access name servers. Programs running on a host that need information from the domain name space use the resolver. The resolver handles the following tasks:

- Querying a name server
- Interpreting responses (which may be resource records or an error)
- Returning the information to the programs that requested it

In BIND, the resolver is just a set of library routines linked into programs such as Telnet and FTP. It's not even a separate process. It has the smarts to put together a query, send it and wait for an answer, and resend the query if it isn't answered, but that's about all. Most of the burden of finding an answer to the query is placed on the name server. The DNS specs call this kind of resolver a *stub resolver.*

Other implementations of DNS have had smarter resolvers, which can do more sophisticated things such as build up a cache of information already retrieved from name servers.* But these aren't nearly as common as the stub resolver implemented in BIND.

Resolution

Name servers are adept at retrieving data from the domain name space. They have to be, given the limited intelligence of most resolvers. Not only can they give you data from zones for which they're authoritative, they can also search through the domain name space to find data for which they're not authoritative. This process is called *name resolution* or simply *resolution.*

Because the namespace is structured as an inverted tree, a name server needs only one piece of information to find its way to any point in the tree: the domain names and addresses of the root name servers (is that more than one piece?). A name server can issue a query to a root name server for any domain name in the domain name space, and the root name server starts the name server on its way.

Root Name Servers

The root name servers know where the authoritative name servers for each of the top-level zones are. (In fact, some of the root name servers are authoritative for the generic top-level zones.) Given a query about any domain name, the root name servers can provide at least the names and addresses of the name servers that are authoritative for the top-level zone that the domain name ends in. And the

---

* Rob Austein's CHIVES resolver for TOPS-20 could cache, for example.

top-level name servers can provide the list of the authoritative name servers for the second-level zone that the domain name ends in. Each name server queried gives the querier information about how to get "closer" to the answer it's seeking, or it provides the answer itself.

The root name servers are clearly important to resolution. Because they're so important, DNS provides mechanisms—such as caching, which we'll discuss a little later—to help offload the root name servers. But in the absence of other information, resolution has to start at the root name servers. This makes the root name servers crucial to the operation of DNS; if all the Internet root name servers were unreachable for an extended period, all resolution on the Internet would fail. To protect against this, the Internet has 13 root name servers (as of this writing) spread across different parts of the network. For example, one is on PSINet, a commercial Internet backbone; one is on the NASA Science Internet; two are in Europe; and one is in Japan.

Being the focal point for so many queries keeps the roots busy; even with 13, the traffic to each root name server is very high. A recent informal poll of root name server administrators showed some roots receiving thousands of queries per second.

Despite the load placed on root name servers, resolution on the Internet works quite well. Figure 2-12 shows the resolution process for the address of a real host in a real domain, including how the process corresponds to traversing the domain name space tree.

The local name server queries a root name server for the address of *girigiri. gbrmpa.gov.au* and is referred to the *au* name servers. The local name server asks an *au* name server the same question, and is referred to the *gov.au* name servers. The *gov.au* name server refers the local name server to the *gbrmpa.gov.au* name servers. Finally, the local name server asks a *gbrmpa.gov.au* name server for the address and gets the answer.

Recursion

You may have noticed a big difference in the amount of work done by the name servers in the previous example. Four of the name servers simply returned the best answer they already had—mostly referrals to other name servers—to the queries they received. They didn't have to send their own queries to find the data requested. But one name server—the one queried by the resolver—had to follow successive referrals until it received an answer.

Why couldn't the local name server simply have referred the resolver to another name server? Because a stub resolver wouldn't have had the intelligence to follow a referral. And how did the name server know not to answer with a referral? Because the resolver issued a recursive query.

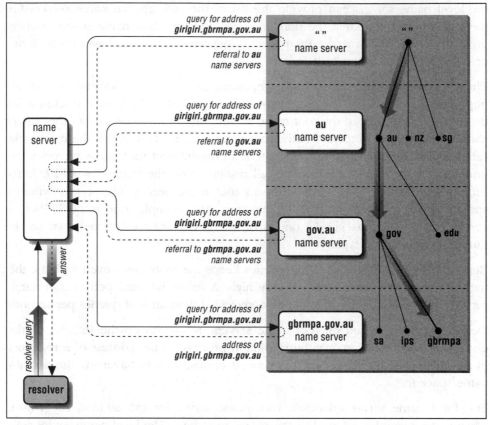

Figure 2-12. Resolution of girigiri.gbrmpa.gov.au on the Internet

Queries come in two flavors, *recursive* and *iterative* (or *nonrecursive*). Recursive queries place most of the burden of resolution on a single name server. *Recursion,* or *recursive resolution,* is just a name for the resolution process used by a name server when it receives recursive queries. As with recursive algorithms in programming, the name server repeats the same basic process (querying a remote name server and following any referrals) until it receives an answer. *Iteration,* or *iterative resolution,* described in the next section, refers to the resolution process used by a name server when it receives iterative queries.

In recursion, a resolver sends a recursive query to a name server for information about a particular domain name. The queried name server is then obliged to respond with the requested data or with an error stating that data of the requested type doesn't exist or that the domain name specified doesn't exist.* The name

---

* BIND 8 name servers can be configured to ignore or refuse recursive queries; see Chapter 11, *Security,* for how and why you'd want to do this.

server can't just refer the querier to a different name server because the query was recursive.

If the queried name server isn't authoritative for the data requested, it will have to query other name servers to find the answer. It could send recursive queries to those name servers, thereby obliging them to find the answer and return it (and passing the buck). Or it could send iterative queries and possibly be referred to other name servers "closer" to the domain name it's looking for. Current implementations are polite and do the latter, following the referrals until an answer is found.*

A name server that receives a recursive query that it can't answer itself will query the "closest known" name servers. The closest known name servers are the servers authoritative for the zone closest to the domain name being looked up. For example, if the name server receives a recursive query for the address of the domain name *girigiri.gbrmpa.gov.au*, it will first check whether it knows which name servers are authoritative for *girigiri.gbrmpa.gov.au*. If it does, it will send the query to one of them. If not, it will check whether it knows the name servers for *gbrmpa.gov.au*, and after that *gov.au*, and then *au*. The default, where the check is guaranteed to stop, is the root zone, since every name server knows the domain names and addresses of the root name servers.

Using the closest known name servers ensures that the resolution process is as short as possible. A *berkeley.edu* name server receiving a recursive query for the address of *waxwing.ce.berkeley.edu* shouldn't have to consult the root name servers; it can simply follow delegation information directly to the *ce.berkeley.edu* name servers. Likewise, a name server that has just looked up a domain name in *ce.berkeley.edu* shouldn't have to start resolution at the roots to look up another *ce.berkeley.edu* (or *berkeley.edu*) domain name; we'll show how this works in the later section "Caching."

The name server that receives the recursive query always sends the same query that the resolver sends it, for example, for the address of *waxwing.ce.berkeley.edu*. It never sends explicit queries for the name servers for *ce.berkeley.edu* or *berkeley. edu*, though this information is also stored in the namespace. Sending explicit queries could cause problems: there may be no *ce.berkeley.edu* name servers (that is, *ce.berkeley.edu* may be part of the *berkeley.edu* zone). Also, it's always possible that an *edu* or *berkeley.edu* name server already knows *waxwing.ce.berkeley.edu*'s address. An explicit query for the *berkeley.edu* or *ce.berkeley.edu* name servers would miss this information.

---

* The exception is a name server configured to forward all unresolved queries to a designated name server, called a forwarder. See Chapter 10, *Advanced Features*, for more information on using forwarders.

Iteration

Iterative resolution, on the other hand, doesn't require nearly as much work on the part of the queried name server. In iterative resolution, a name server simply gives the best answer *it already knows* back to the querier. No additional querying is required. The queried name server consults its local data (including its cache, which we talk about shortly), looking for the data requested. If it doesn't find the answer there, it finds the names and addresses of the name servers closest to the domain name in the query in its local data, and returns that as a referral to help the querier continue the resolution process. Note that the referral includes *all* of the name servers listed in the local data; it's up to the querier to choose which one to query next.

Choosing Between Authoritative Name Servers

Some of the card-carrying Mensa members in our reading audience may be wondering how the name server that receives the recursive query chooses between the name servers authoritative for the zone. For example, we said that there are 13 root name servers on the Internet today. Does the name server simply query the one that appears first in the referral? Does it choose randomly?

BIND name servers use a metric called *roundtrip time*, or RTT, to choose between name servers authoritative for the same zone. Roundtrip time is a measurement of how long a remote name server takes to respond to queries. Each time a BIND name server sends a query to a remote name server, it starts an internal stopwatch. When it receives a response, it stops the stopwatch and makes a note of how long that remote name server took to respond. When the name server must choose which of a group of authoritative name servers to query, it simply chooses the one with the lowest RTT.

Before a BIND name server has queried a name server, it gives it a random RTT value, but lower than any real-world RTT. This ensures that the BIND name server queries all of the name servers authoritative for a given zone in a random order before playing favorites.

On the whole, this simple but elegant algorithm allows BIND name servers to "lock on" to the closest name servers quickly and without the overhead of an out-of-band mechanism to measure performance.

The Whole Enchilada

All of this amounts to a resolution process that, taken as a whole, usually looks something like Figure 2-13.

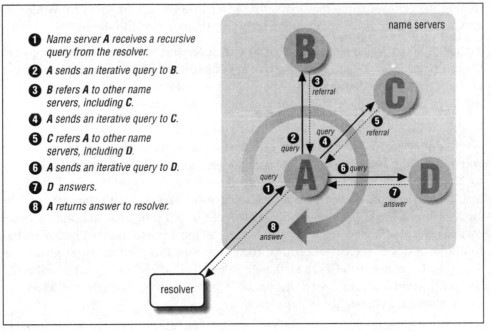

1. Name server **A** receives a recursive query from the resolver.

2. **A** sends an iterative query to **B**.

3. **B** refers **A** to other name servers, including **C**.

4. **A** sends an iterative query to **C**.

5. **C** refers **A** to other name servers, including **D**.

6. **A** sends an iterative query to **D**.

7. **D** answers.

8. **A** returns answer to resolver.

Figure 2-13. The resolution process

A resolver queries a local name server, which sends iterative queries to a number of other name servers in pursuit of an answer for the resolver. Each name server it queries refers it to another name server that is authoritative for a zone further down in the namespace and closer to the domain name sought. Finally, the local name server queries the authoritative name server, which returns an answer. All the while, the local name server uses each response it receives—whether a referral or the answer—to update the RTT of the responding name server, which will help it decide which name servers to query to resolve domain names in the future.

Mapping Addresses to Names

One major piece of functionality missing from the resolution process as explained so far is how addresses get mapped back to domain names. Address-to-name mapping is used to produce output that is easier for humans to read and interpret (in log files, for instance). It's also used in some authorization checks. Unix hosts map addresses to domain names to compare against entries in *.rhosts* and *hosts.equiv* files, for example. When using host tables, address-to-name mapping is trivial. It requires a straightforward sequential search through the host table for an address. The search returns the official host name listed. In DNS, however, address-to-name mapping isn't so simple. Data, including addresses, in the domain name space is indexed by name. Given a domain name, finding an address is relatively easy. But finding the domain name that maps to a given address would seem to require an exhaustive search of the data attached to every domain name in the tree.

Actually, there's a better solution that's both clever and effective. Because it's easy to find data once you're given the domain name that indexes that data, why not create a part of the domain name space that uses addresses as labels? In the Internet's domain name space, this portion is the *in-addr.arpa* domain.

Nodes in the *in-addr.arpa* domain are labeled after the numbers in the dotted-octet representation of IP addresses. (Dotted-octet representation refers to the common method of expressing 32-bit IP addresses as four numbers in the range 0 to 255, separated by dots.) The *in-addr.arpa* domain, for example, could have up to 256 subdomains, one corresponding to each possible value in the first octet of an IP address. Each of these subdomains could have up to 256 subdomains of its own, corresponding to the possible values of the second octet. Finally, at the fourth level down, there are resource records attached to the final octet giving the full domain name of the host at that IP address. That makes for an awfully big domain: *in-addr.arpa*, shown in Figure 2-14, is roomy enough for every IP address on the Internet.

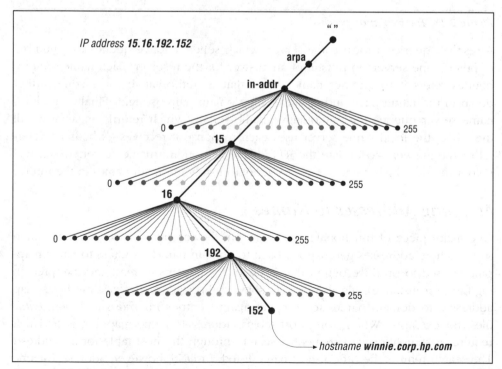

Figure 2-14. The in-addr.arpa domain

Note that when read in a domain name, the IP address appears backward because the name is read from leaf to root. For example, if *winnie.corp.hp.com*'s IP address is 15.16.192.152, the corresponding node in the *in-addr.arpa* domain is *152.192. 16.15.in-addr.arpa*, which maps back to the domain name *winnie.corp.hp.com*.

IP addresses could have been represented the opposite way in the namespace, with the first octet of the IP address at the bottom of the *in-addr.arpa* domain. That way, the IP address would have read correctly (forward) in the domain name.

IP addresses are hierarchical, however, just like domain names. Network numbers are doled out much as domain names are, and administrators can then subnet their address space and further delegate numbering. The difference is that IP addresses get more specific from left to right, while domain names get less specific from left to right. Figure 2-15 shows what we mean.

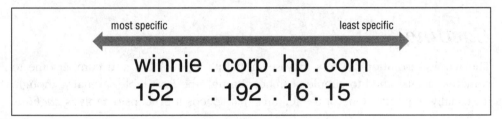

Figure 2-15. Hierarchical names and addresses

Making the first octets in the IP address appear highest in the tree gives administrators the ability to delegate authority for *in-addr.arpa* zones along network lines. For example, the *15.in-addr.arpa* zone, which contains the reverse-mapping information for all hosts whose IP addresses start with 15, can be delegated to the administrators of network 15.0.0.0. This would be impossible if the octets appeared in the opposite order. If the IP addresses were represented the other way around, *15.in-addr.arpa* would consist of every host whose IP address *ended* with 15—not a practical zone to try to delegate.

Inverse Queries

The *in-addr.arpa* domain is clearly useful only for IP address–to–domain name mapping. Searching for a domain name that indexes an *arbitrary* piece of data— something besides an address—in the domain name space would require another specialized namespace, such as *in-addr.arpa*, or an exhaustive search.

That exhaustive search is to some extent possible, and it's called an *inverse query*. An inverse query is a search for the domain name that indexes a given datum. It's processed solely by the name server receiving the query. That name server searches all its local data for the item sought and, if possible, returns the domain name that indexes it. If it can't find the data, it gives up. No attempt is made to consult another name server.

Because any one name server knows about only part of the overall domain name space, an inverse query is never guaranteed to return an answer. For example, if a name server receives an inverse query for an IP address it knows nothing about, it can't return an answer, but it also doesn't know that the IP address doesn't exist, because it holds only part of the DNS database. What's more, the implementation of inverse queries is optional according to the DNS specification; BIND 4.9.8 still contains the code that implements inverse queries, but it's commented out by default. Neither BIND 8 nor BIND 9 includes that code at all, though they do recognize inverse queries and can make up fake responses to them.* That's fine with us, because very little software (such as archaic versions of *nslookup*) actually still uses inverse queries.

Caching

The whole resolution process may seem awfully convoluted and cumbersome to someone accustomed to simple searches through the host table. Actually, though, it's usually quite fast. One of the features that speeds it up considerably is *caching*.

A name server processing a recursive query may have to send out quite a few queries to find an answer. However, it discovers a lot of information about the domain name space as it does so. Each time it's referred to another list of name servers, it learns that those name servers are authoritative for some zone, and it learns the addresses of those servers. And at the end of the resolution process, when it finally finds the data the original querier sought, it can store that data for future reference. With Version 4.9 and all Version 8 and 9 BINDs, name servers even implement *negative caching*: if an authoritative name server responds to a query with an answer that says the domain name or datatype in the query doesn't exist, the local name server will temporarily cache that information, too. Name servers cache all this data to help speed up successive queries. The next time a resolver queries the name server for data about a domain name the name server knows something about, the process is shortened quite a bit. If the name server has cached the answer, positive or negative, it simply returns the answer to the resolver. Even if it doesn't have the answer cached, it may have learned the identities of the name servers that are authoritative for the zone the domain name is in and be able to query them directly.

For example, say our name server has already looked up the address *eecs.berkeley. edu*. In the process, it cached the names and addresses of the *eecs.berkeley.edu*

---

* For details on this functionality, see "Query Refused," in Chapter 12, *nslookup and dig*.

and *berkeley.edu* name servers (plus *eecs.berkeley.edu*'s IP address). Now if a resolver were to query our name server for the address of *baobab.cs.berkeley.edu*, our name server could skip querying the root name servers. Recognizing that *berkeley.edu* is the closest ancestor of *baobab.cs.berkeley.edu* that it knows about, our name server would start by querying a *berkeley.edu* name server, as shown in Figure 2-16. On the other hand, if our name server had discovered that there was no address for *eecs.berkeley.edu*, the next time it receives a query for the address, it could simply respond appropriately from its cache.

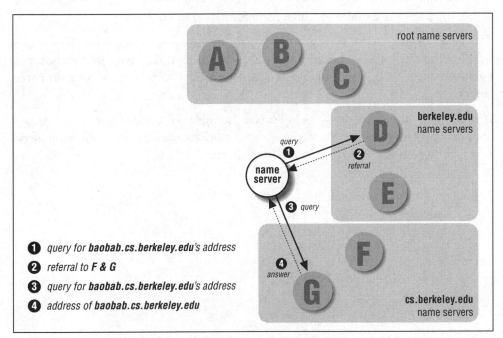

Figure 2-16. Resolving baobab.cs.berkeley.edu

In addition to speeding up resolution, caching obviates a name server's need to query the root name servers to answer queries it can't answer locally. This means that it's not as dependent on the roots, and the roots won't suffer as much from all its queries.

Time to Live

Name servers can't cache data forever, of course. If they did, changes to that data on the authoritative name servers would never reach the rest of the network. Remote name servers would just continue to use cached data. Consequently, the administrator of the zone that contains the data decides on a *time to live*, or TTL, for the data. The time to live is the amount of time that any name server is allowed to cache the data. After the time to live expires, the name server must discard the cached data and get new data from the authoritative name servers. This also applies to negatively cached data; a name server must time out a negative answer after a period, too, in case new data has been added on the authoritative name servers.

Deciding on a time to live for your data is essentially deciding on a trade-off between performance and consistency. A small TTL helps ensure that data in your zones is consistent across the network, because remote name servers will time it out more quickly and be forced to query your authoritative name servers more often for new data. On the other hand, it tends to increase the load on your name servers and lengthen resolution time for information in your zones.

A large TTL shortens the average time it takes to resolve information in your zones because the data can be cached longer. The drawback is that your information will be inconsistent for a longer time if you make changes to your data on your name servers.

But enough of this theory—you're probably antsy to get on with this. There's some homework necessary before you can set up your zones and your name servers, though, and we'll assign it in the next chapter.

3

Where Do I Start?

*"What do you call yourself?" the Fawn said at last.
Such a soft sweet voice it had!*

*"I wish I knew!" thought poor Alice. She answered,
rather sadly, "Nothing, just now."*

"Think again," it said: "that won't do."

*Alice thought, but nothing came of it. "Please,
would you tell me what you call yourself?" she said
timidly. "I think that might help a little."*

*"I'll tell you, if you come a little further on," the
Fawn said. "I can't remember here."*

Now that you understand the theory behind the Domain Name System, we can
attend to more practical matters. Before you set up your zones, you may need to
get the BIND software. Usually, it's included as a standard part of most Unix-based
operating systems. Often, though, you'll want to seek out a more recent version
with all the latest functionality and security enhancements.

Once you've got BIND, you need to decide on a domain name for your main
zone—which may not be quite as easy as it sounds, since it entails finding an
appropriate place in the Internet namespace. That decided, you need to contact
the administrators of the parent of the zone whose domain name you've chosen.

One thing at a time, though. Let's talk about where to get BIND.

Getting BIND

If you plan to set up your own zones and run name servers for them, you'll need
the BIND software first. Even if you're planning on having someone else host your

zones, it's helpful to have the software around. For example, you can use your local name server to test your data files before giving them to the administrator of your remote name servers.

Most commercial Unix vendors ship BIND with the rest of their standard TCP/IP networking software. And the networking software is usually included with the operating system, so you get BIND free. Even if the networking software is priced separately, you've probably already bought it, since you clearly do enough networking to need DNS, right?

If you don't have a version of BIND for your flavor of Unix, though, or if you want the latest, greatest version, you can always get the source code. As luck would have it, it's freely distributed. The source code for the most up-to-date versions of BIND as of this writing (the BIND 8.2.3 and 9.1.0 releases) is available via anonymous FTP from the Internet Software Consortium's web site, *ftp.isc.org*, in */isc/bind/ src/cur/bind-8/bind-src.tar.gz* and */isc/bind9/9.1.0/bind-9.1.0.tar.gz*, respectively. Compiling these releases on most common Unix platforms is relatively straightforward.* The ISC includes a list of Unix-ish operating systems that BIND is known to compile on in the file *src/INSTALL*, including several versions of Linux, Digital Unix, and Solaris 2. There's also a list of other Unix-ish and not-so-Unix-ish (MPE, anyone?) operating systems that BIND has supported in the past and that these most recent versions of BIND will probably compile on without much effort.† Regardless of which category your operating system falls into, we strongly recommend reading all of the sections of *src/INSTALL* relevant to your OS. We also include instructions on compiling BIND 8.2.3 and 9.1.0 on RedHat Linux 6.2 as Appendix C, *Compiling and Installing BIND on Linux*. It's a remarkably short appendix.

Some of you may already have a version of BIND that came with your operating system, but you're wondering whether you need the latest, greatest version of BIND. What does it have to offer that earlier versions of BIND don't? Here's an overview:

Security fixes

Arguably the most important reason to run the newest BIND is that only the most recent versions are patched against most attacks, some of them widely known. BIND 8.2.3 and BIND 9.1.0 are resistant to all well-known attacks, while BIND 4.9.8 can withstand an important subset of them. Earlier versions of BIND have many widely known vulnerabilities. If you're running a name server

---

* Compiling early versions of BIND 9 (before 9.1.0) can be a little tricky, since these versions require *pthreads* and many OSes sport broken *pthreads* implementations. BIND 9.1.0 and later can be built without *pthreads* by running *configure --disable-threads*.

† We know for a fact that BIND 8.2.3 compiles cleanly on several of these operating systems.

on the Internet, we strongly recommend that you run BIND 8.2.3, BIND 9.1.0, at the very least BIND 4.9.8, or whatever the current released version is as you read this.

Security features

BIND 8 and BIND 9 support access lists on queries, zone transfers, and dynamic updates. BIND 4.9 servers support access lists on queries and zone transfers, and earlier versions of BIND don't support access lists at all. Certain name servers, particularly those running on bastion hosts or other security-critical hosts, may require these features.

We cover these features in Chapter 11, *Security*.

DNS UPDATE

BIND 8 and BIND 9 support the Dynamic Update standard described in RFC 2136. This allows authorized agents to update zone data by sending special update messages to add or delete resource records. BIND 4 servers don't support Dynamic Update.

We cover Dynamic Update in Chapter 10, *Advanced Features*.

DNS NOTIFY

BIND 8 and BIND 9 support zone change notification, which allows the primary master name server for a zone to notify the zone's slaves when the serial number has incremented. BIND 4 servers don't support NOTIFY.

We describe NOTIFY in Chapter 10.

Incremental zone transfer

BIND 8.2.3 and BIND 9 support incremental zone transfer, which allows slave name servers to request just the changes to a zone from their master servers. This makes zone transfers faster and more efficient, and is particularly important for large, dynamic zones.

Configuration syntax

The configuration syntax used by BIND 8 and BIND 9 is completely different from BIND 4's. While the new configuration syntax is more flexible and more powerful, it also requires learning a brand-new system for configuring BIND. But then, you have this book to help you through that.

We introduce the BIND 8 and BIND 9 configuration syntax in Chapter 4, *Setting Up BIND*, and describe it throughout the rest of the book.

We've also provided a summary of the capabilities of four popular versions of BIND (4.9.8, 8.1.2, 8.2.3, and 9.1.0) as Appendix B, *BIND Compatibility Matrix*. If you're not sure which version is right for you or if you need some exotic BIND feature you're not sure is supported yet in BIND 9, take a look at the appendix.

If, after reading through this list and checking the appendix, you're convinced you need BIND 8 or BIND 9's features and neither a BIND 8 nor BIND 9 name server comes with your operating system, download the source code and build your own.

Handy Mailing Lists and Usenet Newsgroups

Instructions on how to port BIND to every other version of Unix could consume another book this size, so we'll have to refer you to the BIND users mailing list (*bind-users@isc.org*) or the corresponding Usenet newsgroup (*comp.protocols.dns. bind*) for further help.[*] For BIND 9, there's a separate mailing list, *bind9-users@isc.org*.[†] The folks who read and contribute to the BIND users mailing lists can be enormously helpful in your porting efforts. Before sending mail to the list asking whether a particular port is available, though, be sure to check the searchable archive of the mailing list at *http://www.isc.org/ml-archives/bind-users*. Also, take a look at the ISC's BIND web page at *http://www.isc.org/products/BIND* for notes or links specific to your operating system, and check Andras Salamon's DNS Resource Directory for precompiled BIND software. The directory currently has a short list of precompiled binaries at *http://www.dns.net/dnsrd/bind.html*.

Another mailing list you might be interested in is the *namedroppers* list. Folks on the *namedroppers* mailing list are involved in the IETF working group that develops extensions to the DNS specifications, DNSEXT. For example, the discussion of a new, proposed DNS record type would probably take place on *namedroppers* instead of the BIND mailing list. For more information on DNSEXT's charter, see *http://www.ietf.org/html.charters/dnsext-charter.html*.

The address for the *namedroppers* mailing list is *namedroppers@ops.ietf.org*, and it is gatewayed into the Internet newsgroup *comp.protocols.dns.std*. To join the *namedroppers* mailing list, send mail to *namedroppers-request@ops.ietf.org* with the text "subscribe namedroppers" as the body of the message.

Finding IP Addresses

You'll notice that we gave you a number of domain names of hosts that have FTPable software, and that the mailing lists we mentioned include domain names. That should underscore the importance of DNS: see what valuable software and

---

[*] To ask a question on an Internet mailing list, all you need to do is send a message to the mailing list's address. If you'd like to join the list, however, you have to send a message to the list's maintainer first, requesting that he or she add your electronic mail address to the list. Don't send this request to the list itself—that's considered rude. The Internet convention is that you can reach the maintainer of a mailing list by sending mail to *list-request@domain*, where *list@domain* is the address of the mailing list. So, for example, you can reach the BIND users mailing list's administrator by sending mail to *bind-users-request@isc.org*.

[†] Most of the BIND 9 developers read the *bind9-users* mailing list exclusively.

advice you can get with the help of DNS? Unfortunately, it's also something of a chicken-and-egg problem: you can't send email to an address with a domain name in it unless you've got DNS set up, so how can you ask someone on the list how to set DNS up?

Well, we could give you the IP addresses for all the hosts we mentioned, but since IP addresses change often (in publishing timescales, anyway), we'll show you how you can *temporarily* use someone else's name server to find the information instead. As long as your host has Internet connectivity and the *nslookup* program, you can retrieve information from the Internet namespace. To look up the IP address for *ftp.isc.org*, for example, you could use:

```
% nslookup ftp.isc.org. 207.69.188.185
```

This instructs *nslookup* to query the name server running on the host at the IP address 207.69.188.185 to find the IP address for *ftp.isc.org*, and should produce output like:

```
Server:  ns1.mindspring.com
Address:  207.69.188.185

Name:    isrv4.pa.vix.com
Address: 204.152.184.27
Aliases:  ftp.isc.org
```

Now you can FTP to *ftp.isc.org*'s IP address, 204.152.184.27.

How did we know that the host at IP address 207.69.188.185 runs a name server? Our ISP, Mindspring, told us—it's one of their name servers. If your ISP provides name servers for its customers' use (and most do), use one of them. If your ISP doesn't provide name servers (shame on them!), you can *temporarily* use one of the name servers listed in this book. As long as you use it only to look up a few IP addresses or other data, the administrators probably won't mind. It's considered very rude, however, to point your resolver or query tool at someone else's name server permanently.

Of course, if you already have access to a host with Internet connectivity *and* DNS configured, you can use it to FTP the stuff you need.

Once you've got a working version of BIND, you're ready to start thinking about your domain name.

Choosing a Domain Name

Choosing a domain name is more involved than it may sound because it entails both choosing a name *and* finding out who runs the parent zone. In other words, you need to find out where you fit in the Internet domain name space, then find out who runs that particular corner of that namespace.

The first step in picking a domain name is finding where in the existing domain name space you belong. It's easiest to start at the top and work your way down: decide which top-level domain you belong in, then which of that top-level domain's subdomains you fit into.

Note that to find out what the Internet domain name space looks like (beyond what we've already told you), you'll need access to the Internet. You don't necessarily need access to a host with name service already configured, but it would help a little. If you don't have access to a host with DNS configured, you'll have to "borrow" name service from other name servers (as in our previous *ftp.isc.org* example) to get you going.

On Registrars and Registries

Before we go any further, we need to define a few terms: *registry*, *registrar*, and *registration*. These terms aren't defined anywhere in the DNS specs. Instead, they apply to the way the Internet's namespace is managed today.

A *registry* is an organization responsible for maintaining a top-level domain's (well, zone's, really) data files, which contain the delegation to each subdomain of that top-level domain. Under the current structure of the Internet, a given top-level domain can have no more than one registry. A *registrar* acts as an interface between customers and the registry, providing registration and value-added services. It submits to the registry zone data and other data (including contact information) for each of its customers in a single top-level domain.

Registration, then, is the process by which a customer tells a registrar which name servers to delegate a subdomain to and provides the registrar with contact and billing information. The registrar then makes these changes through the registry.

Network Solutions Inc. acts as both the exclusive registry and as a registrar for the *com*, *net*, *org*, and *edu* top-level domains. And now, back to our story.

Where in the World Do I Fit?

If your organization is attached to the Internet outside of the United States, you first need to decide whether you'd rather request a subdomain of one of the generic top-level domains, such as *com*, *net*, or *org*, or a subdomain of your own country's top-level domain. The generic top-level domains aren't exclusively for U.S. organizations. If your company is a multi- or transnational company that doesn't fit in any one country's top-level domain, or if you'd simply prefer a generic top-level instead of your country's top-level domain, you're welcome to register in one. If you choose this route, skip to the section "The generic top-level domains" later in this chapter.

If you opt for a subdomain under your country's top level, you should check whether your country's top-level domain is registered, and if it is, what kind of structure it has. Consult Appendix D, *Top-Level Domains*, if you're not sure of the name of your country's top-level domain.

Some countries' top-level domains, such as New Zealand's *nz*, Australia's *au*, and the United Kingdom's *uk*, are divided organizationally into second-level domains. The names of their second-level domains, such as *co* or *com* for commercial entities, reflect organizational affiliation. Others, like France's *fr* domain and Denmark's *dk* domain, are divided into a multitude of subdomains managed by individual universities and companies, such as the University of St. Etienne's domain, *univ-st-etienne.fr* and the Danish Unix Users Group's *dkuug.dk*. Many top-level domains have their own web sites that describe their structures. If you're not sure of the URL for your country's top-level domain's web site, start at *http://www.allwhois.com*, a directory of links to such sites.

If your top-level doesn't have a web site explaining how it's organized, you may have to use a tool like *nslookup* to grope around and discover your top-level domain's structure. (If you're uncomfortable with our rushing headlong into *nslookup* without giving it a proper introduction, you might want to skim Chapter 12, *nslookup and dig*.) For example, here's how you could list the *au* domain's subdomains using *nslookup*:

```
% nslookup - 207.69.188.185     —Use the name server at 207.69.188.185
Default Server:  ns1.mindspring.com
Address:  207.69.188.185

> set type=ns                    —Find the name servers (ns)
> au.                            —for the au zone
Server:  ns1.mindspring.com
Address: 207.69.188.185

au       nameserver = MUNNARI.OZ.AU
au       nameserver = MULGA.CS.MU.OZ.AU
au       nameserver = NS.UU.NET
au       nameserver = NS.EU.NET
au       nameserver = NS1.BERKELEY.EDU
au       nameserver = NS2.BERKELEY.EDU
au       nameserver = VANGOGH.CS.BERKELEY.EDU
MUNNARI.OZ.AU       internet address = 128.250.1.21
MULGA.CS.MU.OZ.AU       internet address = 128.250.1.22
MULGA.CS.MU.OZ.AU       internet address = 128.250.37.150
NS.UU.NET       internet address = 137.39.1.3
NS.EU.NET       internet address = 192.16.202.11
NS1.BERKELEY.EDU  internet address = 128.32.136.9
NS1.BERKELEY.EDU  internet address = 128.32.206.9
NS2.BERKELEY.EDU       internet address = 128.32.136.12
NS2.BERKELEY.EDU       internet address = 128.32.206.12
```

```
> server ns.uu.net.    —Now query one of these name servers—preferably a close one!
Default Server:  ns.uu.net
Addresses:  137.39.1.3

> ls -t au. —List the au zone
            —The zone's NS records mark delegation to subdomains and will give you
            —the names of the subdomains
            —Note that not all name servers will allow you to list zones, for security reasons.
 [ns.uu.net]
$ORIGIN au.
@                   3D IN NS        mulga.cs.mu.OZ
                    3D IN NS        vangogh.CS.Berkeley.EDU.
                    3D IN NS        ns1.Berkeley.EDU.
                    3D IN NS        ns2.Berkeley.EDU.
                    3D IN NS        ns.UU.NET.
                    3D IN NS        ns.eu.NET.
                    3D IN NS        munnari.OZ
ORG                 1D IN NS        mulga.cs.mu.OZ
                    1D IN NS        rip.psg.COM.
                    1D IN NS        munnari.OZ
                    1D IN NS        yalumba.connect.COM
info                1D IN NS        ns.telstra.net.
                    1D IN NS        ns1.telstra.net.
                    1D IN NS        munnari.oz
                    1D IN NS        svc01.apnic.net.
otc                 4H IN NS        ns2.telstra.com
                    4H IN NS        munnari.oz
                    4H IN NS        ns.telstra.com
OZ                  1D IN NS        mx.nsi.NASA.GOV.
                    1D IN NS        munnari.OZ
                    1D IN NS        mulga.cs.mu.OZ
                    1D IN NS        dmssyd.syd.dms.CSIRO
                    1D IN NS        ns.UU.NET.
csiro               1D IN NS        steps.its.csiro
                    1D IN NS        munnari.OZ
                    1D IN NS        manta.vic.cmis.csiro
                    1D IN NS        dmssyd.nsw.cmis.csiro
                    1D IN NS        zoiks.per.its.csiro
COM                 1D IN NS        mx.nsi.NASA.GOV.
                    1D IN NS        yalumba.connect.COM
                    1D IN NS        munnari.OZ
                    1D IN NS        mulga.cs.mu.OZ
                    1D IN NS        ns.ripe.NET.
> ^D
```

The basic technique is straightforward: look up the list of name servers for the top-level domain (because they're the only ones with complete information about the corresponding zone), then query one of those name servers and list the name servers for the delegated subdomains.

If you can't tell from the names of the subdomains which one you belong in, you can look up the contact information for the corresponding zone and send email to the technical contact asking, politely, for advice. Similarly, if you think you should be part of an existing subdomain but aren't sure, you can always ask the folks who administer that subdomain to double-check.

To find out who to ask about a particular subdomain, you'll have to look up the corresponding zone's start of authority (SOA) record. In each zone's SOA record, there's a field containing the electronic mail address of the zone's technical contact.* (The other fields in the start of authority record provide general information about a zone—we'll discuss them in more detail later.) You can look up the zone's SOA record with *nslookup*, too.

For example, if you're curious about the purpose of the *csiro* subdomain, you can find out who runs it by looking up *csiro.au*'s SOA record:

```
% nslookup - 207.69.188.185
Default Server: ns1.mindspring.com
Address:  207.69.188.185


> set type=soa      —Look for start of authority data
> csiro.au.         —for csiro.au
Server:  ns1.mindspring.com
Address: 207.69.188.185

csiro.au
        origin = steps.its.csiro.au
        mail addr = hostmaster.csiro.au
        serial = 2000041301
        refresh = 10800  (3H)
        retry   = 3600 (1H)
        expire  = 3600000 (5w6d16h)
        minimum ttl = 86400 (1D)
```

The *mail addr* field is the Internet address of *csiro.au*'s contact. To convert the address into Internet email address format, you'll need to change the first "." in the address to an "@". So *hostmaster.csiro.au* becomes *hostmaster@csiro.au*.†

Using whois

The *whois* service can also help you figure out what a given domain is for. Unfortunately, there are many *whois* servers—most good administrators of top-level domains run one—and they don't talk to each other like name servers do. Consequently, the first step to using *whois* is finding the right *whois* server.

---

* The subdomain and the zone have the same domain name, but the SOA record really belongs to the zone, not the subdomain. The person at the zone's technical contact email address may not manage the whole subdomain (there may be additional delegated subdomains beneath), but he or she should certainly know what the purpose of the subdomain is.

† This form of Internet mail address is a vestige of two former DNS records, MB and MG. MB (mailbox) and MG (mail group) were DNS records specifying Internet mailboxes and mail groups (mailing lists) as subdomains of the appropriate domain. MB and MG never took off, but the address format they would have dictated is used in the SOA record, maybe for sentimental reasons.

One of the easiest places to start your search for the right *whois* server is at *http://www.allwhois.com* (Figure 3-1). We mentioned earlier that this site has a list of web sites for each country code top-level domain; it also has a list of top-level domains with *whois* URLs—pages with HTML-based interfaces to query *whois* servers.

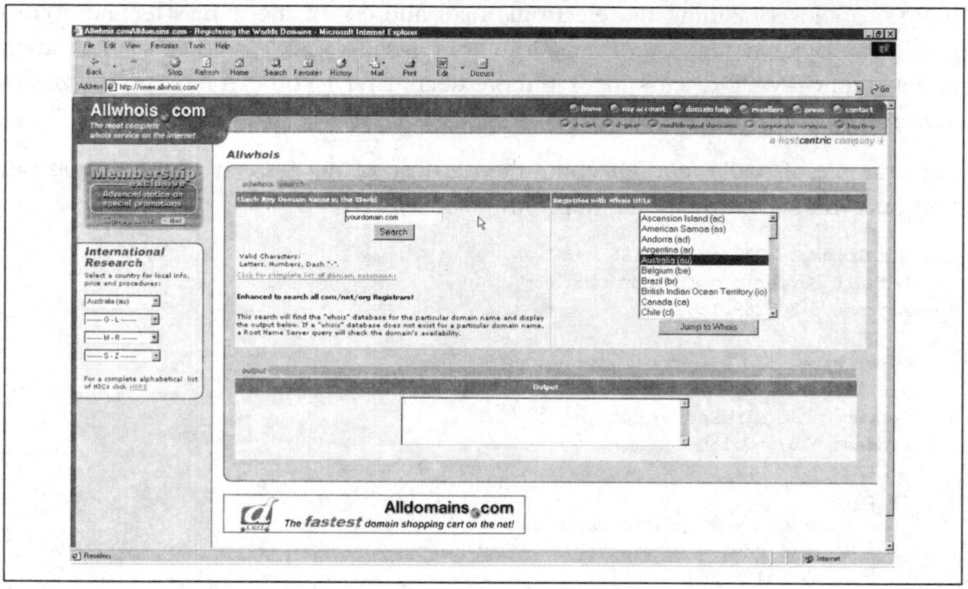

Figure 3-1. The Allwhois.com web site

Scrolling down to "Australia (au)," you can click on "Jump to Whois" and go directly to a page where you can enter *csiro.au*, as shown in Figure 3-2.

Clicking on "Submit" retrieves the information in Figure 3-3 for you.

Perhaps even more interesting for the inertially challenged is the work done by WebMagic to provide a unified *whois* lookup service on the Web. Their web site, *http://www.webmagic.com/whois/index.html*, lets you choose the top-level domain (and sometimes the second-level domain) containing the subdomain you're looking for and then transparently contacts the right *whois* server.

Obviously, these are both very useful web sites if you're looking for the contact for a domain outside of the U.S.

Once you've found the right web site or contact, you've probably found the registrar. Outside the U.S., most domains have a single registrar. A few, though, such as Denmark's *dk* and Great Britain's *co.uk* and *org.uk*, have multiple registrars. However, the process just described will still lead you to them.

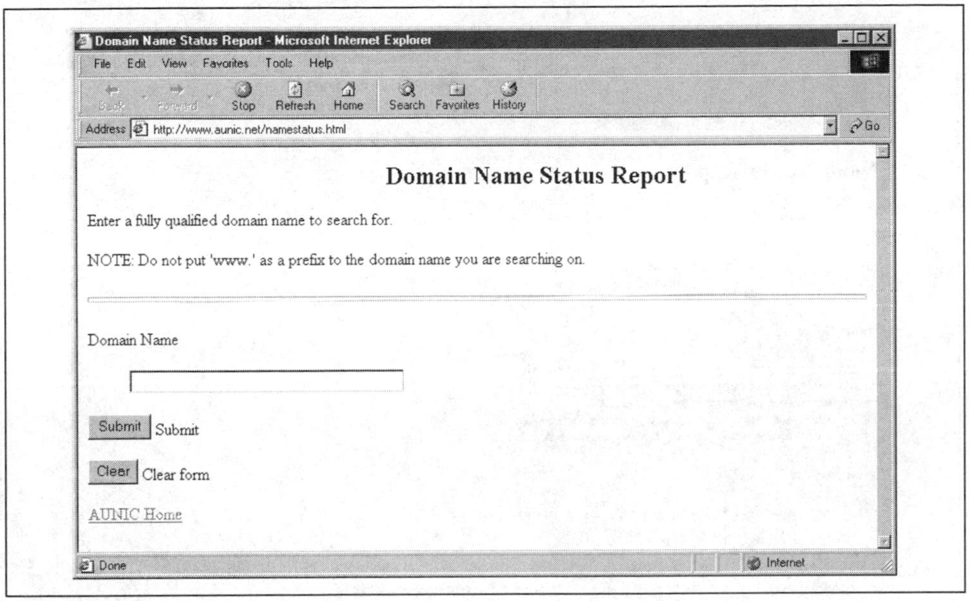

Figure 3-2. Web interface for au's whois server

Back in the U.S.A.

In true cosmopolitan spirit, we covered international domains first. But what if you're from the good ol' U.S. of A.?

If you're in the U.S., where you belong depends mainly upon what your organization does, how you'd like your domain names to look, and how much you're willing to pay. If your organization falls into one of the following categories, you're encouraged to join the *us* top-level domain:

- K-12 (kindergarten through twelfth grade) schools
- Community colleges and technical vocational schools
- State and local government agencies

Even if you don't fall into one of these categories, if you'd like a domain name that indicates your location, like *acme.boulder.co.us*, you can register in the *us* top-level domain. The *us* domain delegates subdomains under third-level domains largely named after "localities" (usually cities or counties); the second-level domains correspond to the appropriate U.S. Postal Service two-letter state abbreviations (recall our discussion in the section "The Internet Domain Name Space" in Chapter 2, *How Does DNS Work?*). So, for example, if all you need is a subdomain to hold the two internetworked hosts in your basement in Colorado Springs, Colorado, you can register *toms-basement.colorado-springs.co.us*.

```
┌─────────────────────────────────────────────────────────────────────────────┐
│ ▓ Name Report for csiro.au - Microsoft Internet Explorer            _ ⊡ ✕   │
│  File   Edit   View   Favorites   Tools   Help                              │
│  ←   →   ✕   ⟳   ⌂      ◎   ☆   ◷                                         │
│  Back Forward Stop Refresh Home  Search Favorites History                   │
│  Address │ http://www.aunic.net/cgi-bin/name-status.p│          ▼  │ ⌀ Go   │
│ ┌─────────────────────────────────────────────────────────────────────────┐│
│ │                                                                          ││
│ │  Name Status Report                                                      ││
│ │                                                                          ││
│ │  Name: csiro.au                                                          ││
│ │  ──────────────────────────────────────────────────────────────────     ││
│ │                                                                          ││
│ │  This name is configured in the DNS:                                     ││
│ │                                                                          ││
│ │  Name Servers:                                                           ││
│ │                                                                          ││
│ │  csiro.au name server zoiks.per.its.csiro.au                             ││
│ │  csiro.au name server steps.its.csiro.au                                 ││
│ │  csiro.au name server munnari.OZ.AU                                      ││
│ │  csiro.au name server manta.vic.cmis.csiro.au                            ││
│ │  csiro.au name server dmssyd.nsw.cmis.csiro.au                           ││
│ │                                                                          ││
│ │  Mail Servers:                                                           ││
│ │                                                                          ││
│ │  csiro.au mail is handled (pri=10) by steps.its.csiro.au                 ││
│ │                                                                          ││
│ │  SOA record:                                                             ││
│ │                                                                          ││
│ │  csiro.au start of authority    steps.its.csiro.au hostmaster.csiro.au(  ││
│ │                  2001011601    ;serial (version)                         ││
│ │                  10800    ;refresh period                                ││
│ │                  3600    ;retry refresh this often                       ││
│ │                  3600000 ;expiration period                              ││
│ │                  86400  ;minimum TTL                                     ││
│ │                  )                                                       ││
│ │  ──────────────────────────────────────────────────────────────────     ││
│ │                                                                          ││
│ │  csiro.au is not in the AUNIC registry.                                  ││
│ │  ──────────────────────────────────────────────────────────────────     ││
│ │  Administrator of parent domain au is hostmaster@munnari.OZ.au.          ││
│ │  ──────────────────────────────────────────────────────────────────     ││
│ └─────────────────────────────────────────────────────────────────────────┘│
│ ▒ Done                                                    🌐 Internet        │
└─────────────────────────────────────────────────────────────────────────────┘
```

Figure 3-3. Information about csiro.au from the au whois server

Finally, there's the issue of cost. It's usually cheaper to register a subdomain of the *us* top-level domain than to register under *com*, *net*, or *org*, and sometimes it's even free.

If you'd like more detailed information on the structure of the *us* domain and the rules that govern it, check out the U.S. NIC's web site, *http://www.nic.us*.

Of course, folks in the U.S. can also ask for a subdomain of one of the generic top-level domains such as *com*, *net*, or *org*. As long as you don't ask for one that's already taken, you should get the one you ask for. We'll cover registration under the generic top-level domains later in this chapter.

The us domain

Let's go through an example to give you an idea of how to comb the *us* domain name space for the perfect domain name. Say you're helping out your son's kindergarten in Boulder, Colorado, and you want to register a domain name for the school.

Using an account you still have on a host at CU (from your undergrad days), you can check to see whether a domain for Boulder exists. (If you didn't have an account there, but you did have Internet connectivity, you could still use *nslookup* to query a well-known name server.)

```
% nslookup
Default Server:  boulder.colorado.edu
Address: 128.138.238.18, 128.138.240.1

> set type=ns           —Look up the name servers
> co.us.                —for co.us
Default Server:  boulder.colorado.edu
Address:  128.138.238.18, 128.138.240.1

co.us    nameserver = VENERA.ISI.EDU
co.us    nameserver = NS.ISI.EDU
co.us    nameserver = RS0.INTERNIC.NET
co.us    nameserver = NS.UU.NET
co.us    nameserver = ADMII.ARL.MIL
co.us    nameserver = EXCALIBUR.USC.EDU
```

This gives you the names of the *co.us* name servers. Now change servers to a *co.us* name server, say *venera.isi.edu*, and check to see if there are any subdomains (you haven't exited out of *nslookup* yet):

```
> server venera.isi.edu.   —Change server to venera.isi.edu
Default Server:  venera.isi.edu
Address:  128.9.0.32

> ls -t co.us.      —List the co.us zone to look for NS records
[venera.isi.edu]
$ORIGIN co.us.
@                      1W IN NS      NS.ISI.EDU.
                       1W IN NS      RS0.INTERNIC.NET.
                       1W IN NS      NS.UU.NET.
                       1W IN NS      ADMII.ARL.MIL.
                       1W IN NS      EXCALIBUR.USC.EDU.
                       1W IN NS      VENERA.ISI.EDU.
officemate1.monument   1W IN NS      ns1.direct.ca.
                       1W IN NS      ns2.direct.ca.
la-junta               1D IN NS      ns2.cw.net.
                       1D IN NS      usdns.beltane.com.
                       1D IN NS      usdns2.beltane.com.
morrison               1W IN NS      NS1.WESTNET.NET.
                       1W IN NS      NS.UTAH.EDU.
littleton              1W IN NS      NS1.WESTNET.NET.
                       1W IN NS      NS.UTAH.EDU.
mus                    1W IN NS      NS1.WESTNET.NET.
                       1W IN NS      NS.UTAH.EDU.
```

```
ci.palmer-lake          1W IN NS        DNS1.REGISTEREDSITE.COM.
                        1W IN NS        DNS2.REGISTEREDSITE.COM.
co.adams                1W IN NS        ns1.rockymtn.net.
                        1W IN NS        ns2.rockymtn.net.
[...]
```

Aha! So there *is* life in Colorado! There are subdomains called *la-junta*, *morrison*, *littleton*, *mus*, and many others. There's even a subdomain for Boulder (called, not surprisingly, *boulder*):

```
boulder                 1W IN NS        NS1.WESTNET.NET.
                        1W IN NS        NS.UTAH.EDU.
```

How do you find out how to contact the administrator of *boulder.co.us*? You can try *whois*, but since *boulder.co.us* isn't a top-level country domain or a subdomain of a generic top-level domain, you won't find much. Fortunately, the U.S. NIC provides a list of email addresses of contacts for each third-level subdomain of *us* at *http://www.isi.edu/in-notes/us-domain-delegated.txt*. If you can't find the information you need there, you can still use *nslookup* to find the SOA record for the *boulder.co.us* zone, just as you did to find out whom to ask about *csiro.au*. Though the people who read mail sent to the address in the SOA record may not handle registration themselves (technical and administrative functions for the zone may be divided), it's a good bet that they know the folks who do and can direct you to them.

Here's how you'd use *nslookup* to dig up the SOA record for *boulder.co.us*:

```
% nslookup
Default Server:  boulder.colorado.edu
Address:  128.138.238.18, 128.138.240.1

> set type=soa       —Look up SOA record
> boulder.co.us.     —for boulder.co.us
Default Server:  boulder.colorado.edu
Address:  128.138.238.18, 128.138.240.1

boulder.co.us
        origin = ns1.westnet.net
        mail addr = cgarner.westnet.net
        serial = 200004101
        refresh = 21600 (6H)
        retry  = 1200 (20M)
        expire = 3600000 (5w6d16h)
        minimum ttl = 432000 (5D)
```

As in the *csiro.au* example, you need to swap the first "." in the *mail addr* field for an "@" before you use it. Thus, *cgarner.westnet.net* becomes *cgarner@westnet.net*.

To request delegation of a subdomain of *boulder.co.us*, you can download a copy of the registration form template from *http://www.nic.us/cgi-bin/template.pl* and mail it to the contact.

If, however, you find that the subdomain for your locality hasn't yet been created, then read through the *us* domain's delegation policy at *http://www.nic.us/register/locality.html* and fill out the registration form at *http://www.nic.us/cgi-bin/template.pl.*

The generic top-level domains

As we mentioned earlier, there are many reasons that you might want to ask for a subdomain of one of the generic top-level domains like *com*, *net*, and *org*: you work for a multi- or transnational company, you like the fact that they're better-known, or you just like the sound of your domain name better with *com* on the end. Let's go through a short example of choosing a domain name under a generic top-level domain.

Imagine you're the network administrator for a think tank in Hopkins, Minnesota. You've just gotten a connection to the Internet through a commercial ISP. Your company has never had so much as a UUCP link, so you're not currently registered in the Internet namespace.

Since you're in the United States, you have the choice of joining either *us* or one of the generic top-level domains. Your think tank is world-renowned, though, so *us* wouldn't be a good choice. A subdomain of *com* would be best.

The think tank is known as The Gizmonic Institute, so you decide *gizmonics.com* might be an appropriate domain name. Now you've got to check whether the name *gizmonics.com* has been taken by anyone, so you use an account you have at UMN:

```
% nslookup
Default Server:  ns.unet.umn.edu
Address:  128.101.101.101

> set type=any     —Look for any records
> gizmonics.com.   —for gizmonics.com
Server:  ns.unet.umn.edu
Address:  128.101.101.101

gizmonics.com   nameserver = NS2.SFO.WENET.NET
gizmonics.com   nameserver = NS1.SFO.WENET.NET
```

Whoops! Looks like *gizmonics.com* is already taken (who would have thought?).[*] Well, *gizmonic-institute.com* is a little longer, but still intuitive:

```
% nslookup
Default Server:  ns.unet.umn.edu
Address:  128.101.101.101
```

---

[*] Actually, *gizmonics.com* is taken by Joel Hodgson, the guy who dreamed up The Gizmonic Institute and Mystery Science Theater 3000 in the first place.

```
> set type=any        —Look for any records
> gizmonic-institute.com.    —for gizmonic-institute.com
Server:  ns.unet.umn.edu
Address:  128.101.101.101
```

```
*** ns.unet.umn.edu can't find gizmonic-institute.com.: Non-existent host/domain
```

Happily, *gizmonic-institute.com* is free, so you can go on to the next step: picking a registrar.

Choosing a registrar

Choose a registrar? Welcome to the brave new world of competition! Before the spring of 1999, a single company, Network Solutions Inc., was both the registry and sole registrar for *com*, *net*, and *org*, as well as *edu*. To register a subdomain of any of the generic top-level domains, you had to go to Network Solutions.

In June 1999, ICANN, the organization that manages the domain name space (we mentioned them in the last chapter) introduced competition to the registrar function of *com*, *net*, and *org*. There are now dozens of *com*, *net*, and *org* registrars you can choose from. There's a list of them at *http://www.internic.net/regist.html*.

We won't presume to tell you how to pick a registrar, but take a look at the price and any other services the registrar provides that might interest you. See if you can get a nice package deal on registration and aluminum siding, for example.

Checking That Your Network Is Registered

Before proceeding, you should also check whether your IP network or networks are registered. Some registrars won't delegate a subdomain to name servers on unregistered networks, and network registries (we'll talk about them shortly) won't delegate an *in-addr.arpa* zone that corresponds to an unregistered network.

An IP network defines a range of IP addresses. For example, the network 15/8 is made up of all IP addresses in the range 15.0.0.0 to 15.255.255.255. The network 199.10.25/24 starts at 199.10.25.0 and ends at 199.10.25.255.

The InterNIC was once the official source of all IP networks: they assigned all IP networks to Internet-connected networks and made sure no two address ranges overlapped. Nowadays, the InterNIC's old role has been largely assumed by Internet service providers (ISPs), who allocate space from their own networks for customers to use. If you know your network came from your ISP, the larger network from which your network was carved is probably registered (to your ISP). You may still want to double-check that your ISP took care of registering their network, but you don't (and probably can't) do anything yourself besides nagging your ISP if they didn't register their network. Once you've verified their registration, you can skip the rest of this section and move on.

A Sidebar on CIDR

Once upon a time, when we wrote the first edition of this book, the Internet's 32-bit address space was divided up into three main classes of networks: class A, class B, and class C. Class A networks were networks in which the first octet (the first eight bits) of the IP address identified the network, and the remaining bits were used by the organization running the network to differentiate hosts on the network. Most organizations with class A networks also subdivided their networks into subnetworks, or subnets, adding another level of hierarchy to the addressing scheme. Class B networks devoted two octets to the network identifier and two to the host; class C networks gave three octets to the network identifier and one to the host.

Unfortunately, this small/medium/large system of networks didn't work well for everyone. Many organizations were large enough to require more than a class C network, which could accommodate at most 254 hosts, but too small to warrant a full class B network, which could serve 65534 hosts. Many of these organizations were allocated class B networks, anyway. Consequently, class B networks quickly became scarce.

To help solve this problem and create networks that were just the right size for all sorts of organizations, *Classless Inter-Domain Routing*, or CIDR (pronounced "cider"), was developed. As the name implies, CIDR does away with the old class A, class B, and class C network designations. Instead of allocating either one, two, or three octets to the network identifier, the allocator could assign any number of contiguous bits of the IP address to the network identifier. So, for example, if an organization needed an address space roughly four times as large as a class B network, the powers-that-be could assign it a network identifier of 14 bits, leaving 18 bits (four class Bs' worth) of space to use.

Naturally, the advent of CIDR made the "classful" terminology outdated— although it's still used a good deal in casual conversation. Now, to designate a particular CIDR network, we specify the particular high-order bit value assigned to an organization, expressed in dotted-octet notation, and how many bits identify the network. The two terms are separated by a slash. So 15/8 is the old class A-sized network that begins with the eight bit pattern 00001111. The old class B-sized network 128.32.0.0 is now 128.32/16. And the network 192.168.0.128/25 consists of the 128 IP addresses from 192.168.0.128 through 192.168.0.255.

If, however, your network was assigned by the InterNIC way back when, or if you *are* an ISP, you should check to see whether your network is registered. Where do you go to check whether your network is registered? Why, to the same organizations that register networks, of course. These organizations, called (what else?) network registries, handle network registration in some part of the world. In the western hemisphere, ARIN, the American Registry of Internet Numbers (*http://www.arin.net*) hands out IP address space and registers networks. In Asia and the Pacific, APNIC, the Asia Pacific Network Information Center (*http://www.apnic.net*) serves the same function. In Europe, it's the RIPE Network Coordination Centre (*http://www.ripe.net*). Each registry may also delegate registration authority for a region; for example, ARIN delegates registration authority for Mexico and Brazil to network registries in each country. Be sure to check for a network registry local to your country.

If you're not sure your network is registered, the best way to find out is to use the *whois* service provided by the various network registries and look for your network. Here are the URLs for each registry's *whois* page:

ARIN
> *http://www.arin.net/whois/index.html*

APNIC
> *http://whois.apnic.net*

RIPE
> *http://www.ripe.net/cgi-bin/whois*

If you find out your network isn't registered, you'll need to get it registered before setting up your *in-addr.arpa* zones. Each registry has a different process for registering networks, but most involve money changing hands (from your hands to theirs, unfortunately).

You may find out that your network is already assigned to your ISP. If this is the case, you don't need to register independently with the network registry.

Once all your Internet-connected hosts are on registered networks, it's time to register your zones.

Registering Your Zones

Different registrars have different registration policies and procedures, but at this point, most handle registration online, through their web sites. Since you found or chose your registrar earlier in the chapter, we'll assume you know which web site to go to.

The basic information that any registrar needs is the domain names and addresses of your name servers and enough information about you to send you a bill or charge your credit card. If you're not connected to the Internet, give them the addresses of the Internet hosts that will act as your name servers. Some registrars also require that you already have operational name servers for your zone. (Those that don't may ask for an estimate of when the name servers will be fully operational.) If that's the case with your registrar, skip ahead to Chapter 4 and set up your name servers. Then contact your registrar with the requisite information.

Most registrars will also ask for some information about your organization, including administrative and technical contacts for your zone (who can be the same person). If your contacts aren't already registered in the registrar's *whois* database, you'll also need to provide information to register them in *whois*. This includes their names, surface mail addresses, phone numbers, and electronic mail addresses. If they are already registered in *whois*, just specify their *whois* "handle" (a unique alphanumeric ID) in the registration.

There's another aspect of registering a new zone that we should mention: cost. Most registrars are commercial enterprises and charge money for registering domain names. Network Solutions, the original registrar for *com, net,* and *org,* charges $35 per year to register subdomains under the generic top-level domains. (If you already have a subdomain under *com, net,* or *org* and haven't received a bill from Network Solutions recently, it'd be a good idea to check your contact information with *whois* to make sure they've got a current address and phone number for you.)

If you're directly connected to the Internet, you should also have the *in-addr.arpa* zones corresponding to your IP networks delegated to you. For example, if your company has been allocated the network 192.201.44/24, you should manage the *44.201.192.in-addr.arpa* zone. This will let you control the IP address-to-name mappings for hosts on your network. Chapter 4 also explains how to set up your *in-addr.arpa* zones.

In the last section, "Checking That Your Network Is Registered," we asked you to find the answers to several questions: is your network a slice of an ISP's network? Is your network, or the ISP's network that your network is part of, registered? In which network registry? You'll need these answers to have your *in-addr.arpa* zones delegated to you.

If your network is part of a larger network registered to an ISP, you should contact the ISP to have the appropriate subdomains of their *in-addr.arpa* zone delegated to you. Each ISP uses a different process for setting up *in-addr.arpa* delegation. Your ISP's web page is a good place to research that process. If you can't find the information there, try looking up the SOA record for the *in-addr. arpa* zone that corresponds to your ISP's network. For example, if your network is part of UUNET's 153.35/16 network, you could look up the SOA record of *35.153. in-addr.arpa* to find the email address of the technical contact for the zone.

If your network is registered directly with one of the regional network registries, contact them to get your *in-addr.arpa* zone registered. Each network registry makes information on its delegation process available on its web site.

Now that you've registered your zones, you'd better take some time to get your house in order. You've got some name servers to set up, and in the next chapter we'll show you how.

4

Setting Up BIND

"It seems very pretty," she said when she had finished it, "but it's rather hard to understand!" (You see she didn't like to confess, even to herself, that she couldn't make it out at all.) "Somehow it seems to fill my head with ideas—only I don't exactly know what they are!"

If you have been diligently reading each chapter of this book, you're probably anxious to get a name server running. This chapter is for you. Let's set up a couple of name servers. Others of you may have read the table of contents and skipped directly to this chapter. (Shame on you!) If you are one of those people, be aware that we may use concepts from earlier chapters and expect you to understand them already.

There are several factors that influence how you should set up your name servers. The biggest is what sort of access you have to the Internet: complete access (e.g., you can FTP to *ftp.uu.net*), limited access (restricted by a security firewall), or no access at all. This chapter assumes you have complete access. We'll discuss the other cases in Chapter 11, *Security*.

In this chapter, we set up two name servers for a few fictitious zones as an example for you to follow in setting up your own zones. We cover the topics in this chapter in enough detail to get your first two name servers running. Subsequent chapters fill in the holes and go into greater depth. If you already have your name servers running, skim through this chapter to familiarize yourself with the terms we use or just to verify that you didn't miss something when you set up your servers.

Our Zone

Our fictitious zone serves a college. Movie University studies all aspects of the film industry and researches novel ways to distribute films. One of our most promising projects involves research into using IP as a film distribution medium. After visiting our registrar's web site, we have decided on the domain name *movie.edu*. A recent grant has enabled us to connect to the Internet.

Movie U. currently has two Ethernets, and we have plans to add another network or two. The Ethernets have network numbers 192.249.249/24 and 192.253.253/24. A portion of our host table contains the following entries:

```
127.0.0.1      localhost

# These are our killer machines

192.249.249.2  robocop.movie.edu robocop
192.249.249.3  terminator.movie.edu terminator bigt
192.249.249.4  diehard.movie.edu diehard dh

# These machines are in horror(ible) shape and will be replaced
# soon.

192.253.253.2  misery.movie.edu misery
192.253.253.3  shining.movie.edu shining
192.253.253.4  carrie.movie.edu carrie

# A wormhole is a fictitious phenomenon that instantly transports
# space travelers over long distances and is not known to be
# stable.  The only difference between wormholes and routers is
# that routers don't transport packets as instantly--especially
# ours.

192.249.249.1  wormhole.movie.edu wormhole wh wh249
192.253.253.1  wormhole.movie.edu wormhole wh wh253
```

And the network is pictured in Figure 4-1.

Setting Up Zone Data

Our first step in setting up the Movie U. name servers is to translate the host table into equivalent DNS zone data. The DNS version of the data has multiple files. One file maps all the host names to addresses. Other files map the addresses back to host names. The name-to-address lookup is sometimes called *forward mapping*, and the address-to-name lookup *reverse mapping*. Each network has its own file for reverse-mapping data.

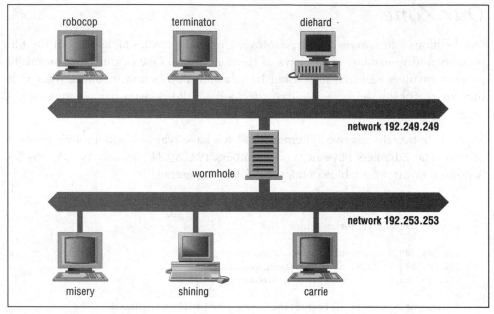

Figure 4-1. The Movie University network

As a convention in this book, a file that maps host names to addresses is called *db.DOMAIN*. For *movie.edu*, this file is called *db.movie.edu*. The files mapping addresses to host names are called *db.ADDR*, where ADDR is the network number without trailing zeros or the specification of a netmask. In our example, the files are called *db.192.249.249* and *db.192.253.253*; there's one for each network. The *db* is short for database. We'll refer to the collection of *db.DOMAIN* and *db.ADDR* files as *zone data files*. There are a few other zone data files: *db.cache* and *db.127.0.0*. These files are overhead. Each name server must have them, and they are more or less the same for each server.

To tie all the zone data files together, a name server needs a configuration file— for BIND Version 4, this file is usually called */etc/named.boot*. For BIND Versions 8 and 9, it is usually called */etc/named.conf*. The format of the zone data files is common to all DNS implementations: it's called the *master file format*. The format of the configuration files, on the other hand, is specific to the name server implementation—in this case, BIND.

The Zone Data Files

Most entries in zone data files are called DNS resource records. DNS lookups are case-insensitive, so you can enter names in your zone data files in uppercase, lowercase, or mixed case. We tend to use all lowercase. However, even though lookups are case-insensitive, case is preserved. That way, if you add records for

Tootsie.movie.edu to your zone data, people looking up *tootsie.movie.edu* will find the records, but with a capital "T" in the domain name.

Resource records must start in the first column of a line. The resource records in the example files in this book do start in the first column, but they may look indented because of the way the book is formatted. In the DNS RFCs, the examples present the resource records in a certain order. Most people have chosen to follow that order, as we have here, but the order is not a requirement. The order of resource records in the zone data files is as follows:

SOA record
> Indicates *authority* for this zone

NS record
> Lists a *name server* for this zone

Other records
> Data about hosts in this zone

Of the other records, this chapter covers:

A
> Name-to-address mapping

PTR
> Address-to-name mapping

CNAME
> Canonical name (for aliases)

Those of you who have some experience with the master file format will no doubt look at our data and say to yourselves, "It would have been shorter to specify it this other way…." We're not using abbreviations or shortcuts in our zone data, at least not initially, so that you'll understand the full syntax of each resource record. Once you understand the long version, we'll go back and "tighten up" the files.

Comments

The zone data files are easier to read if they contain comments and blank lines. Comments start with a semicolon and finish at the end of the line. As you might guess, the name server ignores comments and blank lines.

Setting the Zone's Default TTL

Before we start writing our zone data file, we have to find out what version of BIND we're running. The version makes a difference because the way you set the default time to live for a zone changed in BIND 8.2. Prior to BIND 8.2, the last field in the SOA record set the default TTL for a zone. But just before BIND 8.2 came out, RFC 2308 was published, which changed the meaning of the final field in the SOA record to the *negative caching TTL*. This is how long a remote name server can cache *negative responses* about the zone, answers that say that a particular domain name or the type of data sought for a particular domain name doesn't exist.

So how do you set a default TTL for a zone in BIND 8.2 and later? With the new $TTL control statement. $TTL specifies the time to live for all records in the file that follow the statement (but precede any other $TTL statements) and don't have an explicit TTL.

The name server supplies this TTL in query responses, allowing other servers to cache the data for the TTL interval. If your data doesn't change much, you might consider using a default TTL of several days. One week is about the longest value that makes sense. You can use a value as short as one hour, but we typically don't recommend TTLs lower than that because of the amount of DNS traffic they cause.

Since we're running a new version of BIND, we need to set a default TTL for our zones with a $TTL statement. Three hours seems about right to us, so we start our zone data files with:

```
$TTL 3h
```

If you're running a name server older than BIND 8.2, don't try adding a $TTL statement—the name server won't understand it and will treat it as a syntax error.

SOA Records

The next entry (the first for pre-8.2 BIND servers) in each of these files is the SOA (start of authority) resource record. The SOA record indicates that this name server is the best source of information for the data within this zone. Our name server is authoritative for the zone *movie.edu* because of the SOA record. An SOA record is required in each *db.DOMAIN* and *db.ADDR* file. There can be one, and only one, SOA record in a zone data file.

We added the following SOA record to the *db.movie.edu* file:

```
movie.edu. IN SOA terminator.movie.edu. al.robocop.movie.edu. (
                        1          ; Serial
                        3h         ; Refresh after 3 hours
                        1h         ; Retry after 1 hour
                        1w         ; Expire after 1 week
                        1h )       ; Negative caching TTL of 1 day
```

The name *movie.edu.* must start in the first column of the file. Make sure the name ends with a trailing dot, as ours does here, or you'll be surprised at the result! (We'll explain later in this chapter.)

The IN stands for Internet. This is one class of data—other classes exist, but none of them is currently in widespread use. Our examples use only the IN class. The class field is optional. If the class is omitted, the name server determines the class from the statement in the configuration file that instructs it to read this file. We'll see this later in the chapter, too.

The first name after SOA (*terminator.movie.edu.*) is the name of the primary master name server for the *movie.edu* zone. The second name (*al.robocop.movie.edu.*) is the mail address of the person in charge of the zone if you replace the first "." with an "@". Often you'll see *root*, *postmaster*, or *hostmaster* as the email address. Name servers won't use this address—it's meant for human consumption. If you have a problem with a zone, you can send a message to the listed email address. BIND 4.9 and later versions provide another resource record type, RP (responsible person), for this purpose also. The RP record is discussed in Chapter 7, *Maintaining BIND*.

The parentheses allow the SOA record to span more than one line. Most of the fields within the parentheses of the SOA record are for use by slave name servers and are discussed when we introduce slave name servers later in this chapter. For now, assume these are reasonable values.

We add similar SOA records to the beginning of the *db.192.249.249* and *db.192. 253.253* files. In these files, we change the first name in the SOA record from *movie.edu.* to the name of the appropriate *in-addr.arpa* zone: *249.249.192.in-addr.arpa.* and *253. 253.192.in-addr.arpa.*, respectively.

NS Records

The next entries we add to each file are NS (name server) resource records. We add one NS record for each name server authoritative for our zone. Here are the NS records from the *db.movie.edu* file:

```
movie.edu.  IN NS  terminator.movie.edu.
movie.edu.  IN NS  wormhole.movie.edu.
```

These records indicate that there are two name servers for the zone *movie.edu.* The name servers are on the hosts *terminator.movie.edu* and *wormhole.movie.edu.* Multihomed hosts, like *wormhole.movie.edu*, are excellent choices for name servers because they are "well-connected." They are directly accessible by hosts on more than one network and, if they also serve as routers, are not often down because they are closely monitored. We'll cover more on where to place your name servers in Chapter 8, *Growing Your Domain*.

As with the SOA record, we add NS records to the *db.192.249.249* and *db.192. 253.253* files, too.

Address and Alias Records

Next, we create the name-to-address mappings. We add the following resource records to the *db.movie.edu* file:

```
;
; Host addresses
;
localhost.movie.edu.   IN A    127.0.0.1
robocop.movie.edu.     IN A    192.249.249.2
terminator.movie.edu.  IN A    192.249.249.3
diehard.movie.edu.     IN A    192.249.249.4
misery.movie.edu.      IN A    192.253.253.2
shining.movie.edu.     IN A    192.253.253.3
carrie.movie.edu.      IN A    192.253.253.4
;
; Multi-homed hosts
;
wormhole.movie.edu.    IN A    192.249.249.1
wormhole.movie.edu.    IN A    192.253.253.1
;
; Aliases
;
bigt.movie.edu.        IN CNAME terminator.movie.edu.
dh.movie.edu.          IN CNAME diehard.movie.edu.
wh.movie.edu.          IN CNAME wormhole.movie.edu.
wh249.movie.edu.       IN A    192.249.249.1
wh253.movie.edu.       IN A    192.253.253.1
```

The first two blocks are probably not a surprise. The A stands for address, and each resource record maps a name to an address. *wormhole.movie.edu* acts as a router. It has two addresses associated with its name and therefore two address records. Unlike host table lookups, a DNS lookup can return more than one address for a name; a lookup of *wormhole.movie.edu* returns two. If the requestor and name server are on the same network, some name servers place the "closest" address first in the response for better performance. This feature is called *address sorting* and is covered in Chapter 10, *Advanced Features*. If address sorting does not apply, the addresses are *rotated* between queries so subsequent responses list them in a different order. This "round robin" feature first shows up in BIND 4.9.

The third block has the host table aliases. For the first three aliases, we created CNAME (canonical name) resource records. However, we created address records for the other two aliases (more on this in a moment). A CNAME record maps an alias to its canonical name. The name server handles CNAME records differently from the way aliases are handled in the host table. When a name server looks up a name and finds a CNAME record, it replaces the name with the canonical name and looks up the new name. For example, when the name server looks up *wh.movie.edu*, it finds a CNAME record pointing to *wormhole.movie.edu*. It then looks up *wormhole.movie.edu* and returns both addresses.

There is one thing to remember about aliases like *bigt.movie.edu*—they should never appear on the right-hand side of a resource record. Stated differently, you should always use the canonical name (e.g., *terminator.movie.edu*) in the data portion of the resource record. Notice that the NS records we just created use the canonical name.

The final two entries solve a special problem. Suppose you have a router, like *wormhole.movie.edu*, and you want to check one of the interfaces. One common troubleshooting technique is to *ping* the interface to verify that it is responding. If you *ping* the name *wormhole.movie.edu*, the name server returns both addresses for the name. *ping* uses the first address in the list. But which address is first?

With the host table, we choose the address we want by using either *wh249.movie. edu* or *wh253.movie.edu*; each name referred to *one* of the host's addresses. To provide an equivalent capability with DNS, we don't make *wh249.movie.edu* and *wh253.movie.edu* into aliases (CNAME records). That would result in both addresses for *wormhole.movie.edu* being returned when the alias was looked up. Instead, we use address records. Now, to check the operation of the 192.253.253.1 interface on *wormhole.movie.edu*, we *ping wh253.movie.edu* since it refers to only one address. The same applies to *wh249.movie.edu*.

To state this as a general rule: if a host is multihomed (has more than one network interface), create an address (A) record for each alias unique to one address. Create a CNAME record for each alias common to all the addresses.

Now, don't tell your users about names like *wh249.movie.edu* and *wh253.movie. edu*. Those names are meant for system-administration purposes only. If users learn to use names like *wh249.movie.edu*, they'll be confused when the name doesn't work for them in some places, like *.rhosts* files. That's because these places need the name that results from looking up the address: the canonical name, *wormhole.movie.edu*.

Since we use A (address) records for the *wh249.movie.edu* and *wh253.movie.edu* aliases, you might ask, "Is it okay to use address records instead of CNAME records in *all* cases?" Well, using address records instead of CNAME records doesn't cause problems with most applications, since most applications care only about finding IP addresses. There is one application—*sendmail*—whose behavior changes, though. *sendmail* usually replaces aliases in mail headers with their canonical names; this canonicalization happens only if the names in the mail header have CNAME data associated with them. If you don't use CNAME records for aliases, your *sendmail* will have to understand all the possible aliases your host might be known by, which will require extra *sendmail* configuration on your part.

In addition to the problem with *sendmail*, users might be confused when they try to figure out the canonical name to enter in their *.rhosts* file. Looking up a name that has CNAME data leads them to the canonical name, whereas address data won't. In this case, users *should* instead be looking up the IP address to get the canonical name, as *rlogind* does, but users like these never seem to be on systems we administer.

PTR Records

Next we create the address-to-name mappings. The file *db.192.249.249* maps addresses to host names for the 192.249.249/24 network. The DNS resource records used for this mapping are PTR (pointer) records. There is one record for each network interface on this network. (Recall that addresses are looked up as names in DNS. The address is reversed and *in-addr.arpa* is appended.)

Here are the PTR records we added for network 192.249.249/24:

```
1.249.249.192.in-addr.arpa.    IN PTR wormhole.movie.edu.
2.249.249.192.in-addr.arpa.    IN PTR robocop.movie.edu.
3.249.249.192.in-addr.arpa.    IN PTR terminator.movie.edu.
4.249.249.192.in-addr.arpa.    IN PTR diehard.movie.edu.
```

There are a couple of things you should notice about this data. First, addresses should point to only a single name: the canonical name. Thus, 192.249.249.1 maps to *wormhole.movie.edu*, not to *wh249.movie.edu*. You *can* create two PTR records, one for *wormhole.movie.edu* and one for *wh249.movie.edu*, but most systems are not prepared to see more than one name for an address. Second, even though *wormhole.movie.edu* has two addresses, you see only one of them here. That's because this file shows only the direct connections to network 192.249.249/24, and *wormhole.movie.edu* has only one connection there.

We created similar data for the 192.253.253/24 network.

The Completed Zone Data Files

Now that we've explained the various resource records in the zone data files, we'll show you what they look like with all the data in one place. Again, the actual order of these resource records does not matter.

Here are the contents of the file *db.movie.edu*:

```
$TTL 3h
movie.edu. IN SOA terminator.movie.edu. al.robocop.movie.edu. (
                    1          ; Serial
                    3h         ; Refresh after 3 hours
                    1h         ; Retry after 1 hour
                    1w         ; Expire after 1 week
                    1h )       ; Negative caching TTL of 1 hour


;
; Name servers
```

```
;
movie.edu.   IN NS   terminator.movie.edu.
movie.edu.   IN NS   wormhole.movie.edu.


;
; Addresses for the canonical names
;
localhost.movie.edu.    IN A     127.0.0.1
robocop.movie.edu.      IN A     192.249.249.2
terminator.movie.edu.   IN A     192.249.249.3
diehard.movie.edu.      IN A     192.249.249.4
misery.movie.edu.       IN A     192.253.253.2
shining.movie.edu.      IN A     192.253.253.3
carrie.movie.edu.       IN A     192.253.253.4
wormhole.movie.edu.     IN A     192.249.249.1
wormhole.movie.edu.     IN A     192.253.253.1


;
; Aliases
;
bigt.movie.edu.         IN CNAME terminator.movie.edu.
dh.movie.edu.           IN CNAME diehard.movie.edu.
wh.movie.edu.           IN CNAME wormhole.movie.edu.


;
; Interface specific names
;
wh249.movie.edu.        IN A     192.249.249.1
wh253.movie.edu.        IN A     192.253.253.1
```

Here are the contents of the file *db.192.249.249*:

```
$TTL 3h
249.249.192.in-addr.arpa. IN SOA terminator.movie.edu. al.robocop.movie.edu.(
                          1         ; Serial
                          3h        ; Refresh after 3 hours
                          1h        ; Retry after 1 hour
                          1w        ; Expire after 1 week
                          1h )      ; Negative caching TTL of 1 hour


;
; Name servers
;
249.249.192.in-addr.arpa.   IN NS   terminator.movie.edu.
249.249.192.in-addr.arpa.   IN NS   wormhole.movie.edu.


;
; Addresses point to canonical name
;
1.249.249.192.in-addr.arpa.  IN PTR wormhole.movie.edu.
2.249.249.192.in-addr.arpa.  IN PTR robocop.movie.edu.
3.249.249.192.in-addr.arpa.  IN PTR terminator.movie.edu.
4.249.249.192.in-addr.arpa.  IN PTR diehard.movie.edu.
```

And here are the contents of the file *db.192.253.253*:

```
$TTL 3h
253.253.192.in-addr.arpa. IN SOA terminator.movie.edu. al.robocop.movie.edu.(
                          1       ; Serial
                          3h      ; Refresh after 3 hours
                          1h      ; Retry after 1 hour
                          1w      ; Expire after 1 week
                          1h )    ; Negative caching TTL of 1 hour
;
; Name servers
;
253.253.192.in-addr.arpa.  IN NS  terminator.movie.edu.
253.253.192.in-addr.arpa.  IN NS  wormhole.movie.edu.


;
; Addresses point to canonical name
;
1.253.253.192.in-addr.arpa.  IN PTR wormhole.movie.edu.
2.253.253.192.in-addr.arpa.  IN PTR misery.movie.edu.
3.253.253.192.in-addr.arpa.  IN PTR shining.movie.edu.
4.253.253.192.in-addr.arpa.  IN PTR carrie.movie.edu.
```

The Loopback Address

A name server needs one additional *db.ADDR* file to cover the loopback network: the special address that hosts use to direct traffic to themselves. This network is (almost) always 127.0.0/24, and the host number is (almost) always 127.0.0.1. Therefore, the name of this file is *db.127.0.0*. No surprise here; it looks like the other *db.ADDR* files.

Here are the contents of the file *db.127.0.0*:

```
$TTL 3h
0.0.127.in-addr.arpa. IN SOA terminator.movie.edu. al.robocop.movie.edu. (
                      1       ; Serial
                      3h      ; Refresh after 3 hours
                      1h      ; Retry after 1 hour
                      1w      ; Expire after 1 week
                      1h )    ; Negative caching TTL of 1 hour

0.0.127.in-addr.arpa.  IN NS  terminator.movie.edu.
0.0.127.in-addr.arpa.  IN NS  wormhole.movie.edu.

1.0.0.127.in-addr.arpa.  IN PTR localhost.
```

Why do name servers need this silly little file? Think about it for a second. No one was given responsibility for network 127.0.0/24, yet systems use it for a loopback address. Since no one has direct responsibility, everyone who uses it is responsible for it individually. You could omit this file and your name server would operate. However, a lookup of 127.0.0.1 might fail because the root name server

contacted wasn't itself configured to map 127.0.0.1 to a name. You should provide the mapping yourself so there are no surprises.

The Root Hints Data

Besides your local information, the name server also needs to know where the
name servers for the root zone are. You must retrieve this information from the
Internet host *ftp.rs.internic.net* (198.41.0.6). Use anonymous FTP to retrieve the file
named.root from the *domain* subdirectory. (*named.root* is the same file we've
been calling *db.cache*. Just rename it *db.cache* after you've retrieved it.)

```
;         This file holds the information on root name servers needed to
;         initialize cache of Internet domain name servers
;         (e.g. reference this file in the "cache  .  <file>"
;         configuration file of BIND domain name servers).
;
;         This file is made available by InterNIC registration services
;         under anonymous FTP as
;              file               /domain/named.root
;              on server          FTP.RS.INTERNIC.NET
;         -OR- under Gopher at    RS.INTERNIC.NET
;              under menu         InterNIC Registration Services (NSI)
;                submenu          InterNIC Registration Archives
;              file               named.root
;
;         last update:    Aug 22, 1997
;         related version of root zone:   1997082200
;
;
; formerly NS.INTERNIC.NET
;
.                         3600000  IN  NS   A.ROOT-SERVERS.NET.
A.ROOT-SERVERS.NET.       3600000      A    198.41.0.4
;
; formerly NS1.ISI.EDU
;
.                         3600000      NS   B.ROOT-SERVERS.NET.
B.ROOT-SERVERS.NET.       3600000      A    128.9.0.107
;
; formerly C.PSI.NET
;
.                         3600000      NS   C.ROOT-SERVERS.NET.
C.ROOT-SERVERS.NET.       3600000      A    192.33.4.12
;
; formerly TERP.UMD.EDU
;
.                         3600000      NS   D.ROOT-SERVERS.NET.
D.ROOT-SERVERS.NET.       3600000      A    128.8.10.90
;
; formerly NS.NASA.GOV
;
```

```
.                                3600000     NS    E.ROOT-SERVERS.NET.
E.ROOT-SERVERS.NET.              3600000     A     192.203.230.10
;
; formerly NS.ISC.ORG
;
.                                3600000     NS    F.ROOT-SERVERS.NET.
F.ROOT-SERVERS.NET.              3600000     A     192.5.5.241
;
; formerly NS.NIC.DDN.MIL
;
.                                3600000     NS    G.ROOT-SERVERS.NET.
G.ROOT-SERVERS.NET.              3600000     A     192.112.36.4
;
; formerly AOS.ARL.ARMY.MIL
;
.                                3600000     NS    H.ROOT-SERVERS.NET.
H.ROOT-SERVERS.NET.              3600000     A     128.63.2.53
;
; formerly NIC.NORDU.NET
;
.                                3600000     NS    I.ROOT-SERVERS.NET.
I.ROOT-SERVERS.NET.              3600000     A     192.36.148.17
;
; temporarily housed at NSI (InterNIC)
;
.                                3600000     NS    J.ROOT-SERVERS.NET.
J.ROOT-SERVERS.NET.              3600000     A     198.41.0.10
;
; housed in LINX, operated by RIPE NCC
;
.                                3600000     NS    K.ROOT-SERVERS.NET.
K.ROOT-SERVERS.NET.              3600000     A     193.0.14.129
;
; temporarily housed at ISI (IANA)
;
.                                3600000     NS    L.ROOT-SERVERS.NET.
L.ROOT-SERVERS.NET.              3600000     A     198.32.64.12
;
; housed in Japan, operated by WIDE
;
.                                3600000     NS    M.ROOT-SERVERS.NET.
M.ROOT-SERVERS.NET.              3600000     A     202.12.27.33
; End of File
```

The domain name "." refers to the root zone. Since the root zone's name servers change over time, don't assume this list is current. Download a new version of *named.root.*

How is this file kept up to date? As the network administrator, that's your responsibility. Some old versions of BIND did update this file periodically. That feature was disabled, though; apparently, it didn't work as well as the authors had hoped. Sometimes the changed *db.cache* file is mailed to the *bind-users* or *namedroppers* mailing list. If you are on one of these lists, you are likely to hear about changes.

Can you put data other than root name server data in this file? You can, but it won't be used. Originally, the name server installed this data in its cache. However, the use of the file has changed (subtly) though the name "cache file" stuck. The name server stores the data in this file in a special place in memory as the *root hints*. It does not discard the hints if their TTLs drop to zero, as it would with cached data. The name server uses the hint data to query the root name servers for the current list of root name servers, which it caches. When the cached list of root name servers times out, the name server again uses the hints to get a new list.

Why does the name server bother querying a name server in the root hints file— probably itself a root name server—for a list of root name servers when it already has a list? Because that name server almost certainly knows the *current* list of root name servers, while the file may be out of date.

What are the 3600000s for? That's an explicit time to live for the records in the file. In older versions of this file, this number was 99999999. Since the contents of this file were originally cached, the name server needed to know how long to keep those records active. 99999999 seconds was just a very long time—the root name server data was to be kept in cache for as long as the server ran. Since the name server now stores this data in a special place and doesn't discard it if it times out, the TTL is unnecessary. But it's not harmful to have the 3600000s, and it makes for interesting BIND folklore when you pass responsibility to the next name server administrator.

Setting Up a BIND Configuration File

Now that we've created the zone data files, a name server must be instructed to read each of the files. For BIND, the mechanism for pointing the server to its zone data files is the configuration file. Up to this point, we've been discussing files whose data and format are described in the DNS specifications. The configuration file, though, is specific to BIND and is not defined in the DNS RFCs.

The BIND configuration file syntax changed significantly between Version 4 and Version 8. Mercifully, it didn't change at all between BIND 8 and BIND 9. We'll first show you the BIND 4 syntax, and then the equivalent BIND 8 and 9 syntax. You'll have to check the *named** manual page to find out which you need to use. If you already have a BIND 4 configuration file, you can convert it to a BIND 8 or 9 configuration file by running the program *named-bootconf,* which is distributed with the BIND source code. In BIND 8, the program is in *src/bin/named-bootconf.* In BIND 9, it's in *contrib/named-bootconf.*

---

* *named* is pronounced "name-dee" and stands for "name server daemon." BIND is pronounced to rhyme with "kind." Some creative people have noticed the similarities in the names and choose to mispronounce them "bin-dee" and "named" (like "tamed").

In BIND 4, comments in the configuration file are the same as in the zone data files—they start with a semicolon and stop at the end of the line:

```
; This is a comment
```

In BIND 8 and 9, you can use any of three styles of comments: C-style, C++-style, or shell-style:

```
/* This is a C-style comment */
// This is a C++-style comment
# This is a shell-style comment
```

Don't use a BIND 4–style comment in a BIND 8 or 9 configuration file—it won't work. The semicolon ends a configuration statement instead of starting a comment.

Usually, configuration files contain a line indicating the directory in which the zone data files are located. The name server changes its directory to this location before reading the zone data files. This allows the filenames to be specified relative to the current directory instead of as full pathnames. Here's how a BIND 4 directory line looks:

```
directory /var/named
```

Here's how a BIND 8 or 9 directory line looks:

```
options {
        directory "/var/named";
        // Place additional options here.
};
```

Only one *options* statement is allowed in the configuration file, so any additional options mentioned later in this book must be added along with the *directory* option.

On a primary master server, the configuration file contains one line for each zone data file to be read. For BIND 4, this line comprises three fields—the word *primary* (starting in the first column), the domain name of the zone, and the filename:

```
primary movie.edu                    db.movie.edu
primary 249.249.192.in-addr.arpa db.192.249.249
primary 253.253.192.in-addr.arpa db.192.253.253
primary 0.0.127.in-addr.arpa      db.127.0.0
```

For BIND 8 or 9, the line starts with the keyword *zone* followed by the domain name and the class (*in* stands for Internet). The type *master* is the same as the BIND 4 *primary*. The last field is the filename:

```
zone "movie.edu" in {
        type master;
        file "db.movie";
};
```

Earlier in this chapter, we mentioned that if we omitted the class field from a resource record, the name server would determine the right class to use from the configuration file. The *in* in the *zone* statement sets that class to the Internet class. The *in* is also the default for a BIND 8 or 9 *zone* statement, so you can leave out the field entirely for Internet class zones. Since the BIND 4 syntax doesn't have a place to specify the class of a zone, the default is *in* for BIND 4, too.

Here is the BIND 4 configuration file line to read the root hints file:

```
cache   .   db.cache
```

and the equivalent BIND 8 or 9 configuration file line:[*]

```
zone "." in {
        type hint;
        file "db.cache";
};
```

As mentioned earlier, this file is not for general cache data. It contains only the root name server *hints*.

By default, BIND 4 expects the configuration file to be named */etc/named.boot*, but it can be changed with a command-line option. BIND 8 and 9 expect the configuration file to be named */etc/named.conf* instead of */etc/named.boot*. The zone data files for our example are in the directory */var/named*. Which directory you use doesn't really matter. Just avoid putting the directory in the root filesystem if the root filesystem is short on space, and make sure that the filesystem the directory is in is mounted before the name server starts. Here is the complete BIND 4 */etc/named.boot* file:

```
; BIND configuration file

directory /var/named

primary  movie.edu                   db.movie.edu
primary  249.249.192.in-addr.arpa db.192.249.249
primary  253.253.192.in-addr.arpa db.192.253.253
primary  0.0.127.in-addr.arpa        db.127.0.0
cache    .                           db.cache
```

Here is the complete BIND 8 or 9 */etc/named.conf* file:

```
// BIND configuration file

options {
        directory "/var/named";
        // Place additional options here.
};
```

---

[*] Actually, BIND 9 has a built-in *hints* zone, so you don't need to include a *zone* statement for the hints zone in *named.conf*. Including one doesn't hurt, though, and it gives us the willies not to see one in the configuration file, so we include one anyway.

```
zone "movie.edu" in {
        type master;
        file "db.movie.edu";
};

zone "249.249.192.in-addr.arpa" in {
        type master;
        file "db.192.249.249";
};

zone "253.253.192.in-addr.arpa" in {
        type master;
        file "db.192.253.253";
};

zone "0.0.127.in-addr.arpa" in {
        type master;
        file "db.127.0.0";
};

zone "." in {
        type hint;
        file "db.cache";
};
```

Abbreviations

At this point, we have created all the files necessary for a primary master name server. Let's go back and revisit the zone data files; there are shortcuts we didn't use. Unless you see and understand the long form first, though, the short form can look very cryptic. Now that you know the long form and have seen the BIND configuration file, we'll show you the shortcuts.

Appending Domain Names

The second field of a *primary* directive (BIND 4) or *zone* statement (BIND 8 and 9) specifies a domain name. This domain name is the key to the most useful shortcut. This domain name is the *origin* of all the data in the zone data file. The origin is appended to all names in the zone data file that don't end in a dot, and will be different for each zone data file since each file describes a different zone.

Since the origin is appended to names, instead of entering *robocop.movie.edu*'s address in *db.movie.edu* like this:

```
robocop.movie.edu.    IN A     192.249.249.2
```

we could have entered it like this:

```
robocop     IN A     192.249.249.2
```

In the *db.192.24.249* file we entered this:

```
2.249.249.192.in-addr.arpa.  IN PTR robocop.movie.edu.
```

Since *249.249.192.in-addr.arpa* is the origin, we could have entered:

```
2  IN PTR robocop.movie.edu.
```

Remember our earlier warning not to omit the trailing dot when using the fully qualified domain names? Suppose you forget the trailing dot. An entry like:

```
robocop.movie.edu    IN A    192.249.249.2
```

turns into an entry for *robocop.movie.edu.movie.edu*, not what you intended at all.

The @ Notation

If a domain name is the *same* as the origin, the name can be specified as "@". This is most often seen in the SOA record in the zone data files. The SOA records could have been entered this way:

```
@ IN SOA terminator.movie.edu. al.robocop.movie.edu. (
                    1          ; Serial
                    3h         ; Refresh after 3 hours
                    1h         ; Retry after 1 hour
                    1w         ; Expire after 1 week
                    1h )       ; Negative caching TTL of 1 hour
```

Repeat Last Name

If a resource record name (that starts in the first column) is a space or tab, then the name from the last resource record is used. You use this if there are multiple resource records for a name. Here's an example in which there are two address records for one name:

```
wormhole   IN A    192.249.249.1
           IN A    192.253.253.1
```

In the second address record, the name *wormhole* is implied. You can use this shortcut even if the resource records are of different types.

The Shortened Zone Data Files

Now that we have shown you the abbreviations, we'll repeat the zone data files, making use of these shortcuts.

Here are the contents of the file *db.movie.edu*:

```
$TTL 3h
;
; Origin added to names not ending
; in a dot: movie.edu
;
```

```
@ IN SOA terminator.movie.edu. al.robocop.movie.edu. (
                        1          ; Serial
                        3h         ; Refresh after 3 hours
                        1h         ; Retry after 1 hour
                        1w         ; Expire after 1 week
                        1h )       ; Negative caching TTL of 1 hour

;
; Name servers (The name '@' is implied)
;
            IN NS   terminator.movie.edu.
            IN NS   wormhole.movie.edu.


;
; Addresses for the canonical names
;
localhost   IN A       127.0.0.1
robocop     IN A       192.249.249.2
terminator  IN A       192.249.249.3
diehard     IN A       192.249.249.4
misery      IN A       192.253.253.2
shining     IN A       192.253.253.3
carrie      IN A       192.253.253.4

wormhole    IN A       192.249.249.1
            IN A       192.253.253.1


;
; Aliases
;
bigt        IN CNAME terminator
dh          IN CNAME diehard
wh          IN CNAME wormhole


;
; Interface specific names
;
wh249       IN A       192.249.249.1
wh253       IN A       192.253.253.1
```

Here are the contents of the file *db.192.249.249*:

```
$TTL 3h
;
; Origin added to names not ending
; in a dot: 249.249.192.in-addr.arpa
;


@ IN SOA terminator.movie.edu. al.robocop.movie.edu. (
                        1          ; Serial
                        3h         ; Refresh after 3 hours
                        1h         ; Retry after 1 hour
                        1w         ; Expire after 1 week
                        1h )       ; Negative caching TTL of 1 hour
```

```
;
; Name servers (The name '@' is implied)
;
     IN NS  terminator.movie.edu.
     IN NS  wormhole.movie.edu.


;
; Addresses point to canonical names
;
1  IN PTR wormhole.movie.edu.
2  IN PTR robocop.movie.edu.
3  IN PTR terminator.movie.edu.
4  IN PTR diehard.movie.edu.
```

Here are the contents of the file *db.192.253.253*:

```
$TTL 3h
;
; Origin added to names not ending
; in a dot: 253.253.192.in-addr.arpa
;

@ IN SOA terminator.movie.edu. al.robocop.movie.edu. (
                        1         ; Serial
                        3h        ; Refresh after 3 hours
                        1h        ; Retry after 1 hour
                        1w        ; Expire after 1 week
                        1h )      ; Negative caching TTL of 1 hour


;
; Name servers (The name '@' is implied)
;
     IN NS   terminator.movie.edu.
     IN NS   wormhole.movie.edu.


;
; Addresses point to canonical names
;
1  IN PTR wormhole.movie.edu.
2  IN PTR misery.movie.edu.
3  IN PTR shining.movie.edu.
4  IN PTR carrie.movie.edu.
```

Here are the contents of the file *db.127.0.0*:

```
$TTL 3h
@ IN SOA terminator.movie.edu. al.robocop.movie.edu. (
                        1         ; Serial
                        3h        ; Refresh after 3 hours
                        1h        ; Retry after 1 hour
                        1w        ; Expire after 1 week
                        1h )      ; Negative caching TTL of 1 hour


     IN NS  terminator.movie.edu.
     IN NS  wormhole.movie.edu.


1  IN PTR localhost.
```

While looking at the new *db.movie.edu* file, you may notice that we could have removed *movie.edu* from the host names of the SOA and NS records like this:

```
@ IN SOA terminator al.robocop (
                        1         ; Serial
                        3h        ; Refresh after 3 hours
                        1h        ; Retry after 1 hour
                        1w        ; Expire after 1 week
                        1h )      ; Negative caching TTL of 1 day


        IN NS   terminator
        IN NS   wormhole
```

You can't do this in the other zone data files because their origins are different. In *db.movie.edu*, we leave these names as fully qualified domain names so that the NS and SOA records are exactly the same for *all* the zone data files.

Host Name Checking (BIND 4.9.4 and Later Versions)

If your name server is older than BIND 4.9.4 or is BIND 9 through 9.1.0,[*] skip to the next section.

If your name server is BIND 4.9.4 or newer, you have to pay extra attention to how your hosts are named. Starting with Version 4.9.4, BIND checks host names for conformance to RFC 952. If a host name does not conform, BIND considers it a syntax error.

Before you panic, you need to know that this checking applies only to names that are considered host names. Remember, resource records have a name field and a data field; for example:

```
    <name>      <class> <type>  <data>
    terminator  IN      A       192.249.249.3
```

Host names are in the name fields of A (address) and MX (covered in Chapter 5, *DNS and Electronic Mail*) records. Host names are also in the data fields of SOA and NS records. CNAMEs do not have to conform to the host naming rules because they can point to names that are not host names.

Let's look at the host naming rules. Host names are allowed to contain alphabetic characters and numeric characters in each label. The following are valid host names:

```
    ID4            IN A 192.249.249.10
    postmanring2x  IN A 192.249.249.11
```

---

[*] Name checking isn't implemented in BIND 9 through 9.1.0. It may be implemented in a future version of BIND 9, though, so you may still need to read this section.

A hyphen is allowed if it is in the middle of a label:

```
fx-gateway     IN A 192.249.249.12
```

 Underscores are not allowed in host names.

Names that are not host names can consist of any printable ASCII character.

If a resource record data field calls for a mail address (as in SOA records), the first label, since it is not a host name, can contain any printable character, but the rest of the labels must follow the host name syntax just described. For example, a mail address has the following syntax:

```
<ASCII-characters>.<hostname-characters>
```

For example, if your mail address is *key_grip@movie.edu*, you can use it in an SOA record even with the underscore. Remember, in a mail address you replace the "@" with a "." like this:

```
movie.edu. IN SOA terminator.movie.edu. key_grip.movie.edu. (
                    1          ; Serial
                    3h         ; Refresh after 3 hours
                    1h         ; Retry after 1 hour
                    1w         ; Expire after 1 week
                    1h )       ; Negative caching TTL of 1 hour
```

This extra level of checking can cause dramatic problems at sites that upgrade from a liberal version of BIND to a conservative one, and especially sites that have standardized on host names containing an underscore. If you need to postpone changing names until later (you will still change them, right?), this feature can be toned down to produce warning messages instead of errors or to simply ignore illegal names altogether. The following BIND 4 configuration file statement turns the errors into warning messages:

```
check-names primary warn
```

Here is the equivalent BIND 8 or BIND 9 line:

```
options {
        check-names master warn;
};
```

The warning messages are logged with *syslog*, which we'll explain shortly. The following BIND 4 configuration file statement ignores the errors entirely:

```
check-names primary ignore
```

Here is the equivalent BIND 8 or BIND 9 line:

```
options {
        check-names master ignore;
};
```

If the nonconforming names came from a zone that you back up (and have no control over), then add a similar statement that specifies *secondary* instead of *primary*:

```
check-names secondary ignore
```

For BIND 8 or 9, use *slave* instead of *secondary*:

```
options {
        check-names slave ignore;
};
```

And if the names come in responses to queries and not in zone transfers, specify response instead:

```
check-names response ignore
```

For BIND 8:

```
options {
        check-names response ignore;
};
```

Here are the 4.9.4 defaults:

```
check-names primary fail
check-names secondary warn
check-names response ignore
```

Here are BIND 8's defaults:

```
options {
        check-names master fail;
        check-names slave warn;
        check-names response ignore;
};
```

In BIND 8, name checking can be specified on a per-zone basis, in which case it overrides name checking behavior specified in the *options* statement for this particular zone:

```
zone "movie.edu" in {
        type master;
        file "db.movie.edu";
        check-names fail;
};
```

The *options* line contains three fields (*check-names master fail*), whereas the zone line check contains only two fields (*check-names fail*). This is because the *zone* line already specifies the context (the zone named in the *zone* statement).

Tools

Wouldn't it be handy to have a tool to translate your host table into master file format? There is such a beast, written in Perl: *h2n*, a host table–to–master file converter. You can use *h2n* to create your zone data files the first time and then maintain your data manually. Or you can use *h2n* over and over again. As you've seen, the host table's format is much simpler to understand and modify correctly than master file format. So, you could maintain */etc/hosts* and rerun *h2n* to update your zone data files after each modification.

If you plan to use *h2n*, you might as well start with it, since it uses */etc/hosts*—not your hand-crafted zone data—to generate the new zone data files. We could have saved ourselves a lot of work by generating the sample zone data files in this chapter with the following:

```
% h2n -d movie.edu -s terminator -s robocop \
    -n 192.249.249 -n 192.253.253 \
    -u al.robocop.movie.edu
```

(To generate a BIND 8 or 9 configuration file, add *–v 8* to the option list.)

The *–d* and *–n* options specify the domain name of your forward-mapping zone and your network numbers. You'll notice that the names of the zone data files are derived from these options. The *–s* options list the authoritative name servers for the zones to use in the NS records. The *–u* (user) is the email address in the SOA record. We cover *h2n* in more detail in Chapter 7, after we've covered how DNS affects email.

Running a Primary Master Name Server

Now that you've created your zone data files, you are ready to start a couple of name servers. You'll need to set up two name servers: a primary master name server and a slave name server. Before you start a name server, though, make sure that the *syslog* daemon is running. If the name server reads the configuration file and zone data files and sees an error, it logs a message to the *syslog* daemon. If the error is bad enough, the name server exits.

Starting Up the Name Server

At this point, we assume the machine you are running on has the BIND name server and the support tool *nslookup* installed. Check the *named* manual page to find the directory the name server executable is in and verify that the executable is on your system. On BSD systems, the name server started its life in */etc*, but may have migrated to */usr/sbin*. Other places to look for *named* are */usr/etc/in.named* and */usr/sbin/in.named*. The following descriptions assume that the name server is in */usr/sbin*.

To start up the name server, you must become root. The name server listens for queries on a reserved port, so it requires root privileges. The first time you run it, start the name server from the command line to test that it is operating correctly. Later, we'll show you how to start up the name server automatically when your system boots.

The following command starts the name server. We ran it on the host *terminator. movie.edu*:

```
# /usr/sbin/named
```

This command assumes that your configuration file is */etc/named.boot* (BIND 4) or */etc/named.conf* (BIND 8 or 9). You can put your configuration file elsewhere, but you have to tell the name server where it is using the *–c* command-line option:

```
# /usr/sbin/named -c conf-file
```

Check for Syslog Errors

The first thing to do after starting your name server is to check the *syslog* file for error messages. If you are not familiar with *syslog*, look at the *syslog.conf* manual page for a description of the *syslog* configuration file, or the *syslogd* manual page for a description of the *syslog* daemon. The name server logs messages with facility *daemon* under the name *named*. You might be able to find out where *syslog* messages are logged by looking for the *daemon* facility in */etc/syslog.conf*:

```
% grep daemon /etc/syslog.conf
*.err;kern.debug;daemon,auth.notice /var/adm/messages
```

On this host, the name server *syslog* messages are logged to */var/adm/messages*, and *syslog* saves only the ones that are at severity LOG_NOTICE or higher. Some useful messages are sent at severity LOG_INFO—you might like to see some of these. You can decide if you want to change the log level after reading Chapter 7, where we cover *syslog* messages in more detail.

When the name server starts, it logs a starting message:

```
% grep named /var/adm/messages
Jan 10 20:48:32 terminator named[3221]: starting.
```

The *starting* message is not an error message, but there might be other messages with it that are error messages. (If your server said *restarted* instead of *starting*, that's okay too. The message changed at BIND 4.9.3.) The most common errors are syntax errors in the zone data files or configuration file. For example, if you forget the resource record type in an address record:

```
robocop  IN  192.249.249.2
```

you'll see the following *syslog* error messages:

```
Jan 10 20:48:32 terminator named[3221]: Line 24: Unknown type:
                192.249.249.2
Jan 10 20:48:32 terminator named[3221]: db.movie.edu Line 24:
                Database error near (192.249.249.2)
Jan 10 20:48:32 terminator named[3221]: master zone "movie.edu" (IN) rejected due
to errors (serial 1)
```

Or, if you misspell the word "zone" in */etc/named.conf:*

```
zne "movie.edu" in {
```

you'll see the following *syslog* error message:

```
Mar 22 20:14:21 terminator named[1477]: /etc/named.conf:10:
                syntax error near `zne'
```

If BIND Version 4.9.4 or later finds a name that doesn't conform to RFC 952, you'll see the following *syslog* error message:

```
Jul 24 20:56:26 terminator named[1496]: owner name "ID_4.movie.edu IN"
                                (primary) is invalid - rejecting
Jul 24 20:56:26 terminator named[1496]: db.movie.edu:33: owner name error
Jul 24 20:56:26 terminator named[1496]: db.movie.edu:33: Database error near (A)
Jul 24 20:56:26 terminator named[1496]: master zone "movie.edu" (IN) rejected due
to errors (serial 1)
```

If you have a syntax error, check the line numbers mentioned in the *syslog* error message to see if you can figure out the problem. You've seen what the zone data files are supposed to look like; that should be enough to figure out most simple syntax errors. Otherwise, you'll have to go through Appendix A, *DNS Message Format and Resource Records*, to see the gory syntactic details of all the resource records. If you can fix the syntax error, do so and then reload the name server with *ndc,* the name daemon controller:

```
# ndc reload
```

so that it rereads the zone data files.* You'll see more information in Chapter 7 on using *ndc* to control the name server.

Testing Your Setup with nslookup

If you have set up your local zones correctly and your connection to the Internet is up, you should be able to look up a local and a remote domain name. We'll now step you through the lookups with *nslookup*. There is a whole chapter in this

---

* For a BIND 9 name server, you'd need to use *rndc,* but we haven't shown you how to configure that yet. Skip ahead to Chapter 7 if you'd like to see how that's done. *ndc* works without much configuration, though.

book on *nslookup* (Chapter 12, *nslookup and dig*), but we cover it in enough detail here to do basic name server testing.

Set the local domain name

Before running *nslookup*, you need to set the host's local domain name. With this configured, you can look up a name like *carrie* instead of having to spell out *carrie.movie.edu*—the system adds the domain name *movie.edu* for you.

There are two ways to set the local domain name: *hostname(1)* or */etc/resolv.conf*. Some people say that, in practice, more sites set the local domain in */etc/resolv. conf.* You can use either. Throughout the book, we assume the local domain name comes from *hostname(1)*.

Create a file called */etc/resolv.conf* with the following line starting in the first column (substitute your local domain name for *movie.edu*):

```
domain movie.edu
```

Or, set *hostname(1)* to a domain name. On the host *terminator*, we set *hostname(1)* to *terminator.movie.edu*. Don't add a trailing dot to the name.

Look up a local domain name

nslookup can be used to look up any type of resource record, and it can be directed to query any name server. By default, it looks up A (address) records using the first name server specified in *resolv.conf*. (Without a name specified in *resolv.conf*, the resolver defaults to querying the local name server.) To look up a host's address with *nslookup*, run *nslookup* with the host's domain name as the only argument. A lookup of a local domain name should return almost instantly.

We ran *nslookup* to look up *carrie*:

```
% nslookup carrie
Server:  terminator.movie.edu
Address: 192.249.249.3

Name:    carrie.movie.edu
Address: 192.253.253.4
```

If looking up a local domain name works, your local name server has been configured properly for your forward-mapping zone. If the lookup fails, you'll see something like this:

```
*** terminator.movie.edu can't find carrie: Non-existent domain
```

This means that either *carrie* is not in your zone data—check your zone data file—or you didn't set your local domain name in *hostname(1)*, or some name server error occurred (though you should have caught the error when you checked the *syslog* messages).

Look up a local address

When *nslookup* is given an address to look up, it knows to make a PTR query instead of an address query. We ran *nslookup* to look up *carrie*'s address:

```
% nslookup 192.253.253.4
Server: terminator.movie.edu
Address: 192.249.249.3

Name:    carrie.movie.edu
Address: 192.253.253.4
```

If looking up an address works, your local name server has been configured properly for your *in-addr.arpa* (reverse-mapping) zones. If the lookup fails, you'll see the same error messages as when you looked up a domain name.

Look up a remote domain name

The next step is to try using the local name server to look up a remote domain name, like *ftp.uu.net*, or another system you know of on the Internet. This command may not return as quickly as the last one. If *nslookup* fails to get a response from your name server, it will wait a little longer than a minute before giving up:

```
% nslookup ftp.uu.net.
Server: terminator.movie.edu
Address: 192.249.249.3

Name:     ftp.uu.net
Addresses: 192.48.96.9
```

If this works, your name server knows where the root name servers are and how to contact them to find information about domain names in zones other than your own. If it fails, either you forgot to configure the root hints file (and a *syslog* message will show up) or the network is broken somewhere and you can't reach the name servers for the remote zone. Try a different remote domain name.

If these first lookups succeeded, congratulations! You have a primary master name server up and running. At this point, you are ready to start configuring your slave name server.

One more test

While you're testing, though, run one more test. Try having a remote name server look up a domain name in one of your zones. This will work only if your parent zone's name servers have already delegated your zones to the name server you just set up. If your parent required you to have your two name servers running before delegating your zones, skip ahead to the next section.

To make *nslookup* use a remote name server to look up a local domain name, give the local host's domain name as the first argument and the remote server's domain name as the second argument. Again, if this doesn't work, it may take a little longer than a minute before *nslookup* gives you an error message. Here, for instance, *gatekeeper.dec.com* looks up *carrie.movie.edu*:

```
% nslookup carrie gatekeeper.dec.com.
Server: gatekeeper.dec.com.
Address: 204.123.2.2

Name:    carrie.movie.edu
Address: 192.253.253.4
```

If the first two lookups worked, but using a remote name server to look up a local name failed, your zones may not be registered with your parent name servers. That's not a problem, at first, because systems within your zones can look up the domain names of other systems both within and outside of your zones. You'll be able to send email and to FTP to local and remote systems, though some systems won't allow FTP connections if they can't map your hosts' addresses back to domain names. But not being registered will shortly become a problem. Hosts outside your zones can't look up domain names in your zones—you can send email to friends in remote zones but you won't get their responses. To fix this problem, contact the administrators of your parent zones and have them check the delegation of your zones.

Editing the Startup Files

Once you have confirmed that your name server is running properly and can be used from here on, you'll need to configure it to start automatically and set *hostname(1)* to a domain name in your system's startup files. Check to see if your vendor has already set up the name server to start on bootup. You may have to remove comment characters from the startup lines, or the startup file may test to see if */etc/named.conf* or */etc/named.boot* exists. To look for automatic startup lines, use:

```
% grep named /etc/*rc*
```

or, if you have System V–style *rc* files, use:

```
% grep named /etc/rc.d/*/S*
```

If you don't find anything, add lines like the following to the appropriate startup file somewhere after your interfaces are initialized by *ifconfig*:

```
if test -x /etc/named -a -f /etc/named.conf
then
        echo "Starting named"
        /etc/named
fi
```

You may want to wait to start the name server until after the default route is installed or your routing daemon (*routed* or *gated*) is started, depending upon whether these services need the name server or can get by with */etc/hosts*.

Find out which startup file initializes the host name. Change *hostname(1)* to a domain name. For example, we changed:

```
hostname terminator
```

to:

```
hostname terminator.movie.edu
```

Running a Slave Name Server

You need to set up another name server for robustness. You can (and probably will eventually) set up more than two authoritative name servers for your zones. Two name servers are the minimum—if you have only one name server and it goes down, no one can look up domain names. A second name server splits the load with the first server or handles the whole load if the first server is down. You *could* set up another primary master name server, but we don't recommend it. Instead, set up a slave name server. You can always change a slave name server into a primary master name server later if you decide to expend the extra effort it takes to run multiple primary master name servers.

How does a server know if it's the primary master or a slave for a zone? The *named.conf* file tells the name server whether it is the primary master or a slave on a per-zone basis. The NS records don't tell us which server is the primary master for a zone and which servers are slaves—they only say who the servers are. (Globally, DNS doesn't care; as far as the actual name resolution goes, slave servers are as good as primary master servers.)

What's the difference between a primary master name server and a slave name server? The crucial difference is where the server gets its data. A primary master name server reads its data from zone data files. A slave name server loads its data over the network from another name server. This process is called a *zone transfer*.

A slave name server is not limited to loading zones from a primary master name server; it can also load from another slave server.

The big advantage of slave name servers is that you maintain only one set of zone data files for a zone, the ones on the primary master name server. You don't have to worry about synchronizing the files among name servers; the slaves do that for you. The caveat is that a slave does not resynchronize instantly—it polls to see if its zone data is current. The polling interval is one of those numbers in the SOA record that we haven't explained yet. (BIND Versions 8 and 9 support a mechanism to speed up the distribution of zone data, which we'll describe later.)

A slave name server doesn't need to retrieve all its zone data over the network; the overhead files, *db.cache* and *db.127.0.0*, are the same as on a primary master, so keep a local copy on the slave. That means that a slave name server is a primary master for *0.0.127.in-addr.arpa*. Well, you *could* make it a slave for *0.0.127.in-addr.arpa*, but that zone's data never changes—it may as well be a primary master.

Setup

To set up your slave name server, create a directory for the zone data files on the slave name server host (e.g., */var/named*) and copy over the files */etc/named.conf*, *db.cache*, and *db.127.0.0*:

```
# rcp /etc/named.conf host:/etc
# rcp db.cache db.127.0.0 host:db-file-directory
```

You must modify */etc/named.conf* on the slave name server host. For BIND 4, change every occurrence of *primary* to *secondary* except for the *0.0.127.in-addr.arpa* zone. Before the filename on each of these lines, add the IP address of the primary master server you just set up. For example, if the original BIND 4 configuration file line was this:

```
primary movie.edu       db.movie.edu
```

then the modified line looks like this:

```
secondary movie.edu     192.249.249.3 db.movie.edu
```

If the original BIND 8 or 9 configuration file line was:

```
zone "movie.edu" in {
     type master;
     file "db.movie.edu";
};
```

change *master* to *slave* and add a *masters* line with the IP address of the master server:

```
zone "movie.edu" in {
     type slave;
     file "bak.movie.edu";
     masters { 192.249.249.3; };
};
```

This tells the name server that it is a slave for the zone *movie.edu* and that it should track the version of this zone kept on the name server at 192.249.249.3. The slave name server keeps a backup copy of this zone in the local file *bak.movie.edu*.

For Movie U., we set up our slave name server on *wormhole.movie.edu*. Recall that the configuration file on *terminator.movie.edu* (the primary master) looks like this:

```
directory /var/named

primary movie.edu                       db.movie.edu
```

```
primary   249.249.192.in-addr.arpa  db.192.249.249
primary   253.253.192.in-addr.arpa  db.192.253.253
primary   0.0.127.in-addr.arpa      db.127.0.0
cache     .                         db.cache
```

We copy */etc/named.conf, db.cache*, and *db.127.0.0* to *wormhole.movie.edu*, and edit the configuration file as previously described. The BIND 4 configuration file on *wormhole.movie.edu* now looks like this:

```
directory /var/named

secondary  movie.edu                192.249.249.3 bak.movie.edu
secondary  249.249.192.in-addr.arpa 192.249.249.3 bak.192.249.249
secondary  253.253.192.in-addr.arpa 192.249.249.3 bak.192.253.253
primary    0.0.127.in-addr.arpa     db.127.0.0
cache      .                        db.cache
```

The equivalent BIND 8 or 9 configuration file looks like this:

```
options {
        directory "/var/named";
};

zone "movie.edu" in {
        type slave;
        file "bak.movie.edu";
        masters { 192.249.249.3; };
};

zone "249.249.192.in-addr.arpa" in {
        type slave;
        file "bak.192.249.249";
        masters { 192.249.249.3; };
};

zone "253.253.192.in-addr.arpa" in {
        type slave;
        file "db.192.253.253";
        masters { 192.249.249.3; };
};

zone "0.0.127.in-addr.arpa" in {
        type master;
        file "db.127.0.0";
};

zone "." in {
        type hint;
        file "db.cache";
};
```

This causes the name server on *wormhole.movie.edu* to load *movie.edu, 249.249. 192.in-addr.arpa*, and *253.253.192.in-addr.arpa* over the network from the name server at 192.249.249.3 (*terminator.movie.edu*). It also saves a backup copy of these files in */var/named*. You may find it handy to isolate the backup zone data files in a subdirectory. We name them with a unique prefix like *bak*, since on rare occasions, we may have to delete all of the backup files manually. It's also helpful to be able to tell at a glance that they're backup zone data files so that we're not tempted to edit them. We'll cover more on backup files later.

Now start up the slave name server. Check for error messages in the *syslog* file as you did for the primary master server. As on the primary master, the command to start up a name server is:

```
# /usr/sbin/named
```

One extra check to make on the slave that you didn't have to make on the primary master is to see that the name server created the backup files. Shortly after we started our slave name server on *wormhole.movie.edu*, we saw *bak.movie.edu*, *bak.192.249.249*, and *bak.192.253.253* appear in the */var/named* directory. This means the slave has successfully loaded these zones from the primary master and saved a backup copy.

To complete setting up your slave name server, try looking up the same domain names you looked up after you started the primary master server. This time, you must run *nslookup* on the host running the slave name server so that the slave server is queried. If your slave is working fine, add the proper lines to your system startup files so that the slave name server is started when your system boots up and *hostname(1)* is set to a domain name.

Backup Files

Slave name servers are not *required* to save a backup copy of the zone data. If there is a backup copy, the slave server reads it on startup and later checks with the master server to see if the master server has a newer copy instead of loading a new copy of the zone immediately. If the master server has a newer copy, the slave pulls it over and saves it in the backup file.

Why save a backup copy? Suppose the master name server is down when the slave starts up. The slave will be unable to transfer the zone and therefore won't function as a name server for that zone until the master server is up. With a backup copy, the slave has zone data, although it might be slightly out of date. Since the slave does not have to rely on the master server always being up, it's a more robust setup.

To run without a backup copy, omit the filename at the end of the *secondary* lines in the BIND 4 configuration file. In BIND 8 or 9, remove the *file* line. However, we recommend configuring all your slave name servers to save backup copies. There is very little extra cost to saving a backup zone data file, but there is a very high cost if you get caught without a backup file when you need it most.

SOA Values

Remember this SOA record?

```
movie.edu. IN SOA terminator.movie.edu. al.robocop.movie.edu. (
                    1          ; Serial
                    3h         ; Refresh after 3 hours
                    1h         ; Retry after 1 hour
                    1w         ; Expire after 1 week
                    1h )       ; Negative caching TTL of 1 day
```

We never explained what the values between the parentheses were for.

The serial number applies to all the data within the zone. We chose to start our serial number at 1, a logical place to start. But many people find it more useful to use the date in the serial number instead, like 1997102301. This format is YYYY-MMDDNN, where YYYY is the year, MM is the month, DD is the day, and NN is a count of how many times the zone data was modified that day. These fields won't work in any other order, since no other order gives a value that always increases as the date changes. This is critical: whatever format you choose, it's important that the serial number always increase when you update your zone data.

When a slave name server contacts a master server for zone data, it first asks for the serial number on the data. If the slave's serial number for the zone is lower than the master server's, the slave's zone data is out of date. In this case, the slave pulls a new copy of the zone. If a slave starts up and there is no backup file to read, it will always load the zone. As you might guess, when you modify the zone data files on the primary master, you must increment the serial number. Updating your zone data files is covered in Chapter 7.

The next four fields specify various time intervals, in seconds by default:

refresh

> The refresh interval tells a slave for the zone how often to check that the data for this zone is up to date. To give you an idea of the system load this feature causes, a slave makes one SOA query per zone per refresh interval. The value we chose, three hours, is reasonably aggressive. Most users will tolerate a delay of half a working day for things like zone data to propagate when they are waiting for their new workstation to become operational. If you provide one-day service for your site, you could consider raising this value to eight hours. If your zone data doesn't change very often or if all of your slaves are spread over long distances (as the root name servers are), consider a value that is even longer, say 24 hours.

retry

> If the slave fails to reach the master name server after the refresh interval (the host could be down), it starts trying to connect every *retry* seconds. Normally, the retry interval is shorter than the refresh interval, but it doesn't have to be.

expire

> If the slave fails to contact the master name server for *expire* seconds, the slave expires the zone. Expiring the zone means that the slave stops giving out answers about the zone because the zone data is too old to be useful. Essentially, this field says that at some point, the data is so old that giving out no data is better than giving out stale data. Expire times on the order of a week are common—longer (up to a month) if you frequently have problems reaching your updating source. The expiration time should always be much larger than the retry and refresh intervals; if the expire time is smaller than the refresh interval, your slaves will expire the zone before trying to load new data.

negative caching TTL

> TTL stands for *time to live*. This value applies to all negative responses from the name servers authoritative for the zone.

 On versions of BIND before BIND 8.2, the last field in the SOA record is *both* the default time to live and the negative caching time to live for the zone.

Those of you who have read earlier versions of this book may have noticed the change in the format we used for the SOA record's numeric fields. Once upon a time, BIND only understood units of seconds for the four fields we just described. (Consequently, a whole generation of administrators know that there are 608400 seconds in a week.) Now, with all but the oldest BIND name servers (4.8.3), you can specify units besides seconds for these fields and as arguments to the TTL control statement, as we saw early in this chapter. For example, you can specify a three-hour refresh interval with *3h, 180m,* or even *2h60m.* You can also use *d* for days and *w* for weeks.

The right values for your SOA record depend upon the needs of your site. In general, longer times cause less load on your name servers and can delay the propagation of changes; shorter times increase the load on your name servers and speed up the propagation of changes. The values we use in this book should work well for most sites. RFC 1537 recommends the following values for top-level name servers:

```
Refresh        24 hours
Retry           2 hours
Expire         30 days
Default TTL     4 days
```

There is one implementation feature you should be aware of. Older versions (pre-4.8.3) of BIND slaves stop answering queries during a zone load. As a result, BIND was modified to spread out the zone loads, reducing the periods of unavailability. So, even if you set a low refresh interval, your slaves may not check as often as you request. BIND attempts a certain number of zone loads and then waits 15 minutes before trying another batch.

Now that we've told you all about how slave name servers poll to keep their data up to date, BIND 8 and 9 change how zone data propagates! The polling feature is still there, but BIND 8 and 9 add a notification when zone data changes. If both your primary master server and your slaves run BIND 8 or 9, the primary master notifies the slave that a zone has changed within 15 minutes of loading a new copy of that zone. The notification causes the slave server to shorten the refresh interval and attempt to load the zone immediately. We'll discuss this more in Chapter 10.

Multiple Master Servers

Are there other ways to make your slave name server's configuration more robust? Yes—you can specify up to 10 IP addresses of master servers. In a BIND 4 configuration file, just add them after the first IP address and before the backup filename. In a BIND 8 or 9 configuration file, add them after the first IP address and separate them with semicolons:

```
masters { 192.249.249.3; 192.249.249.4; };
```

The slave will query the master server at each IP address in the order listed until it gets a response. Through BIND 8.1.2, the slave would always transfer the zone from the first master name server to respond if that master had a higher serial number. The slave would try successive master servers only if the previous master didn't respond. From BIND 8.2 on, however, the slave actually queries all of the master name servers listed and transfers the zone from the one with the highest serial number. If multiple master servers tie for the highest serial number, the slave transfers the zone from the first of those masters in the list.

The original intent of this feature was to allow you to list all the IP addresses of the host running the primary master name server for the zone if that host were multihomed. But since there is no check to determine whether the contacted server is a primary master or a slave, you can list the IP addresses of hosts running slave servers for the zone if that makes sense for your setup. That way, if the first master server is down or unreachable, your slave can transfer the zone from another master name server.

Adding More Zones

Now that you have your name servers running, you might want to support more zones. What needs to be done? Nothing special, really. All you need to do is add more *primary* or *secondary* statements (BIND 4) or *zone* statements (BIND 8 and 9) to your configuration file. You can even add *secondary* lines to your primary master server and *primary* lines to your slave server. (You may have already noticed that your slave server is primary master for *0.0.127.in-addr.arpa.*)

At this point, it's useful to repeat something we said earlier in this book. Calling a *given* name server a primary master name server or a slave name server is a little silly. Name servers can be—and usually are—authoritative for more than one zone. A name server can be a primary master for one zone and a slave for another. Most name servers, however, are either primary master for most of the zones they load or slave for most of the zones they load. So if we call a particular name server a primary master or a slave, we mean that it's the primary master or a slave for *most* of the zones it loads.

What Next?

In this chapter, we showed you how to create name server zone data files by translating */etc/hosts* to equivalent name server data, and also how to set up a primary master and a slave name server. There is more work to do to complete setting up your local zones, however: you need to modify your zone data for email and configure the other hosts in your zone to use your name servers. You may also need to start up more name servers. These topics are covered in the next few chapters.

5

DNS and Electronic Mail

> *And here Alice began to get rather sleepy, and went on saying to herself, in a dreamy sort of way, "Do cats eat bats? Do cats eat bats?" and sometimes "Do bats eat cats?" for, you see, as she couldn't answer either question, it didn't much matter which way she put it.*

I'll bet you're drowsy, too, after that looong chapter. Thankfully, this chapter discusses a topic that should be very interesting to you system administrators and postmasters: how DNS impacts electronic mail. And even if it isn't interesting to you, at least it's shorter than the last chapter.

One of the advantages of the Domain Name System over host tables is its support of advanced mail routing. When mailers had only the *HOSTS.TXT* file (and its derivative, */etc/hosts*) to work with, the best they could do was to attempt delivery to a host's IP address. If that failed, they could either defer delivery of the message and try again later, or bounce the message back to the sender.

DNS offers a mechanism for specifying backup hosts for mail delivery, and also for allowing hosts to assume mail handling responsibilities for other hosts. This lets diskless hosts that don't run mailers, for example, have mail addressed to them processed by their server.

DNS, unlike host tables, allows arbitrary names to represent electronic mail destinations. You can—and most organizations on the Internet do—use the domain name of your main forward-mapping zone as an email destination. Or you can add domain names to your zone that are purely email destinations and don't represent any particular host. A single logical email destination may also represent several mail servers. With host tables, mail destinations were hosts, period.

Taken all together, these features give administrators much more flexibility in configuring electronic mail on their networks.

MX Records

DNS uses a single type of resource record to implement enhanced mail routing: the MX record. Originally, the MX record's function was split between two records, the MD (mail destination) and MF (mail forwarder) records. MD specified the final destination to which a message addressed to a given domain name should be delivered; MF specified a host that would forward mail on to the eventual destination, should that destination be unreachable.

Early experience with DNS on the ARPAnet showed that separating the functions didn't work very well. A mailer needed both the MD and MF records attached to a domain name (if both existed) to decide where to send mail—one or the other alone wouldn't do. But an explicit lookup of one type or another (either MD or MF) would cause a name server to cache just that record type. So mailers either had to do two queries, one for MD and one for MF records, or they could no longer accept cached answers. This meant that the overhead of running mail was higher than that of running other services, which was eventually deemed unacceptable.

The two records were integrated into a single record type, MX, to solve this problem. Now a mailer just needed all the MX records for a particular domain name destination to make a mail routing decision. Using cached MX records was fine, as long as the TTLs matched.

MX records specify a *mail exchanger* for a domain name; this is a host that will process *or* forward mail for the domain name (through a firewall, for example). "Processing" the mail means either delivering it to the individual it's addressed to or gatewaying it to another mail transport, like X.400 or Microsoft Exchange. "Forwarding" means sending it to its final destination or to another mail exchanger "closer" to the destination via SMTP, the Internet's Simple Mail Transfer Protocol. Sometimes, forwarding the mail involves queuing it for some amount of time, too.

In order to prevent mail routing loops, the MX record has an extra parameter besides the domain name of the mail exchanger: a *preference value*. The preference value is an unsigned 16-bit number (between 0 and 65535) that indicates the mail exchanger's priority. For example, the MX record:

```
peets.mpk.ca.us.    IN    MX    10 relay.hp.com.
```

specifies that *relay.hp.com* is a mail exchanger for *peets.mpk.ca.us* at preference value 10.

Taken together, the preference values of a destination's mail exchangers determine the order in which a mailer should use them. The preference value itself isn't important, only its relationship to the values of other mail exchangers: is it higher or lower than the values of this destination's other mail exchangers? Unless there are other records involved:

```
plange.puntacana.dr.   IN  MX  1 listo.puntacana.dr.
plange.puntacana.dr.   IN  MX  2 hep.puntacana.dr.
```

does exactly the same thing as:

```
plange.puntacana.dr.   IN  MX  50  listo.puntacana.dr.
plange.puntacana.dr.   IN  MX  100 hep.puntacana.dr.
```

Mailers should attempt delivery to the mail exchangers with the *lowest* preference values first. It may seems a little counterintuitive at first that the most preferred mail exchanger has the lowest preference value. But since the preference value is an unsigned quantity, this lets you specify a "best" mail exchanger at preference value 0.

If delivery to the most preferred mail exchanger(s) fails, mailers should attempt delivery to less preferred mail exchangers (those with higher preference values) in order of increasing preference value. That is, mailers should try more preferred mail exchangers before they try less preferred mail exchangers. More than one mail exchanger may share the same preference value, too, giving the mailer its choice of which to send to first.* The mailer must try all the mail exchangers at a given preference value before proceeding to the next higher value.

For example, the MX records for *oreilly.com* might be:

```
oreilly.com.    IN    MX    0  ora.oreilly.com.
oreilly.com.    IN    MX    10 ruby.oreilly.com.
oreilly.com.    IN    MX    10 opal.oreilly.com.
```

Interpreted together, these MX records instruct mailers to attempt delivery to *oreilly.com* by sending to:

1. *ora.oreilly.com* first

2. Either *ruby.oreilly.com* or *opal.oreilly.com* next, and finally

3. The remaining preference 10 mail exchanger (the one not used in step 2)

Of course, once the mailer successfully delivers the mail to one of *oreilly.com*'s mail exchangers, it can stop. A mailer successfully delivering *oreilly.com* mail to *ora.oreilly.com* doesn't need to try *ruby.oreilly.com* or *opal.oreilly.com*.

Note that *oreilly.com* isn't a particular host; it's the domain name of O'Reilly & Associates' main forward-mapping zone. O'Reilly & Associates uses the domain name as the email destination for everyone who works there. It's much easier for correspondents to remember the single email destination *oreilly.com* than to

---

* The newest version of *sendmail*, Version 8, will actually choose randomly among mail exchangers with the same preference.

remember which host—*ruby.oreilly.com? amber.oreilly.com?*—each employee has an email account on.

This requires, of course, that the mailer on *ora.oreilly.com* keep track of which host each user at O'Reilly & Associates has an email account on. That's usually done by maintaining a master *aliases* file on *ora.oreilly.com* that forwards email from *ora.oreilly.com* to its eventual destination.

What if a destination doesn't have any MX records, but it has one or more A records? Will a mailer simply not deliver mail to that destination? Actually, you can compile recent versions of *sendmail* to do just that. Most vendors, however, have compiled their *sendmail*s to be more forgiving: if no MX records exist but one or more A records do, they'll at least attempt delivery to the address. Version 8 of *sendmail* compiled "out of the box" will try the address of a mail destination without MX records. Check your vendor's documentation if you're not sure whether your mail server will send mail to destinations with only address records. Even though nearly all mailers deliver mail to a destination with just an address record and no MX records, it's still a good idea to have at least one MX record for each legitimate mail destination. When it has mail to deliver, *sendmail* always looks up the MX records for a destination *first*. If the destination doesn't have any MX records, a name server—usually one of your authoritative name servers—still must answer that query, and then *sendmail* goes on to look up A records. That takes extra time, slows mail delivery, and adds a little load to your zone's authoritative name servers. If you simply add an MX record for each destination pointing to a domain name that maps to the same address that an address lookup would return, *sendmail* has to send only one query, and the mailer's local name server caches the MX record for future use.

What's a Mail Exchanger, Again?

The idea of a mail exchanger is probably new to many of you, so let's go over it in a little more detail. A simple analogy should help here. Imagine that a mail exchanger is an airport, and instead of setting up MX records to instruct mailers where to send messages, you're advising your in-laws on which airport to fly into when they come visit you.

Say you live in Los Gatos, California. The closest airport for your in-laws to fly into is San Jose, the second closest is San Francisco, and the third Oakland. (We'll ignore other factors like price of the ticket, Bay Area traffic, etc.) Don't see the parallel? Then picture it like this:

```
los-gatos.ca.us.    IN    MX    1 san-jose.ca.us.
los-gatos.ca.us.    IN    MX    2 san-francisco.ca.us.
los-gatos.ca.us.    IN    MX    3 oakland.ca.us.
```

The MX list is just an ordered list of destinations that tells mailers (your in-laws) where to send messages (fly) if they want to reach a given email destination (your house). The preference value tells them how desirable it is to use that destination—you can think of it as a logical "distance" from the eventual destination (in any units you choose), or simply as a "top-10"–style ranking of the proximity of those mail exchangers to the final destination.

With this list, you're saying, "Try to fly into San Jose, and if you can't get there, try San Francisco and Oakland, in that order." It *also* says that if you reach San Francisco, you should take a commuter flight to San Jose. If you wind up in Oakland, you should try to get a commuter to San Jose or at least to San Francisco.

What makes a good mail exchanger, then? The same qualities that make a good airport:

Size

You wouldn't want to fly into tiny Reid-Hillview Airport to get to Los Gatos because the airport's not equipped to handle large planes or many people. (You'd probably be better off landing a big jet on Interstate 280 than at Reid-Hillview.) Likewise, you don't want to use an emaciated, underpowered host as a mail exchanger; it won't be able to handle the load.

Uptime

You know better than to fly through Denver International Airport in the winter, right? Then you should know better than to use a host that's rarely up or available as a mail exchanger.

Connectivity

If your relatives are flying in from far away, you've got to make sure they're able to get a direct flight to at least one of the airports in the list you give them. You can't tell them their only choices are San Jose and Oakland if they're flying in from Helsinki. Similarly, you've got to make sure that at least one of your hosts' mail exchangers is reachable to anyone who might conceivably send you mail.

Management and administration

How well an airport is managed has a bearing on your safety when flying into or just through the airport, and on how easy it is to use. Think of these factors when choosing a mail exchanger. The privacy of your mail, the speed of its delivery during normal operations, and how well your mail is treated when your hosts go down all hinge upon the quality of the administrators who manage your mail exchangers.

Keep this example in mind, because we'll use it again later.

The MX Algorithm

That's the basic idea behind MX records and mail exchangers, but there are a few more wrinkles you should know about. To avoid routing loops, mailers need to use a slightly more complicated algorithm than what we've described when they determine where to send mail.*

Imagine what would happen if mailers didn't check for routing loops. Let's say you send mail from your workstation to *nuts@oreilly.com*, raving (or raging) about the quality of this book. Unfortunately, *ora.oreilly.com* is down at the moment. No problem! Recall *oreilly.com*'s MX records:

```
oreilly.com.    IN    MX    0 ora.oreilly.com.
oreilly.com.    IN    MX    10 ruby.oreilly.com.
oreilly.com.    IN    MX    10 opal.oreilly.com.
```

Your mailer falls back and sends your message to *ruby.oreilly.com*, which is up. The mailer of *ruby.oreilly.com* then tries to forward the mail on to *ora.reilly.com*, but can't, because *ora.oreilly.com* is down. Now what? Unless *ruby.oreilly.com* checks the sanity of what it's doing, it'll try to forward the message to *opal.oreilly. com*, or maybe even to itself. That's certainly not going to help get the mail delivered. If *ruby.oreilly.com* sends the message to itself, we have a mail routing loop. If *ruby.oreilly.com* sends the message to *opal.oreilly.com*, *opal.oreilly.com* will either send it back to *ruby.oreilly.com* or send it to itself, and we again have a mail routing loop.

To prevent this from happening, mailers discard certain MX records before they decide where to send a message. A mailer sorts the list of MX records by preference value and looks in the list for the canonical domain name of the host it's running on. If the local host appears as a mail exchanger, the mailer discards that MX record and all MX records in which the preference value is equal or higher (that is, equally or less preferred mail exchangers). That prevents the mailer from sending messages to itself or to mailers "farther" from the eventual destination.

Let's think about this in the context of our airport analogy. This time, imagine you're an airline passenger (a message), and you're trying to get to Greeley, Colorado. You can't get a direct flight to Greeley, but you can fly to either Fort Collins or Denver (the two next highest mail exchangers). Since Fort Collins is closer to Greeley, you opt to fly to Fort Collins.

Now, once you've arrived in Fort Collins, there's no sense in flying to Denver, away from your destination (a lower preference mail exchanger). (And flying from Fort Collins to Fort Collins would be pretty silly, too.) So the only acceptable flight

---

* This algorithm is based on RFC 974, which describes how Internet mail routing works.

to get you to your destination is now a Fort Collins–Greeley flight. You eliminate flights to less preferred destinations to prevent frequent flyer looping and wasteful travel time.

One caveat: most mailers will *only* look for their local host's *canonical* domain name in the list of MX records. They don't check for aliases (domain names on the left side of CNAME records). Unless you always use canonical names in your MX records, there's no guarantee that a mailer will be able to find itself in the MX list, and you'll run the risk of having your mail loop.

If you do list a mail exchanger by an alias and it unwittingly tries to deliver mail to itself, it will detect the loop and bounce the mail with the error:

```
554 MX list for movie.edu points back to relay.isp.com
554 <root@movie.edu>... Local configuration error
```

This replaces the quainter "I refuse to talk to myself" error in newer versions of *sendmail.* The moral: in an MX record, always use the mail exchanger's canonical name.

One more caveat: the hosts you list as mail exchangers *must* have address records. A mailer needs to find an address for each mail exchanger you name or else it can't attempt delivery there.

To go back to our *oreilly.com* example, when *ruby.oreilly.com* receives the message from your workstation, its mailer checks the list of MX records:

```
oreilly.com.     IN     MX     0  ora.oreilly.com.
oreilly.com.     IN     MX     10 ruby.oreilly.com.
oreilly.com.     IN     MX     10 opal.oreilly.com.
```

Finding the local host's domain name in the list at preference value 10, *ruby. oreilly.com*'s mailer discards all the records at preference value 10 or higher (the records in bold):

```
oreilly.com.     IN     MX     0  ora.oreilly.com.
oreilly.com.     IN     MX     10 ruby.oreilly.com.
oreilly.com.     IN     MX     10 opal.oreilly.com.
```

leaving only:

```
oreilly.com.     IN     MX     0  ora.oreilly.com.
```

Since *ora.oreilly.com* is down, *ruby.oreilly.com* defers delivery until later and queues the message.

What happens if a mailer finds *itself* at the highest preference (lowest preference value) and has to discard the whole MX list? Some mailers attempt delivery directly to the destination host's IP address as a last-ditch effort. In most mailers, however, it's an error. It may indicate that DNS thinks the mailer should be processing (not just forwarding) mail for the destination, but the mailer hasn't been configured to know that. Or it may indicate that the administrator has ordered the MX records incorrectly by using the wrong preference values.

Say, for example, the folks who run *acme.com* add a mail exchanger record to direct mail addressed to *acme.com* to a mailer at their Internet Service Provider:

```
acme.com.    IN    MX    10 mail.isp.net.
```

Most mailers need to be configured to identify their aliases and the names of other hosts they process mail for. Unless the mailer on *mail.isp.net* is configured to recognize email addressed to *acme.com* as local mail, it will assume it's being asked to relay the mail and attempt to forward the mail to a mail exchanger closer to the final destination.* When it looks up the MX records for *acme.com*, it finds itself as the most preferred mail exchanger and bounces the mail back to the sender with the familiar error:

```
554 MX list for acme.com points back to mail.isp.com
554 <root@acme.com>... Local configuration error
```

Many versions of *sendmail* use class *w* or fileclass *w* as the list of "local" destinations. Depending on your *sendmail.cf* file, adding an alias can be as easy as adding the line:

```
Cw acme.com
```

to *sendmail.cf.* If your mailer uses another mail transport, such as UUCP, to deliver mail to the hosts for which it acts as a mail exchanger, this will probably require more involved configuration.

You may have noticed that we tend to use multiples of 10 for our preference values. This is convenient because it allows you to insert other MX records temporarily at intermediate values without changing the other preferences, but otherwise there's nothing magical about it. We could just as easily use increments of 1 or 100 —the effect would be the same.

---

* Unless, of course, *mail.isp.net*'s mailer is configured not to relay mail for unknown domain names. In this case, it would simply reject the mail.

Configuring Hosts

They were indeed a queer-looking party that assembled on the bank—the birds with draggled feathers, the animals with their fur clinging close to them, and all dripping wet, cross, and uncomfortable.

Now that you or someone else in your organization has set up name servers for your zones, you'll want to configure the hosts on your network to use them. That involves configuring those hosts' resolvers. You should also check files such as *hosts.equiv* and *.rhosts* and make any changes dictated by using DNS; you may need to convert some of the host names in these files to domain names. And you may also want to add aliases, both for your users' convenience and to minimize the shock of the conversion to DNS.

This chapter covers these topics and describes configuring the resolver in many common versions of Unix and in Microsoft's Windows 95, NT, and 2000.

The Resolver

We introduced resolvers way back in Chapter 2, *How Does DNS Work?*, but we didn't say much more about them. The resolver, you'll remember, is the client half of the Domain Name System. It's responsible for translating a program's request for host information into a query to a name server and for translating the response into an answer for the program.

We haven't done any resolver configuration yet, because the occasion for it hasn't arisen. When we set up our name servers in Chapter 4, *Setting Up BIND*, the resolver's default behavior worked just fine for our purposes. But if we'd needed the resolver to do more than what it does by default or to behave differently from the default, we would have had to configure the resolver.

There's one thing we should mention up front: what we'll be describing in the next few sections is the behavior of the vanilla BIND 8.2.3 resolver in the absence of other naming services. Not all resolvers behave quite this way; some vendors still ship resolvers based on earlier versions of the DNS code, and some have implemented special resolver functionality that lets you modify the resolver algorithm. Whenever we think it's important, we'll point out differences between the behavior of the 8.2.3 BIND resolver and that of earlier resolvers, particularly the 4.8.3 and 4.9 resolvers, which many vendors were shipping when we last updated this book. We'll cover various vendors' extensions later in this chapter.

So what exactly does the resolver allow you to configure? Most resolvers let you configure at least three aspects of the resolver's behavior: the local domain name, the search list, and the name server(s) that the resolver queries. Many Unix vendors also allow you to configure other resolver behavior through nonstandard extensions to DNS. Sometimes these extensions are necessary to cope with other software, such as Sun's Network Information Service (NIS); sometimes they're simply value added by the vendor.*

Almost all resolver configuration is done in the file */etc/resolv.conf* (this might be */usr/etc/resolv.conf* or something similar on your host—check the *resolver* manual page, usually in section 4 or 5, to make sure). There are five main *directives* you can use in *resolv.conf*: the *domain* directive, the *search* directive, the *nameserver* directive, the *sortlist* directive, and the *options* directive. These directives control the behavior of the resolver. There are other, vendor-specific directives available on some versions of Unix—we'll discuss them at the end of this chapter.

The Local Domain Name

The local domain name is the domain name in which the resolver resides. In most situations, it's the domain name of the zone in which you'd find the host running the resolver. For example, the resolver on the host *terminator.movie.edu* would probably use *movie.edu* as its local domain name.

The resolver uses the local domain name to interpret domain names that aren't fully qualified. For example, when you add an entry like:

    relay bernie

to your *.rhosts* file, the name *relay* is assumed to be in your local domain. This makes a lot more sense than allowing access to a user called *bernie* on every host on the Internet whose domain name starts with *relay*. Other authorization files like *hosts.equiv* and *hosts.lpd* work the same way.

---

* NIS used to be called "Yellow Pages" or "YP," but its name was changed to NIS because the British phone company had a copyright on the name Yellow Pages.

Normally, the local domain name is determined from the host's *hostname*; the local domain name is everything after the first "." in the name. If the name doesn't contain a ".", the local domain is assumed to be the root domain. So the *hostname asylum.sf.ca.us* implies a local domain name of *sf.ca.us*, while the *hostname dogbert* implies a root local domain—which probably isn't correct, given that there are very few hosts with single-label domain names.*

You can also set the local domain name with the *domain* directive in *resolv.conf.* If you specify the *domain* directive, it overrides deriving the local domain name from the *hostname*.

The *domain* directive has a very simple syntax, but you've got to get it right since the resolver doesn't report errors. The keyword *domain* starts the line in column one, followed by whitespace (one or more blanks or tabs), then the name of the local domain. The local domain name should be written without a trailing dot, like this:

```
domain colospgs.co.us
```

In older versions of the BIND resolver (those before BIND 4.8.3), trailing spaces *are not allowed* on the line and will cause your local domain to be set to a name ending with one or more spaces, which is almost certainly not what you want. And there's yet another way to set the local domain name—via the LOCALDOMAIN environment variable. LOCALDOMAIN is handy because you can set it on a per-user basis. For example, you might have a big, massively parallel box in your corporate computing center that employees from all over the world access. Each employee may do most of her work in a different company subdomain. With LOCALDOMAIN, each employee can set her local domain name appropriately in her shell startup file.

Which method should you use—*hostname*, the *domain* directive, or LOCAL-DOMAIN? We prefer using *hostname* primarily because that's the way Berkeley does it and it seems "cleaner" in that it requires less explicit configuration. Also, some Berkeley software, particularly software that uses the *ruserok()* library call to authenticate users, allows short host names in files like *hosts.equiv* only if *hostname* is set to the full domain name.

If you run software that can't tolerate long *hostnames*, though, you can use the *domain* directive. The *hostname* command will continue to return a short name, and the resolver will fill in the domain from *resolv.conf.* You may even find occasion to use LOCALDOMAIN on a host with lots of users.

---

* There are actually some single-label domain names that point to addresses, like *cc*.

The Search List

The local domain name, whether derived from *hostname* or *resolv.conf*, also determines the default *search list*. The search list was designed to make users' lives a little easier by saving them some typing. The idea is to search one or more domains for names typed at the command line that might be incomplete—that is, that might not be fully qualified domain names.

Most Unix networking commands that take a domain name as an argument, like *telnet*, *ftp*, *rlogin*, and *rsh*, apply the search list to those arguments.

Both the way the default search list is derived and the way it is applied changed from BIND 4.8.3 to BIND 4.9. If your resolver is an older make, you'll still see the 4.8.3 behavior, but if you've got a newer model, including BIND 8.2.3,* you'll see the improvements in the 4.9 resolver.

With any BIND resolver, a user can indicate that a domain name is fully qualified by adding a trailing dot to it.† For example, the trailing dot in the command:

```
% telnet ftp.ora.com.
```

means "don't bother searching any other domains; this domain name is fully qualified." This is analogous to the leading slash in full pathnames in the Unix and MS-DOS filesystems. Pathnames without a leading slash are interpreted as relative to the current working directory while pathnames with a leading slash are absolute, anchored at the root.

The BIND 4.8.3 search list

With BIND 4.8.3 resolvers, the default search list includes the local domain name and the domain names of each of its parent domains with two or more labels. Therefore, on a host running a 4.8.3 resolver and configured with:

```
domain cv.hp.com
```

the default search list would contain first *cv.hp.com*, the local domain name; then *hp.com*, the local domain's parent; but not *com*, as it has only one label.‡ The

---

* Though the ISC added lots of new server functionality in BIND 8, the resolver is nearly identical to the BIND 4.9 resolver.

† Note that we said that the resolver can handle a trailing dot. Some programs, particularly some Unix mail user agents, don't deal correctly with a trailing dot in email addresses. They choke even before they hand the domain name in the address to the resolver.

‡ One reason older BIND resolvers didn't append just the top-level domain name is that there were—and still are—very few hosts at the second level of the Internet's name space, so tacking on just *com* or *edu* to *foo* is unlikely to result in the domain name of a real host. Also, looking up the address of a *foo.com* or *foo.edu* might well require sending a query to a root name server, which taxes the roots and can be time-consuming.

name is looked up as-is, after the resolver appends each element of the search list, and only if the name typed contains at least one dot. Thus, a user typing:

```
% telnet pronto.cv.hp.com
```

causes lookups of *pronto.cv.hp.com.cv.hp.com* and *pronto.cv.hp.com.hp.com* before the resolver looks up *pronto.cv.hp.com* by itself. A user typing:

```
% telnet asap
```

on the same host causes the resolver to look up *asap.cv.hp.com* and *asap.hp.com*, but not just *asap*, since the name typed ("asap") contains no dots.

Note that application of the search list stops as soon as a prospective domain name turns up the data being looked up. In the *asap* example, the search list would never get around to appending *hp.com* if *asap.cv.hp.com* resolved to an address.

The BIND 4.9 and later search list

With BIND 4.9 and later resolvers, the default search list includes just the local domain name. So, if you configure a host with:

```
domain cv.hp.com
```

the default search list would contain just *cv.hp.com*. Also, in a change from earlier resolvers, the search list is usually applied *after* the name is tried as-is. As long as the argument you type has at least one dot in it, it's looked up exactly as you typed it *before* any element of the search list is appended. If that lookup fails, the search list is applied. Even if the argument has no dots in it (that is, it's a single label name), it's tried as-is after the resolver appends the elements of the search list.

Why is it better to try the argument *literatim* first? From experience, the designers of DNS found that, more often than not, if a user bothered to type in a name with even a single dot in it, he was probably typing in a fully qualified domain name without the trailing dot. With older search list behavior, the resolver sent several fruitless queries before ever trying the name as typed.

Therefore, with a 4.9 or newer resolver, a user typing:

```
% telnet pronto.cv.hp.com
```

causes *pronto.cv.hp.com* to be looked up first (there are three dots in the argument). If that query fails, the resolver tries *pronto.cv.hp.com.cv.hp.com*. A user who types:

```
% telnet asap
```

on the same host causes the resolver to look up *asap.cv.hp.com* first, since the name doesn't contain a dot, and then just *asap*.

The search Directive

What if you don't like the default search list you get when you set your local domain name? In BIND 4.8.3 and all newer resolvers, you can set the search list explicitly, domain name by domain name, in the order you want the domains searched. You do this with the *search* directive.

The syntax of the *search* directive is very similar to that of the *domain* directive, except that it can take multiple domain names as arguments. The keyword *search* starts the line in column one, followed by a space or a tab, followed in turn by one to six domain names in the order you want them searched.* The first domain name in the list is interpreted as the local domain name, so the *search* and *domain* directives are mutually exclusive. If you use both in *resolv.conf,* the one that appears last will override the other.

For example, the directive:

```
search corp.hp.com paloalto.hp.com hp.com
```

instructs the resolver to search the *corp.hp.com* domain first, then *paloalto.hp.com,* and then the parent of both domains, *hp.com.*

This directive might be useful on a host whose users access hosts in both *corp.hp. com* and *paloalto.hp.com* frequently. On the other hand, on a BIND 4.8.3 resolver, the directive:

```
search corp.hp.com
```

causes the resolver to skip searching the local domain's parent domain when the search list is applied. (On a 4.9 or later resolver, the parent domain's name usually isn't in the search list, so this is no different from the default behavior.) This might be useful if the host's users only access hosts in the local domain, or if connectivity to the parent name servers isn't good (since it minimizes unnecessary queries to the parent name servers).

If you use the *domain* directive and update your resolver to BIND Version 4.9 or later, users who relied on your local domain's parent being in the search list may believe the resolver has suddenly broken. You can restore the old behavior by using the *search* directive to configure your resolver to use the same search list that it would have built before. For example, under BIND 4.9, BIND 8, or BIND 9, you can replace *domain nsr.hp.com* with *search nsr.hp.com hp.com* and get the same functionality.

---

* BIND 9 resolvers actually support eight elements in the search list.

The nameserver Directive

Back in Chapter 4, we talked about two types of name servers: primary master name servers and slave name servers. But what if you don't want to run a name server on a host, yet still want to use DNS? Or, for that matter, what if you *can't* run a name server on a host (because the operating system doesn't support it, for example)? Surely you don't have to run a name server on *every* host, right?

No, of course you don't. By default, the resolver looks for a name server running on the local host—which is why we could use *nslookup* on *terminator.movie.edu* and *wormhole.movie.edu* right after we configured their name servers. You can, however, instruct the resolver to look to another host for name service. This configuration is called a *DNS client* in the *BIND Operations Guide*.

The *nameserver* directive (yep, all one word) tells the resolver the IP address of a name server to query. For example, the line:

```
nameserver 15.32.17.2
```

instructs the resolver to send queries to the name server running at the IP address 15.32.17.2 instead of to the local host. This means that on hosts not running name servers, you can use the *nameserver* directive to point them at a remote name server. Typically, you configure the resolvers on your hosts to query your own name servers.

However, since name servers before BIND 4.9 don't have any notion of access control and many administrators of newer servers don't restrict queries, you can configure your resolver to query almost anyone's name server. Of course, configuring your host to use someone else's name server without first asking permission is presumptuous, if not downright rude, and using one of your own usually gives you better performance, so we'll consider this only an emergency option.

You can also configure the resolver to query the host's local name server by using either the local host's IP address or the zero address. The zero address, 0.0.0.0, is interpreted by most TCP/IP implementations to mean "this host." The host's real IP address, of course, also means "this host." On hosts that don't understand the zero address, you can use the loopback address, 127.0.0.1.

Now what if the name server your resolver queries is down? Isn't there any way to specify a backup? Do you just fall back to using the host table?

The resolver also allows you to specify up to three (count 'em, three) name servers using multiple *nameserver* directives. The resolver queries those name servers, in the order listed, until it receives an answer or times out. For example, the lines:

```
nameserver 15.32.17.2
nameserver 15.32.17.4
```

tell the resolver to first query the name server at 15.32.17.2, and if it doesn't respond, to query the name server at 15.32.17.4. Be aware that the number of name servers you configure dictates other aspects of the resolver's behavior, too.

> If you use multiple *nameserver* directives, *don't* use the loopback address! There's a bug in some Berkeley-derived TCP/IP implementations that can cause problems with BIND if the local name server is down. The resolver's connected datagram socket won't rebind to a new local address if the local name server isn't running, and consequently the resolver sends query packets to the fallback remote name servers with a source address of 127.0.0.1. When the remote name servers try to reply, they end up sending the reply packets to themselves.

One name server configured

If there's only one name server configured,[*] the resolver queries that name server with a timeout of five seconds. The timeout is the length of time the resolver will wait for a response from the name server before sending another query. If the resolver encounters an error that indicates the name server is really down or unreachable, or if it times out, it doubles the timeout and queries the name server again. The errors that could cause this include:

- Receipt of an *ICMP port unreachable* message, which means that no name server is listening on the name server port

- Receipt of an *ICMP host unreachable* or *network unreachable* message, which means that queries can't be sent to the destination IP address

If the domain name or data doesn't exist, the resolver doesn't retry the query. Theoretically, at least, each name server should have an equivalent "view" of the name space; there's no reason to believe one and not another. So if one name server tells you that a given domain name doesn't exist or that the type of data you're looking for doesn't exist for the domain name you specified, any other name server should give you the same answer.[†] If the resolver receives a network

---

[*] When we say "one name server configured," that means either one *nameserver* directive in *resolv.conf* or no *nameserver* directive with a name server running locally.

[†] The built-in latency of DNS makes this a small fib—a primary master name server can have authority for a zone and have different data from a slave that also has authority for the zone. The primary master may have just loaded new zone data from disk, while the slave may not have had time to transfer the new zone data from its master. Both name servers return authoritative answers for the zone, but the primary master may know about a brand-new host that the slave doesn't yet know about.

error each time it sends a query (for a total of four errors[*]), it falls back to using the host table. Note that these are *errors*, not timeouts. If it times out on even one query, the resolver returns a null answer and does not fall back to */etc/hosts*.

More than one name server configured

With more than one name server configured, the behavior is a little different. Here's what happens: the resolver starts by querying the first name server in the list, with a timeout of five seconds, just as in the single name server case. If the resolver times out or receives a network error, it falls back to the next name server, waiting the same five seconds for that name server. Unfortunately, the resolver won't receive many of the possible errors; the socket the resolver uses is "unconnected" since it must be able to receive responses from any of the name servers it queries, and unconnected sockets don't receive ICMP error messages. If the resolver queries all the configured name servers to no avail, it updates the timeouts and cycles through them again.

The resolver timeout for the next round of queries is based on the number of name servers configured in *resolv.conf.* The timeout for the second round of queries is 10 seconds divided by the number of name servers configured, rounded down. Each successive round's timeout is double the previous timeout. After three sets of retransmissions (a total of four timeouts for every name server configured), the resolver gives up trying to query name servers.

In BIND 8.2.1, the ISC changed the resolver to send only one set of retries, or a total of two queries to each name server in *resolv.conf.* This was intended to reduce the amount of time a user would have to wait for the resolver to return if none of the name servers was responding.

For you mathophobes, Table 6-1 shows what the timeouts look like when you have one, two, or three name servers configured.

Table 6-1. Resolver Timeouts in BIND 4.9 to 8.2

Retry	Name Servers Configured		
	1	2	3
0	5s	(2x) 5s	(3x) 5s
1	10s	(2x) 5s	(3x) 3s
2	20s	(2x) 10s	(3x) 6s
3	40s	(2x) 20s	(3x) 13s
Total	75s	80s	81s

---

[*] Two for BIND 8.2.1 and newer resolvers.

For BIND 8.2 and later resolvers, Table 6-2 shows the default timeout behavior.

Table 6-2. Resolver Timeouts in BIND 8.2.1 and Later

Retry	Name Servers Configured		
	1	2	3
0	5s	(2x) 5s	(3x) 5s
1	10s	(2x) 5s	(3x) 3s
Total	15s	20s	24s

So if you configure three servers, the resolver queries the first server with a time-out period of five seconds. If that query times out, the resolver queries the second server with the same timeout, and similarly for the third. If the resolver cycles through all three servers, it doubles the timeout period and divides by three (to three seconds, 10/3 rounded down) and queries the first server again.

Do these times seem awfully long? Remember, this describes a worst-case scenario. With properly functioning name servers running on tolerably fast hosts, your resolvers should get their answers back in well under a second. Only if all the configured name servers are really busy or they or your network is down will the resolver ever make it all the way through the retransmission cycle and give up.

What does the resolver do after it gives up? It times out and returns an error. Typically this results in an error message like:

```
% telnet tootsie
tootsie: Host name lookup failure
```

Of course, it may take 75 or so seconds of waiting to see this message, so be patient.

The sortlist Directive

The *sortlist* directive is a mechanism in BIND 4.9 and later resolvers that lets you specify subnets and networks for the resolver to prefer if it receives multiple addresses as the result of a query. In some cases, you'll want your host to use a particular network to get to certain destinations. For example, say your workstation and your NFS server have two network interfaces each: one on an Ethernet, subnet 128.32.1/24; and one on an FDDI ring, subnet 128.32.42/24. If you leave your workstation's resolver to its own devices, it's anybody's guess which of the NFS server's IP addresses you'll use when you mount a filesystem from the server—presumably, the first one in a reply packet from the name server. To make sure you try the interface on the FDDI ring first, you can add a *sortlist* directive to *resolv.conf* that sorts the address on 128.32.42/24 to the preferred position in the structure passed back to programs:

```
sortlist 128.32.42.0/255.255.255.0
```

The argument after the slash is the subnet mask for the subnet in question. To prefer an entire network, you can omit the slash and the subnet mask:

```
sortlist 128.32.0.0
```

The resolver then assumes you mean the entire network 128.32/16. (The resolver derives the default unsubnetted net mask for the network from the first two bits of the IP address.)

And, of course, you can specify several (up to 10) subnets and networks to prefer over others:

```
sortlist 128.32.42.0/255.255.255.0 15.0.0.0
```

The resolver sorts any addresses in a reply that match these arguments into the order in which they appear in the directive, and appends addresses that don't match to the end.

The options Directive

The *options* directive was introduced with BIND 4.9 and lets you tweak several internal resolver settings. The first is the debug flag, RES_DEBUG. The directive:

```
options debug
```

sets RES_DEBUG, producing lots of exciting debugging information on standard output, assuming your resolver was configured with DEBUG defined. (Actually, that may not be a good assumption, since most vendors compile their stock resolvers without DEBUG defined.) This is very useful if you're attempting to diagnose a problem with your resolver or with name service in general, but very annoying otherwise.

The second setting you can modify is *ndots*, which sets the minimum number of dots a domain name argument must have for the resolver to look it up before applying the search list. By default, one or more dots will do; this is equivalent to *ndots:1*. The resolver first tries the domain name as typed as long as the name has any dots in it. You can raise the threshold if you believe your users are more likely to type partial domain names that will need the search list applied. For example, if your local domain name is *mit.edu* and your users are accustomed to typing:

```
% ftp prep.ai
```

and having *mit.edu* automatically appended to produce *prep.ai.mit.edu*, you may want to raise *ndots* to two so that your users won't unwittingly cause lookups to the root name servers for names in the top-level *ai* domain. You could do this with:

```
options ndots:2
```

BIND 8.2 introduced four new resolver options: *attempts*, *timeout*, *rotate*, and *no-check-names*. *attempts* allows you to specify how many queries the resolver should send to each name server in *resolv.conf* before giving up. If you think the new default value, two, is too low for your name servers, you can boost it back to four, the default value before BIND 8.2.1, with:

```
options attempts:4
```

The maximum value is five.

timeout allows you to specify the initial timeout for a query to a name server in *resolv.conf.* The default value is five seconds. If you'd like your resolver to retransmit more quickly, you could lower the timeout to two seconds with:

```
options timeout:2
```

The maximum value is 30 seconds. For the second and successive rounds of queries, the resolver still doubles the initial timeout and divides by the number of name servers in *resolv.conf.*

rotate lets your resolver make use of all the name servers in *resolv.conf*, not just the first one. As long as your resolver's first name server is healthy, it'll service all of your resolver's queries. Unless that name server gets very busy or goes down, your resolver will never query the second or third name servers in *resolv.conf.* If you'd like to spread the load around, you can set:

```
options rotate
```

to have each instance of the resolver rotate the order in which it uses the name servers in *resolv.conf.* In other words, an instance of the resolver still queries the first name server in *resolv.conf* first, but for the next domain name it looks up, it queries the second name server first, and so on.

Note that many programs can't take advantage of this since most programs initialize the resolver, look up a name, then exit. Rotation has no effect on repeated *ping* commands, for example, because each *ping* process initializes the resolver, queries the first name server in *resolv.conf*, and then exits before using the resolver again. Each successive invocation of *ping* has no idea which name server the previous one used—or even that *ping* was run earlier. But long-lived processes that send lots of queries, such as a *sendmail* daemon, can take advantage of rotation.

Rotation can also make debugging trickier. If you use it, you'll never be sure which name server in *resolv.conf* your *sendmail* daemon queried when it received that funky response.

no-check-names, finally, allows you to turn off the resolver's name checking, which is on by default.* These routines examine domain names in responses to make sure they adhere to Internet host naming standards, which allow only alphanumerics and dashes in host names. You'll need to set this if you want your users to be able to resolve domain names with underscores or other illegal characters in them.

---

* In all resolvers that support it, from BIND 4.9.4 on.

If you want to specify multiple options, you can combine them on a single line in *resolv.conf*, like so:

```
options attempts:4 timeout:2 ndots:2
```

Comments

Also introduced with BIND 4.9 resolvers (and it's about time, if you ask us), is the ability to put comments in the *resolv.conf* file. Lines that begin with a pound sign or semicolon in the first column are interpreted as comments and ignored by the resolver.

A Note on the 4.9 Resolver Directives

If you're just moving to a BIND 4.9 resolver, be careful when using the new directives. You may still have older resolver code statically linked into programs on your host. Often, this isn't a problem because Unix resolvers ignore directives they don't understand. But don't count on all programs on your host obeying the new directives.

If you're running on a host with programs that include really old resolver code (before 4.8.3) and you still want to use the *search* directive with programs that can take advantage of it, here's a trick: use both a *domain* directive and a *search* directive in *resolv.conf*, with the *domain* directive first. Old resolvers will read the *domain* directive and ignore the *search* directive because they won't recognize it. New resolvers will read the *domain* directive, but the *search* directive will override its behavior.

Sample Resolver Configurations

So much for theory—let's now go over what *resolv.conf* files look like on real hosts. Resolver configuration needs vary depending on whether or not a host runs a local name server, so we'll cover both cases: hosts with local name servers and hosts with remote name servers.

Resolver Only

We, as the administrators of *movie.edu*, have just been asked to configure a professor's new standalone workstation, which doesn't run a name server. Deciding which domain the workstation belongs in is easy—there's only *movie.edu* to choose from. However, she *is* working with researchers at Pixar on new shading algorithms, so perhaps it'd be wise to put *pixar.com* in her workstation's search list. The *search* directive:

```
search movie.edu pixar.com
```

makes *movie.edu* her workstation's local domain name and searches *pixar.com* for names not found in *movie.edu*.

The new workstation is on the 192.249.249/24 network, so the closest name servers are *wormhole.movie.edu* (192.249.249.1) and *terminator.movie.edu* (192.249.249.3). As a rule, you should configure hosts to use the closest name server available first. (The closest possible name server is a name server on the local host; the next closest is a name server on the same subnet or network.) In this case, both name servers are equally close, but we know that *wormhole.movie.edu* is bigger (it's a faster host, with more capacity). So the first *nameserver* directive in *resolv. conf* should be:

```
nameserver 192.249.249.1
```

Since this particular professor is known to get awfully vocal when she has problems with her computer, we'll also add *terminator.movie.edu* (192.249.249.3) as a backup name server. That way, if *wormhole.movie.edu* is down for any reason, the professor's workstation can still get name service (assuming *terminator.movie.edu* and the rest of the network are up).

The *resolv.conf* file ends up looking like this:

```
search movie.edu pixar.com
nameserver 192.249.249.1
nameserver 192.249.249.3
```

Local Name Server

Next, we have to configure the university mail hub, *postmanrings2x.movie.edu*, to use domain name service. *postmanrings2x.movie.edu* is shared by all groups in *movie.edu*. We've recently configured a name server on the host to help cut down the load on the other name servers, so we should make sure the resolver queries the name server on the local host first.

The simplest resolver configuration for this case is no configuration at all: don't create a *resolv.conf* file, and let the resolver default to using the local name server. The *hostname* should be set to the full domain name of the host so that the resolver can determine the local domain name.

If we decide we need a backup name server—a prudent decision—we can use *resolv.conf*. Whether or not we configure a backup name server depends largely on the reliability of the local name server. A good implementation of the BIND name server will keep running for longer than some operating systems, so there may be no need for a backup. If the local name server has a history of problems, though—say it hangs occasionally and stops responding to queries—it'd be a good idea to add a backup name server.

To add a backup name server, just list the local name server first in *resolv.conf* (at the host's IP address or the zero address, 0.0.0.0—either will do), then one or two backup name servers. Remember not to use the loopback address unless you know your system's TCP/IP stack doesn't have the problem we mentioned earlier.

Since we'd rather be safe than sorry, we're going to add two backup name servers. *postmanrings2x.movie.edu* is on the 192.249.249/24 network, too, so *terminator.movie.edu* and *wormhole.movie.edu* are its closest name servers (besides its own). We'll reverse the order in which they're queried from the previous resolver-only example to help balance the load between the two. And because we'd rather not wait the full five seconds for the resolver to try the second name server, we'll lower the timeout to two seconds. The *resolv.conf* file ends up looking like this:

```
domain movie.edu
nameserver 0.0.0.0
nameserver 192.249.249.3
nameserver 192.249.249.1
options timeout:2
```

Minimizing Pain and Suffering

Now that you've configured your host to use DNS, what's going to change? Will your users be forced to type long domain names? Will they have to change their mail addresses and mailing lists?

Thanks to the search list, much of this will continue working as before. There are some exceptions, though, and some notable differences in the way that some programs behave when they use DNS. We'll try to cover all the common ones.

Differences in Service Behavior

As you've seen earlier in this chapter, programs such as *telnet*, *ftp*, *rlogin*, and *rsh* apply the search list to domain name arguments that aren't dot-terminated. That means that if you're in *movie.edu* (i.e., your local domain name is *movie.edu* and your search list includes *movie.edu*), you can type either:

```
% telnet misery
```

or:

```
% telnet misery.movie.edu
```

or even:

```
% telnet misery.movie.edu.
```

and get to the same place. The same holds true for the other services, too. There's one other behavioral difference you may benefit from: because a name server may return more than one IP address when you look up an address, modern versions

of Telnet, FTP, and web browsers try to connect to the first address returned, and
if the connection is refused or times out, for example, they try the next, and so on:

```
% ftp tootsie
ftp: connect to address 192.249.249.244: Connection timed out
Trying 192.253.253.244...
Connected to tootsie.movie.edu.
220 tootsie.movie.edu FTP server (Version 16.2 Fri Apr 26
    18:20:43 GMT 1991) ready.
Name (tootsie: guest):
```

And remember that with the *resolv.conf sortlist* directive, you can even control the
order in which your applications try those IP addresses.

One oddball service is NFS. The *mount* command can handle domain names just
fine, and you can put domain names into */etc/fstab* (your vendor may call it */etc/
checklist*), too. But watch out for */etc/exports* and */etc/netgroup*. */etc/exports* controls which filesystems you allow various clients to NFS-mount. You can also
assign a name to a group of hosts in *netgroup* and then allow them access via
exports by using the name of the group.

Unfortunately, older versions of NFS don't really use DNS to check *exports* or
netgroup—the client tells the NFS server its identity in an RPC (Remote Procedure
Call) packet. Consequently, the client's identity is whatever the client claims it is,
and the identity a host uses in Sun RPC is the local host's *hostname*. So the name
you use in either file needs to match the client's *hostname*, which isn't necessarily
its domain name.

Electronic Mail

Some electronic mail programs, including *sendmail*, also don't work as expected;
sendmail doesn't use the search list quite the same way that other programs do.
Instead, when configured to use a name server, it uses a process called *canonicalization* to convert names in electronic mail addresses to full, canonical domain
names.

In canonicalization, *sendmail* applies the search list to a name and looks up data
of type ANY, which matches any type of record. *sendmail* uses the same rule
newer resolvers do: if the name to canonicalize has at least one dot in it, check the
name as-is first. If the name server queried finds a CNAME record (an alias),
sendmail replaces the name looked up with the canonical name the alias points to
and canonicalizes *that* (in case the target of the alias is itself an alias). If the name
server queried finds an A record (an address), *sendmail* uses the domain name
that resolved to the address as the canonical name. If the name server doesn't find
an address but does find one or more MX records, one of the following actions is
performed:

- If the search list has not yet been appended, *sendmail* uses the domain name that resolved to the MX record(s) as the canonical name.

- If one or more elements of the search list have been appended, *sendmail* notes that the domain name is a potential canonical name and continues appending elements of the search list. If a subsequent element of the search list turns up an address, the domain name that turned up the address is the canonical name. Otherwise, the domain name that found the first MX record is used as the canonical name.*

sendmail uses canonicalization several times when processing an SMTP message; it canonicalizes the destination address and several fields in the SMTP headers.†

sendmail also sets macro *$w* to the canonicalized *hostname* when the *sendmail* daemon starts up. So even if you set your *hostname* to a short, single-part name, *sendmail* canonicalizes the *hostname* using the search list defined in *resolv.conf*. *sendmail* then adds macro *$w* and all aliases for *$w* encountered during canonicalization to class *$=w*, the list of the mail server's other names.

This is important because class *$=w* names are the only names *sendmail* recognizes, by default, as the local host's name. *sendmail* will attempt to forward mail that's addressed to a domain name it thinks isn't local. So, for example, unless you configure *sendmail* to recognize all of the host's aliases (by adding them to class *w* or fileclass *w*, as we showed in Chapter 5, *DNS and Electronic Mail*), the host will try to forward messages that arrive addressed to anything other than the canonical domain name.

There's another important implication of class *$=w*, which is that *sendmail* recognizes only the contents of class *$=w* as the local host's name in MX lists. Consequently, if you use anything other than a name you're sure is in *$=w* in the right side of an MX record, you run the risk that the host will not recognize it. This can cause mail to loop and then be returned to the sender.

One last note on *sendmail*: when you start running a name server, if you're running an older version of *sendmail* (before Version 8), you should set the *I* option in your *sendmail.cf* file. Option *I* determines what *sendmail* does if a lookup for a destination host fails. When using */etc/hosts*, a failed lookup is fatal. If you search the host table once for a name and don't find it, it's doubtful it'll miraculously

---

* All this complexity is necessary to deal with wildcard MX records, which we'll discuss in Chapter 16, *Miscellaneous*.

† Some older versions of *sendmail* use a different technique for doing canonicalization: they apply the search list and query the name server for CNAME records for the name in question. CNAME matches only CNAME records. If a record is found, the name is replaced with the domain name on the right-hand side of the CNAME record.

appear later, so the mailer may as well return the message. When using DNS, however, a lookup failure may be temporary, because of intermittent networking problems, for example. Setting option *I* instructs *sendmail* to queue mail if a lookup fails instead of returning it to the sender. Just add *OI* to your *sendmail.cf* file to set option *I*.

Updating .rhosts, hosts.equiv, etc.

Once you start using DNS, you may also need to disambiguate host names in your host's authorization files. Entries that use simple, one-part host names will now be assumed to be in the local domain. For example, the *lpd.allow* file on *wormhole. movie.edu* might include:

```
wormhole
terminator
diehard
robocop
mash
twins
```

If we move *mash* and *twins* into the *comedy.movie.edu* zone, though, they won't be allowed to access *lpd*; the entries in *lpd.allow* allow only *mash.movie.edu* and *twins.movie.edu*. So we'd have to add the proper domain names to host names outside the *lpd* server's local domain:

```
wormhole
terminator
diehard
robocop
mash.comedy.movie.edu
twins.comedy.movie.edu
```

Some other files you should check for host names in need of domain-ification are:

```
hosts.equiv
.rhosts
X0.hosts
sendmail.cf
```

Sometimes, simply running these files through a canonicalization filter—a program that translates host names to domain names using the search list—is enough to disambiguate them. Here's a very short canonicalization filter in Perl to help you out:

```
#!/usr/bin/perl -ap
# Expects one hostname per line, in the first field (a la .rhosts,
# X0.hosts)

s/$F[0]/$d/ if ($d)=gethostbyname $F[0];
```

Providing Aliases

Even if you cover all your bases and convert all your *.rhosts, hosts.equiv,* and *sendmail.cf* files after you configure your host to use DNS, your users will still have to adjust to using domain names. Hopefully, the confusion they feel will be minimal and more than offset by the benefits of DNS.

One way to make your users' lives less confusing after configuring DNS is to provide aliases for well-known hosts that are no longer reachable using their familiar names. For example, our users are accustomed to typing *telnet doofy* or *rlogin doofy* to get to the bulletin board system run by the movie studio on the other side of town. Now they'll have to start using *doofy*'s full domain name, *doofy.maroon. com.* But most of our users don't know the full domain name, and it'll be some time before we can tell all of them and they get used to it.

Luckily, BIND lets you define aliases for your users. All we need to do is set the environment variable HOSTALIASES to the pathname of a file that contains mappings between aliases and domain names. For example, to set up a system-wide alias for *doofy*, we could set HOSTALIASES to */etc/host.aliases* in the system's shell startup files and add:

```
doofy    doofy.maroon.com
```

to */etc/host.aliases*. The alias file format is simple: the alias starts the line in column one, followed by whitespace and then the domain name that corresponds to the alias. The domain name is written without a trailing dot, and the alias can't contain any dots.

Now when our users type *telnet doofy* or *rlogin doofy*, the resolver transparently substitutes *doofy.maroon.com* for *doofy* in the name server query. The message the users see now looks something like:

```
Trying...
Connected to doofy.maroon.com.
Escape character is '^]'.
IRIX System V.3 (sgi)
login:
```

If the resolver falls back to using */etc/hosts*, though, our HOSTALIASES won't have any effect. So we should also keep a similar alias in */etc/hosts*.

With time, and perhaps a little instruction, the users will start to associate the full domain name they see in the *telnet* banner with the bulletin board they use.

With HOSTALIASES, if you know the domain names your users are likely to have trouble with, you can save them a little frustration. If you don't know which hosts they're trying to get to, you can let your users create their own alias files, and having each user point the HOSTALIASES variable in his shell startup file to his personal alias file.

Vendor-Specific Options

Unix is ostensibly a standard operating system, but there are almost as many Unix standards as flavors of Unix. Likewise, there are almost as many different styles of resolver configuration as there are versions of Unix. Almost all support the original Berkeley syntax, but most add nonstandard enhancements or variations, too. We'll cover as many of the major styles of resolver configuration as we can.

Sun's SunOS 4.x

Configuring a host running SunOS can be a challenge. The behavior of the SunOS resolver is arguably as different from that of standard BIND as major vendors get— primarily because SunOS's resolver is integrated with Sun's Network Information Service, or NIS (née Yellow Pages).

Briefly, NIS provides a mechanism for keeping important files synchronized between hosts on a network. This includes not just */etc/hosts* but also */etc/services*, */etc/passwd*, and others. Sun positions DNS as a backup option to NIS; if the NIS resolver can't find a host name (or IP address) in the NIS *hosts* map, you can configure it to query a name server.

Note that the resolver functionality is implemented as part of the *ypserv* program, which also handles other types of NIS queries. So if *ypserv* isn't running, neither is your resolver! (Mercifully, the resolver in Solaris 2 doesn't require that you run *ypserv*.) One benefit of using *ypserv* to resolve all queries is that you don't need to configure the resolvers on NIS clients, only on NIS servers.* The NIS clients will query an NIS server for host data, and the NIS server will query DNS, if necessary.

If you run SunOS 4.x (Solaris 1), you can either (1) follow the party line and configure your resolver to use DNS as a backup to NIS, (2) choose to run NIS without the *hosts* map, or (3) buck convention and recompile your resolver to use DNS exclusively—or you can pick up free copies of modified resolvers on the Internet. However, we must warn you that, according to our sources, Sun will *not* support the modified resolver option.

If you run Solaris 2, you can simply configure the resolver like a normal human being and use the *nsswitch.conf* file to specify that you want to use DNS for name resolution.

Modified resolvers

We won't go into much detail about this option here, primarily because this process was well-documented and nearly automated in the BIND 4 distributions. The

---

* Actually, you also need to configure the resolver on hosts on which you use *sendmail.mx*, Sun's MX record–smart version of *sendmail.*

process itself usually involves creating a new *libc.so*—the standard, shared C library—by pulling out routines that call NIS and replacing them with pure DNS versions. Although Sun generously provides the necessary replacement routines, they don't support them. Worse, the routines supplied with SunOS 4.x were based on BIND 4.8.1.

BIND 4 source distributions contained instructions on installing the BIND resolver routines under SunOS 4.x in the package's *shres/sunos* subdirectory in a file called *INSTALL*. As of BIND 8, however, the instructions don't work (and as of BIND 8.2.2, they're not included). You can still get older BIND source distributions via anonymous FTP from *ftp.isc.org* in */isc/bind/src*, though. If you want to build a replacement SunOS 4.x resolver from the source code, we recommend using the source code from BIND 4.9.7, available from *ftp.isc.org* in */isc/bind/src/4.9.7/bind-4.9.7-REL.tar.gz*.

If you'd rather skip the potentially edifying experience of creating your own shared C library and leverage someone else's efforts, you can check out *resolv+*, which is based on the BIND 4.8.3 resolver. *resolv+* is an enhanced version of the 4.8.3 resolver routines for SunOS. It was written by Bill Wisner and allows administrators to choose the order in which NIS and DNS are queried (much like the extensions other vendors have added to Unix, which we'll discuss later). The new routines are available, with instructions on how to build them into the file *libc.so*, from *ftp.uu.net* as the file */networking/ip/dns/resolv+2.1.1.tar.Z*. For more information on the functionality *resolv+* provides, see the Linux section later in this chapter.

Using DNS with NIS

If you go the socially acceptable route, though, you'll need to make NIS and DNS coexist peacefully. That's a little tricky, so let's go over it in some detail. We won't cover how to set up NIS—that's already been covered in gory detail in Hal Stern's *Managing NFS and NIS* (O'Reilly). Note that these instructions apply only to versions of SunOS after 4.1. If you run an older version of SunOS, consider the replacement libraries on *ftp.uu.net*. Or upgrade.

First, you'll need to modify the *Makefile* NIS uses to build its maps—the files that it distributes to other hosts on the network. You should make this modification on the master NIS server, not on the slaves.

The NIS *Makefile* lives in */var/yp/Makefile* on a SunOS host. The change you need to make is simple: you need to uncomment one line and comment another. Find the lines that read:

```
#B=-b
B=
```

and change them to read:

```
B=-b
#B=
```

Then rebuild your NIS hosts map:

```
# cd /var/yp
# rm hosts.time
# make hosts.time
updated hosts
pushed hosts
```

This will insert a "magic cookie" into the *hosts* map that instructs NIS to query DNS if it can't find a host name in the *hosts* map. Now, when the *ypserv* program looks up a name, it checks the appropriate *hosts* map for the local NIS domain, and if it can't find the name there, it queries a name server. The search list *ypserv* uses when it queries the name server is derived from either the local NIS *domainname* or from the *domain* directive in *resolv.conf.*

Next, you should create a *resolv.conf* file, if you need one. The rules for configuring the resolver change slightly with SunOS:

- You can't set the *hostname* to a domain name and have the resolver infer the local domain.

- You also can't use the *search* directive in *resolv.conf,* since the SunOS 4.x resolver is based on BIND 4.8.1. The resolver will silently ignore it.

- You *can* set the NIS *domainname* to a domain name (you have to set it to the name of your NIS domain if you're using NIS), and the resolver will derive the name of the local DNS domain from it. However, this doesn't work in quite the same way it does with BIND; if you set *domainname* to *fx.movie.edu,* for example, the search list will include only *movie.edu.* Why doesn't the search list include *fx.movie.edu?* Because NIS assumes it's already checked an authoritative source of *fx.movie.edu* host data—the *fx.movie.edu* hosts map.

- If you want to set the local domain name to the same name as your NIS *domainname,* you can prepend a dot or a plus sign (+) to the *domainname.* To set your local domain name to *fx.movie.edu,* you could set *domainname* to either +*fx.movie.edu* or .*fx.movie.edu.*

- You can also override NIS's normal behavior by setting the local domain name with the *domain* directive in *resolv.conf.* So if you wanted to force the resolver to include *fx.movie.edu* in the search list, you could add *domain fx.movie.edu* to *resolv.conf.*

- You can even set the *domain* directive in *resolv.conf* to a DNS domain name totally unrelated to your NIS *domainname.* In some unfortunate situations, the local NIS *domainname* isn't the same as, or even similar to, the local DNS domain name. Say the Information Technology Department at Movie U. had originally set up the NIS domain *it.dept.movieu,* and still uses it. To prevent spurious DNS queries in the nonexistent *dept.movieu* domain, hosts in this NIS domain should be configured with *domain movie.edu* (or something similar) in *resolv.conf.*

Finally, Sun's *resolv.conf* treats the *nameserver* directive just as vanilla BIND does. So once you're done with inserting magic cookies and configuring your NIS *domainname* and possibly your local DNS domain name, you can add any name servers to *resolv.conf* and be done.

Ignoring NIS

If you want to retain Sun's support but would rather not use icky NIS, you still have an option: you can run NIS with an empty *hosts* map. First, set up your *resolv.conf* file, insert the magic cookie into the NIS *Makefile* as we described in the last section, and create an empty *hosts* map. Creating an empty *hosts* map just requires moving the NIS master server's */etc/hosts* file aside temporarily, generating your NIS *hosts* map, then replacing the */etc/hosts* file:

```
% mv /etc/hosts /etc/hosts.tmp
% touch /etc/hosts # to keep make from complaining
% cd /var/yp
% make hosts.time
updated hosts
pushed hosts
% mv /etc/hosts.tmp /etc/hosts
```

Now, when the resolver checks NIS, it doesn't find anything and goes directly to querying a name server.

If you periodically rebuild your NIS maps, you should make sure the *hosts* map doesn't accidentally get rebuilt from */etc/hosts.* The best way to do this is to remove the *hosts* target from the NIS *Makefile.* You can just comment out everything in the *Makefile* from the line that begins with:

```
hosts.time: $(DIR)/hosts
```

to the next blank line.

Sun's Solaris 2.x

The resolver in Solaris 2 through 2.5.1 is based on the BIND 4.8.3 resolver. The Solaris 2.6, 7, and 8 resolvers are based on BIND 4.9.4-P1. Interestingly, Sun chose not to follow RFC 1535's advice and trim the search list to just the local domain name, so even the BIND 2.6 and later resolvers include the names of all parent domains with at least two labels in the search list. Patches are available to upgrade Solaris 2.5 and 2.5.1 resolvers to BIND 4.9.3.*

---

* Check *http://sunsolve.sun.com/pub-cgi/show.pl?target=patches/patch-access* for current patch numbers.

All Solaris 2.x resolvers support extensions to give you the ability to determine the order in which the resolver consults various sources of host information, including DNS, NIS, NIS+, and */etc/hosts*. This service order is configured in a file called *nsswitch.conf*, which lives in the */etc* directory.

Actually, *nsswitch.conf* is used to configure the order in which a number of different sources are checked. You select the database you want to configure by specifying a keyword. For naming services, the database name is *hosts*. The possible sources for the *hosts* database are *dns*, *nis*, *nisplus*, and *files* (which refers to */etc/hosts* in this case). Configuring the order in which the sources are consulted is a simple matter of listing them after the database name in that order. For example:

```
hosts:  dns files
```

has the resolver try DNS (i.e., query a name server) first, then check */etc/hosts*. By default, resolution moves from one source to the next (e.g., falls back to */etc/hosts* from DNS) if the first source isn't available or the name being looked up isn't found. You can modify this behavior by specifying a *condition* and an *action* in square brackets between the sources. The possible conditions are:

UNAVAIL
> The source hasn't been configured (in DNS's case, there is no *resolv.conf* file and there is no name server running on the local host).

NOTFOUND
> The source can't find the name in question (for DNS, the name looked up or the type of data looked up doesn't exist).

TRYAGAIN
> The source is busy, but might respond next time (for example, the resolver has timed out while trying to look up a name).

SUCCESS
> The requested name was found in the specified source.

For each of these criteria, you can specify that the resolver should either *continue* and fall back to the next source or simply *return*. The default action is *return* for *SUCCESS* and *continue* for all the other conditions.

For example, if you want your resolver to stop looking up a domain name if it receives an NXDOMAIN (no such domain name) answer, but to check */etc/hosts* if DNS isn't available, you could use:

```
hosts:  dns [NOTFOUND=return] files
```

The default Solaris *nsswitch.conf* configuration, by the way, is determined by the answers you give *SunInstall*. Believe it or not, though, none of the default *nsswitch.conf* configurations includes *dns* as a source. This from the dot in *.com*?

nscd

In Solaris 2.x, Sun introduced a name service cache daemon called *nscd*. *nscd* caches the results of lookups in the *passwd*, *group*, and *hosts* sources. You can think of *nscd* as very similar to a caching-only name server, except that it also works for information in *passwd* and *group* sources. Sun's intent with *nscd* was to speed up performance by caching frequently looked-up names. Unfortunately, word on the street is that *nscd* sometimes actually slows DNS lookups, so many people disable it. Moreover, *nscd* interferes with round robin (*nscd* caches records in one order and doesn't rotate them).

nscd is started by default during a multiuser bootup and reads the configuration file */etc/nscd.conf*. Administrators can tune a number of parameters in *nscd.conf*. The most important of these are:

enable-cache hosts (yes | no)
> Determines whether or not *nscd* caches the results of host lookups

positive-time-to-live hosts value
> Determines how long *nscd* caches positive results (e.g., addresses), in seconds

negative-time-to-live hosts value
> Determines how long *nscd* caches negative results (e.g., NXDOMAIN), in seconds

But if you're not convinced of *nscd*'s usefulness, at least with DNS lookups, you can use:

```
enable-cache hosts no
```

to turn caching off for the *hosts* source.

HP's HP-UX

HP's resolver implementation is basically straight BIND; the HP-UX 8.0 through 10.00 resolvers are based on BIND 4.8.3 and support the standard *domain*, *nameserver*, and *search* directives. The order in which a host consults DNS, NIS, and the host table is hard-wired. The host uses DNS if DNS is configured (i.e., if there's a *resolv.conf* file or a name server is running locally). If DNS isn't configured and NIS is running, the host uses NIS. If neither DNS nor NIS is running, the host uses the host table. The host falls back to using the other services only under the circumstances described earlier in the chapter (i.e., the resolver uses only one name server—either listed in *resolv.conf* or on the local host by default—and four errors are received while contacting that name server).

The hard-wired algorithm is less flexible than what other vendors provide, but it's easy to troubleshoot. When you can consult DNS, NIS, and the host table in any order, diagnosing user problems can be awfully difficult.

The HP-UX 10.10 through 11.00 resolvers are based on BIND 4.9.x. Therefore, they support the BIND 4.9.x search list behavior and the *options ndots* directive.

Patches are available for all versions of HP-UX 10.x and later to upgrade the name server and ancillary programs to BIND 4.9.7. To gain access to the patches, visit the HP-UX patch archive at *http://us-support.external.hp.com* and register. Then you can search the patch database for the latest patches.

The HP-UX 11.10 resolver is based on BIND 8.1.2. The configuration of a BIND 8.1.2 resolver is nearly identical, from a configuration perspective, to the previous BIND 4.9.x–based resolvers: they understand the same configuration directives and derive their default search list the same way.

HP-UX 10.00 introduced Solaris's *nsswitch.conf* functionality; that is, you can use *nsswitch.conf* to control the order in which the resolver consults the various naming services.* The syntax is exactly the same as that used in Solaris's *nsswitch.conf*. The default settings for the hosts database under HP-UX are:

```
hosts: dns [NOTFOUND=return] nis [NOTFOUND=return] files
```

The *nsswitch.conf* functionality, as well as the BIND 4.9.7 name server upgrade, is also available in patches for versions of HP-UX as old as 9.0. Check the web-based HP-UX patch archive for these. You may need quite a few patches:

- One for the standard, shared C library, *libc.so*, which contains the resolver routines in HP-UX

- One for the *mount* command, which is statically linked

- One for *nslookup*

- One for the *ifconfig* and *route* commands

- One for HP's Visual User Environment (VUE) or the Common Desktop Environment (CDE), which are shipped statically linked

IBM's AIX

The resolver shipped with the recent versions of AIX, including 4.3 and 4.2.1, is also relatively standard. The code is based on BIND 4.9.x, so it understands the *domain, search, nameserver, options,* and *sortlist* directives; AIX supports up to three *nameserver* directives. AIX Versions 4 and 4.1 were based on BIND 4.8.3, so they handle all the directives AIX 4.2.1's resolver does except *options* and *sortlist*.

---

* Before HP-UX 10.10, you could only use *nsswitch.conf* to configure the order of resolution for the *hosts* source. From 10.10 on, you can also use *nsswitch.conf* to configure resolution order for the *services, networks, protocols, rpc,* and *netgroup* sources.

One difference between AIX's behavior and the stock BSD behavior is that AIX uses the existence of the *resolv.conf* file to determine whether to query a name server. If *resolv.conf* doesn't exist on the local host, the resolver reads */etc/hosts*. This means that on a host running a name server, you should create a zero-length */etc/resolv.conf* file even if you don't intend to put any directives in it.

AIX 4.3

The AIX 4.3 resolver also supports two environment variables, RES_TIMEOUT and RES_RETRY, that allow you to control the resolver's initial timeouts (à la the *options timeout* directive) and number of attempts (à la *options attempts*). You can set these in a shell startup script or on the command line, as in:

```
# RES_TIMEOUT=2 /usr/sbin/sendmail -bd -q1h
```

AIX 4.3 supports a mechanism to control resolution order called *irs.conf*, similar to Solaris's *nsswitch.conf*. The syntax is slightly different, though. Like *nsswitch.conf*, *irs.conf* calls the database *hosts*. The names of the sources are nearly the same (*dns*, *nis*, and *local*, as opposed to *files*) but AIX uses the keyword *continue* at the end of a line to signal that the resolver should try the next source of information, listed on the next line. To indicate that a source of information is authoritative and that the resolver should not try the next source if the previous returns a negative answer (like *[NOTFOUND=return]*), add the tag *=auth* after the argument. So to tell the resolver to try DNS and go on to try */etc/hosts* only if DNS isn't configured, you could use the following *irs.conf* file:

```
hosts dns=auth continue
hosts local
```

If you need to specify the order on a user-by-user basis or override the system's default, you can use the NSORDER environment variable. NSORDER takes the same arguments as *irs.conf* but formatted as a comma-separated list, as in:

```
NSORDER=dns,local
```

As with *irs.conf*, you can specify that a source is authoritative using *=auth*:

```
NSORDER=dns=auth,local
```

AIX 4.2.1

The AIX 4.2.1 mechanism to control resolution order is similar but more limited. AIX 4.2.1 uses a file called */etc/netsvc.conf*. The *netsvc.conf* file also calls the database *hosts*, but it uses an equals sign between the database name and the sources instead of a colon, uses commas between sources, and uses *bind* for DNS and *local* for */etc/hosts*. So:

```
hosts = local,nis,bind
```

has the AIX resolver check the local */etc/hosts* first, then check the NIS *hosts* map, and finally try DNS. As with AIX 4.3, individual users or processes can override the systemwide resolution order configured with *netsvc.conf* by setting the *NSORDER* environment variable.

We should also note that you can configure the resolver using AIX's System Management Interface Tool (SMIT).

Compaq's Tru64 Unix and Digital Unix

The resolver shipped with Tru64 Unix 5.0 is based on the BIND 8.1.2 resolver. The resolver shipped with Digital Unix 4.0 is based on the BIND 4.9.x resolver. As such, both understand all five main resolver directives covered in this chapter, but not BIND 8.2 additions such as *options timeout*.

The Tru64 Unix 5.0 resolver does name checking but also lets you specify certain otherwise-illegal characters that you want to allow in domain names. To do this, simply list the characters, backslash-quoted, after the *allow_special* directive. To allow underscores, for example, you could use:

```
allow_special \_
```

You can also specify the argument *all* to allow any character, but that's probably not a good idea.

Both of Compaq's versions of Unix allow you to configure the order in which the resolver checks NIS, DNS, and the host table via a file called *svc.conf* (check out the *svc.conf(4)* manpage).* *svc.conf* also allows you to configure which services are consulted for other databases, including mail aliases, authentication checks (mapping from IP address to host or domain names), password and group information, and a slew of other things.

To configure the resolver with *svc.conf*, use the database name *hosts*, followed by an equals sign and the keywords for the services you want checked, separated by commas in the order you want them checked. The legal keywords for the *hosts* database are *local (/etc/hosts)*, *yp* (for "Yellow Pages," the old name for NIS), and *bind* (for DNS). *local* must be the first service listed for *hosts*. Don't use any whitespace on the line, except (optionally) after commas and at the end of the line. For example, the line:

```
hosts=local,bind
```

instructs the resolver to check */etc/hosts* for host names first and, if no match is found, to use domain name service. This is very useful when the host has a small

---

* Poor old Ultrix also supports *svc.conf*.

local host table that includes the local host's domain name and IP address, the host's default router, and any other hosts referenced during startup. Checking the local host table first avoids any problems using domain name service during startup, when networking and *named* may not have started.

Compaq's Unixes also include a utility called *svcsetup* (see the *svcsetup(8)* manpage), which allows you to set up the *svc.conf* file interactively, without the aid of an editor. Typing *svcsetup* will throw you into a mode where you can choose the database you'd like to configure. *svcsetup* will prompt you for the order of the services you want checked.

Silicon Graphics' IRIX

As of IRIX 6.5, IRIX has a BIND 4.9.x resolver and name server. The resolver understands the *domain, search, nameserver, options,* and *sortlist* directives. The previous version of IRIX, 6.4, had a BIND 4.9.x–based name server, but a 4.8.3-based resolver. There are also patches available for versions of IRIX as old as 5.3 to bring the name server up to BIND 4.9.7. For the current patch numbers, see *http://support.sgi.com/colls/patches/tools/browse.*

In IRIX 6.x, the *resolv.conf* file moved from */usr/etc/resolv.conf,* its former location, to the more standard */etc/resolv.conf.* (For compatibility with software compiled under older versions of IRIX, you may need to create a link from */usr/etc/resolv.conf* to */etc/resolv.conf.*)

Like Solaris 2.x and HP-UX, IRIX 6.5 supports the *nsswitch.conf* file. IRIX's *nsswitch.conf* has the same format as Solaris's, but adds *noperm* (no permission to use the service) to the list of conditions. The default for the *hosts* database is:

```
hosts: nis dns files
```

The IRIX name service daemon, *nsd,* reads *nsswitch.conf.* Like Sun's *nscd, nsd* maintains a systemwide cache of previously looked-up data, including host information derived from DNS and NIS. *nsd* supports many attribute settings in *nsswitch.conf* that Solaris and HP-UX don't support. For example, you can also add a timeout setting in parentheses to determine how long *nsd* will cache records learned from DNS:

```
hosts: files dns (timeout=600)      # cache timeout of 10 minutes
```

You can also specify a negative caching timeout with *negative_timeout.* For a complete list of attributes, see the *nsd(1m)* manpage.

Older IRIX resolvers (until 6.4) support a *hostresorder* directive instead of *nsswitch. conf.* Like *nsswitch.conf,* the *hostresorder* directive allows the administrator to determine the order in which NIS, DNS, and the local host table are searched. Individual users can set the environment variable *HOSTRESORDER* to determine the order in which the services are used for their commands. The IRIX 6.5 resolver ignores the *hostresorder* directive.

hostresorder takes one or more of the keywords *nis*, *bind*, and *local* as arguments. (The keywords correspond to the obvious services.) The keywords may be separated by either whitespace or a slash. Whitespace indicates that the next service should be tried if the previous service doesn't return an answer (e.g., the name isn't found in the host table or the name server returns "no such domain name") or isn't available (e.g., the name server isn't running). A slash indicates that the preceding service is authoritative, and if no answer is returned, resolution should stop. The next service is tried only if the previous isn't available.

Linux

Since we first published this book, Linux has taken the computing world by storm. A couple of the reasons are that Linux is freeware and that it does a better job of keeping up with developments in the Unix and Internet communities than any vendor's version of Unix. Attesting to that is the fact that Red Hat Linux 7.0, the latest version of one of the predominant strains of Linux, ships with a BIND 8.2.2-P5 name server. The resolver, however, is still based on the BIND 4.9.x resolver. It supports the *nsswitch.conf* file.

However, some older Linux resolvers are based on Bill Wisner's *resolv+* library, which is in turn based on BIND 4.8.3. Consequently, the *resolv.conf* file can include any legit 4.8.3 resolver directives (*domain*, *search*, and *nameserver*, but not *options* or *sortlist*) and has the older default search list described in this chapter.

resolv+, as the name suggests, also provides several enhancements over the standard 4.8.3 resolver. These include the ability to determine the order in which DNS, NIS, and */etc/hosts* are consulted (replaced by the more standard *nsswitch.conf* in newer versions), the ability to detect certain types of DNS spoofing, and the ability to reorder address records in replies to favor local subnets.

All of these enhancements are controlled by the */etc/host.conf* file. The most interesting keywords that *host.conf* accepts are:

order
>   Controls the order in which the various name services are consulted; the valid arguments are *bind*, *hosts*, and *nis*, at least one of which must follow the keyword. Multiple arguments must be separated by commas.

nospoof
>   Takes the single argument *on* or *off*. *nospoof* instructs the resolver to check any reverse-mapping (PTR) information it gets from remote name servers by issuing a forward (address) query for the domain name in the reply. If the

address returned by the address query isn't the same as the address the resolver originally tried to reverse map, the PTR record is ignored.

reorder

Takes the single argument *on* or *off*. With reorder on, the resolver sorts the addresses of multihomed hosts so that any address on a local subnet appears first.

Windows 95

Windows 95 includes its own TCP/IP stack with a DNS resolver. In fact, Windows 95 actually includes *two* TCP/IP stacks: one for TCP/IP over LANs and another for TCP/IP over dialup connections. Configuration of the resolver in Windows 95 is, naturally enough, graphical. To get to the main DNS configuration panel, go to the Control Panel, select *Network*, then choose *TCP/IP protocol*. This brings up a new dialog, which looks similar to the one in Figure 6-1. Choose the tab labeled *DNS Configuration*.

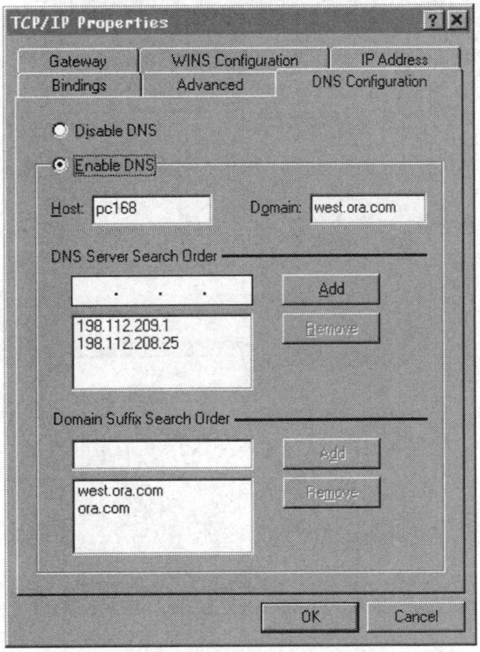

Figure 6-1. Resolver configuration under Windows 95

Configuration using this panel is fairly self-explanatory: you check *Enable DNS* to turn on DNS resolution, then fill in the PC's hostname (in this case, the first label of its domain name) in the *Host* field and the local domain name (everything after the first dot) in the *Domain* field. You add the IP addresses of up to three name servers you want to query, in the order in which you want to query them, under *DNS Server Search Order*. Finally, you fill in the domain names in the search list under *Domain Suffix Search Order* in the order in which you want them appended. If you leave out the *Domain Suffix Search Order*, the Windows 95 resolver derives a search list from the local domain name in the same way a BIND 4.8.3 resolver would.

One interesting note about the current version of Windows 95: you can configure a different set of name servers for each dialup connection you might have to an Internet service provider (ISP) in the Dial-up Networking (DUN) configuration. To configure DUN-specific resolver settings, double-click on the *My Computer* icon on your desktop, then double-click on *Dial-up Networking*, right-click on the name of the connection whose resolver settings you'd like to configure, then select *Properties*. Select the *Server Types* tab and click on *TCP/IP Settings*. You'll see the window shown in Figure 6-2.

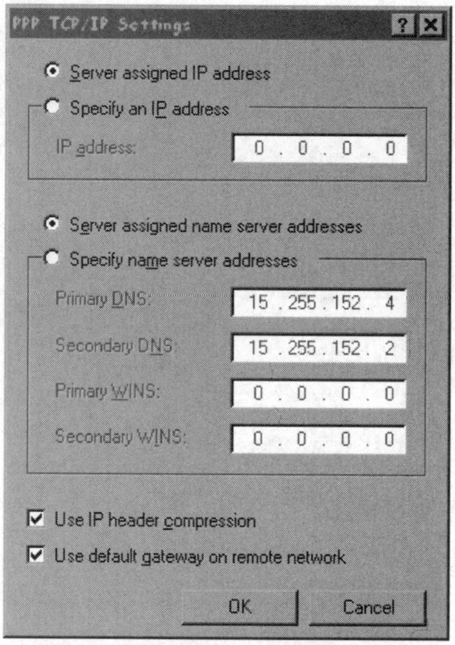

Figure 6-2. DUN resolver configuration under Windows 95

If you leave the *Server assigned name server addresses* radio button checked, the resolver will retrieve the name servers it should query from the server you dial into. If you check *Specify name server addresses* and specify the addresses of one or two name servers, Windows 95 will try to use those name servers when the DUN connection is active.

This is really useful if you use multiple ISPs and each has its own name servers. However, configuring name servers in the *TCP/IP Properties* panel overrides the DUN-specific name servers. To use the DUN-specific name server feature, you must leave the *TCP/IP Properties* panel blank except for enabling DNS and specifying the local hostname. This limitation is due to a lack of integration between the dialup and LAN TCP/IP stacks and is corrected in DUN 1.3. See Knowledge Base article Q191494 for details.*

Windows 98

The resolver in Windows 98 is almost identical to Windows 95's resolver. (Graphically, in fact, it *is* identical, so we won't show you any screen shots.) The major differences between the two resolvers are due to the fact that Windows 98 ships with Winsock 2.0.†

Winsock 2.0, for example, sorts responses according to the local routing table. So if a name server returns multiple addresses in a response and one of those addresses is on a network that the local host has an explicit (not default) route to, the resolver sorts that address to the beginning of the response. For details, see Knowledge Base article Q182644.

Configuring DUN-specific name servers also works with Windows 98. The resolver queries both the name servers listed in the *TCP/IP Properties* panel and the DUN-specific name servers simultaneously, and takes the first positive answer it receives from either set. If the resolver receives only negative answers, it returns that.

Windows NT 4.0

In Windows NT, LAN resolver configuration is done from a single panel that looks remarkably similar to Windows 95's since NT 4.0 incorporated the Windows 95 "shell." In fact, other than the new *Edit* button and the presence of handy little arrows that allow you to reorder name servers and elements of the search list, there's really no semantic difference between them, as shown in Figure 6-3.

To get to the *DNS Configuration* panel, go to the Control Panel, click on *Network*, and select the *Protocols* tab. Double-click on *TCP/IP Protocol*, then select the tab for DNS.

---

* To access a Microsoft Knowledge Base article by article ID number, go to *http://search.support. microsoft.com/kb* and check the *Specific article ID number* radio button, then type the article ID number in the search field.

† The version of Winsock in Windows 95 can be upgraded to 2.0; see Knowledge Base article Q182108.

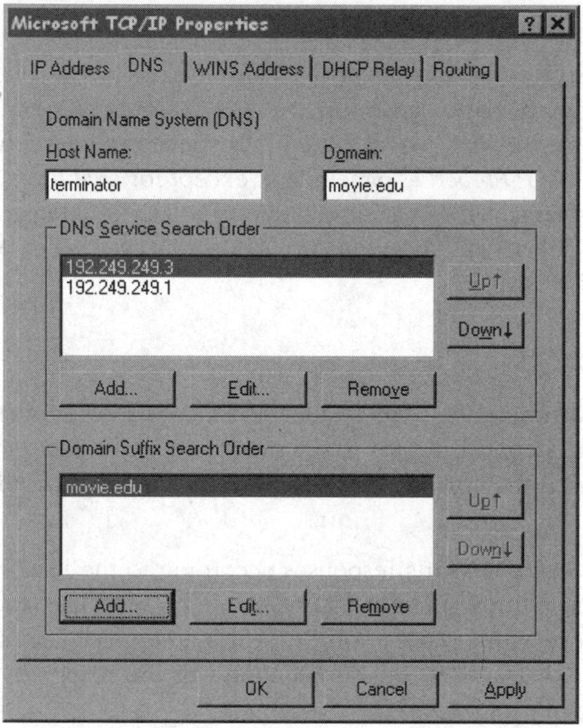

Figure 6-3. Resolver configuration under Windows NT

Windows NT also allows the user to configure resolver settings specific to particular dialup networking connections. To configure these, click on the *My Computer* icon, select *Dial-Up Networking*, pull down the top selection box, and choose the name of the DUN connection whose resolver you'd like to configure. Then click on the *More* pull-down and select *Edit Entry* and *Modem Properties*. Select the *Server* tab on the resulting window, and click on the *TCP/IP Settings* button. You'll see the very same window you'd see in Windows 95 (shown earlier). If you leave the *Server assigned name server addresses* radio button checked, the resolver retrieves the name servers it should query from the server you dial into. If you check *Specify name server addresses* and specify the addresses of one or two name servers, Windows NT uses those name servers when the DUN connection is active. When you drop the DUN connection, NT reverts to using the LAN resolver's settings.

The Windows NT 4.0 resolver caches name-to-address mappings on a per-process basis, according to the time to live on the returned address records. Good for Microsoft!

Microsoft updated the resolver fairly extensively in Windows NT 4.0, Service Pack 4. The SP4 resolver supports a sortlist, like a BIND 4.9.x resolver does, though the sortlist isn't configurable. Instead, the sortlist is based on the computer's routing table: addresses on networks that the computer has direct routes to are sorted to the beginning of responses. If you don't like this behavior—for example, because it interferes with round robin—you can disable it using a new registry value. See Microsoft Knowledge Base article Q196500 for details.

The SP4 resolver also gives you the ability to turn off caching in the resolver using (guess what?) a registry value. For details, see Knowledge Base article Q187709.

The SP4 resolver sports a new retransmission algorithm, too. The resolver still sends its first query to the first name server in the *DNS Server Search Order*. However, the resolver waits only one second before retransmitting the query, and it retransmits to *all* of the name servers it knows about—name servers it has learned about via static configuration, DHCP, and RAS. If none of these name servers responds in two seconds, the resolver retransmits to all the name servers again. It keeps doubling the timeout and retransmitting for a total of four retransmissions and 15 seconds. See Knowledge Base article Q198550 for details.

For you name server administrators, this behavior may mean significantly higher load on your name servers, so take care that the first name server listed in your SP4 resolvers' *DNS Server Search Order* is fast (usually responds in less than a second) and that you don't unnecessarily configure an SP4 resolver to query a name server (i.e., trim the *DNS Server Search Order* down to the minimum).

Windows 2000

The resolver in Windows 2000 is a little tough to find. To get to it, click on *Start*, then *Settings*, then *Network and Dial-up Connections*. This brings up the window shown in Figure 6-4.

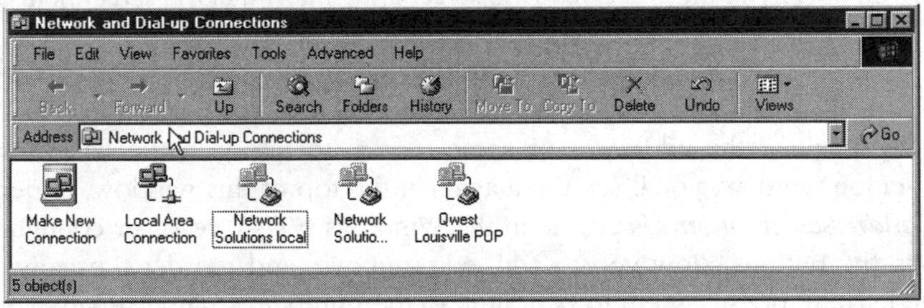

Figure 6-4. Windows 2000 Network and Dial-up Connections

Right-click on *Local Area Connection* and choose *Properties*. This brings up a window like the one shown in Figure 6-5.

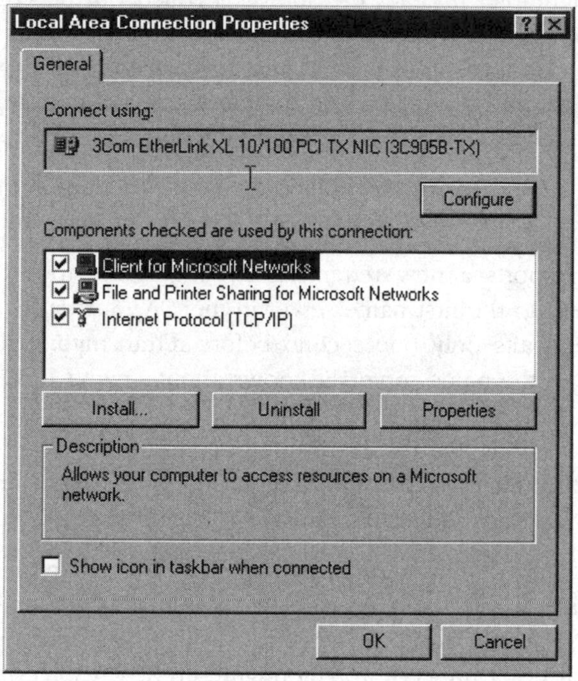

Figure 6-5. Windows 2000 Local Area Connection Properties

Double-click on *Internet Protocol (TCP/IP)*. This posts the basic resolver configuration window shown in Figure 6-6.

If you check the *Obtain DNS server address automatically* radio button, the resolver queries the name servers that the local DHCP server tells it to use. If you check the *Use the following DNS server addresses* radio button, the resolver queries the name servers you specify in the *Preferred DNS server* and *Alternate DNS server* fields.*

To get at more advanced resolver configuration, click on (what else?) the *Advanced...* button. Click on the *DNS* tab and you'll see the window in Figure 6-7.

If you've specified the addresses of name servers to query in the basic resolver configuration window, you'll see them again at the top of this window, under *DNS server addresses, in order of use:*. As in the Windows NT 4.0 resolver configuration window, the buttons allow you to add, edit, remove, and reorder the name servers listed. There doesn't seem to be a limit to the number of name servers you can list, but it doesn't make much sense to list more than three.

---

* More kudos to Microsoft for clarifying their labels. In previous versions of Windows, name servers were sometimes labeled *Primary DNS* and *Secondary DNS*. This sometimes misled users into listing the primary master and slave (secondary master) name servers for some zone or another in those fields. Besides, "DNS" is an abbreviation for "Domain Name System," not "domain name server."

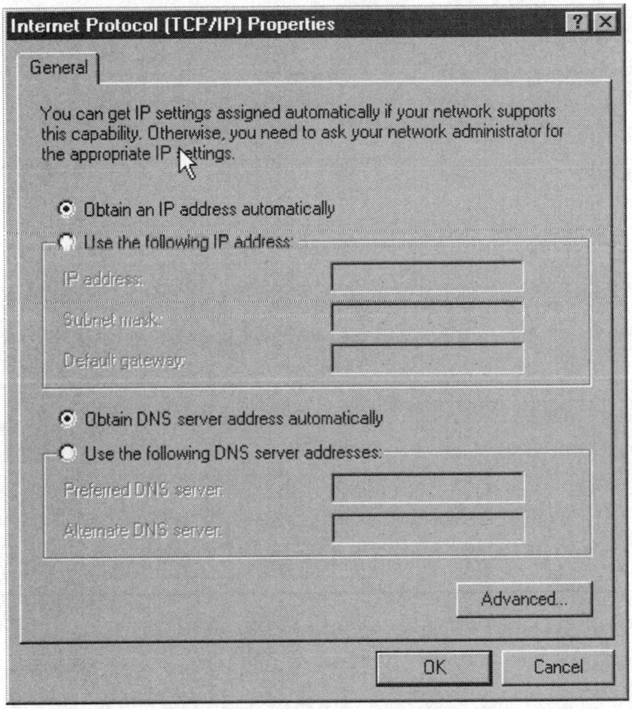

Figure 6-6. Basic Windows 2000 resolver configuration

The Windows 2000 resolver uses the same retransmission algorithm that the Windows NT 4.0 SP4 resolver does: it retransmits to all of the name servers configured. And since you can have a different set of name servers configured for each network interface (or adapter, in Microsoft's parlance), that can be quite a few name servers. For details, see Knowledge Base article Q217769.

Since it's possible, in these days of split namespaces, to get two different answers from two different name servers, the Windows 2000 resolver temporarily ignores negative answers (no such domain name and no such data) while querying multiple name servers. Only if it receives a negative answer from a name server configured for each interface does it return a negative answer. If the resolver receives even a single positive answer from a name server, it returns that.

Checking the *Append primary and connection specific DNS suffixes* radio button has the resolver use the primary DNS suffix and the connection-specific DNS suffixes as the search list. The DNS suffix specific to this connection is set in this window, in the field to the right of *DNS suffix for this connection*. The primary DNS suffix, on the other hand, is set in the Control Panel by clicking on *System*, choosing the *Network Identification* tab, clicking on the *Properties* button, and then clicking on *More….* This brings up the window shown in Figure 6-8.

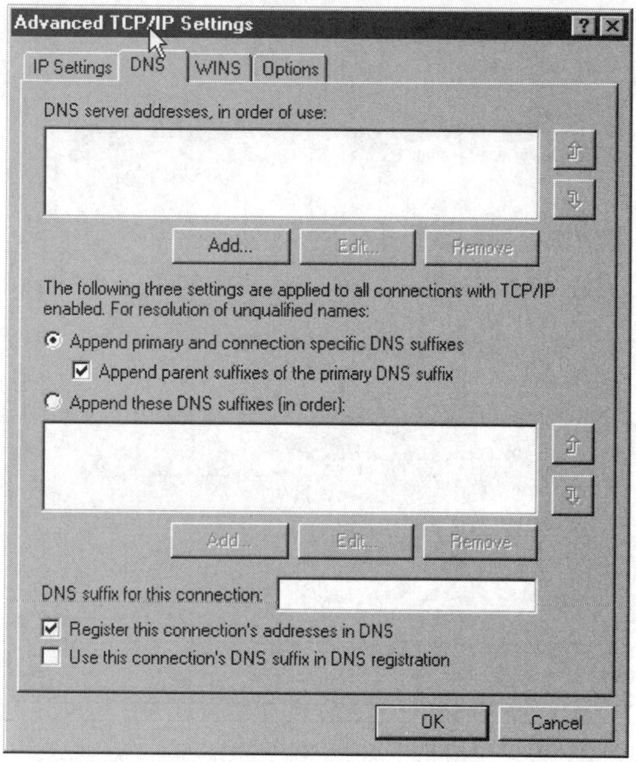

Figure 6-7. Advanced Windows 2000 resolver configuration

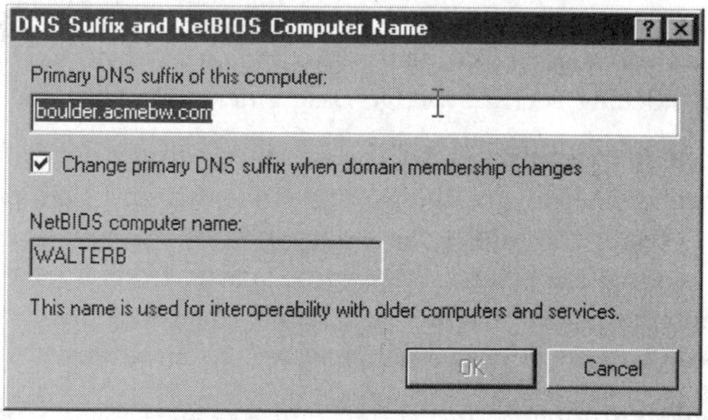

Figure 6-8. Configuring the primary DNS suffix in Windows 2000

To set the *Primary DNS suffix of this computer*, enter it in the field below that label.

The checkbox labeled *Append parent suffixes of the primary domain suffix* (see Figure 6-7) configures the resolver to use a BIND 4.8.3–style search list derived from the primary DNS suffix. So if your primary DNS suffix is *fx.movie.edu*, the search list will contain *fx.movie.edu* and *movie.edu*. Note that the connection-specific DNS suffix isn't "devolved" (in Microsoft's words) into a search list, but if it's configured, the connection-specific suffix is included in the search list.

Checking the *Append these DNS suffixes (in order)* button configures the resolver to use the search list specified in the fields below. As with the list of name servers, you can add, edit, remove, and reorder these with the buttons and arrows.

Finally, it's worth mentioning the two checkboxes at the bottom of the window. *Register this connection's addresses in DNS* determines whether or not this client will try to use dynamic update to add an address record mapping its name to the address of this connection. *Use this connection's suffix in DNS registration* controls whether that update will use the domain name associated with this connection or the primary DNS suffix for this computer.

This feature—automatic registration—is designed to ensure that the domain name of your Windows 2000 client always points to its current IP address, even if that address was delivered by a DHCP server. (The DHCP server actually adds the PTR record mapping the client's IP address back to its domain name.) It's also the death knell of WINS, the Windows Internet Name Service, the proprietary—and much maligned—Microsoft NetBIOS naming service. Once all of your clients are running Windows 2000, they'll all use dynamic update to keep their name-to-address mappings current, and you can drive a wooden stake through the heart of WINS.

Allowing clients to dynamically update zones presents certain, er, challenges, though, which we'll explore in the last chapter of this book.

7

In this chapter:
- *Controlling the Name Server*
- *Updating Zone Data Files*
- *Organizing Your Files*
- *Changing System File Locations in BIND 8 and 9*
- *Logging in BIND 8 and 9*
- *Keeping Everything Running Smoothly*

Maintaining BIND

"Well, in our country," said Alice, still panting a little, "you'd generally get to somewhere else—if you ran very fast for a long time as we've been doing."

"A slow sort of country!" said the Queen. "Now, here, you see, it takes all the running you can do, to keep in the same place. If you want to get somewhere else, you must run at least twice as fast as that!"

This chapter discusses a number of related topics pertaining to name server maintenance. We'll talk about controlling name servers, modifying zone data files, and keeping the root hints file up to date. We'll list common *syslog* error messages and explain the statistics BIND keeps.

This chapter doesn't cover troubleshooting problems. Maintenance involves keeping your data current and watching over your name servers as they operate. Troubleshooting involves putting out fires—those little DNS emergencies that flare up periodically. Firefighting is covered in Chapter 14, *Troubleshooting DNS and BIND*.

Controlling the Name Server

Traditionally, administrators have controlled the BIND name server, *named*, with Unix signals. The name server interprets the receipt of certain signals as an instruction to take a particular action, such as reloading all of the primary master zones that have changed. However, there are a limited number of signals available, and signals offer no means of passing along additional information such as the domain name of a particular zone to reload.

In BIND 8.2, the ISC introduced a method of controlling the name server by sending messages to it on a special control channel. The control channel can be either a Unix domain socket or a TCP port that the name server listens on for messages. Because the control channel isn't limited to a finite number of discrete signals, it's more flexible and powerful. The ISC says that the control channel is the way of the future and that administrators should use it, rather than signals, for all name server management.

You send messages to a name server via the control channel using a program called *ndc* (in BIND 8) or *rndc* (in BIND 9). *ndc* has been around since BIND 4.9, but prior to BIND 8.2, it was simply a shell script that allowed you to substitute convenient arguments (such as *reload*) for signals (such as *HUP*). We'll talk about that version of *ndc* later in this chapter.

ndc and controls (BIND 8)

Executed without arguments, *ndc* will try to communicate with a name server running on the local host by sending messages through a Unix domain socket. The socket is usually called */var/run/ndc*, though some operating systems use a different pathname. The socket is normally owned by root and readable and writable only by the owner. BIND 8.2 and later name servers create the Unix domain socket when they start up. You can specify an alternate pathname or permissions for the socket using the *controls* statement. For example, to change the socket's path to */etc/ndc* and group ownership to *named*, and to make the socket readable and writable by both owner and group, you could use:

```
controls {
    unix "/etc/ndc" perm 0660 owner 0 group 53;  // group 53 is "named"
};
```

The permission value must be specified as an octal quantity (with a leading zero to indicate its octalness). If you're not familiar with this format, see the *chmod(1)* manpage. The owner and group values must also be numeric.

The ISC recommends, and we agree, that you restrict access to the Unix domain socket to administrative personnel authorized to control the name server.

You can also use *ndc* to send messages across a TCP socket to a name server, possibly remote from the host that you're running *ndc* on. To use this mode of operating, run *ndc* with the *–c* command-line option, specifying the name or address of the name server, a slash, and the port on which it's listening for control messages. For example:

```
# ndc -c 127.0.0.1/953
```

To configure your name server to listen on a particular TCP port for control messages, use the *controls* statement:

```
controls {
        inet 127.0.0.1 port 953 allow { localhost; };
};
```

By default, BIND 8 name servers don't listen on any TCP ports. BIND 9 name servers listen on port 953 by default, so we're using that port here. We're configuring the name server to listen only on the local loopback address for messages, and to allow only messages from the local host. Even this isn't especially prudent, since anyone with a login on the local host will be able to control the name server. If we felt even more imprudent (and we don't advise this), we could widen the allow access list and let the name server listen on all local network interfaces by specifying:

```
controls {
        inet * port 953 allow { localnets; };
};
```

ndc supports two modes of operation, interactive and noninteractive. In noninteractive mode, you specify the command to the name server on the command line, for example:

 # ndc reload

If you don't specify a command on the command line, you enter interactive mode:

```
# ndc
Type    help -or-   /h   if you need help.
ndc>
```

/h gives you a list of commands that *ndc* (not the name server) understands. These apply to *ndc*'s operation, not the name server's:

```
ndc> /h
        /h(elp)                 this text
        /e(xit)                 leave this program
        /t(race)                toggle tracing (protocol and system events)
        /d(ebug)                toggle debugging (internal program events)
        /q(uiet)                toggle quietude (prompts and results)
        /s(ilent)               toggle silence (suppresses nonfatal errors)
ndc>
```

For example, the */d* command induces *ndc* to produce debugging output (e.g., what it's sending to the name server and what it's getting in response). It has no effect on the name server's debugging level. For that, see the *debug* command, described later.

Note that */e,* not */x or /q,* exits *ndc.* That's a little counterintuitive.

help tells you the commands at your disposal. These control the name server:

```
ndc> help
getpid
status
stop
exec
reload [zone] ...
reconfig [-noexpired] (just sees new/gone zones)
dumpdb
stats
trace [level]
notrace
querylog
qrylog
help
quit
ndc>
```

There are two commands that aren't listed here, though you can still use them: *start* and *restart*. They're not listed because *ndc* is telling you what commands the name server—as opposed to *ndc*—understands. The name server can't perform a *start* command, since to do so it would need to be running (and if it's running, it doesn't need to be started). It can't perform a *restart* command, either, because if it exited, it would have no way to start a new instance of itself (it wouldn't be around to do it). None of this prevents *ndc* from doing a *start* or *restart*, though.

Here's what those commands do:

getpid
> Prints the name server's current process ID.

status
> Prints lots of useful status information about the name server, including its version, its debug level, the number of zone transfers running, and whether query logging is on.

start
> Starts the name server. If you need to start *named* with any command-line arguments, you can specify these after *start*. For example, *start –c /usr/local/ etc/named.conf.*

stop
> Causes the name server to exit, writing dynamic zones to their zone data files.

restart
> Stops and then starts the name server. As with *start*, you can specify command-line arguments for *named* after the command.

exec

Stops and then starts the name server. Unlike *restart*, however, you can't specify command-line options for *named*; the name server just starts a new copy of itself with the same command-line arguments.

reload

Reloads the name server. Send this command to a primary master name server after modifying its configuration file or one or more of its zone data files. Send this command to a 4.9 or later slave name server to have it update its slave zones if they are not current. You can also specify one or more domain names of zones as arguments to *reload*; if you do, the name server will reload only these zones.

reconfig [–noexpired]

Tells the name server to check its configuration file for new or deleted zones. Send this command to a name server if you've added or deleted zones but haven't changed any existing zones' data. Specifying the *–noexpired* flag tells the name server not to bother you with error messages about zones that have expired. This can come in handy if your name server is authoritative for thousands of zones and you want to avoid seeing a flurry of expiration messages you already know about.

dumpdb

Dumps a copy of the name server's internal database to *named_dump.db* in */usr/tmp* (Version 4) or in the name server's current directory (Version 8).

stats

Appends the name server's statistics to *named.stats* in */usr/tmp* (Version 4) or in the name server's current directory (Version 8).

trace [level]

Appends debugging information to *named.run* in */usr/tmp* (Version 4) or in the name server's current directory (Version 8). Specifying higher debug levels increases the amount of detail in the debugging information. For information on what is logged at each level, see Chapter 13, *Reading BIND Debugging Output*.

notrace

Turns off debugging.

querylog (or qrylog)

Toggle logging all queries with *syslog*. Logging takes place at priority LOG_INFO. *named* must be compiled with QRYLOG defined (it is defined by default). This feature was added in Version 4.9.

quit

Ends the control session.

rndc and controls (BIND 9)

BIND 9, like BIND 8, uses the *controls* statement to determine how the name server listens for control messages. The syntax is the same, except that only the *inet* substatement is allowed. (BIND 9.1.0 doesn't support Unix domain sockets for the control channel, and the ISC suggests BIND 9 probably never will.)

With BIND 9, you can leave out the port specification and the name server will default to listening on port 953. You must also add a *keys* specification:

```
controls {
        inet * allow { any; } keys { "rndc-key"; };
};
```

This determines which cryptographic key *rndc* users must authenticate themselves with to send control messages to the name server. If you leave the *keys* specification out, you'll see this message after the name server starts:

```
Jan 13 18:22:03 terminator named[13964]: type 'inet' control channel
has no 'keys' clause; control channel will be disabled
```

The key or keys specified in the *keys* substatement must be defined in a *key* statement:

```
key "rndc-key" {
        algorithm hmac-md5;
        secret "Zm9vCg==";
};
```

The *key* statement can go directly in *named.conf*, but if your *named.conf* file is world-readable, it's safer to put it in a different file that's not world-readable and include that file in *named.conf*:

```
include "/etc/rndc.key";
```

The only algorithm currently supported is HMAC-MD5, a technique for using the fast MD5 secure hash algorithm to do authentication.* The secret is simply the base 64 encoding of a password that *named* and authorized *rndc* users will share. You can generate the secret using programs like *mmencode* or *dnssec-keygen* from the BIND distribution, as described in Chapter 11, *Security*.

For example, you can use *mmencode* to generate the base 64 encoding of *foobarbaz*:

```
% mmencode
foobarbaz
CmZvb2JhcmJh
```

---

* See RFCs 2085 and 2104 for more information on HMAC-MD5.

To use *rndc*, you need to create an *rndc.conf* file to tell *rndc* which authentication keys to use and which name servers to use them with. *rndc.conf* usually lives in */etc*. Here's a simple *rndc.conf* file:

```
options {
        default-server localhost;
        default-key "rndc-key";
};

key "rndc-key" {
        algorithm hmac-md5;
        secret "Zm9vCg==";
};
```

The syntax of the file is very similar to the syntax of *named.conf*. In the *options* statement, you define the default name server to send control messages to (which you can override on the command line) and the name of the default key to present to remote name servers (which you can also override on the command line).

The syntax of the *key* statement is the same as that used in *named.conf*, described earlier. The name of the key in *rndc.conf*, as well as the secret, must match the key definition in *named.conf*.

 Remember that since you're storing keys (which are essentially passwords) in *rndc.conf* and *named.conf*, you should make sure that neither file is readable by users who aren't authorized to control the name server.

If you're using *rndc* to control only a single name server, its configuration is straightforward. You define an authentication key using identical *key* statements in *named.conf* and *rndc.conf*. Then you define your name server as the default server to control with the *default-server* substatement in the *rndc.conf options* statement, and define the key as the default key using the *default-key* substatement. Then run *rndc* as:

```
% rndc reload
```

If you have multiple name servers to control, you can associate each with a different key. Define the keys in separate *key* statements, and then associate each key with a different server in a *server* statement:

```
server localhost {
    key "rndc-key";
};

server wormhole.movie.edu {
    key "wormhole-key";
};
```

Then run *rndc* with the −*s* option to specify the server to control:

```
% rndc -s wormhole.movie.edu reload
```

If you haven't associated a key with a particular name server, you can still specify which key to use on the command line with the −*y* option:

```
% rndc -s wormhole.movie.edu -y rndc-wormhole reload
```

Finally, if your name server is listening on a nonstandard port for control messages (i.e., a port other than 953), you must use the −*p* option to tell *rndc* which port to connect to:

```
% rndc -s terminator.movie.edu -p 54 reload
```

Now the bad news: in BIND 9.0.0, *rndc* supports only the *reload* command—and not single-zone reloads, which aren't supported until 9.1.0. Though BIND 9.1.0 doesn't support all the commands that BIND 8 does, it does support the *reload, stop, stats, querylog,* and *dumpdb* commands, as well as the new *refresh* and *halt* commands:

refresh
> Schedules immediate maintenance for a slave zone

halt
> Stops the name server without saving pending updates to journal files

Using Signals

Now, back in the old days, all we had to control the name server with were signals. If you're stuck in the past (with a version of BIND older than 8.2), you'll need to use signals to manage your name server. We'll give you a list of the signals you can send to a name server and tell you which modern *ndc* command each is equivalent to. If you have the shell script version of *ndc* (from BIND 4.9 to 8.1.2), you don't have to pay attention to the signal names because *ndc* will translate the commands into the appropriate signals. Be careful not to use a BIND 4 version of *ndc* with a BIND 8 name server, since the signal to send for statistics has changed.

Command	Signal
reload	HUP
dumpdb	INT
stats	ABRT (BIND 4) or ILL (BIND 8)
trace	USR1
notrace	USR2
querylog	WINCH
stop (BIND 8)	TERM

So to toggle query logging with an older version of *ndc*, you could use:

```
# ndc querylog
```

just as you would with the newer version of *ndc*. Under the hood, though, this *ndc* is tracking down *named*'s PID and sending it the WINCH signal.

If you don't have *ndc*, you'll have to do what *ndc* does by hand: find *named*'s process ID and send it the appropriate signal. The BIND name server leaves its process ID in a disk file called the *pid file*, making it easier to chase the critter down—you don't have to use *ps*. The most common path for the *pid* file is */var/ run/named.pid*. On some systems, the *pid* file is */etc/named.pid*. Check the *named* manual page to see which directory *named.pid* is in on your system. Since the name server's process ID is the only thing in the *pid* file, sending a HUP signal can be as simple as:

```
# kill -HUP `cat /var/run/named.pid`
```

If you can't find the *pid* file, you can always find the process ID with *ps*. On a BSD-based system, use:

```
% ps -ax | grep named
```

On a SYS V–based system, use:

```
% ps -ef | grep named
```

However, you may find more than one *named* process running if you use *ps*, since BIND name servers spawn children to perform zone transfers. During a zone transfer, the name server pulling the zone data—the slave—may start a child process, and the name server providing the zone data—its master—may also start a child process. We'll digress a little here and explain why child processes are used.

BIND 4 and BIND 8 slave name servers start a child process to perform a zone transfer. This allows the slave name server to keep answering queries while the zone data is being transferred from the master server to the local disk by the child process. Once the zone is on the local disk, the slave name server reads in the new data. Using a child process to do the zone transfer fixed a problem with pre-4.8.3 versions of BIND in which slave name servers wouldn't answer queries during a zone transfer. This could be a real nuisance on name servers that loaded lots of zones or large zones: they'd go silent for long periods of time.

BIND 9 slave name servers, with their new architecture, don't need to spawn a child process to prevent the name server from going silent while transferring a zone. A name server can transfer a zone while it answers queries.

Version 8 and 9 master name servers do *not* spawn a child process to provide a zone to a slave name server. Instead, the master server transfers the zone at the same time that it answers queries. If the master server loads a new copy of the zone from a zone data file while a transfer of that zone is in progress, it aborts that zone transfer and loads the new zone from the zone data file. The slave server will have to attempt the zone transfer again after the master has completed loading the new zone.

A Version 4 master name server starts a child process to provide a zone to a slave name server. This creates an additional load on the host running the master server, especially if the zones are very large or many zone transfers are active at one time.

If the *ps* output shows multiple name servers, you should be able to easily tell which name server process is the parent and which processes are children. A child name server started by a slave server to pull a copy of a zone is called *named-xfer* instead of *named*:

```
root  548 547  0 22:03:17 ?     0:00 named-xfer -z movie.edu
     -f /usr/tmp/NsTmp0 -s 0 -P 53 192.249.249.3
```

A child name server started by a master name server changes its command-line options to indicate which slave server it is providing the zone to:

```
root 1137 1122 6 22:03:18 ?     0:00 /etc/named -zone XFR
     to [192.249.249.1]
```

You may encounter a version of *named* that doesn't change its command line, but you can still figure out the relationship between multiple *named* processes by examining their process IDs and parent process IDs. All the child processes will have the parent name server's process ID as their parent process ID. This may seem like stating the obvious, but you should only send signals to the *parent* name server process. The child processes go away after the zone transfers complete.

Updating Zone Data Files

Something is always changing on your network—new workstations arrive, you finally retire or sell the relic, or you move a host to a different network. Each change means that zone data files must be modified. Should you make the changes manually? Or should you wimp out and use a tool to help you?

First we'll discuss how to make the changes manually. Then we'll talk about a tool to help out: *h2n*. Actually, we recommend that you use a tool to create the zone data files—we were kidding about that wimp stuff, okay? Or at least use a tool to increment the serial number for you. The syntax of zone data files lends itself to making mistakes. It doesn't help that the address and pointer records are in different files, which must agree with each other. However, even when you use a tool, it is critical to know what goes on when the files are updated, so we'll start with the manual method.

Adding and Deleting Hosts

After creating your zone data files initially, it should be fairly apparent what you need to change when you add a new host. We'll go through the steps here in case you weren't the one to set up those files or if you'd just like a checklist to follow. Make these changes to your *primary* master name server's zone data files. If you make the changes to your *slave* name server's backup zone data files, the slave's data will change, but the next zone transfer will overwrite it.

1. Update the serial number in *db.DOMAIN*. The serial number is likely to be at the top of the file, so it's easy to do first and reduces the chance that you'll forget.

2. Add any A (address), CNAME (alias), and MX (mail exchanger) records for the host to the *db.DOMAIN* file. We added the following resource records to the *db.movie.edu* file when a new host (*cujo*) was added to our network:

   ```
   cujo  IN  A   192.253.253.5  ; cujo's internet address
         IN MX  10 cujo         ; if possible, mail directly to cujo
         IN MX  20 terminator   ; otherwise, deliver to our mail hub
   ```

3. Update the serial number and add PTR records to each *db.ADDR* file for which the host has an address. *cujo* only has one address, on network 192. 253.253/24; therefore, we added the following PTR record to the *db.192.253. 253* file:

   ```
   5  IN PTR cujo.movie.edu.
   ```

4. Reload the primary master name server; this forces it to load the new information:

   # ndc reload

   If you've got a snazzy BIND 8.2 or newer name server, you can reload just the zones you changed:

   # ndc reload movie.edu 253.253.192.in-addr.arpa

The primary master name server will load the new zone data. Slave name servers will load this new data sometime within the time interval defined in the SOA record for refreshing their data.

Sometimes your users won't want to wait for the slaves to pick up the new zone data—they'll want it available right away. (Are you wincing or nodding knowingly as you read this?) Can you force a slave to load the new information right away? With Version 8 or 9 masters and slaves, the slaves pick up the new data quickly because the primary master notifies the slaves of changes within 15 minutes of the change. If your name server is 4.9 or later, you can reload it just as you did for your primary master name server. The reload induces the name server to refresh all of its slave zones. If your name server is 4.8.3 or earlier, remove all the slave's backup zone data files (or just the ones you want to force), kill the slave server, and start up a new one. Since the backup files are gone, the slave must immediately pull new copies of the zones.

To delete a host, remove the resource records from the *db.DOMAIN* and from each *db.ADDR* file pertaining to that host. Increment the serial number in each zone data file you changed and reload your primary master name server.

SOA Serial Numbers

Each of the zone data files has a serial number. Every time you change the data in a zone data file, you must increment the serial number. If you don't increment the serial number, slave name servers for the zone won't pick up the updated data.

Incrementing the serial number is simple. If the original zone data file had this SOA record:

```
movie.edu. IN SOA terminator.movie.edu. al.robocop.movie.edu. (
                        100      ; Serial
                        3h       ; Refresh
                        1h       ; Retry
                        1w       ; Expire
                        1h )     ; Negative caching TTL
```

the updated zone data file would have this SOA record:

```
movie.edu. IN SOA terminator.movie.edu. al.robocop.movie.edu. (
                        101      ; Serial
                        3h       ; Refresh
                        1h       ; Retry
                        1w       ; Expire
                        1h )     ; Negative caching TTL
```

This simple change is the key to distributing the zone data to all of your slaves. Failing to increment the serial number is the most common mistake made when updating a zone. The first few times you make a change to a zone data file, you'll remember to update the serial number because the process is new and you're paying close attention. After modifying the zone data file becomes second nature, you'll make some "quickie" little change, forget to update the serial number . . . and none of the slaves will pick up the new zone data. That's why you should use a tool that updates the serial number for you! It could be *h2n* or something you write yourself, but it's a good idea to use a tool.

BIND does allow you to use a decimal serial number like 1.1, but we recommend that you use only integer values. Here's how BIND Version 4 handles decimal serial numbers: if there is a decimal point in the serial number, BIND multiplies the digits to the left of the decimal by 1000. The digits to the right of the decimal point are then *concatenated* to the digits on the left. Therefore, a number like 1.1

is converted to 10001 internally, and 1.10 is converted to 100010. This creates certain anomalies; for example, 1.1 is "greater" than 2, and 1.10 is "greater" than 2.1. Because this is so counterintuitive, we think it's best to stick with integer serial numbers.

There are several good ways to manage integer serial numbers. The most obvious is just to use a counter: increment the serial number by one each time you modify the file. Another method is to derive the serial number from the date. For example, you could use the eight-digit number formed by YYYYMMDD. Suppose today is January 15, 1997. In this form, your serial number would be 19970115. This scheme allows only one update per day, though, and that may not be enough. Add another two digits to this number to indicate how many times the file has been updated that day. The first number for January 15, 1997 would then be 1997011500. The next modification that day would change the serial number to 1997011501. This scheme allows 100 updates per day. It also has the advantage of leaving you an indication in the zone data file of when you last incremented the serial number. *h2n* will generate the serial number from the date if you use the *−y* option. Whatever scheme you choose, the serial number must fit in a 32-bit integer.

Starting Over with a New Serial Number

What do you do if the serial number on one of your zones accidentally becomes very large and you want to change it back to a more reasonable value? There is a way that works with all versions of BIND, a way that works with Version 4.8.1 and later, and one that works with 4.9 and later.

The way that always works with all versions is to purge your slaves of any knowledge of the old serial number. Then you can start numbering from one (or any convenient point). Here's how. First, change the serial number on your primary master server and restart it; now the primary master server has the new integer serial number. Log onto one of your slave name server hosts and kill the *named* process with the command *ndc stop*. Remove its backup zone data files (e.g., *rm bak.movie.edu bak.192.249.249 bak.192.253.253*) and start up your slave name server. Since the backup copies were removed, the slave must load a new version of the zone data files—picking up the new serial numbers. Repeat this process for each slave server. If any of your slave name servers aren't under your control, you'll have to contact their administrators to get them to do the same.

If all your slaves run a version of BIND newer than 4.8.1 (and we pray you're not using 4.8.1) but older than BIND 9, you can take advantage of the special serial number zero. If you set a zone's serial number to zero, each slave will transfer the zone the next time it checks. In fact, the zone will be transferred *every* time the slave checks, so don't forget to increment the serial number once all the slaves have synchronized on serial number zero. But there is a limit to how far you can increment the serial number. Read on.

The other method of fixing the serial number (with 4.9 and later slaves) is easier to understand if we first cover some background material. The DNS serial number is a 32-bit unsigned integer whose value ranges from 0 to 4,294,967,295. The serial number uses *sequence space arithmetic*, which means that for any serial number, half the numbers in the number space (2,147,483,647 numbers) are less than the serial number and half the numbers are larger.

Let's go over an example of sequence space numbers. Suppose the serial number is 5. Serial numbers 6 through (5 + 2,147,483,647) are larger than serial number 5 and serial numbers (5 + 2,147,483,649) through 4 are smaller. Notice that the serial number wrapped around to 4 after reaching 4,294,967,295. Also notice that we didn't include the number (5 + 2,147,483,648), because this is exactly halfway around the number space and could be larger or smaller than 5, depending on the implementation. To be safe, don't use it.

Now back to the original problem. If your zone serial number is 25,000 and you want to start numbering at 1 again, you can speed through the serial number space in two steps. First, add the largest increment possible to your serial number (25,000 + 2,147,483,647 = 2,147,508,647). If the number you come up with is larger than 4,294,967,295 (the largest 32-bit value), you'll have wrap around to the beginning of the number space by subtracting 4,294,967,296 from it. After changing the serial number, you must wait for all of your slaves to pick up a new copy of the zone. Second, change the zone serial number to its target value (1), which is now *larger* than the current serial number (2,147,508,647). After the slaves pick up a new copy of the zone, you're done!

Additional Zone Data File Entries

After you've been running a name server for a while, you may want to add data to your name server to help you manage your zone. Have you ever been stumped when someone asked you *where* one of your hosts is? Maybe you don't even remember what kind of host it is. Administrators have to manage larger and larger populations of hosts these days, making it easy to lose track of this information. The name server can help you out. And if one of your hosts is acting up and someone notices remotely, the name server can help them get in touch with you.

So far in the book, we've covered SOA, NS, A, CNAME, PTR, and MX records. These records are critical to everyday operation—name servers need them to operate, and applications look up data of these types. DNS defines many more datatypes, though. The next most useful resource record types are TXT and RP; these can be used to tell you a host's location and responsible person. For a list of common (and not-so-common) resource records, see Appendix A, *DNS Message Format and Resource Records*.

General text information

TXT stands for TeXT. These records are simply a list of strings, each less than 256 characters in length. Versions of BIND prior to 4.8.3 do not support TXT records. In Version 4, BIND limits the zone data file TXT record to a single string of almost 2K of data.

TXT records can be used for anything you want; one use is to list a host's location:

```
cujo  IN  TXT  "Location: machine room dog house"
```

BIND 8 and 9 have the same 2K limit, but you can specify the TXT record as multiple strings:

```
cujo  IN  TXT  "Location:" "machine room dog house"
```

Responsible Person

Domain administrators will undoubtedly develop a love/hate relationship with the Responsible Person, or RP, record. The RP record can be attached to any domain name, internal or leaf, and indicates who is responsible for that host or zone. This enables you to locate the miscreant responsible for the host peppering you with DNS queries, for example. But it also leads people to you when one of your hosts acts up.

The record takes two arguments as its record-specific data: an electronic mail address in domain name format, and a domain name pointing to additional data about the contact. The electronic mail address is in the same format the SOA record uses: it substitutes a "." for the "@". The next argument is a domain name, which must have a TXT record associated with it. The TXT record then contains free-format information about the contact, like full name and phone number. If you omit either field, you must specify the root domain (".") as a placeholder instead.

Here are some example RP (and associated) records:

```
robocop     IN  RP   root.movie.edu.  hotline.movie.edu.
            IN  RP   richard.movie.edu.  rb.movie.edu.
hotline     IN  TXT  "Movie U. Network Hotline, (415) 555-4111"
rb          IN  TXT  "Richard Boisclair, (415) 555-9612"
```

Note that TXT records for *root.movie.edu* and *richard.movie.edu* aren't necessary, since they're only the domain name encoding of electronic mail addresses, not real domain names.

This resource record didn't exist when BIND 4.8.3 was implemented, but BIND 4.9 supports it. Check the documentation for your version of the name server to see if it supports RP before trying to use it.

Generating Zone Data Files from the Host Table

As you saw in Chapter 4, *Setting Up BIND*, we defined a process for converting host table information into zone data. We've written a tool in Perl to automate this process, called *h2n*.* Using a tool to generate your data has one big advantage: there will be no syntax errors or inconsistencies in your zone data files—assuming we wrote *h2n* correctly! One common inconsistency is to have an A (address) record for a host but no corresponding PTR (pointer) record, or the other way around. Because this data is in separate zone data files, it is easy to err.

What does *h2n* do? Given the */etc/hosts* file and some command-line options, *h2n* creates the data files for your zones. As a system administrator, you keep the host table current. Each time you modify the host table, you run *h2n* again. *h2n* rebuilds each zone data file from scratch, assigning each new file the next higher serial number. It can be run manually or from *cron* each night. If you use *h2n*, you'll never again have to worry about forgetting to increment the serial number.

First, *h2n* needs to know the domain name of your forward-mapping zone and your network numbers. (*h2n* can figure out the names of your reverse-mapping zones from your network numbers.) These map conveniently into the zone data filenames: *movie.edu* zone data goes in *db.movie*, and network 192.249.249/24 data goes into *db.192.249.249*. The domain name of your forward-mapping zone and your network number are specified with the −*d* and −*n* options, as follows:

−*d domain name*
> The domain name of your forward-mapping zone.

−*n network number*
> The network number of your network. If you are generating files for several networks, use several −*n* options on the command line. Omit trailing zeros and netmask specifications from the network numbers.

The *h2n* command requires the −*d* flag and at least one −*n* option; they have no default values. For example, to create the data file for the zone *movie.edu*, which consists of two networks, give the command:

```
% h2n -d movie.edu -n 192.249.249 -n 192.253.253
```

---

* In case you've forgotten how to get *h2n*, see "Obtaining the Example Programs" in the Preface.

For greater control over the data, you can use other options:

−s server

> The name servers for the NS records. As with *−n*, use several *−s* options if you have multiple primary master or slave name servers. A Version 8 or 9 server will NOTIFY this list of servers when a zone changes. The default is the host on which you run *h2n*.

−h host

> The host for the MNAME field of the SOA record. *host* must be the primary master name server to ensure proper operation of the NOTIFY feature. The default is the host on which you run *h2n*.

−u user

> The mail address of the person in charge of the zone data. This defaults to *root* on the host on which you run *h2n*.

−o other

> Other SOA values, not including the serial number, as a colon-separated list. These default to 10800:3600:604800:86400.

−f file

> Read the *h2n* options from the named *file* rather than from the command line. If you have lots of options, keep them in a file.

−v 4|8

> Generate configuration files for BIND 4 or 8; Version 4 is the default. Since BIND 9's configuration file format is basically the same as BIND 8's, you can use *−v 8* for a BIND 9 name server.

−y

> Generate the serial number from the date.

Here is an example that uses all the options mentioned so far:

```
% h2n -f opts
```

Contents of file *opts*:

```
-d movie.edu
-n 192.249.249
-n 192.253.253
-s terminator.movie.edu
-s wormhole
-u al
-h terminator
-o 10800:3600:604800:86400
-v 8
-y
```

If an option requires a host name, you can provide either a full domain name (e.g., *terminator.movie.edu*) or just the host's name (e.g., *terminator*). If you give the host name only, *h2n* forms a complete domain name by adding the domain name given with the *−d* option. (If a trailing dot is necessary, *h2n* adds it too.)

There are more options to *h2n* than we've shown here. For the complete list of options, you'll have to look at the manpage.

Of course, some kinds of resource records aren't easy to generate from */etc/hosts*— the necessary data simply isn't there. You may need to add these records manually. But since *h2n* always rewrites zone data files, won't your changes be overwritten?

Well, *h2n* provides a "back door" for inserting this kind of data. Put these special records in a file named *spcl.DOMAIN*, where *DOMAIN* is the first label of the domain name of your zone. When *h2n* finds this file, it will "include" it by adding the line:

```
$INCLUDE spcl.DOMAIN
```

to the end of the *db.DOMAIN* file. (The $INCLUDE statement is described later in this chapter.) For example, the administrator of *movie.edu* may add extra MX records into the file *spcl.movie* so that users can mail to *movie.edu* directly instead of sending mail to hosts within *movie.edu*. Upon finding this file, *h2n* would put the line:

```
$INCLUDE spcl.movie
```

at the end of the zone data file *db.movie*.

Keeping the Root Hints Current

As we explained in Chapter 4, the root hints file tells your name server where the servers for the root zone are. It must be updated periodically. The root name servers don't change very often, but they do change. A good practice is to check your root hints file every month or two. In Chapter 4, we told you to get the file by FTPing to *ftp.rs.internic.net*. And that's probably the best way to keep current.

If you have a copy of *dig*, a utility that works a lot like *nslookup* and is included in the BIND distribution, you can retrieve the current list of root name servers just by running:

```
% dig @a.root-servers.net  .  ns > db.cache
```

Organizing Your Files

Back when you first set up your zones, organizing your files was simple—you put them all in a single directory. There was one configuration file and a handful of zone data files. Over time, though, your responsibilities grew. More networks were added and hence more *in-addr.arpa* zones. Maybe you delegated a few subdomains. You started backing up zones for other sites. After a while, an *ls* of your name server directory no longer fit on a single screen. It's time to reorganize. BIND has a few features that will help with this reorganization.

BIND 4.9 and later name servers support a configuration file statement, called *include*, which allows you to insert the contents of a file into the current configuration file. This lets you take a very large configuration file and break it into smaller pieces.

Zone data files (for all BIND versions) support two* control statements: $ORIGIN and $INCLUDE. The $ORIGIN statement changes a zone data file's origin, and $INCLUDE inserts a new file into the current zone data file. These control statements are not resource records; they facilitate the maintenance of DNS data. In particular, they make it easier for you to divide your zone into subdomains by allowing you to store the data for each subdomain in a separate file.

Using Several Directories

One way to organize your zone data files is to store them in separate directories. If your name server is a primary master for several sites' zones (both forward- and reverse-mapping), you could store each site's zone data files in its own directory. Another arrangement might be to store all the primary master zones' data files in one directory and all the backup zone data files in another. Let's look at what the BIND 4 configuration file might look like if you chose to split up your primary master and slave zones:

```
directory /var/named
;
; These files are not specific to any zone
;
cache      .                        db.cache
primary    0.0.127.in-addr.arpa     db.127.0.0
;
; These are our primary zone files
;
primary    movie.edu                primary/db.movie.edu
primary    249.249.192.in-addr.arpa primary/db.192.249.249
primary    253.253.192.in-addr.arpa primary/db.192.253.253
;
; These are our slave zone files
;
secondary ora.com                   198.112.208.25 slave/bak.ora.com
secondary 208.112.198.in-addr.arpa 198.112.208.25 slave/bak.198.112.208
```

---

* Three if you count $TTL, which BIND 8.2 and later name servers support.

Here's the same configuration file in BIND 8 format:

```
options { directory "/var/named"; };
//
// These files are not specific to any zone
//
zone "." {
        type hint;
        file "db.cache";
};
zone "0.0.127.in-addr.arpa" {
        type master;
        file "db.127.0.0";
};
//
// These are our primary zone files
//
zone "movie.edu" {
        type master;
        file "primary/db.movie.edu";
};
zone "249.249.192.in-addr.arpa" {
        type master;
        file "primary/db.192.249.249";
};
zone "253.253.192.in-addr.arpa" {
        type master;
        file "primary/db.192.253.253";
};
//
// These are our slave zone files
//
zone "ora.com" {
        type slave;
        file "slave/bak.ora.com";
        masters { 198.112.208.25; };
};
zone "208.112.192.in-addr.arpa" {
        type slave;
        file "slave/bak.198.112.208";
        masters { 198.112.208.25; };
};
```

Another variation on this division is to break the configuration file into three files: the main file, a file that contains all the *primary* entries, and a file that contains all the *secondary* entries. Here's what the main BIND 4 configuration file might look like:

```
directory /var/named
;
; These files are not specific to any zone
;
cache   .                        db.cache
primary 0.0.127.in-addr.arpa     db.127.0.0
```

```
;
include  named.boot.primary
include  named.boot.slave
```

Here is *named.boot.primary* (BIND 4):

```
;
; These are our primary zone files
;
primary  movie.edu                   primary/db.movie.edu
primary  249.249.192.in-addr.arpa  primary/db.192.249.249
primary  253.253.192.in-addr.arpa  primary/db.192.253.253
```

Here is *named.boot.slave* (BIND 4):

```
;
; These are our slave zone files
;
secondary ora.com                  198.112.208.25 slave/bak.ora.com
secondary 208.112.198.in-addr.arpa 198.112.208.25 slave/bak.198.112.208
```

Here are the same files in BIND 8 or 9 format:

```
options { directory "/var/named"; };
//
// These files are not specific to any zone
//
zone "." {
        type hint;
        file "db.cache";
};
zone "0.0.127.in-addr.arpa" {
        type master;
        file "db.127.0.0";
};

include "named.conf.primary";
include "named.conf.slave";
```

Here is *named.conf.primary* (BIND 8 or 9):

```
//
// These are our primary zone files
//
zone "movie.edu" {
        type master;
        file "primary/db.movie.edu";
};
zone "249.249.192.in-addr.arpa" {
        type master;
        file "primary/db.192.249.249";
};
zone "253.253.192.in-addr.arpa" {
        type master;
        file "primary/db.192.253.253";
};
```

Here is *named.conf.slave* (BIND 8 or 9):

```
//
// These are our slave zone files
//
zone "ora.com" {
        type slave;
        file "slave/bak.ora.com";
        masters { 198.112.208.25; };
};
zone "208.112.192.in-addr.arpa" {
        type slave;
        file "slave/bak.198.112.208";
        masters { 198.112.208.25; };
};
```

You might think the organization would be better if you put the configuration file with the *primary* directives into the *primary* subdirectory by adding a new *directory* directive to change to this directory, and remove the *primary/* from each of the filenames since the name server is now running in that directory. Then you could make comparable changes in the configuration file with the *secondary* lines. Unfortunately, that doesn't work. BIND 8 and 9 name servers allow you to define only a single working directory. BIND 4 name servers let you redefine the working directory with multiple *directory* directives, but that's more of an oversight than a feature. Things get rather confused when the name server keeps switching around to different directories—backup zone data files end up in the last directory the name server changed to, and when the name server is reloaded, it may not be able to find the main configuration file if it isn't left in the directory where it started (if the configuration file is specified with a relative pathname).

Changing the Origin in a Zone Data File

With BIND, the default origin for the zone data files is the second field of the *primary* or *secondary* directive in a BIND 4 *named.boot* file, or the second field of the *zone* statement in a BIND 8 or 9 *named.conf* file. The origin is a domain name that is automatically appended to all names in the file that don't end in a dot. This origin can be changed in the zone data file with the $ORIGIN control statement. In the zone data file, $ORIGIN is followed by a domain name. (Don't forget the trailing dot if you use the full domain name!) From this point on, all names that don't end in a dot have the new origin appended. If your zone (e.g., *movie.edu*) has a number of subdomains, you can use the $ORIGIN statement to reset the origin and simplify the zone data file. For example:

```
$ORIGIN classics.movie.edu.
maltese       IN  A  192.253.253.100
casablanca    IN  A  192.253.253.101
```

```
$ORIGIN comedy.movie.edu.
mash          IN  A  192.253.253.200
twins         IN  A  192.253.253.201
```

We'll cover creating subdomains in more depth in Chapter 9, *Parenting*.

Including Other Zone Data Files

Once you've subdivided your zone like this, you might find it more convenient to keep each subdomain's records in separate files. The $INCLUDE control statement lets you do this:

```
$ORIGIN classics.movie.edu.
$INCLUDE db.classics.movie.edu

$ORIGIN comedy.movie.edu.
$INCLUDE db.comedy.movie.edu
```

To simplify the file even further, you can specify the included file and the new origin on a single line:

```
$INCLUDE db.classics.movie.edu classics.movie.edu.
$INCLUDE db.comedy.movie.edu    comedy.movie.edu.
```

When you specify the origin and the included file on a single line, the origin change applies only to the particular file that you're including. For example, the *comedy.movie.edu* origin applies only to the names in *db.comedy.movie.edu*. After *db.comedy.movie.edu* has been included, the origin returns to what it was before $INCLUDE, even if there was an $ORIGIN statement within *db.comedy.movie.edu*.

Changing System File Locations in BIND 8 and 9

BIND 8 and 9 allow you to change the name and location of the following system files: *named.pid*, *named-xfer*, *named_dump.db*, and *named.stats*. Most of you will not need to use this feature—don't feel obligated to change the names or locations of these files just because you can.

If you do change the location of the files written by the name server (*named.pid*, *named_dump.db*, or *named.stats*), for security reasons, you should choose a directory that is not world-writable. While we don't know of any break-ins caused by writing these files, you should follow this guideline just to be safe.

named.pid's full path is usually */var/run/named.pid* or */etc/named.pid*. One reason you might change the default location of this file is if you find yourself running more than one name server on a single host. (Yikes! Why would someone do that?) Chapter 10, *Advanced Features*, gives an example of running two name servers on one host. You can specify a different *named.pid* file in the configuration file for each server:

```
options { pid-file "server1.pid"; };
```

named-xfer's path is usually */usr/sbin/named-xfer* or */etc/named-xfer*. You'll remember that *named-xfer* is used by a slave name server for inbound zone transfers. One reason you might change the default location is to build and test a new version of BIND in a local directory—your test version of *named* can be configured to use the local version of *named-xfer*:

```
options { named-xfer "/home/rudy/named/named-xfer"; };
```

Since BIND 9 doesn't use *named-xfer*, of course, there's not much call for this substatement with BIND 9.

The name server writes *named_dump.db* into its current directory (BIND 8 or 9) when you tell it to dump its database. Here's an example of how to change the location of the dump file:

```
options { dump-file "/home/rudy/named/named_dump.db"; };
```

The name server writes *named.stats* into its current directory (BIND 8 or 9.1.0 and later) when you tell it to dump statistics. Here's an example of how to change its location:

```
options { statistics-file "/home/rudy/named/named.stats"; };
```

Logging in BIND 8 and 9

BIND 4 had an extensive logging system, writing information to a debug file and sending information to *syslog*. But BIND 4 gave you limited control over this logging process—you could turn debugging up to a certain level, but that was it. BIND 8 and 9 have the same logging system as BIND 4, but both of the new BINDs give you control you didn't have with BIND 4.

This control has its costs though—there's a lot to learn before you can effectively configure this subsystem. If you don't have some time you can spend to experiment with logging, use the defaults and come back to this topic later. Most of you won't need to change the default logging behavior.

There are two main concepts in logging: *channels* and *categories*. A channel specifies where logged data goes: to *syslog*, to a file, to *named*'s standard error output, or to the bit bucket. A category specifies what data is logged. In the BIND source code, most messages that the name server logs are categorized according to the function of the code they relate to. For example, a message produced by the part of BIND that handles dynamic updates is probably in the *update* category. We'll give you a list of the categories shortly.

Each category of data can be sent to a single channel or to multiple channels. In Figure 7-1, queries are logged to a file while statistics data is both logged to a file and to *syslog*.

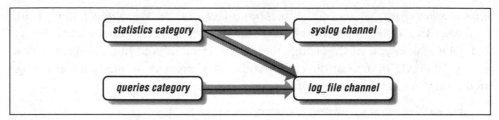

Figure 7-1. Logging categories to channels

Channels allow you to filter by message severity. Here's the list of severities, from most severe to least:

```
critical
error
warning
notice
info
debug [level]
dynamic
```

The top five severities (*critical, error, warning, notice,* and *info*) are the familiar severity levels used by *syslog*. The other two (*debug* and *dynamic*) are unique to BIND 8 and 9.

debug is name server debugging for which you can specify a debug level. If you omit the debug level, then the level is assumed to be 1. If you specify a debug level, you will see messages of that level when name server debugging is turned on (e.g., if you specify "debug 3", then you will see level 3 debugging messages even when you send only one trace command to the name server). If you specify *dynamic* severity, then the name server will log messages that match its debug level (e.g., if you send one trace command to the name server, it will log messages from level 1. If you send three trace commands to the name server, it will log messages from levels 1 through 3.) The default severity is *info*, which means that you won't see debug messages unless you specify the severity.

You can configure a channel to log both debug messages and *syslog* messages to a file. However, the converse is not true: you cannot configure a channel to log both debug messages and *syslog* messages with *syslog*—debug messages can't be sent to *syslog*.

Let's configure a couple of channels to show you how this works. The first channel will go to *syslog* and log with facility *daemon*, sending those messages of
severity *info* and above. The second channel will go to a file, logging debug messages at any level as well as *syslog* messages. Here is the *logging* statement for the
BIND 8 or 9 configuration file:

```
logging {
  channel my_syslog {
      syslog daemon;
      // Debug messages will not be sent to syslog, so
      // there is no point to setting the severity to
      // debug or dynamic; use the lowest syslog level: info.
      severity info;
  };
  channel my_file {
      file "log.msgs";
      // Set the severity to dynamic to see all the debug messages.
      severity dynamic;
  };
};
```

Now that we've configured a couple of channels, we have to tell the name server
exactly what to send to those channels. Let's implement what was pictured in
Figure 7-1, with statistics going to *syslog* and to the file, and queries going to the
file. The category specification is part of the *logging* statement, so we'll build on
the previous *logging* statement:

```
logging {
  channel my_syslog {
      syslog daemon;
      severity info;
  };
  channel my_file {
      file "log.msgs";
      severity dynamic;
  };

  category statistics { my_syslog; my_file; };
  category queries { my_file; };
};
```

With this *logging* statement in your configuration file, start your name server and
send it a few queries. But nothing is written to *log.msgs*! (Well, if you wait long
enough, the name server's statistics will show up in *log.msgs*.) You expected queries to be logged. Alas, you have to turn on name server debugging to get queries
logged:

```
# ndc trace
```

Now if you send your name server some queries they're logged to *log.msgs*. But look around the name server's working directory—there's a new file called *named.run*. It has all the other debugging information written to it. You didn't want all this other debugging, though; you just wanted the statistics and queries. How do you get rid of *named.run?*

There's a special category we haven't told you about: *default*. If you don't specify any channels for a category, BIND sends those messages to whichever channel the *default* category is assigned to. Let's change the *default* category to discard all logging messages (there's a channel called *null* for this purpose):

```
logging {
  channel my_syslog {
     syslog daemon;
     severity info;
  };
  channel my_file {
     file "log.msgs";
     severity dynamic;
  };

  category default { null; };
  category statistics { my_syslog; my_file; };
  category queries { my_file; };
};
```

Now, start your server, turn on debugging to level 1, and send some queries. The queries end up in *log.msgs*, and *named.run* is created but stays empty. Great! We're getting the hang of this after all.

A few days pass. One of your coworkers notices that the name server is sending many fewer messages to *syslog* than it used to. In fact, the only *syslog* messages are statistics messages. The ones your coworker watched, the zone transfer messages, are gone. What happened?

Well, the *default* category is set up, by default, to send messages to both *syslog* and to the debug file (*named.run*). When you assigned the *default* category to the *null* channel, you turned off the other *syslog* messages, too. Here's what we should have used:

```
category default { my_syslog; };
```

This sends the *syslog* messages to *syslog*, but does not write debug or *syslog* messages to a file.

Remember, we said you'd have to experiment for a while with logging to get exactly what you want. We hope this example gives you a hint of what you might run into. Now, let's go over the details of logging.

The Logging Statement

Here's the syntax of the *logging* statement. It's rather intimidating. We'll go over some more examples as we explain what each substatement means:

```
logging {
  [ channel channel_name {
    ( file path_name
      [ versions ( number | unlimited ) ]
      [ size size_spec ]
    | syslog ( kern | user | mail | daemon | auth | syslog | lpr |
               news | uucp | cron | authpriv | ftp |
               local0 | local1 | local2 | local3 |
               local4 | local5 | local6 | local7 )
    | stderr
    | null );

    [ severity ( critical | error | warning | notice |
                 info  | debug [ level ] | dynamic ); ]
    [ print-category yes_or_no; ]
    [ print-severity yes_or_no; ]
    [ print-time yes_or_no; ]
  }; ]

  [ category category_name {
    channel_name; [ channel_name; ... ]
  }; ]
  ...
};
```

Here are the default channels. The name server creates these channels even if you don't want them. You can't redefine these channels; you can only add more of them:

```
channel default_syslog {
    syslog daemon;        // send to syslog's daemon facility
    severity info;        // only send severity info and higher
};

channel default_debug {
    file "named.run";     // write to named.run in the
                          // working directory
    severity dynamic;     // log at the server's current debug level
};

channel default_stderr {  // writes to stderr
    stderr;               // only BIND 9 lets you define your own stderr
                          // channel, though BIND 8 has the built-in
                          // default_stderr channel.
    severity info;        // only send severity info and higher
};

channel null {
    null;                 // toss anything sent to this channel
};
```

If you don't assign channels to the categories *default, panic, packet,* and *eventlib,* a BIND 8 name server assigns them these channels by default:

```
logging {
    category default { default_syslog; default_debug; };
    category panic { default_syslog; default_stderr; };
    category packet { default_debug; };
    category eventlib { default_debug; };
};
```

A BIND 9 name server uses this as the default logging statement:

```
logging {
    category default {
        default_syslog;
        default_debug;
    };
};
```

As we mentioned earlier, the *default* category logs to both *syslog* and to the debug file (which by default is *named.run*). This means that all *syslog* messages of severity *info* and above are sent to *syslog,* and when debugging is turned on, the *syslog* messages and debug messages are written to *named.run.* This more or less matches the BIND 4 behavior.

Channel Details

A channel may be defined to go to a file, to *syslog,* or to null.

File channels

If a channel goes to a file, you must specify the file's pathname. Optionally, you can specify how many versions of the file can exist at one time and how big the file may grow.

If you specify that there can be three versions, BIND 8 or 9 will keep *file, file.0, file.1,* and *file.2* around. After the name server starts or after it is reloaded, it will move *file.1* to *file.2, file.0* to *file.1, file* to *file.0,* and start writing to a new copy of *file.* If you specify unlimited versions, BIND will keep 99 versions.

If you specify a maximum file size, the name server will stop writing to the file after it reaches the specified size. Unlike the *versions* substatement (mentioned in the last paragraph), the file will not be rolled over and a new file opened when the specified size is reached. The name server just stops writing to the file. If you do not specify a file size, the file will grow indefinitely.

Here is an example file channel using the *versions* and *size* substatements:

```
logging{
  channel my_file {
    file "log.msgs" versions 3 size 10k;
```

```
        severity dynamic;
    };
};
```

The size can include a scaling factor as in the example. *K* or *k* is kilobytes. *M* or *m* is megabytes. *G* or *g* is gigabytes.

It's important to specify the severity as either *debug* or *dynamic* if you want to see debug messages. The default severity is *info*, which will show you only *syslog* messages.

Syslog channels

If a channel goes to *syslog*, you can specify the facility to be any of the following: *kern, user, mail, daemon, auth, syslog, lpr, news, uucp, cron, authpriv, ftp, local0, local1, local2, local3, local4, local5, local6,* or *local7*. The default is *daemon*, and we recommend that you use that.

Here's an example *syslog* channel using the facility *local0* instead of *daemon*:

```
logging {
    channel my_syslog {
        syslog local0;         // send to syslog's local0 facility
        severity info;         // only send severity info and higher
    };
};
```

Stderr channel

There is a predefined channel called *default_stderr* for any messages you'd like written to the *stderr* file descriptor of the name server. With BIND 8, you cannot configure any other file descriptors to use *stderr*. With BIND 9, you can.

Null channel

There is a predefined channel called *null* for messages you want to throw away.

Data formatting for all channels

The BIND 8 and 9 logging facility also allows you some control over the formatting of messages. You can add a timestamp, a category, and a severity level to the messages.

Here's an example debug message that has all the extra goodies:

```
01-Feb-1998 13:19:18.889 config: debug 1: source = db.127.0.0
```

The category for this message is *config*, and the severity is *debug* level one.

Here's an example channel configuration that includes all three additions:

```
logging {
  channel my_file {
```

```
        file "log.msgs";
        severity debug;
        print-category yes;
        print-severity yes;
        print-time yes;
    };
};
```

There isn't much point in adding a timestamp for messages to a *syslog* channel because *syslog* adds the time and date itself.

Category Details

Both BIND 8 and BIND 9 have lots of categories—lots! Unfortunately, they're different categories. We'll list them here so you can see them all. Rather than trying to figure out which you want to see, we recommend that you configure your name server to print out all of its log messages with their category and severity, and then pick out the ones you want to see. We'll show you how to do this after describing the categories.

BIND 8 categories

default

> If you don't specify any channels for a category, the *default* category is used. In that sense, *default* is synonymous with all categories. However, there are some messages that didn't end up in a category. So even if you specify channels for each category individually, you'll still want to specify a channel for the *default* category for all the uncategorized messages.
>
> If you do not specify a channel for the *default* category, one will be specified for you:
>
> ```
> category default { default_syslog; default_debug; };
> ```

cname

> CNAME errors (e.g., "… has CNAME and other data").

config

> High-level configuration file processing.

db

> Database operations.

eventlib

> System events; must point to a single file channel. The default is:
>
> ```
> category eventlib { default_debug; };
> ```

insist

> Internal consistency check failures.

lame-servers

Detection of bad delegation.

load

Zone loading messages.

maintenance

Periodic maintenance events (e.g., system queries).

ncache

Negative caching events.

notify

Asynchronous zone change notifications.

os

Problems with the operating system.

packet

Decodes of packets received and sent; must point to a single file channel. The default is:

```
category packet { default_debug; };
```

panic

Problems that cause the shutdown of the server. These problems are logged both in the *panic* category and in their native category. The default is:

```
category panic { default_syslog; default_stderr; };
```

parser

Low-level configuration file processing.

queries

Analogous to BIND 4's query logging.

response-checks

Malformed responses, unrelated additional information, etc.

security

Approved/unapproved requests.

statistics

Periodic reports of activities.

update

Dynamic update events.

xfer-in

Zone transfers from remote name servers to the local name server.

xfer-out

Zone transfers from the local name server to remote name servers.

BIND 9 categories

default

As with BIND 8, BIND 9's *default* category matches all categories not specifically assigned to channels. However, BIND 9's *default* category, unlike BIND 8's, doesn't match BIND's messages that aren't categorized. Those are part of the category listed next.

general

The *general* category contains all of the BIND messages that aren't explicitly classified.

client

Processing client requests.

config

Configuration file parsing and processing.

database

Messages relating to BIND's internal database; used to store zone data and cache records.

dnssec

Processing DNSSEC-signed responses.

lame-servers

Detection of bad delegation (re-added in BIND 9.1.0; before that, lame server messages were logged to *resolver*).

network

Network operations.

notify

Asynchronous zone change notifications.

queries

Analogous to BIND 8's query logging (added in BIND 9.1.0).

resolver

Name resolution, including the processing of recursive queries from resolvers.

security

Approved/unapproved requests.

update

Dynamic update events.

xfer-in

Zone transfers from remote name servers to the local name server.

xfer-out

Zone transfers from the local name server to remote name servers.

Viewing all category messages

A good way to start your foray into logging is to configure your name server to log all its messages to a file, including the category and severity, and then pick out which messages you are interested in.

Earlier, we listed the categories that are configured by default. For BIND 8, that's:

```
logging {
    category default { default_syslog; default_debug; };
    category panic { default_syslog; default_stderr; };
    category packet { default_debug; };
    category eventlib { default_debug; };
};
```

For BIND 9, it's:

```
logging {
    category default { default_syslog; default_debug; };
};
```

By default, the category and severity are not included with messages written to the *default_debug* channel. In order to see all the log messages, with their category and severity, you'll have to configure each of these categories yourself.

Here's a BIND 8 *logging* statement that does just that:

```
logging {
    channel my_file {
        file "log.msgs";
        severity dynamic;
        print-category yes;
        print-severity yes;
    };

    category default  { default_syslog; my_file; };
    category panic    { default_syslog; my_file; };
    category packet   { my_file; };
    category eventlib { my_file; };
    category queries  { my_file; };
};
```

(A BIND 9 *logging* statement wouldn't have *panic*, *packet*, or *eventlib* categories.)

Notice that we've defined each category to include the channel *my_file*. We also added one category that wasn't in the previous default logging statement: *queries*. Queries aren't printed unless you configure the *queries* category.

Start your server and turn on debugging to level one. You'll then see messages in *log.msgs* that look like the following:

```
queries: info: XX /192.253.253.4/foo.movie.edu/A
default: debug 1: req: nlookup(foo.movie.edu) id 4 type=1 class=1
default: debug 1: req: found 'foo.movie.edu' as 'foo.movie.edu' (cname=0)
default: debug 1: ns_req: answer -> [192.253.253.4].2338 fd=20 id=4 size=87
```

Once you've determined the messages that interest you, configure your server to log only those messages.

Keeping Everything Running Smoothly

A significant part of maintenance is being aware that something is wrong before it becomes a real problem. If you catch a problem early, chances are it'll be that much easier to fix. As the old adage says, an ounce of prevention is worth a pound of cure.

This isn't quite troubleshooting—we'll devote an entire chapter to troubleshooting later—think of it more as "pre-troubleshooting." Troubleshooting (the pound of cure) is what you have to do after your problem has developed complications, and then you need to identify the problem by its symptoms.

The next two sections deal with preventative maintenance: looking periodically at the *syslog* file and at the BIND name server statistics to see whether any problems are developing. Consider this a name server's medical checkup.

Common Syslog Messages

There are a large number of *syslog* messages that *named* can emit. In practice, you'll see only a few of them. We'll cover the most common *syslog* messages here, excluding reports of syntax errors in zone data files.

Every time you start *named*, it sends out a message at priority LOG_NOTICE. For a BIND 8 name server, it looks like this:

```
Jan 10 20:48:32 terminator named[3221]: starting.  named 8.2.3 Tue May 16 09:39:40
MDT 2000 ^Icricket@huskymo.boulder.acmebw.com:/usr/local/src/bind-8.2.3/src/bin/
named
```

For BIND 9, it's significantly abridged:

```
Jul 27 16:18:41 terminator named[7045]: starting BIND 9.1.0
```

This message logs the fact that *named* started at this time and tells you the version of BIND you're running as well as who built it and where (for BIND 8). Of course, this is nothing to be concerned about. It *is* a good place to look if you're not sure what version of BIND your operating system supports. (Older versions of BIND used the message "restarted" instead of "starting.")

Every time you send the name server a reload command, a BIND 8 name server sends out this message at priority LOG_NOTICE:

```
Jan 10 20:50:16 terminator named[3221]: reloading nameserver
```

BIND 9 name servers log:

```
Jul 27 16:27:45 terminator named[7047]: loading configuration from '/etc/named.
conf
```

These messages simply tell you that *named* reloaded its database (as a result of a reload command) at this time. Again, this is nothing to be concerned about. This message will most likely be of interest when you are tracking down how long a bad resource record has been in your zone data or how long a whole zone has been missing because of a mistake during an update.

Another message you may see shortly after your name server starts is:

```
Jan 10 20:50:20 terminator named[3221]: cannot set resource limits on
                this system
```

This means that your name server thinks your operating system does not support the *getrlimit()* and *setrlimit()* system calls, which are used when you try to define *coresize, datasize, stacksize,* or *files* on a BIND 8 or 9 name server. It doesn't matter whether you're actually using any of these substatements in your configuration file; BIND will print the message anyway. If you are not using these substatements, ignore the message. If you are, and you think your operating system actually does support *getrlimit()* and *setrlimit()*, you'll have to recompile BIND with HAVE_GETRUSAGE defined. This message is logged at priority LOG_INFO.

If you run your name server on a host with many network interfaces (especially virtual network interfaces), you may see this message soon after startup or even after your name server has run well for a while:

```
Jan 10 20:50:31 terminator named[3221]: fcntl(dfd, F_DUPFD, 20): Too
                many open files
Jan 10 20:50:31 terminator named[3221]: fcntl(sfd, F_DUPFD, 20): Too
                many open files
```

This means that BIND has run out of file descriptors. BIND uses a fair number of file descriptors: two for each network interface it's listening on (one for UDP and one for TCP), and one for opening zone data files. If that's more than the limit your operating system places on processes, BIND won't be able to get any more file descriptors and you'll see this message. The priority depends on which part of BIND fails to get the file descriptor: the more critical the subsystem, the higher the priority.

The next step is either to get BIND to use fewer file descriptors, or to raise the limit the operating system places on the number of file descriptors BIND can use:

- If you don't need BIND listening on all your network interfaces (particularly the virtual ones), use the *listen-on* substatement to configure BIND to listen only on those interfaces it needs to. See Chapter 10 for details on the syntax of *listen-on*.

- If your operating system supports *getrlimit()* and *setrlimit()* (as just described), configure your name server to use a larger number of files with the *files* substatement. See Chapter 10 for details on using the *files* substatement.

- If your operating system places too restrictive a limit on open files, raise that limit before you start *named* with the *ulimit* command.

Every time a BIND 8 name server loads a zone, it sends out a message at priority LOG_INFO:

```
Jan 10 21:49:50 terminator named[3221]: master zone "movie.edu" (IN)
               Loaded (serial 1996011000)
```

(BIND 4.9 name servers call it a "primary zone" instead of a "master zone.") This tells you when the name server loaded the zone, the class of the zone (in this case, IN), and the serial number in the zone's SOA record. BIND 9 name servers, as of 9.1.0, don't tell you when they load a zone.

About every hour, a BIND 8 name server sends a snapshot of the current statistics at priority LOG_INFO:

```
Feb 18 14:09:02 terminator named[3565]: USAGE 824681342 824600158
               CPU=13.01u/3.26s CHILDCPU=9.99u/12.71s
Feb 18 14:09:02 terminator named[3565]: NSTATS 824681342 824600158
               A=4 PTR=2
Feb 18 14:09:02 terminator named[3565]: XSTATS 824681342 824600158
               RQ=6 RR=2 RIQ=0 RNXD=0 RFwdQ=0 RFwdR=0 RDupQ=0 RDupR=0
               RFail=0 RFErr=0 RErr=0 RTCP=0 RAXFR=0 RLame=0 Ropts=0
               SSysQ=2 SAns=6 SFwdQ=0 SFwdR=0 SDupQ=5 SFail=0 SFErr=0
               SErr=0 RNotNsQ=6 SNaAns=2 SNXD=1
```

(This feature was also present in BIND 4.9 through 4.9.3, and was turned off in the 4.9.4 server. BIND 9 doesn't support it as of 9.1.0.) The first two numbers for each message are times. If you subtract the second number from the first number, you'll find out how many seconds your server has been running. (You'd think the name server could do that for you.) The CPU entry tells you how much time your server has spent in user mode (13.01 seconds) and system mode (3.26 seconds). Then it tells you the same statistic for child processes. The NSTATS message lists the types of queries your server has received and the counts for each. The XSTATS message lists additional statistics. The statistics under NSTATS and XSTATS are explained in more detail later in this chapter.

If BIND Version 4.9.4 or later (but not BIND 9 as of 9.1.0—it doesn't implement name checking yet) finds a name that doesn't conform to RFC 952, it logs a *syslog* error:

```
Jul 24 20:56:26 terminator named[1496]: owner name "ID_4.movie.edu IN"
               (primary) is invalid - rejecting
```

This message is logged at level LOG_NOTICE. See Chapter 4 for the host naming rules.

Another *syslog* message, sent at priority LOG_INFO, is a warning message about the zone data:

```
Jan 10 20:48:38 terminator named[3221]: terminator2 has CNAME
               and other data (invalid)
```

This message means that there's a problem with your zone data. For example, you may have entries like these:

```
terminator2   IN   CNAME t2
terminator2   IN   MX    10 t2
t2            IN   A     192.249.249.10
t2            IN   MX    10 t2
```

The MX record for *terminator2* is incorrect and would cause the message just listed. *terminator2* is an alias for *t2*, which is the canonical name. As described earlier, when a name server looks up a name and finds a CNAME, it replaces the original name with the canonical name, and then tries looking up the canonical name. Thus, when the server looks up the MX data for *terminator2*, it finds a CNAME record and then looks up the MX record for *t2*. Since the server follows the CNAME record for *terminator2*, it never uses the MX record for *terminator2*; in fact, this record is illegal. In other words, all resource records for a host have to use the canonical name; it's an error to use an alias in place of the canonical name.

We realize this is getting repetitive, but BIND 9 doesn't detect this error until 9.1.0.

The following message indicates that a BIND 4 or 8 slave was unable to reach any master server when it tried to do a zone transfer:

```
Jan 10 20:52:42 wormhole named[2813]: zoneref: Masters for
               secondary zone "movie.edu" unreachable
```

BIND 9 slaves say:

```
Jul 27 16:50:55 terminator named[7174]: refresh_callback: zone movie.edu/IN:
failure for 10.0.0.1#53: timed out
```

This message is sent at priority LOG_NOTICE on BIND 4 or 8, and LOG_INFO on BIND 9, and is sent only the first time the zone transfer fails. When the zone transfer finally succeeds, a 4.9 or later name server tells you that the zone transferred by issuing another *syslog* message. Older servers don't tell you when the zone transferred. When this message first appears, you don't need to take any immediate action. The name server will continue to attempt to transfer the zone according to the retry period in the SOA record. After a few days (or half the expire time), you might check that the server was able to transfer the zone. On servers that don't issue the *syslog* message when the zone transfers, you can verify that the zone transferred by checking the timestamp on the backup zone data file. When a zone transfer succeeds, a new backup file is created. When a name server finds a zone is up to date, it "touches" the backup file (à la the Unix *touch* command). In both cases, the timestamp on the backup file is updated, so go to the slave and give the command *ls –l /usr/local/named/db**. This will tell you when the slave last synchronized each zone with the master server. We'll cover how to troubleshoot slaves failing to transfer zones in Chapter 14.

If you are watching the *syslog* messages on your 4.9 or later master name server, you'll see a LOG_INFO *syslog* message when the slave picks up the new zone data or when a tool such as *nslookup* transfers a zone:

```
Mar  7 07:30:04 terminator named[3977]: approved AXFR from
                              [192.249.249.1].2253 for "movie.edu"
```

Once again, BIND 9 doesn't log anything as of 9.1.0.

If you're using the BIND 4 *xfrnets* configuration file directive or BIND 8 *allow-transfer* substatement (explained in Chapter 10) to limit which servers can load zones, you may see this message saying *unapproved* instead of *approved*. A BIND 9 name server reports:

```
Jul 27 16:59:26 terminator named[7174]: client 192.249.249.1#1386: zone transfer
denied
```

You'd see this *syslog* message only if you capture LOG_INFO *syslog* messages:

```
Jan 10 20:52:42 wormhole named[2813]: Malformed response
                       from 192.1.1.1
```

Most often, this message means that some bug in a name server caused it to send an erroneous response packet. The error probably occurred on the remote name server (192.1.1.1) rather than the local server (*wormhole*). Diagnosing this kind of error involves capturing the response packet in a network trace and decoding it. Decoding DNS packets manually is beyond the scope of this book, so we won't go into much detail. You'd see this type of error if the response packet said it contained several answers in the answer section (like four address resource records), yet the answer section contained only a single answer. The only course of action is to notify the administrator of the offending host via email (assuming you can get the name of the host by looking up the address). You would also see this message if the underlying network altered (damaged) the UDP response packets in some way. Checksumming UDP packets is optional, so this error might not be caught at a lower level.

A BIND 4.9 or 8 *named* logs this message when you try to sneak records into your zone data file that belong in another zone:

```
Jun 13 08:02:03 terminator named[2657]: db.movie.edu:28: data "foo.bar.edu"
                       outside zone "movie.edu" (ignored)
```

A BIND 9 *named* logs:

```
Jul 27 17:07:01 terminator named[7174]: dns_master_load: db.movie.edu:28: ignoring
out-of-zone data
```

For instance, if we tried to use this zone data:

```
robocop       IN A  192.249.249.2
terminator    IN A  192.249.249.3


; Add this entry to the name server's cache
foo.bar.edu.  IN A  10.0.7.13
```

we'd be adding data for the *bar.edu* zone into our *movie.edu* zone data file. A 4.8.3 vintage name server would blindly add *foo.bar.edu* to its cache, and wouldn't check that all the data in the *db.movie.edu* file was in the *movie.edu* zone. You can't fool a name server newer than 4.9, though. This *syslog* message is logged at priority LOG_INFO.

Earlier in the book, we said that you couldn't use a CNAME in the data portion of a resource record. BIND Versions 4.9 and 8 will catch this misuse:

```
Jun 13 08:21:04 terminator named[2699]: "movie.edu IN NS" points to a
                                        CNAME (dh.movie.edu)
```

BIND 9 doesn't catch it as of 9.1.0.

Here is an example of the offending resource records:

```
@                      NS      terminator.movie.edu.
                       NS      dh.movie.edu.
terminator.movie.edu.  IN A    192.249.249.3
diehard.movie.edu.     IN A    192.249.249.4
dh                     IN CNAME diehard
```

The second NS record should have listed *diehard.movie.edu* instead of *dh.movie. edu*. This *syslog* message won't show up immediately when you start your name server.

 You'll only see the *syslog* message when the offending data is looked up. This *syslog* message is logged by a BIND 4.9.3 or BIND 8 server at priority LOG_INFO, and by a 4.9.4 to 4.9.7 server at priority LOG_DEBUG.

The following message indicates that your name server may be guarding itself against one type of network attack:

```
Jun 11 11:40:54 terminator named[131]: Response from unexpected source
                                      ([204.138.114.3].53)
```

Your name server sent a query to a remote name server, but the response that came wasn't returned from any of the addresses your name server had listed for the remote name server. The potential security breach is this: an intruder causes your name server to query a remote name server, and at the same time the intruder sends responses (pretending the responses are from the remote name server) that the intruder hopes your name server will add to its cache. Perhaps he sends along a false PTR record, pointing the IP address of one of his hosts to the domain name of a host you trust. Once the false PTR record is in your cache, the intruder uses one of the BSD "r" commands (e.g., *rlogin*) to gain access to your system.

Less paranoid admins will realize that this situation can also happen if a parent zone's name server knows about only one of the IP addresses of a multihomed name server for a child zone. The parent tells your name server the one IP address it knows about, and when your server queries the remote name server, the remote name server responds from the other IP address. This shouldn't happen if BIND is running on the remote name server host, because BIND makes every effort to use the same IP address in the response as the query was sent to. This *syslog* message is logged at priority LOG_INFO.

Here's an interesting *syslog* message:

```
Jun 10 07:57:28 terminator named[131]: No root nameservers for
                class 226
```

The only classes defined to date are: class 1, Internet (IN); class 3, Chaos (CH); and class 4, Hesiod (HS). What's class 226? That's exactly what your name server is saying with this *syslog* message—something is wrong because there's no class 226. What can you do about it? Nothing, really. This message doesn't give you enough information—you don't know who the query is from or what the query was for. Then again, if the class field is corrupted, the domain name in the query may be garbage too. The actual cause of the problem could be a broken remote name server or resolver, or a corrupted UDP datagram. This *syslog* message is logged at priority LOG_INFO.

This message might appear if you are backing up some other zone:

```
Jun  7 20:14:26 wormhole named[29618]: Zone "253.253.192.in-addr.arpa"
                (class 1) SOA serial# (3345) rcvd from [192.249.249.10]
                is < ours (563319491)
```

Ah, the pesky admin for *253.253.192.in-addr.arpa* changed the serial number format and neglected to tell you about it. Some thanks you get for running a slave for this zone, huh? Drop the admin a note to see if this change was intentional or just a typo. If the change was intentional or if you don't want to contact the admin, then you have to deal with it locally—kill your slave, remove the backup copy of this zone, and restart your server. This procedure removes all knowledge your slave had of the old serial number, at which point it's quite happy with the new serial number. This *syslog* message is logged at priority LOG_NOTICE.

By the way, if that pesky admin was running a BIND 8 or 9 name server, then he must have missed (or ignored) a message his server logged, telling him that he'd rolled the zone's serial number back. On a BIND 8 name server, the message looks like:

```
Jun 7 19:35:14 terminator named[3221]: WARNING: new serial number < old
                (zp->z_serial < serial)
```

On a BIND 9 name server, it looks like:

```
Jun 7 19:36:41 terminator named[9832]: dns_zone_load: zone movie.edu/IN: zone
serial has gone backwards
```

This message is logged at LOG_NOTICE.

You might want to remind him of the wisdom of checking *syslog* after making any changes to the name server.

This BIND 8 message will undoubtedly become familiar to you:

```
Aug 21 00:59:06 terminator named[12620]: Lame server on 'foo.movie.edu'
        (in 'MOVIE.EDU'?): [10.0.7.125].53 'NS.HOLLYWOOD.LA.CA.US':
        learnt (A=10.47.3.62,NS=10.47.3.62)
```

Under BIND 9, it looks like this:

```
Jan 15 10:20:16 terminator named[14205]: lame server on 'foo.movie.edu' (in
'movie.EDU'?): 10.0.7.125#53
```

"Aye, Captain, she's sucking mud!" There's some mud out there in the Internet waters in the form of bad delegations. A parent name server is delegating a subdomain to a child name server, and the child name server is not authoritative for the subdomain. In this case, the *edu* name server is delegating *movie.edu* to 10.0.7.125, and the name server on this host is not authoritative for *movie.edu*. Unless you know the admin for *movie.edu*, there's probably nothing you can do about this. The *syslog* message is logged by a 4.9.3 server at priority LOG_WARNING, by a 4.9.4 to 4.9.7 server at priority LOG_DEBUG, and by a BIND 8 or 9 server at LOG_INFO.

If your BIND 4.9 or later name server's configuration file has:

```
options query-log
```

or your BIND 8 or 9 configuration file has:

```
logging { category queries { default_syslog; }; };
```

you will get a LOG_INFO *syslog* message for every query your name server receives:

```
Feb 20 21:43:25 terminator named[3830]:
            XX /192.253.253.2/carrie.movie.edu/A
Feb 20 21:43:32 terminator named[3830]:
            XX /192.253.253.2/4.253.253.192.in-addr.arpa/PTR
```

BIND 9 name servers support query logging as of 9.1.0. The format has changed slightly, though:

```
Jan 13 18:32:25 terminator named[13976]: client 192.253.253.2#1702: query: carrie.
movie.edu IN A
Jan 13 18:32:42 terminator named[13976]: client 192.253.253.2#1702: query: 4.253.
253.192.in-addr.arpa IN PTR
```

These messages include the IP address of the host that made the query as well as the query itself. On a BIND 8.2.1 or later name server, recursive queries are marked with XX+ instead of XX. Make sure you have lots of disk space if you log all the queries to a busy name server. (On a running server, you can toggle query logging on and off with the *querylog* command.)

Starting with BIND 8.1.2, you might see this set of *syslog* messages:

```
May 19 11:06:08 named[21160]: bind(dfd=20, [10.0.0.1].53):
                Address already in use
May 19 11:06:08 named[21160]: deleting interface [10.0.0.1].53
May 19 11:06:08 named[21160]: bind(dfd=20, [127.0.0.1].53):
                Address already in use
May 19 11:06:08 named[21160]: deleting interface [127.0.0.1].53
May 19 11:06:08 named[21160]: not listening on any interfaces
May 19 11:06:08 named[21160]: Forwarding source address
                is [0.0.0.0].1835
May 19 11:06:08 named[21161]: Ready to answer queries.
```

On BIND 9 name servers, that looks like:

```
Jul 27 17:15:58 terminator named[7357]: listening on IPv4 interface lo, 127.0.0.
1#53
Jul 27 17:15:58 terminator named[7357]: binding TCP socket: address in use
Jul 27 17:15:58 terminator named[7357]: listening on IPv4 interface eth0, 206.168.
194.122#53
Jul 27 17:15:58 terminator named[7357]: binding TCP socket: address in use
Jul 27 17:15:58 terminator named[7357]: listening on IPv4 interface eth1, 206.168.
194.123#53
Jul 27 17:15:58 terminator named[7357]: binding TCP socket: address in use
Jul 27 17:15:58 terminator named[7357]: couldn't add command channel 0.0.0.0#953:
address in use
```

What has happened is that you had a name server running and you started up a second name server without killing the first one. Unlike what you might expect, the second name server continues to run; it just isn't listening on any interfaces.

Understanding the BIND Statistics

Periodically, you should look over the statistics on some of your name servers, if only to see how busy they are. We'll now show you an example of the name server statistics and discuss what each line means. Name servers handle many queries and responses during normal operation, so first we need to show you what a typical exchange might look like.

Reading the explanations for the statistics is hard without a mental picture of what goes on during a lookup. To help you understand the name server's statistics, Figure 7-2 shows what might happen when an application tries to look up a domain name. The application, FTP, queries a local name server. The local name server had previously looked up data in this zone and knows where the remote name servers are. It queries each of the remote name servers—one of them twice—trying to find the answer. In the meantime, the application times out and sends yet another query, asking for the same information.

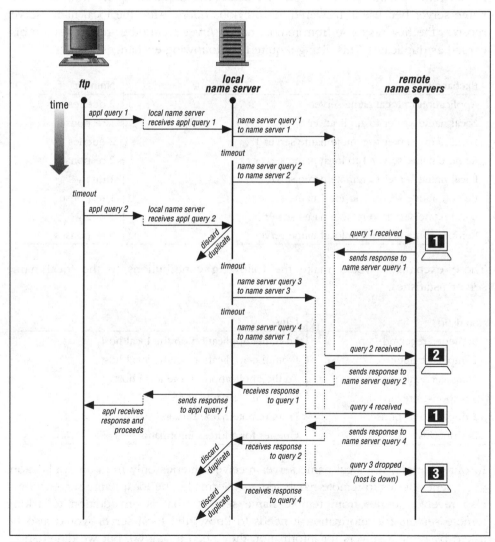

Figure 7-2. Example query/response exchange

Keep in mind that even though a name server has sent a query to a remote name server, the remote name server may not receive the query right away. The query might be delayed or lost by the underlying network, or perhaps the remote name server host might be busy with another application.

Notice that a BIND name server is able to detect duplicate queries only while it is still trying to answer the original query. The local name server detects the duplicate query from the application because the local name server is still working on it. But remote name server 1 does not detect the duplicate query from the local name server because it answered the previous query. After the local name server receives the first response from remote name server 1, all other responses are discarded as duplicates. This dialog required the following exchanges:

Exchange	Number
Application to local name server	2 queries
Local name server to application	1 response
Local name server to remote name server 1	2 queries
Remote name server 1 to local name server	2 responses
Local name server to remote name server 2	1 query
Remote name server 2 to local name server	1 response
Local name server to remote name server 3	1 query
Remote name server 3 to local name server	0 responses

These exchanges would make the following contributions to the local name server's statistics:

Statistic	Cause
2 queries received	From the application on the local host
1 duplicate query	From the application on the local host
1 answer sent	To the application on the local host
3 responses received	From remote name servers
2 duplicate responses	From remote name servers
2 A queries	Queries for address information

In our example, the local name server received queries only from an application, yet it sent queries to remote name servers. Normally, the local name server would also receive queries from remote name servers (that is, in addition to asking remote servers for information it needs to know, the local server would also be asked by remote servers for information they need to know), but we didn't show any remote queries for the sake of simplicity.

BIND 4.9 and 8 statistics

Now that you've seen a typical exchange between applications and name servers, as well as the statistics it generated, let's go over a more extensive example of the statistics. To get the statistics from your BIND 8 name server, use *ndc*:

```
# ndc stats
```

On older BIND 4 name servers without *ndc*, send *named* the ABRT signal:

```
# kill -ABRT `cat /var/run/named.pid`
```

(The process ID is stored in */etc/named.pid* on pre-SVR4 filesystems.) Wait a few seconds and look at the file *named.stats* in the name server's working directory (for BIND 8) or at */var/tmp/named.stats* or */usr/tmp/named.stats* (for BIND 4). If the statistics are not dumped to this file, your server may not have been compiled with STATS defined and, thus, may not be collecting statistics. Following are the statistics from one of Paul Vixie's BIND 4.9.3 name servers. BIND 8 name servers have all of the same items listed here except for RnotNsQ, and the items are arranged in a different order. BIND 9 name servers, as of 9.1.0, keep an entirely different set of statistics, which we'll show you in the next section.

```
+++ Statistics Dump +++ (800708260) Wed May 17 03:57:40 1995
746683     time since boot (secs)
392768     time since reset (secs)
14         Unknown query types
268459     A queries
3044       NS queries
5680       CNAME queries
11364      SOA queries
1008934    PTR queries
44         HINFO queries
680367     MX queries
2369       TXT queries
40         NSAP queries
27         AXFR queries
8336       ANY queries
++ Name Server Statistics ++
(Legend)
        RQ      RR     RIQ    RNXD    RFwdQ
        RFwdR  RDupQ  RDupR  RFail   RFErr
        RErr   RTCP   RAXFR  RLame   ROpts
        SSysQ  SAns   SFwdQ  SFwdR   SDupQ
        SFail  SFErr  SErr   RNotNsQ SNaAns
        SNXD
(Global)
    1992938 112600 0 19144 63462 60527 194 347 3420 0   5 2235 27 35289 0
    14886 1927930 63462 60527 107169   10025 I19 0 1785426 805592   35863
[15.255.72.20]
    485 0 0 0 0   0 0 0 0   0 0 0 0   0 485 0 0 0   0 0 0 0 485   0
[15.255.152.2]
    441 137 0 1 2 108 0 0 0   0 0 0 0   13 439 85 7 84   0 0 0 0 431   0
```

```
[15.255.152.4]
   770 89 0 1 4  69 0 0 0 0  0 0 0 0 0  14 766 68 5 7  0 0 0 0 755  0
...  <lots of entries deleted>
```

If your BIND 8 name server doesn't include any per–IP address sections after "(Global)," you'll need to set *host-statistics* to yes in your *options* statement if you want to track per-host statistics:

```
options {
    host-statistics yes;
};
```

However, keeping host statistics requires a fair amount of memory, so you may not want to do it routinely unless you're trying to build a profile of your name server's activity.

Let's look at these statistics one line at a time.

```
+++ Statistics Dump +++ (800708260) Wed May 17 03:57:40 1995
```

This is when this section of the statistics was dumped. The number in parentheses (800708260) is the number of seconds since the Unix epoch, which was January 1, 1970. Mercifully, BIND converts that into a real date and time for you: May 17, 1995, 3:57:40 a.m.

```
746683    time since boot (secs)
```

This is how long the local name server has been running. To convert to days, divide by 86400 ($60 \times 60 \times 24$, the number of seconds in a day). This server has been running for about 8.5 days.

```
392768    time since reset (secs)
```

This is how long the local name server has run since the last reload. You'll probably see this number differ from the time since boot only if the server is a primary master name server for one or more zones. Name servers that are slaves for a zone automatically pick up new data with zone transfers and are not usually reloaded. Since *this* server has been reset, it is probably the primary master name server for some zone.

```
14        Unknown query types
```

This name server received 14 queries for data of a type it didn't recognize. Either someone is experimenting with new types, there is a defective implementation somewhere, or Paul needs to upgrade his name server.

```
268459    A queries
```

There have been 268459 address lookups. Address queries are normally the most common type of query.

```
3044      NS queries
```

There have been 3044 name server queries. Internally, name servers generate NS queries when they are trying to look up servers for the root zone. Externally, applications like *dig* and *nslookup* can also be used to look up NS records.

    5680   CNAME queries

Some versions of *sendmail* make CNAME queries in order to canonicalize a mail address (replace an alias with the canonical name). Other versions of *sendmail* use ANY queries instead (we'll get to those shortly). Otherwise, the CNAME lookups arc most likcly from *dig* or *nslookup*.

    11364   SOA queries

SOA queries are made by slave name servers to check if their zone data is current. If the data is not current, an AXFR query follows to cause the zone transfer. Since this set of statistics does show AXFR queries, we can conclude that slave name servers load zone data from this server.

    1008934 PTR queries

The pointer queries map addresses to names. Many kinds of software look up IP addresses: *inetd*, *rlogind*, *rshd*, network management software, and network tracing software.

    44   HINFO queries

The host-information queries are most likely from someone interactively looking up HINFO records.

    680367 MX queries

Mailers like *sendmail* make mail exchanger queries as part of the normal electronic mail delivery process.

    2369   TXT queries

Some application must be making text queries for this number to be this large. It might be a tool like *Harvest*, which is an information search and retrieval technology developed at the University of Colorado.

    40   NSAP queries

This is a relatively new record type used to map domain names to OSI Network Service Access Point addresses.

    27   AXFR queries

Slave name servers make AXFR queries to initiate zone transfers.

    8336   ANY queries

ANY queries request records of any type for a name. *sendmail* is the most common program to use this query type. Since *sendmail* looks up CNAME, MX, and address records for a mail destination, it will make a query for ANY record type so that all the resource records are cached right away at the local name server.

The rest of the statistics are kept on a per-host basis. If you look over the list of hosts your name server has exchanged packets with, you'll find out just how garrulous your name server is—you'll see hundreds or even thousands of hosts in the list. While the size of the list is impressive, the statistics themselves are only somewhat interesting. We'll explain *all* the statistics, even the ones with zero counts, although you'll probably find only a handful of the statistics useful. To make the statistics easier to read, you'll need a tool to expand the statistics because the output format is rather compact. We wrote a tool called *bstat* to do just this. Here's what its output looks like:

```
hpcvsop.cv.hp.com
        485 queries received
        485 responses sent to this name server
        485 queries answered from our cache
relay.hp.com
        441 queries received
        137 responses received
          1 negative response received
          2 queries for data not in our cache or authoritative data
        108 responses from this name server passed to the querier
         13 system queries sent to this name server
        439 responses sent to this name server
         85 queries sent to this name server
          7 responses from other name servers sent to this name server
         84 duplicate queries sent to this name server
        431 queries answered from our cache
hp.com
        770 queries received
         89 responses received
          1 negative response received
          4 queries for data not in our cache or authoritative data
         69 responses from this name server passed to the querier
         14 system queries sent to this name server
        766 responses sent to this name server
         68 queries sent to this name server
          5 responses from other name servers sent to this name server
          7 duplicate queries sent to this name server
        755 queries answered from our cache
```

In the raw statistics (not the *bstat* output), each host's IP address is followed by a table of counts. The column heading for this table is the cryptic legend at the beginning. The legend is broken into several lines, but the host statistics are all on a single line. In the following section, we'll explain briefly what each column means as we look at the statistics for one of the hosts this name server conversed with—15.255.152.2 (*relay.hp.com*). For the sake of our explanation, we'll first show you the column heading from the legend (e.g., RQ) followed by the count for this column for *relay*.

```
RQ 441
```

RQ is the count of queries received from *relay*. These queries were made because *relay* needed information about a zone served by this name server.

```
RR 137
```

RR is the count of responses received from *relay*. These are responses to queries made from this name server. Don't try to correlate this number to RQ, because they are not related. RQ counts questions asked by *relay*; RR counts answers that *relay* gave to this name server (because this name server asked *relay* for information).

```
RIQ 0
```

RIQ is the count of inverse queries received from *relay*. Inverse queries were originally intended to map addresses to names, but that function is now handled by PTR records. Older versions of *nslookup* use an inverse query on startup, so you may see a nonzero RIQ count.

```
RNXD 1
```

RNXD is the count of "no such domain" answers received from *relay*.

```
RFwdQ 2
```

RFwdQ is the count of queries received (RQ) from *relay* that needed further processing before they could be answered. This count is much higher for hosts that configure their resolver (with *resolv.conf*) to send all queries to your name server.

```
RFwdR 108
```

RFwdR is the count of responses received (RR) from *relay* that answered the original query and were passed back to the application that made the query.

```
RDupQ 0
```

RDupQ is the count of duplicate queries from *relay*. You'll see duplicates only when the resolver is configured (with *resolv.conf*) to query this name server.

```
RDupR 0
```

RDupR is the count of duplicate responses from *relay*. A response is a duplicate when the name server can no longer find the original query in its list of pending queries that caused the response.

```
RFail 0
```

RFail is the count of SERVFAIL responses from *relay*. A SERVFAIL response indicates some sort of server failure. Server failure responses often occur because the remote server read a zone data file and found a syntax error. Any queries for data in the zone with the erroneous zone data file will result in a server failure answer from the remote name server. This is probably the most common cause of SERVFAIL responses. Server failure responses also occur when the remote name server tries to allocate more memory and can't, or when the remote slave name server's zone data expires.

    RFErr 0

RFErr is the count of FORMERR responses from *relay*. FORMERR means that the remote name server said the local name server's query had a format error.

    RErr 0

RErr is the count of errors that weren't either SERVFAIL or FORMERR.

    RTCP 0

RTCP is the count of queries received on TCP connections from *relay*. (Most queries use UDP.)

    RAXFR 0

RAXFR is the count of zone transfers initiated. The 0 count indicates that *relay* is not a slave for any zones served by this name server.

    RLame 0

RLame is the count of lame delegations received. If this count is not 0, it means that some zone is delegated to the name server at this IP address, and the name server is not authoritative for the zone.

    ROpts 0

ROpts is the count of packets received with IP options set.

    SSysQ 13

SSysQ is the count of system queries sent to *relay*. System queries are queries that are *initiated* by the local name server. Most system queries will go to root name servers because system queries are used to keep the list of root name servers up to date. But system queries are also used to find out the address of a name server if the address record timed out before the name server record did. Since *relay* is not a root name server, these queries must have been sent for the latter reason.

    SAns 439

SAns is the count of answers sent to *relay*. This name server answered 439 out of the 441 (RQ) queries *relay* sent to it. I wonder what happened to the two queries it didn't answer . . . .

    SFwdQ 85

SFwdQ is the count of queries that were sent (forwarded) to *relay* when the answer was not in this name server's zone data or cache.

    SFwdR 7

SFwdR is the count of responses from some name server that were sent (forwarded) to *relay*.

```
SDupQ 84
```

SDupQ is the count of duplicate queries sent to *relay*. It's not as bad as it looks, though. The duplicate count is incremented if the query was sent to any other name server first. So *relay* might have answered all the queries it received the first time it received them, and the query still counted as a duplicate because it was sent to some other name server before *relay*.

```
SFail 0
```

SFail is the count of SERVFAIL responses sent to *relay*.

```
SFErr 0
```

SFErr is the count of FORMERR responses sent to *relay*.

```
SErr  0
```

SErr is the count of *sendto()* system calls that failed when the destination was *relay*.

```
RNotNsQ 0
```

RNotNsQ is the count of queries received that were not from port 53, the name server port. Prior to BIND 8, all name server queries came from port 53. Any queries from ports other than 53 came from a resolver. BIND 8 name servers query from ports other than 53, however, which makes this statistic useless since you can no longer distinguish resolver queries from name server queries. Hence, BIND 8 dropped RNotNsQ from its statistics.

```
SNaAns 431
```

SNaAns is the count of nonauthoritative answers sent to *relay*. Out of the 439 answers (SAns) sent to *relay*, 431 were from cached data.

```
SNXD  0
```

SNXD is the count of "no such domain" answers sent to *relay*.

BIND 9 statistics

BIND 9.1.0 is the first version of BIND 9 to keep statistics. You use *rndc* to induce BIND 9 to dump its statistics:

```
% rndc stats
```

The name server dumps statistics, as a BIND 8 name server would, to a file called *named.stats* in its working directory. However, those statistics look completely different from BIND 8's. Here are the contents of the stats file from one of our BIND 9 name servers:

```
+++ Statistics Dump +++ (979436130)
success 9
referral 0
nxrrset 0
```

```
nxdomain 1
recursion 1
failure 1
--- Statistics Dump --- (979436130)
+++ Statistics Dump +++ (979584113)
success 651
referral 10
nxrrset 11
nxdomain 17
recursion 296
failure 217
--- Statistics Dump --- (979584113)
```

The name server appends a new statistics block (the section between "+++ Statistics Dump +++" and "--- Statistics Dump ---") each time it receives a stats command. The number in parentheses (979436130) is, as in earlier stats files, the number of seconds since the Unix epoch. Unfortunately, BIND doesn't convert the value for you, but you can use the date command to convert it to something more readable. For example, to convert 979584113 seconds since the Unix epoch (January 1, 1970), you could use:

```
% date -d '1970-01-01 979584113 sec'
Mon Jan 15 18:41:53 MST 2001
```

Let's now go through these statistics one line at a time.

```
success 651
```

This is the number of successful queries the name server handled. Successful queries are those that didn't result in referrals or errors.

```
referral 10
```

This is the number of queries the name server handled that resulted in referrals.

```
nxrrset 11
```

This is the number of queries the name server handled that resulted in responses saying that the type of record the querier requested didn't exist for the domain name it specified.

```
nxdomain 17
```

This is the number of queries the name server handled that resulted in responses saying that the domain name the querier specified didn't exist.

```
recursion 296
```

This is the number of queries the name server received that required recursive processing to answer.

```
failure 217
```

This is the number of queries the name server received that resulted in errors other than those covered by *nxrrset* and *nxdomain*.

These are obviously not nearly as many statistics as a BIND 8 name server keeps, but future versions of BIND 9 will probably record more.

Using the BIND statistics

Is your name server "healthy"? How do you know what "healthy" operation looks like? From a single snapshot, you can't really say whether a name server is healthy. You have to watch the statistics generated by your server over a period of time to get a feel for what sorts of numbers are normal for your configuration. These numbers will vary markedly among name servers depending on the mix of applications generating lookups, the type of server (primary master, slave, caching-only), and the level of the zones in the namespace it is serving.

One thing to watch for in the statistics is how many queries per second your name server receives. Take the number of queries received and divide by the number of seconds the name server has been running. Paul's BIND 4.9.3 name server received 1992938 queries in 746683 seconds, or approximately 2.7 queries per second—not a very busy server.* If the number you come up with for your name server seems out of line, look at which hosts are making all the queries and decide if it makes sense for them to be making all those queries. At some point you may decide that you need more name servers to handle the load. We'll cover that situation in the next chapter.

---

* Recall that the root name servers, which run plain vanilla BIND, can handle thousands of queries per second.

8

Growing Your Domain

In this chapter:
- *How Many Name Servers?*
- *Adding More Name Servers*
- *Registering Name Servers*
- *Changing TTLs*
- *Planning for Disasters*
- *Coping with Disaster*

"What size do you want to be?" it asked.

"Oh, I'm not particular as to size," Alice hastily replied; "only one doesn't like changing so often, you know..."

"Are you content now?" said the Caterpillar.

"Well, I should like to be a little larger, sir, if you wouldn't mind...."

How Many Name Servers?

We set up two name servers in Chapter 4, *Setting Up BIND*. Two servers are as few as you'll ever want to run. Depending on the size of your network, you may need to run many more than just two servers. It is not uncommon to run from five to seven servers, with one of them off-site. How many name servers are enough? You'll have to decide that based on your network. Here are some guidelines to help out:

- Run at least one name server on each network or subnet you have. This removes routers as a point of failure. Make the most of any multihomed hosts you have, since they are (by definition) attached to more than one network.

- If you have a file server and some diskless nodes, run a name server on the file server to serve this group of machines.

- Run name servers near, but not necessarily on, large multiuser computers. The users and their processes probably generate a lot of queries, and as an administrator, you will work harder to keep a multiuser host up. But balance their needs against the risk of running a name server—a security-critical server—on a system that lots of people have access to.

- Run at least one name server off-site. This makes your data available when your network isn't. You might argue that it's useless to look up an address when you can't reach the host. Then again, the off-site name server may be available if your network is reachable, but your other name servers are down. If you have a close relationship with an organization on the Internet—say another university or a business partner—they may be willing to run a slave for you.

Figure 8-1 shows a sample topology and a brief analysis to show you how this might work.

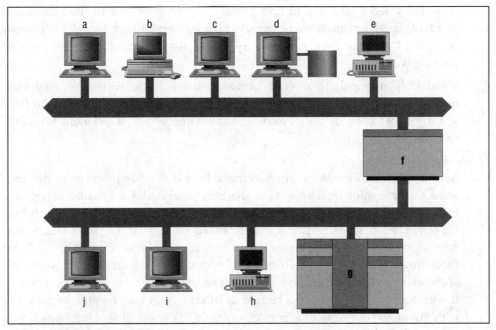

Figure 8-1. Sample network topology

Notice that if you follow our guidelines, there are still a number of places you could choose to run a name server. Host *d*, the file server for hosts *a*, *b*, *c*, and *e*, could run a name server. Host *g*, a big, multiuser host, is another good candidate. But probably the best choice is host *f*, the smaller host with interfaces on both networks. You'll need to run only one name server instead of two, and it'll run on a closely watched host. If you want more than one name server on either network, you can also run one on *d* or *g*.

Where Do I Put My Name Servers?

In addition to giving you a rough idea of how many name servers you'll need, these criteria should also help you decide *where* to run name servers (e.g., on file servers and multihomed hosts). But there are other important considerations when choosing the right host.

Other factors to keep in mind are the host's connectivity, the software it runs (BIND and otherwise), maintaining the homogeneity of your name servers, and security:

Connectivity

It's important that name servers be well-connected. Having a name server running on the fastest, most reliable host on your network won't do you any good if the host is mired in some backwater subnet of your network behind a slow, flaky serial line. Try to find a host close to your link to the Internet (if you have one), or find a well-connected Internet host to act as a slave for your zone. And on your own network, try to run name servers near the hubs of your network.

It's doubly important that your primary master name server be well connected. The primary needs good connectivity to all the slaves that update from it, for reliable zone transfers. And, like any name server, it'll benefit from fast, reliable networking.

Software

Another factor to consider in choosing a host for a name server is the software the host runs. Software-wise, the best candidate for a name server is a host running a vendor-supported version of BIND 8.2.3 or 9.1.0 and a robust implementation of TCP/IP (preferably based on 4.3 or 4.4 BSD Unix's networking—we're Berkeley snobs). You can compile your own 8.2.3 or 9.1.0 BIND from the sources—it's not hard, and the latest versions are very reliable—but you'll probably have a tough time getting your vendor to support it. If you don't absolutely need a feature of BIND 8, you may be able to get away with running your vendor's port of older BIND code, like 4.9.7, which will give you the benefit of your vendor's support, for what that's worth.

Homogeneity

One last thing to take into account is the homogeneity of your name servers. As much as you might believe in "open systems," hopping between different versions of Unix can be frustrating and confusing. Avoid running name servers on lots of different platforms, if you can. You can waste a lot of time porting your scripts (or ours!) from one operating system to another or looking for the location of *nslookup* or *named.conf* on three different Unixes. Moreover, different vendors' versions of Unix tend to support different versions of BIND, which can cause all sorts of frustration. If you need the security features of BIND 8 or 9 on all your name servers, for example, choose a platform that supports BIND 8 or 9 for all your name servers.

Security

Since you would undoubtedly prefer that hackers not commandeer your name server to assist them in attacking your own hosts or other networks across the Internet, it's important to run your name server on a secure host. Don't run a name server on a big, multiuser system if you can't trust its users. If you have certain computers that are dedicated to hosting network services but don't permit general logins, those are good candidates for running name servers. If you have only one or a few really secure hosts, consider running the primary master name server on one of those, since its compromise would be more significant than the compromise of the slaves.

Though these are really secondary considerations—it's more important to have a name server on a given subnet than to have it running on the perfect host—do keep these criteria in mind when making a choice.

Capacity Planning

If you have heavily populated networks or users who do a lot of name server–intensive work, you may find that you need more name servers than we've recommended to handle the load. Or our recommendations may be fine for a little while, but as people add hosts to your nets or install new name server–intensive programs, you may find your name servers bogged down by queries.

Just which tasks are "name server–intensive"? Surfing the Web can be name server–intensive. Sending electronic mail, especially to large mailing lists, can be name server–intensive. Programs that make lots of remote procedure calls to different hosts can be name server–intensive. Even running certain graphical user environments can tax your name server. X Windows–based user environments, for example, query the name server to check access lists (among other things).

The astute (and precocious) among you may be asking, "But how do I know when my name servers are overloaded? What do I look for?" An excellent question!

Memory utilization is probably the most important aspect of a name server's operation to monitor. *named* can get very large on a name server that is authoritative for many zones. If *named*'s size, plus the size of the other processes you run, exceeds the size of your host's real memory, your host may swap furiously ("thrash") and not get anything done. Even if your host has more than enough memory to run all its processes, large name servers are slow to start and slow to spawn new *named* processes (e.g., to handle zone transfers). Another problem, peculiar to BIND 4: since a BIND 4 name server creates new *named* processes to handle zone transfers, it's quite possible to have more than one *named* process running at one time—one answering queries and one or more servicing zone transfers. If your BIND 4 master name server already consumes 5 or 10 megabytes of memory, count on two or three times that amount being used occasionally.

Another criterion you can use to measure the load on your name server is the load the *named* process places on the host's CPU. Correctly configured name servers don't use much CPU time, so high CPU usage is often symptomatic of a configuration error. Programs such as *top* can help you characterize your name server's average CPU utilization.* Unfortunately, there are no absolute rules when it comes to acceptable CPU utilization. We offer a rough rule of thumb, though: 5% average CPU utilization is probably acceptable; 10% is a bit high, unless the host is dedicated to providing name service.

To get an idea of what normal figures are, here's what *top* might show for a relatively quiet name server:

```
last pid: 14299; load averages: 0.11, 0.12, 0.12         18:19:08
68 processes: 64 sleeping, 3 running, 1 stopped
Cpu states: 11.3% usr, 0.0% nice, 15.3% sys, 73.4% idle, 0.0% intr, 0.0% ker
Memory: Real: 8208K/13168K act/tot Virtual: 16432K/30736K act/tot Free: 4224K


  PID USERNAME PRI NICE   SIZE   RES STATE  TIME   WCPU    CPU COMMAND
   89 root        1    0 2968K 2652K sleep  5:01  0.00%  0.00% named
```

Okay, that's *really* quiet. Here's what *top* shows on a busy (though not overloaded) name server:

```
load averages: 0.30, 0.46, 0.44                  system: relay 16:12:20
39 processes: 38 sleeping, 1 waiting
Cpu states: 4.4% user, 0.0% nice, 5.4% system, 90.2% idle, 0.0% unk5, 0.0% unk6,
0.0% unk7, 0.0% unk8
Memory: 31126K (28606K) real, 33090K (28812K) virtual, 54344K free Screen #1/ 3


   PID USERNAME PRI NICE  SIZE   RES   STATE   TIME WCPU   CPU  COMMAND
 21910 root        1    0 2624K 2616K sleep 146:21 0.00% 1.42% /etc/named
```

Another statistic to look at is the number of queries the name server receives per minute (or second, if you have a busy name server). Again, there are no absolutes here: a fast Pentium III running NetBSD can probably handle thousands of queries per second without breaking a sweat, while an older Unix host might have problems with more than a few queries a second.

To check the volume of queries your name server is receiving, it's easiest to look at the name server's internal statistics, which you can configure the server to write

---

* *top* is a very handy program, written by Bill LeFebvre, that gives you a continuous report of which processes are sucking up the most CPU time on your host. The most recent version of *top* is available via anonymous FTP from *eecs.nwu.edu* as file */pub/top/top-3.4.tar.Z*.

to *syslog* at regular intervals.* For example, you could configure your name server to dump statistics every hour (actually, that's the default for BIND 8 servers), and compare the number of queries received between hours:

```
options {
        statistics-interval 60;
};
```

BIND 9 name servers don't support the *statistics-interval* substatement, but you can use *rndc* to tell a BIND 9 name server to dump statistics on the hour, for example in *crontab*:

```
0 * * * *  /usr/local/sbin/rndc stats
```

You should pay special attention to peak periods. Monday morning is often busy, because many people like to respond to mail they've received over the weekend first thing on Mondays.

You might also want to take a sample starting just after lunch, when people are returning to their desks and getting back to work—all at about the same time. Of course, if your organization is spread across several time zones, you'll have to use your own good judgment to determine a busy time.

Here's a snippet from the *syslog* file on a BIND 8.2.3 name server:

```
Aug  1 11:00:49 terminator named[103]: NSTATS 965152849 959476930 A=8 NS=1
SOA=356966 PTR=2 TXT=32 IXFR=9 AXFR=204
Aug  1 11:00:49 terminator named[103]: XSTATS 965152849 959476930 RR=3243 RNXD=0
RFwdR=0 RDupR=0 RFail=20 RFErr=0 RErr=11 RAXFR=204 RLame=0 ROpts=0 SSysQ=3356

SAns=391191 SFwdQ=0 SDupQ=1236 SErr=0 RQ=458031 RIQ=25 RFwdQ=0 RDupQ=0 RTCP=101316
SFwdR=0 SFail=0 SFErr=0 SNaAns=34482 SNXD=0 RUQ=0 RURQ=0 RUXFR=10 RUUpd=34451
Aug  1 12:00:49 terminator named[103]: NSTATS 965156449 959476930 A=8 NS=1
SOA=357195 PTR=2 TXT=32 IXFR=9 AXFR=204
Aug  1 12:00:49 terminator named[103]: XSTATS 965156449 959476930 RR=3253 RNXD=0
RFwdR=0 RDupR=0 RFail=20 RFErr=0 RErr=11 RAXFR=204 RLame=0 ROpts=0 SSysQ=3360

SAns=391444 SFwdQ=0 SDupQ=1244 SErr=0 RQ=458332 RIQ=25 RFwdQ=0 RDupQ=0 RTCP=101388
SFwdR=0 SFail=0 SFErr=0 SNaAns=34506 SNXD=0 RUQ=0 RURQ=0 RUXFR=10 RUUpd=34475
```

The number of queries received is dumped in the *RQ* field (in bold). To calculate the number of queries received in the hour, just subtract the first *RQ* value from the second one: $458332 - 458031 = 301$.

Even if your host is fast enough to handle the number of queries it receives, you should make sure that the DNS traffic isn't placing an undue load on your network.

---

* Some older BIND name servers need coercion to dump their statistics: the ABRT signal (IOT on older systems). BIND 4.9 name servers automatically dump stats every hour, but 4.9.4 through 4.9.7 name servers, once again, need to be coerced with ABRT.

On most LANs, DNS traffic is too small a proportion of the network's bandwidth to worry about. Over slow leased lines or dialup connections, though, DNS traffic could consume enough bandwidth to merit concern.

For a rough estimate of the volume of DNS traffic on your LAN, multiply the number of queries received (RQ) plus the number of answers sent (SAns) in an hour by 800 bits (100 bytes, a rough average size for a DNS message), and divide by 3600 (seconds per hour) to find the bandwidth utilized. This should give you a feeling for how much of your network's bandwidth is consumed by DNS traffic.[*]

To give you an idea of what's normal, the last NSFNET traffic report (in April 1995) showed that DNS traffic constituted just over 5% of the total traffic volume (in bytes) on their backbone. The NSFNET's figures were based upon actual traffic sampling, not calculations like ours using the name server's statistics.[†] If you want to get a more accurate idea of the traffic your name server is receiving, you can always do your own traffic sampling with a LAN protocol analyzer.

Once you've found that your name servers are overworked, what then? First, it's a good idea to make sure your name servers aren't being bombarded with queries by a misbehaving program. To do that, you'll need to find out where all the queries are coming from.

If you're running a BIND 4.9 or 8.1.2 name server, you can find out which resolvers and name servers are querying your name server just by dumping the statistics. These name servers keep statistics on a host-by-host basis, which is really useful in tracking down heavy users of your name server. BIND 8.2 or newer name servers don't keep these statistics by default; to induce them to keep host-by-host statistics, use the *host-statistics* substatement in your *options* statement, like this:[‡]

```
options {
    host-statistics yes;
};
```

For example, take these statistics:

```
+++ Statistics Dump +++ (829373099) Fri Apr 12 23:24:59 1996
970779   time since boot (secs)
471621   time since reset (secs)
0    Unknown query types
185108   A queries
```

---

[*] For a nice package that automates the analysis of BIND's statistics, look for Nigel Campbell's *bindgraph* in the DNS Resources Directory's tools page, *http://www.dns.net/dnsrd/tools.html*.

[†] We're not sure how representative of the current state of the Internet these numbers are, but it's extremely difficult to wheedle equivalent numbers out of the commercial backbone providers that succeeded the NSFNET.

[‡] BIND 9 doesn't support the *host-statistics* substatement—or keeping per-host statistics, for that matter—as of 9.1.0.

```
     6     NS queries
     69213     PTR queries
     669     MX queries
     2361     ANY queries
     ++ Name Server Statistics ++
     (Legend)
          RQ        RR        RIQ       RNXD      RFwdQ
          RFwdR     RDupQ     RDupR     RFail     RFErr
          RErr      RTCP      RAXFR     RLame     ROpts
          SSysQ     SAns      SFwdQ     SFwdR     SDupQ
          SFail     SFErr     SErr      RNotNsQ   SNaAns
          SNXD
     (Global)
          257357 20718 0 8509 19677   19939 1494 21 0 0   0 7 0 1 0
          824 236196 19677 19939 7643   33 0 0 256064 49269   155030
      [15.17.232.4]
          8736 0 0 0 717  24 0 0 0 0   0 0 0 0 0   0 8019 0 717 0
          0 0 0 8736 2141   5722
      [15.17.232.5]
          115 0 0 0 8   0 21 0 0 0   0 0 0 0 0   0 86 0 1 0   0 0 0 115 0   7
      [15.17.232.8]
          66215 0 0 0 6910   148 633 0 0 0   0 5 0 0 0   0 58671 0 6695 0
          15 0 0 66215 33697   6541
      [15.17.232.16]
          31848 0 0 0 3593   209 74 0 0 0   0 0 0 0 0   0 28185 0 3563 0
          0 0 0 31848 8695   15359
      [15.17.232.20]
          272 0 0 0 0   0 0 0 0 0   0 0 0 0 0   0 272 0 0 0   0 0 0 272 7   0
      [15.17.232.21]
          316 0 0 0 52   14 3 0 0 0   0 0 0 0 0   0 261 0 51 0   0 0 0 316 30   30
      [15.17.232.24]
          853 0 0 0 65   1 3 0 0 0   0 2 0 0 0   0 783 0 64 0   0 0 0 853 125   337
      [15.17.232.33]
          624 0 0 0 47   1 0 0 0 0   0 0 0 0 0   0 577 0 47 0   0 0 0 624 2   217
      [15.17.232.94]
          127640 0 0 0 1751   14 449 0 0 0   0 0 0 0 0   0 125440 0 1602 0
          0 0 0 127640 106   124661
      [15.17.232.95]
          846 0 0 0 38   1 0 0 0 0   0 0 0 0 0   0 809 0 37 0   0 0 0 846 79   81
     -- Name Server Statistics --
     --- Statistics Dump --- (829373099) Fri Apr 12 23:24:59 1996
```

After the *Global* entry, each host is broken out by IP address in brackets. Looking at the legend, you can see that the first field in each record is RQ, or queries received. That gives us a good reason to look at hosts 15.17.232.8, 15.17.232.16, and 15.17.232.94, which appear to be responsible for about 88% of our queries.

If you're running an older name server, the only way to find out which resolvers and name servers are sending all those darned queries is to turn on name server debugging. (We'll cover this in depth in Chapter 13, *Reading BIND Debugging Output.*) All you're really interested in is the source IP addresses of the queries your name server is receiving. When poring over the debugging output, look for hosts sending repeated queries, especially for the same or similar information. That may indicate a misconfigured or buggy program running on the host, or a foreign name server pelting your name server with queries.

If all the queries appear legitimate, add a new name server. Don't put the name server just anywhere, though; use the information from the debugging output to help you decide where best to run one. In cases where DNS traffic is gobbling up your Ethernet, it won't help to choose a host at random and create a name server there. You need to consider which hosts are sending all the queries, then figure out how to best provide them name service. Here are some hints to help you decide:

- Look for queries from resolvers on hosts that share the same file server. You could run a name server on the file server.

- Look for queries from resolvers on large, multiuser hosts. You could run a name server there.

- Look for queries from resolvers on another subnet. Those resolvers should be configured to query a name server on their local subnet. If there isn't one on that subnet, create one.

- Look for queries from resolvers on the same bridged segment (assuming you use bridging). If you run a name server on the bridged segment, the traffic won't need to be bridged to the rest of the network.

- Look for queries from hosts connected to each other via another, lightly loaded network. You could run a name server on the other network.

Adding More Name Servers

When you need to create new name servers for your zones, the simplest recourse is to add slaves. You already know how—we went over it in Chapter 4—and once you've set up one slave, cloning it is a piece of cake. But you can run into trouble by adding slaves indiscriminately.

If you run a large number of slave servers for a zone, the primary master name server can take quite a beating just keeping up with the slaves' polling to check that their zone data is current. There are a number of courses of action to take for this problem:

- Make more primary master name servers

- Increase the refresh interval so that the slaves don't check so often

- Direct some of the slave name servers to load from other slave name servers

- Create caching-only name servers (described later)

- Create "partial-slave" name servers (also described later)

Primary Master and Slave Servers

Creating more primaries means extra work for you, since you have to keep */etc/ named.conf* and the zone data files synchronized manually. Whether or not this is preferable to your other alternatives is your call. You can use tools like *rdist* or *rsync** to simplify the process of distributing the files. A *distfile†* to synchronize files between primaries might be as simple as the following:

```
dup-primary:

# copy named.conf file to dup'd primary

/etc/named.conf  -> wormhole
    install ;

# copy contents of /var/named (zone data files, etc.) to dup'd primary

/var/named -> wormhole
    install ;
```

or for multiple primaries:

```
dup-primary:

primaries =  ( wormhole carrie )
/etc/named.conf  -> {$primaries}
    install ;

/var/named -> {$primaries}
    install ;
```

You can even have *rdist* trigger your name server's reload using the *special* option by adding lines like:

```
special /var/named/* "ndc reload" ;
special /etc/named.conf "ndc reload" ;
```

These tell *rdist* to execute the quoted command if any of the files change.

Increasing your zone's refresh interval is another option. This slows down the propagation of new information, however. In some cases, this is not a problem. If you rebuild your zone data with *h2n* only once each day at 1 a.m. (run from *cron*) and then allow six hours for the data to distribute, all the slaves will be current by 7 a.m.‡ That may be acceptable to your user population. See the section called "Changing Other SOA Values" later in this chapter for more detail.

---

* *rsync* is a remote file synchronization program that transmits only the differences between files. You can find out more about it at *http://rsync.samba.org*.

† The file *rdist* reads to find out which files to update.

‡ And, of course, if you're using NOTIFY, they'll catch up much sooner than that.

You can even have some of your slaves load from other slaves. Slave name servers *can* load zone data from other slave name servers instead of loading from a primary master name server. The slave name server can't tell if it is loading from a primary or from another slave. It's important only that the name server serving the zone transfer is authoritative for the zone. There's no trick to configuring this. Instead of specifying the IP address of the primary in the slave's configuration file, you simply specify the IP address of another slave.

Here are the contents of the file *named.conf*:

```
// this slave updates from wormhole, another
// slave
zone "movie.edu" {
            type slave;
            masters { 192.249.249.1; };
            file "bak.movie.edu";
};
```

For a BIND 4 server, this would look slightly different.

Here are the contents of the file *named.boot*:

```
; this slave updates from wormhole, another slave
secondary   movie.edu   192.249.249.1   bak.movie.edu
```

When you go to this second level of distribution, though, it can take up to twice as long for the data to percolate from the primary master name server to all the slaves. Remember that the *refresh interval* is the period after which the slave name servers will check to make sure that their zone data is still current. Therefore, it can take the first-level slave servers the entire refresh interval before they get a new copy of the zone from the primary master server. Similarly, it can take the second-level slave servers the entire refresh interval to get a new copy of the zone from the first-level slave servers. The propagation time from the primary master server to all of the slave servers can therefore be twice the refresh interval.

One way to avoid this is to use the NOTIFY feature in BIND 8 and 9. This is on by default, and will trigger zone transfers soon after the zone is updated on the primary master. Unfortunately, it works only on Version 8 and 9 BIND slaves.* We'll discuss NOTIFY in more detail in Chapter 10, *Advanced Features*.

If you decide to configure your network with two (or more) tiers of slave name servers, be careful to avoid updating loops. If we were to configure *wormhole* to update from *diehard* and then accidentally configure *diehard* to update from *wormhole*, neither would ever get data from the primary master. They would merely check their out-of-date serial numbers against each other and perpetually decide that they were both up to date.

---

* And, incidentally, on the Microsoft DNS Server.

Caching-Only Servers

Creating *caching-only* name servers is another alternative when you need more servers. Caching-only name servers are name servers not authoritative for any zones (except *0.0.127.in-addr.arpa*). The name doesn't imply that primary master and slave name servers don't cache—they do. The name implies that the *only* function this server performs is looking up data and caching it. As with primary master and slave name servers, a caching-only name server needs a root hints file and a *db.127.0.0* file. The *named.conf* file for a caching-only server contains these lines:

```
options {
    directory "/var/named";  // or your data directory
};

zone "0.0.127.in-addr.arpa" {
    type master;
    file "db.127.0.0";
};

zone "." {
    type hint;
    file "db.cache";
};
```

On a BIND 4 server, the *named.boot* file looks like this:

```
directory /var/named  ; or your data directory

primary 0.0.127.in-addr.arpa  db.127.0.0  ; for loopback address
cache   .                     db.cache
```

A caching-only name server can look up domain names inside and outside your zone, as can primary master and slave name servers. The difference is that when a caching-only name server initially looks up a name within your zone, it ends up asking one of the primary master or slave name servers for your zone for the answer. A primary or slave would answer the same question out of its authoritative data. Which primary or slave does the caching-only server ask? As with name servers outside your zone, it finds out which name servers serve your zone from one of the name servers for your parent zone. Is there any way to prime a caching-only name server's cache so it knows which hosts run primary master and slave name servers for your zone? No, there isn't. You can't use *db.cache*—the *db. cache* file is only for root name server hints. And actually, it's better that your caching-only name servers find out about your authoritative name servers from your parent zone's name servers: you keep your zone's delegation information up to date. If you hard-wired a list of authoritative name servers on your caching-only name servers, you might forget to update it.

A caching-only name server's real value comes after it builds up its cache. Each time it queries an authoritative name server and receives an answer, it caches the records in the answer. Over time, the cache will grow to include the information most often requested by the resolvers querying the caching-only name server. And you avoid the overhead of zone transfers—a caching-only name server doesn't need to do them.

Partial-Slave Servers

In between a caching-only name server and a slave name server is another variation: a name server that is a slave for only a few of the local zones. We call this a *partial-slave* name server (and probably nobody else does). Suppose *movie.edu* had 20 of the /24-sized (the old class C) networks and a corresponding 20 *in-addr.arpa* zones. Instead of creating a slave server for all 21 zones (all the *in-addr.arpa* subdomains plus *movie.edu*), we could create a partial-slave server for *movie.edu* and only those *in-addr.arpa* zones the host itself is in. If the host had two network interfaces, its name server would be a slave for three zones: *movie.edu* and the two *in-addr.arpa* zones.

Let's say we scare up the hardware for another name server. We'll call the new host *zardoz.movie.edu*, with IP addresses 192.249.249.9 and 192.253.253.9. We'll create a partial-slave name server on *zardoz*, with this *named.conf* file:

```
options {
    directory "/var/named";
};

zone "movie.edu" {
    type slave;
    masters { 192.249.249.3; };
    file "bak.movie.edu";
};

zone "249.249.192.in-addr.arpa" {
    type slave;
    masters { 192.249.249.3; };
    file "bak.192.249.249";
};

zone "253.253.192.in-addr.arpa" {
    type slave;
    masters { 192.249.249.3; };
    file "bak.192.253.253";
};

zone "0.0.127.in-addr.arpa" {
    type master;
    file "db.127.0.0";
};
```

```
zone "." {
    type hint;
    file "db.cache";
};
```

For a BIND 4 server, the *named.boot* file would look like this:

```
directory    /var/named
secondary    movie.edu                       192.249.249.3 bak.movie.edu
secondary    249.249.192.in-addr.arpa 192.249.249.3 bak.192.249.249
secondary    253.253.192.in-addr.arpa 192.249.249.3 bak.192.253.253
primary      0.0.127.in-addr.arpa        db.127.0.0
cache        .                           db.cache
```

This server is a slave for *movie.edu* and only two of the 20 *in-addr.arpa* zones. A "full" slave would have 21 different *zone* statements in *named.conf.*

What's so useful about a partial-slave name server? They're not much work to administer because their *named.conf* files don't change much. On a name server authoritative for all the *in-addr.arpa* zones, we'd need to add and delete *in-addr. arpa* zones (and their corresponding entries in *named.conf*) as our network changed. That can be a surprising amount of work on a large network.

A partial slave can still answer most of the queries it receives, though. Most of these queries will be for data in *movie.edu* and the two *in-addr.arpa* zones. Why? Because most of the hosts querying the name server are on the two networks it's connected to, 192.249.249 and 192.253.253. And those hosts probably communicate primarily with other hosts on their own network. This generates queries for data within the *in-addr.arpa* zone that corresponds to the local network.

Registering Name Servers

When you get around to setting up more and more name servers, a question may strike you—do I need to register *all* of my primary master and slave name servers with my parent zone? No, only those servers you want to make available to name servers outside your zone need to be registered with your parent. For example, if you run nine name servers for your zone, you may choose to tell the parent zone about only four of them. Within your network, you use all nine servers. Five of those nine servers, however, are queried only by resolvers on hosts that are configured to query them (in *resolv.conf*, for example). Their parent zone's name servers don't delegate to them, so they'll never be queried by remote name servers. Only the four servers registered with your parent zone are queried by other name servers, including caching-only and partial-slave name servers on your network. This setup is shown in Figure 8-2.

Besides being able to pick and choose which of your name servers are hammered by outside queries, there's a technical motivation for registering only some of your

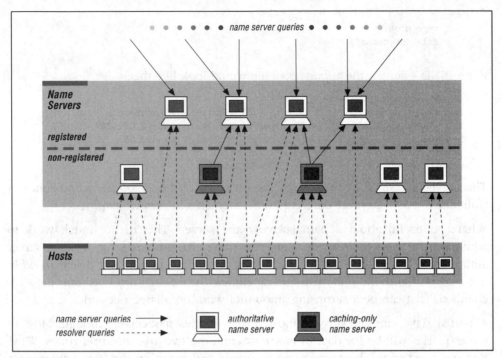

Figure 8-2. Registering only some of your name servers

zone's name servers: there's a limit to how many servers will fit in a UDP response message. In practice, around 10 name server records should fit. Depending on the data (how many servers are in the same domain), you could get more or fewer.* There's not much point in registering more than 10 name servers, anyway—if none of the 10 servers can be reached, it's unlikely the destination host can be reached.

If you set up a new authoritative name server and decide it should be registered, make a list of the parents of the zones it's authoritative for. You'll need to contact the administrators for each of these parent zones. For example, let's say we want to register the name server we just set up on *zardoz.movie.edu*. In order to get this slave registered in all the right zones, we'll need to contact the administrators of *edu* and *in-addr.arpa*. (For help determining who runs your parent zones, turn back to Chapter 3, *Where Do I Start?*)

When you contact the administrators of a parent zone, be sure to follow the process they specify (if any) on their web site. If there's no standard modification process, you'll have to send them the domain name of the zone (or zones) that the

---

* The domain names of the Internet's root name servers were changed because of this. All of the roots were moved into the same domain, *root-servers.net*, to take the most advantage of domain name compression and store information about as many roots as possible in a single UDP packet.

new name server is authoritative for. If the new name server is in the new zone,
you'll also need to give them the IP address(es) of the new name server. In fact, if
there's no official format for submitting the information, it's often best just to send
your parent the complete list of registered name servers for the zone, plus any
addresses necessary, in zone data file format. That avoids any potential confusion.

Since our networks were originally assigned by the InterNIC, we used the web-
based process at *http://www.arin.net/cgi-bin/amt.pl* to change our registration. (If
we'd preferred to do things manually, we could have sent them the form at *http://
www.arin.net/regserv/templates/modifytemplate.txt*.) If they hadn't had a template
for us to use, our message to the administrator of *in-addr.arpa* might have read
something like this:

```
Howdy!

I've just set up a new slave name server on
zardoz.movie.edu for the 249.249.192.in-addr.arpa
and 253.253.192.in-addr.arpa zones.  Would you
please add NS records for this name server to the
in-addr.arpa zone?  That would make our delegation
information look like:

253.253.192.in-addr.arpa. 86400 IN NS terminator.movie.edu.
253.253.192.in-addr.arpa. 86400 IN NS wormhole.movie.edu.
253.253.192.in-addr.arpa. 86400 IN NS zardoz.movie.edu.

249.249.192.in-addr.arpa. 86400 IN NS terminator.movie.edu.
249.249.192.in-addr.arpa. 86400 IN NS wormhole.movie.edu.
249.249.192.in-addr.arpa. 86400 IN NS zardoz.movie.edu.

Thanks!

Albert LeDomaine
al@robocop.movie.edu
```

Notice that we specified explicit TTLs on the NS and A records? That's because our
parent name servers aren't authoritative for those records; *our* name servers are.
By including them, we're indicating our choice of a TTL for our zone's delegation.
Of course, our parent may have other ideas about what the TTL should be.

In this case, glue data—A records for each of the name servers—isn't necessary,
since the domain names of the name servers aren't within the *in-addr.arpa* zones.
They're within *movie.edu*, so a name server that was referred to *terminator.movie.
edu* or *wormhole.movie.edu* could still find their addresses by following delegation to the *movie.edu* name servers.

Is a partial-slave name server a good name server to register with your parent
zone? Actually, it's not ideal, because it's only authoritative for some of your *in-
addr.arpa* zones. Administratively, it may be easier to register only servers that

back up *all* the local zones; that way, you don't need to keep track of which name servers are authoritative for which zones. All of your parent zones can delegate to the same set of name servers: your primary master and your "full" slaves.

However, if you don't have many name servers or if you're good at remembering which name servers are authoritative for what, go ahead and register a partial-slave.

Caching-only name servers, on the other hand, must *never* be registered. A caching-only name server rarely has complete information for any given zone, just the bits and pieces of it that it has looked up recently. If a parent zone's name server were mistakenly to refer a foreign name server to a caching-only name server, the foreign name server would send the caching-only name server a nonrecursive query. The caching-only name server might have the data cached, but then again, it might not. If it didn't have the data, it would refer the querier to the best name servers it knew (those closest to the domain name in the query)—which might include the caching-only name server itself! The poor foreign name server might never get an answer. This kind of misconfiguration—actually, delegating a zone to any name server not authoritative for that zone—is known as *lame delegation*.

Changing TTLs

An experienced administrator needs to know how to set the time to live on his zone's data to his best advantage. The TTL on a resource record, remember, is the length of time any name server can cache that record. So if the TTL for a particular resource record is 3600 seconds and a server outside your network caches that record, it has to remove the entry from its cache after an hour. If it needs the same data after the hour is up, it has to query one of your name servers again.

When we introduced TTLs, we emphasized that your choice of a TTL dictates how current you keep copies of your data at the cost of increased load on your name servers. A low TTL means that name servers outside your network have to get data from your name servers often and therefore keep current. However, your name servers are then peppered by their queries.

You don't *have* to choose a TTL once and for all, though. You can—and experienced administrators do—change TTLs periodically to suit your needs.

Suppose we know that one of our hosts is about to be moved to another network. This host houses the *movie.edu* film library, a large collection of files our site makes available to Internet users. During normal operation, outside name servers cache the address of our host according to the default TTL set in the $TTL control statement, or for pre–BIND 8.2 name servers, in the SOA record. We set the default TTL for *movie.edu* to three hours in our sample files. A name server caching the old address record just before the change could have the wrong address for as long as three hours. A loss of connectivity for three hours is unacceptable, though. What can we do to minimize the loss of connectivity? We can lower the TTL so that outside servers cache the address record for a shorter period. By reducing the TTL, we force the outside servers to update their data more frequently, which means that any changes we make when we actually move the system are propagated to the outside world quickly. How long can we make the TTL? Unfortunately, we can't safely use a TTL of zero, which should mean "don't cache this record at all." Some older BIND 4 name servers can't return records with a TTL of zero, instead returning null answers or SERVFAIL errors. Small TTLs, like 30 seconds, are okay, though. The easiest change is to lower the TTL in the $TTL control statement in the *db.movie.edu* file. If you don't place an explicit TTL on resource records in the zone data files, the name server applies this *default TTL* to each resource record. If you lower the default TTL, though, the new, lower default applies to all zone data, not just the address of the host being moved. The drawback to this approach is that your name server will be answering a lot more queries since the querying servers will cache *all* the data in your zone for a shorter period. A better alternative is to put a different TTL only on the affected address record.

To add an explicit TTL on an individual resource record, place it before the IN in the class field. The TTL value is in seconds by default, but you can also specify units of *m* (minutes), *h* (hours), *d* (days), and *w* (weeks), just as you could in the $TTL control statement. Here's an example of an explicit TTL from *db.movie.edu*:

```
cujo  1h IN A    192.253.253.5  ; explicit TTL of 1 hour
```

If you're observant and have read RFC 1034, you may have noticed a potential problem when loading this record on an older name server: the explicit TTL on *cujo*'s address is one hour, but the TTL field in the SOA record—ostensibly the minimum TTL for the zone on pre–BIND 8.2 name servers—is higher. Which takes precedence?

If older BINDs followed the original DNS RFCs to the letter, the TTL field in the SOA record would really define the minimum TTL for all resource records in the zone. Thus, you could specify only explicit TTLs larger than this minimum. Older BIND name servers don't work this way, though. In other words, in BIND, "minimum" is not really minimum. Instead, BIND interprets the minimum TTL field in the SOA record as a "default" TTL. (Newer BINDs, of course, have the explicit default TTL set with $TTL to go by.) If there is no TTL on a record, the minimum applies. If there is a TTL on the resource record, BIND allows it even if it is smaller than the minimum. That one record is sent out in responses with the smaller TTL, while all other records are sent out with the "minimum" TTL from the SOA record.

You should also know that when giving out answers, a slave supplies the same TTL a primary master does—that is, if a primary gives out a TTL of one hour for a particular record, a slave will, too. The slave doesn't decrement the TTL according to how long it's been since it loaded the zone. So, if the TTL of a single resource record is set smaller than the default, both the primary and slave name servers give out the resource record with the same, smaller TTL. If the slave name server has reached the expiration time for the zone, it expires the whole zone. It will never expire an individual resource record within a zone.

So BIND does allow you to put a small TTL on an individual resource record if you know that the data is going to change shortly. Thus, any name server caching that data caches it only for a brief time. Unfortunately, while BIND makes tagging records with a small TTL possible, most administrators don't spend the time to do it. When a host's address changes, you often lose connectivity to it for a while.

More often than not, the host having its address changed is not one of the main hubs on the site, so the outage affects few people. If one of the mail hubs or a major web server or FTP archive—like the film library—is moving, though, a day's loss of connectivity may be unacceptable. In cases like this, the administrator should plan ahead and reduce the TTL on the data to be changed.

Remember that the TTL on the affected data needs to be lowered *before* the change takes place. Reducing the TTL on a workstation's address record and changing the workstation's address simultaneously may do you little or no good; the address record may have been cached seconds before you made the change and linger until the old TTL times out. *And* be sure to factor in the time it'll take your slaves to load from your primary master. For example, if your default TTL is 12 hours and your refresh interval is 3 hours, be sure to lower the TTLs at least 15 hours ahead of time, so that by the time you move the host, all the old, longer–TTL records will have timed out. Of course, if all your slaves are BIND 8 or 9 name servers that use NOTIFY, the slaves shouldn't take the full refresh interval to synch up.

Changing Other SOA Values

We briefly mentioned increasing the refresh interval as a way of offloading your primary master name server. Let's discuss refresh in a little more detail and go over the remaining SOA values, too.

The *refresh* value, you'll remember, controls how often a slave checks whether its zone data is up to date. The *retry* value then becomes the refresh time after the first failure to reach a master name server. The *expire* value determines how long zone data can be held before it's discarded, when a master is unreachable. Finally, on pre–BIND 8.2 name servers, the *default TTL* sets how long zone information may be cached. On newer name servers, the last SOA field is the negative caching TTL.

Suppose we've decided we want the slaves to pick up new information every hour instead of every three hours. We change the refresh value to *1h* in each of the zone data files (or with the *–o* option to *h2n*). Since retry is related to refresh, we should probably reduce retry, too—to every 15 minutes or so. Typically, retry is less than refresh, but that's not required.* Although lowering the refresh value will speed up the distribution of zone data, it will also increase the load on the name server being loaded from, since the slaves will check more often. The added load isn't much, though; each slave makes a single SOA query during each zone's refresh interval to check its master's copy of the zone. So with two slave name servers, changing the refresh time from three hours to one hour will generate only four more queries (per zone) to the primary master in any three-hour span.

Of course, if all of your slaves run BIND 8 or 9 and you use NOTIFY, refresh doesn't mean as much. But if you have even one BIND 4 slave, your zone data may take up to the refresh interval to reach it.

Some older versions of BIND slaves stopped answering queries during a zone load. As a result, BIND was modified to spread out the zone loads, reducing the periods of unavailability. So, even if you set a low refresh interval, your slaves may not check exactly as often as you request. BIND 4 name servers attempt a certain number of zone loads, and then wait 15 minutes before trying another batch. On the other hand, BIND 4.9 and later may also refresh more often than the refresh interval. These newer BINDs wait a random number of seconds between one-half the refresh interval and the full refresh interval to check serial numbers.

Expiration times on the order of a week are common—longer if you frequently have problems reaching your updating source. The expiration time should always be much larger than the retry and refresh intervals; if the expire time is smaller than the refresh interval, your slaves will expire their data before trying to load new data. BIND 8 will complain if you set an expire time less than refresh plus retry, less than twice retry, less than seven days, or greater than six months. (BIND 9.1.0 doesn't complain yet.) Choosing an expire time that meets all BIND 8's criteria is a good idea in most situations.

If your zone's data doesn't change much, you might consider raising its default TTL. Default TTLs are commonly a few hours to one day, but you can use longer values. One week is about the longest value that makes sense for a TTL. Longer than that and you may find yourself unable to change bad, cached data in a reasonable amount of time.

---

* Actually, BIND 8 servers will warn you if refresh is set to less than 10 times the retry interval.

Planning for Disasters

It's a fact of life on a network that things go wrong. Hardware fails, software has bugs, and people very occasionally make mistakes. Sometimes this results in minor inconveniences, like having a few users lose connections. Sometimes the results are catastrophic and involve the loss of important data and valuable jobs.

Because the Domain Name System relies so heavily on the network, it is vulnerable to network outages. Thankfully, the design of DNS takes into account the imperfection of networks: it allows for multiple, redundant name servers, retransmission of queries, retrying zone transfers, and so on.

The Domain Name System doesn't protect itself from every conceivable calamity, though. There are types of network failures—some of them quite common—that DNS doesn't or can't protect against. But with a small investment of time and money, you can minimize the threat of these outages.

Outages

Power outages, for example, are relatively common in many parts of the world. In some parts of the U.S., thunderstorms or tornadoes may cause a site to lose power, or to have only intermittent power, for an extended period. Elsewhere, typhoons, volcanoes, or construction work may interrupt your electrical service.

If all your hosts are down, of course, you don't need name service. Quite often, however, sites have problems when power is *restored.* Following our recommendations, they run their name servers on file servers and big multiuser machines. And when the power comes up, those machines are naturally the last to boot— because all those disks need to be *fsck*'d first! Which means that all the on-site hosts that are quick to boot do so without the benefit of name service.

This can cause all sorts of wonderful problems, depending on how your hosts' startup files are written. Unix hosts often execute some variant of:

```
/usr/sbin/ifconfig lan0 inet `hostname` netmask 255.255.128.0 up
/usr/sbin/route add default site-router 1
```

to bring up their network interface and add a default route. Using host names in the commands (`hostname` expands to the local host name and *site-router* is the name of the local router) is admirable for two reasons:

- It lets the administrators change the router's IP address without changing all the startup files on-site.

- It lets the administrators change the host's IP address by changing the IP address in only one file.

Unfortunately, the *route* command fails without name service. The *ifconfig* command fails only if the local host's name and IP address don't appear in the host's */etc/hosts* file, so it's a good idea to leave at least that data in each host's */etc/hosts*.

By the time the startup sequence reaches the *route* command, the network interface will be up, and the host will try to use name service to map the name of the router to an IP address. And since the host has no default route until the *route* command is executed, the only name servers it can reach are those on the local subnet.

If the booting host can reach a working name server on its local subnet, it can execute the *route* command successfully. Quite often, however, one or more of the name servers it can reach aren't yet running. What happens then depends on the contents of *resolv.conf*.

BIND resolvers fall back to the host table only if there is just one name server listed in *resolv.conf* (or if no name server is listed, and the resolver defaults to using a name server on the local host). If only one name server is configured, the resolver queries it, and if the network returns an error each time the resolver sends a query, the resolver falls back to searching the host table. The errors that cause the resolver to fall back include:

- Receipt of an ICMP port unreachable message
- Receipt of an ICMP network unreachable message
- Inability to send the UDP packet (e.g., because networking is not yet running on the local host)[*]

If the host running the one configured name server isn't running at all, though, the resolver doesn't receive any errors. The name server is effectively a black hole. After about 75 seconds of trying, the resolver just times out and returns a null answer to the application that called it. Only if the name server host has actually started networking—but not yet started the name server—does the resolver get an error: an ICMP port unreachable message.

Overall, the single name server configuration does work if you have name servers available on each network, but not as elegantly as we might like. If the local name server hasn't come up when a host on its network reboots, the *route* command fails.

This may seem awkward, but it's not nearly as bad as what happens with multiple name servers. With multiple servers listed in *resolv.conf*, BIND *never* falls back to the host table after the primary network interface has been *ifconfig*'d. The resolver simply loops through the name servers, querying them until one answers or the 75-plus second timeout is reached.

---

[*] Check Chapter 6, *Configuring Hosts*, for vendor-specific enhancements to and variants of this resolver algorithm.

This is especially problematic during bootup. If none of the configured name servers is available, the resolver times out without returning an IP address, and adding the default route fails.

Recommendations

Our recommendation, as primitive as it sounds, is to hardcode the IP address of the default router into the startup file or an external file (many systems use */etc/ defaultrouter*). This ensures that your host's networking starts correctly.

An alternative is to list just a single, reliable name server on your host's local network in *resolv.conf*. This allows you to use the name of the default router in the startup file, as long as you make sure that the router's name appears in */etc/hosts* (in case your reliable name server isn't running when the host reboots). Of course, if the host running the reliable name server isn't running when your host reboots, all bets are off. You won't fall back to */etc/hosts* because there won't be any networking running to return an error to your host.

If your vendor's version of BIND allows configuration of the order in which services are queried or falls back from DNS to */etc/hosts* if DNS doesn't find an answer, take advantage of it! In the former case, you can configure the resolver to check */etc/hosts* first, and then keep a "stub" */etc/hosts* file on each host, including the default router and the local host's name. In the latter situation, just make sure such a "stub" */etc/hosts* exists; no other configuration should be necessary.

A last, promising prospect is to do away with setting the default route manually by using *ICMP Router Discovery Messages*. This extension to the ICMP protocol, described in RFC 1256, uses broadcast or multicast messages to dynamically discover and advertise routers on a network. Windows NT 4.0 supports it, though it's disabled by default. To enable it, follow the instructions in Knowledge Base article Q223756. Sun includes an implementation of this protocol in recent versions of Solaris as */usr/sbin/in.rdisc,* and Cisco's Internetwork Operating System (IOS) supports it too.

And what if your default route is added correctly but the name servers still haven't come up? This can affect *sendmail*, NFS, and a slew of other services. *sendmail* won't canonicalize host names correctly without DNS, and your NFS mounts may fail.

The best solution to this problem is to run a name server on a host with uninterruptible power. If you rarely experience extended power loss, battery backup might be enough. If your outages are longer and name service is critical to you, you should consider an uninterruptible power system (UPS) with a generator of some kind.

If you can't afford luxuries like these, you might just try to track down the fastest booting host around and run a name server on it. Hosts with filesystem journaling should boot especially quickly since they don't need to *fsck*. Hosts with small filesystems should boot quickly, too, since they don't have as much filesystem to check.

Once you've located the right host, you'll need to make sure the host's IP address appears in the *resolv.conf* files of all the hosts that need full-time name service. You'll probably want to list the backed-up host last, since during normal operation hosts should use the name server closest to them. Then, after a power failure, your critical applications will still have name service, albeit at a small sacrifice in performance.

Coping with Disaster

When disaster strikes, it really helps to know what to do. Knowing to duck under a sturdy table or desk during an earthquake can save you from being pinned under a toppling monitor. Knowing how to turn off your gas can save your house from conflagration.

Likewise, knowing what to do in a network disaster (or even just a minor mishap) can help you keep your network running. Living out in California, as we do, we have some experience and some suggestions.

Short Outages (Hours)

If your network is cut off from the outside world (whether "the outside world" is the rest of the Internet or the rest of your company), your name servers may start to have trouble resolving names. For example, if your domain, *corp.acme.com*, is cut off from the rest of the Acme Internet, you may not have access to your parent (*acme.com*) name servers or to the root name servers.

You'd think this wouldn't affect communication between hosts in your local domain, but it can. For example, if you type:

```
% telnet selma.corp.acme.com
```

on a host running an older version of the resolver, the first domain name the resolver looks up is *selma.corp.acme.com.corp.acme.com* (assuming your host is using the default search list—remember this from Chapter 6?). The local name server, if it's authoritative for *corp.acme.com*, can tell that's not a kosher domain name. The next lookup, however, is for *selma.corp.acme.com.acme.com*. This prospective domain name is no longer in the *corp.acme.com* zone, so the query is sent to the *acme.com* name servers. Or rather, your local name server *tries* to send the query there and keeps retransmitting until it times out.

You can avoid this problem by making sure the first domain name the resolver looks up is the right one. Instead of typing:

```
% telnet selma.corp.acme.com
```

it's better to type:

```
% telnet selma
```

or:

```
% telnet selma.corp.acme.com.
```

(Note the trailing dot.) These result in a lookup of *selma.corp.acme.com* first.

BIND 4.9 and later resolvers don't have this problem, at least not by default. 4.9 and newer resolvers check the domain name as-is first, as long as the name has more than one dot in it. So, if you type:

```
% telnet selma.corp.acme.com
```

even without the trailing dot, the first name looked up is *selma.corp.acme.com*.

If you are stuck running a 4.8.3 BIND or older resolver, you can avoid querying off-site name servers by taking advantage of the configurable search list. You can use the *search* directive to define a search list that doesn't include your parent zone's domain name. For example, to work around the problem *corp.acme.com* is having, you could temporarily set your hosts' search lists to just:

```
search corp.acme.com
```

Now, when a user types:

```
% telnet selma.corp.acme.com
```

the resolver looks up *selma.corp.acme.com.corp.acme.com* first (which the local name server can answer), then *selma.corp.acme.com*, the correct domain name. And this works fine, too:

```
% telnet selma
```

Longer Outages (Days)

If you lose network connectivity for a long time, your name servers may have other problems. If they lose connectivity to the root name servers for an extended period, they'll stop resolving queries outside their authoritative zone data. If the slaves can't reach their master, sooner or later they'll expire the zone.

In case your name service really goes haywire because of the connectivity loss, it's a good idea to keep a site-wide or workgroup */etc/hosts* around. In times of dire need, you can move *resolv.conf* to *resolv.bak*, kill the local name server (if there is one), and just use */etc/hosts*. It's not flashy, but it'll get you by.

As for slaves, you can reconfigure a slave that can't reach its master to temporarily run as a primary master. Just edit *named.conf* and change the *type* substatement in the *zone* statement from *slave* to *master*, then delete the *masters* substatement. If more than one slave for the same zone is cut off, you can configure one as a primary master temporarily and reconfigure the others to load from the temporary primary.

Alternatively, you can just increase the expire time in all of your slaves' backup zone data files, and then signal the slaves to reload the files.

Really Long Outages (Weeks)

If an extended outage cuts you off from the Internet   say for a week or more—you may need to restore connectivity to root name servers artificially to get things working again. Every name server needs to talk to a root name server occasionally. It's a bit like therapy: the name server needs to contact a root to regain its perspective on the world.

To provide root name service during a long outage, you can set up your own root name servers, *but only temporarily.* Once you're reconnected to the Internet, you *must* shut off your temporary root servers. The most obnoxious vermin on the Internet are name servers that believe they're root name servers but don't know anything about most top-level domains. A close second is the Internet name server configured to query—and report—a false set of root name servers.

That said, and our alibis in place, here's what you have to do to configure your own root name server. First, you need to create *db.root*, the root zone data file. The *db.root* file will delegate to the highest-level zones in your isolated network. For example, if *movie.edu* were to be isolated from the Internet, we might create a *db.root* file for *terminator* that looked like this:

```
$TTL 1d
. IN SOA terminator.movie.edu. al.robocop.movie.edu. (
                1       ; Serial
                3h      ; Refresh
                1h      ; Retry
                1w      ; Expire
                1h )    ; Negative TTL

   IN NS terminator.movie.edu. ; terminator is the temp. root

; Our root only knows about movie.edu and our two
; in-addr.arpa domains

movie.edu. IN NS terminator.movie.edu.
           IN NS wormhole.movie.edu.

249.249.192.in-addr.arpa. IN NS terminator.movie.edu.
                          IN NS wormhole.movie.edu.
```

```
253.253.192.in-addr.arpa. IN NS terminator.movie.edu.
                          IN NS wormhole.movie.edu.

terminator.movie.edu.  IN A 192.249.249.3
wormhole.movie.edu.    IN A 192.249.249.1
                       IN A 192.253.253.1
```

Then we need to add the appropriate line to *terminator*'s *named.conf* file:

```
// Comment out hints zone
// zone . {
//              type hint;
//                     file "db.cache";
//              };

zone "." {
                type master;
                file "db.root";
};
```

Or, for BIND 4's *named.boot* file:

```
; cache    .   db.cache  (comment out the cache directive)
primary  .   db.root
```

We then update all of our name servers (except the new, temporary root) with a *db.cache* file that includes just the temporary root name server (it's best to move the old root hints file aside—we'll need it later, once connectivity is restored).

Here are the contents of the file *db.cache*:

```
.  99999999  IN  NS  terminator.movie.edu.

terminator.movie.edu.  99999999   IN  A  192.249.249.3
```

That will keep *movie.edu* name resolution going during the outage. Then, once Internet connectivity is restored, we can delete the new master *zone* statement from *named.conf*, uncomment the hint *zone* statement on *terminator*, and restore the original root hints files on all our other name servers.

9

Parenting

The way Dinah washed her children's faces was this: first she held the poor thing down by its ear with one paw, and then with the other paw she rubbed its face all over, the wrong way, beginning at the nose: and just now, as I said, she was hard at work on the white kitten, which was lying quite still and trying to purr—no doubt feeling that it was all meant for its good.

Once your domain reaches a certain size, or you decide you need to distribute the management of parts of your domain to various entities within your organization, you'll want to divide the domain into subdomains. These subdomains will be the children of your current domain in the namespace; your domain will be the parent. If you delegate responsibility for your subdomains to another organization, each becomes its own zone, separate from its parent zone. We like to call the management of your subdomains—your children—*parenting*.

Good parenting starts with carving up your domain sensibly, choosing appropriate names for your subdomains, and delegating the subdomains to create new zones. A responsible parent also works hard at maintaining the relationship between his zone and its children; he ensures that delegation from parent to child is current and correct.

Good parenting is vital to the success of your network, especially as name service becomes critical to navigating between sites. Incorrect delegation to a child zone's name servers can render a site effectively unreachable, while the loss of connectivity to the parent zone's name servers can leave a site unable to reach any hosts outside the local zone.

In this chapter we present our views on when to create subdomains, and we go over how to create and delegate them in some detail. We also discuss management of the parent-child relationship and, finally, how to manage the process of carving up a large domain into smaller subdomains with a minimum of disruption and inconvenience.

When to Become a Parent

Far be it from us to *tell* you when you should become a parent, but we will be so bold as to offer you some guidelines. You may find some compelling reason to implement subdomains that isn't on our list, but here are some of the most common reasons:

- A need to delegate or distribute management of your domain to a number of organizations

- The large size of your domain—dividing it would make it easier to manage and reduce the load on your authoritative name servers

- A need to distinguish hosts' organizational affiliation by including them in particular subdomains

Once you've decided to have children, the next question to ask yourself is, naturally, how many children to have.

How Many Children?

Of course, you won't simply say, "I want to create four subdomains." Deciding how many subdomains to implement is really choosing the organizational affiliation of those subdomains. For example, if your company has four branch offices, you might decide to create four subdomains, each of which corresponds to a branch office.

Should you create subdomains for each site, for each division, or even for each department? You have a lot of latitude in your choice because of DNS's scalability. You can create a few large subdomains or many small subdomains. There are trade-offs whichever you choose, though.

Delegating to a few large subdomains isn't much work for the parent because there's not much delegation to keep track of. However, you wind up with larger subdomains, which require more memory to load and faster name servers, and administration isn't as distributed. If you implement site-level subdomains, for example, you may force autonomous or unrelated groups at a site to share a single zone and a single point of administration.

Delegating to many smaller subdomains can be a headache for the administrator of the parent. Keeping delegation data current involves keeping track of which hosts run name servers and which zones they're authoritative for. The data changes each time a subdomain adds a new name server, or when the address of a name server for the subdomain changes. If the subdomains are all administered by different people, that means more administrators to train, more relationships for the parent's administrator to maintain, and more overhead for the organization overall. On the other hand, the subdomains are smaller and easier to manage, and the administration is more widely distributed, allowing closer management of zone data.

Given the advantages and disadvantages of either alternative, it may seem difficult to make a choice. Actually, though, there's probably a natural division in your organization. Some companies manage computers and networks at the site level; others have decentralized, relatively autonomous workgroups that manage everything themselves. Here are a few basic rules to help you find the right way to carve up your namespace:

- Don't shoehorn your organization into a weird or uncomfortable structure. Trying to fit 50 independent, unrelated U.S. divisions into four regional subdomains may save you work (as the administrator of the parent zone), but it won't help your reputation. Decentralized, autonomous operations demand different zones—that's the raison d'être of the Domain Name System.

- The structure of your domain should mirror the structure of your organization, especially your organization's *support* structure. If departments run networks, assign IP addresses, and manage hosts, then departments should manage the subdomains.

- If you're not sure or can't agree about how the namespace should be organized, try to come up with guidelines for when a group within your organization can carve off its own subdomain (e.g., how many hosts you need to create a new subdomain, what level of support the group must provide) and grow the namespace organically, only as needed.

What to Name Your Children

Once you've decided how many subdomains you'd like to create and what they correspond to, you should choose good names for them. Rather than unilaterally deciding on your subdomains' names, it's considered polite to involve your future subdomain administrators and their constituencies in the decision. In fact, you can leave the decision entirely to them, if you like.

This can lead to problems, though. It's nice to use a relatively consistent naming scheme across your subdomains. It makes it easier for users in one subdomain, or outside your domain entirely, to guess or remember your subdomain names, and to figure out in which domain a particular host or user lives.

Leaving the decision to the locals can result in naming chaos. Some will want to use geographical names, others will insist on organizational names. Some will want to abbreviate, others will want to use full names.

Therefore, it's often best to establish a naming convention before choosing sub-domain names. Here are some suggestions from our experience:

- In a dynamic company, the names of organizations can change frequently. Naming subdomains organizationally in a climate like this can be disastrous. One month the Relatively Advanced Technology group seems stable enough, the next month they've been merged into the Questionable Computer Systems organization, and the following quarter they're all sold to a German conglomerate. Meanwhile, you're stuck with well-known hosts in a subdomain whose name no longer has any meaning.

- Geographical names are more stable than organizational names, but sometimes not as well known. You may know that your famous Software Evangelism Business Unit is in Poughkeepsie or Waukegan, but people outside your company may have no idea where it is (and might have trouble spelling either name).

- Don't sacrifice readability for convenience. Two-letter subdomain names may be easy to type, but they can be impossible to recognize. Why abbreviate "Italy" to "it" and have it confused with your Information Technology organization, when for a paltry three more letters you can use the full name and eliminate any ambiguity?

- Too many companies use cryptic, inconvenient domain names. The general rule seems to be: the larger the company, the more indecipherable the domain names. Buck the trend—make the names of your subdomains obvious!

- Don't use existing or reserved top-level domain names as subdomain names. It might seem sensible to use two-letter country abbreviations for your international subdomains or to use organizational top-level domain names like *net* for your networking organization, but it can cause nasty problems. For example, naming your Communications department's subdomain *com* might impede your ability to communicate with hosts in the top-level *com* domain. Imagine the administrators of your *com* subdomain naming their new Sun workstation *sun* and their new HP 9000 *hp* (they aren't the most imaginative folks)—users anywhere within your domain sending mail to friends at *sun.com* or *hp.com* could have their letters end up in your *com* subdomain* since the domain name of your parent zone may be in some of your hosts' search lists.

---

* Actually, not all mailers have this problem, but some popular versions of *sendmail* do. It all depends on which form of canonicalization they do, as we discussed in the section entitled "Electronic Mail" in Chapter 6, *Configuring Hosts*.

How to Become a Parent: Creating Subdomains

Once you've decided on names, creating the child domains is easy. But first, you've got to decide how much autonomy you're going to give your subdomains. Odd that you have to decide that *before* you actually create them . . . .

Thus far, we've assumed that if you create a subdomain, you'll want to delegate it to another organization, thereby making it a separate zone from the parent. Is this always true, though? Not necessarily.

Think carefully about how the computers and networks within a subdomain are managed when deciding whether or not to delegate it. It doesn't make sense to delegate a subdomain to an entity that doesn't manage its own hosts or networks. For example, in a large corporation, the personnel department probably doesn't run its own computers: the MIS (Management Information Systems) or IT (Information Technology—same animal as MIS) department manages them. So while you may want to create a subdomain for personnel, delegating management for that subdomain to them is probably wasted effort.

Creating a Subdomain in the Parent's Zone

You can create a subdomain without delegating it, however. How? By creating resource records that refer to the subdomain within the parent's zone. For example, *movie.edu* has a host that stores its complete database of employee and student records, called *brazil*. To put *brazil* in the *personnel.movie.edu* domain, we could add records to *db.movie.edu*.

Partial contents of file *db.movie.edu*:

```
brazil.personnel        IN  A      192.253.253.10
                        IN  MX     10 brazil.personnel.movie.edu.
                        IN  MX     100 postmanrings2x.movie.edu.
employeedb.personnel    IN  CNAME  brazil.personnel.movie.edu.
db.personnel            IN  CNAME  brazil.personnel.movie.edu.
```

Now users can log into *db.personnel.movie.edu* to get to the employee database. We could make this setup especially convenient for personnel department employees by adding *personnel.movie.edu* to their PCs' or workstations' search lists; they'd need to type only *telnet db* to get to the right host.

We can make this more convenient for ourselves by using the $ORIGIN control statement to change the origin to *personnel.movie.edu* so that we can use shorter names.

Partial contents of file *db.movie.edu*:

```
$ORIGIN personnel.movie.edu.
brazil      IN A    192.253.253.10
            IN MX   10 brazil.personnel.movie.edu.
            IN MX   100 postmanrings2x.movie.edu.
employeedb IN CNAME brazil.personnel.movie.edu.
db          IN CNAME brazil.personnel.movie.edu.
```

If we had a few more records, we could create a separate file for them and use $INCLUDE to include it in *db.movie.edu* and change the origin at the same time.

Notice that there's no SOA record for *personnel.movie.edu*? There's no need for one, since the *movie.edu* SOA record indicates the start of authority for the entire *movie.edu* zone. Since there's no delegation to *personnel.movie.edu*, it's part of the *movie.edu* zone.

Creating and Delegating a Subdomain

If you decide to delegate your subdomains—to send your children out into the world, as it were—you'll need to do things a little differently. We're in the process of doing it now, so you can follow along with us.

We need to create a new subdomain of *movie.edu* for our special effects lab. We've chosen the name *fx.movie.edu*—short, recognizable, unambiguous. Because we're delegating *fx.movie.edu* to administrators in the lab, it'll be a separate zone. The hosts *bladerunner* and *outland*, both within the special effects lab, will serve as the zone's name servers (*bladerunner* will serve as the primary master). We've chosen to run two name servers for the zone for redundancy—a single *fx.movie. edu* name server would be a single point of failure that could effectively isolate the entire special effects lab. Since there aren't many hosts in the lab, though, we feel two name servers should be enough.

The special effects lab is on *movie.edu*'s new 192.253.254/24 network.

Partial contents of */etc/hosts*:

```
192.253.254.1 movie-gw.movie.edu movie-gw
# fx primary
192.253.254.2 bladerunner.fx.movie.edu bladerunner br
# fx secondary
192.253.254.3 outland.fx.movie.edu outland
192.253.254.4 starwars.fx.movie.edu starwars
192.253.254.5 empire.fx.movie.edu empire
192.253.254.6 jedi.fx.movie.edu jedi
```

First, we create a zone data file that includes records for all the hosts that will live in *fx.movie.edu*.

Contents of file *db.fx.movie.edu*:

```
$TTL 1d
@ IN SOA bladerunner.fx.movie.edu. hostmaster.fx.movie.edu. (
                1       ; serial
                3h      ; refresh
                1h      ; retry
                1w      ; expire
                1h )    ; negative caching TTL


        IN NS bladerunner
        IN NS outland

; MX records for fx.movie.edu
        IN MX 10 starwars
        IN MX 100 wormhole.movie.edu.


; starwars handles bladerunner's mail
; wormhole is the movie.edu mail hub

bladerunner IN A    192.253.254.2
            IN MX   10 starwars
            IN MX   100 wormhole.movie.edu.

br          IN  CNAME    bladerunner

outland     IN A    192.253.254.3
            IN MX   10 starwars
            IN MX   100 wormhole.movie.edu.

starwars    IN A    192.253.254.4
            IN MX   10 starwars
            IN MX   100 wormhole.movie.edu.

empire      IN A    192.253.254.5
            IN MX   10 starwars
            IN MX   100 wormhole.movie.edu.

jedi        IN A    192.253.254.6
            IN MX   10 starwars
            IN MX   100 wormhole.movie.edu.
```

Then we create the *db.192.253.254* file:

```
$TTL 1d
@ IN SOA bladerunner.fx.movie.edu. hostmaster.fx.movie.edu. (
                1       ; serial
                3h      ; refresh
                1h      ; retry
                1w      ; expire
                1h )    ; negative caching TTL


        IN  NS  bladerunner.fx.movie.edu.
        IN  NS  outland.fx.movie.edu.
```

```
1       IN      PTR     movie-gw.movie.edu.
2       IN      PTR     bladerunner.fx.movie.edu.
3       IN      PTR     outland.fx.movie.edu.
4       IN      PTR     starwars.fx.movie.edu.
5       IN      PTR     empire.fx.movie.edu.
6       IN      PTR     jedi.fx.movie.edu.
```

Notice that the PTR record for *1.254.253.192.in-addr.arpa* points to *movie-gw. movie.edu*. That's intentional. The router connects to the other *movie.edu* networks, so it really doesn't belong in *fx.movie.edu*, and there's no requirement that all the PTR records in *254.253.192.in-addr.arpa* map into a single zone—though they should correspond to the canonical names for those hosts.

Next, we create an appropriate *named.conf* file for the primary master name server:

```
options {
                directory "/var/named";
};

zone "0.0.127.in-addr.arpa" {
                type master;
                file "db.127.0.0";
};

zone "fx.movie.edu" {
                type master;
                file "db.fx.movie.edu";
};

zone "254.253.192.in-addr.arpa" {
                type master;
                file "db.192.253.254";
};

zone "." {
                type hint;
                file "db.cache";
};
```

Here are the contents of the corresponding *named.boot* file for BIND 4:

```
directory       /var/named

primary         0.0.127.in-addr.arpa      db.127.0.0  ; loopback
primary         fx.movie.edu              db.fx.movie.edu
primary         254.253.192.in-addr.arpa  db.192.253.254

cache           .                         db.cache
```

Of course, if we'd used *h2n*, we could have just run:

```
% h2n -d fx.movie.edu -n 192.253.254 -s bladerunner -s outland \
-u hostmaster.fx.movie.edu -m 10:starwars -m 100:wormhole.movie.edu
```

and saved ourselves some typing. *h2n* would have created essentially the same *db.fx.movie.edu*, *db.192.253.254*, and *named.boot* files.

Now we need to configure *bladerunner's* resolver. Actually, this may not require creating *resolv.conf*. If we set *bladerunner's hostname* to its new domain name, *bladerunner.fx.movie.edu*, the resolver can derive the local domain name from the fully qualified domain name.

Next we start up the *named* process on *bladerunner* and check for *syslog* errors. If *named* starts okay and there are no *syslog* errors that need tending to, we'll use *nslookup* to look up a few hosts in *fx.movie.edu* and in *254.253.192.in-addr.arpa*:

```
Default Server: bladerunner.fx.movie.edu
Address: 192.253.254.2


> jedi
Server: bladerunner.fx.movie.edu
Address: 192.253.254.2


Name:   jedi.fx.movie.edu
Address: 192.253.253.6


> set type=mx
> empire
Server: bladerunner.fx.movie.edu
Address: 192.253.254.2


empire.fx.movie.edu       preference = 10,
                          mail exchanger = starwars.fx.movie.edu
empire.fx.movie.edu       preference = 100,
                          mail exchanger = wormhole.movie.edu
fx.movie.edu     nameserver = outland.fx.movie.edu
fx.movie.edu     nameserver = bladerunner.fx.movie.edu
starwars.fx.movie.edu   internet address = 192.253.254.4
wormhole.movie.edu      internet address = 192.249.249.1
wormhole.movie.edu      internet address = 192.253.253.1
bladerunner.fx.movie.edu       internet address = 192.253.254.2
outland.fx.movie.edu    internet address = 192.253.254.3
> ls -d fx.movie.edu
[bladerunner.fx.movie.edu]
$ORIGIN fx.movie.edu.
@                      1D IN SOA     bladerunner hostmaster (
                                     1              ; serial
                                     3H             ; refresh
                                     1H             ; retry
                                     1W             ; expiry
                                     1H )           ; minimum

                       1D IN NS      bladerunner
                       1D IN NS      outland
                       1D IN MX      10 starwars
                       1D IN MX      100 wormhole.movie.edu.
```

```
bladerunner          1D IN A       192.253.254.2
                     1D IN MX      10 starwars
                     1D IN MX      100 wormhole.movie.edu.
br                   1D IN CNAME   bladerunner
empire               1D IN A       192.253.254.5
                     1D IN MX      10 starwars
                     1D IN MX      100 wormhole.movie.edu.
jedi                 1D IN A       192.253.254.6
                     1D IN MX      10 starwars
                     1D IN MX      100 wormhole.movie.edu.
outland              1D IN A       192.253.254.3
                     1D IN MX      10 starwars
                     1D IN MX      100 wormhole.movie.edu.
starwars             1D IN A       192.253.254.4
                     1D IN MX      10 starwars
                     1D IN MX      100 wormhole.movie.edu.
@                    1D IN SOA     bladerunner hostmaster (
                                   1              ; serial
                                   3H             ; refresh
                                   1H             ; retry
                                   1W             ; expiry
                                   1H )           ; minimum

  > set type=ptr
  > 192.253.254.3
Server:  bladerunner.fx.movie.edu
Address:  192.253.254.2


3.254.253.192.in-addr.arpa      name = outland.fx.movie.edu

  > ls -d 254.253.192.in-addr.arpa.
[bladerunner.fx.movie.edu]
$ORIGIN 254.253.192.in-addr.arpa.
@         1D IN SOA     bladerunner.fx.movie.edu. hostmaster.fx.movie.edu. (
                        1              ; serial
                        3H             ; refresh
                        1H             ; retry
                        1W             ; expiry
                        1H )           ; minimum


          1D IN NS      bladerunner.fx.movie.edu.
          1D IN NS      outland.fx.movie.edu.
1         1D IN PTR     movie-gw.movie.edu.
2         1D IN PTR     bladerunner.fx.movie.edu.
3         1D IN PTR     outland.fx.movie.edu.
4         1D IN PTR     starwars.fx.movie.edu.
5         1D IN PTR     empire.fx.movie.edu.
6         1D IN PTR     jedi.fx.movie.edu.
@         1D IN SOA     bladerunner.fx.movie.edu. hostmaster.fx.movie.edu. (
                        1              ; serial
                        3H             ; refresh
                        1H             ; retry
                        1W             ; expiry
                        1H )           ; minimum

  > exit
```

The output looks reasonable, so it's now safe to set up a slave name server for *fx.movie.edu* and then delegate *fx.movie.edu* from *movie.edu*.

An fx.movie.edu Slave

Setting up the slave name server for *fx.movie.edu* is simple: copy *named.conf*, *db. 127.0.0*, and *db.cache* over from *bladerunner*, and edit *named.conf* and *db.127.0.0* according to the instructions in Chapter 4, *Setting Up BIND*.

Contents of file *named.conf*:

```
options {
            directory "/var/named";
};

zone "0.0.127.in-addr.arpa" {
            type master;
            file "db.127.0.0";
};

zone "fx.movie.edu" {
            type slave;
            masters { 192.253.254.2; };
            file "bak.fx.movie.edu";
};

zone "254.253.192.in-addr.arpa" {
            type slave;
            masters { 192.253.254.2; };
            file "bak.192.253.254";
};

zone "." {
            type hint;
            file "db.cache";
};
```

Or, the equivalent *named.boot* file:

```
directory   /var/named

primary     0.0.127.in-addr.arpa        db.127.0.0
secondary   fx.movie.edu                192.253.254.2  bak.fx.movie.edu
secondary   254.253.192.in-addr.arpa  192.253.254.2  bak.192.253.254

cache       .                           db.cache
```

Like *bladerunner*, *outland* really doesn't need a *resolv.conf* file, as long as its *hostname* is set to *outland.fx.movie.edu*.

Again, we start *named* and check for errors in the *syslog* output. If the *syslog* output is clean, we'll look up a few records in *fx.movie.edu*.

On the movie.edu Primary Master Name Server

All that's left now is to delegate the *fx.movie.edu* subdomain to the new *fx.movie.edu* name servers on *bladerunner* and *outland*. We add the appropriate NS records to *db.movie.edu*.

Partial contents of file *db.movie.edu*:

```
fx      86400     IN    NS    bladerunner.fx.movie.edu.
        86400     IN    NS    outland.fx.movie.edu.
```

According to RFC 1034, the domain names in the resource record–specific portion of these two lines (*bladerunner.fx.movie.edu* and *outland.fx.movie.edu*) must be the canonical domain names for the name servers. A remote name server following delegation expects to find one or more address records attached to that domain name, not an alias (CNAME) record. Actually, the RFC extends this restriction to any type of resource record that includes a domain name as its value—all must specify the canonical domain name.

These two records alone aren't enough, though. Do you see the problem? How can a name server outside *fx.movie.edu* look up information within *fx.movie.edu*? Well, a *movie.edu* name server would refer it to the name servers authoritative for *fx.movie.edu*, right? That's true, but the NS records in *db.movie.edu* give only the *names* of the *fx.movie.edu* name servers. The foreign name server needs the IP addresses of the *fx.movie.edu* name servers in order to send queries to them. Who can give it those addresses? Only the *fx.movie.edu* name servers. A real chicken-and-egg problem!

The solution is to include the addresses of the *fx.movie.edu* name servers in the *movie.edu* zone data file. While these aren't strictly part of the *movie.edu* zone, they're necessary for delegation to *fx.movie.edu* to work. Of course, if the name servers for *fx.movie.edu* weren't within *fx.movie.edu*, these addresses—called glue records—wouldn't be necessary. A foreign name server would be able to find the address it needed by querying other name servers.

So, with the glue records, the records added look like the following.

Partial contents of file *db.movie.edu*:

```
fx      86400     IN    NS    bladerunner.fx.movie.edu.
        86400     IN    NS    outland.fx.movie.edu.
bladerunner.fx.movie.edu.   86400  IN  A  192.253.254.2
outland.fx.movie.edu.       86400  IN  A  192.253.254.3
```

Be sure you don't include unnecessary glue records in the file. Older BIND name servers (pre-4.9) load these records into their caches and give them out in referrals to other name servers. If the name server listed in the address record changes IP addresses and you forget to update the glue, your name server will continue giving out the outdated address information, resulting in poor resolution performance for name servers looking for data in the delegated zone or even rendering them unable to resolve names in the delegated zone.

A BIND 4.9 or later name server automatically ignores any glue you include that isn't strictly necessary and logs the fact that it has ignored the record(s) to *syslog* on the primary master or in the slave's backup copy of the zone data. For example, if we had an NS record for *movie.edu* that pointed to an off-site name server, *ns-1.isp.net*, and we made the mistake of including its address in *db.movie.edu* on the *movie.edu* primary master name server, we'd see a message like this in *named*'s *syslog* output:

```
Aug  9 14:23:41 terminator named[19626]: dns_master_load: db.movie.edu:55:
ignoring out-of-zone data
```

If we were running a pre-4.9 name server as our primary master and it mistakenly included an unnecessary glue record in a zone transfer to a newer name server, we'd see a message like this in the backup zone data file:

```
; Ignoring info about ns-1.isp.net, not in zone movie.edu
; ns-1.isp.net 258983  IN     A      10.1.2.3
```

Note that the extraneous A record has been commented out.

Also, remember to keep the glue up to date. If *bladerunner* gets a new network interface, and hence another IP address, then you should add another A record to the glue data.

We might also want to include aliases for any hosts moving into *fx.movie.edu* from *movie.edu*. For example, if we were to move *plan9.movie.edu*, a server with an important library of public domain special effects algorithms, into *fx.movie.edu*, we should create an alias in *movie.edu* pointing the old domain name to the new one:

```
plan9          IN     CNAME    plan9.fx.movie.edu.
```

This will allow people outside *movie.edu* to reach *plan9* even though they're using its old domain name, *plan9.movie.edu*.

You shouldn't put any information about domain names in *fx.movie.edu* into the *db.movie.edu* file. The *plan9* alias is actually in the *movie.edu* zone (the owner of the record is *plan9.movie.edu*), so it belongs in *db.movie.edu*. An alias pointing *p9.fx.movie.edu* to *plan9.fx.movie.edu*, on the other hand, is in the *fx.movie.edu* zone, and belongs in *db.fx.movie.edu*. If you were to put a record in the zone data file that was outside the zone the file described, a BIND 4.9 or later name server would ignore it, as shown earlier in the unnecessary glue example. An older name server might load it into cache or even into authoritative data, but since the behavior is unpredictable and is eliminated in newer versions of BIND, it's best to do it the right way even if the software doesn't force you to.

Delegating an in-addr.arpa Zone

We almost forgot to delegate the *254.253.192.in-addr.arpa* zone! This is a little trickier than delegating *fx.movie.edu* because we don't manage the parent zone.

First, we need to figure out what *254.253.192.in-addr.arpa*'s parent zone is and who runs it. Figuring this out may take some sleuthing; we covered how to do this in Chapter 3, *Where Do I Start?*

As it turns out, the *in-addr.arpa* zone is *254.253.192.in-addr.arpa*'s parent. And, if you think about it, that makes some sense. There's no reason for the administrators of *in-addr.arpa* to delegate *253.192.in-addr.arpa* or *192.in-addr.arpa* to a separate authority, because unless 192/8 or 192.253/16 is all one big CIDR block, networks like 192.253.253/24 and 192.253.254/24 don't have anything in common with each other. They may be managed by totally unrelated organizations.

You might have remembered (from Chapter 3) that the *in-addr.arpa* zone is managed by ARIN, the American Registry of Internet Numbers. (Of course, if you didn't remember, you could always use *nslookup* to find the contact address in *in-addr.arpa*'s SOA record, like we showed you in that chapter.) All that's left is for us to use the web-based "Modify Tool" at *http://www.arin.net/cgi-bin/amt.pl* to request registration of our reverse-mapping zone.

Adding a movie.edu Slave

If the special effects lab gets big enough, it may make sense to put a *movie.edu* slave somewhere on the 192.253.254/24 network. That way, a larger proportion of DNS queries from *fx.movie.edu* hosts can be answered locally. It seems logical to make one of the existing *fx.movie.edu* name servers into a *movie.edu* slave, too— that way, we can make better use of an existing name server instead of setting up a brand-new name server.

We've decided to make *bladerunner* a slave for *movie.edu*. This won't interfere with *bladerunner*'s primary mission: acting as the primary master name server for *fx.movie.edu*, that is. A single name server, given enough memory, can be authoritative for literally thousands of zones. One name server can load some zones as a primary master and others as a slave.[*]

The configuration change is simple: we add one statement to *bladerunner*'s *named.conf* file to tell *named* to load the *movie.edu* zone from the IP address of the *movie.edu* primary master name server, *terminator.movie.edu*.

---

[*] Clearly, though, a name server can't be both the primary master and a slave for a single zone. Either the name server gets the data for a given zone from a local zone data file (and is a primary master for the zone) or from another name server (and is a slave for the zone).

Contents of file *named.conf*:

```
options {
    directory "/var/named";
};

zone "0.0.127.in-addr.arpa" {
    type master;
    file "db.127.0.0";
};

zone "fx.movie.edu" {
    type master;
    file "db.fx.movie.edu";
};

zone "254.253.192.in-addr.arpa" {
    type master;
    file "db.192.253.254";
};

zone "movie.edu" {
    type slave;
    masters { 192.249.249.3; };
    file "bak.movie.edu";
};

zone "." {
    type hint;
    file "db.cache";
};
```

Or, if you're using a BIND 4 name server, here are the contents of the *named.boot* file:

```
directory      /var/named

primary        0.0.127.in-addr.arpa        db.127.0.0  ; loopback
primary        fx.movie.edu                db.fx.movie.edu
primary        254.253.192.in-addr.arpa    db.192.253.254
secondary      movie.edu                   192.249.249.3      bak.movie.edu

cache          .                           db.cache
```

Subdomains of in-addr.arpa Domains

Forward-mapping domains aren't the only domains that you can divide into subdomains and delegate. If your *in-addr.arpa* namespace is large enough, you may need to divide it, too. Typically, you divide the domain that corresponds to your network number into subdomains that correspond to your subnets. How that works depends on the type of network you have and on your network's subnet mask.

Subnetting on an Octet Boundary

Since Movie U. has just three /24 (class C-sized) networks, one per segment, there's no particular need to subnet those networks. However, our sister university, Altered State, has a class B-sized network, 172.20/16. Their network is subnetted between the third and fourth octet of the IP address; that is, their subnet mask is 255.255.255.0. They've already created a number of subdomains of their domain, *altered.edu*, including *fx.altered.edu* (okay, we copied them), *makeup.altered.edu*, and *foley.altered.edu*. Since each of these departments also runs its own subnet (their Special Effects department runs subnet 172.20.2/24, Makeup runs 172.20.15/24, and Foley runs 172.20.25/24), they'd like to divvy up their *in-addr.arpa* namespace appropriately, too.

Delegating *in-addr.arpa* subdomains is no different from delegating subdomains of forward-mapping domains. Within their *db.172.20* zone data file, they need to add NS records like these:

```
2     86400    IN    NS    gump.fx.altered.edu.
2     86400    IN    NS    toystory.fx.altered.edu.
15    86400    IN    NS    prettywoman.makeup.altered.edu.
15    86400    IN    NS    priscilla.makeup.altered.edu.
25    86400    IN    NS    blowup.foley.altered.edu.
25    86400    IN    NS    muppetmovie.foley.altered.edu.
```

delegating the subdomain that corresponds to each subnet to the correct name server in each subdomain.

A few important notes: the Altered States administrators could only use the third octet of the subnet in the owner name field because the default origin in this file is *20.172.in-addr.arpa*. They needed to use the fully qualified domain names of the name servers in the right side of the NS records, though, to avoid having the origin appended. And they *didn't* need glue address records, since the names of the name servers they delegated the zone to didn't end in the domain name of the zone.

Subnetting on a Non-Octet Boundary

What do you do about networks that aren't subnetted neatly on octet boundaries, like subnetted /24 (class C-sized) networks? In these cases, you can't delegate along lines that match the subnets. This forces you into one of two situations: you have multiple subnets per *in-addr.arpa* zone, or you have multiple *in-addr.arpa* zones per subnet. Neither is particularly pleasing.

Class A and B networks

Let's take the case of the /8 (class A-sized) network 15/8, subnetted with the subnet mask 255.255.248.0 (a 13-bit subnet field and an 11-bit host field, or 8192 subnets of 2048 hosts). In this case, the subnet 15.1.200.0, for example, extends from

15.1.200.0 to 15.1.207.255. Therefore, the delegation for that single subdomain in *db.15*, the zone data file for *15.in-addr.arpa*, might look like this:

```
200.1.15.in-addr.arpa.    86400   IN   NS   ns-1.cns.hp.com.
200.1.15.in-addr.arpa.    86400   IN   NS   ns-2.cns.hp.com.
201.1.15.in-addr.arpa.    86400   IN   NS   ns-1.cns.hp.com.
201.1.15.in-addr.arpa.    86400   IN   NS   ns-2.cns.hp.com.
202.1.15.in-addr.arpa.    86400   IN   NS   ns-1.cns.hp.com.
202.1.15.in-addr.arpa.    86400   IN   NS   ns-2.cns.hp.com.
203.1.15.in-addr.arpa.    86400   IN   NS   ns-1.cns.hp.com.
203.1.15.in-addr.arpa.    86400   IN   NS   ns-2.cns.hp.com.
204.1.15.in-addr.arpa.    86400   IN   NS   ns-1.cns.hp.com.
204.1.15.in-addr.arpa.    86400   IN   NS   ns-2.cns.hp.com.
205.1.15.in-addr.arpa.    86400   IN   NS   ns-1.cns.hp.com.
205.1.15.in-addr.arpa.    86400   IN   NS   ns-2.cns.hp.com.
206.1.15.in-addr.arpa.    86400   IN   NS   ns-1.cns.hp.com.
206.1.15.in-addr.arpa.    86400   IN   NS   ns-2.cns.hp.com.
207.1.15.in-addr.arpa.    86400   IN   NS   ns-1.cns.hp.com.
207.1.15.in-addr.arpa.    86400   IN   NS   ns-2.cns.hp.com.
```

That's a lot of delegation for one subnet!

Luckily, BIND 8.2 and later as well as BIND 9.1.0 and later name servers support a control statement called $GENERATE. $GENERATE lets you create a group of resource records that differ only by a numerical iterator. For example, you could create the 16 NS records just listed using these two $GENERATE control statements:

```
$GENERATE 200-207 $.1.15.in-addr.arpa.   86400   IN   NS   ns-1.cns.hp.com.
$GENERATE 200-207 $.1.15.in-addr.arpa.   86400   IN   NS   ns-1.cns.hp.com.
```

The syntax is fairly simple: when the name server reads the control statement, it iterates over the range specified as the first argument, replacing any dollar signs ($) in the template that follows the first argument with the current iterator.

Class C networks

Now let's look at the case of a subnetted /24 (class C-sized) network, say 192.253. 254/24, subnetted with the mask 255.255.255.192. Here, you have a single *in-addr. arpa* zone, *254.253.192.in-addr.arpa*, that corresponds to subnets 192.253.254.0/ 26, 192.253.254.64/26, 192.253.254.128/26, and 192.253.254.192/26. This can be a problem if you want to let different organizations manage the reverse-mapping information corresponding to each subnet. You can solve this in one of three ways, none of them pretty.

Solution 1. The first solution is to administer the *254.253.192.in-addr.arpa* zone as a single entity and not even try to delegate. This requires either cooperation between the administrators of the four subnets involved or the use of a tool like Webmin (*http://www.webmin.com/webmin*) to allow each of the four administrators to take care of his or her own data.

Solution 2. The second is to delegate at the *fourth* octet. That's even nastier than the /8 delegation we just showed you. You'll need at least a couple of NS records per IP address in the file *db.192.253.254*, like this:

```
1.254.253.192.in-addr.arpa.    86400    IN    NS    ns1.foo.com.
1.254.253.192.in-addr.arpa.    86400    IN    NS    ns2.foo.com.

2.254.253.192.in-addr.arpa.    86400    IN    NS    ns1.foo.com.
2.254.253.192.in-addr.arpa.    86400    IN    NS    ns2.foo.com.

...

65.254.253.192.in-addr.arpa.    86400    IN    NS    relay.bar.com.
65.254.253.192.in-addr.arpa.    86400    IN    NS    gw.bar.com.

66.254.253.192.in-addr.arpa.    86400    IN    NS    relay.bar.com.
66.254.253.192.in-addr.arpa.    86400    IN    NS    gw.bar.com.

...

129.254.253.192.in-addr.arpa.    86400    IN    NS    mail.baz.com.
129.254.253.192.in-addr.arpa.    86400    IN    NS    www.baz.com.

130.254.253.192.in-addr.arpa.    86400    IN    NS    mail.baz.com.
130.254.253.192.in-addr.arpa.    86400    IN    NS    www.baz.com.
```

and so on, all the way down to *254.254.253.192.in-addr.arpa.*

You can pare that down substantially by using $GENERATE:

```
$GENERATE 0-63 $.254.253.192.in-addr.arpa 86400 IN NS ns1.foo.com.
$GENERATE 0-63 $.254.253.192.in-addr.arpa 86400 IN NS ns2.foo.com.

$GENERATE 64-127 $.254.253.192.in-addr.arpa. 86400 IN NS relay.bar.com.
$GENERATE 64-127 $.254.253.192.in-addr.arpa. 86400 IN NS gw.bar.com.

$GENERATE 128-191 $.254.253.192.in-addr.arpa. 86400 IN NS mail.baz.com.
$GENERATE 128-191 $.254.253.192.in-addr.arpa. 86400 IN NS www.baz.com.
```

Of course, in *ns1.foo.com*'s *named.conf*, you'd also expect to see:

```
zone "1.254.253.192.in-addr.arpa" {
            type master;
            file "db.192.253.254.1";
};

zone "2.254.253.192.in-addr.arpa" {
            type master;
            file "db.192.253.254.2";
};
```

Or, if *ns1.foo.com* were running BIND 4, you'd expect to see these directives in *named.boot*:

```
primary    1.254.253.192.in-addr.arpa    db.192.253.254.1
primary    2.254.253.192.in-addr.arpa    db.192.253.254.2
```

and in *db.192.253.254.1*, just the one PTR record:

```
$TTL 1d
@   IN   SOA   ns1.foo.com.   root.ns1.foo.com.   (
                       1       ; Serial
                       3h      ; Refresh
                       1h      ; Retry
                       1w      ; Expire
                       1h      ; Negative caching TTL


       IN   NS    ns1.foo.com.
       IN   NS    ns2.foo.com.

       IN   PTR   thereitis.foo.com.
```

Notice that the PTR record is attached to the zone's domain name since the zone's domain name corresponds to just one IP address. Now, when a *254.253.192.in-addr.arpa* name server receives a query for the PTR record for *1.254.253.192.in-addr.arpa*, it refers the querier to *ns1.foo.com* and *ns2.foo.com*, which respond with the one PTR record in the zone.

Solution 3. Finally, there's a clever technique that obviates the need to maintain a separate zone data file for each IP address.* The organization responsible for the overall /24 network creates CNAME records for each of the domain names in the zone, pointing to domain names in new subdomains, which are then delegated to the proper servers. These new subdomains can be called just about anything, but names like *0-63*, *64-127*, *128-191*, and *192-255* clearly indicate the range of addresses each subdomain will reverse map. Each subdomain then contains only the PTR records in the range the subdomain is named for.

Partial contents of file *db.192.253.254*:

```
1.254.253.192.in-addr.arpa.   IN   CNAME   1.0-63.254.253.192.in-addr.arpa.
2.254.253.192.in-addr.arpa.   IN   CNAME   2.0-63.254.253.192.in-addr.arpa.

. . .

0-63.254.253.192.in-addr.arpa.   86400   IN   NS   ns1.foo.com.
0-63.254.253.192.in-addr.arpa.   86400   IN   NS   ns2.foo.com.

65.254.253.192.in-addr.arpa. IN  CNAME 65.64-127.254.253.192.in-addr.arpa.
66.254.253.192.in-addr.arpa. IN  CNAME 66.64-127.254.253.192.in-addr.arpa.

. . .

64-127.254.253.192.in-addr.arpa.   86400   IN   NS   relay.bar.com.
64-127.254.253.192.in-addr.arpa.   86400   IN   NS   gw.bar.com.
```

---

* We first saw this explained by Glen Herrmansfeldt of CalTech in the newsgroup *comp.protocols.tcp-ip. domains*. It's now codified as RFC 2317.

```
129.254.253.192.in-addr.arpa.   IN   CNAME  129.128-191.254.253.192.in-addr. arpa.
130.254.253.192.in-addr.arpa.   IN   CNAME  130.128-191.254.253.192.in-addr. arpa.


...


128-191.254.253.192.in-addr.arpa.      86400   IN   NS   mail.baz.com.
128-191.254.253.192.in-addr.arpa.      86400   IN   NS   www.baz.com.
```

Again, you can abbreviate this with $GENERATE:

```
$GENERATE 1-63 $ IN CNAME $.0-63.254.253.192.in-addr.arpa.


0-63.254.253.192.in-addr.arpa.      86400   IN   NS   ns1.foo.com.
0-63.254.253.192.in-addr.arpa.      86400   IN   NS   ns2.foo.com.


$GENERATE 65-127 $ IN CNAME $.64-127.254.253.192.in-addr.arpa.


64-127.254.253.192.in-addr.arpa.      86400   IN   NS   relay.bar.com.
64-127.254.253.192.in-addr.arpa.      86400   IN   NS   gw.bar.com.
```

The zone data file for *0-63.254.253.192.in-addr.arpa*, *db.192.253.254.0-63*, can contain just PTR records for IP addresses 192.253.254.1 through 192.253.254.63.

Partial contents of file *db.192.253.254.0-63*:

```
$TTL 1d
@    IN    SOA    ns1.foo.com.    root.ns1.foo.com.    (
                          1       ; Serial
                          3h      ; Refresh
                          1h      ; Retry
                          1w      ; Expire
                          1h )    ; Negative caching TTL


     IN    NS    ns1.foo.com.
     IN    NS    ns2.foo.com.


1    IN    PTR    thereitis.foo.com.
2    IN    PTR    setter.foo.com.
3    IN    PTR    mouse.foo.com.
...
```

The way this setup works is a little tricky, so let's go over it. A resolver requests the PTR record for *1.254.253.192.in-addr.arpa*, causing its local name server to look that up. The local name server ends up asking a *254.253.192.in-addr.arpa* name server, which responds with the CNAME record indicating that *1.254.253.192.in-addr.arpa* is actually an alias for *1.0-63.254.253.192.in-addr.arpa* and that the PTR record is attached to that name. The response will also include NS records telling the local name server that the authoritative name servers for *0-63.254.253.192.in-addr.arpa* are *ns1.foo.com* and *ns2.foo.com*. The local name server then queries either *ns1.foo.com* or *ns2.foo.com* for the PTR record for *1.0-63.254.253.192.in-addr.arpa*, and receives the PTR record.

Good Parenting

Now that the delegation to the *fx.movie.edu* name servers is in place, we—responsible parents that we are—should check that delegation using *host*. What? We haven't given you *host* yet? A version of *host* for Unix is available via anonymous FTP from *ftp.nikhef.nl* as */pub/network/host.tar.Z*.

To build *host*, first extract it:

```
% zcat host.tar.Z | tar -xvf -
```

Then build it on your system:

```
% make
```

host makes it easy to check delegation. With *host,* you can look up the NS records for your zone on your parent zone's name servers. If those look good, you can use *host* to query each name server listed for the zone's SOA record. The query is nonrecursive, so the name server queried doesn't query other name servers to find the SOA record. If the name server replies, *host* checks the reply to see whether the *aa*—authoritative answer—bit in the reply message is set. If it is, the name server checks to make sure that the message contains an answer. If both these criteria are met, the name server is flagged as authoritative for the zone. Otherwise, the name server is not authoritative, and *host* reports an error.

Why all the fuss over bad delegation? Incorrect delegation can slow name resolution or cause the propagation of old and erroneous root name server information. When a name server is queried for data in a zone it isn't authoritative for, it does its best to provide useful information to the querier. This "useful information" comes in the form of NS records for the closest ancestor zone the name server knows. (We mentioned this briefly in Chapter 8, *Growing Your Domain*, when we discussed why you shouldn't register a caching-only name server.)

For example, say one of the *fx.movie.edu* name servers mistakenly receives an iterative query for the address of *carrie.horror.movie.edu*. It knows nothing about the *horror.movie.edu* zone (except for what it might have cached), but it likely has NS records for *movie.edu* cached, since those are its parent name servers. So it would return those records to the querier.

In that scenario, the NS records may help the querying name server get an answer. However, it's a fact of life on the Internet that not all administrators keep their root hints files up to date. If one of your name servers follows a bad delegation and queries a remote name server for records it doesn't have, look what can happen:

```
% nslookup
Default Server: terminator.movie.edu
Address: 192.249.249.3
```

```
> set type=ns
> .
Server:  terminator.movie.edu
Address:  192.249.249.3

Non-authoritative answer:
(root)   nameserver = D.ROOT-SERVERS.NET
(root)   nameserver = E.ROOT-SERVERS.NET
(root)   nameserver = I.ROOT-SERVERS.NET
(root)   nameserver = F.ROOT-SERVERS.NET
(root)   nameserver = G.ROOT-SERVERS.NET
(root)   nameserver = A.ROOT-SERVERS.NET
(root)   nameserver = H.ROOT-SERVERS.NET
(root)   nameserver = B.ROOT-SERVERS.NET
(root)   nameserver = C.ROOT-SERVERS.NET
(root)   nameserver = A.ISI.EDU              —These three name
(root)   nameserver = SRI-NIC.ARPA           —servers are no longer
(root)   nameserver = GUNTER-ADAM.ARPA       —roots
```

A remote name server tried to "help out" our local name server by sending it the current list of roots. Unfortunately, the remote name server was corrupt and returned NS records that were incorrect. And our local name server, not knowing any better, cached that data.

BIND 4.9 and later name servers are resistant to this.

Queries to misconfigured *in-addr.arpa* name servers often result in bad root NS records, because the *in-addr.arpa* and *arpa* zones are the closest ancestors of most *in-addr.arpa* subdomains, and name servers very seldom cache NS records of either *in-addr.arpa* or *arpa*. (The roots seldom give them out, since they delegate directly to lower-level subdomains.) Once your name server has cached bad root NS records, your name resolution may suffer.

Those root NS records may have your name server querying a root name server that is no longer at that IP address, or a root name server that no longer exists at all. If you're having an especially bad day, the bad root NS records may point to a real, nonroot name server that is close to your network. Even though it won't return authoritative root data, your name server will favor it because of its proximity to your network.

Using host

If our little lecture has convinced you of the importance of maintaining correct delegation, you'll be eager to learn how to use *host* to ensure that you don't join the ranks of the miscreants.

The first step is to use *host* to look up your zone's NS records on a name server for your parent zone and make sure they're correct. Here's how we would check the *fx.movie.edu* NS records on one of the *movie.edu* name servers:

```
% host -t ns fx.movie.edu. terminator.movie.edu.
```

If everything's okay with the NS records, we'll simply see them in the output:

```
fx.movie.edu    NS    bladerunner.fx.movie.edu
fx.movie.edu    NS    outland.fx.movie.edu
```

This tells us that all the NS records delegating *fx.movie.edu* from *terminator.movie. edu* are correct.

Next, we'll use *host*'s "SOA check" mode to query each of the name servers in the NS records for the *fx.movie.edu* zone's SOA record. This will also check whether the response was authoritative:

```
% host -C fx.movie.edu.
```

Normally, this produces the NS records just listed, along with the contents of the *fx.movie.edu* zone's SOA record:

```
fx.movie.edu            NS          bladerunner.fx.movie.edu
bladerunner.fx.movie.edu        hostmaster.fx.movie.edu    (1 10800 3600 608400 3600)
fx.movie.edu            NS          outland.fx.movie.edu
bladerunner.fx.movie.edu        hostmaster.fx.movie.edu    (1 10800 3600 608400 3600)
```

If one of the *fx.movie.edu* name servers—say *outland*—were misconfigured, we might see this:

```
fx.movie.edu    NS    bladerunner.fx.movie.edu
fx.movie.edu    NS    outland.fx.movie.edu
fx.movie.edu SOA record currently not present at outland.fx.movie.edu
fx.movie.edu has lame delegation to outland.fx.movie.edu
```

This indicates that the name server on *outland* is running, but it's not authoritative for *fx.movie.edu*.

If one of the *fx.movie.edu* name servers weren't running at all, we'd see:

```
fx.movie.edu    NS    bladerunner.fx.movie.edu
bladerunner.fx.movie.edu        hostmaster.fx.movie.edu    (1 10800 3600 608400 3600)
fx.movie.edu    NS    outland.fx.movie.edu
fx.movie.edu SOA record not found at outland.fx.movie.edu, try again
```

In this case, the *try again* message indicates that *host* sent *outland* a query and didn't get a response back in an acceptable amount of time.

While we could have checked the *fx.movie.edu* delegation using *nslookup,* *host*'s powerful command-line options make the task especially easy.

Managing Delegation

If the special effects lab gets bigger, we may find that we need additional name servers. We dealt with setting up new name servers in Chapter 8 and even went over what information to send to the parent zone's administrator. But we never explained what the parent needed to do.

It turns out that the parent's job is relatively easy, especially if the administrators of the subdomain send complete information. Imagine that the special effects lab expands to a new network, 192.254.20/24. This network has a passel of new, high-powered graphics workstations. One of them, *alien.fx.movie.edu,* will act as the new network's name server.

The administrators of *fx.movie.edu* (we delegated it to the folks in the lab) send their parent zone's administrators (that's us) a short note:

```
Hi!

We've just set up alien.fx.movie.edu (192.254.20.3) as a name
server for fx.movie.edu.  Would you please update your
delegation information?  I've attached the NS records you'll
need to add.

Thanks,

Arty Segue
ajs@fx.movie.edu

----- cut here -----

fx.movie.edu.   86400   IN  NS  bladerunner.fx.movie.edu.
fx.movie.edu.   86400   IN  NS  outland.fx.movie.edu.
fx.movie.edu.   86400   IN  NS  alien.fx.movie.edu.

bladerunner.fx.movie.edu.   86400   IN  A  192.253.254.2
outland.fx.movie.edu.       86400   IN  A  192.253.254.3
alien.fx.movie.edu.         86400   IN  A  192.254.20.3
```

Our job as the *movie.edu* administrators is straightforward: add the NS and A records to *db.movie.edu.*

What if we're using *h2n* to create our name server data? We can stick the delegation information into the *spcl.movie* file, which *h2n* $INCLUDEs at the end of the *db.movie* file it creates.

The final step for the *fx.movie.edu* administrator is to send a similar message to *noc@netsol.com* (the administrator of the *in-addr.arpa* zone), requesting that the *20.254.192.in-addr.arpa* subdomain be delegated to *alien.fx.movie.edu*, *bladerunner.fx.movie.edu*, and *outland.fx.movie.edu*.

Stubs: another way to manage delegation

If you're running BIND 4.9 or later name servers, you don't have to manage delegation information manually. BIND 4.9 and later name servers support an experimental feature called *stub zones*, which enables a name server to pick up changes to delegation information automatically.

Name servers that act as stubs for a zone periodically perform discrete queries for the zone's SOA and NS records, as well as any necessary glue A records. The name server uses the NS records to delegate the zone from its parent, and the SOA record governs how often the name server does these queries. Now, when the administrators of a subdomain make changes to the subdomain's name servers, they simply update their NS records. The parent zone's authoritative name servers pick up the updated records within the refresh interval.

On the *movie.edu* name servers, here's what we'd add to *named.conf*:

```
zone "fx.movie.edu" {
            type stub;
            masters { 192.253.254.2; };
            file "stub.fx.movie.edu";
};
```

On a BIND 4.9 name server, we'd use this directive:

```
stub     fx.movie.edu     192.253.254.2     stub.fx.movie.edu
```

Note that we should configure all *movie.edu* name servers as stubs for *fx.movie.edu*, because if the *fx.movie.edu* delegation information changes, that won't change the *movie.edu* zone's serial number.* Making all the *movie.edu* name servers stubs for the subdomain will keep them synchronized.

Managing the Transition to Subdomains

We won't lie to you—the *fx.movie.edu* example we showed you was unrealistic for several reasons. The main one is the magical appearance of the special effects lab's hosts. In the real world, the lab would start out with a few hosts, probably in the *movie.edu* zone. After a generous endowment, an NSF grant, or a corporate gift, they might expand the lab a little and buy a few more computers. Sooner or later, the lab would have enough hosts to warrant the creation of a new subdomain. By

---

* BIND 9 name servers also don't promote the NS records into the parent zone, so they wouldn't be included in the zone transfer.

that point, however, many of the original hosts would be well known by their names in *movie.edu.*

We briefly touched on using CNAME records in the parent zone (in our *plan9. movie.edu* example) to help people adjust to a host's change of domain. But what happens when you move a whole network or subnet into a new subdomain?

The strategy we recommend uses CNAME records in much the same way, but on a larger scale. Using a tool such as *h2n*, you can create CNAMEs for hosts en masse. This allows users to continue using the old domain names for any of the hosts that have moved. When they telnet or FTP (or whatever) to those hosts, however, the command will report that they're connected to a host in *fx.movie.edu*:

```
% telnet plan9
Trying...
Connected to plan9.fx.movie.edu.
Escape character is '^]'.

HP-UX plan9.fx.movie.edu A.09.05 C 9000/735 (ttyu1)

login:
```

Some users, of course, don't notice subtle changes like this, so you should also do some public relations work and notify folks of the change.

On *fx.movie.edu* hosts running old versions of *sendmail,* we may also need to configure *sendmail* to accept mail addressed to the new domain names. Modern versions of *sendmail* canonicalize the host names in addresses in message headers using a name server before sending the messages. This will turn a *movie.edu* alias into a canonical name in *fx.movie.edu.* If, however, the *sendmail* on the receiving end is older and hardcodes the local host's domain name, we have to change the name to the new domain name by hand. This usually requires a simple change to class *w* or fileclass *w* in *sendmail.cf;* see the section "The MX Algorithm" in Chapter 5, *DNS and Electronic Mail.*

How do you create all these aliases? You simply tell *h2n* to create the aliases for hosts on the *fx.movie.edu* networks (192.253.254/24 and 192.254.20/24) and indicate (in the */etc/hosts* file) the new domain names for the hosts. For example, using the *fx.movie.edu* host table, we could easily generate the aliases in *movie.edu* for all the hosts in *fx.movie.edu.*

Partial contents of file */etc/hosts*:

```
192.253.254.1 movie-gw.movie.edu movie-gw
# fx primary
192.253.254.2 bladerunner.fx.movie.edu bladerunner br
# fx secondary
192.253.254.3 outland.fx.movie.edu outland
192.253.254.4 starwars.fx.movie.edu starwars
```

```
192.253.254.5 empire.fx.movie.edu empire
192.253.254.6 jedi.fx.movie.edu jedi
192.254.20.3  alien.fx.movie.edu alien
```

h2n's *–c* option takes a zone's domain name as an argument. When *h2n* finds any hosts in that zone on networks it's building data for, it'll create aliases for them in the current zone (specified with *–d*). So by running:

```
% h2n -d movie.edu -n 192.253.254 -n 192.254.20 \
-c fx.movie.edu -f options
```

(where *options* contains other command-line options for building data from other *movie.edu* networks), we could create aliases in *movie.edu* for all *fx.movie.edu* hosts.

Removing Parent Aliases

Although parent-level aliases are useful for minimizing the impact of moving your hosts, they're also a crutch of sorts. Like a crutch, they'll restrict your freedom. They'll clutter up your parent namespace when one of your motivations for implementing a subdomain may have been making the parent zone smaller. And they'll prevent you from using the names of hosts in the subdomain as names for hosts in the parent zone.

After a grace period—which should be well advertised to users—you should remove all the aliases, with the possible exception of aliases for extremely well-known Internet hosts. During the grace period, users can adjust to the new domain names and modify scripts, *.rhosts* files, and the like. But don't get suckered into leaving all those aliases in the parent zone; they defeat part of the purpose of DNS, as they prevent you and your subdomain administrator from naming hosts autonomously.

You might want to leave CNAME records for well-known Internet hosts or central network resources intact because of the potential impact of a loss of connectivity. On the other hand, rather than moving the well-known host or central resource into a subdomain at all, it might be better to leave it in the parent zone.

h2n gives you an easy way to delete the aliases you created so simply with the *–c* option, even if the records for the subdomain's hosts are mixed in the host table or on the same network as hosts in other zones. The *–e* option takes a zone's domain name as an argument and tells *h2n* to exclude (hence *e*) all records containing that domain name on networks it would otherwise create data for. This command line, for example, would delete all the CNAME records for *fx.movie.edu* hosts created earlier while still creating an A record for *movie-gw.movie.edu* (which is on the 192.253.254/24 network):

```
% h2n -d movie.edu -n 192.253.254 -n 192.254.20 \
-e fx.movie.edu -f options
```

The Life of a Parent

That's a lot of parental advice to digest in one sitting, so let's recap the highlights of what we've talked about. The life cycle of a typical parent goes something like this:

1. You have a single zone, with all of your hosts in that zone.

2. You break your zone into a number of subdomains, some of them in the same zone as the parent, if necessary. You provide CNAME records in the parent zone for well-known hosts that have moved into subdomains.

3. After a grace period, you delete any remaining CNAME records.

4. You handle subdomain delegation updates, either manually or by using stub zones, and periodically check delegation.

Okay, now that you know all there is to parenting, let's go on to talk about more advanced name server features. You may need some of these tools to keep those kids in line.

10

Advanced Features

"What's the use of their having names," the Gnat said, "if they won't answer to them?"

The latest BIND name servers, Versions 8.2.3 and 9.1.0, have *lots* of new features. Some of the most prominent introductions are support for dynamic updates, asynchronous zone change notification (called "NOTIFY" for short), and incremental zone transfer. Of the rest, the most important are related to security: they let you tell your name server whom to answer queries from, whom to offer zone transfers to, and whom to permit dynamic updates from. Many of the security features aren't necessary inside a corporate network, but the other mechanisms will help out the administrators of any name servers.

In this chapter, we'll cover these features and suggest how they might come in handy in your DNS infrastructure. (We do save some of the hardcore firewall material 'til the next chapter, though.)

Address Match Lists and ACLs

Before we introduce the new features, however, we'd better cover address match lists. BIND 8 and 9 use address match lists for nearly every security feature and for some features that aren't security-related at all.

An address match list is a list (what else?) of terms that specifies one or more IP addresses. The elements in the list can be individual IP addresses, IP prefixes, or a named address match list (more on those shortly).* An IP prefix has the format:

```
network in dotted-octet format/bits in netmask
```

For example, the network 15.0.0.0 with the network mask 255.0.0.0 (eight contiguous ones) would be written 15/8. Traditionally, this would have been thought of as the "class A" network 15. The network consisting of IP addresses 192.168.1.192 through 192.168.1.255, on the other hand, would be written 192.168.1.192/26 (network 192.168.1.192 with the netmask 255.255.255.192, which has 26 contiguous ones). Here's an address match list comprising those two networks:

```
15/8; 192.168.1.192/26;
```

A named address match list is just that: an address match list with a name. To be used within another address match list, a named address match list must have been previously defined in *named.conf* with an *acl* statement. The *acl* statement has a simple syntax:

```
acl name { address_match_list; };
```

This just makes the name equivalent to that address match list from now on. Although the name of the statement, *acl*, suggests "access control list," you can use the named address match list anywhere an address match list is accepted, including some places that don't have anything to do with access control.

Any time you're going to use one or more of the same terms in a few access control lists, it's a good idea to use an *acl* statement to associate them with a name. You can then refer to the name in the address match list. For example, let's call 15/8 what it is: "HP-NET." And we'll call 192.168.1.192/26 "internal":

```
acl "HP-NET" { 15/8; };

acl "internal" { 192.168.1.192/26; };
```

Now we can refer to these address match lists by name in other address match lists. This not only cuts down on typing, but it makes the resulting *named.conf* file more readable.

We prudently enclosed the names of our ACLs in quotes to avoid collisions with words BIND reserves for its own use. If you're sure your ACL names don't conflict with reserved words, you don't need the quotes.

---

* And if you're running BIND 9, address match lists can include IPv6 addresses and IPv6 prefixes. These are described later in the chapter.

There are four predefined named address match lists:

none
No IP addresses

any
All IP addresses

localhost
Any of the IP addresses of the local host (i.e., the one running the name server)

localnets
Any of the networks the local host has a network interface on (found by using each network interface's IP address and using the netmask to mask off the host bits in the address)

DNS Dynamic Update

The world of the Internet—and of TCP/IP networking in general—has become a much more dynamic place. Most large corporations use DHCP to assign IP addresses dynamically. Nearly all ISPs assign addresses to dialup and cable modem customers using DHCP. To keep up, DNS needed to support the dynamic addition and deletion of records. RFC 2136 introduced this mechanism, called DNS Dynamic Update.

BIND 8 and 9 support the dynamic update facility described in RFC 2136. This permits authorized updaters to add and delete resource records from a zone for which a name server is authoritative. An updater can find the authoritative name servers for a zone by retrieving the zone's NS records. If the name server receiving an authorized update message is not the primary master for the zone, it forwards the update "upstream" to its master server, a process referred to as "update forwarding." If this next server, in turn, is a slave for the zone, it also forwards the update upstream. Only the primary master name server for a zone, after all, has a "writable" copy of the zone data; all of the slaves get their copies of the zone data from the primary master, either directly or indirectly (through other slaves). Once the primary master has processed the dynamic update and modified the zone, the slaves can get a new copy of it via zone transfers.

Dynamic update permits more than the simple addition and deletion of records. Updaters can add or delete individual resource records, delete RRsets (a set of resource records with the same domain name, class, and type, such as all the addresses of *www.movie.edu*), or even delete all records associated with a given domain name. An update can also stipulate that certain records exist or not exist in the zone as a prerequisite to the update's taking effect. For example, an update can add the address record:

```
armageddon.fx.movie.edu.  300  IN  A  192.253.253.15
```

only if the domain name *armageddon.fx.movie.edu* isn't currently being used or only if *armageddon.fx.movie.edu* currently has no address records.

> A note on update forwarding: BIND name servers didn't implement update forwarding before 9.1.0, so it's particularly important when using BIND name servers older than 9.1.0 that you make sure the update is sent directly to the primary master name server for the zone you're trying to update. You can do this by ensuring that the primary master name server for the zone is listed in the MNAME field of the zone's SOA record. Most dynamic update routines use the MNAME field as a hint to tell them which of the authoritative name servers to send the update to.

For the most part, dynamic update functionality is used by programs like DHCP servers that assign IP addresses automatically to computers and then need to register the resulting name-to-address and address-to-name mappings. Some of these programs use the new *ns_update( )* resolver routine to create update messages and send them to an authoritative server for the zone that contains the domain name.

It's also possible to create updates manually with the command-line program *nsupdate*, which is part of the standard BIND distribution. *nsupdate* reads one-line commands and translates them into an update message. Commands can be specified on standard input (the default) or in a file, whose name must be given as an argument to *nsupdate*. Commands not separated by a blank line are incorporated into the same update message, as long as there's room.

nsupdate understands the following commands:

prereq yxrrset domain name type [rdata]
> Makes the existence of an RRset of type *type* owned by *domain name* a prerequisite for performing the update specified in successive *update* commands. If *rdata* is specified, it must also exist.

prereq nxrrset
> Makes the nonexistence of an RRset of type *type* owned by *domain name* a prerequisite for performing the update specified.

prereq yxdomain domain name
> Makes the existence of the specified domain name a prerequisite for performing the update.

prereq nxdomain

Makes the nonexistence of the specified domain name a prerequisite for performing the update.

update delete domain name [type] [rdata]

Deletes the domain name specified or, if *type* is also specified, deletes the RRset specified or, if *rdata* is also specified, deletes the record matching *domain name*, *type*, and *rdata*.

update add domain name ttl [class] type rdata

Adds the record specified to the zone. Note that the TTL, in addition to the type and resource record–specific data, must be included, but the class is optional and defaults to IN.

So, for example, the command:

```
% nsupdate
> prereq nxdomain mib.fx.movie.edu.
> update add mib.fx.movie.edu. 300 A 192.253.253.16
>
```

tells the server to add an address for *mib.fx.movie.edu* only if the domain name does not already exist. Note that the last blank line is *nsupdate*'s cue to send the update. Subtle, eh?

The command:

```
% nsupdate
> prereq yxrrset mib.fx.movie.edu. MX
> update delete mib.fx.movie.edu. MX
> update add mib.fx.movie.edu. 600 MX 10 mib.fx.movie.edu.
> update add mib.fx.movie.edu. 600 MX 50 postmanrings2x.movie.edu.
>
```

checks to see whether *mib.fx.movie.edu* already has MX records and, if it does, deletes them and adds two in their place.

There are some limitations to what you can do with dynamic update: you can't delete a zone entirely (though you can delete everything in it except the SOA record and one NS record), and you can't add new zones.

Dynamic Update and Serial Numbers

When a name server processes a dynamic update, it's changing a zone and must increment that zone's serial number to signal the change to the zone's slaves. This is done automatically. However, the name server doesn't necessarily increment the serial number for each dynamic update.

BIND 8 name servers defer updating a zone's serial number for as long as five minutes or 100 updates, whichever comes first. The deferral is intended to deal with a mismatch between a name server's ability to process dynamic updates and its ability to transfer zones: the latter may take significantly longer for large zones. When the name server does finally increment the zone's serial number, it sends a NOTIFY announcement (described later in this chapter) to tell the zone's slaves that the serial number has changed.

BIND 9 name servers update the serial number once for each dynamic update that is processed.

Dynamic Update and Zone Data Files

Since a dynamic update makes a permanent change to a zone, a record of it needs to be kept on disk. But rewriting a zone data file each time a record is added to or deleted from the zone could be prohibitively onerous for a name server. Writing a zone data file takes time, and the name server could conceivably receive tens or hundreds of dynamic updates each second.

Instead, when they receive dynamic updates, both BIND 8 and 9 name servers simply append a short record of the update to a log file.* The change takes effect immediately in the copy of the zone the name servers maintain in memory, of course. But the name servers can wait and write the entire zone to disk only at a designated interval (hourly, usually). BIND 8 name servers then delete the log file, as it's no longer needed. (At that point, the copy of the zone in memory is the same as that on disk.) BIND 9 name servers, however, leave the log file because they also use it for incremental zone transfers, which we'll cover later in this chapter. (BIND 8 name servers keep incremental zone transfer information in another file.)

On BIND 8 name servers, the name of the log file is constructed by appending *.log* to the name of the zone data file. On BIND 9 name servers, the name of the log file—also called a *journal file*—is the name of the zone data file concatenated with *.jnl*. So when you start using dynamic update, don't be surprised to see these files appear alongside your zone data files—it's totally normal.

On a BIND 8 name server, the log files should disappear hourly (though they may reappear very quickly if your name server receives lots of updates) as well as when the name server exits gracefully. On a BIND 9 name server, the log files won't disappear at all. Both name servers incorporate the record of the changes in the log file into the zone if the log file exists when the name server starts.

In case you're interested, BIND 8's log files are human-readable and contain entries like this:

```
;BIND LOG V8
[DYNAMIC_UPDATE] id 8761 from [192.249.249.3].1148 at 971389102 (named pid 17602):
```

---

* This idea will seem familiar to anyone who's ever used a journaling filesystem.

```
zone:   origin movie.edu class IN serial 2000010957
update: {add} almostfamous.movie.edu. 600 IN A 192.249.249.215
```

BIND 9's log files, unfortunately, aren't human-readable. Well, not to these humans, anyway.

Update Access Control Lists

Given the fearsome control that dynamic updates obviously give an updater over a zone, you clearly need to restrict them, if you use them at all. By default, neither BIND 8 nor BIND 9 name servers allow dynamic updates to authoritative zones. In order to use dynamic updates, you add an *allow-update* or *update-policy* substatement to the *zone* statement of the zone that you'd like to allow updates to.

allow-update takes an address match list as an argument. The address or addresses matched by the list are the only addresses allowed to update the zone. It's prudent to make this access control list as restrictive as possible:

```
zone "fx.movie.edu" {
    type master;
    file "db.fx.movie.edu";
    allow-update { 192.253.253.100; }; // just our DHCP server
};
```

TSIG-Signed Updates

Given that BIND 9.1.0 and later slave name servers can forward updates, what's the use of an IP address–based access control list? If the primary master name server allows updates from its slaves' addresses, then any forwarded update will be allowed, regardless of the original sender. That's not good.[*]

Well, first, you can control *which* updates are forwarded. The *allow-update-forwarding* substatement takes an address match list as an argument. Only updates from IP addresses that match the address match list will be forwarded. So the following *zone* statement forwards only those updates from the Special Effects Department's subnet:

```
zone "fx.movie.edu" {
    type slave;
    file "bak.fx.movie.edu";
    allow-update-forwarding { 192.253.254/24; };
};
```

Still, when you use update forwarding, you should also use TSIG-signed dynamic updates. We won't cover TSIG in depth until Chapter 11, *Security*, but all you

---

[*] BIND 9.1.0 goes so far as to warn you that IP address–based access control lists are insecure if you try to use them.

need to know for now is that TSIG-signed dynamic updates bear the cryptographic signature of the signer. If they're forwarded, the signature is forwarded
with them. The signature, when verified, tells you the name of the key used to
sign the update. The name of the key looks like a domain name, and it's often just
the domain name of the host the key is installed on.

With BIND 8.2 and later name servers, an address match list can include the name
of one or more TSIG keys:

```
zone "fx.movie.edu"
    type master;
    file "db.fx.movie.edu";
    allow-update { key dhcp-server.fx.movie.edu.; }; // allow only updates
                                                     // signed by the DHCP
                                                     // server's TSIG key
};
```

This allows an updater who signs an update with the TSIG key *dhcp-server.fx.
movie.edu* to make any change to the *fx.movie.edu* zone. Unfortunately, there's no
way to further restrict the updater with that TSIG key to a list of source IP
addresses.

BIND 9 supports a finer-grained access control mechanism than *allow-update*, also
based on TSIG signatures. This mechanism uses the new *update-policy zone* substatement. *update-policy* lets you specify which keys are allowed to update which
records in the zone. It's meaningful only for primary master zones, since the slaves
are expected to forward the updates.

The update is specified by the name of the key used to sign it and by the domain
name and type of records it attempts to update. *update-policy*'s syntax looks like
the following:

```
(grant | deny) identity nametype name [types]
```

grant and *deny* have the obvious meanings: allow or disallow the specified
dynamic update. *identity* refers to the *name* of the key used to sign the update.
nametype is one of:

name
> Matches when the domain name being updated is the same as the name in the
> *name* field.

subdomain
> Matches when the domain name being updated is a subdomain of (i.e., ends
> in) the name in the *name* field. (The domain name must still be in the zone,
> of course.)

wildcard
> Matches when the domain name being updated matches the wildcard expres-
> sion in the *name* field.

self

> Matches when the domain name being updated is the same as the name in the *identity* (not *name*) field, that is, when the domain name being updated is the same as the name of the key used to sign the update. If *nametype* is *self*, then the *name* field is ignored. And even though it looks redundant (as we'll see in the example in a moment), you still have to include the *name* field when using a *nametype* of *self*.

name, naturally, is a domain name appropriate to the *nametype* specified. For example, if you specify *wildcard* as the *nametype*, the *name* field should contain a wildcard label.

The *types* field is optional and can contain any valid record type (or multiple types, separated by spaces) except NXT. (ANY is a convenient shorthand for "all types but NXT.") If you leave *types* out, it matches all record types except SOA, NS, SIG, and NXT.

 A note on the precedence of *update-policy* rules: the first match (not the closest match) in an *update-policy* substatement is the one that applies to a dynamic update.

So, if *mummy.fx.movie.edu* uses a key called *mummy.fx.movie.edu* to sign its dynamic updates, we could restrict *mummy.fx.movie.edu* to updating its own records with the following:

```
zone "fx.movie.edu" {
    type master;
    file "db.fx.movie.edu";
    update-policy { grant mummy.fx.movie.edu. self mummy.fx.movie.edu.; };
};
```

or just its own address records with this:

```
zone "fx.movie.edu" {
    type master;
    file "db.fx.movie.edu";
    update-policy { grant mummy.fx.movie.edu. self mummy.fx.movie.edu. A; };
};
```

More generally, we could restrict all of our clients to updating only their own address records by using:

```
zone "fx.movie.edu" {
    type master;
    file "db.fx.movie.edu";
    update-policy { grant *.fx.movie.edu. self fx.movie.edu. A; };
};
```

Here's a more complicated example: to allow all clients the ability to change any records, except SRV records, that are owned by the same domain name as their key name, but to allow *matrix.fx.movie.edu* to update SRV records associated with Windows 2000 (in the *_udp.fx.movie.edu*, *_tcp.fx.movie.edu*, *_sites.fx.movie.edu*, and *_msdcs.fx.movie.edu* subdomains), you could use:

```
zone "fx.movie.edu" {
    type master;
    file "db.fx.movie.edu";
    update-policy {
        deny *.fx.movie.edu. self *.fx.movie.edu. SRV;
        grant *.fx.movie.edu. self *.fx.movie.edu. ANY;
        grant matrix.fx.movie.edu. subdomain _udp.fx.movie.edu. SRV;
        grant matrix.fx.movie.edu. subdomain _tcp.fx.movie.edu. SRV;
        grant matrix.fx.movie.edu. subdomain _sites.fx.movie.edu. SRV;
        grant matrix.fx.movie.edu. subdomain _msdcs.fx.movie.edu. SRV;
    };
};
```

Since the rules in the *update-policy* substatement are evaluated in the order in which they appear, clients can't update their SRV records, though they can update any other record types they own.

In case you're wondering, the difference between:

```
grant identity subdomain fx.movie.edu
```

and:

```
grant identity wildcard fx.movie.edu:
```

is that the former allows the key specified by *identity* to modify records attached to *fx.movie.edu* (say, the zone's NS records) while the latter doesn't.

If you'd like to take advantage of TSIG-signed dynamic updates but don't have any software that can send them, you can use newer versions of *nsupdate*; see the next chapter for that.

DNS NOTIFY (Zone Change Notification)

Traditionally, BIND slaves have used a polling scheme to determine when they need a zone transfer. The polling interval is called the *refresh interval*. Other parameters in the zone's SOA record govern other aspects of the polling mechanism.

But with this polling scheme, it can take up to the refresh interval before a slave detects and transfers new zone data from its master name server. That kind of latency could wreak havoc in a dynamically updated environment. Wouldn't it be nice if the primary master name server could *tell* its slave servers when the information in the zone changed? After all, the primary master name server *knows* the data has changed; someone reloaded the data, and the server checked the *mtime* (the Unix file modification time) of all its zone data files to determine which had been changed,* or it received and processed a dynamic update. The primary master could send notification right after processing the reload or update instead of waiting for the refresh interval to pass.

RFC 1996 proposed a mechanism that would allow primary master name servers to notify their slaves of changes to a zone's data. BIND 8 and 9 implement this scheme, which is called DNS NOTIFY.

DNS NOTIFY works like this: when a primary master name server notices that the serial number of a zone has changed, it sends a special announcement to all of the slave name servers for that zone. The primary master name server determines which servers are the slaves for the zone by looking at the list of NS records in the zone and taking out the record that points to the name server listed in the MNAME field of the zone's SOA record as well as the domain name of the local host.

When does the name server notice a change? Restarting a primary master name server causes it to notify all of its slaves of the current serial number of all of its zones because the primary master has no way of knowing whether its zone data files were edited before it started. Reloading one or more zones with new serial numbers causes a name server to notify the slaves of those zones. And a dynamic update that causes a zone's serial number to increment also causes notification.

The special NOTIFY announcement is identified by its opcode in the DNS header. The opcode for most queries is QUERY. NOTIFY messages, including announcements and responses, have a special opcode, NOTIFY (duh). Other than that, NOTIFY messages look very much like queries for the SOA record for a zone: they specify the domain name of the zone whose serial number has changed, its class, and a type of SOA. The authoritative answer bit is also set.

When a slave receives a NOTIFY announcement for a zone from one of its configured master name servers, it responds with a NOTIFY response. The response tells the master that the slave received the NOTIFY announcement so that the master can stop sending it NOTIFY announcements for the zone. Then the slave proceeds just as if the refresh timer for that zone had expired: it queries the master name server for the SOA record for the zone that the master claims has changed. If the serial number is higher, the slave transfers the zone.

Why doesn't the slave simply take the master's word that the zone has changed? It's possible that a miscreant could forge NOTIFY announcements to slaves, causing lots of unnecessary zone transfers and amounting to a denial-of-service attack against a master name server.

---

* Except in the case of a single-zone reload, when the name server checks the *mtime* of the data file only of the zone being reloaded.

If the slave actually transfers the zone, RFC 1996 says that it should issue its own NOTIFY announcements to the other authoritative name servers for the zone. The idea is that the primary master may not be able to notify all of the slave name servers for the zone itself, since it's possible some slaves can't communicate directly with the primary master (they use another slave as their master). However, while BIND 8.2.3 and BIND 9 implement this, earlier versions of BIND 8 don't. Older BIND 8 slaves don't send NOTIFY messages unless explicitly configured to do so.

Here's how that works in practice. On our network, *terminator.movie.edu* is the primary master name server for *movie.edu*, and *wormhole.movie.edu* and *zardoz.movie.edu* are slaves, as shown in Figure 10-1.

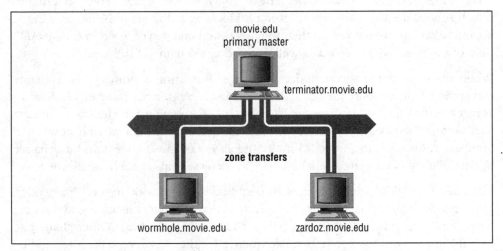

Figure 10-1. movie.edu zone transfers

When we edit and reload or dynamically update *movie.edu* on *terminator.movie.edu*, *terminator.movie.edu* sends NOTIFY announcements to *wormhole.movie.edu* and *zardoz.movie.edu*. Both slaves respond to *terminator.movie.edu*, telling it that they've received the notification. They then check to see whether *movie.edu*'s serial number has incremented and, when they find it has, perform a zone transfer. If *wormhole.movie.edu* and *zardoz.movie.edu* are running BIND 8.2.3 or BIND 9, after they transfer the new version of the zone, they also send NOTIFY announcements to tell each other about the change. But since *wormhole.movie.edu* isn't *zardoz.movie.edu*'s master name server for *movie.edu*, and the converse isn't true either, both slaves just ignore each other's NOTIFY announcements.

BIND 8 name servers log information about NOTIFY messages to *syslog*. Here's what *terminator.movie.edu* logged after we reloaded *movie.edu*:

```
Oct 14 22:56:34 terminator named[18764]: Sent NOTIFY for "movie.edu IN SOA
2000010958" (movie.edu); 2 NS, 2 A
```

```
Oct 14 22:56:34 terminator named[18764]: Received NOTIFY answer (AA) from 192.249.
249.1 for "movie.edu IN SOA"
Oct 14 22:56:34 terminator named[18764]: Received NOTIFY answer (AA) from 192.249.
249.9 for "movie.edu IN SOA"
```

The first message shows us the NOTIFY announcement that *terminator.movie.edu* sent, informing the two slaves (2 NS) that the serial number of *movie.edu* is now 2000010958. The next two lines show the slave name servers confirming their receipt of the notification. (BIND 9 name servers don't usually log NOTIFY activity.)

Let's also look at a more complicated zone transfer scheme. Here, *a* is the primary master name server for the zone and *b*'s master server, but *b* is *c*'s master server. Moreover, *b* has two network interfaces. This setup is shown in Figure 10-2.

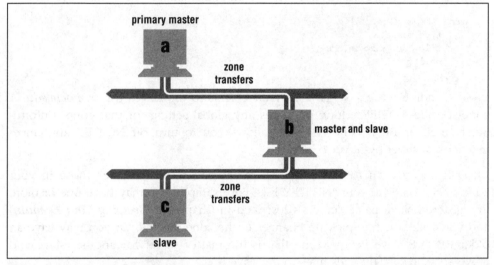

Figure 10-2. Complex zone transfer example

In this scenario, *a* notifies both *b* and *c* after the zone is updated. Then, *b* checks to see whether the zone's serial number has incremented and initiates a zone transfer. However, *c* ignores *a*'s NOTIFY announcement because *a* is not *c*'s configured master name server (*b* is). If *b* is running BIND 8.2.3 or BIND 9 or is explicitly configured to notify *c*, then after *b*'s zone transfer completes, it sends a NOTIFY announcement to *c*, which prompts *c* to check the serial number *b* holds for the zone. If *c* is also running BIND 8.2.3 or BIND 9, it sends *b* a NOTIFY announcement after its zone transfer finishes, which *b*, naturally, ignores.

Note also that if there's any possibility that *c* will receive a NOTIFY announcement from *b*'s other network interface, *c* must be configured with both network interfaces' addresses in the zone's *masters* substatement, or else *c* will ignore NOTIFY announcements from the unknown interface.

BIND 4 slave name servers and other name servers that don't support NOTIFY will respond with a Not Implemented (NOTIMP) error. Note that the Microsoft DNS Server *does* support DNS NOTIFY.

In both BIND 8 and 9, DNS NOTIFY is on by default, but you can turn NOTIFY off globally with the substatement:

```
options {
        notify no;
};
```

You can also turn NOTIFY on or off for a particular zone. For example, say we know that all the slave name servers for our *fx.movie.edu* zone are running BIND 4 and therefore don't understand NOTIFY announcements. The *zone* statement:

```
zone "fx.movie.edu" {
    type master;
    file "db.fx.movie.edu";
    notify no;
};
```

avoids sending useless NOTIFY announcements to the slaves for *fx.movie.edu*. A zone-specific NOTIFY setting overrides any global setting for that zone. Unfortunately, neither BIND 8 nor BIND 9 allows you to turn off NOTIFY announcements on a server-by-server basis.

BIND 8 and 9 even have a provision for adding servers besides those in your zone's NS records to your "NOTIFY list." For example, you may have one or more unregistered slave name servers (described in Chapter 8, *Growing Your Domain*) and you'd like them to pick up changes to the zone quickly. Or you may have an older BIND 8 slave for the zone that is the master server for another slave and needs to send NOTIFY messages to the slave.

To add a server to your NOTIFY list, use the *also-notify* substatement of the *zone* statement:

```
zone "fx.movie.edu" {
    type slave;
    file "bak.fx.movie.edu";
    notify yes;
    also-notify { 15.255.152.4; }; // This is a BIND 8 slave, which
                                   // must be explicitly configured
                                   // to notify its slave
};
```

In BIND 8.2.2 and later name servers, you can specify *also-notify* as an *options* substatement as well. This will apply to all zones for which NOTIFY is on (and that don't have their own *also-notify* substatements).

Beginning in BIND 9.1.0, you can specify *explicit* as an argument to the *notify* substatement; this suppresses NOTIFY messages to all name servers *except* those in the *also-notify* list. You can also use the *allow-notify* substatement to tell your name server to accept NOTIFY messages from name servers other than just the configured master name servers for a zone:

```
options {
     allow-notify { 192.249.249.17; }; // let 192.249.249.17 send NOTIFY msgs
};
```

As an *options* substatement, *allow-notify* affects all slave zones. When specified as a *zone* substatement, *allow-notify* overrides any global *allow-notify* for just that zone.

Incremental Zone Transfer (IXFR)

With dynamic update and NOTIFY, our zones are updated according to the changing state of the network, and those changes quickly propagate to all the authoritative name servers for those zones. The picture's complete, right?

Not quite. Imagine you run a large zone that's dynamically updated with frightening frequency. That's easy to envision: you might have a big zone to begin with, including thousands of clients, when all of a sudden management decides to implement Windows 2000 and DHCP. Now each of your clients updates its own address record in the zone, and the Domain Controllers update the records that tell clients which services they run. (There's much more to come on Windows 2000 in Chapter 16, *Miscellaneous.*)

Each time your primary master name server receives an update that increments the zone's serial number, it sends a NOTIFY announcement to its slaves. And each time they receive NOTIFY announcements, the slaves check the serial number of the zone on their master server and, possibly, transfer the zone. If that zone is large, the transfer will take some time—another update could arrive in the interim. Your slaves could be transferring zones in perpetuity! At the very least, your name servers will spend a lot of time transferring the whole zone when the change to the zone is probably very small (e.g., the addition of a client's address record).

Incremental zone transfer, or IXFR for short, solves this problem by allowing slave name servers to tell their master servers which version of a zone they currently hold and to request just the changes to the zone between that version and the current one. This can reduce the size and duration of a zone transfer dramatically.

An incremental zone transfer request has a query type of IXFR instead of AXFR (the type of query that initiates a full zone transfer), and it contains the slave's current SOA record from the zone in the authority section of the message. When the master name server receives an incremental zone transfer request, it looks for the record of the changes to the zone between the slave's version of the zone and the version the master holds. If that record is missing, the master sends a full zone transfer. Otherwise, it sends just the differences between the versions of the zone.

IXFR Limitations

Sound good? It is! But IXFR has a few limitations that you should know about. First, IXFR didn't work well until BIND 8.2.3. All BIND 9 name servers have IXFR implementations that work well and interoperate with BIND 8.2.3.

Next, IXFR works best when you're only modifying your zone data with dynamic updates. Dynamic updates leave a record of the changes made to the zone and the serial number changes they correspond to—exactly what a master name server needs to send to a slave that requests IXFR. But a BIND primary master name server that reloads an entire zone data file can't compute the differences between that zone and the previous zone. Nor can a BIND slave that gets a full zone transfer figure out what changed between that zone and the last.

This means that, to take maximum advantage of IXFR, you should modify your zone only by using dynamic update, and never edit the zone data file by hand.

IXFR Files

BIND 8 name servers maintain an IXFR log of changes to the zone separate from the dynamic update log file. Like the dynamic update log file, the IXFR log file is updated every time the name server receives an update. Unlike the dynamic update log file, the IXFR log file is never deleted, though the name server can be configured to trim it when it exceeds a particular size. The name of the BIND 8 IXFR log file, by default, is the name of the zone data file with *.ixfr* appended to it.

BIND 9 name servers use the dynamic update log file, or *journal file*, to assemble IXFR responses and to maintain the integrity of the zone. Since a primary master name server never knows when it may need the record of a particular change to the zone, it doesn't delete the journal file. A BIND 9 slave deletes the journal file if it receives an AXFR of the zone, since it now has a fresh full zone transfer and no longer needs to keep track of incremental changes to the last full zone transfer.

BIND 8 IXFR Configuration

Configuring IXFR in BIND 8 is fairly straightforward. First, you need an *options* substatement called *maintain-ixfr-base* on your master name server that tells it to maintain IXFR log files for all zones—even those the name server is a slave for, since those in turn may have slaves that want IXFRs:

```
options {
    directory "/var/named";
    maintain-ixfr-base yes;
};
```

Then you need to tell your slaves to request IXFRs from that master name server. You do that with a new *server* substatement, *support-ixfr*:

```
server 192.249.249.3 {
    support-ixfr yes;
};
```

That's about it, unless you want to rename the IXFR log file on the master. That's done with a new *zone* statement, *ixfr-base*:

```
zone "movie.edu" {
    type master;
    file "db.movie.edu";
    ixfr-base "ixfr.movie.edu";
};
```

Oh, and you can configure the name server to trim the IXFR log file after it exceeds a particular size:*

```
options {
    directory "/var/named";
    maintain-ixfr-base yes;
    max-ixfr-log-size 1M;      // trim IXFR log to 1 megabyte
};
```

Once the IXFR log file exceeds the specified limit by 100 KB, the name server trims it back to that size. The 100 KB of "slush" prevents the log file from reaching the limit and then being trimmed back after each successive update.

Using the *many-answers* zone transfer format can make zone transfers even more efficient. Take a look at the later section "More efficient zone transfers" for details.

BIND 9 IXFR Configuration

It's even easier to configure IXFR in a BIND 9 master name server because you don't have to do a thing: it's on by default. If you need to turn it off for a particular slave server (and you probably won't, since a slave must *request* an incremental zone transfer), use the *provide-ixfr server* substatement, which defaults to *yes*:

```
server 192.249.249.1 {
    provide-ixfr no;
};
```

You can also use *provide-ixfr* as an *options* substatement, in which case it applies to all slaves that don't have an explicit *provide-ixfr* substatement of their own in a *server* statement.

Since BIND 9 master name servers send *many-answers* zone transfers by default, you don't need any special *transfer-format* configuration.

---

* Before BIND 8.2.3, you need to specify the number of bytes, rather than just "1M," because of a bug.

More useful is the *request-ixfr* substatement, which can be used in either an *options* or a *server* statement. If you have a mix of IXFR-capable and IXFR-impaired masters, you can tailor your slave's zone transfer requests to match the capabilities of its masters:

```
options {
    directory "/var/named";
    request-ixfr no;
};

server 192.249.249.3 {
    request-ixfr yes;      // of our masters, only terminator supports IXFR
};
```

BIND 9 doesn't support the *max-ixfr-log-size* substatement.

Forwarding

Certain network connections discourage sending large volumes of traffic off-site, either because the network connection is billed by volume or because it's a slow link with high delay, like a remote office's satellite connection to the company's network. In these situations, you'll want to limit the off-site DNS traffic to the bare minimum. BIND provides a mechanism to do this: *forwarders*.

Forwarders are also useful if you need to shunt name resolution to a particular name server. For example, if only one of the hosts on your network has Internet connectivity and you run a name server on that host, you can configure your other name servers to use it as a forwarder so that they can look up Internet domain names. (More on this use of forwarders when we discuss firewalls in Chapter 11.)

If you designate one or more servers at your site as forwarders, your name servers will send all their off-site queries to the forwarders first. The idea is that the forwarders handle all the off-site queries generated at the site, building up a rich cache of information. For any given query in a remote zone, there is a high probability that the forwarder can answer the query from its cache, avoiding the need for the other servers to send queries off-site. You don't do anything to a name server to make it a forwarder; you modify all the *other* servers at your site to direct their queries through the forwarders.

A primary master or slave name server's mode of operation changes slightly when it is configured to use a forwarder. If a resolver requests records that are already in the name server's authoritative data or cached data, the name server answers with that information; this part of its operation hasn't changed. However, if the records aren't in its database, the name server sends the query to a forwarder and waits a short period for an answer before resuming normal operation and contacting the remote name servers itself. What the name server is doing differently here is sending a *recursive* query to the forwarder, expecting it to find the answer. At all other times, the name server sends out *nonrecursive* queries to other name servers and deals with responses that only refer it to other name servers.

For example, here is the BIND 8 and 9 *forwarders* substatement—and the equivalent BIND 4 boot file directive—for name servers in *movie.edu*. Both *wormhole. movie.edu* and *terminator.movie.edu* are the site's forwarders. We add this *forwarders* substatement to every name server's configuration file except the ones for the forwarders themselves:

```
options {
    forwarders { 192.249.249.1; 192.249.249.3; };
};
```

The equivalent BIND 4 directive is:

```
forwarders 192.249.249.1 192.249.249.3
```

When you use forwarders, try to keep your site configuration simple. You could end up with configurations that are really twisted.

Avoid chaining your forwarders. Don't configure name server A to forward to server B, and server B to forward to server C (or worse yet, back to server A). This can cause long resolution delays and creates a brittle configuration, in which the failure of any forwarder in the chain impairs or breaks name resolution.

A More Restricted Name Server

You may want to restrict your name servers even further—stopping them from even *trying* to contact an off-site server if their forwarder is down or doesn't respond. You can do this by configuring your name servers to use *forward-only* mode. A name server in forward-only mode is a variation on a name server that uses forwarders. It still answers queries from its authoritative data and cached data. However, it relies *completely* on its forwarders; it doesn't try to contact other name servers to find information if the forwarders don't give it an answer. Here is an example of what the configuration file of a name server in forward-only mode would contain:

```
options {
    forwarders { 192.249.249.1; 192.249.249.3; };
    forward only;
};
```

On a BIND 4 name server, that would look like:

```
forwarders 192.249.249.1 192.249.249.3
options forward-only
```

BIND name servers before 4.9 provide the same functionality using the *slave* directive instead of the *options forward-only* directive:

```
forwarders 192.249.249.1 192.249.249.3
slave
```

Don't confuse this old use of the term "slave" with the modern use. In BIND 4 name servers, "slave" was synonymous with "forward-only." "Slave" now means a name server that gets zone data from a master server via a zone transfer.

If you use forward-only mode, you must have forwarders configured. Otherwise, it doesn't make sense to have forward-only mode set. If you configure a name server in forward-only mode and run a version of BIND older than 8.2.3, you might want to consider including the forwarders' IP addresses more than once. On a BIND 8 server, that would look like:

```
options {
    forwarders { 192.249.249.1; 192.249.249.3;
            192.249.249.1; 192.249.249.3; };
    forward only;
};
```

On a BIND 4 server, it would be:

```
forwarders 192.249.249.1 192.249.249.3 192.249.249.1 192.249.249.3
options forward-only
```

This name server contacts each forwarder only once, and it waits a short time for the forwarder to respond. Listing the forwarders multiple times directs the name server to *retransmit* queries to the forwarders and increases the overall length of time that the forward-only name server will wait for an answer from forwarders.

However, you have to ask yourself if it *ever* makes sense to use a name server in forward-only mode. Such a name server is completely dependent on its forwarders. You can achieve much the same results by not running a name server at all; instead, create a *resolv.conf* file that contains *nameserver* directives pointing to the forwarders you were using. This way, you're still relying on the forwarders, but now your applications are querying the forwarders directly instead of having a name server query them on the applications' behalf. You lose the local caching and address sorting that the name server would have done, but you reduce the overall complexity of your site's configuration by running fewer name servers.

Forward Zones

Traditionally, using forwarders has been an all-or-nothing proposition: either you use forwarders to resolve every query your name server can't answer itself or you don't use forwarders at all. However, there are some situations in which it would be nice to have more control over forwarding. For example, maybe you'd like to resolve certain domain names using a particular forwarder, but other domain names iteratively.

BIND 8.2 introduced a new feature, *forward zones*, that allows you to configure your name server to use forwarders only when looking up certain domain names. (BIND 9's support for forward zones was added in 9.1.0.) For example, you can configure your name server to shunt all queries for domain names ending in *pixar.com* to a pair of Pixar's name servers:

```
zone "pixar.com" {
    type forward;
    forwarders { 138.72.10.20; 138.72.30.28; };
};
```

Why would you ever configure this explicitly rather than letting your name server follow delegation from the *com* name servers to the *pixar.com* name servers? Well, imagine that you have a private connection to Pixar and you're told to use a special set of name servers, reachable only from your network, to resolve all *pixar. com* domain names.

Even though forwarding rules are specified in the *zone* statement, they apply to all domain names that end in the domain name specified. That is, regardless of whether the domain name you're looking up, *foo.bar.pixar.com*, is in the *pixar.com* zone, the rule applies to it because it ends in *pixar.com* (or is in the *pixar.com* domain, if you prefer).

There's another variety of forward zone, in a way the opposite of the kind we just showed you. These allow you to specify which queries *don't* get forwarded. Therefore, it applies only to name servers with forwarders specified in the *options* statement, which would normally apply to all queries.

These forward zones are configured using a *zone* statement, but not of type *forward*. Instead, these are normal zones—master, slave, or stub—with a *forwarders* substatement. To "undo" the forwarding configured in the *options* statement, we specify an empty list of forwarders:

```
options {
    directory "/var/named";
    forwarders { 192.249.249.3; 192.249.249.1; };
};

zone "movie.edu" {
    type slave;
    masters { 192.249.249.3; };
    file "bak.movie.edu";
    forwarders {};
};
```

Wait a minute—why would you need to disable forwarding in a zone you're authoritative for? Wouldn't you just answer the query and not use a forwarder?

Remember, the forwarding rules apply to queries for all domain names that end in the domain name of the zone. So this forwarding rule really applies only to queries for domain names in delegated subdomains of *movie.edu*, like *fx.movie.edu*. Without the forwarding rule, this name server would have forwarded a query for *matrix.fx.movie.edu* to the name servers at 192.249.249.3 and 192.249.249.1. With the forwarding rule, it instead uses the subdomain's NS records from the *movie.edu* zone and queries the *fx.movie.edu* name servers directly.

Forward zones are enormously helpful in dealing with Internet firewalls, as we'll see in the next chapter.

Forwarder Selection

On BIND 8.2.3 name servers, you don't need to list forwarders more than once. These name servers don't necessarily query the forwarders in the order listed; they interpret the name servers in the list as "candidate" forwarders and choose which one to query first based on roundtrip time, the time it took to respond to previous queries.

This is a real benefit if a forwarder fails, especially the first one in the list. Older versions of BIND would keep blindly querying the failed forwarder and waiting before querying the next in the list. BIND 8.2.3 quickly realizes that the forwarder isn't responding and tries another first.

BIND 9 doesn't yet implement this more intelligent form of forwarder selection, unfortunately, though it will retransmit queries to forwarders when necessary.

Views

BIND 9 introduced *views*, another mechanism that's very useful in firewalled environments. Views allow you to present one name server configuration to one community of hosts and a different configuration to another community. This is particularly handy if you're running a name server on a host that receives queries from both your internal hosts and hosts on the Internet (we'll cover this in the next chapter).

If you don't configure any views, BIND 9 automatically creates a single, implicit view that it shows to all hosts that query it. To explicitly create a view, you use the *view* statement, which takes the name of the view as an argument:

```
view "internal" {
};
```

Although the name of the view can be just about anything, using a descriptive name is always a good idea. And while quoting the name of the view isn't necessary, it's helpful to do so to avoid conflict with words BIND reserves for its own use (like "internal," for example). The *view* statement must come after any *options* statement, though not necessarily right after it.

You select which hosts "see" a particular view using the *match-clients view* substatement, which takes an address match list as an argument. If you don't specify a community of hosts with *match-clients*, the view applies to all hosts.

Let's say we're setting up a special view of the *fx.movie.edu* zone on our name servers that we want only the Special Effects Department to see. We could create a view visible only to hosts on our subnet:

```
view "internal" {
    match-clients { 192.253.254/24; };
};
```

If you want to make that a little more readable, you can use an *acl* statement:

```
acl "fx-subnet" { 192.253.254/24; };

view "internal" {
    match-clients { "fx-subnet"; };
};
```

Just be sure you define the ACL *outside* of the view, since you can't use *acl* statements inside views yet.

What can you put inside a *view* statement? Nearly anything else. You can define zones with *zone* statements, describe remote name servers with *server* statements, and configure TSIG keys with *key* statements. You can use most *options* substatements within a view, but if you do, don't enclose them in an *options* statement; just use them "raw" in the *view* statement:

```
acl "fx-subnet" { 192.253.254/24; };

view "internal" {
    match-clients { "fx-subnet"; };
    recursion yes;  // turn recursion on for this view
                    // (it's off globally, in the options statement)
};
```

Any configuration option you specify within a view overrides the like-named global option (e.g., one in the *options* statement) for hosts that match *match-clients*.

For a complete list of what's supported inside the *view* statement on the version of BIND 9 you run (because it changes from release to release), see the file *doc/misc/options* in the BIND distribution.

Here's the Special Effects Lab's full *named.conf* file, to give you an idea of the power of views:

```
options {
        directory "/var/named";
};

acl "fx-subnet" { 192.253.254/24; };

view "internal" {  // internal view of our zones

    match-clients { "fx-subnet"; };

    zone "fx.movie.edu" {
        type master;
        file "db.fx.movie.edu";
    };

    zone "254.253.192.in-addr.arpa" {
        type master;
        file "db.192.253.254";
    };
};

view "external" {  // view of our zones for the rest of the world

    match-clients { any; };  // implicit
    recursion no;            // outside of our subnet, they shouldn't be
                             // requesting recursion
    zone "fx.movie.edu" {
        type master;
        file "db.fx.movie.edu.external";  // external zone data file
    };

    zone "254.254.192.in-addr.arpa" {
        type master;
        file "db.192.253.254.external";   // external zone data file
    };
};
```

Notice that each view has an *fx.movie.edu* and a *254.253.192.in-addr.arpa* zone, but the zone data files are different in the "internal" and "external" views. This allows us to show the outside world a different "face" than we see internally.

The order of the *view* statements is important because the first view that a host's IP address matches is the one that dictates what it sees. If the "external" view were listed first in the configuration file, it would occlude the "internal" view because the "external" view matches all addresses.

One last note on views (before we use them in the next chapter, anyway): if you configure even one *view* statement, all of your *zone* statements must appear within explicit views.

Round Robin Load Distribution

Name servers released since BIND 4.9 have formalized some load distribution functionality that has existed in patches to BIND for some time. Bryan Beecher wrote patches to BIND 4.8.3 to implement what he called "shuffle address records." These were address records of a special type that the name server rotated between responses. For example, if the domain name *foo.bar.baz* had three "shuffled" IP addresses, 192.168.1.1, 192.168.1.2, and 192.1.168.3, an appropriately patched name server would give them out first in the order:

```
192.168.1.1 192.168.1.2 192.168.1.3
```

then in the order:

```
192.168.1.2 192.168.1.3 192.168.1.1
```

and then in the order:

```
192.168.1.3 192.168.1.1 192.168.1.2
```

before starting all over with the first order and repeating the rotation ad infinitum.

The functionality is enormously useful if you have a number of equivalent network resources, such as mirrored FTP servers, web servers, or terminal servers, and you'd like to spread the load among them. You establish one domain name that refers to the group of resources and configure clients to access that domain name, and the name server distributes requests among the IP addresses you list.

BIND 4.9 and later versions do away with the shuffle address record as a separate record type, subject to special handling. Instead, a modern name server rotates addresses for any domain name that has more than one A record. (In fact, the name server will rotate any type of record as long as a given domain name has more than one of them.[*]) So the records:

```
foo.bar.baz.    60    IN    A    192.168.1.1
foo.bar.baz.    60    IN    A    192.168.1.2
foo.bar.baz.    60    IN    A    192.168.1.3
```

accomplish on a 4.9 or later name server just what the shuffle address records did on a patched 4.8.3 server. The BIND documentation calls this process *round robin*.

It's a good idea to reduce the records' time to live, too, as we did in this example. This ensures that if the addresses are cached on an intermediate name server that doesn't support round robin, they'll time out of the cache quickly. If the intermediate name server looks up the name again, your authoritative name server can round robin the addresses again.

---

[*] Actually, until BIND 9, PTR records weren't rotated. BIND 9 rotates all record types.

Note that this is really load distribution, not load balancing, since the name server gives out the addresses in a completely deterministic way without regard to the actual load or capacity of the servers servicing the requests. In our example, the server at address 192.168.1.3 could be a 486DX33 running Linux and the other two servers HP9000 Superdomes, and the Linux box would still get a third of the queries. Listing a higher-capacity server's address multiple times won't help because BIND eliminates duplicate records.

Multiple CNAMEs

Back in the heyday of BIND 4 name servers, some folks set up round robin using multiple CNAME records instead of multiple address records:

```
foo1.bar.baz.    60   IN   A       192.168.1.1
foo2.bar.baz.    60   IN   A       192.168.1.2
foo3.bar.baz.    60   IN   A       192.168.1.3
foo.bar.baz.     60   IN   CNAME   foo1.bar.baz.
foo.bar.baz.     60   IN   CNAME   foo2.bar.baz.
foo.bar.baz.     60   IN   CNAME   foo3.bar.baz.
```

This probably looks odd to those of you who are used to our harping on the evils of mixing anything with a CNAME record. But BIND 4 name servers didn't recognize this as the configuration error it is and simply returned the CNAME records for *foo.bar.baz* in round robin order.

BIND 8 name servers, on the other hand, are more vigilant and catch this error. You can, however, explicitly configure them to allow multiple CNAME records for a single domain name with:

```
options {
     multiple-cnames yes;
};
```

BIND 9 name servers don't notice the multiple CNAME problem until 9.1.0. BIND 9.1.0 detects the problem but doesn't support the *multiple-cnames* statement.

The rrset-order Substatement

There are certain times when you'd rather the name server didn't use round robin. For example, maybe you'd like to designate one web server as a backup to another. To do this, the name server should always return the backup's address after the primary web server's address. But you can't do that with round robin; it'll just rotate the order of the addresses in successive responses.

BIND 8.2 and later name servers—but not BIND 9 name servers, as of 9.1.0—allow you to turn off round robin for certain domain names and types of records. For example, if we wanted to ensure that the address records for *www.movie.edu* were always returned in the same order, we could use this *rrset-order* substatement:

```
options {
    rrset-order {
        class IN type A name "www.movie.edu" order fixed;
    };
};
```

We should probably lower the TTL on *www.movie.edu*'s address records, too, so a name server that cached the records wouldn't round robin them for long.

The *class*, *type*, and *name* settings determine which records the specified order applies to. The class defaults to IN, type to ANY, and name to *—in other words, any records. So the statement:

```
options {
    rrset-order {
        order random;
    };
};
```

applies a random order to all records returned by the name server. The name setting may contain a wildcard as its leftmost label, as in:

```
options {
    rrset-order {
        type A name "*.movie.edu" order cyclic;
    };
};
```

Only one *rrset-order* substatement is permitted, but it can contain multiple order specifications. The first order specification to match a set of records in a response applies.

rrset-order supports three (count 'em, three!) different orders:

fixed

Always return matching records in the same order

random

Return matching records in random order

cyclic

Return matching records in cyclic (round robin) order

The default behavior is:

```
options {
    rrset-order {
        class IN type ANY name "*" order cyclic;
    };
};
```

Configuring *rrset-order* is far from a complete solution, unfortunately, because resolver and name server caching can interfere with its operation. A better long-term solution is the SRV record, which we'll discuss in Chapter 16.

Name Server Address Sorting

Sometimes, neither round robin nor another configurable order is what you want. When you are contacting a host that has multiple network interfaces and hence multiple IP addresses, choosing a particular interface based on your host's address may give you better performance. No *rrset-order* substatement can do that for you.

If the multihomed host is local and shares a network or subnet with your host, one of the multihomed host's addresses is "closer." If the multihomed host is remote, you may see better performance using one interface instead of another, but often it doesn't matter much which address is used. In days long past, net 10 (the former ARPAnet "backbone") was always closer than any other remote address. The Internet has improved drastically since those days, so you won't often see a marked performance improvement when using one network over another for remote multihomed hosts, but we'll cover that case anyway.

Before we get into address sorting by a name server, you should first look at whether address sorting by the resolver better suits your needs. (See "The sortlist Directive" in Chapter 6, *Configuring Hosts.*) Since your resolver and name server may be on different networks, it often makes more sense for the resolver to sort addresses optimally for its host. Address sorting at the name server works fairly well, but it can be hard to optimize for every resolver it services. Resolver address sorting was added in BIND 4.9, though, so if your resolver (not your name server) is older than 4.9 or isn't BIND at all, you're out of luck. You'll have to make do with address sorting at the name server, which was introduced in 4.8.3.

In an uncommon turn of events, the name server's address sorting feature was *removed* in early versions of BIND 8, primarily because of the developers' insistence that it had no place in the name server. The feature was restored—and in fact enhanced—in BIND 8.2. BIND 9.1.0 is the first BIND 9 release to support address sorting.

BIND 4 Address Sorting

BIND 4's address sorting, while simpler to configure than BIND 8's, is more complex to describe because it does quite a bit automatically, without any configuration. Let's cover it first.

Local multihomed hosts

Let's deal with the local multihomed host first. Suppose you have a source host (i.e., a host that keeps your master source code) on two networks, cleverly called network A and network B, and this host uses NFS to export filesystems to hosts on both networks. Hosts on network A experience better performance if they use the source host's interface to network A. Likewise, hosts on network B benefit from using the source host's interface to network B for the address of the NFS mount.

In Chapter 4, *Setting Up BIND*, we mentioned that BIND returns all the addresses for a multihomed host. There was no guarantee of the order in which a DNS server would return the addresses, so we assigned aliases (*wh249.movie.edu* and *wh253.movie.edu* for *wormhole.movie.edu*) to the individual interfaces. If one interface was preferable, you (or more realistically, a DNS client) could use an appropriate alias to get the correct address. You can use aliases to choose the "closer" interface (e.g., for setting up NFS mounts), but because of address sorting, that's not always necessary.

BIND 4 servers, by default, sort addresses if one condition holds: if the host that sent the query to the name server shares a network with the name server host (e.g., both are on network A), then BIND sorts the addresses in the response. How does BIND know when it shares a network with the querier? It knows because when BIND starts up, it finds all the interface addresses of the host it's running on. BIND extracts the network numbers from these addresses to create the default sort list. When a query is received, BIND checks whether the sender's address is on a network in the default sort list. If it is, then the query is local and BIND sorts the addresses in the response.

In Figure 10-3, let's assume that there is a BIND 4 name server on *notorious*. The name server's default sort list would contain network A and network B. When *spellbound* sends a query to *notorious* looking up the addresses of *notorious*, it gets an answer back with *notorious*'s network A address first. That's because *notorious* and *spellbound* share network A. When *charade* looks up the addresses of *notorious*, it gets an answer back with *notorious*'s network B address first, because both hosts are on network B. In both these cases, the name server sorts the addresses in the response because the hosts share a network with the name server host. The sorted address list has the "closer" interface first.

Let's change the situation slightly. Suppose the name server is running on *gaslight*. When *spellbound* queries *gaslight* for *notorious*'s address, *spellbound* sees the same response as in the last case because *spellbound* and *gaslight* share network A, which means that the name server will sort the response. However, *charade* may see a differently ordered response, since it does not share a network with *gaslight*. The closer address for *notorious* may still be first in the response to *charade*, but

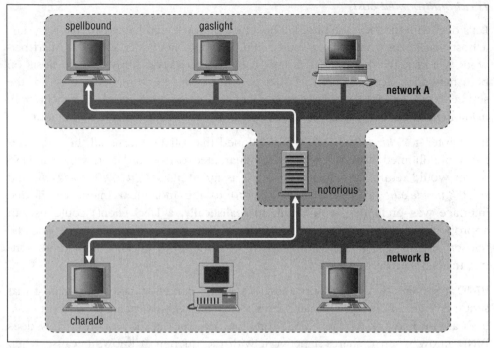

Figure 10-3. Communicating with a local multihomed host

only because of luck, not name server address sorting. In this case, you'd have to run an additional name server on network B for *charade* to benefit from BIND 4's default address sorting.

As you can see, you benefit by running a name server on each network; not only is your name server available if your router goes down, it also sorts addresses of multihomed hosts. Because the name server sorts addresses, you do not need to specify aliases for NFS mounts or network logins to get the best response.

Remote multihomed hosts

Suppose that your site often contacts a particular remote site or a "distant" local site, and that you get better performance by favoring addresses on one of the remote site's networks. For instance, the *movie.edu* zone comprises the networks 192.249.249/24 and 192.253.253/24. Let's add a connection to network 10/8 (the old ARPAnet). The remote host being contacted has two network connections, one to network 10/8 and one to network 26/8. This host does not route to 26/8, but for special reasons it has a connection to it. Since the router to 26/8 is always overloaded, you'll get better performance using the remote host's 10/8 address. Figure 10-4 shows this situation.

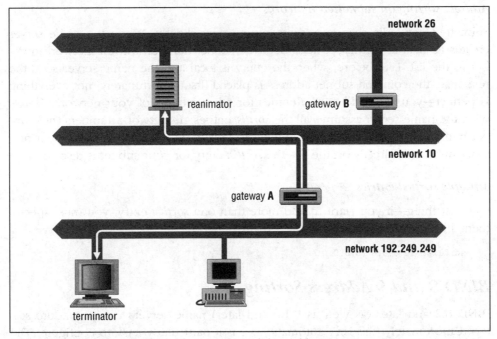

Figure 10-4. Communicating with a remote multihomed host

If a user on *terminator.movie.edu* contacts *reanimator.movie.edu*, it's preferable to use the 10/8 address because access through gateway B to the 26/8 address is slower than the direct route. Unfortunately, the name server running on *terminator.movie.edu* will not intentionally place a 10/8 address first in the list when it looks up the addresses for *reanimator.movie.edu*; the only network that *terminator.movie.edu* is attached to is 192.249.249/24, so it doesn't know that 10/8 is "closer" than 26/8. This is where the *sortlist* directive comes into play. To indicate a preference for addresses on network 10/8, add the following line to *named.boot*:

```
sortlist 10.0.0.0
```

The *sortlist* arguments are *appended* to the default sort list. With this *sortlist* directive, the sort list on *terminator.movie.edu* now contains networks 192.249.249/24 and 10/8. Now, when a user on *terminator.movie.edu* queries the name server on *terminator.movie.edu* and the name server sorts the response because the query is local, the name server will check for addresses on the 192.249.249/24 network and place them first in the response. If there are no addresses on 192.249.249/24, it will check for 10/8 addresses and place them first in the response. This solves the problem we described earlier; now when *reanimator.movie.edu* is looked up, its address on network 10/8 will be placed first in the response.

Address sorting on subnetted networks

Subnetted networks change address sorting only slightly. When the name server creates its default sort list, it adds both the subnet number and the network number to the list. Like before, when the query is local and the name server sorts the response, the common subnet address is placed first. Unfortunately, not everything is perfect—you can't add *sortlist* entries for other subnets of your network. Here's why: the name server assumes all the *sortlist* entries are network numbers (not subnet numbers), and your network number is already on the sort list. Since your network number is already on the list, the *sortlist* entry for your subnet is discarded.

Multiple sortlist entries

One last thing—if you want to add more than one *sortlist* entry, you must specify them all on the same line, like this:

```
sortlist 10.0.0.0 26.0.0.0
```

BIND 8 and 9 Address Sorting

BIND 8.2 and later (as well as 9.1.0 and later) name servers can sort addresses, too. Unfortunately, this isn't automatic, nor is it particularly easy to configure. The key is an *options* substatement called, naturally, *sortlist*.

The *sortlist* substatement takes an address match list as an argument. Unlike address match lists used as access control lists, though, *sortlist*'s has a very specialized interpretation. Each entry in the address match list is itself an address match list with either one or two elements.

If an entry has only one element, it's used to check the IP address of a querier. If the querier's address matches, then the name server sorts addresses in a response to that querier so that any addresses that match the element are first. Confusing? Here's an example:

```
options {
    sortlist {
        { 192.249.249/24; };
    };
};
```

The only entry in this sort list has just one element. This sort list sorts addresses on the network 192.249.249/24 to the front of responses to queriers that are also on that network.

If an entry has two elements, the first element is used to match the IP address of a querier. If the querier's address matches, the name server sorts addresses in a response to that querier so that any addresses that match the second element come first. The second element can actually be a whole address match list of several elements, in which case the first address added to the response is the one that matches first in the list. Here's a simple example:

```
options {
    sortlist {
        { 192.249.249/24; { 192.249.249/24; 192.253.253/24; }; };
    };
};
```

This sort list applies to queriers on 192.249.249/24 and sends them addresses on their own network first, followed by addresses on 192.253.253/24.

The elements in the sort list specification can just as easily be subnets or even individual hosts:

```
options {
    sortlist {
        { 15.1.200/21;         // if the querier is on 15.1.200/21
            { 15.1.200/21;      // then prefer addresses on that subnet
            15/8; };            // or at least on 15/8
        };
    };
};
```

Preferring Name Servers on Certain Networks

BIND 8's topology feature is somewhat similar to *sortlist*, but it applies only to the process of choosing name servers. (BIND 9 doesn't support topology as of 9.1.0.) Earlier in the book, we described how BIND chooses between a number of name servers that are authoritative for the same zone by selecting the name server with the lowest roundtrip time (RTT). But we lied—a little. BIND 8 actually places remote name servers in 64-millisecond bands when comparing RTT. The first band is actually only 32 milliseconds wide (there! we did it again), from zero to 32 milliseconds. The next extends from 33 to 96 milliseconds, and so on. The bands are designed so that name servers on different continents are always in different bands.

The idea is to favor name servers in lower bands but to treat servers in the same band as equivalent. If a name server compares two remote servers' RTTs and one is in a lower band, the name server chooses to query the name server in the lower band. But if the remote servers are in the same band, the name server checks to see whether one of the remote servers is topologically closer.

So topology lets you introduce an element of fudge into the process of choosing a name server to query. It lets you favor name servers on certain networks over others. Topology takes as an argument an address match list, where the entries are networks, listed in the order in which the local name server should prefer them (highest to lowest). Therefore:

```
topology {
    15/8;
    172.88/16;
};
```

tells the local name server to prefer name servers on the network 15/8 over other name servers, and name servers on the network 172.88/16 over name servers on networks other than 15/8. So if the name server has a choice between a name server on network 15/8, a name server on 172.88/16, and a name server on 192. 168.1/24, assuming all three have RTT values in the same band, it will choose to query the name server on 15/8.

You can also negate entries in the topology address match list to penalize name servers on certain networks. The earlier in the address match list the negated entry matches, the greater the penalty. You might use this to keep your name server from querying remote name servers on a network that's particularly flaky, for example.

A Nonrecursive Name Server

By default, BIND resolvers send recursive queries, and by default BIND name servers do the work required to answer them. (If you don't remember how recursion works, look in Chapter 2, *How Does DNS Work?*) In the process of finding the answers to recursive queries, the name server builds up a cache of nonauthoritative information from other zones.

In some situations, it's undesirable for name servers to do the extra work required to answer a recursive query or to build up a cache of data. The root name servers are an example of one of these situations. The root name servers are so busy that they can't expend the extra effort necessary to find the answers to recursive queries. Instead, they send a response based only on the authoritative data they have. The response may contain the answer, but it more likely contains a referral to other name servers. And since the root servers do not support recursive queries, they don't build up a cache of nonauthoritative data, which is good because their caches would be huge.[*]

---

[*] Note that a root name server doesn't normally receive recursive queries unless a name server's administrator configured it to use a root server as a forwarder, a host's administrator configured its resolver to use the root server as a name server, or a user pointed *nslookup* at the root server. All of these happen more often than you'd expect, though.

You can induce a BIND name server to run in nonrecursive mode with the following conf file statement:

```
options {
    recursion no;
};
```

On a BIND 4.9 server, that's the directive:

```
options no-recursion
```

Now the server will respond to recursive queries as if they were nonrecursive.

In conjunction with *recursion no*, there is one more configuration option necessary if you want to prevent your name server from building a cache:

```
options {
    fetch-glue no;
};
```

Or, on BIND 4.9:

```
options no-fetch-glue
```

This stops the server from fetching missing glue when constructing the additional data section of a response. BIND 9 name servers don't fetch glue, so the *fetch-glue* substatement is obsolete in BIND 9.

If you choose to make one of your servers nonrecursive, don't list that name server in any host's *resolv.conf* file. While you can make your name server nonrecursive, there is no corresponding option to make your resolver work with a nonrecursive name server.* If your name server needs to continue to serve one or more resolvers, you can use the *allow-recursion* substatement, available in BIND 8.2.1 and later (including BIND 9). *allow-recursion* takes an address match list as an argument; any queriers that match can send recursive queries, but everyone else is treated as if recursion were off:

```
options {
    allow-recursion { 192.253.254/24; };  // Only resolvers on the FX
                                           // subnet should be sending
                                           // recursive queries
};
```

allow-recursion's default is to provide recursion to any IP address.

Also, don't list a nonrecursive name server as a forwarder. When a name server is using another server as a forwarder, it forwards *recursive* queries to the forwarder. Use *allow-recursion* to permit just authorized name servers to use your forwarder instead.

---

* In general. Of course, programs designed to send nonrecursive queries, or programs that can be configured to send nonrecursive queries, like *nslookup*, will still work.

You *can* list a nonrecursive name server as one of the servers authoritative for your zone data (i.e., you can tell a parent name server to refer queries about your zone to this server). This works because name servers send nonrecursive queries between themselves.

Avoiding a Bogus Name Server

In your term as name server administrator, you might find some remote name server that responds with bad information—old, incorrect, badly formatted, or even deliberately deceptive. You can attempt to find an administrator to fix the problem. Or you can save yourself some grief and configure your name server not to ask questions of this server, which is possible with BIND 4.9, BIND 8, and BIND 9.1.0 and later. Here is the configuration file statement:

```
server 10.0.0.2 {
    bogus yes;
};
```

Or, on a BIND 4.9 server:

```
bogusns 10.0.0.2
```

Of course, you fill in the correct IP address.

If you tell your name server to stop talking to a server that is the only server for a zone, don't expect to be able to look up names in that zone. Hopefully, there are other servers for that zone that can provide good information.

An even more potent way of shutting out a remote name server is to put it on your *blackhole* list. Your name server won't query name servers on the list *and* it won't respond to their queries.* *blackhole* is an *options* substatement that takes an address match list as an argument:

```
options {

    /* Don't waste your time trying to respond to queries from RFC 1918
       private addresses */

    blackhole {
        10/8;
        172.16/12;
        192.168/16;
    };
};
```

---

* And we really mean *won't respond*. Whereas queriers disallowed by an *allow-query* access control list get a response back indicating that their query was refused, queries on the *blackhole* list get nothing back. Nada.

This will prevent your name server from trying to respond to any queries it might receive from RFC 1918 private addresses. There are no routes on the Internet to these addresses, so trying to reply to them is a waste of CPU cycles and bandwidth.

The *blackhole* substatement is supported on BIND 8 versions after 8.2 and on BIND 9 after 9.1.0.

System Tuning

While for many name servers BIND's default configuration values work just fine, yours may be one of those that need some further tuning. In this section, we discuss all the various dials and switches available to you to tune your name server.

Zone Transfers

Zone transfers can place a heavy load on a name server. On BIND 4 name servers, outbound zone transfers (transfers of a zone the server is master for) require *fork()*ing the *named* process, thereby using a significant amount of extra memory. BIND 4.9 introduced mechanisms for limiting the zone transfer load that your name server places on its master servers. BIND 8 and 9 have these mechanisms and more.

Limiting transfers requested per name server

With BIND 4.9 and later, you can limit the number of zones your name server requests from a single remote name server. This will make the administrator of the remote name server happy because his host won't be pounded for zone transfers if all of the zones change—important if hundreds of zones are involved.

In BIND 8 and 9, the config file statement is:

```
options {
    transfers-per-ns 2;
};
```

The equivalent BIND 4 boot file directive is:

```
limit transfers-per-ns 2
```

In BIND 9, you can also set the limit on a server-by-server basis instead of globally. To do this, use the *transfers* substatement inside a *server* statement, where the server is the name server you'd like to specify the limit for:

```
server 192.168.1.2 {
    transfers 2;
};
```

This overrides any global limit set in the *options* statement. The default limit is two active zone transfers per name server. That limit may seem small, but it works.

Here's what happens: suppose your name server needs to load four zones from a remote name server. Your name server starts transferring the first two zones and wait to transfer the third and fourth zones. After one of the first two zone transfers completes, the name server begins transferring the third zone. After another transfer completes, the name server starts transferring the fourth zone. The net result is the same as before there were limits—all the zones are transferred—but the work is spread out.

When might you need to increase this limit? You might notice that it is taking too long to synch up with the remote name server, and you know that the reason is the serializing of transfers—not just that the network between the hosts is slow. This probably matters only if you're maintaining hundreds or thousands of zones. You also need to make sure that the remote name server and the networks in between can handle the additional workload of more simultaneous zone transfers.

Limiting the total number of zone transfers requested

The last limit dealt with the zone transfers requested from a single remote name server. This limit deals with multiple remote name servers. BIND Versions 4.9 and later let you limit the total number of zones your name server can request at any one time. The default limit is 10. As we explained previously, your name server will pull only two zones from any single remote server by default. If your name server is transferring two zones from each of five remote servers, your server has hit the limit and will postpone any further transfers until one of the current transfers finishes.

The BIND 8 and 9 *named.conf* file statement is:

```
options {
    transfers-in 10;
};
```

The equivalent BIND 4 boot file directive is:

```
limit transfers-in 10
```

If your host or network cannot handle 10 active zone transfers, you should decrease this number. If you run a server that supports hundreds or thousands of zones and your host and network can support the load, you might want to raise this limit. If you raise this limit, you may also need to raise the limit for the number of transfers per name server. (For example, if your name server loads from only four remote name servers and your name server will start only two transfers per remote name server, then your server will have at most eight active zone transfers. Increasing the limit for the total number of zone transfers won't have any effect unless you also increase the per-name server limit.)

Limiting the total number of zone transfers served

BIND 9 name servers can also limit the number of zone transfers they'll *serve* simultaneously. This is arguably more useful than limiting the number you'll request, since without it you'd have to rely on the kindness of the administrators who run your slave name servers not to overload your master server. The BIND 9 statement is:

```
options {
    transfers-out 10;
};
```

The default limit is 10.

Limiting the duration of a zone transfer

BIND 8 and 9 also let you limit the duration of an inbound zone transfer. By default, zone transfers are limited to 120 minutes, or two hours. The idea is that a zone transfer taking longer than 120 minutes is probably hung and won't complete, and the process is taking up resources unnecessarily. If you'd like a smaller or larger limit, perhaps because you know that your name server is a slave for a zone that normally takes more than 120 minutes to transfer, you can use this statement:

```
options {
    max-transfer-time-in 180;
};
```

You can even place a limit on transfers of a particular zone by using the *max-transfer-time-in* substatement inside a *zone* statement. For example, if you know that the *rinkydink.com* zone always takes a long time (say three hours) to transfer, either because of its size or because the links to the master name server are so slow, but you'd still like a shorter time limit (maybe an hour) on other zone transfers, you could use:

```
options {
    max-transfer-time-in 60;
};

zone "rinkydink.com" {
    type slave;
    file "bak.rinkydink.com";
    masters { 192.168.1.2; };
    max-transfer-time-in 180;
};
```

In BIND 9, there's also a *max-transfer-time-out* substatement that can be used the same way (either within an *options* statement or a *zone* statement). It controls how long an outbound zone transfer (i.e., a transfer to a slave) can run and has the same default value (120 minutes) as *max-transfer-time-in*.

BIND 9 name servers even let you limit zone transfer idle time, the length of time since the zone transfer made any progress. The two configuration substatements, *max-transfer-idle-in* and *max-transfer-idle-out*, control how long an inbound and an outbound zone transfer can be idle, respectively. Like the transfer time limits, both can be used as either an *options* substatement or a *zone* substatement. The default limit on idle time is 60 minutes.

Limiting the frequency of zone transfers

It's possible to set a zone's refresh interval so low as to cause slave name servers for that zone undue work. For example, if your name server is a slave for thousands of zones and the administrators of some of those zones set their refresh intervals to very small values, your name server may not be able to keep up with all the refreshing it needs to do. (If you run a name server that's a slave for that many zones, be sure to read the later section "Limiting the number of SOA queries"; you may also need to tune the number of SOA queries allowed.) On the other hand, it's possible for an inexperienced administrator to set her zone's refresh interval so high as to cause prolonged inconsistencies between the zone's primary master and slave name servers.

BIND Versions 9.1.0 and later let you limit the refresh interval with *max-refresh-time* and *min-refresh-time*. These substatements bracket the refresh value for all master, slave, and stub zones if used as an *options* substatement, or just for a particular zone if used as a *zone* substatement. Both take a number of seconds as an argument:

```
options {
    max-refresh-time 86400;    // refresh should never be more than a day
    min-refresh-time 1800;     // or less than 30 minutes
};
```

BIND 9.1.0 and later name servers also let you limit the retry interval with the *max-retry-time* and *min-retry-time* substatements, which use the same syntax.

More efficient zone transfers

A zone transfer, as we said earlier, is composed of many DNS messages sent end-to-end over a TCP connection. Traditional zone transfers put only a single resource record in each DNS message. That's a waste of space: you need a full header on each DNS message, even though you're carrying only a single record. It's like being the only person in a Chevy Suburban. A TCP-based DNS message could carry many more records: its maximum size is a whopping 64 KB!

BIND 8 and 9 name servers understand a new zone transfer format, called *many-answers*. The *many-answers* format puts as many records as possible into a single DNS message. The result is that a *many-answers* zone transfer takes less bandwidth because there's less overhead, and less CPU time because less time is spent unmarshaling DNS messages.

The *transfer-format* substatement controls which zone transfer format the name server uses for zones for which it is a master. That is, it determines the format of the zones that your name server transfers to its slaves. *transfer-format* is both an *options* substatement and a *server* substatement; as an *options* substatement, *transfer-format* controls the name server's global zone transfer format. BIND 8's default is to use the old *one-answer* zone transfer format for interoperability with BIND 4 name servers. BIND 9's default is to use the *many-answers* format. The statement:

```
options {
    transfer-format many-answers;
};
```

changes the name server's settings to use the *many-answers* format for zone transfers to all slave servers, unless a *server* statement like the following explicitly says otherwise:

```
server 192.168.1.2 {
    transfer-format one-answer;
};
```

The one downside to using the *many-answers* format is that zone transfers can actually take longer to complete using the new format, despite being more efficient from a bandwidth and CPU utilization point of view.

If you'd like to take advantage of the new, more efficient zone transfers, do one of the following:

- Set your name server's global zone transfer format to *many-answers* (or don't add one at all if you're running BIND 9) if most of your slaves run BIND 8, BIND 9, or Microsoft's DNS Server, which also understands the format.

- Set your name server's global zone transfer format to *one-answer*, if most of your slaves run BIND 4. Then use the *transfer-format server* substatement to adjust the global setting for exceptional servers.

Remember that if you run BIND 9, you'll need to add an explicit *server* statement for all BIND 4 slaves to change their transfer formats to *one-answer*.

Resource Limits

Sometimes you just want to tell the name server to stop being so greedy: don't use more than this much memory, don't open more than this many files. BIND 4.9 introduced these limits, and, as with so many features, BIND 8 and 9 give you several new variations.

Changing the data segment size limit

Some operating systems place a default limit on the amount of memory a process can use. If your OS ever prevents your name server from allocating additional memory, the server will panic or exit. Unless your name server handles an extremely large amount of data or the limit is very small, you won't run into this limit. But if you do, BIND 4.9 and 8 as well as BIND 9.1.0 and later name servers have configuration options to change the system's default limit on data segment size. You might use these options to set a higher limit for *named* than the default system limit.

For BIND 8 and 9, the statement is:

```
options {
    datasize size
};
```

For BIND 4, the directive is:

```
limit datasize size
```

size is an integer value, specified in bytes by default. You can specify a unit other than bytes by appending a character: k (kilobyte), m (megabyte), or g (gigabyte). For example, "64m" is 64 megabytes.

 Not all systems support increasing the data segment size for individual processes. If your system doesn't, the name server will issue a *syslog* message at level LOG_WARNING to tell you that this feature is not implemented.

Changing the stack size limit

In addition to allowing you to change the limit on the size of the name server's data segment, BIND 8 and BIND 9.1.0 and later name servers let you adjust the limit the system places on the amount of memory the *named* process's stack can use. The syntax is:

```
options {
    stacksize size;
};
```

where *size* is specified as in *datasize*. Like *datasize*, this feature works only on systems that permit a process to modify the stack size limit.

Changing the core size limit

If you don't appreciate *named*'s leaving huge core files lying around on your filesystem, you can at least make them smaller by using *coresize*. Conversely, if *named* hasn't been able to dump an entire core file because of a tight operating system limit, you may be able to raise that limit with *coresize*.

coresize's syntax is:

```
options {
    coresize size;
};
```

Again, as with *datasize*, this feature works only on operating systems that let processes modify the limit on core file size, and doesn't work on versions of BIND 9 before 9.1.0.

Changing the open files limit

If your name server is authoritative for a lot of zones, the *named* process opens lots of files when it starts up—one per authoritative zone, assuming you use backup zone data files on the zones you're a slave for. Likewise, if the host running your name server has lots of virtual network interfaces,* *named* requires one file descriptor per interface. Most Unix operating systems place a limit on the number of files any process can open concurrently. If your name server tries to open more files than this limit permits, you'll see this message in your *syslog* output:

```
named[pid]: socket(SOCK_RAW): Too many open files
```

If your operating system also permits changing that limit on a per-process basis, you can increase it using BIND's *files* substatement:

```
options {
    files number;
};
```

The default is *unlimited* (which is also a valid value), although this just means that the name server doesn't place a limit on the number of concurrently open files; the operating system may, however. And though we know you're sick of our saying it, BIND 9 doesn't support this until 9.1.0.

Limiting the number of clients

BIND 9 gives you the ability to restrict the number of clients your name server will serve concurrently. You can apply a limit to the number of recursive clients (resolvers plus name servers using your name server as a forwarder) with the *recursive-clients* substatement:

```
options {
    recursive-clients 10;
};
```

---

* Chapter 14, *Troubleshooting DNS and BIND*, describes better solutions to the "Too many open files" problem than bumping up the limit on files.

The default limit is 1000. If you find your name server refusing recursive queries and logging, as shown by an error message like this one:

```
Sep 22 02:26:11 terminator named[13979]: client 192.249.249.151#1677: no more
recursive clients: quota reached
```

you may want to increase the limit. Conversely, if you find your name server struggling to keep up with the deluge of recursive queries it receives, you could lower the limit.

You can also apply a limit to the number of concurrent TCP connections your name server will process (for zone transfers and TCP-based queries) with the *tcp-clients* substatement. TCP connections consume considerably more resources than UDP because the host needs to track the state of the TCP connection. The default limit is 100.

Limiting the number of SOA queries

BIND 8.2.2 and later name servers let you limit the number of outstanding SOA queries your name server allows. If your name server is a slave for thousands of zones, it may have many queries for the SOA records of those zones pending at any one time. Tracking each of those queries requires a small but finite amount of memory, so by default BIND 8 name servers limit outstanding SOA queries to four. If you find that your name server can't keep up with its duties as a slave, you may need to raise the limit with the *serial-queries* substatement:

```
options {
    serial-queries 1000;
};
```

serial-queries is obsolete in BIND 9. BIND 9 limits the rate at which serial queries are sent (to 20 per second), not the number of outstanding queries.

Maintenance Intervals

BIND name servers have always done periodic housekeeping, such as refreshing zones for which the server is a slave. With BIND 8 and 9, you can now control how often these chores happen or whether they happen at all.

Cleaning interval

Name servers older than BIND 4.9 only passively remove stale entries from the cache. Before such a name server returns a record to a querier, it checks to see whether the TTL on that record has expired. If it has, the name server starts the resolution process to find more current data. This means that a BIND 4 server may cache a lot of records in a flurry of name resolution and then just let those records spoil in the cache, taking up valuable memory even though the records are stale.

BIND 8 and 9 actively walk through the cache and remove stale records once per cleaning interval. This means that BIND 8 and 9 name servers tend to use less memory for caching than a BIND 4 server in the same role. On the other hand, the cleaning process takes CPU time, and on very slow or very busy name servers, you may not want it running every hour.

By default, the cleaning interval is 60 minutes. You can tune the interval with the *cleaning-interval* substatement to the *options* statement. For example:

```
options {
    cleaning-interval 120;
};
```

sets the cleaning interval to 120 minutes. To turn off cache cleaning entirely, set the cleaning interval to zero.

Interface interval

We've said already that BIND, by default, listens on all of a host's network interfaces. BIND 8 and 9 name servers are actually smart enough to notice when a network interface on the host they're running on comes up or goes down. To do this, they periodically scan the host's network interfaces. This happens once each interface interval, which is 60 minutes by default. If you know that the host your name server runs on has no dynamic network interfaces, you can disable scanning for new interfaces to avoid the unnecessary hourly overhead by setting the interface interval to zero:

```
options {
    interface-interval 0;
};
```

On the other hand, if your host brings up or tears down network interfaces more often than every hour, you may want to reduce the interval.

Statistics interval

Okay, adjusting the statistics interval—the frequency with which the BIND 8 name server dumps statistics to the statistics file—won't have much effect on performance. But it fits better here, with the other maintenance intervals, than anywhere else in the book.

The syntax of the *statistics-interval* substatement is exactly analogous to the other maintenance intervals:

```
options {
    statistics-interval 60;
};
```

And as with the other maintenance intervals, the default is 60 minutes and a setting of zero disables the periodic dumping of statistics. Because BIND 9 doesn't write statistics to *syslog*, it doesn't have a configurable statistics interval either.

TTLs

Internally, BIND has trimmed TTL values on cached records to reasonable values for some time. BIND 8 and 9 name servers make the limits configurable.

In BIND 8.2 or later name servers, you can limit the TTL on cached negative information with the *max-ncache-ttl options* substatement. This was designed as a safety net for people who upgraded to 8.2 and its new negative caching scheme (RFC 2308 and all that, described in Chapter 4). This new name server caches negative information according to the last field of the zone's SOA record, and many zone admins still use that field for the default TTL for the zone—probably much too long for negative information. So a prudent name server administrator can use a substatement like:

```
options {
    max-ncache-ttl 3600;  // 3600 seconds is one hour
};
```

to trim larger negative caching TTLs to one hour. The default is 10800 seconds (three hours). Without this precaution, it's possible that someone looking up a brand-new record could get a negative answer (maybe because the new record hadn't yet reached the zone's slaves), and her name server would cache that answer for an inordinately long time, rendering the record unresolvable.

BIND 9 name servers also let you configure the upper limit of the TTL on cached records with the *max-cache-ttl* substatement. The default is one week. BIND 8 name servers trim TTLs to one week, too, but they don't let you configure the limit.

Finally, there's what's referred to as the *lame TTL*, which isn't really a TTL at all. Instead, it's the amount of time your name server remembers that a given remote name server isn't authoritative for a zone that's delegated to it. This prevents your name server from wasting valuable time and resources asking that name server for information about a domain name it knows nothing about. BIND 8 name servers after 8.2 and BIND 9 name servers newer than 9.1.0 let you tune the lame TTL with the *lame-ttl options* substatement. The default lame TTL is 600 seconds (10 minutes), with a maximum of 30 minutes. You can even turn off the caching of lame name servers with a value of zero, though that strikes us as a Very Bad Thing.

Compatibility

Now, to wrap things up, we'll cover some configuration substatements related to your name server's compatibility with resolvers and other name servers.

The *rfc2308-type1* substatement controls the format of the negative answers your name server sends. By default, BIND 8 and 9 name servers include only the SOA record in a negative response from a zone. Another legitimate format for that response includes the zone's NS records, too, but some older name servers misinterpret such a response as a referral. If for some odd reason (odd because we can't think of one) you want to send those NS records as well, use:

```
options {
     rfc2308-type1 yes;
};
```

rfc2308-type1 is first supported in BIND 8.2; BIND 9 doesn't support it.

Older name servers can also cause problems when you send them cached negative responses. Before the days of negative caching, all negative responses were, naturally, authoritative. But some name server implementors added a check to their servers: they'd accept only authoritative negative responses. Then, with the advent of negative caching, negative responses could be nonauthoritative. Oops!

The *auth-nxdomain options* substatement lets your name server falsely claim that a negative answer from its cache is actually authoritative, just so one of these older name servers will believe it. By default, BIND 8 name servers have *auth-nxdomain* on (set to yes); BIND 9 name servers turn it off by default.

Finally, when some adventurous souls ported BIND 8.2.2 to Windows NT, they found they needed the name server to treat a carriage return and a newline at the end of a line (Windows' end-of-line sequence) the same way it treated just a newline (Unix's end-of-line). For that behavior, use:

```
options {
     treat-cr-as-space yes;
};
```

BIND 9 ignores this option because it always treats carriage return and newline and a newline alone the same way.

The ABCs of IPv6 Addressing

Before we cover the next two topics, which include how domain names map to IPv6 addresses and vice versa, we'd better describe the representation and structure of IPv6 addresses. As you probably know, IPv6 addresses are 128 bits long.

The preferred representation of an IPv6 address is eight groups of as many as four hexadecimal digits, separated by colons; for example:

```
0123:4567:89ab:cdef:0123:4567:89ab:cdef
```

The first group of hex digits (0123, in this example) represents the most significant (or highest order) four bits of the address.

Groups of digits that begin with one or more zeros don't need to be padded to four places, so you can also write the previous address as:

```
123:4567:89ab:cdef:123:4567:89ab:cdef
```

Each group must contain at least one digit, though, unless you're using the :: notation. The :: notation allows you to compress sequential groups of zeros. This comes in handy when you're specifying just an IPv6 prefix. For example:

```
dead:beef::
```

specifies the first 32 bits of an IPv6 address as *dead:beef* and the remaining 96 as zeros.

You can also use :: at the beginning of an IPv6 address to specify a suffix. For example, the IPv6 loopback address is commonly written as:

```
::1
```

or 127 zeros followed by a single one. You can even use :: in the middle of an address as a shorthand for contiguous groups of zeros:

```
dead:beef::1
```

You can use the :: shorthand only once in an address, since more than one could be ambiguous.

IPv6 prefixes are specified in a format similar to IPv4's CIDR notation. As many bits of the prefix as are significant are expressed in the standard IPv6 notation, followed by a slash and a decimal count of exactly how many significant bits there are. So the following three prefix specifications are equivalent (though obviously not equivalently terse):

```
dead:beef:0000:00f1:0000:0000:0000:0000/64
dead:beef::00f1:0:0:0:0/64
dead:beef:0:f1::/64
```

IP Version 4 addresses are hierarchical, mirroring the nature of IPv4 networks: individual networks connect to Internet service providers, which in turn connect to other ISPs or to the core of the Internet. Each provider assigns a few bits of the overall 32-bit IP address: providers closer to the core of the Internet assign bits earlier in the address, and finally the administrator of the network assigns the remaining bits.

IPv6 was designed to accommodate a much larger Internet, so IPv6 addresses have even more levels of hierarchy. Each level corresponds to one of the levels of networks in an IPv6-based internet.

At the core of an IPv6 internet, there are *Top-Level Aggregators*, or TLAs. TLAs are networks that connect directly to the backbone of the internet and provide connectivity to *Next-Level Aggregators*, or NLAs. NLA networks connect site networks to an IPv6 internet. The whole arrangement is depicted in Figure 10-5.

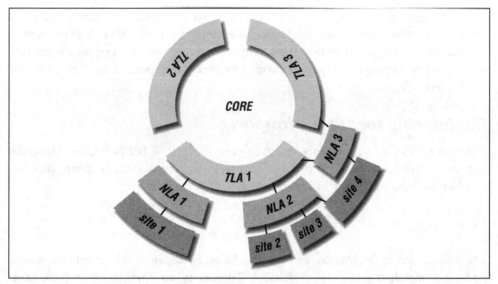

Figure 10-5. The structure of an IPv6 internet

As with IPv4 networks, each of these organizations assigns certain bits of an IPv6 address. To help you picture the addressing hierarchy within IPv6, here's a diagram of the most common structure of an IPv6 address, as described in RFC 2374:

```
| 3|  13  | 8 |   24    |   16    |          64 bits                   |
+--+------+---+---------+---------+-----------------------------------+
|FP| TLA  |RES|  NLA    |  SLA    |          Interface ID             |
|  | ID   |   |  ID     |  ID     |                                   |
+--+------+---+---------+---------+-----------------------------------+
```

FP is the *Format Prefix*, the first three bits of the address, which determine the format of the rest of the address. The Format Prefix for this particular format, called (take a breath) the *IPv6 Aggregatable Global Unicast Address Format*, is 001. The next 13 bits identify the Top-Level Aggregator, followed by three reserved bits (set to zero), then 24 bits specifying the Next-Level Aggregator. The remaining bits are used by the site: the *Site-Level Aggregator ID*, or *SLA ID*, is basically like the subnet bits in an IPv4 address, and the *Interface ID* uniquely identifies a particular interface on the site's network.

In this address format, each ID is assigned by the entity at the next level up in the hierarchy. For example, a single, top-level address registry assigns TLA IDs to the Top-Level Aggregators. TLAs, in turn, assign NLA IDs to their NLA customers, who assign SLA IDs to their customers. NLA IDs need only be unique within a TLA ID, just as SLA IDs need only be unique within a particular NLA ID.

Addresses and Ports

BIND 9 name servers can use both IPv4 and IPv6 as a transport; that is, they can send and receive queries and responses over IPv4 and IPv6. BIND 8 name servers support only IPv4 as a transport. However, both name servers support similar substatements to configure which network interfaces and ports they listen on and send queries from.

Configuring the IPv4 Transport

You can specify which network interface your BIND 8 or BIND 9 name server listens on for queries using the *listen-on* substatement. In its simplest form, *listen-on* takes an address match list as an argument:

```
options {
    listen-on { 192.249.249/24; };
};
```

The name server listens on any of the local host's network interfaces whose addresses match the address match list. To specify an alternate port (one other than 53) to listen on, use the *port* modifier:

```
options {
    listen-on port 5353 { 192.249.249/24; };
};
```

In BIND 9, you can even specify a different port for each network interface:

```
options {
    listen-on { 192.249.249.1 port 5353; 192.253.253.1 port 1053; };
};
```

Note that there's no way to configure most resolvers to query a name server on an alternate port, so this name server might not be as useful as you'd think. Still, it can serve zone transfers, because you can specify an alternate port in a *masters* substatement:

```
zone "movie.edu" {
    type slave;
    masters port 5353 { 192.249.249.1; };
    file "bak.movie.edu";
};
```

Or, if your BIND 9 name server has multiple master name servers, each listening on a different port, you can use something like:

```
zone "movie.edu" {
    type slave;
    masters { 192.249.249.1 port 5353; 192.253.253.1 port 1053; };
    file "bak.movie.edu";
};
```

BIND 9 even allows you to send your NOTIFY messages to alternate ports. To tell your master name server to notify all its slave name servers on the same oddball port, use:

```
also-notify port 5353 { 192.249.249.9; 192.253.253.9; }; // zardoz's two addresses
```

To notify each on a different port, use:

```
also-notify { 192.249.249.9 port 5353; 192.249.249.1 port 1053; };
```

If your slave name server needs to use a particular local network interface to send queries—perhaps because one of its master name servers recognizes it by only one of its many addresses—use the *query-source* substatement:

```
options {
    query-source address 192.249.249.1;
};
```

Note that the argument isn't an address match list; it's a single IP address. You can also specify a particular source port to use for queries:

```
options {
    query-source address 192.249.249.1 port 53;
};
```

BIND's default behavior is to use whichever network interface the route to the destination points out and a random, unprivileged port, i.e.:

```
options {
    query-source address * port *;
};
```

Note that *query-source* applies only to UDP-based queries; TCP-based queries always choose the source address according to the routing table and use a random source port.

There's an analogous *transfer-source* substatement that controls the source address to use for zone transfers. In BIND 9, it also applies to a slave name server's SOA queries and to forwarded dynamic updates:

```
options {
    transfer-source 192.249.249.1;
};
```

As with *query-source*, the argument is just a single IP address, but with no *address* keyword. With BIND 8, there's no *port* modifier. With BIND 9, you can specify a source port:

```
options {
    transfer-source 192.249.249.1 port 1053;
};
```

However, that source port applies only to UDP-based traffic (i.e., SOA queries and forwarded dynamic updates).

transfer-source can also be used as a *zone* substatement, in which case it applies only to transfers (and, for BIND 9, SOA queries and dynamic updates) of that zone:

```
zone "movie.edu" {
    type slave;
    masters { 192.249.249.3; };
    file "bak.movie.edu";
    transfer-source 192.249.249.1; // always use IP address on same network
                                   // for transfers of movie.edu
};
```

Finally, as of BIND 9.1.0, there's even a substatement that lets you control which address you send NOTIFY messages from, called *notify-source*. This comes in handy with multihomed name servers since slaves only accept NOTIFY messages for a zone from IP addresses in that zone's *masters* substatement. *notify-source*'s syntax is similar to the syntax of the other *-source* substatements; for example:

```
options {
    notify-source 192.249.249.1;
};
```

As with *transfer-source*, *notify-source* can specify a source port and can be used as a *zone* statement to apply only to that zone:

```
zone {
    type slave;
    masters { 192.249.249.3; };
    file "bak.movie.edu";
    notify-source 192.249.249.1 port 5353;
};
```

Configuring the IPv6 Transport

By default, a BIND 9 name server won't listen for IPv6-based queries. To configure it to listen on the local host's IPv6 network interfaces, use the *listen-on-v6* substatement:

```
options {
    listen-on-v6 { any; };
};
```

Unlike its IPv4 counterpart, the *listen-on-v6* substatement accepts only *any* and *none* as arguments. You can, however, configure a BIND 9 name server to listen on an alternate port—or even multiple ports—with the *port* modifier:

```
options {
    listen-on-v6 port 1053 { any; };
};
```

The default port is, of course, 53.

You can also determine which IPv6 address your name server uses as the source port for outgoing queries with the *transfer-source-v6* substatement, as in:

```
options {
    transfer-source-v6 222:10:2521:1:210:4bff:fe10:d24;
};
```

or:

```
options {
    transfer-source-v6 port 53 222:10:2521:1:210:4bff:fe10:d24;
};
```

The default is to use the source address corresponding to whichever network interface the route points out and a random, unprivileged source port. As with *transfer-source*, you can use *transfer-source-v6* as a *zone* substatement. And the source port applies only to SOA queries and forwarded dynamic updates.

Finally, BIND 9.1.0 and later let you determine which IPv6 address to use in NOTIFY messages, à la the *notify-source* substatement. The IPv6 substatement is called, not surprisingly, *notify-source-v6*:

```
options {
    notify-source-v6 222:10:2521:1:210:4bff:fe10:d24;
};
```

As with *transfer-source-v6*, you can specify a source port and use the substatement in a *zone* statement.

IPv6 Forward and Reverse Mapping

Clearly, the existing A record won't accommodate IPv6's 128-bit addresses; BIND expects an A record's record-specific data to be a 32-bit address in dotted-octet format.

The IETF came up with a simple solution to this problem, described in RFC 1886. A new address record, AAAA, is used to store a 128-bit IPv6 address, and there's a new IPv6 reverse-mapping domain, *ip6.int*. This solution was straightforward enough to implement in BIND 4.9. Unfortunately, not everyone liked the simple solution, so they came up with a much more complicated one. This solution, which we'll describe shortly, involves the new A6 and DNAME records and required a complete overhaul of the BIND name server to implement.

Use of the old AAAA record and *ip6.int* is now deprecated, but there's enough IPv6 software out there still using it—and not the new stuff—that it's important to understand both methods.

AAAA and ip6.int

Now the simple way to handle this, described in RFC 1886, is with an address record that's four times as long as an A record. That's the AAAA (pronounced "quad A") record. The AAAA record takes as its record-specific data the textual format of an IPv6 record as described earlier. So for example, you'd see AAAA records like this one:

```
ipv6-host    IN    AAAA    4321:0:1:2:3:4:567:89ab
```

RFC 1886 also established *ip6.int*, a new reverse-mapping name space for IPv6 addresses. Each level of subdomain under *ip6.int* represents four bits of the 128-bit address, encoded as a hexadecimal digit just like in the record-specific data of the AAAA record. The least significant (lowest order) bits appear at the far left of the domain name. Unlike the format of addresses in AAAA records, omitting leading zeros is not allowed, so there are always 32 hexadecimal digits and 32 levels of subdomain below *ip6.int* in a domain name corresponding to a full IPv6 address. The domain name that corresponds to the address in the previous example is:

```
b.a.9.8.7.6.5.0.4.0.0.0.3.0.0.0.2.0.0.0.1.0.0.0.0.0.0.0.1.2.3.4.ip6.int.
```

These domain names have PTR records attached, just as the domain names under *in-addr.arpa* do:

```
b.a.9.8.7.6.5.0.4.0.0.0.3.0.0.0.2.0.0.0.1.0.0.0.0.0.0.0.1.2.3.4.ip6.int.  IN  PTR
mash.ip6.movie.edu.
```

A6, DNAMEs, Bitstring Labels, and ip6.arpa

That's the easy way. The more difficult—and now official—way of handling IPv6 forward and reverse mapping uses two new record types, A6 and DNAME records. A6 and DNAME records are described in RFCs 2874 and 2672, respectively. Version 9.0.0 is the first version of BIND to support these records.

The main reason the AAAA record and the *ip6.int* reverse-mapping scheme were replaced was because they made network renumbering difficult. For example, if an organization were to change Next-Level Aggregators, it would have to change all the AAAA records in its zone data files since 24 of the bits of an IPv6 address are an identifier for the NLA.* Or imagine an NLA changing TLAs: this would wreak havoc with its customers' zone data.

A6 records and forward mapping

To make renumbering easier, A6 records can specify only a part of an IPv6 address, such as the last 64 bits (the interface ID) assigned to a host's network interface, and then refer to the remainder of the address by a symbolic domain name. This allows zone administrators to specify only the part of the address under their control. To build an entire address, a resolver or name server must follow the chain of A6 records from a host's domain name to the TLA ID. And that chain may branch if a site network is connected to multiple NLAs or if an NLA is connected to multiple TLAs.

For example, the A6 record:

```
$ORIGIN movie.edu.
drunkenmaster IN  A6  64  ::0210:4bff:fe10:0d24  subnet1.v6.movie.edu.
```

specifies the final 64 bits of *drunkenmaster.movie.edu*'s IPv6 address (64 is the number of bits of the prefix *not* specified in this A6 record) and that the remaining 64 bits can be found by looking up an A6 record at *subnet1.v6.movie.edu*.

subnet1.v6.movie.edu, in turn, specifies the last 16 bits of the 64-bit prefix (the SLA ID) that we didn't specify in *drunkenmaster.movie.edu*'s A6 address as well as the domain name of the next A6 record to look up:

```
$ORIGIN v6.movie.edu.
subnet1 IN A6  48  0:0:0:1::  movie-u.nla-a.net.
subnet1 IN A6  48  0:0:0:1::  movie.nlab.net.
```

The first 48 bits of the prefix in *subnet1.v6.movie.edu*'s record-specific data are set to zero, since they're not significant here.

In fact, these records tell us to look up *two* A6 records next, one at *movie-u.nla-a. net* and one at *movie.nlab.net*. That's because Movie U. has connections to two NLAs, NLA A and NLA B. In NLA A's zone, we'd find:

```
$ORIGIN nla-a.net.
movie-u IN A6  40  0:0:21::  nla-a.tla-1.net.
```

indicating the eight-bit *Site ID* pattern within the NLA ID field set by NLA A for the Movie University network. You see, the NLA ID field is hierarchical, too, comprising both an identifier for our Next-Level Aggregator assigned to it by its TLA, *and* its identifier for our network. Since the NLA assigns our Site ID but has the rest of their NLA ID assigned by its TLA, we'd expect to see only our Site ID in our NLA's zone data. The remainder of its NLA ID would appear in an A6 record in its TLA's zone.

---

* And, of course, the new NLA might use a different TLA, which would mean 16 more bits to change . . .

In NLA B's zone, we'd find the following record showing us their Site ID for our network:

```
$ORIGIN nlab.net.
movie IN A6 40 0:0:42:: nlab.tla-2.net.
```

In the TLAs' zones, we'd find:

```
$ORIGIN tla-1.net.
nla-a IN A6 16 0:10:2500:: tla-1.top-level-v6.net.
```

and:

```
$ORIGIN tla-2.net.
nlab  IN A6 16 0:19:6600:: tla-2.top-level-v6.net.
```

Finally, in the top-level IPv6 address registry's zone, we'd find this record showing us the TLA IDs assigned to TLA 1 and TLA 2:

```
$ORIGIN top-level-v6.net.
tla-1 IN A6 0 222::
tla-2 IN A6 0 242::
```

By following this chain of A6 records, a name server can assemble all 128 bits of *drunkenmaster.movie.edu*'s two IPv6 addresses. These turn out to be:

```
222:10:2521:1:210:4bff:fe10:d24
242:19:6642:1:210:4bff:fe10:d24
```

The first of these uses a route through TLA 1 and NLA A to the Movie U. network, and the second uses a route through TLA 2 and NLA B. (We're connected to two NLAs for redundancy.) Note that if TLA 1 changes its NLA assignment for NLA A, it only needs to change the A6 record for *nla-a.tla-1.net* in its zone data; the change "cascades" into all A6 chains that go through NLA A. This makes the management of addressing on IPv6 networks very convenient, and makes changing NLAs easy, too.

 If a name server appears in an NS record and owns one or more A6 records, those A6 records should specify all 128 bits of the IPv6 address. This helps avoid deadlock problems, where a resolver or name server needs to talk to a remote name server to resolve part of that name server's IPv6 address.

DNAME records and reverse mapping

Now that you've seen how forward mapping works with A6 records, let's look at how reverse mapping IPv6 addresses works. As with A6 records, unfortunately, this isn't nearly as simple as *ip6.int*.

Reverse mapping IPv6 addresses involves DNAME records, described in RFC 2672, and bitstring labels, introduced in RFC 2673. DNAME records are a little like wildcard CNAME records. They're used to substitute one suffix of a domain name with another. For example, if we had previously used the domain name *movieu.edu* at Movie University but had since changed to *movie.edu*, we could have replaced the old *movieu.edu* zone with this one:

```
$TTL 1d
@    IN  SOA    terminator.movie.edu.  root.movie.edu. (
     2000102300
     3h
     30m
     30d
     1h  )

     IN  NS     terminator.movie.edu.
     IN  NS     wormhole.movie.edu.

     IN  MX     10 postmanrings2x.movie.edu.

     IN  DNAME  movie.edu.
```

The DNAME record in the *movieu.edu* zone applies to any domain name that ends in *movieu.edu* except *movieu.edu* itself. Unlike the CNAME record, the DNAME record can coexist with other record types owned by the same domain name as long as they aren't CNAME or other DNAME records. The owner of the DNAME record may *not* have any subdomains, though.

When the *movieu.edu* name server receives a query for any domain name that ends in *movieu.edu*, say *cuckoosnest.movieu.edu*, the DNAME record tells it to "synthesize" an alias from *cuckoosnest.movieu.edu* to *cuckoosnest.movie.edu*, replacing *movieu.edu* with *movie.edu*:

```
cuckoosnest.movieu.edu.  IN  CNAME  cuckoosnest.movie.edu.
```

It's a little like *sed*'s "s" (substitute) command. The *movieu.edu* name server replies with this CNAME record. If it's responding to a newer name server, it also sends the DNAME record in the response, and the recipient name server can then synthesize its own CNAME records from the cached DNAME.

Bitstring labels are the other half of the magic involved in IPv6 reverse mapping. Bitstring labels are simply a compact way of representing a long sequence of binary (i.e., one-bit) labels in a domain name. Say you wanted to permit delegation between any two bits of an IP address. That might compel you to represent each bit of the address as a label in a domain name. But that would require over 128 labels for a domain name that represented an IPv6 address! Oy!

Bitstring labels concatenate the bits in successive labels into a shorter hexadecimal, octal, binary or dotted-octet string. The string is encapsulated between the tokens

"\[" and "]" to distinguish it from a traditional label, and begins with one letter that determines the base of the string: *b* for binary, *o* for octal, and *x* for hexadecimal.

Here are the bitstring labels that correspond to *drunkenmaster.movie.edu*'s two IPv6 addresses:

```
\[x02220010252100010210bfffe100d24]
\[x02420019664200010210bfffe100d24]
```

Notice that the most significant bit begins the string, as in the text representation of an IPv6 address, but in the opposite order of the labels in the *in-addr.arpa* domain. Despite this, these two bitstring labels are simply a different encoding of traditional domain names that begin:

```
0.0.1.0.0.1.0.0.1.0.1.1.0.0.0.0.0.0.0.0.1.0.0.0.0.1.1.1.1.1.1.1...
```

Also note that all 32 hex digits in the address are present—you can't drop leading zeros, because there are no colons to separate groups of four digits.

Bitstring labels can also represent parts of IPv6 addresses, in which case you need to specify the number of significant bits in the string, separated from the string by a slash. So TLA 1's TLA ID is *\[x0222/16]*.

Together, DNAMEs and bitstring labels are used to match portions of a long domain name that encodes an IPv6 address and to iteratively change the domain name looked up to a domain name in a zone under the control of the organization that manages the host with that IPv6 address.

Imagine we're reverse mapping *\[x02420019664200010210bfffe100d24].ip6.arpa*, the domain name that corresponds to *drunkenmaster.movie.edu*'s network interface (when reached through TLA 2 and NLA B). The root name servers would probably refer our name server to the *ip6.arpa* name servers, which contain these records:

```
$ORIGIN ip6.arpa.
\[x0222/16]     IN      DNAME       ip6.tla-1.net.
\[x0242/16]     IN      DNAME       ip6.tla-2.net.
```

The first of these matches the beginning of the domain name we're looking up, so the *ip6.arpa* name servers reply to our name server with an alias that says:

```
\[x02420019664200010210bfffe100d24].ip6.arpa.  IN  CNAME
\[x0019664200010210bfffe100d24].ip6.tla-2.net.
```

Notice that the first four hex digits (the most significant 16 bits) of the address are stripped off, and the end of the target of the alias is now *ip6.tla-2.net*, since we know this address belongs to TLA 2. In *ip6.tla-2.net*, we find:

```
$ORIGIN ip6.tla-2.net.
\[x00196600/24]   IN   DNAME      ip6.nlab.net.
```

This turns the domain name in our new query:

```
\[x00196642000102104bfffe100d24].ip6.tla-2.net
```

into:

```
\[x42000102104bfffe100d24].ip6.nlab.net
```

Next, our name server queries the *ip6.nlab.net* name servers for the new domain name. This record in the *ip6.nlab.net* zone:

```
$ORIGIN ip6.nlab.net.
\[x0042/8]    IN   DNAME    ip6.movie.edu.
```

turns the domain name we're looking up into:

```
\[x000102104bfffe100d24].ip6.movie.edu
```

The *ip6.movie.edu* zone, finally, contains the PTR record that gives us the domain name of the host we're after:

```
$ORIGIN ip6.movie.edu.
\[x000102104bfffe100d24/80]  IN   PTR   drunkenmaster.ip6.movie.edu.
```

Mercifully, as a zone administrator you'll probably only be responsible for maintaining PTR records like the ones in *ip6.movie.edu*. Even if you work for a Top-Level or Next-Level Aggregator, creating DNAME records that "extract" the appropriate NLA ID or Site ID from your customers' addresses isn't too tough. And you gain the convenience of using a single zone data file for your reverse-mapping information, even though each of your hosts has multiple addresses, and of being able to switch NLAs without changing all of your zone data files.

11

Security

In this chapter:
- *TSIG*
- *Securing Your Name Server*
- *DNS and Internet Firewalls*
- *The DNS Security Extensions*

"I hope you've got your hair well fastened on?"
he continued, as they set off.

"Only in the usual way," Alice said, smiling.

"That's hardly enough," he said, anxiously.
"You see the wind is so very strong here.
It's as strong as soup."

"Have you invented a plan for keeping the hair
from being blown off?" Alice enquired.

"Not yet," said the Knight. "But I've got a plan
for keeping it from falling off."

Why should you care about DNS security? Why go to the trouble of securing a service that mostly maps names to addresses? Let us tell you a story.

In July 1997, during two periods of several days, users around the Internet who typed *www.internic.net* into their web browsers thinking they were going to the InterNIC's web site instead ended up at a web site belonging to the AlterNIC. (The AlterNIC runs an alternate set of root name servers that delegate to additional top-level domains with names like *med* and *porn.*) How'd it happen? Eugene Kashpureff, then affiliated with the AlterNIC, had run a program to "poison" the caches of major name servers around the world, making them believe that *www.internic.net*'s address was actually the address of the AlterNIC web server.

Kashpureff hadn't made any attempt to disguise what he had done; the web site that users reached was plainly the AlterNIC's, not the InterNIC's. But imagine someone poisoning your name server's cache to direct *www.amazon.com* or *www.wellsfargo.com* to his own web server, conveniently well outside local law enforcement jurisdiction. Further, imagine your users typing in their credit card numbers and expiration dates. Now you get the idea.

Protecting your users against these kinds of attacks requires DNS security. DNS security comes in several flavors. You can secure transactions—the queries, responses, and other messages your name server sends and receives. You can secure your name server, refusing queries, zone transfer requests, and dynamic updates from unauthorized addresses, for example. You can even secure zone data by digitally signing it.

Since DNS security is one of the most complicated topics in DNS, we'll start you off easy and build up to the hard stuff.

TSIG

BIND 8.2 introduced a new mechanism for securing DNS messages called *transaction signatures*, or TSIG for short. TSIG uses shared secrets and a one-way hash function to authenticate DNS messages, particularly responses and updates.

TSIG, now codified in RFC 2845, is relatively simple to configure, lightweight for resolvers and name servers to use, and flexible enough to secure DNS messages (including zone transfers) and dynamic updates. (Contrast this with the DNS Security Extensions, which we'll discuss at the end of this chapter.)

With TSIG configured, a name server or updater adds a TSIG record to the additional data section of a DNS message. The TSIG record "signs" the DNS message, proving that the message's sender had a cryptographic key shared with the receiver and that the message wasn't modified after it left the sender.*

One-Way Hash Functions

TSIG provides authentication and data integrity through the use of a special type of mathematical formula called a *one-way hash function*. A one-way hash function, also known as a cryptographic checksum or message digest, computes a fixed-size hash value based on arbitrarily large input. The magic of a one-way hash function is that each bit of the hash value depends on each and every bit of the input. Change a single bit of the input and the hash value changes dramatically and unpredictably—so unpredictably that it's "computationally infeasible" to reverse the function and find an input that produces a given hash value.

TSIG uses a one-way hash function called MD5. In particular, it uses a variant of MD5 called HMAC-MD5. HMAC-MD5 works in a keyed mode in which the 128-bit hash value depends not only on the input, but also on a key.

---

* Cryptography wonks may argue that TSIG "signatures" aren't really signatures in a cryptographic sense because they don't provide nonrepudiation. Since either holder of the shared key can create a signed message, the recipient of a signed message can't claim that only the sender could have sent it (the recipient could have forged it himself).

The TSIG Record

We won't cover the TSIG record's syntax in detail because you don't need to know it: TSIG is a "meta-record" that never appears in zone data and is never cached by a resolver or name server. A signer adds the TSIG record to a DNS message, and the recipient removes and verifies the record before doing anything further, such as caching the data in the message.

You should know, however, that the TSIG record includes a hash value computed over the entire DNS message as well as some additional fields. (When we say "computed over," we mean that the raw, binary DNS message and the additional fields are fed through the HMAC-MD5 algorithm to produce the hash value.) The hash value is keyed with a secret shared between the signer and the verifier. Verifying the hash value proves both that the DNS message was signed by a holder of the shared secret and that it wasn't modified after it was signed.

The additional fields in the TSIG record include the time the DNS message was signed. This helps combat replay attacks, in which a hacker captures a signed, authorized transaction (say a dynamic update deleting an important resource record) and replays it later. The recipient of a signed DNS message checks the time signed to make sure it's within the allowable "fudge" (another field in the TSIG record).

Configuring TSIG

Before using TSIG for authentication, we need to configure one or more TSIG keys on either end of the transaction. For example, if we want to use TSIG to secure zone transfers between the master and slave name servers for *movie.edu*, we need to configure both name servers with a common key:

```
key terminator-wormhole.movie.edu. {
    algorithm hmac-md5;
    secret "skrKc4Twy/cIgIykQu7JZA==";
};
```

The argument to the *key* statement in this example, *terminator-wormhole.movie. edu.*, is actually the name of the key, though it looks like a domain name. (It's encoded in the DNS message in the same format as a domain name.) The TSIG RFC suggests you name the key after the two hosts that use it. The RFC also suggests that you use different keys for each pair of hosts.

It's important that the name of the key—not just the binary data the key points to—be identical on both ends of the transaction. If it's not, the recipient tries to verify the TSIG record and finds it doesn't know the key that the TSIG record says was used to compute the hash value. That causes errors like the following:

```
Nov 21 19:43:00 wormhole named-xfer[30326]: SOA TSIG verification from server
[192.249.249.1], zone movie.edu: message had BADKEY set (17)
```

The algorithm, for now, is always *hmac-md5*. The secret is the base 64 encoding of the binary key. You can create a base 64–encoded key using the *dnssec-keygen* program included in BIND 9 or the *dnskeygen* program included in BIND 8. Here's how you'd create a key using *dnssec-keygen*, the easier of the two to use:

```
# dnssec-keygen -a HMAC-MD5 -b 128 -n HOST terminator-wormhole.movie.edu.
Kterminator-wormhole.movie.edu.+157+28446
```

The *−a* option takes as an argument the name of the algorithm the key will be used with. (That's necessary because *dnssec-keygen* can generate other kinds of keys, as we'll see in the DNSSEC section.) *−b* takes the length of the key as its argument; the RFC recommends using keys 128 bits long. *−n* takes as an argument HOST, the type of key to generate. (DNSSEC uses ZONE keys.) The final argument is the name of the key.

dnssec-keygen and *dnskeygen* both create files in their working directories that contain the keys generated. *dnssec-keygen* prints the base name of the files to its standard output. In this case, *dnssec-keygen* created the files *Kterminator-wormhole.movie.edu.+157+28446.key* and *Kterminator-wormhole.movie.edu.+157+28446.private*. You can extract the key from either file. The funny numbers (157 and 28446), in case you're wondering, are the key's DNSSEC algorithm number (157 is HMAC-MD5) and the key's fingerprint (28446), a hash value computed over the key to identify it. The fingerprint isn't particularly useful in TSIG, but DNSSEC supports multiple keys per zone, so identifying which key you mean by its fingerprint is important.

Kterminator-wormhole.movie.edu.+157+28446.key contains:

```
terminator-wormhole.movie.edu. IN KEY 512 3 157 skrKc4Twy/cIgIykQu7JZA==
```

and *Kterminator-wormhole.movie.edu.+157+28446.private* contains:

```
Private-key-format: v1.2
Algorithm: 157 (HMAC_MD5)
Key: skrKc4Twy/cIgIykQu7JZA==
```

You can also choose your own key and encode it in base 64 using *mmencode*:

```
% mmencode
foobarbaz
Zm9vYmFyYmF6
```

Since the actual binary key is, as the substatement implies, a secret, we should take care in transferring it to our name servers (e.g., by using *ssh*) and make sure that not just anyone can read it. We can do that by making sure our *named.conf* file isn't world-readable or by using the *include* statement to read the *key* statement from another file, which isn't world-readable:

```
include "/etc/dns.keys.conf";
```

There's one last problem that we see cropping up frequently with TSIG: time synchronization. The timestamp in the TSIG record is useful for preventing replay attacks, but it tripped us up initially because the clocks on our name servers weren't synchronized. That produced error messages like the following:

```
Nov 21 19:56:36 wormhole named-xfer[30420]: SOA TSIG verification from server
[192.249.249.1], zone movie.edu: BADTIME (-18)
```

We quickly remedied the problem using NTP, the network time protocol.*

Using TSIG

Now that we've gone to the trouble of configuring our name servers with TSIG keys, we should probably configure them to use those keys for something. In BIND 8.2 and later name servers, we can secure queries, responses, zone transfers, and dynamic updates with TSIG.

The key to configuring this is the *server* statement's *keys* substatement, which tells a name server to sign queries and zone transfer requests sent to a particular remote name server. This *server* substatement, for example, tells the local name server, *wormhole.movie.edu*, to sign all such requests sent to 192.249.249.1 (*terminator.movie.edu*) with the key *terminator-wormhole.movie.edu*:

```
server 192.249.249.1 {
    keys { terminator-wormhole.movie.edu.; };
};
```

Now, on *terminator.movie.edu*, we can restrict zone transfers to those signed with the *terminator-wormhole.movie.edu* key:

```
zone "movie.edu" {
    type master;
    file "db.movie.edu";
    allow-transfer { key terminator-wormhole.movie.edu.; };
};
```

terminator.movie.edu also signs the zone transfer, which allows *wormhole.movie. edu* to verify it.

You can also restrict dynamic updates with TSIG by using the *allow-update* and *update-policy* substatements, as we showed you in the last chapter.

---

* See the Time Synchronization Server web site at *http://www.eecis.udel.edu/~ntp* for information on NTP.

The *nsupdate* programs shipped with BIND 8.2 and later support sending TSIG-signed dynamic updates. If you have the key files created by *dnssec-keygen* lying around, you can specify either of those as an argument to *nsupdate*'s *−k* option. Here's how you'd do that with BIND 9's version of *nsupdate*:

```
% nsupdate -k Kterminator-wormhole.movie.edu.+157+28446.key
```

or:

```
% nsupdate -k Kterminator-wormhole.movie.edu.+157+28446.private
```

With the BIND 8.2 or later *nsupdate*, the syntax is a little different: *−k* takes a directory and a key name as an argument, separated by a colon:

```
% nsupdate -k /var/named:terminator-wormhole.movie.edu.
```

If you don't have the files around (maybe you're running *nsupdate* from another host), you can still specify the key name and the secret on the command line with the BIND 9 *nsupdate*:

```
% nsupdate -y terminator-wormhole.movie.edu.:skrKc4Twy/cIgIykQu7JZA==
```

The name of the key is the first argument to the *−y* option, followed by a colon and the base 64–encoded secret. You don't need to quote the secret since base 64 values can't contain shell metacharacters, but you can if you like.

Michael Fuhr's Net::DNS Perl module also lets you send TSIG-signed dynamic updates and zone transfer requests. For more information on Net::DNS, see Chapter 15, *Programming with the Resolver and Name Server Library Routines.*

Now that we've got a handy mechanism for securing DNS transactions, let's talk about securing our whole name server.

Securing Your Name Server

BIND 4.9 introduced several important security features that help you protect your name server. BIND 8 and 9 continued the tradition by adding several more. These features are particularly important if your name server is running on the Internet, but they're also useful on purely internal name servers.

We'll start by discussing measures you should take on all name servers for which security is important. Then we'll describe a model in which your name servers are split into two communities, one for serving only resolvers and one for answering other name servers' queries.

BIND Version

One of the most important ways you can enhance the security of your name server is to run a recent version of BIND. All versions of BIND before 8.2.3 are susceptible to at least a few known attacks. Check the ISC's list of vulnerabilities in various BIND versions at *http://www.isc.org/products/BIND/bind-security.html* for updates.

But don't stop there: new attacks are being thought up all the time, so you'll have to do your best to keep abreast of BIND's vulnerabilities and the latest "safe" version of BIND. One good way to do that is to read the *comp.protocols.dns.bind* newsgroup regularly.

There's another aspect of BIND's version relevant to security: if a hacker can easily find out which version of BIND you're running, he may be able to tailor his attacks to that version of BIND. And, wouldn't you know it, since about BIND 4.9, BIND name servers have replied to a certain query with their version. If you look up TXT records in the CHAOSNET class attached to the domain name *version. bind*, BIND graciously returns something like this:

```
% dig txt chaos version.bind.

; <<>> DiG 9.1.0 <<>> txt chaos version.bind.
;; global options:  printcmd
;; Got answer:
;; ->>HEADER<<- opcode: QUERY, status: NOERROR, id: 34772
;; flags: qr aa rd; QUERY: 1, ANSWER: 1, AUTHORITY: 0, ADDITIONAL: 0

;; QUESTION SECTION:
;version.bind.                    CH        TXT

;; ANSWER SECTION:
version.bind.          0          CH        TXT       "9.1.0"
```

To address this, BIND Versions 8.2 and later let you tailor your name server's response to the *version.bind* query:

```
options {
    version "None of your business";
};
```

Of course, receiving a response like "None of your business" will tip off the alert hacker to the fact that you're likely running BIND 8.2 or better, but that still leaves a number of possibilities.

Restricting Queries

Before BIND 4.9, administrators had no way to control who could look up names on their name servers. That makes a certain amount of sense; the original idea behind DNS was to make information easily available all over the Internet.

The neighborhood is not such a friendly place anymore, though. In particular, people who run Internet firewalls may have a legitimate need to hide certain parts of their namespace from most of the world while making it available to a limited audience.

The BIND 8 and 9 *allow-query* substatement lets you apply an IP address–based access control list to queries. The access control list can apply to queries for data in a particular zone or to any queries received by the name server. In particular, the access control list specifies which IP addresses are allowed to send queries to the server.

Restricting all queries

The global form of the *allow-query* substatement looks like this:

```
options {
        allow-query { address_match_list; };
};
```

So to restrict our name server to answering queries from the three main Movie U. networks, we'd use:

```
options {
        allow-query { 192.249.249/24; 192.253.253/24; 192.253.254/24; };
};
```

Restricting queries in a particular zone

BIND 8 and 9 also allow you to apply an access control list to a particular zone. In this case, just use *allow-query* as a substatement to the *zone* statement for the zone you want to protect:

```
acl "HP-NET" { 15/8; };

zone "hp.com" {
        type slave;
        file "bak.hp.com";
        masters { 15.255.152.2; };
        allow-query { "HP-NET"; };
};
```

Any kind of authoritative name server, master or slave, can apply an access control list to the zone. Zone-specific access control lists take precedence over a global ACL for queries in that zone. The zone-specific access control list may even be more permissive than the global ACL. If there's no zone-specific access control list defined, any global ACL will apply.

In BIND 4.9, this functionality is provided by the *secure_zone* record. Not only does it limit queries for individual resource records, it limits zone transfers, too. (In BIND 8 and 9, restricting zone transfers is done separately.) However, BIND 4.9 name servers have no mechanism for restricting who can send your server queries for data in zones your server is *not* authoritative for; the *secure_zone* mechanism works only with authoritative zones.

To use *secure_zone*, include one or more special TXT records in your zone data on the primary master name server. Conveniently, these records are transferred to the zone's slave servers automatically. Of course, only BIND 4.9 slaves will understand them.

The TXT records are special because they're attached to the pseudo–domain name *secure_zone*, and the resource record–specific data has a special format, too:

    address:mask

or:

    address:H

In the first form, *address* is the dotted-octet form of the IP network to which you want to allow access to the data in this zone. The *mask* is the netmask for that network. If you want to allow all of 15/8 access to your zone data, use 15.0.0.0:255.0.0.0. If you want to allow only the range of IP addresses from 15.254.0.0 to 15.255.255.255 access to your zone data, use 15.254.0.0:255.254.0.0.

The second form specifies the address of a particular host you'd like to allow access to your zone data. The *H* is equivalent to the mask 255.255.255.255; in other words, each bit in the 32-bit address is checked. Therefore, 15.255.152.4:H gives the host with the IP address 15.255.152.4 the ability to look up data in the zone.

If we want to restrict queries for information in *movie.edu* to hosts on Movie U.'s networks, but our name servers run BIND 4.9 instead of BIND 8 or 9, we could add the following lines to *db.movie.edu* on the *movie.edu* primary master:

```
secure_zone     IN     TXT     "192.249.249.0:255.255.255.0"
secure_zone     IN     TXT     "192.253.253.0:255.255.255.0"
secure_zone     IN     TXT     "192.253.254.0:255.255.255.0"
secure_zone     IN     TXT     "127.0.0.1:H"
```

Notice that we included the loopback address (127.0.0.1) in our access control list. That's so a resolver running on the same host as a name server can query the local name server.

If you forget the *:H*, you'll see the following *syslog* message:

```
Aug 17 20:58:22 terminator named[2509]: build_secure_netlist
    (movie.edu): addr (127.0.0.1) is not in mask (0xff000000)
```

Also, note that the *secure_zone* records here apply only to the zone they're in—that is, *movie.edu*. If you wanted to prevent unauthorized queries for data in other zones on this server, you'd have to add *secure_zone* records to those zones on their primary master name servers, too.

Preventing Unauthorized Zone Transfers

Arguably even more important than controlling who can query your name server is ensuring that only your real slave name servers can transfer zones from your name server. Users on remote hosts that can query your name server's zone data can only look up records (e.g., addresses) for domain names they already know, one at a time. Users who can start zone transfers from your server can list all of the records in your zones. It's the difference between letting random folks call your company's switchboard and ask for John Q. Cubicle's phone number and sending them a copy of your corporate phone directory.

BIND 8 and 9's *allow-transfer* substatement and 4.9's *xfrnets* directive let administrators apply an access control list to zone transfers. *allow-transfer* restricts transfers of a particular zone when used as a *zone* substatement, and restricts all zone transfers when used as an *options* substatement. It takes an address match list as an argument.

The slave servers for our *movie.edu* zone have the IP addresses 192.249.249.1 and 192.253.253.1 (*wormhole.movie.edu*) and 192.249.249.9 and 192.253.253.9 (*zardoz. movie.edu*). The following *zone* statement:

```
zone "movie.edu" {
        type master;
        file "db.movie.edu";
        allow-transfer { 192.249.249.1; 192.253.253.1; 192.249.249.9; 192.253.253.9; };
};
```

allows only those slaves to transfer *movie.edu* from the primary master name server. Note that because the default for BIND 8 or 9 is to allow zone transfer requests from any IP address, and because hackers can just as easily transfer the zone from your slaves, you should probably also have a *zone* statement like this on your slaves:

```
zone "movie.edu" {
        type slave;
        masters { 192.249.249.3; };
        file "bak.movie.edu";
        allow-transfer { none; };
};
```

BIND 8 and 9 also let you apply a global access control list to zone transfers. This applies to any zones that don't have their own explicit access control lists defined as *zone* substatements. For example, we might want to limit all zone transfers to our internal IP addresses:

```
options {
        allow-transfer { 192.249.249/24; 192.253.253/24; 192.253.254/24; };
};
```

The BIND 4.9 *xfrnets* directive also applies an access control list to all zone transfers. *xfrnets* takes as its arguments the networks or IP addresses you'd like to allow to transfer zones from your name server. Networks are specified by the dotted-octet form of the network number. For example:

```
xfrnets 15.0.0.0 128.32.0.0
```

allows only hosts on the network 15/8 or the network 128.32/16 to transfer zones from this name server. Unlike the *secure_zone* TXT record, this restriction applies to any zones the server is authoritative for.

If you want to specify just a part of a network, down to a single IP address, you can add a network mask. *network&netmask* is the syntax for including a network mask. Note that spaces aren't allowed between the network and the ampersand or between the ampersand and the netmask.

To pare down the addresses allowed to transfer zones in the previous example to just the IP address 15.255.152.4 and the subnet 128.32.1/24, use the *xfrnets* directive:

```
xfrnets 15.255.152.4&255.255.255.255 128.32.1.0&255.255.255.0
```

Finally, as we mentioned earlier in the chapter, those newfangled BIND 8.2 and later name servers let you restrict zone transfers to slave name servers that include a correct transaction signature with their request. On the master name server, you need to define the key in a key statement and then specify the key in the address match list:

```
key terminator-wormhole. {
    algorithm hmac-md5;
    secret "UNd5xYLjz0FPkoqWRymtgI+paxW927LU/gTrDyulJRI=";
};

zone "movie.edu" {
    type master;
    file "db.movie.edu";
    allow-transfer { key terminator-wormhole.; };
};
```

On the slave's end, you need to configure the slave to sign zone transfer requests with the same key:

```
key terminator-wormhole. {
    algorithm hmac-md5;
    secret "UNd5xYLjz0FPkoqWRymtgI+paxW927LU/gTrDyulJRI=";
};

server 192.249.249.3 {
    keys { terminator-wormhole.; };  // sign all requests to 192.249.249.3
                                     // with this key
};

zone "movie.edu" {
    type slave;
    masters { 192.249.249.3; };
    file "bak.movie.edu";
};
```

For a primary master name server accessible from the Internet, you probably want to limit zone transfers to just your slave name servers. You probably don't need to worry about name servers inside your firewall, unless you're worried about your own employees listing your zone data.

Running BIND with Least Privilege

Running a network server such as BIND as the root user can be dangerous—and BIND normally runs as root. If a hacker finds a vulnerability in the name server through which he can read or write files, he'll have unfettered access to the filesystem. If he can exploit a flaw that allows him to execute commands, he'll execute them as root.

BIND 8.1.2 and later include code that allows you to change the user and group the name server runs as. This allows you to run the name server with what's known as *least privilege*: the minimal set of rights it needs to do its job. That way, if someone breaks into your host through the name server, at least that person won't have root privileges.

BIND 8.1.2 and later also include an option that allows you to *chroot()* the name server: to change its view of the filesystem so that its root directory is actually a particular directory on your host's filesystem. This effectively traps your name server in this directory, along with any attackers who successfully compromise your name server's security.

The command-line options that implement these features are:

−*u* Specifies the username or user ID the name server changes to after starting, e.g., *named −u bin.*

−*g* Specifies the group or group ID the name server changes to after starting, e.g., *named −g other.* If you specify −*u* without −*g*, the name server uses the user's primary group. BIND 9 name servers always change to the user's primary group, so they don't support −*g*.

−*t* Specifies the directory for the name server to *chroot()* to.

If you opt to use the −*u* and −*g* options, you'll have to decide what user and group to use. Your best bet is to create a new user and group for the name server to run as, such as *named.* Since the name server reads *named.conf* before giving up root privileges, you don't have to change that file's permissions. However, you may have to change the permissions and ownership of your zone data files so that the user the name server runs as can read them. If you use dynamic update, you'll have to make the zone data files for dynamically updated zones writable by the name server.

If your name server is configured to log to files (instead of to *syslog*), make sure that those files exist and are writable by the name server before starting the server.

The *–t* option takes a little more specialized configuration. In particular, you need to make sure that all the files *named* uses are present in the directory you're restricting the server to. Here's a procedure to follow to set up your *chroot*ed environment, which we'll assume lives under */var/named:**

1. Create the */var/named* directory, if it doesn't exist. Create *dev*, *etc*, *lib*, *usr*, and *var* subdirectories. Within *usr*, create an *sbin* subdirectory. Within *var*, create subdirectories named *named* and *run*:

   ```
   # mkdir /var/named
   # cd /var/named
   # mkdir -p dev etc lib usr/sbin var/named var/run
   ```

2. Copy *named.conf* to */var/named/etc/named.conf*:

   ```
   # cp /etc/named.conf etc
   ```

3. If you're running BIND 8, copy the *named-xfer* binary to the *usr/sbin/* or *etc* subdirectory (depending on whether you found it in */usr/sbin* or */etc*).

   ```
   # cp /usr/sbin/named-xfer usr/sbin
   ```

   Alternately, you can put it wherever you like under */var/named* and use the *named-xfer* substatement to tell *named* where to find it. Just remember to strip */var/named* off of the pathname, since when *named* reads *named.conf*, */var/named* will look like the root of the filesystem. (If you're running BIND 9, skip this step because BIND 9 doesn't use *named-xfer*.)

4. Create *dev/null* in the *chroot*ed environment:

   ```
   # mknod dev/null c 1 3
   ```

5. If you're running BIND 8, copy the standard, shared C library and the loader to the *lib* subdirectory:

   ```
   # cp /lib/libc.so.6 /lib/ld-2.1.3.so lib
   # ln -s lib/ld-2.1.3.so lib/ld-linux.so.2
   ```

   The pathnames may vary on your operating system. BIND 9 name servers are self-contained.

6. Edit your startup files to start *syslogd* with an additional option and option argument: *–a /var/named/dev/log*. On many modern versions of Unix, *syslogd* is started from */etc/rc.d/init.d/syslog*. When *syslogd* restarts next, it will create */var/named/dev/log*, and *named* will log to it.

   If your *syslogd* doesn't support the *–a* option, use the *logging* statement described in Chapter 7, *Maintaining BIND*, to log to files in the *chroot*ed directory.

---

* This procedure is based on Red Hat Linux 6.2, so if you use a different operating system, your mileage may vary.

7. If you're running BIND 8 and use the *–u* or *–g* options, create *passwd* and *group* files in the *etc* subdirectory to map the arguments of *–u* and *–g* to their numeric values (or just use numeric values as arguments):

```
# echo "named:x:42:42:named:/:" > etc/passwd
# echo "named::42" > etc/group
```

Then add the entries to the system's */etc/passwd* and */etc/group* files. If you're running BIND 9, you can *just* add the entries to the system's */etc/passwd* and */etc/group* files, since BIND 9 name servers read the information they need before calling *chroot( )*.

8. Finally, edit your startup files to start *named* with the *–t* option and option argument: *–t /var/named*. Similarly to *syslogd*, many modern versions of Unix start *named* from */etc/rc.d/init.d/named*.

If you're hooked on using *ndc* to control your BIND 8 name server, you can continue to do so as long as you specify the pathname to the Unix domain socket as the argument to *ndc*'s *–c* option:

```
# ndc -c /var/named/var/run/ndc reload
```

rndc will continue to work as before with your BIND 9 name server since it just talks to the server via port 953.

Split-Function Name Servers

Name servers really have two major roles: answering iterative queries from remote name servers and answering recursive queries from local resolvers. If we separate these roles, dedicating one set of name servers to answering iterative queries and another to answering recursive queries, we can more effectively secure those name servers.

"Delegated" name server configuration

Some of your name servers answer nonrecursive queries from other name servers on the Internet because these name servers appear in NS records delegating your zones to them. We'll call these name servers "delegated" name servers.

There are special measures you can take to secure your delegated name servers. But first, you should make sure that these name servers don't receive any recursive queries (that is, you don't have any resolvers configured to use these servers and no name servers use them as forwarders). Some of the precautions we'll take—like making the server respond nonrecursively even to recursive queries—preclude your resolvers from using these servers. If you do have resolvers using your delegated name servers, consider establishing another class of name servers to serve just your resolvers or using the "Two Name Servers in One" configuration, both described later in this chapter.

Once you know your name server only answers queries from other name servers, you can turn off recursion. This eliminates a major vector of attack: the most common spoofing attacks involve inducing the target name server to query name servers under the hacker's control by sending the target a recursive query for a domain name in a zone served by the hacker's servers. To turn off recursion, use the following statement on a BIND 8 or 9 name server:

```
options {
      recursion no;
};
```

or, on a BIND 4.9 server, use:

```
options no-recursion
```

You should also restrict zone transfers of your zones to known slave servers, as described in the section "Preventing Unauthorized Zone Transfers" earlier in this chapter. Finally, you might also want to turn off glue fetching. Some name servers will automatically try to resolve the domain names of any name servers in NS records; to prevent this from happening and keep your name server from sending any queries of its own, use this on a BIND 8 name server (BIND 9 name servers have glue fetching turned off by default):

```
options {
      fetch-glue no;
};
```

or, on a BIND 4.9 server, use:

```
options no-fetch-glue
```

"Resolving" name server configuration

We'll call a name server that serves one or more resolvers or that is configured as another name server's forwarder a "resolving" name server. Unlike a delegated name server, a resolving name server can't refuse recursive queries. Consequently, we have to configure it a little differently to secure it. Since we know our name server should receive queries only from our own resolvers, we can configure it to deny queries from any but our resolvers' IP addresses.

Only BIND 8 and 9 allow us to restrict which IP addresses can send our name server arbitrary queries. (BIND 4.9 name servers let us restrict which IP addresses can send the server queries in authoritative zones, via the *secure_zone* TXT record, but we're actually more worried about recursive queries in others' zones.) This *allow-query* substatement restricts queries to just our internal network:

```
options {
      allow-query { 192.249.249/24; 192.253.253/24; 192.253.254/24; };
};
```

With this configuration, the only resolvers that can send our name server recursive queries and induce them to query other name servers are our own internal resolvers, which are presumably relatively benevolent.

There's one other option we can use to make our resolving name server a little more secure—*use-id-pool*:

```
options {
    use-id-pool yes;
};
```

use-id-pool was introduced in BIND 8.2. It tells our name server to take special care to use random message IDs in queries. Normally, the message IDs aren't random enough to prevent brute-force attacks that try to guess the IDs our name server has outstanding in order to spoof a response.

The ID pool code became a standard part of BIND 9, so you don't need to specify it on a BIND 9 name server.

Two Name Servers in One

What if you have only one name server to advertise your zones and serve your resolvers, and you can't afford the additional expense of buying another computer to run a second name server on? There are still a few options open to you. Two are single-server solutions that take advantage of the flexibility of BIND 8 and 9. One of these configurations allows anyone to query the name server for information in zones it's authoritative for, but only our internal resolvers can query the name server for other information. While this doesn't prevent remote resolvers from sending our name server recursive queries, those queries have to be in its authoritative zones so they won't induce our name server to send additional queries.

Here's a *named.conf* file to do that:

```
acl "internal" {
    192.249.249/24; 192.253.253/24; 192.253.254/24;
};

acl "slaves" {
    192.249.249.1; 192.253.253.1; 192.249.249.9; 192.253.253.9;
};

options {
    directory "/var/named";
    allow-query { "internal"; };
    use-id-pool yes;
};

zone "movie.edu" {
    type master;
    file "db.movie.edu";
```

```
        allow-query { any; };
        allow-transfer { "slaves"; };
    };

    zone "249.249.192.in-addr.arpa" {
        type master;
        file "db.192.249.249";
        allow-query { any; };
        allow-transfer { "slaves"; };
    };
```

Here, the more permissive zone-specific access control lists apply to queries in the name server's authoritative zones, but the more restrictive global access control list applies to all other queries.

If we were running BIND 8.2.1 or newer, we could simplify this configuration somewhat using the *allow-recursion* substatement:

```
    acl "internal" {
        192.249.249/24; 192.253.253/24; 192.253.254/24;
    };

    acl "slaves" {
        192.249.249.1; 192.253.253.1; 192.249.249.9; 192.253.253.9;
    };

    options {
        directory "/var/named";
        allow-recursion { "internal"; };
        use-id-pool yes;
    };

    zone "movie.edu" {
        type master;
        file "db.movie.edu";
        allow-transfer { "slaves"; };
    };

    zone "249.249.192.in-addr.arpa" {
        type master;
        file "db.192.249.249";
        allow-transfer { "slaves"; };
    };
```

We don't need the *allow-query* substatements anymore: although the name server may receive queries from outside our internal network, it'll treat those queries as nonrecursive, regardless of whether they are or not. Consequently, external queries won't induce our name server to send any queries. This configuration also doesn't suffer from a gotcha the previous setup is susceptible to: if your name server is authoritative for a parent zone, it may receive queries from remote name servers resolving domain names in a subdomain of the zone. The *allow-query* solution will refuse those legitimate queries, but the *allow-recursion* solution won't.

Another option is to run two *named* processes on a single host. One is configured as a delegated name server, another as a resolving name server. Since we have no way of telling remote servers or configuring resolvers to query one of our name servers on a port other than 53, the default DNS port, we have to run these servers on different IP addresses.

Of course, if your host already has more than one network interface, that's no problem. Even if it has only one, the operating system may support IP address aliases. These allow you to attach more than one IP address to a single network interface. One *named* process can listen on each. Finally, if the operating system doesn't support IP aliases, you can still bind one *named* against the network interface's IP address and one against the loopback address. Only the local host will be able to send queries to the instance of *named* listening on the loopback address, but that's fine if the local host's resolver is the only one you need to serve.

First, here's the *named.conf* file for the delegated name server, listening on the network interface's IP address:

```
acl "slaves" {
    192.249.249.1; 192.253.253.1; 192.249.249.9; 192;253.253.9; };
};

options {
    directory "/var/named-delegated";
    recursion no;
    fetch-glue no;
    listen-on { 192.249.249.3; };
    pid-file "/var/run/named.delegated.pid";
};

zone "movie.edu" {
    type master;
    file "db.movie.edu";
    allow-transfer { "slaves"; };
};

zone "249.249.192.in-addr.arpa" {
    type master;
    file "db.192.249.249";
    allow-transfer { "slaves"; };
};

zone "." {
    type hint;
    file "db.cache";
};
```

Next, here's the *named.conf* file for the resolving name server, listening on the loopback address:

```
options {
    directory "/var/named-resolving";
    listen-on { 127.0.0.1; };
```

```
        pid-file "/var/run/named.resolving.pid";
        use-id-pool yes;
};

zone "." {
        type hint;
        file "db.cache";
};
```

Note that we didn't need an access control list for the resolving name server, since it's only listening on the loopback address and can't receive queries from other hosts. (If our resolving name server were listening on an IP alias or a second network interface, we could use *allow-query* to prevent others from using our name server.) We turn recursion off on the delegated name server, but we must leave it on on the resolving name server. We also give each name server its own PID file and its own directory so that the servers don't try to use the same default filename for their PID files, debug files, and statistics files.

To use the resolving name server listening on the loopback address, the local host's *resolv.conf* file must include the following:

```
nameserver 127.0.0.1
```

as the first *nameserver* directive.

If you're running BIND 9, you can even consolidate the two name server configurations into one using views:

```
options {
        directory "/var/named";
};

acl "internal" {
        192.249.249/24; 192.253.253/24; 192.253.254/24;
};

view "internal" {
        match-clients { "internal"; };
        recursion yes;

        zone "movie.edu" {
                type master;
                file "db.movie.edu";
        };

        zone "249.249.192.in-addr.arpa" {
                type master;
                file "db.192.249.249";
        };

        zone "." {
                type hint;
                file "db.cache";
```

```
        };
    };

    view "external" {
        match-clients { any; };
        recursion no;

        zone "movie.edu" {
            type master;
            file "db.movie.edu";
        };

        zone "249.249.192.in-addr.arpa" {
            type master;
            file "db.192.249.249";
        };

        zone "." {
            type hint;
            file "db.cache";
        };
    };
```

It's a fairly simple configuration: two views, internal and external. The internal view, which applies only to our internal network, has recursion on. The external view, which applies to everyone else, has recursion off. The zones *movie.edu* and *249.249.192.in-addr.arpa* are defined identically in both zones. You could do a lot more with it—define different versions of the zones internally and externally, for example—but we'll hold off on that until the next section.

DNS and Internet Firewalls

The Domain Name System wasn't designed to work with Internet firewalls. It's a testimony to the flexibility of DNS and of its BIND implementation that you can configure DNS to work with, or even through, an Internet firewall.

That said, configuring BIND to work in a firewalled environment, although not difficult, takes a good, complete understanding of DNS and a few of BIND's more obscure features. Describing it also requires a large portion of this chapter, so here's a roadmap.

We'll start by describing the two major families of Internet firewall software—packet filters and application gateways. The capabilities of each family have a bearing on how you'll need to configure BIND to work through the firewall. Next, we'll detail the two most common DNS architectures used with firewalls, forwarders and internal roots, and describe the advantages and disadvantages of each. We'll then introduce a solution using a new feature, forward zones, which combines the best of internal roots and forwarders. Finally, we'll discuss split namespaces and the configuration of the bastion host, the host at the core of your firewall system.

Types of Firewall Software

Before you start configuring BIND to work with your firewall, it's important to understand what your firewall is capable of. Your firewall's capabilities will influence your choice of DNS architecture and determine how you implement it. If you don't know the answers to the questions in this section, track down someone in your organization who does know and ask. Better yet, work with your firewall's administrator when designing your DNS architecture to ensure it will coexist with the firewall.

Note that this is far from a complete explanation of Internet firewalls. These few paragraphs describe only the two most common types of Internet firewalls and only in enough detail to show how the differences in their capabilities affect name servers. For a comprehensive treatment of Internet firewalls, see Elizabeth D. Zwicky, Simon Cooper, and D. Brent Chapman's *Building Internet Firewalls* (O'Reilly).

Packet filters

The first type of firewall we'll cover is the packet-filtering firewall. Packet-filtering firewalls operate largely at the transport and network levels of the TCP/IP stack (layers three and four of the OSI reference model, if you dig that). They decide whether to route a packet based on packet-level criteria like the transport protocol (e.g., whether it's TCP or UDP), the source and destination IP address, and the source and destination port (see Figure 11-1).

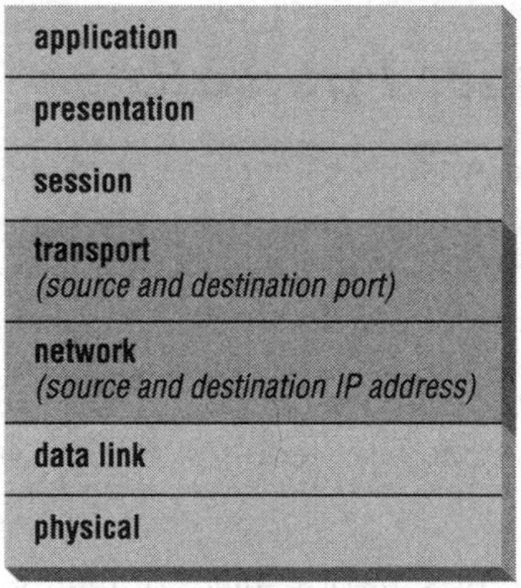

Figure 11-1. Packet filters operate at the network and transport layers of the stack

What's most important to us about packet-filtering firewalls is that you can typically configure them to allow DNS traffic selectively between hosts on the Internet and your internal hosts. That is, you can let an arbitrary set of internal hosts communicate with Internet name servers. Some packet-filtering firewalls can even permit your name servers to query name servers on the Internet, but not vice versa.

All router-based Internet firewalls are packet-filtering firewalls. Checkpoint's Fire-Wall-1, Cisco's PIX, and Sun's SunScreen are popular commercial packet-filtering firewalls.

A Gotcha with BIND 8 or 9
and Packet-Filtering Firewalls

BIND 4 name servers always send queries from port 53, the well-known port for DNS servers, to port 53. Resolvers, on the other hand, usually send queries from high-numbered ports (above 1023) to port 53. Though name servers clearly have to send their queries *to* the DNS port on a remote host, there's no reason they have to send the queries *from* the DNS port. And, wouldn't you know it, BIND 8 and 9 name servers don't send queries from port 53 by default. Instead, they send queries from high-numbered ports, the same as resolvers do.

This can cause problems with packet-filtering firewalls that are configured to allow name server–to–name server traffic but not resolver–to–name server traffic, because they typically expect name server–to–name server traffic to originate from port 53 and terminate at port 53.

There are two solutions to this problem:

- Reconfigure the firewall to allow your name server to send and receive queries from ports other than 53 (assuming this doesn't compromise the security of the firewall by allowing packets from Internet hosts to high-numbered ports on internal name servers).

- Configure BIND to revert to its old behavior with the *query-source* substatement.

query-source takes as arguments an address specification and an optional port number. For example, the statement:

```
options { query-source address * port 53; };
```

tells BIND to use port 53 as the source port for queries sent from all local network interfaces. You can use a nonwildcard address specification to limit the addresses that BIND will send queries from. For example, on *wormhole.movie. edu*, the statement:

```
options { query-source address 192.249.249.1 port *; };
```

tells BIND to send all queries from the 192.249.249.1 address (i.e., not from 192.253.253.1) and to use dynamic, high-numbered ports.

The use of *query-source* with a wildcard address is broken in BIND 9 before 9.1.0, though you can tell an early BIND 9 name server to send all queries from a particular address's port 53.

Application gateways

Application gateways operate at the application protocol level, several layers higher in the OSI reference model than most packet filters (see Figure 11-2). In a sense, they "understand" the application protocol in the same way a server for that particular application would. An FTP application gateway, for example, can make the decision to allow or deny a particular FTP operation, such as a *RETR* (a *get*) or a *STOR* (a *put*).

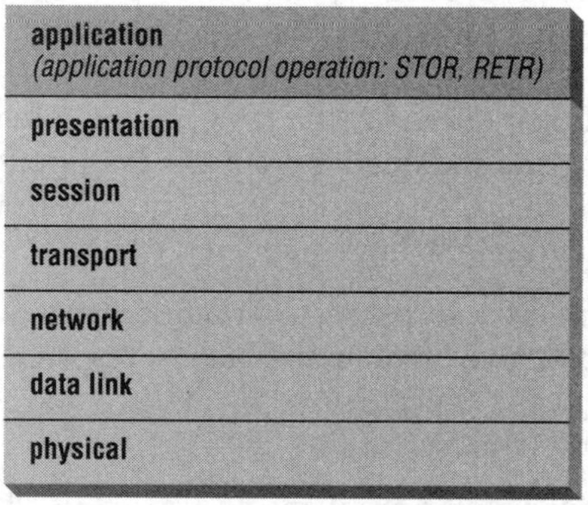

Figure 11-2. Application gateways operate at the application layer of the stack

The bad news, and what's important for our purposes, is that most application gateway–based firewalls handle only TCP-based application protocols. DNS, of course, is largely UDP-based, and we know of no application gateways for DNS. This implies that if you run an application gateway–based firewall, your internal hosts will likely not be able to communicate directly with name servers on the Internet.

The popular Firewall Toolkit from Trusted Information Systems (TIS, now part of Network Associates) is a suite of application gateways for common Internet protocols such as Telnet, FTP, and HTTP. Network Associates' Gauntlet product is also based on application gateways, as is Axent's Eagle Firewall.

Note that these two categories of firewall are really just generalizations. The state of the art in firewalls changes very quickly, and by the time you read this, you may have a firewall that includes an application gateway for DNS. Which family your firewall falls into is important only because it suggests what that firewall is capable of; what's more important is whether your particular firewall will let you permit DNS traffic between arbitrary internal hosts and the Internet.

A Bad Example

The simplest configuration is to allow DNS traffic to pass freely through your firewall (assuming you can configure your firewall to do that). That way, any internal name server can query any name server on the Internet, and any Internet name server can query any of your internal name servers. You don't need any special configuration.

Unfortunately, this is a really bad idea, for a number of reasons:

Version control
> The developers of BIND are constantly finding and fixing security-related bugs in the BIND code. Consequently, it's important to run a recent version of BIND, especially on name servers directly exposed to the Internet. If one or just a few of your name servers communicate directly with name servers on the Internet, upgrading them to a new version is easy. If any of the name servers on your network can communicate directly with name servers on the Internet, upgrading all of them is vastly more difficult.

Possible vector for attack
> Even if you're not running a name server on a particular host, a hacker might be able to take advantage of your allowing DNS traffic through your firewall and attack that host. For example, a co-conspirator working on the inside could set up a Telnet daemon listening on the host's DNS port, allowing the hacker to *telnet* right in.

For the rest of this chapter, we'll try to set a good example.

Internet Forwarders

Given the dangers of allowing bidirectional DNS traffic through the firewall unrestricted, most organizations limit the internal hosts that can "talk DNS" to the Internet. In an application gateway firewall, or any firewall without the ability to pass DNS traffic, the only host that can communicate with Internet name servers is the bastion host (see Figure 11-3).

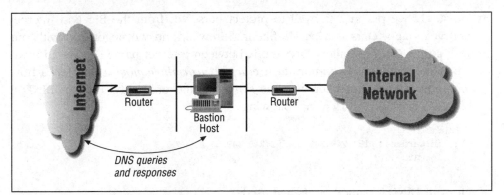

Figure 11-3. A small network, showing the bastion host

In a packet-filtering firewall, the firewall's administrator can configure the firewall to let any set of internal name servers communicate with Internet name servers.

Often, this is a small set of hosts that run name servers under the direct control of the network administrator (see Figure 11-4).

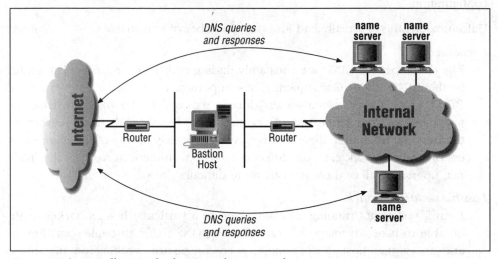

Figure 11-4. A small network, showing select internal name servers

Internal name servers that can directly query name servers on the Internet don't require any special configuration. Their root hints files contain the Internet's root name servers, which enables them to resolve Internet domain names. Internal name servers that *can't* query name servers on the Internet, however, need to know to forward queries they can't resolve to one of the name servers that can. This is done with the *forwarders* directive or substatement, introduced in Chapter 10, *Advanced Features*.

Figure 11-5 illustrates a common forwarding setup, with internal name servers forwarding queries to a name server running on a bastion host.

At Movie U., we put in a firewall to protect ourselves from the Big Bad Internet several years ago. Ours is a packet-filtering firewall, and we negotiated with our firewall administrator to allow DNS traffic between Internet name servers and two of our name servers, *terminator.movie.edu* and *wormhole.movie.edu*. Here's how we configured the other internal name servers at the university. For our BIND 8 and 9 name servers, we used the following:

```
options {
    forwarders { 192.249.249.1; 192.249.249.3; };
    forward only;
};
```

and for our BIND 4 name servers, we used:

```
forwarders 192.249.249.3 192.249.249.1
options forward-only
```

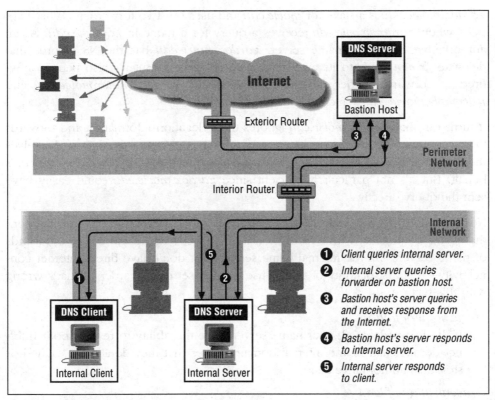

Figure 11-5. Using forwarders

We vary the order in which the forwarders appear to help spread the load between them, though that's not necessary with BIND 8.2.3 name servers, which choose which forwarder to query according to roundtrip time.

When an internal name server receives a query for a name it can't resolve locally, such as an Internet domain name, it forwards that query to one of our forwarders, which can resolve the name using name servers on the Internet. Simple!

The trouble with forwarding

Unfortunately, it's a little too simple. Forwarding starts to get in the way once you delegate subdomains or build an extensive network. To explain what we mean, take a look at part of the configuration file on *zardoz.movie.edu*:

```
options {
    directory "/var/named";
    forwarders { 192.249.249.1; 192.253.253.3; };
};

zone "movie.edu" {
    type slave;
    masters { 192.249.249.3; };
    file "bak.movie.edu";
};
```

zardoz.movie.edu is a slave for *movie.edu* and uses our two forwarders. What happens when *zardoz.movie.edu* receives a query for a name in *fx.movie.edu*? As an authoritative *movie.edu* name server, *zardoz.movie.edu* has the NS records that delegate *fx.movie.edu* to its authoritative name servers. But it's also been configured to forward queries it can't resolve locally to *terminator.movie.edu* and *wormhole.movie.edu*. Which will it do?

It turns out that *zardoz.movie.edu* ignores the delegation information and forwards the query to *terminator.movie.edu*. That works since *terminator.movie.edu* receives the recursive query and asks an *fx.movie.edu* name server on *zardoz.movie.edu*'s behalf. But it's not particularly efficient since *zardoz.movie.edu* could easily have sent the query directly.

Now imagine that the scale of the network is much larger: a corporate network that spans continents, with tens of thousands of hosts and hundreds or thousands of name servers. All the internal name servers that don't have direct Internet connectivity—the vast majority of them—use a small set of forwarders. What's wrong with this picture?

Single point of failure

If the forwarders fail, your name servers lose the ability to resolve both Internet domain names and internal domain names that they don't have cached or stored as authoritative data.

Concentration of load

The forwarders have an enormous query load placed on them. This is both because of the large number of internal name servers that use them, and because the queries are recursive and require a good deal of work to answer.

Inefficient resolution

Imagine two internal name servers, authoritative for *west.acmebw.com* and *east.acmebw.com*, respectively, both on the same network segment in Boulder, Colorado. Both are configured to use the company's forwarder in Bethesda, Maryland. For the *west.acmebw.com* name server to resolve a name in *east.acmebw.com*, it sends a query to the forwarder in Bethesda. The forwarder in Bethesda then sends a query back to Boulder to the *east.acmebw. com* name server, the original querier's neighbor. The *east.acmebw.com* name server replies by sending a response back to Bethesda, which the forwarder sends back to Boulder.

In a traditional configuration with root name servers, the *west.acmebw.com* name server would have learned quickly that an *east.acmebw.com* name server was next door and would favor it (because of its low roundtrip time). Using forwarders "short-circuits" the normally efficient resolution process.

The upshot is that forwarding is fine for small networks and simple namespaces, but probably inadequate for large networks and complex namespaces. We found this out the hard way at Movie U., as our network grew and we were forced to find an alternative.

Using forward zones

We can solve this problem by using the forward zones introduced in BIND 8.2. We change *zardoz.movie.edu*'s configuration to this:

```
options {
    directory "/var/named";
    forwarders { 192.249.249.1; 192.253.253.3; };
};

zone "movie.edu" {
    type slave;
    masters { 192.249.249.3; };
    file "bak.movie.edu";
    forwarders {};
};
```

Now, if *zardoz.movie.edu* receives a query for a domain name ending in *movie.edu* but outside the *movie.edu* zone (e.g., in *fx.movie.edu*), it ignores the forwarders and sends iterative queries.

With this configuration, *zardoz.movie.edu* still sends queries for domain names in our reverse-mapping zones to our forwarders. To relieve that load, we can add a few *zone* statements to *named.conf*:

```
zone "249.249.192.in-addr.arpa" {
    type stub;
    masters { 192.249.249.3; };
    file "stub.192.249.249";
    forwarders {};
};

zone "253.253.192.in-addr.arpa" {
    type stub;
    masters { 192.249.249.3; };
    file "stub.192.253.253";
    forwarders {};
};

zone "254.253.192.in-addr.arpa" {
    type stub;
    masters { 192.253.254.2; };
    file "stub.192.253.254";
    forwarders {};
};
```

```
zone "20.254.192.in-addr.arpa" {
    type stub;
    masters { 192.253.254.2; };
    file "stub.192.254.20";
    forwarders {};
};
```

These new *zone* statements bear some explaining: first of all, they configure Movie U.'s reverse-mapping zones as stubs. That makes our name server track the NS records for those zones by periodically querying the master name servers for those zones. The *forwarders* substatement then turns off forwarding for domain names in the reverse-mapping domains. Now, instead of querying the forwarders for, say, the PTR record for *2.254.253.192.in-addr.arpa, zardoz.movie.edu* will query one of the *254.253.192.in-addr.arpa* name servers directly.

We'll need *zone* statements like these on all of our internal name servers, which also implies that we'll need all of our name servers to run some version of BIND 8 after 8.2.*

This gives us a fairly robust resolution architecture that minimizes our exposure to the Internet: it uses efficient, robust iterative name resolution to resolve internal domain names, and forwarders only when necessary to resolve Internet domain names. If our forwarders fail or we lose our connection to the Internet, we lose only our ability to resolve Internet domain names.

Internal Roots

If you want to avoid the scalability problems of forwarding, you can set up your own root name servers. These internal roots will serve only the name servers in your organization. They'll know about only the portions of the namespace relevant to your organization.

What good are they? By using an architecture based on root name servers, you gain the scalability of the Internet's namespace (which should be good enough for most companies), plus redundancy, distributed load, and efficient resolution. You can have as many internal roots as the Internet has roots—13 or so—whereas having that many forwarders may be an undue security exposure and a configuration burden. Most of all, the internal roots don't get used frivolously. Name servers need to consult an internal root only when they time out the NS records for your top-level zones. Using forwarders, name servers may have to query a forwarder once *per resolution*.

The moral of our story is that if you have, or intend to have, a large namespace and lots of internal name servers, internal root name servers will scale better than any other solution.

---

* As we mentioned in the last chapter, BIND 9 doesn't support forward zones until BIND 9.1.0.

Where to put internal root name servers

Since name servers "lock on" to the closest root name server by favoring the one with the lowest roundtrip time, it pays to pepper your network with internal root name servers. If your organization's network spans the U.S., Europe, and the Pacific Rim, consider locating at least one internal root name server on each continent. If you have three major sites in Europe, give each of them an internal root.

Forward-mapping delegation

Here's how an internal root name server is configured. An internal root delegates directly to any zones you administer. For example, on the *movie.edu* network, the root zone's data file would contain:

```
movie.edu.    86400   IN   NS   terminator.movie.edu.
              86400   IN   NS   wormhole.movie.edu.
              86400   IN   NS   zardoz.movie.edu.
terminator.movie.edu.   86400   IN   A   192.249.249.3
wormhole.movie.edu.     86400   IN   A   192.249.249.1
                        86400   IN   A   192.253.253.1
zardoz.movie.edu.       86400   IN   A   192.249.249.9
                        86400   IN   A   192.253.253.9
```

On the Internet, this information would appear in the *edu* name servers' zone data files. On the *movie.edu* network, of course, there aren't any *edu* name servers, so you delegate directly to *movie.edu* from the root.

Notice that this doesn't contain delegation to *fx.movie.edu* or to any other subdomain of *movie.edu*. The *movie.edu* name servers know which name servers are authoritative for all *movie.edu* subdomains, and all queries for information in those subdomains pass through the *movie.edu* name servers, so there's no need to delegate them here.

in-addr.arpa delegation

We also need to delegate from the internal roots to the *in-addr.arpa* zones that correspond to the networks at the university:

```
249.249.192.in-addr.arpa.   86400   IN   NS   terminator.movie.edu.
                            86400   IN   NS   wormhole.movie.edu.
                            86400   IN   NS   zardoz.movie.edu.
253.253.192.in-addr.arpa.   86400   IN   NS   terminator.movie.edu.
                            86400   IN   NS   wormhole.movie.edu.
                            86400   IN   NS   zardoz.movie.edu.
254.253.192.in-addr.arpa.   86400   IN   NS   bladerunner.fx.movie.edu.
                            86400   IN   NS   outland.fx.movie.edu.
                            86400   IN   NS   alien.fx.movie.edu.
20.254.192.in-addr.arpa.    86400   IN   NS   bladerunner.fx.movie.edu.
                            86400   IN   NS   outland.fx.movie.edu.
                            86400   IN   NS   alien.fx.movie.edu.
```

Notice that we *did* include delegation for the *254.253.192.in-addr.arpa* and the *20.254.192.in-addr.arpa* zones, even though they correspond to the *fx.movie.edu* zone. We don't need to delegate to *fx.movie.edu* because we'd already delegated to its parent, *movie.edu*. The *movie.edu* name servers delegate to *fx.movie.edu*, so by transitivity the roots delegate to *fx.movie.edu*. Since neither of the other *in-addr.arpa* zones is a parent of *254.253.192.in-addr.arpa* or *20.254.192.in-addr.arpa*, we need to delegate both zones from the root. As we explained earlier, we don't need to add address records for the three Special Effects name servers, *bladerunner.fx.movie.edu*, *outland.fx.movie.edu*, and *alien.fx.movie.edu*, because a remote name server can already find their addresses by following delegation from *movie.edu*.

The db.root file

All that's left is to add an SOA record for the root zone and NS records for this internal root name server and any others:

```
$TTL 1d
. IN SOA rainman.movie.edu. hostmaster.movie.edu. (
            1    ; serial
            3h   ; refresh
            1h   ; retry
            1w   ; expire
            1h ) ; negative caching TTL

    IN NS rainman.movie.edu.
    IN NS awakenings.movie.edu.

rainman.movie.edu.    IN A 192.249.249.254
awakenings.movie.edu. IN A 192.253.253.254
```

rainman.movie.edu and *awakenings.movie.edu* are the hosts running the internal root name servers. We shouldn't run an internal root on a bastion host, because if a name server on the Internet accidentally queries it for data it's not authoritative for, the internal root will respond with its list of roots—all internal!

So the whole *db.root* file (by convention, we call the root zone's data file *db.root*) looks like this:

```
$TTL 1d
. IN SOA rainman.movie.edu. hostmaster.movie.edu. (
            1    ; serial
            3h   ; refresh
            1h   ; retry
            1w   ; expire
            1h ) ; negative caching TTL

    IN NS rainman.movie.edu.
    IN NS awakenings.movie.edu.
```

```
rainman.movie.edu.     IN  A  192.249.249.254
awakenings.movie.edu.  IN  A  192.253.253.254

movie.edu.   IN  NS  terminator.movie.edu.
             IN  NS  wormhole.movie.edu.
             IN  NS  zardoz.movie.edu.

terminator.movie.edu.  IN  A  192.249.249.3
wormhole.movie.edu.    IN  A  192.249.249.1
                       IN  A  192.253.253.1
zardoz.movie.edu.      IN  A  192.249.249.9
                       IN  A  192.253.253.9

249.249.192.in-addr.arpa.  IN  NS  terminator.movie.edu.
                           IN  NS  wormhole.movie.edu.
                           IN  NS  zardoz.movie.edu.
253.253.192.in-addr.arpa.  IN  NS  terminator.movie.edu.
                           IN  NS  wormhole.movie.edu.
                           IN  NS  zardoz.movie.edu.
254.253.192.in-addr.arpa.  IN  NS  bladerunner.fx.movie.edu.
                           IN  NS  outland.fx.movie.edu.
                           IN  NS  alien.fx.movie.edu.
20.254.192.in-addr.arpa.   IN  NS  bladerunner.fx.movie.edu.
                           IN  NS  outland.fx.movie.edu.
                           IN  NS  alien.fx.movie.edu.
```

The *named.conf* file on both the internal root name servers, *rainman.movie.edu* and *awakenings.movie.edu,* contains the lines:

```
zone "." {
    type master;
    file "db.root";
};
```

Or, for a BIND 4 server's *named.boot* file:

```
primary    .    db.root
```

This replaces a *zone* statement of type *hint* or a *cache* directive—a root name server doesn't need a root hints file to tell it where the other roots are; it can find that in *db.root.* Did we really mean that each root name server is a primary master for the root zone? Not unless you're running an ancient version of BIND. All BIND versions after 4.9 let you declare a server as a slave for the root zone, but BIND 4. 8.3 and earlier insist that all root name servers load the root zone as primaries.

If you don't have a lot of idle hosts sitting around that you can turn into internal roots, don't despair! Any internal name server (i.e., one that's not running on a bastion host or outside your firewall) can serve double duty as an internal root *and* as an authoritative name server for whatever other zones you need it to load. Remember, a single name server can be authoritative for many, many zones, including the root zone.

Configuring other internal name servers

Once you've set up internal root name servers, configure all your name servers on hosts anywhere on your internal network to use them. Any name server running on a host without direct Internet connectivity (i.e., behind the firewall) should list the internal roots in its root hints file:

```
; Internal root hints file, for Movie U. hosts without direct
; Internet connectivity
;
; Don't use this file on a host with Internet connectivity!
;

.   99999999  IN  NS  rainman.movie.edu.
    99999999  IN  NS  awakenings.movie.edu.

rainman.movie.edu.      99999999  IN  A  192.249.249.254
awakenings.movie.edu.   99999999  IN  A  192.253.253.254
```

Name servers running on hosts using this root hints file will be able to resolve domain names in *movie.edu* and in Movie U.'s *in-addr.arpa* domains, but not outside those domains.

How internal name servers use internal roots

To tie together how this whole scheme works, let's go through an example of name resolution on an internal caching-only name server using these internal root name servers. First, the internal name server receives a query for a domain name in *movie.edu*, say the address of *gump.fx.movie.edu*. If the internal name server doesn't have any "better" information cached, it starts by querying an internal root name server. If it has communicated with the internal roots before, it has a roundtrip time associated with each, telling it which of the internal roots is responding to it most quickly. It then sends a nonrecursive query to that internal root for *gump.fx.movie.edu*'s address. The internal root answers with a referral to the *movie.edu* name servers on *terminator.movie.edu*, *wormhole.movie.edu*, and *zardoz.movie.edu*. The caching-only name server follows up by sending another nonrecursive query to one of the *movie.edu* name servers for *gump.fx.movie.edu*'s address. The *movie.edu* name server responds with a referral to the *fx.movie.edu* name servers. The caching-only name server sends the same nonrecursive query for *gump.fx.movie.edu*'s address to one of the *fx.movie.edu* name servers and finally receives a response.

Contrast this with the way a forwarding setup would work. Let's imagine that instead of using internal root name servers, our caching-only name server were configured to forward queries first to *terminator.movie.edu* and then to *wormhole. movie.edu*. In that case, the caching-only name server would check its cache for the address of *gump.fx.movie.edu* and, not finding it, would forward the query to *terminator.movie.edu*. Then, *terminator.movie.edu* would query an *fx.movie.edu* name server on the caching-only name server's behalf and return the answer. Should the caching-only name server need to look up another name in *fx.movie. edu*, it would still ask the forwarder, even though the forwarder's response to the query for *gump.fx.movie.edu*'s address probably contains the names and addresses of the *fx.movie.edu* name servers.

Mail from internal hosts to the Internet

But wait! That's not all internal roots will do for you. We talked about getting mail to the Internet without changing *sendmail*'s configuration all over the network.

Wildcard records are the key to getting mail to work—specifically, wildcard MX records. Let's say that we want mail to the Internet to be forwarded through *postmanrings2x.movie.edu*, the Movie U. bastion host, which has direct Internet connectivity. Adding the following records to *db.root* will get the job done:

```
*        IN    MX    5 postmanrings2x.movie.edu.
*.edu.   IN    MX    10 postmanrings2x.movie.edu.
```

We need the **.edu* MX record in addition to the *** record because of wildcard production rules, which you can read more about in the "Wildcards" section of Chapter 16, *Miscellaneous*. Basically, since there is explicit data for *movie.edu* in the zone, the first wildcard won't match *movie.edu* or any other subdomains of *edu*. We need another, explicit wildcard record for *edu* to match subdomains of *edu* besides *movie.edu*.

Now mailers on our internal *movie.edu* hosts will send mail addressed to Internet domain names to *postmanrings2x.movie.edu* for forwarding. For example, mail addressed to *nic.ddn.mil* will match the first wildcard MX record:

```
% nslookup -type=mx nic.ddn.mil.   —Matches the MX record for *
Server:  rainman.movie.edu
Address:  192.249.249.19

nic.ddn.mil
      preference = 5, mail exchanger = postmanrings2x.movie.edu
postmanrings2x.movie.edu    internet address = 192.249.249.20
```

Mail addressed to *vangogh.cs.berkeley.edu* will match the second MX record:

```
% nslookup -type=mx vangogh.cs.berkeley.edu.   —Matches the MX record for *.edu
Server:  rainman.movie.edu
Address:  192.249.249.19

vangogh.cs.berkeley.edu
      preference = 10, mail exchanger = postmanrings2x.movie.edu
postmanrings2x.movie.edu    internet address = 192.249.249.20
```

Once the mail has reached *postmanrings2x.movie.edu*, our bastion host, *postmanrings2x.movie.edu*'s mailer will look up the MX records for these addresses itself. Since *postmanrings2x.movie.edu* will resolve the destination's domain name using the Internet's namespace instead of the internal namespace, it will find the real MX records for the domain name and deliver the mail. No changes to *sendmail*'s configuration are necessary.

Mail to specific Internet domain names

Another nice perk of this internal root scheme is that it gives you the ability to forward mail addressed to certain Internet domain names through particular bastion hosts, if you have more than one. We can choose, for example, to send all mail addressed to recipients in the *uk* domain to our bastion host in London first and then out onto the Internet. This can be very useful if we want our mail to travel across our own network as far as possible or if we're billed for our usage of some network in the U.K.

Movie U. has a private network connection to our sister university in London near Pinewood Studios. For security reasons, we'd like to send mail addressed to correspondents in the U.K. across our private link and then through the Pinewood host. So we add the following wildcard records to *db.root*:

```
; holygrail.movie.ac.uk is at the other end of our U.K. Internet link
*.uk.    IN    MX    10 holygrail.movie.ac.uk.
holygrail.movie.ac.uk.    IN    A    192.168.76.4
```

Now, mail addressed to users in subdomains of *uk* will be forwarded to the host *holygrail.movie.ac.uk* at our sister university, which presumably has facilities to forward that mail to other points in the U.K.

The trouble with internal roots

Unfortunately, just as forwarding has its problems, internal root architectures have their limitations. Chief among these is the fact that your internal hosts can't see the Internet namespace. On some networks, this isn't an issue because most internal hosts don't have any direct Internet connectivity. The few that do can have their resolvers configured to use a name server on the bastion host. Some of these hosts will probably need to run proxy servers to allow other internal hosts access to services on the Internet.

On other networks, however, the Internet firewall or other software may require that all internal hosts have the ability to resolve names in the Internet's namespace. For these networks, an internal root architecture won't work.

A Split Namespace

Many organizations would like to advertise different zone data to the Internet than they advertise internally. In most cases, much of the internal zone data is irrelevant to the Internet because of the organization's Internet firewall. The firewall may not allow direct access to most internal hosts, and may also translate internal, unregistered IP addresses into a range of IP addresses registered to the organization. Therefore, the organization might need to trim out irrelevant information from the external view of the zone or change internal addresses to their external equivalents.

Unfortunately, BIND doesn't support automatic filtering and translation of zone data. Consequently, many organizations manually create what have become known as "split namespaces." In a split namespace, the real namespace is available only internally, while a pared-down, translated version of it called the *shadow namespace* is visible to the Internet.

The shadow namespace contains the name-to-address and address-to-name mappings of only those hosts accessible from the Internet through the firewall. The addresses advertised may be the translated equivalents of internal addresses. The shadow namespace may also contain one or more MX records to direct mail from the Internet through the firewall to a mail server.

Since Movie U. has an Internet firewall that greatly limits access from the Internet to the internal network, we elected to create a shadow namespace. For the zone *movie.edu*, the only information we need to give out is about the domain name *movie.edu* (an SOA record and a few NS records), the bastion host (*postmanrings2x.movie.edu*), and our new external name server, *ns.movie.edu*, which also functions as an external web server, *www.movie.edu*. The address of the external interface on the bastion host is 200.1.4.2, and the address of the name/web server is 200.1.4.3. The shadow *movie.edu* zone data file looks like this:

```
$TTL 1d
@       IN   SOA    ns.movie.edu.    hostmaster.movie.edu. (
                              1    ; Serial
                              3h   ; Refresh
                              1h   ; Retry
                              1w   ; Expire
                              1h ) ; Negative caching TTL


        IN   NS     ns.movie.edu.
        IN   NS     ns1.isp.net.         ; our ISP's name server is a movie.edu slave

        IN   A      200.1.4.3
        IN   MX     10 postmanrings2x.movie.edu.
        IN   MX     100 mail.isp.net.

www             IN   CNAME movie.edu.

postmanrings2x  IN   A      200.1.4.2
                IN   MX     10 postmanrings2x.movie.edu.
                IN   MX     100 mail.isp.net.
```

```
;postmanrings2x.movie.edu handles mail addressed to ns.movie.edu
ns              IN   A    200.1.4.3
                IN   MX   10 postmanrings2x.movie.edu.
                IN   MX   100 mail.isp.net.

*               IN   MX   10 postmanrings2x.movie.edu.
                IN   MX   100 mail.isp.net.
```

Note that there's no mention of any of the subdomains of *movie.edu*, including any delegation to the name servers for those subdomains. The information simply isn't necessary since there's nothing in any of the subdomains that you can get to from the Internet, and inbound mail addressed to hosts in the subdomains is caught by the wildcard.

The *db.200.1.4* file, which we need in order to reverse map the two Movie U. IP addresses that hosts on the Internet might see, looks like this:

```
$TTL 1d
@   IN   SOA   ns.movie.edu.   hostmaster.movie.edu. (
                        1    ; Serial
                        3h   ; Refresh
                        1h   ; Retry
                        1w   ; Expire
                        1h ) ; Negative caching TTL

    IN   NS    ns.movie.edu.
    IN   NS    ns.isp.net.

2   IN   PTR   postmanrings2x.movie.edu.
3   IN   PTR   ns1.movie.edu.
```

One precaution we have to take is to make sure that the resolver on our bastion host isn't configured to use the server on *ns.movie.edu*. Since that server can't see the real, internal *movie.edu*, using it would render *postmanrings2x.movie.edu* unable to map internal domain names to addresses or internal addresses to names.

Configuring the bastion host

The bastion host is a special case in a split namespace configuration. It has a foot in each environment: one network interface connects it to the Internet and another connects it to the internal network. Now that we have split our namespace in two, how can our bastion host see both the Internet namespace and our real internal namespace? If we configure it with the Internet's root name servers in its root hints file, it will follow delegation from the Internet's *edu* name servers to an external *movie.edu* name server with shadow zone data. It would be blind to our internal namespace, which it needs to see to log connections, deliver inbound mail, and more. On the other hand, if we configure it with our internal roots, then it won't see the Internet's namespace, which it clearly needs to do in order to function as a bastion host. What to do?

If we have internal name servers that can resolve both internal and Internet domain names—using forward zones per the configuration earlier in this chapter, for example—we can simply configure the bastion host's resolver to query those name servers. But if we use forwarding internally, depending on the type of firewall we're running, we may also need to run a forwarder on the bastion host itself. If the firewall won't pass DNS traffic, we'll need to run at least a caching-only name server, configured with the Internet roots, on the bastion host so that our internal name servers will have somewhere to forward their unresolved queries.

If our internal name servers don't support forward zones, the name server on our bastion host must be configured as a slave for *movie.edu* and any *in-addr.arpa* zones in which it needs to resolve addresses. This way, if it receives a query for a domain name in *movie.edu*, it uses its local authoritative data to resolve the name. (If our internal name servers support forward zones and are configured correctly, the name server on our bastion host will never receive queries for names in *movie. edu.*) If the domain name is in a delegated subdomain of *movie.edu*, it follows NS records in the zone data to query an internal name server for the name. Therefore, it doesn't need to be configured as a slave for any *movie.edu* subdomains, such as *fx.movie.edu*, just the "topmost" zone (see Figure 11-6).

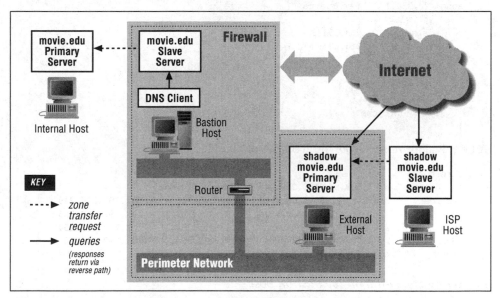

Figure 11-6. A split DNS solution

The *named.conf* file on our bastion host looks like this:

```
options {
    directory "/var/named";
};
```

```
zone "movie.edu" {
    type slave;
    masters { 192.249.249.3; };
    file "bak.movie.edu";
};

zone "249.249.192.in-addr.arpa" {
    type slave;
    masters { 192.249.249.3; };
    file "bak.192.249.249";
};

zone "253.253.192.in-addr.arpa" {
    type slave;
    masters { 192.249.249.3; };
    file "bak.192.253.253";
};

zone "254.253.192.in-addr.arpa" {
    type slave;
    masters { 192.253.254.2; };
    file "bak.192.253.254";
};

zone "20.254.192.in-addr.arpa" {
    type slave;
    masters { 192.253.254.2; };
    file "bak.192.254.20";
};

zone "." {
    type hint;
    file "db.cache";
};
```

An equivalent *named.boot* file would look like this:

```
directory    /var/named
secondary    movie.edu      192.249.249.3    bak.movie.edu
secondary    249.249.192.in-addr.arpa    192.249.249.3    bak.192.249.249
secondary    253.253.192.in-addr.arpa    192.249.249.3    bak.192.253.253
secondary    254.253.192.in-addr.arpa    192.253.254.2    bak.192.253.254
secondary    20.254.192.in-addr.arpa     192.253.254.2    bak.192.254.20
cache    .    db.cache    ; lists Internet roots
```

Protecting zone data on the bastion host

Unfortunately, loading these zones on the bastion host also exposes them to the possibility of disclosure on the Internet, which we were trying to avoid by splitting the namespace in the first place. But as long as we're running BIND 4.9 or better, we can protect the zone data using the *secure_zone* TXT record or the *allow-query* substatement, both discussed earlier in the chapter. With *allow-query,* we can place a global access list on our zone data. Here's the new *options* statement from our *named.conf* file:

```
options {
    directory "/var/named";
    allow-query { 127/8; 192.249.249/24; 192.253.253/24;
        192.253.254/24; 192.254.20/24; };
};
```

With BIND 4.9's *secure_zone* feature, we can turn off all external access to our zone data by including these TXT records in each zone data file:

```
secure_zone     IN     TXT     "192.249.249.0:255.255.255.0"
                IN     TXT     "192.253.253.0:255.255.255.0"
                IN     TXT     "192.253.254.0:255.255.255.0"
                IN     TXT     "192.254.20.0:255.255.255.0"
                IN     TXT     "127.0.0.1:H"
```

Don't forget to include the loopback address in the list, or the bastion host's resolver may not get answers from its own name server!

The final configuration

Finally, we need to apply the other security precautions we discussed earlier to our bastion host's name server. In particular, we should:

- Restrict zone transfers
- Use the ID pool feature (on BIND 8.2 or newer name servers but not BIND 9)
- (Optionally) Run BIND *chroot*ed and with least privilege

In the end, our *named.conf* file ends up looking like this:

```
acl "internal" {
    127/8; 192.249.249/24; 192.253.253/24;
    192.253.254/24; 192.254.20/24;
};

options {
    directory "/var/named";
    allow-query { "internal"; };
    allow-transfer { none; };
    use-id-pool yes;
};

zone "movie.edu" {
    type slave;
    masters { 192.249.249.3; };
    file "bak.movie.edu";
};

zone "249.249.192.in-addr.arpa" {
    type slave;
    masters { 192.249.249.3; };
```

```
        file "bak.192.249.249";
    };

    zone "253.253.192.in-addr.arpa" {
        type slave;
        masters { 192.249.249.3; };
        file "bak.192.253.253";
    };

    zone "254.253.192.in-addr.arpa" {
        type slave;
        masters { 192.253.254.2; };
        file "bak.192.253.254";
    };

    zone "20.254.192.in-addr.arpa" {
        type slave;
        masters { 192.253.254.2; };
        file "bak.192.254.20";
    };

    zone "." {
        type hint;
        file "db.cache";
    };
```

Using views on the bastion host

If we're running BIND 9 on our bastion host, we can use views to safely present
the shadow *movie.edu* to the outside world on the same name server that resolves
Internet domain names. That may obviate the need to run an external name server
on the same host as our web server, *www.movie.edu*. If not, it'll give us two name
servers to advertise the external *movie.edu*.

This configuration is very similar to one shown in the section on "Views" in
Chapter 10:

```
    options {
        directory "/var/named";
    };

    acl "internal" {
        127/8; 192.249.249/24; 192.253.253/24; 192.253.254/24; 192.254.20/24;
    };

    view "internal" {
        match-clients { "internal"; };
        recursion yes;

        zone "movie.edu" {
            type slave;
            masters { 192.249.249.3; };
            file "bak.movie.edu";
        };
```

```
        zone "249.249.192.in-addr.arpa" {
            type slave;
            masters { 192.249.249.3; };
            file "bak.192.249.249";
        };

        zone "253.253.192.in-addr.arpa" {
            type slave;
            masters { 192.249.249.3; };
            file "bak.192.253.253";
        };

        zone "254.253.192.in-addr.arpa" {
            type slave;
            masters { 192.253.254.2; };
            file "bak.192.253.254";
        };

        zone "20.254.192.in-addr.arpa" {
            type slave;
            masters { 192.253.254.2; };
            file "bak.192.254.20";
        };

        zone "." {
            type hint;
            file "db.cache";
        };
    };

    view "external" {
        match-clients { any; };
        recursion no;

        acl "ns1.isp.net" { 199.11.28.12; };

        zone "movie.edu" {
            type master;
            file "db.movie.edu.external";
            allow-transfer { "ns1.isp.net"; };
        };

        zone "4.1.200.in-addr.arpa" {
            type master;
            file "db.200.1.4";
            allow-transfer { "ns1.isp.net"; };
        };

        zone "." {
            type hint;
            file "db.cache";
        };
    };
```

Notice that the internal and external views present different versions of *movie.edu*: one loaded from the zone data file *db.movie.edu*, and one loaded from *db.movie. edu.external*. If there were more than a few zones in our external view, we probably would have used a different subdirectory for our external zone data files than we used for the internal zone data files.

The DNS Security Extensions

TSIG, which we described earlier in this chapter, is well suited to securing the communications between two name servers or between an updater and a name server. However, it won't protect you if one of your name servers is compromised: if someone breaks into the host that runs one of your name servers, he may also gain access to its TSIG keys. Moreover, because TSIG uses shared secrets, it isn't practical to configure TSIG among many name servers. You couldn't use TSIG to secure your name servers' communications with arbitrary name servers on the Internet because you can't distribute and manage that many keys.

The most common way to deal with key management problems like these is to use *public key cryptography*. The DNS Security Extensions, described in RFC 2535, use public key cryptography to enable zone administrators to digitally sign their zone data, thereby proving its authenticity.

Note: we'll describe the DNS Security Extensions, or DNSSEC, in their current form as described by RFC 2535. However, the IETF's DNSEXT working group is still working on DNSSEC and may change aspects of it before it becomes a standard.

Another note: though BIND 8 provided preliminary support of DNS-SEC as early as BIND 8.2,* DNSSEC wasn't really usable before BIND 9. Consequently, we'll use BIND 9 in our examples. If you want to use DNSSEC, you really shouldn't use anything older.

Public Key Cryptography and Digital Signatures

Public key cryptography solves the key distribution problem by using asymmetric cryptographic algorithms. In an asymmetric cryptographic algorithm, one key is used to decrypt data that another has encrypted. These two keys—a *key pair*—are

---

* In particular, BIND 8 can't follow a chain of trust. It can verify SIG records only in zones it has *trusted-keys* statements for.

generated at the same time using a mathematical formula. That's the only easy way to find two keys that have this special asymmetry (one decrypts what the other encrypts): it's very difficult to determine one key given the other. (In the most popular asymmetric cryptographic algorithm, RSA, that determination involves factoring very large numbers.)

In public key cryptography, an individual first generates a key pair. Then one key of the key pair is made public (e.g., published in a directory) while the other is kept private. Someone who wants to communicate securely with that individual can encrypt a message with the individual's public key and then send the encrypted message to the individual. (Or he could even post the message to a newsgroup or on a web site.) If the recipient has kept his private key private, only he can decrypt the message.

Conversely, the individual can encrypt a message with his private key and send it to someone. The recipient can verify that it came from the individual by attempting to decrypt it with the individual's public key. If the message decrypts to something reasonable (i.e., not gibberish) and the sender kept his private key to himself, then the individual must have encrypted it. Successful decryption also proves that the message wasn't modified in transit (e.g., while passing through a mail server), because if it had been, it wouldn't have decrypted correctly. So the recipient has authenticated the message.

Unfortunately, encrypting large amounts of data with asymmetric encryption algorithms tends to be slow—much slower than encryption using symmetric encryption algorithms. But when using public key encryption for authentication (and not for privacy), we don't have to encrypt the whole message. Instead, we run the message through a one-way hash function first. Then we can encrypt just the hash value, which represents the original data. We attach the encrypted hash value, now called a *digital signature*, to the message we want to authenticate. The recipient can still authenticate the message by decrypting the digital signature and running the message through her own copy of the one-way hash function. If the hash values match, the message is authentic. The process of signing and verifying a message is shown in Figure 11-7.

The KEY Record

In the DNS Security Extensions, or DNSSEC, each secure zone has a key pair associated with it. The zone's private key is stored somewhere safe, often in a file on the name server's filesystem. The zone's public key is advertised as a new type of record attached to the domain name of the zone, the KEY record.

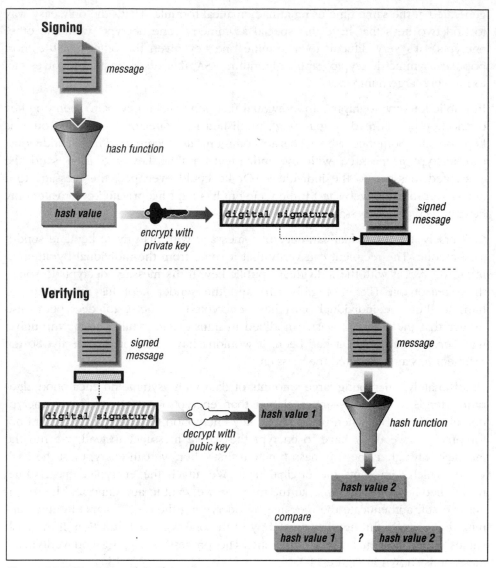

Figure 11-7. Signing and verifying a message

The KEY record is actually a general-purpose record, as we'll see when we dissect one. You can use the KEY record to store different kinds of cryptographic keys, not just zones' public keys for use with DNSSEC. However, the only use we're going to explore in this book is to store a zone's public key.

A KEY record looks like this:

```
movie.edu.  IN KEY 256 3 1 AQPdWbrGbVv1eDhNgRhpJMPonJfA3reyEo82ekwRnjbX7+uBxB11Bq
L7 LAB7/C+eb0vCtI53FwMhkkNkTmA6bI8B
```

The owner is the domain name of the zone that owns this public key. The first field after the type, 256, is the flags field. The flags field is two bytes long and encodes a set of one- and two-bit values:

```
  0   1   2   3   4   5   6   7   8   9   0   1   2   3   4   5
+---+---+---+---+---+---+---+---+---+---+---+---+---+---+---+---+
| A/C   | Z | XT| Z | Z | NAMTYP| Z | Z | Z | Z |     SIG       |
+---+---+---+---+---+---+---+---+---+---+---+---+---+---+---+---+
```

If the value of the first bit is zero, the key can be used for authentication. Clearly, a key that we can't use for authentication isn't very useful in DNSSEC, so that bit is always zero.

If the value of the second bit is zero, the key can be used for confidentiality. DNSSEC doesn't make your zone data private, but also doesn't prohibit you from using your zone's public key for confidentiality, so this bit is always zero for a zone's public key.

A KEY record in which the first two bits are set to one is called a *null key*. Later on, we'll show you how null keys are used in parent zones.

The third bit is reserved for future use. For now, its value must be zero. The fourth bit is a "flag extension" bit. It's designed to provide future expandability. If it's set, the KEY record must include another two-byte field after the algorithm field (the third field after the type) and before the public key itself (normally the fourth field). The meanings of the bits in that additional two-byte field haven't been defined yet, so for now the fourth bit is always zero. Like the third bit, the fifth and sixth bits are reserved and must be zero.

The seventh and eighth bits encode the type of key:

00

> This is a user's key. A mail user agent might use a user's key to encrypt email addressed to that user. This type of key isn't used in DNSSEC.

01

> This is a zone's public key. All DNSSEC keys are this type of key.

10

> This is a host's key. An IPSEC implementation might use a host's key to encrypt all IP packets sent to that host. DNSSEC doesn't use host keys.

11

> Reserved for future use.

The ninth through twelfth bits are reserved and must be zero. The last four bits are the signatory field, which is now obsolete.

In the KEY record shown earlier, the flags field (the first field in the record after the type) says that this KEY is *movie.edu*'s zone key and can be used for authentication and confidentiality.

The next field in the record, which in the example has the value 3, is called the *protocol octet*. Since you can use KEY records for different purposes, you have to specify which purpose a particular key is intended for. The following values are defined:

0   Reserved.

1   This key is used with Transport Layer Security (TLS), as described in RFC 2246.

2   This key is used in connection with email, e.g., an S/MIME key.

3   This key is used with DNSSEC. All DNSSEC keys, obviously, will have a protocol octet of 3.

4   This key is used with IPSEC.

255
      This key is used with any protocol that can use a KEY record.

All of the values between 4 and 255 are available for future assignment.

The next (third) field in the KEY record, which here has the value 1, is the algorithm number. DNSSEC can work with a number of public key encryption algorithms, so you need to identify which algorithm a zone uses and which algorithm this key is used with here. The following values are defined:

0   Reserved.

1   RSA/MD5. RFC 2535 recommends, but doesn't require, the use of RSA/MD5. However, RSA is very popular and the patent covering the RSA algorithm recently ran out, so there has been some discussion of making the use of RSA mandatory.

2   Diffie-Hellman. RFC 2535 makes using Diffie-Hellman optional.

3   DSA. RFC 2535 makes *support* (not use) of DSA mandatory. However, as noted earlier, this may change soon.

4   Reserved for an elliptic curve–based public key algorithm.

We'll use RSA keys in our examples because we think RSA keys are likely to become the standard.

The final field in the KEY record is the public key itself, encoded in base 64. DNSSEC supports keys of many lengths, as we'll see shortly when we generate the *movie.edu* public key. The longer the key, the harder it is to find the corresponding private key, but the longer it takes to sign zone data with the private key and verify it with the public key.

Null keys don't have a public key, though they do have a protocol octet and an algorithm number.

The SIG Record

If the KEY record stores a zone's public key, then there must be a new record to store the corresponding private key's signature, right? Sure enough, that's the SIG record. The SIG record stores the private key's digital signature on an *RRset*. An RRset is a group of resource records with the same owner, class, and type; for example, all of *wormhole.movie.edu*'s address records make up an RRset. Likewise, all of *movie.edu*'s MX records are another RRset.

Why sign RRsets rather than individual records? It saves time. There's no way to look up just one of *wormhole.movie.edu*'s address records; a name server will always return them as a group. So why go to the trouble of signing each one individually when you can sign them together?

Here's the SIG record that "covers" *wormhole.movie.edu*'s address records:

```
wormhole.movie.edu.              SIG    A 1 3 86400 20010102235426 (
                                 20001203235426 27791 movie.edu.
                                 1S/LuuxhSHs2LknPC7K/7v4+PNxESKZnjX6CtgGLZDWf
                                 Rmovkw9VpW7htTNJYhzlFck/BO/k17tRj0fbQ6JWaA== )
```

The owner name is *wormhole.movie.edu*, the same as the owner of the records signed. The first field after the type, which holds the value A, is called the *type covered*. That tells us which of *wormhole.movie.edu*'s records were signed; in this case, its address records. There would be a separate SIG record for each type of record *wormhole.movie.edu* might own.

The second field, which has the value 1, is the algorithm number. This is one of the same values used in the KEY record's algorithm number field, so 1 means RSA/MD5. If you generate an RSA key and use it to sign your zone, you'll get RSA/MD5 signatures, naturally. If you sign your zone with multiple types of keys, say an RSA key and a DSA key, you'll end up with two SIG records for each RRset, one with an algorithm number of 1 (RSA/MD5) and one with an algorithm number of 3 (DSA).[*]

The third field is called the *labels field*. It indicates how many labels there are in the owner name of the records signed. *wormhole.movie.edu* obviously has three labels, so the labels field contains 3. When would the labels field ever differ from the number of labels in the SIG's owner? When the SIG record covered a wildcard

---

[*] You might sign your zone with two different algorithms' keys so that people whose software supported only DSA could verify your data while people who preferred RSA could use RSA.

record of some type. Unfortunately (or maybe fortunately, for our sanity's sake), BIND doesn't support wildcard records in secure zones.

The fourth field is the original TTL on the records in the RRset that was signed. (All the records in an RRset are supposed to have the same TTL.) The TTL needs to be stored here because a name server caching the RRset that this SIG record covers will decrement the TTLs on the cached records. Without the original TTL, it's impossible to feed the original address records through the one-way hash function in their original state to verify the digital signature.

The next two fields are the signature expiration and inception fields, respectively. They're both stored as an unsigned integer number of seconds since the Unix epoch, January 1, 1970, but in the SIG record's text representation, they're presented in the format YYYYMMDDHHMMSS for convenience. (The signature expiration time for the SIG record we showed you earlier is just after 11:54 p.m. on January 2, 2001.) The signature inception time is usually the time you ran the program to sign your zone. You choose the signature expiration time when you run that program, too. After the signature's expiration, the SIG record is no longer valid and can't be used to verify the RRset. Bummer. This means that you have to re-sign your zone data periodically to keep the signatures valid. Fun. Thankfully, re-signing takes much less time than signing it for the first time.

The next (seventh) field in the SIG record, which in this record contains 27791, is the *key tag* field. The key tag is a fingerprint derived from the public key that corresponds to the private key that signed the zone. If the zone has more than one public key (and yours will when you're changing keys), DNSSEC verification software uses the key tag to determine which key to use to verify this signature.

The eighth field, which contains *movie.edu*, is the *signer's name* field. As you'd expect, it's the domain name of the public key that a verifier should use to check the signature. It, together with the key tag, identifies the KEY record to use. In most cases, the signer's name field is the domain name of the zone the signed records are in. In one case, however—which we'll cover soon—the signer's name is the domain name of the parent zone.

The final field is the *signature field*. This is the digital signature of the zone's private key on the signed records and the SIG record itself, minus this field. Like the key in the KEY record, this signature is encoded in base 64.

The NXT Record

DNSSEC introduces one more new record type: the NXT record. We'll explain what it's for.

What happens if you look up a domain name that doesn't exist in a secure zone? If the zone weren't secure, the name server would simply respond with the "no such domain name" response code. But how do you sign a response code? If you signed the whole response message, it would be difficult to cache.

The NXT record solves the problem of signing negative responses. It "spans" a gap between two consecutive domain names in a zone, telling you which domain name comes next after a given domain name—hence the name of the record.

But doesn't the notion of "consecutive domain names" imply a canonical order to the domain names in a zone? Why, yes, it does.

To order the domain names in a zone, you begin by sorting by the rightmost label in those domain names, then by the next label to the left, and so on. Labels are sorted case-insensitively and lexicographically (by dictionary order), with numbers coming before letters and nonexistent labels before numbers (in other words, *movie.edu* would come before *0.movie.edu*). So the domain names in *movie.edu* would sort to the following:

```
movie.edu
bigt.movie.edu
carrie.movie.edu
cujo.movie.edu
dh.movie.edu
diehard.movie.edu
fx.movie.edu
bladerunner.fx.movie.edu
outland.fx.movie.edu
horror.movie.edu
localhost.movie.edu
misery.movie.edu
robocop.movie.edu
shining.movie.edu
terminator.movie.edu
wh.movie.edu
wh249.movie.edu
wh253.movie.edu
wormhole.movie.edu
```

Notice that just as *movie.edu* comes before *bigt.movie.edu*, *fx.movie.edu* precedes *bladerunner.fx.movie.edu*.

Once the zone is in canonical order, the NXT records make sense. Here's one NXT record (the first, in fact) from *movie.edu*:

```
movie.edu.                      NXT    bigt.movie.edu. ( NS SOA MX SIG NXT )
```

This record says that the next domain name in the zone after *movie.edu* is *bigt. movie.edu*, which we could see from our sorted list of domain names. It also says that *movie.edu* has NS records, an SOA record, MX records, a SIG record, and a NXT record.

The last NXT record in a zone is special. Since there's really no next domain name after the last one, the last NXT record "wraps around" to the first record in the zone:

```
wormhole.movie.edu.              NXT      movie.edu. ( A SIG NXT )
```

In other words, to indicate that *wormhole.movie.edu* is the last domain name in the zone, we say that the next domain name is *movie.edu*, the first domain name in the zone.

So how do NXT records provide authenticated negative responses? Well, if you looked up *www.movie.edu* internally, you'd get back the *wormhole.movie.edu* NXT record, telling you that there's no *www.movie.edu* because there are no domain names in the zone after *wormhole.movie.edu*. Similarly, if you tried to look up TXT records for *movie.edu*, you'd get the first NXT record we showed you, which tells you there are no TXT records for *movie.edu*, just NS, SOA, MX, SIG, and NXT records.

A SIG record covering the NXT record accompanies it in the response, authenticating the nonexistence of the domain name or type of data you asked for.

It's important that the NXT records, *in toto*, identify specifically what doesn't exist in the zone. A single catch-all record that simply says "That doesn't exist" could be sniffed off the wire and replayed to claim falsely that existing domain names or records don't actually exist.

For those of you worried about the prospects of adding of these new records to your zone and keeping them up to date manually—uh-oh, now that I've added a host, I've got to adjust my NXT records—take heart: BIND provides a tool to add NXT and SIG records for you automatically.

Some of you may also worry about the information NXT records reveal about your zone. A hacker could, for example, look up the NXT record attached to the domain name of your zone to find the lexicographically next domain name, then repeat the process to learn all the domain names in the zone. That, unfortunately, is an unavoidable side effect of securing your zone. Just repeat this mantra: "My zone data is secure, but public."

The Chain of Trust

There's one more aspect of DNSSEC theory that we should discuss: the chain of trust. (No, this isn't some touchy-feely team-building exercise.) So far, each RRset in our secure zone has a SIG record associated with it. To let others verify those SIG records, our zone advertises its public key to the world in a KEY record. But imagine that someone breaks into our primary master name server. What's to keep him from generating his own key pair? Then he could modify our zone data, re-sign our zone with his newly generated private key, and advertise his newly generated public key in a KEY record.

To combat this problem, our public key is "certified" by a higher authority. This higher authority attests to the fact that the *movie.edu* public key in our KEY record really belongs to the organization that owns and runs the zone, and not to some random yahoo. Before certifying us, this higher authority demanded some sort of proof that we wcrc who we said we were and that we were the duly authorized administrators of *movie.edu*.

This higher authority is our parent zone, *edu*. When we generated our key pair and signed our zone, we also sent our public key to the administrators of *edu*, along with proof of our identity and of our positions as the Two True Administrators of *movie.edu*.* They signed our KEY record with the *edu* zone's private key and sent it back to us so that we could add it to our zone. Here's our KEY record and its accompanying SIG record:

```
movie.edu              IN SIG  KEY 1 2 3600 20010104010141 (
                               20001205010141 65398 edu.
                               aE4sCZKgFtp5RuD1sib0+19dc3MF/y9S2Fr8+h66g+Y2
                               1bc31M4y0493cSoyRpapJrd7qfG+Cr7GK+uY+eLCRA== )
                       KEY     256 3 1 (
                               AQPdWbrGbVv1eDhNgRhpJMPonJfA3reyEo82ekwRnjbX
                               7+uBxB11BqL7LAB7/C+eb0vCtI53FwMhkkNkTmA6bI8B )
```

Note that the signer's name field of the SIG record is *edu,* not *movie.edu*, showing that our KEY record was signed by our parent zone's private key, not our own.

What if someone were to break into the *edu* zone's primary master name server? The *edu* zone's KEY record is signed by the root zone's private key. And the root zone? Well, the root zone's public key is very widely known and configured on every name server that supports DNSSEC.†

That is, the root zone's public key will be configured on every name server once DNSSEC is widely implemented. Right now, neither the root zone nor the *edu* zone is signed, and neither has a key pair. Until DNSSEC is widely implemented, though, it's possible to use DNSSEC piecemeal.

---

* In fact, there aren't any top-level zones signing their child zone's KEY records yet, though some European registries will likely begin signing KEY records soon.

† This reminds us of the tale of the man who asks the priest what holds the Earth up. The priest tells him that the Earth rests on the back of a turtle, which holds it up. The man then asks what the turtle rests on. "On the back of an elephant," replies the priest. "But what," the man asks, "does the elephant rest on?" The frustrated priest snaps back, "It's elephants all the way down!"

Security roots

Let's say we want to begin using DNSSEC at Movie U. to improve the security of our zone data. We've signed the *movie.edu* zone but can't have *edu* sign our KEY record since they haven't secured their zone yet and don't have a key pair. How can other name servers on the Internet verify our zone data? How can our own name servers verify our zone data, for that matter?

BIND 9 name servers provide a mechanism for specifying the public key that corresponds to a particular zone in the *named.conf* file: the *trusted-keys* statement. Here's the *trusted-keys* statement for *movie.edu*:

```
trusted-keys {
      movie.edu. 256 3 1 "AQPdWbrGbVv1eDhNgRhpJMPonJfA3reyEo82ekwRnjbX7+uBxB11Bq
L7 LAB7/C+eb0vCtI53FwMhkkNkTmA6bI8B";
};
```

It's basically the KEY record without the class and type fields and with the key itself quoted. The domain name of the zone may be quoted, but it's not necessary. If *movie.edu* had more than one public key—say a DSA key—we could include it, too:

```
trusted-keys {
      movie.edu. 256 3 1 "AQPdWbrGbVv1eDhNgRhpJMPonJfA3reyEo82ekwRnjbX7+uBxB11Bq
L7 LAB7/C+eb0vCtI53FwMhkkNkTmA6bI8B";
      movie.edu. 256 3 3 "AMnD8GXACuJ5GVnfCJWmRydg2A6JptSm6tjH7QoL81SfBY/kcz1Nbe
Hh z4l9AT1GG2kAZjGLjH07BZHY+joz6iYMPRCDaPOIt9LO+SRfBNZg62P4 aSPT5zVQPahDIMZmTIvv
O7FV6IaTV+cQiKQl6noro8uTk4asCADrAHw0 iVjzjaYpoFF5AsB0cJU18fzDiCNBUb0VqElmKFuRA/K
1KyxM2vJ3U7IS to0IgACiCfHkYK5r3qFbMvF1GrjyVwfwCC4NcMsqEXIT8IEI/YYIgFt4 Ennh";
};
```

This *trusted-keys* statement enables a BIND 9 name server to verify any records in the *movie.edu* zone. The name server can also verify any records in child zones like *fx.movie.edu*, assuming their KEY records are signed by *movie.edu*'s private key and it can verify records in *their* child zones (*movie.edu*'s grandchildren), assuming a valid chain of trust back to the *movie.edu* zone's public key. In other words, *movie.edu* becomes a *security root*, below which our name server can verify any secure zone data.

Null keys

A security root lets your name server verify signed records below a certain point in the namespace. *Null keys* do the opposite: they tell your name server that records below a certain point aren't secured. Let's say the administrators of *fx.movie.edu* haven't secured their zone yet. When we sign *movie.edu*, the BIND 9 signer software adds a special null key to the *movie.edu* zone for *fx.movie.edu*:

```
fx.movie.edu.              KEY      49408 3 3 (
                      )
```

Note that there's no base 64 encoding of a public key in the record. If you look *very* closely (or get out your scientific calculator), you'll see that the flags field indicates that this key should not be used for either authentication or confidentiality; that is, it's a null key. DNSSEC-aware name servers interpret this to mean that the *fx.movie.edu* zone isn't secure and that they shouldn't expect signed data from it.

If BIND 9's signer software finds a file containing *fx.movie.edu*'s KEY record when it runs, it omits the null key, implying that *fx.movie.edu* is secure.

How the Records Are Used

Let's go through what a DNSSEC-capable name server does to verify a record in *movie.edu*. In particular, let's see what happens when it looks up the address of *wormhole.movie.edu*. First, of course, the name server sends a query for the address:

```
% dig +dnssec +norec wormhole.movie.edu.

; <<>> DiG 9.1.0 <<>> +dnssec +norec wormhole.movie.edu.
;; global options:  printcmd
;; Got answer:
;; ->>HEADER<<- opcode: QUERY, status: NOERROR, id: 15766
;; flags: qr aa ra; QUERY: 1, ANSWER: 3, AUTHORITY: 4, ADDITIONAL: 6

;; OPT PSEUDOSECTION:
; EDNS: version:   0, udp=  4096
;; QUESTION SECTION:
;wormhole.movie.edu.            IN      A

;; ANSWER SECTION:
wormhole.movie.edu.     86400   IN      A       192.249.249.1
wormhole.movie.edu.     86400   IN      A       192.253.253.1
wormhole.movie.edu.     86400   IN      SIG     A 1 3 86400 20010215174848
20010116174848 27791 movie.edu.
cYKQvgVksHjwGedNz72iyIpjXBhtSOeUEQA6V0b618asG3mpV6hzrzNf
YwTpLoh9FSjSf0kUzmXkW9aYJmd5Bw==

;; AUTHORITY SECTION:
movie.edu.              86400   IN      NS      outland.fx.movie.edu.
movie.edu.              86400   IN      NS      wormhole.movie.edu.
movie.edu.              86400   IN      NS      terminator.movie.edu.
movie.edu.              86400   IN      SIG     NS 1 2 86400 20010215174848
20010116174848 27791 movie.edu.
ZXRnlbJBWJa4XX3YTWgkYnoQjGLFDN+2JwoGpLpxTidwkJ0FT+N3gMSw anSxa22b+X/
7v4b99t2WMcxCtUIXvw==

;; ADDITIONAL SECTION:
outland.fx.movie.edu.   86400   IN      A       192.253.254.3
terminator.movie.edu.   86400   IN      A       192.249.249.3
```

```
terminator.movie.edu.    86400    IN      SIG     A 1 3 86400 20010215174848
20010116174848 27791 movie.edu.
GSnxseyN4w5sA2Fb9uK9zVNSRJRbbcvr0DaDRwLDO8X2m6ZBbkRssSHJ tZYwoO4ZIFERLKakB//
VTDMhYJmNvw==
movie.edu.               86400    IN      KEY     256 3 1
AQPdWbrGbVv1eDhNgRhpJMPonJfA3reyEo82ekwRnjbX7+uBxB11BqL7 LAB7/
C+eb0vCtI53FwMhkkNkTmA6bI8B
movie.edu.               86400    IN      SIG     KEY 1 2 86400 20010215174837
20010116174837 65398 edu. LW+nc2gmz618u/LjDtlKSorv9OkJOwC8wj/sa/CpzCJJqceB/55JhsWI
t1ADlfQwb4h9hs6oMeN2sU9jHiYQmw==

;; Query time: 3 msec
;; SERVER: 206.168.194.122#53(206.168.194.122)
;; WHEN: Tue Jan 16 10:49:48 2001
;; MSG SIZE  rcvd: 671
```

Notice that we had to specify *+dnssec* on the command line. BIND 9.1.0 and later name servers include DNSSEC records (SIG, NXT, and KEY) in a response only if the querier indicates that it can handle DNSSEC. How do queriers do that? By setting a special flag in a "pseudosection" of the header. It's called a pseudosection because it's not actually part of the bits in the header. Instead, it's a new record type, OPT, that's carried in the DNS message. OPT records usually indicate the capabilities of the querier.

Also notice that the response includes four SIG records: one covering the records in the answer section, one covering the records in the authority section, one covering *terminator.movie.edu*'s address record in the additional section, and one covering *movie.edu*'s KEY record in the additional section. The additional section would have included a SIG record covering *outland.fx.movie.edu*, address records for *wormhole.movie.edu*, and a SIG record covering those addresses if they'd fit in a single UDP datagram, but there wasn't enough room.

To verify the SIG records, the name server must look at *movie.edu*'s KEY record, included in the additional section. But before using the key, it must verify the SIG on that key. That requires at least one additional query: to one of the *edu* name servers for the *edu* zone's public key—unless, of course, the name server already knows the *movie.edu* public key from a *trusted-keys* statement.

DNSSEC and Performance

It should be evident from this *dig* output that DNSSEC increases the average size of a DNS message, that it requires substantially more computational horsepower from name servers verifying zone data, and that signing a zone increases its size substantially—current estimates are that signing multiplies the size of a zone by a factor of seven. Each of these effects has its own consequences, some of which are less obvious:

- Larger DNS messages means more truncated messages, which means more fallback to the use of TCP. Using TCP, of course, is more resource-intensive than using UDP.

- Verifying zone data takes time and slows the resolution process.

- Larger zones mean larger and harder-to-administer *named* processes.

In fact, DNSSEC's complexity meant that BIND 8's architecture couldn't support DNSSEC. DNSSEC also provided part of the impetus for developing BIND 9 and for designing it to run on multiprocessor hosts. If you're planning on signing your zones, make sure your authoritative name servers have enough memory to load the new, larger zones. If your name servers are resolving more records in secure zones, make sure they have enough processor power to verify all those digital signatures—and remember that BIND 9 can take advantage of any processors you can add to the host it runs on.

Signing a Zone

Okay, now you've got the theoretical background you need to actually sign your zone. We'll show you how we signed *movie.edu*. Remember, we used the BIND 9 tools—they're much easier to use than the BIND 8 tools, and of course BIND 9 supports DNSSEC much more completely than BIND 8 does.

Generating your key pair

First, we generated a key pair for *movie.edu*:

```
# cd /var/named
# dnssec-keygen -a RSA -b 512 -n ZONE movie.edu.
Kmovie.edu.+001+27791
```

We ran *dnssec-keygen* in our name server's working directory. That's mostly for convenience: the zone data files are in this directory, so we won't need to use full pathnames as arguments. If we want to use dynamic update with DNSSEC, though, we'd need the keys in the name server's working directory.

Recall *dnssec-keygen*'s options from the TSIG section of this chapter (oh, so long ago):

−*a* The cryptographic algorithm to use, in this case RSA. We could also have used DSA, but RSA is more efficient.

−*b* The length of the keys to generate, in bits. RSA keys can be anywhere from 512 to 2000 bits long. DSA keys can be 512 to 1024 bits long, as long as the length is divisible by 64.

−*n* The type of key. DNSSEC keys are always zone keys.

The only non-option argument is the domain name of the zone, *movie.edu*. The *dnssec-keygen* program prints the basename of the files it's written the keys to. The numbers at the end of the basename (001 and 27791), as we explained in the TSIG section, are the key's DNSSEC algorithm number as used in the KEY record (001 is RSA/MD5), and the key's fingerprint, used to distinguish one key from another when multiple keys are associated with the same zone.

The public key is written to the file *basename.key* (*Kmovie.edu.+001+27791.key*). The private key is written to the file *basename.private* (*Kmovie.edu.+001+27791. private*). Remember to protect the private key; anyone who knows the private key can forge signed zone data. *dnssec-keygen* does what it can to help you: it makes the *.private* file readable and writable only by the user who runs it.

Sending your keys to be signed

Next, we sent our KEY record to the administrator of our parent zone to sign. BIND 9 includes a nice little program to package up the key for transmission, *dnssec-makekeyset*:

```
# dnssec-makekeyset -t 172800 Kmovie.edu.+001+27791.key
```

dnssec-makekeyset created a file called *keyset-movie.edu*,* which contains the following:

```
$ORIGIN .
$TTL 172800     ; 2 days
movie.edu             IN SIG  KEY 1 2 86400 20010104034839 (
                              20001205034839 27791 movie.edu.
                              M7RDKMyc9w1djDc0mQAXQc1PJdmLRBg3nfaGEUZe9Fbi
                              mjiNVaQK33IWhzI95oD8AS0WqRDy5TusTXt4nx1/dQ== )
                      KEY     256 3 1 (
                              AQPdWbrGbVv1eDhNgRhpJMPonJfA3reyEo82ekwRnjbX
                              7+uBxB11BqL7LAB7/C+eb0vCtI53FwMhkkNkTmA6bI8B )
```

The *−t* option takes a TTL for the records to submit. This serves as a suggestion to your parent zone's administrator of the TTL (in seconds) you'd like for your record. They may ignore it, of course. The SIG record actually contains a signature covering your zone's KEY record, generated with your zone's private key. That proves you really have the private key that corresponds to the public key in the KEY record—you're not just submitting a KEY record you found on the street.

The signature expiration and inception fields default to "now" and "30 days from now," respectively. These serve as a suggestion to the signer of the signature lifetime you'd like. You can use the *−s* (start) and *−e* (end) options to adjust the

---

* In versions of *dnssec-makekeyset* shipped with BIND 9.0.1 and earlier, the name of the file would have been *movie.edu.keyset*. However, putting the domain name of the zone first caused problems: the name of the root zone's keyset file was *.keyset*, which is a hidden file on a Unix filesystem.

signature expiration and inception times. Both options accept either an absolute time as an argument, in the form YYYYMMDDHHMMSS, or an offset. For *–s*, the offset is calculated from the current time. For *–e*, the offset is calculated from the start time.

You can also use the signature expiration and inception fields to bundle up several keysets and submit them all at once to your parent zone's administrator to sign. For example, you could submit keysets valid for January, February, and March to your parent zone's administrator all at once, and then put them into production one per month.

Then we sent our file off to our parent zone's administrators to sign. Since the message included proof of our identity,* they signed it with the *dnssec-signkey* program:

```
# dnssec-signkey keyset-movie.edu Kedu.+001+65398.private
```

and sent the resulting file, *movie.edu.signedkey*, back to us:

```
$ORIGIN .
$TTL 172800       ; 1 hour
movie.edu            IN SIG   KEY 1 2 3600 20010104010141 (
                             20001205010141 65398 edu.
                             aE4sCZKgFtp5RuD1sib0+19dc3MF/y9S2Fr8+h66g+Y2
                             1bc31M4y0493cSoyRpapJrd7qfG+Cr7GK+uY+eLCRA== )
                     KEY     256 3 1 (
                             AQPdWbrGbVv1eDhNgRhpJMPonJfA3reyEo82ekwRnjbX
                             7+uBxB11BqL7LAB7/C+eb0vCtI53FwMhkkNkTmA6bI8B )
```

If we didn't care about getting our KEY record signed, we could have skipped this step. But then only name servers with a *trusted-keys* entry for *movie.edu* could verify our data.

Signing your zone

Before signing our zone, we had to add the KEY record to our plain-Jane zone data file:

```
# cat "$INCLUDE Kmovie.edu.+001+27791.key" >> db.movie.edu
```

That gave the signer program the information it needed to know which key to use to sign the zone. It automatically finds and includes the contents of *movie.edu. signedkey*.

Then we signed the zone with *dnssec-signzone*:

```
# dnssec-signzone -o movie.edu. db.movie.edu
```

---

* Since top-level zones haven't started signing zones yet, there's still some question as to how they'll require us to authenticate ourselves. The use of cryptographically signed email messages is a possibility.

We used the *−o* option to specify the origin in the zone data file, because *dnssec-signzone* doesn't read *named.conf* to determine which zone the file describes. The only non-option argument is the name of the zone data file.

This produces a new zone data file, *db.movie.edu.signed*, which begins like this:

```
$ORIGIN .
$TTL 86400        ; 1 day
movie.edu                     IN SOA  terminator.movie.edu. al.robocop.movie.edu. (
                                      2000092603 ; serial
                                      10800      ; refresh (3 hours)
                                      3600       ; retry (1 hour)
                                      604800     ; expire (1 week)
                                      3600       ; minimum (1 hour)
                                      )
                              SIG     SOA 1 2 86400 20010104041530 (
                                      20001205041530 27791 movie.edu.
                                      aO1eZKhGSm99GgC9PfLXfHjl3tAWN/Vn33msppmyhN7a
                                      RlfvJMTpSoJ9XwQCdjqhz01cnCnQiL+jZkqU3uUecg== )
                              NS      terminator.movie.edu.
                              NS      wormhole.movie.edu.
                              NS      outland.fx.movie.edu.
                              SIG     NS 1 2 86400 20010104041530 (
                                      20001205041530 27791 movie.edu.
                                      pkmZJHqFlNmZdNjyupBMMzDDGweGsf9TS1EGci9cwKe5
                                      c0o9h/yncInn2e8QSakjxpwKB8aw9D9uiStxJ/sLvQ== )
                              SIG     MX 1 2 86400 20010104041530 (
                                      20001205041530 27791 movie.edu.
                                      ZcKKeT0XaNlw83eSzRxt74DaLXvQtPYCdgKGOfSiJmYQ
                                      WxI5zZUEWA6ku3w48mo9jbVF+/7nF3QcpFTIiwV1ug== )
$TTL 3600         ; 1 hour
                              SIG     NXT 1 2 3600 20010104041530 (
                                      20001205041530 27791 movie.edu.
                                      upMjK21eD7OQkrHpxSWqkOPcRXbfL8WAgQVK1aGHcTPE
                                      X3JtaLtCLuKLd3YFs7T8BuZoN7aJYRVREWSPVedYPw== )
                              NXT     bigt.movie.edu. ( NS SOA MX SIG KEY NXT )
$TTL 172800       ; 2 days
                              SIG     KEY 1 2 172800 20001205040220 (
                                      20001205040219 65398 edu.
                                      HIReZ98rieIuRI04XsoL+xLRLe8tCQbNKD8US1V35vb4
                                      VsLUGCAEgBq7lLsHty7YCskbxhQu8ncysBKnR/muiA== )
                              KEY     256 3 1 (
                                      AQPdWbrGbVv1eDhNgRhpJMPonJfA3reyEo82ekwRnjbX
                                      7+uBxB11BqL7LAB7/C+eb0vCtI53FwMhkkNkTmA6bI8B )
$TTL 86400        ; 1 day
                              MX      10 postmanrings2x.movie.edu.
```

Believe it or not, those are just the records attached to the domain name *movie.edu*. The zone data file as a whole nearly quadrupled in length and quintupled in size. Oy!

Finally, we changed the *zone* statement in *named.conf* so that *named* would load the new zone data file:

```
zone "movie.edu" {
    type master;
    file "db.movie.edu.signed";
};
```

Then we reloaded the zone and checked *syslog*.

dnssec-signzone does take some options that we didn't use:

−*s*, −*e*
> These options specify the signature inception and expiration times to use in SIG records; they have exactly the same syntax as in *dnssec-makekeyset*.

−*i* Specifies as an option argument the cycle period for resigning records (which we'll cover in a minute). This was the −*c* option before BIND 9.1.0.

−*f* Specifies as an option argument the name of the file to write the signed zone to. The default is the name of the zone data file with *.signed* concatenated.

You can also specify, as a second non-option argument, which private key to use to sign the zone. By default, *dnssec-signzone* signs the zone with each of the zone's private keys in the directory. If you specify the name of one or more files that contain the zone's private keys as arguments, it will sign using only those keys.

Remember, you'll need to re-sign the zone each time you change the zone data, though you certainly don't need to generate a new key pair or have your KEY record re-signed each time. You can re-sign the zone by running *dnssec-signzone* on the signed zone data:

```
# dnssec-signzone -o movie.edu -f db.movie.edu.signed.new db.movie.edu.signed
# mv db.movie.edu.signed db.movie.edu.signed.bak
# mv db.movie.edu.signed.new db.movie.edu.signed
# rndc reload movie.edu
```

The program is smart enough to recalculate NXT records, sign new records, and re-sign records whose signature expiration times are approaching. By default, *dnssec-signzone* re-signs records whose signatures expire within 7.5 days (a quarter of the difference between the default signature inception and expiration times). If you specify different inception and expiration times, *dnssec-signzone* adjusts the re-signing cycle time accordingly. Or you can simply specify a cycle time with the −*i* (formerly the −*c*) option.

DNSSEC and Dynamic Update

dnssec-signzone isn't the only way to sign zone data. The BIND 9 name server is capable of signing dynamically updated records on the fly.* Color us impressed!

---

* Yet another DNSSEC capability BIND 8 doesn't have.

As long as the private key for a secure zone is available in the name server's work-ing directory (in the correctly named *.private* file), a BIND 9 name server signs any records that are added via dynamic update. If any records are added to or deleted from the zone, the name server adjusts (and re-signs) the neighboring NXT records, too.

Let's show you this in action. First, we'll look up a domain name that doesn't yet exist in *movie.edu*:

```
% dig +dnssec perfectstorm.movie.edu.

; <<>> DiG 9.1.0 <<>> +dnssec perfectstorm.movie.edu.
;; global options:  printcmd
;; Got answer:
;; ->>HEADER<<- opcode: QUERY, status: NXDOMAIN, id: 4705
;; flags: qr aa rd ra; QUERY: 1, ANSWER: 0, AUTHORITY: 4, ADDITIONAL: 3

;; OPT PSEUDOSECTION:
; EDNS: version:    0, udp=   4096
;; QUESTION SECTION:
;perfectstorm.movie.edu.                    IN    A

;; AUTHORITY SECTION:
movie.edu.              3600    IN    SOA     terminator.movie.edu. al.robocop.
movie.edu. 2001011600 10800 3600 604800 3600
movie.edu.              3600    IN    SIG     SOA 1 2 86400 20010215174848
20010116174848 27791 movie.edu.
Ea0+xyEsj0Hy4JP115r0D0UFVpWfxqf0NQA8hpKwlLCsxJ3rA+sJBg2Q ZiCTEwfAcwGRfbNsRYu/CcuV/
VJTDA==
misery.movie.edu.       86400   IN    NXT     robocop.movie.edu. A SIG NXT
misery.movie.edu.       86400   IN    SIG     NXT 1 3 86400 20010215174848
20010116174848 27791 movie.edu. ZVfV9KbPb8hKZdZirlpv+WnUxv72di8lUgZiot/
JaWDsZPfNoYqSnKPW ND4H92guwj7oR6CgrhsgLJ9dMDYSpg==
```

(We trimmed the output a little.) Notice *misery.movie.edu*'s NXT record, indicating that the domain name doesn't exist. Now we'll use *nsupdate* to add an address record for *perfectstorm.movie.edu*:

```
% nsupdate
> update add perfectstorm.movie.edu. 3600 IN A 192.249.249.91
>
```

Now, let's look up *perfectstorm.movie.edu* again:

```
% dig +dnssec perfectstorm.movie.edu.

; <<>> DiG 9.1.0 <<>> +dnssec perfectstorm.movie.edu.
;; global options:  printcmd
;; Got answer:
;; ->>HEADER<<- opcode: QUERY, status: NOERROR, id: 11973
;; flags: qr aa rd ra; QUERY: 1, ANSWER: 2, AUTHORITY: 4, ADDITIONAL: 9

;; OPT PSEUDOSECTION:
; EDNS: version:    0, udp=   4096
```

```
;; QUESTION SECTION:
;perfectstorm.movie.edu.                IN      A

;; ANSWER SECTION:
perfectstorm.movie.edu. 3600    IN      A       192.249.249.91
perfectstorm.movie.edu. 3600    IN      SIG     A 1 3 3600 20010215195456
20010116185456 27791 movie.edu. C/
JXdCLUdugxN91v0DZuUDTusi2XNNttb4bdB2nBujLxjwwPAf/D5MJz //
cDtuZ3X+uYzhkN8MDROqOwUQuQSA==

;; AUTHORITY SECTION:
movie.edu.                      86400   IN      NS      terminator.movie.edu.
movie.edu.                      86400   IN      NS      outland.fx.movie.edu.
movie.edu.                      86400   IN      NS      wormhole.movie.edu.
movie.edu.                      86400   IN      SIG     NS 1 2 86400 20010215195301
20010116195301 27791 movie.edu.
1ZR592izM1AjMusJ26e4lvQ0V9lFiFvQh6hCluBxSv7FwNqF7TcJFImc
W52XhXbHUEtiFOzDqYMHOzPV7j23nA==
```

(Again, we trimmed the output a little.) Now not only was an address record generated, but there is also a SIG record generated from *movie.edu*'s private key. The signature expiration is set to 30 days from the update by default, but you can change it with the *sig-validity-interval* substatement, which takes a number of days as an argument:*

```
options {
    sig-validity-interval 7;  // We want SIG on updated records to last a week
};
```

The signature inception is always set to one hour before the update to allow for verifiers with clocks that may be slightly skewed from ours.

If we look up *perfectstorm2.movie.edu* (though how there'd be a sequel to *that* movie I don't know), we find the following:

```
% dig +dnssec perfectstorm2.movie.edu.

; <<>> DiG 9.1.0 <<>> +dnssec perfectstorm2.movie.edu.
;; global options:  printcmd
;; Got answer:
;; ->>HEADER<<- opcode: QUERY, status: NXDOMAIN, id: 11232
;; flags: qr aa rd ra; QUERY: 1, ANSWER: 0, AUTHORITY: 4, ADDITIONAL: 3

;; OPT PSEUDOSECTION:
; EDNS: version:    0, udp=   4096
;; QUESTION SECTION:
;perfectstorm2.movie.edu.        IN      A

;; AUTHORITY SECTION:
```

---

* Before BIND 9.1.0, *sig-validity-interval* interpreted its argument as seconds, not days.

```
movie.edu.              3600    IN      SOA     terminator.movie.edu. al.robocop.
movie.edu. 2001011601 10800 3600 604800 3600
movie.edu.              3600    IN      SIG     SOA 1 2 86400 20010215195456
20010116185456 27791 movie.edu. c1RwtgBX2SO8Q7Hz7vJD0aJfNfA6lsrqH4txHJI/slRpx/
UFYbnz3Gje N0JspZEihdLw0ZYMEiN6hnwRAzB4ag==
perfectstorm.movie.edu. 3600    IN      NXT     robocop.movie.edu. A SIG NXT
perfectstorm.movie.edu. 3600    IN      SIG     NXT 1 3 3600 20010215195456
20010116185456 27791 movie.edu.
qsB9l5AmSrB+qKmv+cKa+htCw84zwaakTmPC2yl+shzSEparrKwIMSR6 x5N69w8cze/
AW+gyFIwQZZkfZInJZA==
```

Notice the NXT record: it was added automatically when we added *perfectstorm. movie.edu*'s address record because *perfectstorm.movie.edu* was a new domain name in the zone. Sweet!

As impressive as this is, you should be careful when allowing dynamic updates to secure zones. You should make sure that you use strong authentication (e.g., TSIG) to authenticate the updates, or you'll give a hacker an easy backdoor to use to modify your "secure" zone. And you should ensure you have enough horse-power for the task: normally, dynamic updates don't take much to process. But dynamic updates to a secure zone require NXT recalculation and, more signifi-cantly, asymmetric encryption (to calculate new SIG records), so you should expect your name server to take longer and need more resources to process them.

Changing Keys

Though we said you don't need to generate a new key each time you sign your zone, there are occasions when you'll need to create a new key, either because you've "used up" your private key or, worse, because your private key has been cracked.

After a certain amount of use, it becomes dangerous to continue signing records with your private key. The larger the pool of available data that's been encrypted using your private key, the easier it is for a hacker to determine your private key using cryptanalysis. While there's no simple rule to tell you when your private key's time is up, here are some guidelines:

- The larger your zone is, the more data your private key encrypts when it signs it. If your zone is very large, change keys more frequently.

- The longer your key, the harder it is to crack. Long keys don't need to be changed as often as short keys.

- The more frequently you update and sign your zone data, the more data encrypted by your private key is available. If you update your zone data fre-quently—and particularly if you dynamically update your secure zone—change keys frequently.

- The more valuable it would be for a hacker to spoof your zone data, the more time and money he will spend trying to crack your private key. If the integrity of your zone data is particularly crucial, change keys frequently.

Since we update *movie.edu* only about once a day and it's not particularly large, we change our key pair every six months. We're only a university, after all. If we were more concerned about our zone data, we would use longer keys or change keys more frequently.

Unfortunately, rolling over to a new key isn't as easy as just generating a new key and replacing the old one with it. If you did that, you'd leave name servers that had cached your zone's data with no way to retrieve your zone's KEY record and verify that data. So rolling over to a new key is a multistep process:

1. Generate a new key pair.

2. Make a new keyset that includes both your new KEY record and your old KEY record, and send it to your parent zone's administrator.

3. Make a keyset that includes just your new KEY record, and send that to your parent zone's administrator, too.

4. If you use *trusted-keys*, add an entry to the statement for your new KEY record. And tell others who use *trusted-keys*, too.

5. Incorporate the signed keyset from your parent zone's administrator that includes both KEY records.

6. Sign your zone data with the new private key, but leave the old KEY record in the zone.

7. After all records signed with the old private key have expired, remove the old KEY record from the zone.

8. Incorporate the signed keyset from your parent zone's administrator that includes just the new KEY record.

9. Sign your zone data with the new private key.

Let's go through the process. First, we generate a new key pair:

```
# dnssec-keygen -a RSA -b 512 -n ZONE movie.edu.
Kmovie.edu.+001+47703
```

Next, we make a new keyset that contains both KEY records and send it to our parent zone's administrator:

```
# dnssec-makekeyset -t 172800 Kmovie.edu.+001+27791.key Kmovie.edu.+001+47703.key
# mail -s "Sign my keys, please" hostmaster@nsiregistry.net < keyset-movie.edu
# mv keyset-movie.edu keyset-movie.edu.2key
```

Then we make a keyset that contains just the new KEY record and send it to our parent zone's administrator, too:

```
% dnssec-makekeyset -t 172800 Kmovie.edu.+001+47703.key
% mail -s "Sign my keys, please" hostmaster@nsiregistry.net < keyset-movie.edu
```

(Okay, it would take a lot more than just those messages to get anyone to sign our keys.)

The first keyset includes both KEY records and SIG records covering both:

```
$ORIGIN .
$TTL 172800      ; 2 days
movie.edu              IN SIG  KEY 1 2 172800 20010104060917 (
                               20001205060917 27791 movie.edu.
                               RyNYoZ/k0tHqnFhUiVs2yjJWPFNeP8BKZ/Jaw+7x09J1
                               ZwJN2ZYQjVNVGLk30rJlxQRjCCdaaYQSq8u81up3xw== )
                       IN SIG  KEY 1 2 172800 20010104060917 (
                               20001205060917 47703 movie.edu.
                               1JGNBQydq6U+qKfq1wxfu1nsu283Zf7mNDDmuBtuuB7o
                               lwaeBL96tzBKpMUAcDYXsM8zxiStF+wTY+I5wfgevA== )
                       KEY     256 3 1 (
                               AQPdWbrGbVv1eDhNgRhpJMPonJfA3reyEo82ekwRnjbX
                               7+uBxB11BqL7LAB7/C+eb0vCtI53FwMhkkNkTmA6bI8B )
                       KEY     256 3 1 (
                               AQPjAfGtDkx6PSgYFs6G2vY1bJEldAMudngn6ZpGJnyg
                               k+LeU5PYiYd48wFLimihjyzlTWMb+C+egtQGpDVQulez )
```

Note that one of the SIG records was generated by the key with key tag 27791 (the old private key) while the other was generated by the key with tag 47703 (the new private key). This proves we have both of the corresponding private keys.

Once we get a response back from our parent zone's administrator, we save it to */var/named* as *movie.edu.signedkey*, the filename we $INCLUDEd into *db.movie. edu.signed*. Here's what *movie.edu.signedkey* looks like:

```
$ORIGIN .
$TTL 172800      ; 2 days
movie.edu              IN SIG  KEY 1 2 172800 20010104060917 (
                               20001205060917 65398 edu.
                               qzvmuTVv9yGZf963ZuN2jxk8brEX/VP3sI5pOM/g2mU/
                               EPa57fyhHDNo7ny8Q2Su5vXnAIoxaaKAR8VmognQ7A== )
                       KEY     256 3 1 (
                               AQPdWbrGbVv1eDhNgRhpJMPonJfA3reyEo82ekwRnjbX
                               7+uBxB11BqL7LAB7/C+eb0vCtI53FwMhkkNkTmA6bI8B )
                       KEY     256 3 1 (
                               AQPjAfGtDkx6PSgYFs6G2vY1bJEldAMudngn6ZpGJnyg
                               k+LeU5PYiYd48wFLimihjyzlTWMb+C+egtQGpDVQulez )
```

edu's SIG record covers both KEY records, so we can use either or both to sign our zone data.

Then we sign our zone data using *only* the new private key:

```
# dnssec-signzone -o movie.edu. db.movie.edu Kmovie.edu.+001+47703.private
```

dnssec-signzone doesn't like re-signing zones that were signed with another key, so we started over from an unsigned version of the *movie.edu* zone. Here's a snippet from the signed zone data file, *db.movie.edu.signed*:

```
$ORIGIN .
$TTL 86400        ; 1 day
movie.edu               IN SOA  terminator.movie.edu. al.robocop.movie.edu. (
                                2000092603 ; serial
                                10800      ; refresh (3 hours)
                                3600       ; retry (1 hour)
                                604800     ; expire (1 week)
                                3600       ; minimum (1 hour)
                                )
                        SIG     SOA 1 2 86400 20010104062430 (
                                20001205062430 47703 movie.edu.
                                LIsndGD5q2VPWb+Ha0ffFP54UE6RYPweqtTp1xhgw4B9
                                Pyb/7z54J8q8LC0NmzQ6SthnfecBQhDBpc72HfNeJQ== )
                        NS      terminator.movie.edu.
                        NS      wormhole.movie.edu.
                        NS      outland.fx.movie.edu.
                        SIG     NS 1 2 86400 20010104062430 (
                                20001205062430 47703 movie.edu.
                                Ktq2mYMzTrBfGjdSb2F7ghyh2nXaLc0iTPV4k8I64j10
                                nJt/hsBZPpeyM2u+Zymvp3mJMWg66E4tirj0AvlGXw== )
                        SIG     MX 1 2 86400 20010104062430 (
                                20001205062430 47703 movie.edu.
                                1/XnJ+JWhmAZLp6YF27YQQl0yT7iZ0qGDXPw860P6U1H
                                NmgDkUKoHfD6CdYwpKz15NyxRKilVmx2ne3oB0TUEQ== )
$TTL 3600         ; 1 hour
                        SIG     NXT 1 2 3600 20010104062430 (
                                20001205062430 47703 movie.edu.
                                2sxN3rQXn/JklugmyGV+on1Io6tV1wEYP6m4oD1xHCP1
                                +NHPR+uT2IknW8SvGc3Kaj16kb2Ej+i3RvleWSI4Tg== )
                        NXT     bigt.movie.edu. ( NS SOA MX SIG KEY NXT )
$TTL 172800       ; 2 days
                        SIG     KEY 1 2 172800 20010104060917 (
                                20001205060917 65398 edu.
                                qzvmuTVv9yGZf963ZuN2jxk8brEX/VP3sI5pOM/g2mU/
                                EPa57fyhHDNo7ny8Q2Su5vXnAIoxaaKAR8VmognQ7A== )
                        KEY     256 3 1 (
                                AQPdWbrGbVv1eDhNgRhpJMPonJfA3reyEo82ekwRnjbX
                                7+uBxB11BqL7LAB7/C+eb0vCtI53FwMhkkNkTmA6bI8B )
                        KEY     256 3 1 (
                                AQPjAfGtDkx6PSgYFs6G2vY1bJEldAMudngn6ZpGJnyg
                                k+LeU5PYiYd48wFLimihjyzlTWMb+C+egtQGpDVQulez )
$TTL 86400        ; 1 day
                        MX      10 postmanrings2x.movie.edu.
```

Although the zone includes two KEY records and *edu*'s SIG record, which covers both, the other records in the zone were signed only by the new private key, with key tag 47703.

We need the second signed keyset when we delete the old KEY record: at that point, the SIG record *edu* sent us that covers both KEYs is no good. If we use the keyset that includes just the new KEY record, we'll be fine.

We're guessing that after reading that, you'll probably decide to use the longest keys available just to avoid ever needing to roll your keys over.

What Was That All About?

We realize that DNSSEC is a bit, er, daunting. (We nearly fainted the first time we saw it.) But it's designed to do something very important: make DNS spoofing much, much harder. And as people do more and more business over the Internet, knowing you're really getting where you thought you were going becomes crucial.

That said, we realize that DNSSEC and the other security measures we've described in this chapter aren't for all of you. (Certainly they're not *all* for all of you.) You should balance your need for security against the cost of implementing it, in terms of the burden it places both on your infrastructure and on your productivity.

12

nslookup and dig

> *"Don't stand chattering to yourself like that,"*
> *Humpty Dumpty said, looking at her for the first*
> *time, "but tell me your name and your business."*
>
> *"My name is Alice, but—"*
>
> *"It's a stupid name enough!" Humpty Dumpty*
> *interrupted impatiently. "What does it mean?"*
>
> *"Must a name mean something?"*
> *Alice asked doubtfully.*
>
> *"Of course it must," Humpty Dumpty said*
> *with a short laugh…*

To be proficient at troubleshooting name server problems, you'll need a troubleshooting tool to send DNS queries, one that gives you complete control. We'll cover *nslookup* in this chapter because it's distributed with BIND and with many vendors' operating systems. That doesn't mean it's the best DNS troubleshooting tool available, though. *nslookup* has its faults—so many, in fact, that it's now deprecated (geekish for "officially out of favor") in the BIND 9 distribution. We'll cover it anyway, since it's pervasive. We'll also cover *dig*, which provides similar functionality and doesn't suffer from *nslookup*'s deficiencies.

Note that this chapter isn't comprehensive; there are aspects of *nslookup* and *dig* (mostly obscure and seldom used) that we won't cover. You can always consult the manual pages for those.

Is nslookup a Good Tool?

Much of the time, you'll use *nslookup* to send queries in the same way the resolver sends them. Sometimes, though, you'll use *nslookup* to query other name servers as a name server would instead. The way you use it will depend on the problem you're trying to debug. You might wonder, "How accurately does *nslookup* emulate a resolver or a name server? Does *nslookup* actually use the BIND resolver library routines?" No, *nslookup* uses its own routines for querying name servers, but those routines are based on the resolver routines. Consequently, *nslookup*'s behavior is very similar to the resolver's behavior, but it does differ slightly. We'll point out some of those differences. As for emulating name server behavior, *nslookup* allows us to query another server with the same query message that a name server would use, but the retransmission scheme is quite different. Like a name server, though, *nslookup* can transfer a copy of the zone data. So *nslookup* doesn't emulate either the resolver or the name server exactly, but it does emulate them well enough to make a decent troubleshooting tool. Let's delve into those differences we alluded to.

Multiple Servers

nslookup talks to only one name server at a time. This is the biggest difference between *nslookup*'s behavior and the resolver's behavior. The resolver makes use of each *nameserver* directive in *resolv.conf*. If there are two *nameserver* directives in *resolv.conf*, the resolver tries the first name server, then the second, then the first, then the second, until it receives a response or gives up. The resolver does this for every query. On the other hand, *nslookup* tries the first name server in *resolv.conf* and keeps retrying until it finally gives up on the first name server and tries the second. Once it gets a response, it locks onto that server and doesn't try the next. However, you *want* your troubleshooting tool to talk to only one name server so you can reduce the number of variables when analyzing a problem. If *nslookup* used more than one name server, you wouldn't have as much control over your troubleshooting session. So talking to only one server is the right thing for a troubleshooting tool to do.

Timeouts

The *nslookup* timeouts match the resolver timeouts when the resolver is querying only one name server. A name server's timeouts, however, are based on how quickly the remote server answered the last query, a dynamic measure. *nslookup*'s timeouts will never match a name server's timeouts, but that's not a problem either. When you're querying remote name servers with *nslookup*, you probably only care what the response was, not how long it took.

The Search List

nslookup implements the search list just as the resolver code does. Versions of *nslookup* shipped with pre–BIND 4.9 name servers tend to use a "full" search list: the local domain name and all ancestor domain names with at least two labels.

Versions of *nslookup* shipped with BIND 4.9 and later name servers use an abridged search list that includes just the local domain name. We'll show you how to determine your type of *nslookup* later, in case you're not sure.

Name servers don't implement search lists, so, to act like a name server, the *nslookup* search function must be turned off—more on that later.

Zone Transfers

nslookup does zone transfers just like a name server. Unlike a name server, however, *nslookup* does not check SOA serial numbers before pulling the zone data; if you want to do that, you'll have to do it manually.

Using NIS and /etc/hosts

This last point doesn't compare *nslookup* to the resolver or name server but to ways of looking up names in general. As distributed from the Internet Software Consortium, *nslookup* uses only DNS; it won't use NIS or */etc/hosts*. Most applications can use DNS, NIS, or */etc/hosts*, depending on how the system is configured. Don't count on *nslookup* to help you find your lookup problem unless your host is really configured to use name servers.*

Interactive Versus Noninteractive

Let's start our tutorial on *nslookup* by looking at how to start it and how to exit from it. You can run *nslookup* either interactively or noninteractively. If you only want to look up one record for one domain name, use the noninteractive form. If you plan on doing something more extensive, such as changing name servers or options, use an interactive session.

To start an interactive session, just type *nslookup*:

```
% nslookup
Default Server:  terminator.movie.edu
Address:  0.0.0.0

> ^D
```

If you need help, type *?* or *help*.† When you want to exit, type ^D (control-D) or *exit*. If you try to exit from *nslookup* by interrupting it with ^C (or whatever your interrupt character is), you won't get very far. *nslookup* catches the interrupt, stops whatever it is doing (like a zone transfer), and gives you the > prompt.

---

* Or your vendor's *nslookup* has been enhanced to query NIS servers and check */etc/hosts*, like the one in HP-UX.

† The help function isn't implemented in BIND 9's *nslookup* as of 9.1.0.

For a noninteractive lookup, include the name you are looking up on the command line:

```
% nslookup carrie
Server:  terminator.movie.edu
Address:  0.0.0.0

Name:    carrie.movie.edu
Address: 192.253.253.4
```

Option Settings

nslookup has its own set of dials and knobs, called *option settings*. All of the option settings can be changed. We'll discuss here what each of the options means, and we'll use the rest of the chapter to show you how to use them.

```
% nslookup
Default Server:  bladerunner.fx.movie.edu
Address:  0.0.0.0

> set all
Default Server:  bladerunner.fx.movie.edu
Address:  0.0.0.0

Set options:
  nodebug          defname          search          recurse
  nod2             novc             noignoretc      port=53
  querytype=A      class=IN         timeout=5       retry=4
  root=a.root-servers.net.
  domain=fx.movie.edu
  srchlist=fx.movie.edu

> ^D
```

Before we get into the options, we need to cover the introductory lines. The default name server is *bladerunner.fx.movie.edu*. This means that *nslookup* will query *bladerunner* unless we specify another name server. The address 0.0.0.0 means "this host." When *nslookup* is using address 0.0.0.0 or 127.0.0.1 as its name server, it is using the server running on the local system—in this case, *bladerunner*.

The options come in two flavors: Boolean and value. The options that do not have an equals sign after them are Boolean options. They have the interesting property of being either "on" or "off." The value options can take on different, well, values. How can we tell which Boolean options are on and which are off? The option is off when a "no" precedes the option's name. *nodebug* means that debugging is off. As you might guess, the *search* option is on.

How you change Boolean or value options depends on whether you are using *nslookup* interactively or not. In an interactive session, you change an option with the *set* command, as in *set debug* or *set domain=classics.movie.edu*. From the command line, you omit the word *set* and precede the option with a hyphen, as in *nslookup -debug* or *nslookup -domain=classics.movie.edu*. The options can be abbreviated to their shortest unique prefix, e.g., *nodeb* for *nodebug*. In addition to its abbreviation, the *querytype* option can also be called simply *type*.

Let's go through each of the options:

[no]debug

Debugging is turned off by default. If it is turned on, the name server shows timeouts and displays the response messages. See *[no]d2* for a discussion of debug level 2.

[no]defname

By default, *nslookup* adds the local domain name to names without a dot in them. Before search lists existed, the BIND resolver code only added the local domain name to names without *any* dots in them; this option reflects that behavior. *nslookup* can implement the pre-search list behavior (with *search* off and *defname* on) or the search list behavior (with *search* on).

[no]search

The search option supersedes the local domain name (*defname*) option. That is, *defname* applies only if *search* is turned off. By default, *nslookup* appends the domain names in the search list (*srchlist*) to names that don't end in a dot.

[no]recurse

nslookup sends recursive queries by default. This turns on the recursion-desired bit in query messages. The BIND resolver sends recursive queries in the same way. Name servers, however, send out nonrecursive queries to other name servers.

[no]d2

Debugging at level 2 is turned off by default. If it is turned on, you see the query messages sent out in addition to the regular debugging output. Turning on *d2* also turns on *debug*. Turning off *d2* turns off *d2* only; *debug* is left on. Turning off *debug* turns off both *debug* and *d2*.

[no]vc

By default, *nslookup* sends queries using UDP datagrams instead of over a Virtual Circuit (TCP). Most BIND resolvers send queries over UDP, so the default *nslookup* behavior matches the resolver. As the resolver can be instructed to use TCP, so can *nslookup*.

[no]ignoretc

By default, *nslookup* doesn't ignore truncated messages. If a message is received that has the "truncated" bit set—indicating that the name server couldn't fit all the important information in the UDP response datagram—*nslookup* doesn't ignore it; it retries the query using a TCP connection instead of UDP. Again, this matches the BIND resolver's behavior. The reason for retrying the query using a TCP connection is that TCP responses can be many times as large as UDP responses.

port=53

Name servers listen on port 53. You can start a name server on another port—for debugging purposes, for example—and *nslookup* can be directed to use that port.

querytype=A

By default, *nslookup* looks up A (address) resource record types. In addition, if you type in an IP address (and the *nslookup* query type is A or PTR), then *nslookup* will invert the address, append *in-addr.arpa*, and look up PTR records instead.

class=IN

The only class that matters is Internet (IN). Well, there is the Hesiod (HS) class, too, if you are an MITer or run Ultrix.

timeout=5

If the name server doesn't respond within 5 seconds, *nslookup* resends the query and doubles the timeout (to 10, 20, and then 40 seconds). Most BIND resolvers use the same timeouts when querying a single name server.

retry=4

Send the query four times before giving up. After each retry, the timeout value is doubled. Again, this matches most BIND resolvers' behavior.

root=a.root-servers.net.

There is a convenience command called *root* that switches your default name server to the server named here. Executing the *root* command from a modern *nslookup*'s prompt is equivalent to executing *server a.root-servers.net*. Older versions use *nic.ddn.mil* (old) or even *sri-nic.arpa* (ancient) as the default root name server. You can change the default "root" server with *set root=server*.

domain=fx.movie.edu

This is the default domain name to append if the *defname* option is on.

srchlist=fx.movie.edu

If *search* is on, these are the domain names appended to names that do not end in a dot. The domain names are listed in the order in which they are tried, separated by a slash. (The BIND 4.8.3 *nslookup*'s search list would have defaulted to *fx.movie.edu/movie.edu*. With 4.9 and later versions, *nslookup*'s default search list includes only the default domain name.* You have

---

* This gives you an easy way to determine which version of *nslookup* you're running: type *set all* and check whether the default search list includes just the local domain name (BIND 4.9 or later) or ancestor domain names, too (BIND 4.8.3 or earlier).

to explicitly set the search list in */etc/resolv.conf* to get both *fx.movie.edu* and *movie.edu*.)

The .nslookuprc File

You can set up new default *nslookup* options in an *.nslookuprc* file. *nslookup* looks for an *.nslookuprc* file in your home directory when it starts up, in both interactive and noninteractive modes. The *.nslookuprc* file can contain any legal *set* commands, one per line. This is useful, for example, if your old *nslookup* still thinks *sri-nic.arpa* is a root name server. You can set the default root name server to a real, current root with a line like this in your *.nslookuprc* file:

```
set root=a.root-servers.net.
```

You might also use *.nslookuprc* to set your search list to something other than your host's default search list or to change the timeouts *nslookup* uses.

Avoiding the Search List

nslookup implements the same search list as the resolver. When you're debugging, though, the search list can get in your way. You may need to turn the search list off completely (*set nosearch*) or add a trailing dot to the fully qualified domain name you are looking up. We prefer the latter, as you'll see in our examples.

Common Tasks

There are little chores you'll come to use *nslookup* for almost every day: finding the IP address or MX records for a given domain name, or querying a particular name server for data. We'll cover these first, before moving on to the more occasional stuff.

Looking Up Different Record Types

By default, *nslookup* looks up the address for a domain name, or the domain name for an address. You can look up any record type by changing the *querytype*, as we show in this example:

```
% nslookup
Default Server:  terminator.movie.edu
Address:  0.0.0.0

>misery                    —Look up address
Server:  terminator.movie.edu
Address:  0.0.0.0

Name:    misery.movie.edu
Address:  192.253.253.2
```

```
> 192.253.253.2              —Look up domain name
Server:  terminator.movie.edu
Address:  0.0.0.0

Name:    misery.movie.edu
Address:  192.253.253.2

> set q=mx                   —Look up MX records
> wormhole
Server:  terminator.movie.edu
Address:  0.0.0.0

wormhole.movie.edu           preference = 10, mail exchanger = wormhole.movie.edu
wormhole.movie.edu           internet address = 192.249.249.1
wormhole.movie.edu           internet address = 192.253.253.1

> set q=any                  —Look up records of any type
> diehard
Server:  terminator.movie.edu
Address:  0.0.0.0

diehard.movie.edu            internet address = 192.249.249.4
diehard.movie.edu            preference = 10, mail exchanger = diehard.movie.edu
diehard.movie.edu            internet address = 192.249.249.4
```

These are only a few of the valid DNS record types, of course. For a more complete list, see Appendix A, *DNS Message Format and Resource Records*.

Authoritative Versus Nonauthoritative Answers

If you've used *nslookup* before, you might have noticed something peculiar—the first time you look up a remote domain name, the answer is authoritative, but the second time you look up the same name it is nonauthoritative. Here's an example:

```
% nslookup
Default Server:  relay.hp.com
Address:  15.255.152.2

> slate.mines.colorado.edu.
Server:  relay.hp.com
Address:  15.255.152.2

Name:    slate.mines.colorado.edu
Address:  138.67.1.3

> slate.mines.colorado.edu.
Server:  relay.hp.com
Address:  15.255.152.2

Non-authoritative answer:
Name:    slate.mines.colorado.edu
Address:  138.67.1.3
```

While this looks odd, it really isn't. What's happening here is that the first time the local name server looks up *slate.mines.colorado.edu*, it contacts the name server for *mines.colorado.edu*, and the *mines.colorado.edu* server then responds with an authoritative answer. The local name server, in effect, passes the authoritative response directly back to *nslookup*. It also caches the response. The second time you look up *slate.mines.colorado.edu*, the name server answers out of its cache, which results in the answer "non-authoritative."[*]

Notice that we terminated the domain name with a trailing dot each time we looked it up. The response would have been the same if we'd left the trailing dot off. There are times when it's critical that you use the trailing dot while debugging, and times when it's not. Rather than stopping to decide if *this* name needs a trailing dot, we always add one if we know the name is fully qualified, except, of course, if we've turned off the search list.

Switching Name Servers

Sometimes you want to query another name server directly—you may think it is misbehaving, for example. You can switch servers with *nslookup* by using the *server* or *lserver* command. The difference between *server* and *lserver* is that *lserver* queries your "local" name server—the one you started out with—to get the address of the server you want to switch to; *server* uses the default name server instead of the local server. This difference is important because the server you just switched to may not be responding, as we'll show in this example:

```
% nslookup
Default Server:  relay.hp.com
Address:  15.255.152.2
```

When we start up, our first name server, *relay.hp.com*, becomes our *lserver*. This will matter later on in this session.

```
> server galt.cs.purdue.edu.
Default Server:  galt.cs.purdue.edu
Address:  128.10.2.39

> cs.purdue.edu.
Server:  galt.cs.purdue.edu
Address:  128.10.2.39

*** galt.cs.purdue.edu can't find cs.purdue.edu.: No response from server
```

---

[*] BIND 9 name servers, interestingly, show even the first responses as nonauthoritative.

At this point, we try to switch back to our original name server. But there is no name server running on *galt.cs.purdue.edu* to look up *relay.hp.com's* address:

```
> server relay.hp.com.

*** Can't find address for server relay.hp.com.: No response from server
```

Instead of being stuck, though, we use the *lserver* command to have our local name server look up *relay.hp.com's* address:

```
> lserver relay.hp.com.
Default Server:  relay.hp.com
Address:  15.255.152.2


> ^D
```

Since the name server on *galt.cs.purdue.edu* did not respond—that host isn't even running a name server—it wasn't possible to look up the address of *relay.hp.com* to switch back to using *relay's* name server. Here's where *lserver* comes to the rescue: the local name server, *relay*, was still responding, so we used it. Instead of using *lserver*, we also could have recovered by using *relay's* IP address directly— *server 15.255.152.2*.

You can even change servers on a per-query basis. To specify that you'd like *nslookup* to query a particular name server for information about a given domain name, you can specify the server as the second argument on the line, after the domain name to look up, like so:

```
% nslookup
Default Server:  relay.hp.com
Address:  15.255.152.2

> saturn.sun.com. ns.sun.com.
Name Server:  ns.sun.com
Address:  192.9.9.3

Name:    saturn.sun.com
Addresses: 192.9.25.2


> ^D
```

And, of course, you can change servers from the command line. You can specify the server to query as the argument after the domain name to look up, like this:

```
% nslookup -type=mx fisherking.movie.edu. terminator.movie.edu.
```

This instructs *nslookup* to query *terminator.movie.edu* for MX records for *fisherking.movie.edu*.

Finally, to specify an alternate default name server and enter interactive mode, you can use a hyphen in place of the domain name to look up:

```
% nslookup - terminator.movie.edu.
```

Less Common Tasks

Let's move on to some tricks you'll probably use less often but are still handy to have in your repertoire. Most of these will be helpful when you are trying to troubleshoot a DNS or BIND problem; they'll enable you to grub around in the messages the resolver sees and mimic a BIND name server querying another name server or transferring zone data.

Showing the Query and Response Messages

If you need to, you can direct *nslookup* to show you the queries it sends out and the responses it receives. Turning on *debug* shows the responses. Turning on *d2* shows the queries as well. When you want to turn off debugging completely, you have to use *set nodebug*, since *set nod2* turns off only level 2 debugging. After the following trace, we'll explain some parts of the output. If you want, pull out your copy of RFC 1035, turn to page 25, and read along with our explanation.

```
% nslookup
Default Server:  terminator.movie.edu
Address:  0.0.0.0

> set debug
> wormhole
Server:  terminator.movie.edu
Address:  0.0.0.0

------------
Got answer:
    HEADER:
        opcode = QUERY, id = 6813, rcode = NOERROR
        header flags:  response, auth. answer, want recursion,
        recursion avail.  questions = 1,  answers = 2,
        authority records = 2,  additional = 3

    QUESTIONS:
        wormhole.movie.edu, type = A, class = IN
    ANSWERS:
    -> wormhole.movie.edu
        internet address = 192.253.253.1
        ttl = 86400 (1D)
    -> wormhole.movie.edu
        internet address = 192.249.249.1
        ttl = 86400 (1D)
    AUTHORITY RECORDS:
    -> movie.edu
        nameserver = terminator.movie.edu
        ttl = 86400 (1D)
    -> movie.edu
        nameserver = wormhole.movie.edu
        ttl = 86400 (1D)
    ADDITIONAL RECORDS:
    -> terminator.movie.edu
```

```
           internet address = 192.249.249.3
           ttl = 86400 (1D)
    ->  wormhole.movie.edu
           internet address = 192.253.253.1
           ttl = 86400 (1D)
    ->  wormhole.movie.edu
           internet address = 192.249.249.1
           ttl = 86400 (1D)


------------
Name:     wormhole.movie.edu
Addresses:  192.253.253.1, 192.249.249.1


> set d2
> wormhole
Server:  terminator.movie.edu
Address:  0.0.0.0
```

This time the query is also shown.

```
------------
SendRequest(), len 36
    HEADER:
        opcode = QUERY, id = 6814, rcode = NOERROR
        header flags:  query, want recursion
        questions = 1,  answers = 0,  authority records = 0,
      additional = 0

    QUESTIONS:
        wormhole.movie.edu, type = A, class = IN


------------
------------
Got answer (164 bytes):
```

The answer is the same as above.

The lines between the dashes are the query and response messages. As promised, we'll go through the contents of the messages. DNS packets comprise five sections: Header, Question, Answer, Authority, and Additional.

Header section

The header section is present in every query and response message. The operation code *nslookup* reports is always QUERY. There are other opcodes for asynchronous notification of zone changes (NOTIFY) and for dynamic updates (UPDATE), but *nslookup* doesn't see those because it just sends regular queries and receives responses.

The ID in the header is used to associate a response with a query and detect duplicate queries or responses. You have to look in the header flags to see which messages are queries and which are responses. The string *want recursion* means that this is a recursive query. The flag is parroted in the response.

The string *auth. answer* means that this response is authoritative. In other words, the response is from the name server's authoritative data, not from its cache. The response code, *rcode*, can be one of *no error, server failure, name error* (also known as *nxdomain* or *nonexistent domain*), *not implemented*, or *refused*. The *server failure, name error, not implemented*, and *refused* response codes cause the *nslookup* "Server failed," "Nonexistent domain," "Not implemented," and "Query refused" errors, respectively. The last four entries in the header section are counters—they indicate how many resource records there are in each of the next four sections.

Question section

There is always one question in a DNS message; it includes the domain name and the requested datatype and class. There is never more than one question in a DNS message—the capability of handling more than one would require a redesign of the message format. For one thing, the single authority bit would have to be changed because the answer section could contain a mix of authoritative and nonauthoritative answers. In the present design, setting the authoritative answer bit means that the name server is authoritative for the zone that contains the domain name in the question section.

Answer section

This section contains the resource records that answer the question. There can be more than one resource record in the response. For example, if the host is multihomed, there will be more than one address resource record.

Authority section

The authority section is where name server records are returned. When a response refers the querier to some other name servers, those name servers are listed here.

Additional section

The additional records section adds information that may complete the information included in other sections. For instance, if a name server is listed in the authority section, the name server's address may be included in the additional records section. After all, to contact the name server, you need to have its address.

For you sticklers for detail, there *is* a time when the number of questions in a DNS message isn't one: in an inverse query, when it's zero. In an inverse query, there is one answer in the query message, and the question section is empty. The name server fills in the question. But, as we said, inverse queries are almost nonexistent.

Querying Like a BIND Name Server

You can make *nslookup* send out the same query message a name server would. Name servers' query messages aren't that much different from resolvers' query messages in the first place. The primary difference in the query messages is that resolvers request recursive resolution and name servers seldom do. Requesting recursion is the default with *nslookup*, so you have to explicitly turn it off. The difference in operation between a resolver and a name server is that the resolver applies the search list, and the name server doesn't. By default, *nslookup* applies the search list, so that must be explicitly turned off as well. Of course, judicious use of the trailing dot will have the same effect.

In raw *nslookup* terms, this means that to query like a resolver, you use *nslookup*'s default settings. To query like a name server, use *set norecurse* and *set nosearch*. On the command line, that's *nslookup -norecurse -nosearch*.

When a BIND name server receives a query, it looks for the answer in its authoritative data and in its cache. If it doesn't have the answer and it is authoritative for the zone, the name server responds that the name doesn't exist or that there are no records of the type sought. If the name server doesn't have the answer and it is *not* authoritative for the zone, it starts walking up the namespace looking for NS records. There are always NS records somewhere higher in the namespace. As a last resort, it uses the NS records for the root zone, the highest level.

If the name server has received a nonrecursive query, it responds to the querier by returning the NS records that it found. On the other hand, if the original query was a recursive query, the name server queries the remote name servers in the NS records that it found. When the name server receives a response from one of the remote name servers, it caches the response and, if necessary, repeats this process. The remote server's response either has the answer to the question or contains a list of name servers lower in the namespace and closer to the answer.

Let's assume for our example that we are trying to satisfy a recursive query and that we didn't find any NS records until we checked the *gov* zone. That is, in fact, the case when we ask the name server on *relay.hp.com* about *www.whitehouse.gov*—it doesn't find any NS records until the *gov* zone. From there we switch servers to a *gov* name server and ask the same question. It directs us to the *whitehouse.gov* servers. We then switch to a *whitehouse.gov* name server and ask the same question:

```
% nslookup
Default Server:  relay.hp.com
Address:  15.255.152.2

> set norec              —Query like a name server: turn off recursion
> set nosearch           —Turn off the search list
> www.whitehouse.gov     —We don't need to dot-terminate since we've turned
                         —search off
Server:  relay.hp.com
Address:  15.255.152.2
```

```
Name:     www.whitehouse.gov
Served by:
- I.ROOT-SERVERS.NET
          192.36.148.17
          gov
- E.ROOT-SERVERS.NET
          192.203.230.10
          gov
- D.ROOT-SERVERS.NET
          128.8.10.90
          gov
- B.ROOT-SERVERS.NET
          128.9.0.107
          gov
- C.ROOT-SERVERS.NET
          192.33.4.12
          gov
- A.ROOT-SERVERS.NET
          198.41.0.4
          gov
- H.ROOT-SERVERS.NET
          128.63.2.53
          gov
- G.ROOT-SERVERS.NET
          192.112.36.4
          gov
- F.ROOT-SERVERS.NET
          192.5.5.241
          gov
```

Switch to a *gov* name server (you may have to turn recursion back on temporarily if your name server doesn't have the address of the *gov* name server already cached):

```
> server e.root-servers.net
Default Server:  e.root-servers.net
Address: 192.203.230.10
```

Ask the same question of the *gov* name server. It will refer us to name servers closer to our desired answer:

```
> www.whitehouse.gov.
Server:  e.root-servers.net
Address:  192.203.230.10

Name:     www.whitehouse.gov
Served by:
- DNSAUTH1.SYS.GTEI.NET

          whitehouse.gov
- DNSAUTH2.SYS.GTEI.NET

          whitehouse.gov
- DNSAUTH3.SYS.GTEI.NET

          whitehouse.gov
```

Switch to a *whitehouse.gov* name server—any of them will do:

```
> server dnsauth2.sys.gtei.net.
Default Server:  dnsauth2.sys.gtei.net
Address:  4.2.49.3

> www.whitehouse.gov.
Server:  sec1.dns.psi.net
Address:  38.8.92.2

Name:     www.whitehouse.gov
Addresses:  198.137.240.91, 198.137.240.92
```

Hopefully, this example gives you a feeling for how name servers look up domain names. If you need to refresh your understanding of what this looks like graphically, flip back to Figures 2-12 and 2-13.

Before we move on, notice that we asked each of the servers the very same question: "What's the address of *www.whitehouse.gov?*" What do you think would happen if the *gov* name server had already cached *www.whitehouse.gov*'s address itself? The *gov* name server would have answered the question out of its cache instead of referring you to the *whitehouse.gov* name servers. Why is this significant? Suppose you messed up a particular host's address in your zone. Someone points it out to you, and you clean up the problem. Even though your name server now has the correct data, some remote sites find the old, messed-up data when they look up the domain name of the host. One of the name servers that serves a zone higher up in the namespace, such as a root name server, has cached the incorrect data; when it receives a query for that host's address, it returns the incorrect data instead of referring the querier to your name servers. What makes this problem hard to track down is that only one of the "higher up" name servers has cached the incorrect data, so only some of the remote lookups get the wrong answer—the ones that use this server. Fun, huh? Eventually, though, the "higher up" name server will time out the old record. If you're pressed for time, you can contact the administrators of the remote name server and ask them to restart *named* to flush the cache. Of course, if the remote name server is an important, much-used name server, they may tell you where to go with that suggestion.

Zone Transfers

nslookup can be used to transfer a whole zone using the *ls* command. This feature is useful for troubleshooting, for figuring out how to spell a remote host's domain name, or just for counting how many hosts are in some remote zone. Since the output can be substantial, *nslookup* allows you to redirect the output to a file. If you want to bail out in the middle of a transfer, you can interrupt it by typing your interrupt character.

Beware: some name servers won't let you pull a copy of their zones, either for security reasons or to limit the load placed on them. The Internet is a friendly place, but administrators must defend their turf.

Let's look at the *movie.edu* zone. As you can see in the following output, all the zone data is listed—the SOA record is listed twice, which is an artifact of how the data is exchanged during the zone transfer. Since some *nslookup*s only show you address and name server records by default, we specify the −*d* option to retrieve the whole zone:

```
% nslookup
Default Server: terminator.movie.edu
Address:  0.0.0.0

> ls -d movie.edu.
[terminator.movie.edu]
$ORIGIN movie.edu.
@                       1D IN SOA       terminator al.robocop (
                                        2000091400      ; serial
                                        3H              ; refresh
                                        1H              ; retry
                                        4W2D            ; expiry
                                        1H )            ; minimum

                        1D IN NS        terminator
                        1D IN NS        wormhole
wormhole                1D IN A         192.249.249.1
                        1D IN A         192.253.253.1
wh249                   1D IN A         192.249.249.1
robocop                 1D IN A         192.249.249.2
bigt                    1D IN CNAME     terminator
cujo                    1D IN TXT       "Location:" "machine" "room" "dog" "house"
wh253                   1D IN A         192.253.253.1
wh                      1D IN CNAME     wormhole
shining                 1D IN A         192.253.253.3
terminator              1D IN A         192.249.249.3
localhost               1D IN A         127.0.0.1
fx                      1D IN NS        bladerunner.fx
bladerunner.fx          1D IN A         192.253.254.2
fx                      1D IN NS        outland.fx
outland.fx              1D IN A         192.253.254.3
fx                      1D IN NS        huskymo.boulder.acmebw.com.
                        1D IN NS        tornado.acmebw.com.
dh                      1D IN CNAME     diehard
carrie                  1D IN A         192.253.253.4
diehard                 1D IN A         192.249.249.4
misery                  1D IN A         192.253.253.2
@                       1D IN SOA       terminator al.robocop (
                                        2000091400      ; serial
                                        3H              ; refresh
                                        1H              ; retry
                                        4W2D            ; expiry
                                        1H )            ; minimum
```

Now let's say you missed a record in the beginning of the zone data, one that flew off the top of your screen. *nslookup* lets you save the listing of a zone to a file:

```
> ls -d movie.edu  > /tmp/movie.edu  —List all data into /tmp/movie.edu
[terminator.movie.edu]
Received 25 answers (25 records).
```

Some versions of *nslookup* even support a built-in *view* command that sorts and displays the contents of a zone listing from interactive mode. In the latest BIND 8 releases, though, *view* is broken, and it isn't supported by BIND 9's *nslookup* as of 9.1.0.

Troubleshooting nslookup Problems

The last thing you want is to have problems with your troubleshooting tool. Unfortunately, some types of failures render *nslookup* nearly useless. Other types of *nslookup* failures are (at best) confusing, because they don't give you any clear information to work with. While there may be a few problems with *nslookup* itself, most of the problems you encounter will be caused by name server configuration and operation. We'll cover these problems here.

Looking Up the Right Data

This isn't really a problem per se, but it can be awfully confusing. If you use *nslookup* to look up a type of record for a domain name, and the domain name exists but records of the type you're looking for don't, you'll get an error like this:

```
% nslookup
Default Server: terminator.movie.edu
Address: 0.0.0.0

> movie.edu.

*** No address (A) records available for movie.edu.
```

So what types of records do exist? Just *set type=any* to find out:

```
> set type=any
> movie.edu.
Server: terminator.movie.edu
Address: 0.0.0.0

movie.edu
        origin = terminator.movie.edu
        mail addr = al.robocop.movie.edu
        serial = 42
        refresh = 10800 (3H)
        retry  = 3600 (1H)
        expire = 604800 (7D)
        minimum ttl = 86400 (1D)
```

```
movie.edu      nameserver = terminator.movie.edu
movie.edu      nameserver = wormhole.movie.edu
movie.edu      nameserver = zardoz.movie.edu
movie.edu      preference = 10, mail exchanger = postmanrings2x.movie.edu
postmanrings2x.movie.edu        internet address = 192.249.249.66
```

No Response from Server

What could have gone wrong if your name server can't look up its own name?

```
% nslookup
Default Server:  terminator.movie.edu
Address:  0.0.0.0

> terminator
Server:  terminator.movie.edu
Address:  0.0.0.0

*** terminator.movie.edu can't find terminator: No response from server
```

The "no response from server" error message means exactly that: the resolver didn't get back a response. *nslookup* doesn't necessarily look up anything when it starts up. If you see that the address of your name server is 0.0.0.0, then *nslookup* grabbed the system's host name (what the *hostname* command returns) for the *Default Server* field and gave you its prompt. It's only when you try to look something up that you find out there is no name server responding. In this case, it's pretty obvious that there's no server running—a name server ought to be able to look up its own name. If you are looking up some remote information, though, the name server could fail to respond because it's still trying to look up the data and *nslookup* gave up waiting. How can you tell the difference between a name server that isn't running and a name server that is running but didn't respond? You can use the *ls* command to figure it out:

```
% nslookup
Default Server:  terminator.movie.edu
Address:  0.0.0.0

> ls foo.        —Try to list a nonexistent zone
*** Can't list domain foo.: No response from server
```

In this case, no name server is running. If the host couldn't be reached, the error would be "timed out." If a name server is running, you'll see the following error message:

```
% nslookup
Default Server:  terminator.movie.edu
Address:  0.0.0.0

> ls foo.
[terminator.movie.edu]
*** Can't list domain foo.: No information
```

That is, unless there's a top-level *foo* zone in your world.

No PTR Record for Name Server's Address

Here's one of *nslookup*'s most annoying problems: something went wrong, and
nslookup exited on startup:

```
% nslookup

*** Can't find server name for address 192.249.249.3: Non-existent host/domain
*** Default servers are not available
```

The "nonexistent domain" message means that the name *3.249.249.192.in-addr.
arpa* doesn't exist. In other words, *nslookup* couldn't map 192.249.249.3, the
address of its name server, to a domain name. But didn't we just say that *nslookup*
doesn't look up anything when it starts up? In the configuration we showed you
before, *nslookup* didn't look up anything, but that's not a rule. If you create a
resolv.conf that includes one or more *nameserver* directives, *nslookup* tries to
reverse map the address to get the name server's domain name. In the preceding
example, there *is* a name server running on 192.249.249.3, but it said there are no
PTR records for the address 192.249.249.3. Obviously, the reverse-mapping zone is
messed up, at least for the domain name *3.49.249.192.in-addr.arpa*.

The "default servers are not available" message in the example is misleading. After
all, there is a name server there to say the address doesn't exist. More often, you'll
see the error "no response from server" if the name server isn't running on the
host or the host can't be reached. Only then does the "default servers are not
available" message make sense.

Query Refused

Refused queries can cause problems at startup, and they can cause lookup failures during a session. Here's what it looks like when *nslookup* exits on startup
because of a refused query:

```
% nslookup
*** Can't find server name for address 192.249.249.3: Query refused
*** Default servers are not available
%
```

This one has two possible causes. Either your name server does not support
inverse queries (older *nslookup*s only) or an access list is preventing the lookup.

Old versions of *nslookup* (pre-4.8.3) used an inverse query on startup. Inverse
queries were never widely used—*nslookup* was one of the few applications that
did use them. In BIND 4.9, support for inverse queries was dropped, which broke

old *nslookup*s. To accommodate these old clients, a new configuration file option was added.

In BIND 4, the directive looks like this:

```
options fake-iquery
```

In BIND 8, the statement looks like this:

```
options { fake-iquery yes; };
```

(BIND 9 doesn't support *fake-iquery* as of 9.1.0.)

This causes your name server to respond to the inverse query with a "fake" response that is good enough to let *nslookup* continue.[*]

Access lists can also cause *nslookup* startup problems. When *nslookup* attempts to find the domain name of its name server (using a PTR query, not an inverse query), the query can be refused. If you think the problem is an access list, make sure you allow the host you're running on to query the name server. Check any *secure_zone* TXT records or *allow-query* substatements for the IP address of the local host or the loopback address, if you're running *nslookup* on the same host as the name server.

Access lists can do more than cause *nslookup* to fail to start up. They can also cause lookups and zone transfers to fail in the middle of a session when you point *nslookup* at a remote name server. This is what you would see:

```
% nslookup
Default Server:  hp.com
Address:  15.255.152.4

> server terminator.movie.edu
Default Server:  terminator.movie.edu
Address:  192.249.249.3

> carrie.movie.edu.
Server:  terminator.movie.edu
Address:  192.249.249.3

*** terminator.movie.edu can't find carrie.movie.edu.: Query refused

>ls movie.edu                    —This attempts a zone transfer
[terminator.movie.edu]
*** Can't list domain movie.edu: Query refused
>
```

---

[*] The fake response to an inverse query for, say, the domain name that owns the address 192.249.249.3 is just the address in square brackets, [192.249.249.3].

First resolv.conf Name Server Not Responding

Here is another twist on the last problem:

```
% nslookup
*** Can't find server name for address 192.249.249.3: No response from server
Default Server: wormhole.movie.edu
Address: 192.249.249.1
```

This time, the first name server listed in *resolv.conf* did not respond. We had a second *nameserver* directive in *resolv.conf*, though, and the second server did respond. From now on, *nslookup* will send queries only to *wormhole.movie.edu*; it won't try the name server at 192.249.249.3 again.

Finding Out What Is Being Looked Up

We've been waving our hands in the last examples, claiming that *nslookup* was looking up the name server's address, but we didn't prove it. Here is our proof. This time, when we started up *nslookup*, we turned on *d2* debugging from the command line. This causes *nslookup* to print out the query messages it sent, as well as printing out when the query timed out and was retransmitted:

```
% nslookup -d2
------------
SendRequest(), len 44
    HEADER:
        opcode = QUERY, id = 1, rcode = NOERROR
        header flags:  query, want recursion
        questions = 1,  answers = 0,  authority records = 0,
        additional = 0

    QUESTIONS:
        3.249.249.192.in-addr.arpa, type = PTR, class = IN

------------
timeout (5 secs)
timeout (10 secs)
timeout (20 secs)
timeout (40 secs)
SendRequest failed

*** Can't find server name for address 192.249.249.3: No response from server
*** Default servers are not available
```

As you can see by the timeouts, it took 75 seconds for *nslookup* to give up. Without the debugging output, you wouldn't have seen anything printed to the screen for 75 seconds; it'd look as if *nslookup* had hung.

Unspecified Error

You can run into a rather unsettling problem called an "unspecified error." We have an example of this error here. We've included only the tail end of the output, since we just want to talk about the error at this point (you'll find the whole *nslookup* session that produced this segment in Chapter 14, *Troubleshooting DNS and BIND*):

```
Authoritative answers can be found from:
(root)   nameserver = NS.NIC.DDN.MIL
(root)   nameserver = B.ROOT-SERVERS.NET
(root)   nameserver = E.ROOT-SERVERS.NET
(root)   nameserver = D.ROOT-SERVERS.NET
(root)   nameserver = F.ROOT-SERVERS.NET
(root)   nameserver = C.ROOT-SERVERS.NET
(root)   nameserver =
*** Error: record size incorrect (1050690 != 65519)

*** relay.hp.com can't find .: Unspecified error
```

What happened here is that there was too much data to fit into a UDP datagram. The name server stopped filling in the response when it ran out of room. The name server didn't set the truncation bit in the response packet, or *nslookup* would have retried the query over a TCP connection; the name server must have decided that enough of the "important" information fit. You won't see this kind of error very often. You'll see it if you create too many NS records for a zone, so don't create too many. (Advice like this makes you wonder why you bought this book, right?) How many is "too many" depends on how well the domain names in the packet can be "compressed," which, in turn, depends on how many name servers' names end in the same domain name. The root name servers were renamed to end in *root-servers.net* for this very reason—this allows more root name servers (13) on the Internet. As a rule of thumb, don't go over 10 NS records. As for what caused *this* error, you'll just have to read Chapter 14. Those of you who just read Chapter 9, *Parenting*, may know already.

Best of the Net

System administrators have a thankless job. There are certain questions, usually quite simple ones, that users ask over and over again. And sometimes, when in a creative mood, sysadmins come up with clever ways to help their users. When the rest of us discover their ingenuity, we can only sit back, smile admiringly, and wish we had thought of it ourselves. Here is one such case, where a system administrator found a way to communicate the solution to the sometimes vexing puzzle of how to end an *nslookup* session:

```
% nslookup
Default Server:  envy.ugcs.caltech.edu
```

```
Address:   131.215.134.135

> quit
Server:   envy.ugcs.caltech.edu
Addresses:   131.215.134.135, 131.215.128.135

Name:    ugcs.caltech.edu
Addresses:   131.215.128.135, 131.215.134.135
Aliases:   quit.ugcs.caltech.edu
           use.exit.to.leave.nslookup.-.-.-.ugcs.caltech.edu

> exit
%
```

Using dig

That's one way to deal with what's arguably a shortcoming in *nslookup*. Another is just to chuck *nslookup* and use *dig*, the Domain Information Groper (a reverse-engineered acronym if we've ever heard one).

We said earlier that *dig* isn't as pervasive as *nslookup*, so we'd better begin by telling you where to get it. You can pick up source for *dig* from the *tools* directory (BIND 4), *src/bin/dig* directory (BIND 8), or *bin/dig* directory (BIND 9) of the BIND distribution. If you build the whole distribution, you'll build a nice, new copy of *dig*, too.

With *dig*, you specify all aspects of the query you'd like to send on the command line; there's no interactive mode. You specify the domain name you want to look up as an argument, and the type of query you want to send (e.g., *a* for address records, *mx* for MX records) as another argument; the default is to look up address records. You specify the name server you'd like to query after an "@." You can use either a domain name or an IP address to designate a name server. The default is to query the name servers in *resolv.conf*.

dig is smart about arguments, too. You can specify the arguments in any order you like, and *dig* will figure out that *mx* is probably the type of records, not the domain name, you want to look up.*

One major difference between *nslookup* and *dig* is that *dig* doesn't apply the search list, so always use fully qualified domain names as arguments to *dig*. So:

    % **dig plan9.fx.movie.edu**

looks up address records for *plan9.fx.movie.edu* using the first name server in *resolv.conf*, while:

---

* Actually, early BIND 9 versions of *dig* (before 9.1.0) are order-impaired and require that you specify the domain name argument before the type. You can specify the server to query anywhere, though.

```
% dig acmebw.com mx
```

looks up MX records for *acmebw.com* on the same name server, and:

```
% dig @wormhole.movie.edu. movie.edu. soa
```

queries *wormhole.movie.edu* for the SOA record of *movie.edu*.

dig's Output Format

dig shows you the complete DNS response message in all its glory, with the various sections (header, question, answer, authority, and additional) clearly called out, and with resource records in those sections printed in master file format. This can come in handy if you need to use some of your troubleshooting tool's output in a zone data file or in your root hints file. For example, the output produced by:

```
% dig @a.root-servers.net ns .
```

looks like this:

```
; <<>> DiG 8.3 <<>> @a.root-servers.net . ns
; (1 server found)
;; res options: init recurs defnam dnsrch
;; got answer:
;; ->>HEADER<<- opcode: QUERY, status: NOERROR, id: 6
;; flags: qr aa rd; QUERY: 1, ANSWER: 13, AUTHORITY: 0, ADDITIONAL: 13
;; QUERY SECTION:
;;      ., type = NS, class = IN

;; ANSWER SECTION:
.                       6D IN NS        A.ROOT-SERVERS.NET.
.                       6D IN NS        H.ROOT-SERVERS.NET.
.                       6D IN NS        C.ROOT-SERVERS.NET.
.                       6D IN NS        G.ROOT-SERVERS.NET.
.                       6D IN NS        F.ROOT-SERVERS.NET.
.                       6D IN NS        B.ROOT-SERVERS.NET.
.                       6D IN NS        J.ROOT-SERVERS.NET.
.                       6D IN NS        K.ROOT-SERVERS.NET.
.                       6D IN NS        L.ROOT-SERVERS.NET.
.                       6D IN NS        M.ROOT-SERVERS.NET.
.                       6D IN NS        I.ROOT-SERVERS.NET.
.                       6D IN NS        E.ROOT-SERVERS.NET.
.                       6D IN NS        D.ROOT-SERVERS.NET.

;; ADDITIONAL SECTION:
A.ROOT-SERVERS.NET.     6D IN A         198.41.0.4
H.ROOT-SERVERS.NET.     6D IN A         128.63.2.53
C.ROOT-SERVERS.NET.     6D IN A         192.33.4.12
G.ROOT-SERVERS.NET.     6D IN A         192.112.36.4
F.ROOT-SERVERS.NET.     6D IN A         192.5.5.241
B.ROOT-SERVERS.NET.     6D IN A         128.9.0.107
J.ROOT-SERVERS.NET.     5w6d16h IN A    198.41.0.10
K.ROOT-SERVERS.NET.     5w6d16h IN A    193.0.14.129
L.ROOT-SERVERS.NET.     5w6d16h IN A    198.32.64.12
M.ROOT-SERVERS.NET.     5w6d16h IN A    202.12.27.33
```

```
    I.ROOT-SERVERS.NET.      6D IN A        192.36.148.17
    E.ROOT-SERVERS.NET.      6D IN A        192.203.230.10
    D.ROOT-SERVERS.NET.      6D IN A        128.8.10.90

;; Total query time: 116 msec
;; FROM: terminator.movie.edu to SERVER: a.root-servers.net  198.41.0.4
;; WHEN: Fri Sep 15 09:47:26 2000
;; MSG SIZE  sent: 17  rcvd: 436
```

Let's examine this output section by section.

The first line, beginning with the master file comment character (;) and <<>> *DiG 8.3* <<>>, simply parrots the options we specified in the command line, namely, that we were interested in the NS records that *a.root-servers.net* had for the root zone.

The next line, *(1 server found)*, tells us that when *dig* looked up the addresses associated with the domain name we specified after the "@", *a.root-servers.net*, it found one. (If *dig* finds more than three, the maximum number of name servers most resolvers can query, it'll report three.)

The line beginning with ->> *HEADER* <<- is the first part of the header of the reply message that *dig* received from the remote name server. The opcode in the header is always QUERY, just as it is with *nslookup*. The status is NOERROR; it can be any of the statuses mentioned earlier in this chapter under "Showing the Query and Response Messages." The ID is the message ID, a 16-bit number used to match responses to queries.

The flags tell us a bit more about the response. *qr* indicates that the message was a response, not a query. *dig* decodes responses, not queries, so *qr* will always be present. Not so with *aa* or *rd*, though. *aa* indicates that the response was authoritative, and *rd* indicates that the recursion desired bit was set in the query (since the responding name server just copies the bit from the query to the response). Most of the time *rd* is set in the query, you'll also see *ra* set in the response, indicating that recursion was available from the remote name server. However, *a.root-servers.net* is a root name server and has recursion disabled, like we showed you in Chapter 11, *Security*, so it handles recursive queries the same as it does iterative queries. So it ignores the *rd* bit and correctly indicates that recursion wasn't available by leaving *ra* unset.

The last fields in the header indicate that *dig* asked one question and received 13 records in the answer section, zero records in the authority section, and 13 records in the additional data section.

The line after the line that contains *QUERY SECTION:* shows us the query *dig* sent: for the NS records in the IN class for the root zone. After *ANSWER SECTION:*, we see the 13 NS records for the root name servers, and after *ADDITIONAL SECTION:*, we have the 13 A records that correspond to those 13 root name servers. If the response had included an authority section, we'd have seen that, too, after *AUTHORITY SECTION:*.

At the very end, *dig* includes summary information about the query and response. The first line shows you how long it took the remote name server to return the response after *dig* sent the query. The second line shows you from which host you sent the query and to which name server you sent it. The third line is a timestamp showing when the response was received. And the fourth line shows you the size of the query and the response, in bytes.

Zone Transfers with dig

As with *nslookup*, you can use *dig* to initiate zone transfers. Unlike *nslookup*, though, *dig* has no special command to request a zone transfer. Instead, you simply specify *axfr* (as the query type) and the domain name of the zone as arguments. Remember that you can only transfer a zone from a name server that's authoritative for the zone.

So to transfer the *movie.edu* zone from *wormhole.movie.edu*, you could use:

```
$ dig @wormhole.movie.edu movie.edu axfr

; <<>> DiG 8.3 <<>> @wormhole.movie.edu movie.edu axfr
; (1 server found)
$ORIGIN movie.edu.
@                       1D IN SOA       terminator al.robocop (
                                        2000091402      ; serial
                                        3H              ; refresh
                                        1H              ; retry
                                        1W              ; expiry
                                        1H )            ; minimum

                        1D IN NS        terminator
                        1D IN NS        wormhole
                        1D IN NS        outland.fx
outland.fx              1D IN A         192.253.254.3
wormhole                1D IN A         192.249.249.1
                        1D IN A         192.253.253.1
wh249                   1D IN A         192.249.249.1
robocop                 1D IN A         192.249.249.2
bigt                    1D IN CNAME     terminator
cujo                    1D IN TXT       "Location:" "machine" "room" "dog" "house"
wh253                   1D IN A         192.253.253.1
wh                      1D IN CNAME     wormhole
shining                 1D IN A         192.253.253.3
terminator              1D IN A         192.249.249.3
localhost               1D IN A         127.0.0.1
fx                      1D IN NS        bladerunner.fx
bladerunner.fx          1D IN A         192.253.254.2
fx                      1D IN NS        outland.fx
outland.fx              1D IN A         192.253.254.3
dh                      1D IN CNAME     diehard
carrie                  1D IN A         192.253.253.4
diehard                 1D IN A         192.249.249.4
```

```
misery                    1D IN A        192.253.253.2
@                         1D IN SOA      terminator al.robocop (
                                         2000091402      ; serial
                                         3H              ; refresh
                                         1H              ; retry
                                         1W              ; expiry
                                         1H )            ; minimum
```

```
;; Received 25 answers (25 records).
;; FROM: terminator.movie.edu to SERVER: wormhole.movie.edu
;; WHEN: Fri Sep 22 11:02:45 2000
```

Note that as with *nslookup*, the SOA record appears twice, at the beginning and the end of the zone. And as with all *dig* output, the results of the zone transfer are printed in master file format, so you can use the output as a zone data file if you need to.*

dig Options

There are too many command-line options to *dig* to show here, so look at *dig*'s manual page for an exhaustive list. Here's a list of the most important ones, though, and what they do:

−x address

> *nslookup* is smart enough to recognize an IP address and look up the appropriate domain name in *in-addr.arpa*, so why not *dig*? If you use the *−x* option, *dig* assumes that the domain name argument you've specified is really an IP address, so it inverts the octets and tacks on *in-addr.arpa*. Using *−x* also changes the default record type looked up to ANY, so you can reverse map an IP address with *dig −x 10.0.0.1*.

−p port

> Send queries to the specified port instead of port 53, the default.

+norec[urse]

> Turn off recursion (recursion is on by default).

+vc

> Send TCP-based queries (queries are UDP by default).

---

* Though you'd need to delete the extra SOA record first.

13

Reading BIND Debugging Output

"O Tiger-lily!" said Alice, addressing herself to one that was waving gracefully about in the wind, "I wish you could talk!"

"We can talk," said the Tiger-lily, "when there's anybody worth talking to."

One of the tools in your troubleshooting toolchest is the name server's debugging output. As long as your name server has been compiled with DEBUG defined, you can get query-by-query reports of its internal operation. The messages you get are often quite cryptic; they were meant for someone who has the source code to follow. We'll explain some of the debugging output in this chapter. Our goal is to cover just enough for you to follow what the name server is doing; we aren't trying to supply an exhaustive compilation of debugging messages.

As you read through the explanations here, think back to material covered in earlier chapters. Seeing this information again, in another context, should help you understand more fully how a name server works.

Debugging Levels

The amount of information the name server provides depends on the debugging level. The lower the debugging level, the less information you get. Higher debugging levels give you more information, but they also fill up your disk faster. After you've read a lot of debugging output, you'll develop a feel for how much information you'll need to solve any particular problem. Of course, if you can easily recreate the problem, you can start at level 1 and increase the debugging level until you have enough information. For the most basic problem—why a name can't be looked up—level 1 will often suffice, so you should start there.

What Information Is at Each Level?

Here's a list of the information that each debugging level produces for BIND 8 and BIND 9 name servers. The debugging information is cumulative; for example, level 2 includes all of level 1's debugging information. The data is divided into the following basic areas: starting up, updating the database, processing queries, and maintaining zones. We won't cover updating the name server's internal database—problems almost always occur elsewhere. However, *what* the name server adds or deletes from its internal database can be a problem, as you'll see in Chapter 14, *Troubleshooting DNS and BIND*.

BIND 8 and 9 have a whopping 99 debug levels, but most of the debugging messages are logged at just a few of those levels. We'll look at those now.

BIND 8 debugging levels

Level 1

The information at this level is necessarily brief. Name servers can process *lots* of queries, which can create *lots* of debugging output. Since the output is condensed, you can collect data over long periods. Use this debugging level for basic startup information and for watching query transactions. You'll see some errors logged at this level, including syntax errors and DNS packet formatting errors. This level also shows referrals.

Level 2

Level 2 provides lots of useful stuff: it lists the IP addresses of remote name servers used during a lookup, along with their roundtrip time values; it calls out bad responses; and it tags a response as to which type of query it is answering, a SYSTEM (sysquery) or a USER query. When you are tracking down a problem with a slave server loading a zone, this level shows you the zone values—serial number, refresh time, retry time, expire time, and time left—as the slave checks if it is up to date with its master.

Level 3

Level 3 debugging becomes much more verbose, because it generates lots of messages about updating the name server database. Make sure you have enough disk space if you are going to collect debugging output at level 3 or above. At level 3, you also see duplicate queries called out, system queries generated (sysquery), the names of the remote name servers used during a lookup, and the number of addresses found for each server.

Level 4

Use level 4 debugging when you want to see the query and response packets *received* by the name server. This level also shows the credibility level for cached data.

Level 5

There are a variety of messages at level 5, but none of them is particularly useful for general debugging. This level includes some error messages, for example when a *malloc()* fails or when the name server gives up on a query.

Level 6

Level 6 shows you the response sent to the original query.

Level 7

Level 7 shows you a few configuration and parsing messages.

Level 8

There is no significant debugging information at this level.

Level 9

There is no significant debugging information at this level.

Level 10

Use level 10 debugging when you want to see the query and response packets *sent* by the name server. The format of these packets is the same format used in level 4. You won't use this level very often since you can see the name server response packet with *nslookup* or *dig*.

Level 11

There are only a couple of debugging messages at and above this level, and they are in seldom-traversed code.

BIND 9 debugging levels

Level 1

Level 1 shows you basic name server operation: zone loading, maintenance (including SOA queries, zone transfers and zone expiration, and cache cleaning), NOTIFY messages, queries received, and high-level tasks dispatched (such as looking up addresses for a name server).

Level 2

Level 2 logs multicast requests.

Level 3

Level 3 shows you low-level task creation and operation. Unfortunately, most of these tasks don't have particularly descriptive names (*requestmgr_detach?*) and the arguments they report are awfully cryptic. Level 3 also shows you journal activity, such as when the name server writes a record of a zone change to the zone's journal or when the name server applies a journal to a zone at startup. Operation of the DNSSEC validator and checking of TSIG signatures also come in at debug level 3.

Level 4

Level 4 logs when a master name server falls back to using AXFR because the transferred zone's journal isn't available.

Level 5

Level 5 logs which view was used while satisfying a particular request.

Level 6

A handful of outbound zone transfer messages are logged at level 6, including checks of the query that initiated the transfer.

Level 7

There are only a couple of new debugging messages at this level (logging of journal adds and deletes, and a count of how many bytes were returned by a zone transfer).

Level 8

Many dynamic update messages are logged at level 8: prerequisite checks, writing journal entries, and rollbacks. Several low-level zone transfer messages also appear here, including a log of resource records sent in a zone transfer.

Level 10

Level 10 reports a couple of messages about zone timer activity.

Level 20

Level 20 reports an update to a zone's refresh timer.

Level 90

Low-level operation of the BIND 9 task dispatcher is logged at level 90.

With BIND 8 and BIND 9, you can configure the name server to print out the debug level with the debug message. Just turn on the logging option *print-severity* as explained in "Logging in BIND 8 and 9" in Chapter 7, *Maintaining BIND*.

Keep in mind that this *is* debugging information—it was used by the authors of BIND to debug the code, so it is not as readable as you might like. You can use it to figure out why the name server isn't doing what you think it should be or just to learn how the name server operates—but don't expect nicely designed, carefully formatted output.

Turning On Debugging

Name server debugging can be started either from the command line or with control messages. If you need to see the startup information to diagnose your current problem, you'll have to use the command-line option. If you want to start debugging on a name server that is already running or if you want to turn off debugging, you'll have to use controls. The name server writes its debugging output to *named.run.* BIND 4 name servers create *named.run* in */usr/tmp* (or */var/tmp*), and BIND 8 and 9 name servers create it in the name server's working directory.

Debugging Command-Line Option

When troubleshooting, you sometimes need to see the sortlist, know which interface a file descriptor is bound to, or find out where in the initialization stage the name server was when it exited (if the *syslog* error message wasn't clear enough). To see this kind of debugging information, you'll have to start debugging with a command-line option; by the time you send a control message, it will be too late. The command-line option for debugging is *–d level.* When you use the command-line option to turn on debugging, a BIND 4 name server will not go into the background as it does normally; you'll have to add the & at the end of your command line to get your shell prompt back. Here's how to start a BIND 4 name server at debugging level 1:

```
# /etc/named -d 1 &
```

BIND 8 and 9 name servers go into the background even when you specify *–d,* so there's no need for the &.

Changing the Debugging Level with Control Messages

If you don't need to see the name server's initialization, start your name server without the debugging command-line option. You can later turn debugging on and off by using *ndc* to send the appropriate control message to the name server process. Here, we set debugging to level 3, then turn debugging off:

```
# ndc trace 3
# ndc notrace
```

And, as you might expect, if you turn on debugging from the command line, you can still use *ndc* to change the name server's debug level.

BIND 9.1.0's *rndc* doesn't implement the *trace* or *notrace* arguments yet (nor does the 9.1.0 *named*), but a future version will. So if you're running BIND 9, use the *–d* command-line option.

Reading Debugging Output

We'll cover five examples of debugging output. The first example shows the name server starting up. The next two examples show successful name lookups. The fourth example shows a secondary name server keeping its zone up to date. And in the last example, we switch from showing you name server behavior to showing you resolver behavior: the resolver search algorithm. After each trace (except the last one) we killed the name server and started it again so that each trace started with a fresh, nearly empty cache.

You might wonder why we've chosen to show normal name server behavior for all our examples; after all, this chapter is about debugging. We're showing you normal behavior because you have to know what normal operation is before you track down abnormal operation. Another reason is to help you understand the concepts (retransmissions, roundtrip times, etc.) we described in earlier chapters.

Name Server Startup (BIND 8, Debug Level 1)

We'll start the debugging examples by watching the name server initialize. This first name server is a BIND 8 name server. We used *–d 1* on the command line, and this is the *named.run* output that resulted:

```
1) Debug level 1
2) Version = named 8.2.3-T7B Mon Aug 21 19:21:21 MDT 2000
3) cricket@abugslife.movie.edu:/usr/local/src/bind-8.2.3-T7B/src/bin/named
4) conffile = ./named.conf
5) starting.  named 8.2.3-T7B Mon Aug 21 19:21:21 MDT 2000
6) cricket@abugslife.movie.edu:/usr/local/src/bind-8.2.3-T7B/src/bin/named
7) ns_init(./named.conf)
8) Adding 64 template zones
9) update_zone_info('0.0.127.in-addr.arpa', 1)
10) source = db.127.0.0
11) purge_zone(0.0.127.in-addr.arpa,1)
12) reloading zone
13) db_load(db.127.0.0, 0.0.127.in-addr.arpa, 1, Nil, Normal)
14) purge_zone(0.0.127.in-addr.arpa,1)
15) master zone "0.0.127.in-addr.arpa" (IN) loaded (serial 2000091500)
16) zone[1] type 1: '0.0.127.in-addr.arpa' z_time 0, z_refresh 0
17) update_zone_info('.', 3)
18) source = db.cache
19) reloading hint zone
20) db_load(db.cache, , 2, Nil, Normal)
21) purge_zone(,1)
22) hint zone "" (IN) loaded (serial 0)
23) zone[2] type 3: '.' z_time 0, z_refresh 0
24) update_pid_file()
25) getnetconf(generation 969052965)
26) getnetconf: considering lo [127.0.0.1]
27) ifp->addr [127.0.0.1].53 d_dfd 20
28) evSelectFD(ctx 0x80d8148, fd 20, mask 0x1, func 0x805e710, uap 0x40114344)
29) evSelectFD(ctx 0x80d8148, fd 21, mask 0x1, func 0x8089540, uap 0x4011b0e8)
30) listening on [127.0.0.1].53 (lo)
31) getnetconf: considering eth0 [192.249.249.3]
32) ifp->addr [192.249.249.3].53 d_dfd 22
33) evSelectFD(ctx 0x80d8148, fd 22, mask 0x1, func 0x805e710, uap 0x401143b0)
34) evSelectFD(ctx 0x80d8148, fd 23, mask 0x1, func 0x8089540, uap 0x4011b104)
35) listening on [206.168.194.122].53 (eth0)
```

```
36) fwd ds 5 addr [0.0.0.0].1085
37) Forwarding source address is [0.0.0.0].1085
38) evSelectFD(ctx 0x80d8148, fd 5, mask 0x1, func 0x805e710, uap 0)
39) evSetTimer(ctx 0x80d8148, func 0x807cbe8, uap 0x40116158, due 969052990.
812648000, inter 0.000000000)
40) exit ns_init()
41) update_pid_file()
42) Ready to answer queries.
43) prime_cache: priming = 0, root = 0
44) evSetTimer(ctx 0x80d8148, func 0x805bc30, uap 0, due 969052969.000000000,
inter 0.000000000)
45) sysquery: send -> [192.33.4.12].53 dfd=5 nsid=32211 id=0 retry=969052969
46) datagram from [192.33.4.12].53, fd 5, len 436
47) 13 root servers
```

We added the line numbers to the debugging output; you won't see them in yours. Lines 2 through 6 give the version of BIND you are running and the name of the configuration file. Version 8.2.3-T7B was released by ISC (Internet Software Consortium) in August 2000. We used the configuration file in the current directory, *./named.conf*, for this run.

Lines 7 through 23 show BIND reading the configuration file and the zone data files. This name server is a caching-only name server—the only files read are *db. 127.0.0* (lines 9 through 16) and *db.cache* (lines 17–23). Line 9 shows the zone being updated (*0.0.127.IN-ADDR.ARPA*) and line 10 shows the file containing the zone data (*db.127.0.0*). Line 11 indicates that any old data for the zone is purged before new data is added. Line 12 says the zone is being reloaded, even though the zone is actually being loaded for the first time. The zone data is loaded during lines 13 through 15. On lines 16 and 23, *z_time* is the time to check when this zone is up to date; *z_refresh* is the zone refresh time. These values matter only if the name server is a slave for the zone.

Lines 25 through 39 show the initialization of file descriptors. (In this case, they're really socket descriptors.) File descriptors 20 and 21 (lines 27–29) are bound to 127.0.0.1, the loopback address. Descriptor 20 is a datagram socket and descriptor 21 is a stream socket. File descriptors 22 and 23 (lines 32–34) are bound to the 192.249.249.3 interface. Each interface address was considered and used—they would not be used if the interface had not been initialized or if the address were already in the list. File descriptor 5 (lines 36–39) is bound to 0.0.0.0, the wildcard address. Most network daemons use only one socket bound to the wildcard address, not sockets bound to individual interfaces. The wildcard address picks up packets sent to any interface on the host. Let's digress for a moment to explain why *named* uses both a socket bound to the wildcard address and sockets bound to specific interfaces.

When *named* receives a request from an application or from another name server, it receives the request on one of the sockets bound to a specific interface. If *named* did not have sockets bound to specific interfaces, it would receive the requests on the socket bound to the wildcard address. When *named* sends back a response, it uses the same socket descriptor that the request came in on. Why does *named* do this? When responses are sent out via the socket bound to the wildcard address, the kernel fills in the sender's address with the address of the interface the response was actually sent out on. This address may or may not be the same address that the request was sent to. When responses are sent out via the socket bound to a specific address, the kernel fills in the sender's address with that specific address—the same address the request was sent to. If the name server gets a response from an IP address it doesn't know about, the response is tagged a "martian" and discarded. *named* tries to avoid martian responses by sending its responses on descriptors bound to specific interfaces, so the sender's address is the same address the request was sent to. However, when *named* sends out *queries*, it uses the wildcard descriptor since there is no need to use a specific IP address.

Lines 43 through 47 show the name server sending out a system query to find out which name servers are currently serving the root zone. This is known as "priming the cache." The first server queried sent a response that included 13 name servers.

The name server is now initialized and ready to answer queries.

Name Server Startup (BIND 9, Debug Level 1)

Here's what a BIND 9 name server looks like starting up:

```
1)   Sep 15 15:34:53.878 starting BIND 9.1.0 -d1
2)   Sep 15 15:34:53.883 using 1 CPU
3)   Sep 15 15:34:53.899 loading configuration from './named.conf'
4)   Sep 15 15:34:53.920 the default for the 'auth-nxdomain' option is now 'no'
5)   Sep 15 15:34:54.141 no IPv6 interfaces found
6)   Sep 15 15:34:54.143 listening on IPv4 interface lo, 127.0.0.1#53
7)   Sep 15 15:34:54.151 listening on IPv4 interface eth0, 192.249.249.3#53
8)   Sep 15 15:34:54.163 command channel listening on 0.0.0.0#953
9)   Sep 15 15:34:54.180 now using logging configuration from config file
10)  Sep 15 15:34:54.181 dns_zone_load: zone 0.0.127.in-addr.arpa/IN: start
11)  Sep 15 15:34:54.188 dns_zone_load: zone 0.0.127.in-addr.arpa/IN: loaded
12)  Sep 15 15:34:54.189 dns_zone_load: zone 0.0.127.in-addr.arpa/IN: dns_journal
_rollforward: no journal
13)  Sep 15 15:34:54.190 dns_zone_maintenance: zone 0.0.127.in-addr.arpa/IN: enter
14)  Sep 15 15:34:54.190 dns_zone_maintenance: zone version.bind/CHAOS: enter
15)  Sep 15 15:34:54.190 running
```

The first difference you probably noticed between BIND 9's debugging output and BIND 8's is BIND 9's terseness. Remember that BIND 8 has been around for three years, and the authors have had plenty of time to add debugging messages to the code. BIND 9 is brand-spanking-new, so there aren't as many debugging messages yet.

You probably also noticed that BIND 9 includes a timestamp for each debugging message, which can be handy if you're trying to correlate messages to real-world events.

Lines 1 and 2 show the version of BIND we're running (9.1.0) and the configuration file it's reading. As with the previous example, we're using *named.conf* in the current directory. Line 3 tells us we're using only one CPU—to be expected on a box with just one processor.

Line 4 gives us a simple warning that the default for the *auth-nxdomain* substatement (covered in Chapter 10, *Advanced Features*) has changed. Line 5 reminds us that our host doesn't have any IP Version 6 network interfaces; if it did, BIND 9 could listen on those interfaces for queries.

Lines 6 and 7 show the name server listening on two network interfaces: *lo*, the loopback interface, and *eth0*, the Ethernet interface. BIND 9 displays the address and port in the format *address#port*, unlike BIND 8, which uses *[address].port*. Line 8 shows *named* listening on port 953, the default port, for control messages.

Lines 10–12 show the name server loading *0.0.127.in-addr.arpa*. The *start* and *loaded* messages are self-explanatory. The *no journal* message indicates that no journal was present. (A journal, described in Chapter 10, is a record of dynamic updates the name server received for the zone.)

Finally, lines 13 and 14 show the name server doing maintenance on the *0.0.127. in-addr.arpa* and *version.bind* zones. (*version.bind* is a built-in CHAOSNET zone that contains a single TXT record, attached to the domain name *version.bind*.) Zone maintenance is the process that schedules periodic tasks, such as SOA queries for slave and stub zones or NOTIFY messages.

A Successful Lookup (BIND 8, Debug Level 1)

Suppose you want to watch the name server look up a name. Your name server wasn't started with debugging. Use *ndc* once to turn on debugging, look up the name, then again to turn off debugging, like this:

```
# ndc trace 1
# /etc/ping galt.cs.purdue.edu.
# ndc notrace
```

We did this; here's the resulting *named.run* file:

```
datagram from [192.249.249.3].1162, fd 20, len 36

req: nlookup(galt.cs.purdue.edu) id 29574 type=1 class=1
req: missed 'galt.cs.purdue.edu' as '' (cname=0)
forw: forw -> [198.41.0.10].53 ds=4 nsid=40070 id=29574 2ms retry 4sec
datagram from [198.41.0.10].53, fd 4, len 343
```

```
;; ->>HEADER<<- opcode: QUERY, status: NOERROR, id: 40070
;; flags: qr; QUERY: 1, ANSWER: 0, AUTHORITY: 9, ADDITIONAL: 9
;;              galt.cs.purdue.edu, type = A, class = IN
EDU.                          6D IN NS    A.ROOT-SERVERS.NET.
EDU.                          6D IN NS    H.ROOT-SERVERS.NET.
EDU.                          6D IN NS    B.ROOT-SERVERS.NET.
EDU.                          6D IN NS    C.ROOT-SERVERS.NET.
EDU.                          6D IN NS    D.ROOT-SERVERS.NET.
EDU.                          6D IN NS    E.ROOT-SERVERS.NET.
EDU.                          6D IN NS    I.ROOT-SERVERS.NET.
EDU.                          6D IN NS    F.ROOT-SERVERS.NET.
EDU.                          6D IN NS    G.ROOT-SERVERS.NET.
A.ROOT-SERVERS.NET.           5w6d16h IN A    198.41.0.4
H.ROOT-SERVERS.NET.           5w6d16h IN A    128.63.2.53
B.ROOT-SERVERS.NET.           5w6d16h IN A    128.9.0.107
C.ROOT-SERVERS.NET.           5w6d16h IN A    192.33.4.12
D.ROOT-SERVERS.NET.           5w6d16h IN A    128.8.10.90
E.ROOT-SERVERS.NET.           5w6d16h IN A    192.203.230.10
I.ROOT-SERVERS.NET.           5w6d16h IN A    192.36.148.17
F.ROOT-SERVERS.NET.           5w6d16h IN A    192.5.5.241
G.ROOT-SERVERS.NET.           5w6d16h IN A    192.112.36.4
resp: nlookup(galt.cs.purdue.edu) qtype=1
resp: found 'galt.cs.purdue.edu' as 'edu' (cname=0)
resp: forw -> [192.36.148.17].53 ds=4 nsid=40071 id=29574 1ms
datagram from [192.36.148.17].53, fd 4, len 202


;; ->>HEADER<<- opcode: QUERY, status: NOERROR, id: 40071
;; flags: qr rd; QUERY: 1, ANSWER: 0, AUTHORITY: 4, ADDITIONAL: 4
;;    galt.cs.purdue.edu, type = A, class = IN
PURDUE.EDU.                   2D IN NS    NS.PURDUE.EDU.
PURDUE.EDU.                   2D IN NS    MOE.RICE.EDU.
PURDUE.EDU.                   2D IN NS    PENDRAGON.CS.PURDUE.EDU.
PURDUE.EDU.                   2D IN NS    HARBOR.ECN.PURDUE.EDU.
NS.PURDUE.EDU.                    2D IN A      128.210.11.5
MOE.RICE.EDU.                     2D IN A      128.42.5.4
PENDRAGON.CS.PURDUE.EDU.             2D IN A 128.10.2.5
HARBOR.ECN.PURDUE.EDU.              2D IN A     128.46.199.76
resp: nlookup(galt.cs.purdue.edu) qtype=1
resp: found 'galt.cs.purdue.edu' as 'cs.purdue.edu' (cname=0)
resp: forw -> [128.46.199.76].53 ds=4 nsid=40072 id=29574 8ms
datagram from [128.46.199.76].53, fd 4, len 234


send_msg -> [192.249.249.3].1162 (UDP 20) id=29574
Debug off
```

First, notice that IP addresses, not domain names, are logged—odd for a *name* server, don't you think? It's really not that odd, though. If you are trying to debug a problem with looking up names, you don't want the name server looking up additional names just to make the debugging output more readable—the extra queries would interfere with the debugging. None of the debugging levels translates IP addresses into domain names. You'll have to use a tool (like the one we provide later) to convert them for you.

Let's go through this debugging output line by line. This detailed approach is important if you want to understand what each line means. If you turn on debugging, you're probably trying to find out why some name can't be looked up, and you're going to have to figure out what the trace means.

```
datagram from [192.249.249.3].1162, fd 20, len 36
```

A datagram came from the host with IP address 192.249.249.3 (*terminator.movie. edu*). You may see the datagram come from 127.0.0.1 if the sender is on the same host as the name server. The sending application used port 1162. The name server received the datagram on file descriptor (fd) 20. The startup debugging output, like the one shown earlier, tells you which interface file descriptor 20 is bound to. The length (len) of the datagram was 36 bytes.

```
req: nlookup(galt.cs.purdue.edu) id 29574 type=1 class=1
```

Since the next debugging line starts with *req*, we know that the datagram was a request. The name looked up in the request was *galt.cs.purdue.edu*. The request id is 29574. The *type=1* means the request is for address information. The *class=1* means the class is IN. You can find a complete list of query types and classes in the header file */usr/ include/arpa/nameser.h*.

```
req: missed 'galt.cs.purdue.edu' as '' (cname=0)
```

The name server looked up the requested name and didn't find it. Then it tried to find a remote name server to ask; none was found until the root zone (the empty quotes). The *cname=0* means the name server didn't encounter a CNAME record. If it does see a CNAME record, the canonical name is looked up instead of the original name, and *cname* will be nonzero.

```
forw: forw -> [198.41.0.10].53 ds=4 nsid=40070 id=29574 2ms retry 4sec
```

The query was forwarded to the name server (port 53) on host 198.41.0.10 (*j.root-servers.net*). The name server used file descriptor 4 (which is bound to the wildcard address) to send the query. The name server tagged this query with ID number 40070 (*nsid=40070*) so that it could match the response to the original question. The application used ID number 29574 (*id=29574*), as you saw on the *nlookup* line. The name server will wait four seconds before trying the next name server.

```
datagram from [198.41.0.10].53, fd 4, len 343
```

The name server on *j.root-servers.net* responded. Since the response was a delegation, it is printed in full in the debug log.

```
resp: nlookup(galt.cs.purdue.edu) qtype=1
```

After the information in the response message is cached, the name is looked up again. As mentioned earlier, *qtype=1* means that the name server is looking for address information.

```
resp: found 'galt.cs.purdue.edu' as 'edu' (cname=0)
resp: forw -> [192.36.148.17].53 ds=4 nsid=40071 id=29574 1ms
datagram from [192.36.148.17].53, fd 4, len 202
```

The root name server responded with a delegation to the *edu* servers. The same query is sent to 192.36.148.17 (*i.root-servers.net*), one of the *edu* servers. *i.root-servers.net* responds with information about the *purdue.edu* servers.

```
resp: found 'galt.cs.purdue.edu' as 'cs.purdue.edu' (cname=0)
```

This time there is some information at the *cs.purdue.edu* level.

```
resp: forw -> [128.46.199.76].53 ds=4 nsid=40072 id=29574 8ms
```

A query was sent to the name server on 128.46.199.76 (*harbor.ecn.purdue.edu*). This time the name server ID is 40072.

```
datagram from [128.46.199.76].53, fd 4, len 234
```

The name server on *harbor.ecn.purdue.edu* responded. We have to look at what happens next to figure out the contents of this response.

```
send_msg -> [192.249.249.3].1162 (UDP 20) id=29574
```

The last response must have contained the address requested, since the name server responded to the application (which used port 1162, if you look back at the original query). The response was in a UDP packet (as opposed to a TCP connection), and it used file descriptor 20.

This name server was "quiet" when we did this trace; it wasn't handling other queries at the same time. When you do a trace on an active name server, though, you won't be so lucky. You'll have to sift through the output and patch together those pieces that pertain to the lookup in which you are interested. It's not that hard, though. Start up your favorite editor, search for the *nlookup* line with the name you looked up, then trace the entries with the same *nsid*. You'll see how to follow the *nsid* in the next BIND 8 trace.

A Successful Lookup (BIND 9, Debug Level 1)

We'll show you the debugging output produced by looking up the same domain name on a BIND 9 name server at debug level 1, but it's almost laughably short. Still, as we said, it's important to know what debugging output looks like under correct operation. Anyway, here goes:

```
Sep 16 17:20:57.193 client 192.249.249.3#1090: query: galt.cs.purdue.edu A
Sep 16 17:20:57.194 createfetch: galt.cs.purdue.edu. A
```

The first line tells us that a client at IP address 192.249.249.3 (that is, the local host), running on port 1090, sent us a query for *galt.cs.purdue.edu*'s address. The second line is logged by the portion of the name server that does name resolution to let us know what it's up to.

A Successful Lookup with Retransmissions (BIND 8, Debug Level 1)

Not all lookups are as "clean" as the last one—sometimes the query must be retransmitted. The user doesn't see any difference as long as the lookup succeeds, although a query involving retransmissions will take longer. Following is a trace where there are retransmissions. We converted the IP addresses to domain names after the trace was done. Notice how much easier it is to read with names!

```
 1)  Debug turned ON, Level 1
 2)
 3)  datagram from terminator.movie.edu port 3397, fd 20, len 35
 4)  req: nlookup(ucunix.san.uc.edu) id 1 type=1 class=1
 5)  req: found 'ucunix.san.uc.edu' as 'edu' (cname=0)
 6)  forw: forw -> i.root-servers.net port 53  ds=4 nsid=2 id=1 0ms retry 4 sec
 7)
 8)  datagram from i.root-servers.net port 53, fd 4, len 240
     <delegation lines removed>
 9)  resp: nlookup(ucunix.san.uc.edu) qtype=1
10)  resp: found 'ucunix.san.uc.edu' as 'san.uc.edu' (cname=0)
11)  resp: forw -> uceng.uc.edu port 53 ds=4 nsid=3 id=1 0ms
12)  resend(addr=1 n=0) - > ucbeh.san.uc.edu port 53 ds=4 nsid=3 id=1 0ms
13)
14)  datagram from terminator.movie.edu port 3397, fd 20, len 35
15)  req: nlookup(ucunix.san.uc.edu) id 1 type=1 class=1
16)  req: found 'ucunix.san.uc.edu' as 'san.uc.edu' (cname=0)
17)  resend(addr=2 n=0) - > uccba.uc.edu port 53 ds=4 nsid=3 id=1 0ms
18)  resend(addr=3 n=0) - > mail.cis.ohio-state.edu port 53 ds=4 nsid=3 id=1 0ms
19)
20)  datagram from mail.cis.ohio-state.edu port 53, fd 4, len 51
21)  send_msg -> terminator.movie.edu (UDP 20 3397) id=1
```

This trace starts out the same way as the last trace (lines 1 through 11): the name server receives a query for *ucunix.san.uc.edu*, sends the query to an *edu* name server (*i.root-servers.net*), receives a response that includes a list of name servers for *uc.edu*, and sends the query to one of the *uc.edu* name servers (*uceng.uc.edu*).

What's new in this trace is the *resend* lines (lines 12, 17, and 18). The *forw* on line 11 counts as *resend(addr=0 n=0)*—we CS dweebs always start counting at zero. Since *uceng.uc.edu* didn't respond, the name server went on to try *ucbeh.san.uc. edu* (line 12), *uccba.uc.edu* (line 17), and *mail.cis.ohio-state.edu* (line 18). The off-site name server on *mail.cis.ohio-state.edu* finally responded (line 20). Notice that you can track all the retransmissions by searching for *nsid=3*; that's important to know, because lots of other queries may be wedged between these.

Also, notice the second datagram from *terminator.movie.edu* (line 14). It has the same port, file descriptor, length, ID, and type as the query on line 3. The application didn't receive a response in time, so it retransmitted its original query. Since the name server is still working on the first query transmitted, this one is a duplicate. It doesn't say so in this output, but the name server detected the duplicate and dropped it. We can tell because there is no *forw:* line after the *req:* lines, as there was on lines 4 through 6.

Can you guess what this output might look like if the name server were having trouble looking up a name? You'd see a lot of retransmissions as the name server kept trying to look up the name (which you could track by matching the *nsid=* lines). You'd see the application send a couple more retransmissions, thinking that the name server hadn't received the application's first query. Eventually the name server would give up, usually after the application itself gave up.

With a BIND 9.1.0 name server, you won't see resends until debug level 3, and at that point they'll be very difficult to pick out from BIND 9's other logged messages. Moreover, even at debug level 3, BIND 9.1.0 doesn't tell you *which* name server it's resending to.

A Slave Name Server Checking Its Zone (BIND 8, Debug Level 1)

In addition to tracking down problems with name server lookups, you may have to track down why a slave server is not loading from its master. Tracking down this problem can often be done by simply comparing the zone's SOA serial numbers on the two servers using *nslookup* or *dig*, as we'll show in Chapter 14. If your problem is more elusive, you may have to resort to looking at the debugging information. We'll show you what the debugging information should look like if your server is running normally.

This debugging output was generated on a "quiet" name server—one not receiving any queries—to show you exactly which lines pertain to zone maintenance. Remember that a BIND 4 or 8 slave name server uses a child process to transfer the zone data to the local disk before reading it in. While the slave logs its debugging information to *named.run*, the slave's child process logs its debugging information to *xfer.ddt.PID*. The *PID* suffix, by default the process ID of the child process, may be changed to ensure that the filename is unique. Beware—turning on debugging on a slave name server will leave *xfer.ddt.PID* files lying around, even if you are only trying to trace a lookup. Our trace is at debugging level 1, and we turned on the BIND 8 logging option *print-time*. Debug level 3 gives you more information, more than you may want if a transfer actually occurs. A debugging level 3 trace of a zone transfer of several hundred resource records can create an *xfer.ddt.PID* file several megabytes in size.

```
21-Feb 00:13:18.026 do_zone_maint for zone movie.edu (class IN)
21-Feb 00:13:18.034 zone_maint('movie.edu')
21-Feb 00:13:18.035 qserial_query(movie.edu)
21-Feb 00:13:18.043 sysquery: send -> [192.249.249.3].53 dfd=5
                        nsid=29790 id=0 retry=888048802
21-Feb 00:13:18.046 qserial_query(movie.edu) QUEUED
21-Feb 00:13:18.052 next maintenance for zone 'movie.edu' in 2782 sec
21-Feb 00:13:18.056 datagram from [192.249.249.3].53, fd 5, len 380
21-Feb 00:13:18.059 qserial_answer(movie.edu, 26739)
21-Feb 00:13:18.060 qserial_answer: zone is out of date
21-Feb 00:13:18.061 startxfer() movie.edu
21-Feb 00:13:18.063 /usr/etc/named-xfer -z movie.edu -f db.movie
                        -s 26738 -C 1 -P 53 -d 1 -l xfer.ddt 192.249.249.3
21-Feb 00:13:18.131 started xfer child 390
21-Feb 00:13:18.132 next maintenance for zone 'movie.edu' in 7200 sec

21-Feb 00:14:02.089 endxfer: child 390 zone movie.edu returned
                        status=1 termsig=-1
21-Feb 00:14:02.094 loadxfer() "movie.edu"
21-Feb 00:14:02.094 purge_zone(movie.edu,1)

21-Feb 00:14:30.049 db_load(db.movie, movie.edu, 2, Nil)
21-Feb 00:14:30.058 next maintenance for zone 'movie.edu' in 1846 sec

21-Feb 00:17:12.478 slave zone "movie.edu" (IN) loaded (serial 26739)
21-Feb 00:17:12.486 no schedule change for zone 'movie.edu'

21-Feb 00:42:44.817 Cleaned cache of 0 RRs

21-Feb 00:45:16.046 do_zone_maint for zone movie.edu (class IN)
21-Feb 00:45:16.054 zone_maint('movie.edu')
21-Feb 00:45:16.055 qserial_query(movie.edu)
21-Feb 00:45:16.063 sysquery: send -> [192.249.249.3].53 dfd=5
                        nsid=29791 id=0 retry=888050660
21-Feb 00:45:16.066 qserial_query(movie.edu) QUEUED
21-Feb 00:45:16.067 next maintenance for zone 'movie.edu' in 3445 sec
21-Feb 00:45:16.074 datagram from [192.249.249.3].53, fd 5, len 380
21-Feb 00:45:16.077 qserial_answer(movie.edu, 26739)
21-Feb 00:45:16.078 qserial_answer: zone serial is still OK
21-Feb 00:45:16.131 next maintenance for zone 'movie.edu' in 2002 sec
```

Unlike the previous traces, each line in this trace has a timestamp. The timestamp makes it clear which debug statements are grouped together.

This name server is a slave for a single zone, *movie.edu*. The line with time 00:13: 18.026 shows that it is time to check with the master server. The server queries for the zone's SOA record and compares serial numbers before deciding to load the zone. The lines with times 00:13:18.059 through 00:13:18.131 show you the zone's serial number (26739), tell you the zone is out of date, and start a child process (pid 390) to transfer the zone. At time 00:13:18.132, a timer is set to expire 7200 seconds later. This is the amount of time the server allows for a transfer to complete. At time 00:14:02.089, you see the exit status of the child process. The status of 1 indicates that the zone data was successfully transferred. The old zone data is purged (time 00:14:02.094), and the new data is loaded.

The next maintenance (see time 00:14:30.058) is scheduled for 1846 seconds later. For this zone, the refresh interval is 3600, but the name server chose to check again in 1846 seconds. Why? The name server is trying to avoid having its refresh timer become synchronized. Instead of using 3600 exactly, it uses a random time between half the refresh interval (1800) and the full refresh interval (3600). At 00:45:16.046, the zone is checked again and this time it is up to date.

If your trace ran long enough, you'd see more lines like the one at 00:42:44.817—one line each hour. What's happening is that the server is making a pass through its cache, freeing any data that has expired to reduce the amount of memory used.

The master server for this zone is a BIND 4 name server. If the master were a BIND 8 name server, the slave would have been notified when the zone changed rather than waiting for the refresh interval to pass. The slave server's debug output would look almost exactly the same, but the trigger to check the zone status is a NOTIFY:

```
rcvd NOTIFY(movie.edu, IN, SOA) from [192.249.249.3].1059
qserial_query(movie.edu)
sysquery: send -> [192.249.249.3].53 dfd=5
          nsid=29790 id=0 retry=888048802
```

A Slave Name Server Checking Its Zone (BIND 9 Debug Level 1)

The equivalent debugging output from a BIND 9.1.0 name server at level 1 is, as usual, more concise. Here's what it looks like:

```
Sep 18 15:05:00.059 zone_timer: zone movie.edu/IN: enter
Sep 18 15:05:00.059 dns_zone_maintenance: zone movie.edu/IN: enter
Sep 18 15:05:00.059 queue_soa_query: zone movie.edu/IN: enter
Sep 18 15:05:00.059 soa_query: zone movie.edu/IN: enter
Sep 18 15:05:00.061 refresh_callback: zone movie.edu/IN: enter
Sep 18 15:05:00.062 refresh_callback: zone movie.edu/IN: Serial: new 2000010923,
old 2000010922
Sep 18 15:05:00.062 queue_xfrin: zone movie.edu/IN: enter
Sep 18 15:05:00.070 zone_xfrdone: zone movie.edu/IN: success
Sep 18 15:05:00.070 transfer of 'movie.edu' from 192.249.249.3#53: end of transfer
Sep 18 15:05:01.089 zone_timer: zone movie.edu/IN: enter
Sep 18 15:05:01.089 dns_zone_maintenance: zone movie.edu/IN: enter
Sep 18 15:05:19.121 notify_done: zone movie.edu/IN: enter
Sep 18 15:05:19.621 notify_done: zone movie.edu/IN: enter
```

The message at 15:05:00.059 shows the refresh timer popping, causing the name server to begin maintenance for the zone on the next line. First the name server queues a query for the SOA record for the IN class zone *movie.edu* (*queue_soa_query* at the same timestamp), which it sends. At 15:05:00.062, the name server finds that the master name server has a higher serial number than it does (2000010923 to its 2000010922), so it queues an inbound zone transfer (*queue_xfrin*). All of eight milliseconds later (at 15:05:00.070) the transfer is done, and at 15:05:01.089 the name server resets the refresh timer (*zone_timer*).

The next three lines show the name server doing maintenance on *movie.edu* again. If, for example, some of *movie.edu*'s name servers were outside the *movie.edu* zone, the name server would use this opportunity to look up their addresses (not just A, but also A6 and AAAA records!) so that it could include them in future responses. On the last two lines, our name server sends NOTIFY messages—two, to be exact—to the name servers listed in the NS records for *movie.edu*.

The Resolver Search Algorithm and Negative Caching (BIND 8)

In this trace, we'll show you what the BIND 4.9 and later resolver search algorithm and negative caching look like from the perspective of a BIND 8 name server. We could look up *galt.cs.purdue.edu* like the last trace, but it wouldn't show you the search algorithm. Instead, we will look up *foo.bar*, a name that doesn't exist. In fact, we'll look it up twice:

```
1)  datagram from cujo.horror.movie.edu 1109, fd 6, len 25
2)  req: nlookup(foo.bar) id 19220 type=1 class=1
3)  req: found 'foo.bar' as '' (cname=0)
4)  forw: forw -> D.ROOT-SERVERS.NET 53 ds=7 nsid=2532 id=19220 0ms retry 4sec
5)
6)  datagram from D.ROOT-SERVERS.NET 53, fd 5, len 25
7)  ncache: dname foo.bar, type 1, class 1
8)  send_msg -> cujo.horror.movie.edu 1109 (UDP 6) id=19220
9)
10) datagram from cujo.horror.movie.edu 1110, fd 6, len 42
11) req: nlookup(foo.bar.horror.movie.edu) id 19221 type=1 class=1
12) req: found 'foo.bar.horror.movie.edu' as 'horror.movie.edu' (cname=0)
13) forw: forw -> carrie.horror.movie.edu 53 ds=7 nsid=2533 id=19221 0ms
                                                          retry 4sec
14) datagram from carrie.horror.movie.edu 53, fd 5, len 42
15) ncache: dname foo.bar.horror.movie.edu, type 1, class 1
16) send_msg -> cujo.horror.movie.edu 1110 (UDP 6) id=19221
```

Look up *foo.bar* again:

```
17) datagram from cujo.horror.movie.edu 1111, fd 6, len 25
18) req: nlookup(foo.bar) id 15541 type=1 class=1
19) req: found 'foo.bar' as 'foo.bar' (cname=0)
```

```
20) ns_req: answer -> cujo.horror.movie.edu 1111 fd=6 id=15541 size=25 Local
21)
22) datagram from cujo.horror.movie.edu 1112, fd 6, len 42
23) req: nlookup(foo.bar.horror.movie.edu) id 15542 type=1 class=1
24) req: found 'foo.bar.horror.movie.edu' as 'foo.bar.horror.movie.edu' (cname=0)
25) ns_req: answer -> cujo.horror.movie.edu 1112 fd=6 id=15542 size=42 Local
```

Let's look at the resolver search algorithm. The first name looked up (line 2) is exactly the name we typed in. Since the name had at least one dot, it is looked up without modification. When that name lookup failed, *horror.movie.edu* was appended to the name and looked up. (Resolvers before BIND 4.9 would have tried appending both *horror.movie.edu* and *movie.edu*.)

Line 7 shows caching the negative answer (*ncache*). If the same name is looked up again in the next few minutes (line 19), the name server still has the negative response in its cache, so the server can answer immediately that the name doesn't exist. (If you don't believe this hand-waving, compare lines 3 and 19. On line 3, nothing was found for *foo.bar*, but line 19 shows the whole name being found.)

The Resolver Search Algorithm and Negative Caching (BIND 9)

Here's what a BIND 9.1.0 name server's debugging output looks like when looking up *foo.bar* twice:

```
Sep 18 15:45:42.944 client cujo.horror.movie.edu#1044: query: foo.bar A
Sep 18 15:45:42.945 createfetch: foo.bar. A
Sep 18 15:45:42.945 createfetch: . NS
Sep 18 15:45:43.425 client cujo.horror.movie.edu#1044: query: foo.bar.horror.
movie.edu A
Sep 18 15:45:43.425 createfetch: foo.bar.horror.movie.edu. A
```

This output is more subtle and succinct than BIND 8's, but you can get the information you need from it. The first line, at 15:45:42.944, shows the initial query for *foo.bar*'s address arriving from the client *cujo.horror.movie.edu* (remember, we ran this through our magic IP-to-name filter, which we'll introduce next). The next two lines show the name server dispatching two tasks (*createfetch*) to look up *foo. bar*: the first is the actual task to look up *foo.bar*'s address, while the second is a subsidiary task to look up NS records for the root zone, necessary to complete the *foo.bar* lookup. Once the name server has current NS records for the root, it queries a root name server for *foo.bar*'s address and gets a response indicating that no top-level domain called *bar* exists. Unfortunately, you don't see that.

The line at 15:45:43.425 shows *cujo.horror.movie.edu* applying the search list, looking up *foo.bar.horror.movie.edu*. This causes the name server to dispatch a task (*createfetch*) to look up that domain name.

When we look up *foo.bar* again we see:

```
Sep 18 15:45:46.557 client cujo.horror.movie.edu#1044: query: foo.bar A
Sep 18 15:45:46.558 client cujo.horror.movie.edu#1044: query: foo.bar.horror.
movie.edu A
```

Notice the absence of *createfetch* entries? That's because our name server has the negative answers cached.

Tools

Let's wrap up a few loose ends. We told you about our tool to convert IP addresses to names so that your debugging output is easier to read. Here is such a tool written in Perl:

```perl
#!/usr/bin/perl -n

use "Socket";

if (/\b)(\d+\.\d+\.\d+\.\d+)\b/) {
    $addr = pack('C4', split(/\./, $1));
    ($name, $rest) = gethostbyaddr($addr, &AF_INET);
    if($name) {s/$1/$name/;
}

print;
```

It's best not to pipe *named.run* output into this script with debugging on, because the script will generate its own queries to the name server.

14

Troubleshooting DNS and BIND

"Of course not," said the Mock Turtle. "Why, if a fish came to me, and told me he was going on a journey, I should say, 'With what porpoise?'"

"Don't you mean 'purpose'?" said Alice.

"I mean what I say," the Mock Turtle replied, in an offended tone. And the Gryphon added, "Come, let's hear some of your adventures."

In the last two chapters, we've demonstrated how to use *nslookup* and *dig*, and how to read the name server's debugging information. In this chapter, we'll show you how to use these tools—plus traditional Unix networking tools like trusty ol' *ping*—to troubleshoot real-life problems with DNS and BIND.

Troubleshooting, by its nature, is a tough subject to teach. You start with any of a world of symptoms and try to work your way back to the cause. We can't cover the whole gamut of problems you may encounter on the Internet, but we will certainly do our best to show how to diagnose the most common of them. And along the way, we hope to teach you troubleshooting techniques that will be valuable in tracking down more obscure problems that we don't document.

Is NIS Really Your Problem?

Before we launch into a discussion of how to troubleshoot a DNS or BIND problem, we should make sure you know how to tell whether a problem is caused by DNS as opposed to NIS. On hosts running NIS, figuring out whether the culprit is DNS or NIS can be difficult. The stock BSD *nslookup*, for example, doesn't pay any attention to NIS. You can run *nslookup* on a Sun and query the name server 'til the cows come home while all the other services are using NIS.

How do you know where to put the blame? Some vendors have modified *nslookup* to use NIS for name service if NIS is configured. The HP-UX *nslookup*, for example, will report that it's querying an NIS server when it starts up:

```
% nslookup
Default NIS Server:  terminator.movie.edu
Address:  192.249.249.3

>
```

On hosts with vanilla versions of *nslookup*, you can often use *ypmatch* to determine whether you're using DNS or NIS. *ypmatch* prints a blank line after the host information if it received the data from a name server. So in this example, the answer came from NIS:

```
% ypmatch ruby hosts
140.186.65.25   ruby ruby.ora.com
%
```

Whereas in this example, the answer came from a name server:

```
% ypmatch harvard.harvard.edu hosts
128.103.1.1       harvard.harvard.edu

%
```

Note that this works with SunOS 4.1.1, but is not guaranteed to work on all future versions of SunOS. For all we know, this is a bug-*cum*-feature that may disappear in the next release.

A more surefire way to decide whether an answer came from NIS is to use *ypcat* to list the *hosts* database. For example, to find out whether *andrew.cmu.edu* is in your NIS hosts map, you could execute:

```
% ypcat hosts | grep andrew.cmu.edu
```

If you find the answer in NIS (and you know NIS is being consulted first), you've found the cause of the problem.

Finally, in the versions of Unix that use the *nsswitch.conf* file, you can determine the order in which the different name services are used by referring to the entry for the *hosts* database in the file. An entry like this, for example, indicates that NIS is being checked first:

```
hosts:    nis dns files
```

while this entry has the name resolver querying DNS first:

```
hosts:    dns nis files
```

For more detailed information on the syntax and semantics of the *nsswitch.conf* file, see Chapter 6, *Configuring Hosts*.

These hints should help you identify the guilty party or at least exonerate one suspect. If you narrow down the suspects and DNS is still implicated, you'll just have to read this chapter.

Troubleshooting Tools and Techniques

We went over *nslookup, dig,* and the name server's debugging output in the last two chapters. Before we go on, let's introduce some new tools that can be useful in troubleshooting: *named-xfer,* name server database dumps, and query logging.

How to Use named-xfer

named-xfer is the program that BIND 4 and 8 name servers start to perform zone transfers. (BIND 9 name servers, you'll remember, are multithreaded, so they don't need a separate program to do inbound zone transfers: they just start a new thread.) *named-xfer* checks whether the slave's copy of the zone data is up to date and transfers a new zone if necessary. (In Versions 4.9 and 8, *named* checks if a zone is up to date first, to avoid starting up a child process when no transfer is necessary.)

In Chapter 13, *Reading BIND Debugging Output,* we showed you the debugging output a BIND 8 slave name server logged as it checked its zone. When the slave server transferred the zone, it started a child process (*named-xfer*) to pull the data to the local filesystem. We didn't tell you, however, that you can also start *named-xfer* manually instead of waiting for *named* to start it, and that you can tell it to produce debugging output independently of *named.*

This can be useful if you're tracking down a problem with zone transfers but don't want to wait for *named* to schedule one. To test a zone transfer manually, you need to specify a number of command-line options:

```
% /usr/sbin/named-xfer
Usage error: no domain
Usage: named-xfer
        -z zone_to_transfer
        -f db_file
        [-i ixfr_file]
        [-s serial_no]
        [-d debug_level]
        [-l debug_log_file]
        [-t trace_file]
        [-p port]
        [-S] [-Z]
        [-C class]
        [-x axfr-src]
        [-T tsig_info_file]
        servers [-ixfr|-axfr]...
```

This is the output from a BIND 8.2.3 version of *named-xfer*. Earlier versions of *named-xfer* won't have all of these options.

When *named* starts *named-xfer*, it specifies the *−z* option (the zone *named* wants to check), the *−f* option (the name of the zone data file that corresponds to the zone, from *named.boot* or *named.conf*), the *−s* option (the zone's serial number on the slave from the current SOA record), and the addresses of the servers the slave was instructed to load from (the IP addresses from the *masters* substatement in the *zone* statement in *named.conf*, or from the *secondary* directive in *named.boot*). If *named* is running in debug mode, it also specifies the debug level for *named-xfer* with the *−d* option. The other options aren't usually necessary to troubleshoot problems; they have to do with incremental zone transfers, TSIG signing zone transfers, and such.

When you run *named-xfer* manually, you can also specify the debug level on the command line with *−d*. (Don't forget, though, that debug levels above 3 will produce tons of debugging output if the transfer succeeds!) You can also specify an alternate filename for the debug file with the *−l* option. The default log file is */var/tmp/xfer.ddt.XXXXXX*, where *XXXXXX* is a suffix appended to preserve uniqueness or a file by the same name in */usr/tmp*. And you can specify the name of the host to load from instead of its IP address.

For example, with the following command line, you can see whether zone transfers from *terminator.movie.edu* are working:

```
% /usr/sbin/named-xfer -z movie.edu -f /tmp/db.movie -s 0 terminator
% echo $?
4
```

In this command, we specified a serial number of zero because we wanted to force *named-xfer* to attempt a zone transfer even if it wasn't needed. Zero is a special serial number—*named-xfer* will transfer the zone regardless of the actual zone serial number. Also, we told *named-xfer* to put the new zone data file in */tmp* rather than overwriting the zone's working zone data file.

We can tell if the transfer succeeded by looking at *named-xfer*'s return value. If you're running BIND Version 8.1.2 or older, your *named-xfer* has four possible return values:

0   The zone data is up to date and no transfer was needed.

1   Indicates a successful transfer.

2   The host(s) *named-xfer* queried can't be reached, or an error occurred and *named-xfer* may have logged an error message to *syslog*.

3   An error occurred and *named-xfer* logged an error message to *syslog*.

As of BIND 8.2, three new return values have been added to accommodate incremental zone transfers:

4   Indicates a successful AXFR (full) zone transfer.

5   Indicates a successful IXFR (incremental) zone transfer.

6   Indicates that the master name server returned an AXFR to *named-xfer*'s IXFR request.

It's perfectly legal for a name server—even one that supports IXFR—to return a full zone transfer to a request for an incremental zone transfer. For example, the master name server may be missing part of the record of the changes made to the zone.

Note that BIND 8.2 and later *named-xfer*s don't use return value 1 anymore. Return value 1 has been replaced by return values 4 through 6.

What If I Don't Have named-xfer?

If you've upgraded to BIND 9 and don't have a *named-xfer* binary, you can still use *nslookup* or *dig* to do a zone transfer. Either query tool will give you some of the information that *named-xfer* would have given you.

For example, to use *dig* to do the same zone transfer we showed you earlier, you could run:

```
% dig @terminator.movie.edu movie.edu axfr
```

With *nslookup*, you could change your name server and use the *ls –d* command from interactive mode.

Unfortunately, both *dig* and *nslookup* are more subtle than *named-xfer* is in reporting errors. If *nslookup* can't transfer a zone, it usually reports an "unspecified error":

```
> ls movie.edu
[terminator.movie.edu]
*** Can't list domain movie.edu: Unspecified error
```

This could be caused by an *allow-transfer* access list, the fact that *terminator. movie.edu* isn't actually authoritative for *movie.edu*, or a number of other problems. To tell which, you may just have to send other, related queries or check the *syslog* output on the master name server.

How to Read a Database Dump

Poring over a dump of the name server's internal database—including cached information—can also help you track down problems. The *ndc dumpdb* or *rndc* *dumpdb* command causes *named* to dump its authoritative data, cached data, and hints data to *named_dump.db* in BIND's working directory (or in */usr/tmp/named_dump.db* or */var/tmp/named_dump.db*, for BIND 4).* An example of a *named_dump.db* file follows. The authoritative data and cached entries, mixed together, appear first in the file. At the end of the file is the hints data:

```
; Dumped at Tue Jan  6 10:49:08 1998
;; ++zone table++
; 0.0.127.in-addr.arpa (type 1, class 1, source db.127.0.0)
;    time=0, lastupdate=0, serial=1,
;    refresh=0, retry=3600, expire=608400, minimum=86400
;    ftime=884015430, xaddr=[0.0.0.0], state=0041, pid=0
;; --zone table--
; Note: Cr=(auth,answer,addtnl,cache) tag only shown for non-auth RR's
; Note: NT=milliseconds for any A RR which we've used as a nameserver
; --- Cache & Data ---
$ORIGIN .
.     518375 IN      NS  G.ROOT-SERVERS.NET.    ;Cr=auth [128.8.10.90]
      518375 IN      NS  J.ROOT-SERVERS.NET.    ;Cr=auth [128.8.10.90]
      518375 IN      NS  K.ROOT-SERVERS.NET.    ;Cr=auth [128.8.10.90]
      518375 IN      NS  L.ROOT-SERVERS.NET.    ;Cr=auth [128.8.10.90]
      518375 IN      NS  M.ROOT-SERVERS.NET.    ;Cr=auth [128.8.10.90]
      518375 IN      NS  A.ROOT-SERVERS.NET.    ;Cr=auth [128.8.10.90]
      518375 IN      NS  H.ROOT-SERVERS.NET.    ;Cr=auth [128.8.10.90]
      518375 IN      NS  B.ROOT-SERVERS.NET.    ;Cr=auth [128.8.10.90]
      518375 IN      NS  C.ROOT-SERVERS.NET.    ;Cr=auth [128.8.10.90]
      518375 IN      NS  D.ROOT-SERVERS.NET.    ;Cr=auth [128.8.10.90]
      518375 IN      NS  E.ROOT-SERVERS.NET.    ;Cr=auth [128.8.10.90]
      518375 IN      NS  I.ROOT-SERVERS.NET.    ;Cr=auth [128.8.10.90]
      518375 IN      NS  F.ROOT-SERVERS.NET.    ;Cr=auth [128.8.10.90]
EDU 86393 IN        SOA A.ROOT-SERVERS.NET.  hostmaster.INTERNIC.NET. (
          1998010500 1800 900 604800 86400 )   ;Cr=addtnl [128.63.2.53]
$ORIGIN  0.127.in-addr.arpa.
0         IN     SOA cujo.movie.edu. root.cujo.movie.edu. (
          1998010600 10800 3600 608400 86400 )         ;Cl=5
          IN     NS cujo.movie.edu.   ;Cl=5
$ORIGIN  0.0.127.in-addr.arpa.
1         IN     PTR localhost.    ;Cl=5
$ORIGIN EDU.
PURDUE    172787 IN NS  NS.PURDUE.EDU.           ;Cr=addtnl [192.36.148.17]
          172787 IN NS  MOE.RICE.EDU.            ;Cr=addtnl [192.36.148.17]
          172787 IN NS  PENDRAGON.CS.PURDUE.EDU. ;Cr=addtnl [192.36.148.17]
          172787 IN NS  HARBOR.ECN.PURDUE.EDU.   ;Cr=addtnl [192.36.148.17]
$ORIGIN movie.EDU.
;cujo     593    IN  SOA A.ROOT-SERVERS.NET. hostmaster.INTERNIC. NET. (
;         1998010500 1800 900 604800 86400 );EDU.; NXDOMAIN  ;-$
   ;Cr=auth [128.63.2.53]
$ORIGIN   RICE.EDU.
MOE       172787 IN A  128.42.5.4        ;NT=84 Cr=addtnl [192.36.148.17]
$ORIGIN   PURDUE.EDU.
```

---

* BIND 9.1.0 is the first version of BIND 9 to support dumping the database.

```
CS        86387    IN  NS  pendragon.cs.PURDUE.edu.    ;Cr=addtnl [128.42.5.4]
          86387    IN  NS  ns.PURDUE.edu.             ;Cr=addtnl [128.42.5.4]
          86387    IN  NS  harbor.ecn.PURDUE.edu.     ;Cr=addtnl [128.42.5.4]
          86387    IN  NS  moe.rice.edu.              ;Cr=addtnl [128.42.5.4]
NS        172787   IN  A   128.210.11.5        ;NT=4 Cr=addtnl [192.36.148.17]
$ORIGIN   ECN.PURDUE.EDU.
HARBOR    172787   IN  A   128.46.199.76       ;NT=6 Cr=addtnl [192.36.148.17]
$ORIGIN   CS.PURDUE.EDU.
galt      86387    IN  A   128.10.2.39                ;Cr=auth [128.42.5.4]
PENDRAGON 172787   IN  A   128.10.2.5          ;NT=20 Cr=addtnl [192.36.148.17]
$ORIGIN   ROOT-SERVERS.NET.
K         604775   IN  A   193.0.14.129        ;NT=10 Cr=answer [128.8.10.90]
A         604775   IN  A   198.41.0.4          ;NT=20 Cr=answer [128.8.10.90]
L         604775   IN  A   198.32.64.12        ;NT=8 Cr=answer [128.8.10.90]
B         604775   IN  A   128.9.0.107         ;NT=9 Cr=answer [128.8.10.90]
M         604775   IN  A   202.12.27.33        ;NT=20 Cr=answer [128.8.10.90]
C         604775   IN  A   192.33.4.12         ;NT=17 Cr=answer [128.8.10.90]
D         604775   IN  A   128.8.10.90         ;NT=11 Cr=answer [128.8.10.90]
E         604775   IN  A   192.203.230.10      ;NT=9 Cr=answer [128.8.10.90]
F         604775   IN  A   192.5.5.241         ;NT=73 Cr=answer [128.8.10.90]
G         604775   IN  A   192.112.36.4        ;NT=14 Cr=answer [128.8.10.90]
H         604775   IN  A   128.63.2.53         ;NT=160 Cr=answer [128.8.10.90]
I         604775   IN  A   192.36.148.17       ;NT=102 Cr=answer [128.8.10.90]
J         604775   IN  A   198.41.0.10         ;NT=21 Cr=answer [128.8.10.90]
; --- Hints ---
$ORIGIN .
.   3600             IN  NS  A.ROOT-SERVERS.NET.     ;Cl=0
    3600             IN  NS  B.ROOT-SERVERS.NET.     ;Cl=0
    3600             IN  NS  C.ROOT-SERVERS.NET.     ;Cl=0
    3600             IN  NS  D.ROOT-SERVERS.NET.     ;Cl=0
    3600             IN  NS  E.ROOT-SERVERS.NET.     ;Cl=0
    3600             IN  NS  F.ROOT-SERVERS.NET.     ;Cl=0
    3600             IN  NS  G.ROOT-SERVERS.NET.     ;Cl=0
    3600             IN  NS  H.ROOT-SERVERS.NET.     ;Cl=0
    3600             IN  NS  I.ROOT-SERVERS.NET.     ;Cl=0
    3600             IN  NS  J.ROOT-SERVERS.NET.     ;Cl=0
    3600             IN  NS  K.ROOT-SERVERS.NET.     ;Cl=0
    3600             IN  NS  L.ROOT-SERVERS.NET.     ;Cl=0
    3600             IN  NS  M.ROOT-SERVERS.NET.     ;Cl=0
$ORIGIN   ROOT-SERVERS.NET.
K   3600             IN  A   193.0.14.129       ;NT=11 Cl=0
L   3600             IN  A   198.32.64.12       ;NT=9 Cl=0
A   3600             IN  A   198.41.0.4         ;NT=10 Cl=0
M   3600             IN  A   202.12.27.33       ;NT=11 Cl=0
B   3600             IN  A   128.9.0.107        ;NT=1288 Cl=0
C   3600             IN  A   192.33.4.12        ;NT=21 Cl=0
D   3600             IN  A   128.8.10.90        ;NT=1288 Cl=0
E   3600             IN  A   192.203.230.10     ;NT=19 Cl=0
F   3600             IN  A   192.5.5.241        ;NT=23 Cl=0
G   3600             IN  A   192.112.36.4       ;NT=18 Cl=0
H   3600             IN  A   128.63.2.53        ;NT=11 Cl=0
I   3600             IN  A   192.36.148.17      ;NT=21 Cl=0
J   3600             IN  A   198.41.0.10        ;NT=13 Cl=0
```

The name server that created this *named_dump.db* file was authoritative only for *0.0.127.in-addr.arpa*. Only two names have been looked up by this server: *galt. cs.purdue.edu* and *cujo.movie.edu*. In the process of looking up *galt.cs.purdue. edu*, this server cached not only the address of *galt*, but also the list of name servers for *purdue.edu* and the addresses for those servers. The name *cujo.movie.edu*, however, doesn't really exist (nor does the zone *movie.edu*, except in our examples), so the server cached the negative response. In the dump file, the negative response is commented out (the line starts with a semicolon), and the reason is listed (NXDOMAIN) instead of real data. You'll notice the TTL is quite low (593). On BIND 8.2 and later name servers, negative responses are cached according to the last field in the SOA record, which is usually much smaller than the default TTL for the zone.

The hints section at the bottom of the file contains the data from the *db.cache* file. The TTL of the hints data is decremented, and it may go to zero, but the hints are never discarded.

Note that some of the resource records are followed by a semicolon and *NT=*. You will only see these on the address records of name servers. The number is the roundtrip time calculation that the name server keeps so that it knows which name servers have responded most quickly in the past; the name server with the lowest roundtrip time will be tried first the next time.

The cached data is easy to pick out—those entries have a *credibility* tag (*Cr=*) and (sometimes) the IP address of the server the data came from.* The zone data and hint data are tagged with *Cl=*, which is just a count of the level in the domain tree (the root is level 0, *foo* would be level 1, *foo.foo* would be level 2, etc.). Let's digress a moment to explain the concept of credibility.

One of the advances between Versions 4.8.3 and 4.9 was the addition of a credibility measure. This allows a name server to make more intelligent decisions about what to do with new data from a remote server.

A 4.8.3 name server had only two credibility levels—locally authoritative data and everything else. The locally authoritative data was data from your zone data files—your name server knew better than to update its internal copy of what came from your zone file. But all data from remote name servers was considered equal.

---

* The name server prints the IP address of the remote name server if it's available. On BIND 8.2 and later name servers, the IP address is available only if you've turned on *host-statistics*, which we introduced in Chapter 8, *Growing Your Domain*. On earlier BIND 4.9 and BIND 8 name servers, it's on by default. *host-statistics* keeps impressive statistics on every name server and resolver you've ever communicated with, which is very useful for some purposes (like figuring out which name server your server got a record from), but consumes a fair amount of memory.

Here is a situation that could happen and the way a 4.8.3 server would deal with it. Suppose that your server looked up an address for *terminator.movie.edu* and received an authoritative answer from the *movie.edu* name server. (Remember, an authoritative answer is the best you can get.) Sometime later, while looking up *foo.oreilly.com*, your server receives another address record for *terminator.movie.edu*, but this time as part of the delegation info for *oreilly.com* (which *terminator.movie.edu* is a slave for). The 4.8.3 name server would update the cached address record for *terminator.movie.edu*, even though the data came from the *com* name server instead of the authoritative *movie.edu* name server. Of course, the *com* and *movie.edu* name servers will have exactly the same data for *terminator.movie.edu*, so this won't be a problem, right? Yeah, and it never rains in southern California, either.

A 4.9 or newer name server is more intelligent. Like a 4.8.3 name server, it still considers your zone data unassailable—beyond any doubt. But a 4.9 or newer name server distinguishes among the different data from remote name servers. Here is the hierarchy of remote data credibility from most credible to least:

auth
> These records are data from authoritative answers—the answer section of a response message with the authoritative answer bit set.

answer
> These records are data from nonauthoritative, or cached, answers—the answer section of a response message without the authoritative answer bit set.

addtnl
> These records are data from the rest of the response message—the *authority* and *additional* sections. The *authority* section of the response contains NS records that delegate a zone to an authoritative name server. The *additional* section contains address records that may complete information in other sections (e.g., address records that go with NS records in the *authority* section).

There is one exception to this rule: when the name server is priming its root name server cache, the records that would be at credibility *addtnl* are bumped up to *answer* to make them harder to change accidentally. Notice in the dump that the address records for root name servers are at credibility *answer*, but the address records for the *purdue.edu* name servers are at credibility *addtnl*.

In the situation just described, a 4.9 or newer name server would not replace the authoritative data (credibility = *auth*) for *terminator.movie.edu* with the delegation data (credibility = *addtnl*) because the authoritative answer has higher credibility.

Logging Queries

BIND Version 4.9 added a feature called *query logging* that can be used to help diagnose certain problems. When query logging is turned on, a running name server will log every query to *syslog*. This feature could help you find resolver configuration errors because you can verify that the name you think is being looked up really is the name being looked up.

First you must make sure that LOG_INFO messages are being logged by *syslog* for the facility *daemon*. Next, you need to turn on query logging. This can be done in several ways: for BIND 4.9, set *options query-log* in your name server boot file; for BIND 4.9 or BIND 8, start the name server with *−q* on the command line or send an *ndc querylog* command to a running name server. For BIND 9.1.0 or later (earlier versions don't support query logging), use *rndc querylog*. You'll start seeing *syslog* messages like this:

```
Feb 20 21:43:25 terminator named[3830]:
                    XX+ /192.253.253.2/carrie.movie.edu/A
Feb 20 21:43:32 terminator named[3830]:
                    XX+ /192.253.253.2/4.253.253.192.in-addr.arpa/PTR
```

Or, if you're running BIND 9, like this:

```
Jan 13 18:32:25 terminator named[13976]: info: client 192.253.253.2#1702: query:
carrie.movie.edu IN A
Jan 13 18:32:42 terminator named[13976]: info: client 192.253.253.2#1702: query:
4.253.253.192.in-addr.arpa IN PTR
```

These messages include the IP address of the host that made the query, as well as the query itself. Since the first example comes from a BIND 8.2.3 name server and these queries are recursive, they begin with XX+. Iterative queries begin with just XX. (Name servers older than BIND 8.2.1 don't distinguish recursive from non-recursive queries.) Inverse queries have a dash before the query type (e.g., an inverse query for an address record is logged as "-A" instead of just "A"). After enough queries have been logged, you can turn off query logging by sending another *ndc querylog* or *rndc querylog* command to your name server.

If you're stuck running an older BIND 9 name server, you can still see the queries received in *named*'s debugging output at level 1.

Potential Problem List

Now that we've given you a nice set of tools, let's talk about how you can use them to diagnose real problems. There are some problems that are easy to recognize and correct. We should cover these as a matter of course—they're some of the most common problems because they're caused by some of the most common mistakes. Here are the contestants, in no particular order. We call 'em our "Unlucky Thirteen."

1. Forgot to Increment Serial Number

The main symptom of this problem is that slave name servers don't pick up any changes you made to the zone's data file on the primary master. The slaves think the zone data hasn't changed since the serial number is still the same.

How do you check whether or not you remembered to increment the serial number? Unfortunately, that's not so easy. If you don't remember what the old serial number was and your serial number gives you no indication of when it was updated, there's no direct way to tell whether it's changed.* When you reload the primary, it loads the updated zone file regardless of whether you've changed the serial number. It checks the file's timestamp, sees that it's been modified since it last loaded the data, and reads the file. About the best you can do is to use *nslookup* to compare the data returned by the primary and by a slave. If they return different data, you probably forgot to increment the serial number. If you can remember a recent change you made, you can look for that data. If you can't remember a recent change, you could try transferring the zone from a primary and from a slave, sorting the results, and using *diff* to compare them.

The good news is that, although determining whether the zone was transferred is tricky, making sure the zone is transferred is simple. Just increment the serial number on the primary master's copy of the zone data file and reload the zone on the primary. The slaves should pick up the new data within their refresh interval, or sooner if they use NOTIFY. If you want to make sure the slaves transfer the new data, you can execute *named-xfer* by hand (on the slaves, naturally):

```
# /usr/sbin/named-xfer -z movie.edu -f db.movie -s 0 terminator.movie.edu
# echo $?
```

If *named-xfer* returns 1 or 4, the zone was transferred successfully. Other return values indicate that no zone was transferred, either because of an error or because the slave thought the zone was up to date. (See "How to Use named-xfer" earlier in this chapter for more details.)

There's another variation of the "forgot to increment the serial number" problem. We see it in environments where administrators use tools like *h2n* to create zone data files from the host table. With scripts like *h2n*, it's temptingly easy to delete old zone data files and create new ones from scratch. Some administrators do this

---

* On the other hand, if you encode the date into the serial number, as many people do (e.g., 2001010500 is the first rev of data on January 5, 2001), you may be able to tell at a glance whether you updated the serial number when you made the change.

occasionally because they mistakenly believe that data in the old zone data files can creep into the new ones. The problem with deleting the zone data files is that, without the old data file to read for the current serial number, *h2n* starts over at serial number 1. If your zone's serial number on the primary master rolls all the way back to 1 from 598 or what-have-you, the slaves (Versions 4.8.3 and earlier) won't complain; they just figure they're all caught up and don't need zone transfers. A 4.9 or later slave server, however, is ever watchful and will emit a *syslog* error message warning you that something might be wrong:

```
Jun  7 20:14:26 wormhole named[29618]: Zone "movie.edu"
                (class 1) SOA serial# (1) rcvd from [192.249.249.3]
                is < ours (112)
```

So if the serial number on the primary master looks suspiciously low, check the serial number on the slaves, too, and compare them:

```
% nslookup
Default Server:  terminator.movie.edu
Address:  192.249.249.3

> set q=soa
> movie.edu.
Server:  terminator.movie.edu
Address:  192.249.249.3

movie.edu
        origin = terminator.movie.edu
        mail addr = al.robocop.movie.edu
        serial = 1
        refresh = 10800 (3 hours)
        retry   = 3600 (1 hour)
        expire  = 604800 (7 days)
        minimum ttl = 86400 (1 day)
> server wormhole.movie.edu.
Default Server:  wormhole.movie.edu
Addresses:  192.249.249.1, 192.253.253.1

> movie.edu.
Server:  wormhole.movie.edu
Addresses:  192.249.249.1, 192.253.253.1

movie.edu
        origin = terminator.movie.edu
        mail addr = al.robocop.movie.edu
        serial = 112
        refresh = 10800 (3 hours)
        retry   = 3600 (1 hour)
        expire  = 604800 (7 days)
        minimum ttl = 86400 (1 day)
```

wormhole.movie.edu, as a *movie.edu* slave, should never have a larger serial number than the primary master, so clearly something's amiss.

This problem is really easy to spot, by the way, with the tool we'll write in Chapter 15, *Programming with the Resolver and Name Server Library Routines*, coming up next.

2. Forgot to Reload Primary Master Name Server

Occasionally, you may forget to reload your primary master name server after making a change to the configuration file or to a zone data file. The name server won't know to load the new configuration or the new zone data—it doesn't automatically check the timestamp of the file and notice that it changed. Consequently, any changes you've made won't be reflected in the name server's data: new zones won't be loaded, and new records won't percolate out to the slaves.

To check when you last reloaded the name server, scan the *syslog* output for the last entry like this for a BIND 9 name server:

```
Mar  8 17:22:08 terminator named[22317]: loading configuration from '/etc/named.
conf'
```

Or like this for a BIND 4.9 or BIND 8 name server:

```
Mar  8 17:22:08 terminator named[22317]: reloading nameserver
```

These messages tell you the last time you sent a reload command to the name server. If you killed and then restarted the name server, you'll see an entry like this on a BIND 9 name server:

```
Mar  8 17:22:08 terminator named[22317]: starting BIND 9.1.0
```

On a BIND 8 name server, it'd look like:

```
Mar  8 17:22:08 terminator named[22317]: restarted
```

or, on a 4.9 name server:

```
Mar  8 17:22:08 terminator named[22317]: starting
```

If the time of the restart or reload doesn't correlate with the time you made the last change, reload the name server again. And check that you incremented the serial numbers in zone data files you changed, too. If you're not sure when you edited the zone data file, you can check the file modification time by doing a long listing of the file with *ls −l*.

3. Slave Name Server Can't Load Zone Data

If a slave name server can't get the current serial number for a zone from its master name server, it logs a message via *syslog*. On a BIND 9 name server, that looks like:

```
Sep 25 22:02:38 wormhole named[21246]: refresh_callback: zone movie.edu/IN:
failure for 192.249.249.3#53: timed out
```

On BIND 8, look for:

```
Jan  6 11:55:25 wormhole named[544]: Err/TO getting serial# for "movie.edu"
```

On BIND 4, it looks like this:

```
Mar  3 8:19:34 wormhole named[22261]: zoneref: Masters for secondary
        zone movie.edu unreachable
```

If you let this problem fester, the slave will expire the zone. A BIND 9 name server will report:

```
Sep 25 23:20:20 wormhole named[21246]: zone_expire: zone movie.edu/IN: expired
```

A BIND 4.9 or 8 name server will log:

```
Mar  8 17:12:43 wormhole named[22261]: secondary zone
        "movie.edu" expired
```

Once the zone has expired, you'll start getting SERVFAIL errors when you query the name server for data in the zone:

```
% nslookup robocop wormhole.movie.edu.
Server:  wormhole.movie.edu
Addresses:  192.249.249.1, 192.253.253.1

*** wormhole.movie.edu can't find robocop.movie.edu: Server failed
```

There are three leading causes of this problem: a loss in connectivity to the master server due to network failure, an incorrect IP address for the master server in the configuration file, or a syntax error in the zone data file on the master server. First check the configuration file's entry for the zone and see what IP address the slave is attempting to load from:

```
zone "movie.edu" {
            type slave;
            masters { 192.249.249.3; };
            file "bak.movie.edu";
};
```

On a BIND 4 server, the directive looks like this:

```
secondary        movie.edu        192.249.249.3        bak.movie.edu
```

Make sure that's really the IP address of the master name server. If it is, check connectivity to that IP address:

```
% ping 192.249.249.3 -n 10
PING 192.249.249.3: 64 byte packets

----192.249.249.3 PING Statistics----
10 packets transmitted, 0 packets received, 100% packet loss
```

If the master server isn't reachable, make sure that the host the name server runs on is really running (e.g., is powered on, etc.) or look for a network problem. If the host is reachable, make sure *named* is running on the host and that you can manually transfer the zone:

```
# /usr/sbin/named-xfer -z movie.edu -f /tmp/db.movie.edu -s 0 192.249.249.3
# echo $?
2
```

A return code of 2 means that an error occurred. Check to see if there is a *syslog* message. In this case, there was a message:

```
Jan  6 14:56:07 zardoz named-xfer[695]: record too short from [192.249.249.3],
zone movie.edu
```

At first glance, this error looks like a truncation problem. The real problem is easier to see if you use *nslookup*:

```
% nslookup - terminator.movie.edu
Default Server:  terminator.movie.edu
Address:  192.249.249.3

> ls movie.edu                    —This attempts a zone transfer
[terminator.movie.edu]
*** Can't list domain movie.edu: Query refused
```

What's happening here is that *named* is refusing to allow you to transfer its zone data. The remote server has secured its zone data with an *allow-transfer* substatement, the *secure_zone* resource record, or the *xfrnets* boot file directive.

If the master server is responding as not authoritative for the zone, you'll see a message like this from your BIND 9 name server:

```
Sep 26 13:29:23 zardoz named[21890]: refresh_callback: zone movie.edu/IN:
non-authoritative answer from 192.249.249.3#53
```

Or on BIND 8, like this:

```
Jan  6 11:58:36 zardoz named[544]: Err/TO getting serial# for "movie.edu"
Jan  6 11:58:36 zardoz named-xfer[793]: [192.249.249.3] not authoritative for
    movie.edu, SOA query got rcode 0, aa 0, ancount 0, aucount 0
```

If this is the correct master server, the server *should* be authoritative for the zone. This probably indicates that the master had a problem loading the zone, usually because of a syntax error in the zone data file. Contact the administrator of the master server and have her check her *syslog* output for indications of a syntax error (see problem 5, coming up).

4. Added Name to Zone Data File but Forgot to Add PTR Record

Because mappings of host names to IP addresses are disjointed from mappings of IP addresses to host names in DNS, it's easy to forget to add a PTR record for a new host. Adding the A record is intuitive, but many people who are used to host tables assume that adding an address record takes care of the reverse mapping, too. That's not true—you need to add a PTR record for the host to the appropriate reverse-mapping zone.

Forgetting to add the PTR record for a host's address usually causes that host to fail authentication checks. For example, users on the host won't be able to *rlogin* to other hosts without specifying a password, and *rsh* or *rcp* to other hosts simply won't work. The servers these commands talk to must be able to map a client's IP address to a domain name to check *.rhosts* and *hosts.equiv*. These users' connections will cause entries like this to be *syslogged*:

```
Aug 15 17:32:36 terminator inetd[23194]: login/tcp:
      Connection from unknown (192.249.249.23)
```

Also, many large FTP archives, including *ftp.uu.net*, refuse anonymous FTP access to hosts whose IP addresses don't map back to domain names. *ftp.uu.net*'s FTP server emits a message that reads, in part:

```
530- Sorry, we're unable to map your IP address 140.186.66.1 to a hostname
530- in the DNS.  This is probably because your nameserver does not have a
530- PTR record for your address in its tables, or because your reverse
530- nameservers are not registered.  We refuse service to hosts whose
530- names we cannot resolve.
```

That makes the reason you can't use anonymous FTP pretty evident. Other FTP sites, however, don't bother printing informative messages; they simply deny service.

nslookup is handy for checking whether you've forgotten the PTR record or not:

```
% nslookup
Default Server:  terminator.movie.edu
Address:  192.249.249.3

>beetlejuice        —Check for a name-to-address mapping
Server:  terminator.movie.edu
Address:  192.249.249.3

Name:    beetlejuice.movie.edu
Address:  192.249.249.23

>192.249.249.23   —Now check for a corresponding address-to-name mapping
Server:  terminator.movie.edu
Address:  192.249.249.3

*** terminator.movie.edu can't find 192.249.249.23: Non-existent domain
```

On the primary master for *249.249.192.in-addr.arpa*, a quick check of the *db.192. 249.249* file will tell you if the PTR record hasn't been added to the zone data file yet or if the name server hasn't been reloaded. If the name server having trouble is a slave for the zone, check that the serial number was incremented on the primary master and that the slave has had enough time to load the zone.

5. Syntax Error in Configuration File or Zone Data File

Syntax errors in a name server's configuration file and in zone data files are also relatively common (more or less, depending on the experience of the administrator). Generally, an error in the config file will cause the name server to fail to load one or more zones. Some typos in the *options* statement will cause the name server to fail to start at all and to log an error like this via *syslog* (BIND 9):

```
Sep 26 13:39:30 terminator named[21924]: change directory to '/var/name' failed:
file not found
Sep 26 13:39:30 terminator named[21924]: options configuration failed: file not
found
Sep 26 13:39:30 terminator named[21924]: loading configuration: failure
Sep 26 13:39:30 terminator named[21924]: exiting (due to fatal error)
```

A BIND 8 name server logs:

```
Jan  6 11:59:29 terminator named[544]: can't change directory to /var/name: No
    such file or directory
```

Note that you won't see an error message when you try to start *named* on the command line or at boot time, but *named* won't stay running for long.

If the syntax error is in a less important line in the config file—say, in a *zone* statement—only that zone will be affected. Usually, the name server won't be able to load the zone at all (say, you misspell "masters" or the name of the zone data file, or you forget to put quotes around the filename or domain name). This would produce *syslog* output from BIND 9 like this:

```
Sep 26 13:43:03 terminator named[21938]: /etc/named.conf:80: parse error near
'masters'
Sep 26 13:43:03 terminator named[21938]: loading configuration: failure
Sep 26 13:43:03 terminator named[21938]: exiting (due to fatal error)
```

Or from BIND 8:

```
Jan  6 12:01:36 terminator named[841]: /etc/named.conf:10: syntax error near
    'movie.edu'
```

If a zone data file contains a syntax error yet the name server succeeds in loading the zone, it will either answer as nonauthoritative for *all* data in the zone or return a SERVFAIL error for lookups in the zone:

```
% nslookup carrie
Server:  terminator.movie.edu
Address:  192.249.249.3
```

```
Non-authoritative answer:
Name:    carrie.movie.edu
Address:  192.253.253.4
```

Here's the BIND 9 *syslog* message produced by the syntax error that caused this problem:

```
Sep 26 13:45:40 terminator named[21951]: error: dns_rdata_fromtext: db.movie.edu:
11: near 'postmanrings2x': unexpected token
Sep 26 13:45:40 terminator named[21951]: error: dns_zone_load: zone movie.edu/IN:
database db.movie.edu: dns_db_load failed: unexpected token
Sep 26 13:45:40 terminator named[21951]: critical: loading zones: unexpected token
Sep 26 13:45:40 terminator named[21951]: critical: exiting (due to fatal error)
```

Here's BIND 8's error:

```
Jan  6 15:07:46 terminator named[693]: db.movie.edu:11: Priority error
      (postmanrings2x.movie.edu.)
Jan  6 15:07:46 terminator named[693]: master zone "movie.edu" (IN) rejected due
      to errors (serial 1997010600)
```

If you looked in the zone data file for the problem, you'd find this record:

```
postmanrings2x    IN    MX       postmanrings2x.movie.edu.
```

The MX record is missing the preference field, which causes the error.

Note that unless you correlate the lack of authority (when you expect the name server to be authoritative) with a problem or scan your *syslog* file assiduously, you might never notice the syntax error!

Starting with BIND 4.9.4, an "invalid" host name can be a syntax error:

```
Jan  6 12:04:10 terminator named[841]: owner name "ID_4.movie.edu" IN (primary)
      is invalid - rejecting
Jan  6 12:04:10 terminator named[841]: db.movie.edu:11: owner name error
Jan  6 12:04:10 terminator named[841]: db.movie.edu:11: Database error near (A)
Jan  6 12:04:10 terminator named[841]: master zone "movie.edu" (IN) rejected
      due to errors (serial 1997010600)
```

BIND 9, however, doesn't implement name checking as of 9.1.0. A future version of BIND 9 may.

6. Missing Dot at the End of a Domain Name in a Zone Data File

It's *very* easy to leave off trailing dots when editing a zone data file. Since the rules for when to use them change so often (don't use them in the configuration file, don't use them in *resolv.conf*, do use them in zone data files to override $ORIGIN . . .), it's hard to keep them straight. These resource records:

```
zorba        IN    MX     10 zelig.movie.edu
movie.edu    IN    NS     terminator.movie.edu
```

really don't look that odd to the untrained eye, but they probably don't do what they're intended to. In the *db.movie.edu* file, they'd be equivalent to:

```
zorba.movie.edu.        IN    MX    10 zelig.movie.edu.movie.edu.
movie.edu.movie.edu.    IN    NS    terminator.movie.edu.movie.edu.
```

unless the origin were explicitly changed.

If you omit a trailing dot after a domain name in the resource record's data (as opposed to leaving off a trailing dot in the resource record's *name*), you usually end up with wacky NS or MX records:

```
% nslookup -type=mx zorba.movie.edu.
Server:  terminator.movie.edu
Address:  192.249.249.3

zorba.movie.edu         preference = 10, mail exchanger
                        = zelig.movie.edu.movie.edu
zorba.movie.edu         preference = 50, mail exchanger
                        = postmanrings2x.movie.edu.movie.edu
```

The cause of this should be fairly clear from the *nslookup* output. But if you forget the trailing dot on the domain name field in a record (as in the *movie.edu* NS record just listed), spotting your mistake might not be as easy. If you try to look up the record with *nslookup*, you won't find it under the domain name you thought you used. Dumping your name server's database may help you root it out:

```
$ORIGIN edu.movie.edu.
movie    IN    NS    terminator.movie.edu.movie.edu.
```

The $ORIGIN line looks odd enough to stand out.

7. Missing Root Hints Data

If, for some reason, you forget to install a root hints file on your name server or if you accidentally delete it, your name server will be unable to resolve names outside of its authoritative data. This behavior is easy to recognize using *nslookup*, but be careful to use full, dot-terminated domain names or else the search list may cause misleading failures:

```
% nslookup
Default Server:  terminator.movie.edu
Address:  192.249.249.3

> ftp.uu.net.        —A lookup of a name outside your name server's authoritative data
                     —causes a SERVFAIL error...
Server:  terminator.movie.edu
Address:  192.249.249.3

*** terminator.movie.edu can't find ftp.uu.net.: Server failed
```

A lookup of a name in your name server's authoritative data returns a response:

```
> wormhole.movie.edu.
Server:  terminator.movie.edu
Address:  192.249.249.3

Name:    wormhole.movie.edu
Addresses:  192.249.249.1, 192.253.253.1

> ^D
```

To confirm your suspicion that the root hints data is missing, check the *syslog* output for an error like this:

```
Jan  6 15:10:22 terminator named[764]: No root nameservers for class IN
```

Class 1, you'll remember, is the IN, or Internet, class. This error indicates that because no root hints data was available, no root name servers were found.

You're unlikely to run into this problem with BIND 9, since it has built-in root hints.

8. Loss of Network Connectivity

Though the Internet is more reliable today than it was back in the wild and woolly days of the ARPAnet, network outages are still relatively common. Without "lifting the hood" and poking around in debugging output, these failures usually look like poor performance:

```
% nslookup nisc.sri.com.
Server:  terminator.movie.edu
Address:  192.249.249.3

*** Request to terminator.movie.edu timed out ***
```

If you turn on name server debugging, though, you may see that your name server, anyway, is healthy. It received the query from the resolver, sent the necessary queries, and waited patiently for a response. It just didn't get one. Here's what the debugging output might look like on a BIND 8 name server:

```
Debug turned ON, Level 1
```

Here, *nslookup* sends the first query to our local name server for the IP address of *nisc.sri.com*. Then the query is forwarded to another name server, and, when no answer is received, it is resent to a different name server:

```
datagram from [192.249.249.3].1051, fd 5, len 30
req: nlookup(nisc.sri.com) id 18470 type=1 class=1
req: missed 'nisc.sri.com' as 'com' (cname=0)
forw: forw -> [198.41.0.4].53 ds=7 nsid=58732 id=18470 0ms retry 4 sec
resend(addr=1 n=0) -> [128.9.0.107].53 ds=7 nsid=58732 id=18470 0ms
```

Now *nslookup* is getting impatient, and it queries our local name server again. Notice that it uses the same source port. The local name server ignores the duplicate query and tries forwarding the query two more times:

```
datagram from [192.249.249.3].1051, fd 5, len 30
req: nlookup(nisc.sri.com) id 18470 type=1 class=1
req: missed 'nisc.sri.com' as 'com' (cname=0)
resend(addr=2 n=0) -> [192.33.4.12].53 ds=7 nsid=58732 id=18470 0ms
resend(addr=3 n=0) -> [128.8.10.90].53 ds=7 nsid=58732 id=18470 0ms
```

nslookup queries the local name server again, and the name server fires off more queries:

```
datagram from [192.249.249.3].1051, fd 5, len 30
req: nlookup(nisc.sri.com) id 18470 type=1 class=1
req: missed 'nisc.sri.com' as 'com' (cname=0)
resend(addr=4 n=0) -> [192.203.230.10].53 ds=7 nsid=58732 id=18470 0ms
resend(addr=0 n=1) -> [198.41.0.4].53 ds=7 nsid=58732 id=18470 0ms
resend(addr=1 n=1) -> [128.9.0.107].53 ds=7 nsid=58732 id=18470 0ms
resend(addr=2 n=1) -> [192.33.4.12].53 ds=7 nsid=58732 id=18470 0ms
resend(addr=3 n=1) -> [128.8.10.90].53 ds=7 nsid=58732 id=18470 0ms
resend(addr=4 n=1) -> [192.203.230.10].53 ds=7 nsid=58732 id=18470 0ms
resend(addr=0 n=2) -> [198.41.0.4].53 ds=7 nsid=58732 id=18470 0ms
Debug turned OFF
```

On a BIND 9 name server, there's considerably less detail at debug level 1. Still, you can see that the name server is trying repeatedly to look up *nisc.sri.com*:

```
Sep 26 14:33:27.486 client 192.249.249.3#1028: query: nisc.sri.com A
Sep 26 14:33:27.486 createfetch: nisc.sri.com. A
Sep 26 14:33:32.489 client 192.249.249.3#1028: query: nisc.sri.com A
Sep 26 14:33:32.490 createfetch: nisc.sri.com. A
Sep 26 14:33:42.500 client 192.249.249.3#1028: query: nisc.sri.com A
Sep 26 14:33:42.500 createfetch: nisc.sri.com. A
Sep 26 14:34:02.512 client 192.249.249.3#1028: query: nisc.sri.com A
Sep 26 14:34:02.512 createfetch: nisc.sri.com. A
```

At higher debug levels, you can actually see the timeouts, but BIND 9.1.0 still doesn't show the addresses of the remote name servers tried.

From the BIND 8 debugging output, you can extract a list of the IP addresses of the name servers that your name server tried to query, and then check your connectivity to them. Odds are, *ping* won't have much better luck than your name server did:

```
% ping 198.41.0.4 -n 10  —ping first name server queried
PING 198.41.0.4: 64 byte packets

----198.41.0.4 PING Statistics----
10 packets transmitted, 0 packets received, 100% packet loss
% ping 128.9.0.107 -n 10  —ping second name server queried
PING 128.9.0.107: 64 byte packets

----128.9.0.107 PING Statistics----
10 packets transmitted, 0 packets received, 100% packet loss
```

If it does, you should check that the remote name servers are really running. You might also check whether your Internet firewall is inadvertently blocking your name server's queries. If you've upgraded to BIND 8 or 9 recently, see the sidebar "A Gotcha with BIND 8 or 9 and Packet-Filtering Firewalls" in Chapter 11, *Security*, and see if it applies to you.

If *ping* can't get through either, all that's left to do is to locate the break in the network. Utilities like *traceroute* and *ping*'s record route option can be very helpful in determining whether the problem is on your network, the destination network, or somewhere in the middle.

Also, use your own common sense when tracking down the break. In this trace, for example, the remote name servers your name server tried to query are all root name servers. (You might have had their PTR records cached somewhere, so you could find out their domain names.) Now it's not very likely that each root's local network went down, nor that the Internet's backbone networks collapsed entirely. Occam's razor says that the simplest condition that could cause this behavior— namely, the loss of *your* network's link to the Internet—is the most likely cause.

9. Missing Subdomain Delegation

Even though registrars do their very best to process your requests as quickly as possible, it may take a day or two for your subdomain's delegation to appear in your parent zone's name servers. If your parent zone isn't one of the generic top-level domains, your mileage may vary. Some parents are quick and responsible, others are slow and inconsistent. Just like in real life, though, you're stuck with them.

Until your zone's delegation appears in your parent zone's name servers, your name servers will be able to look up data in the Internet's namespace, but no one out on the Internet (outside of your domain) will know how to look up data in *your* namespace.

That means that even though you can send mail outside of your domain, the recipients won't be able to reply to it. Furthermore, no one will be able to *telnet* to, *ftp* to, or even *ping* your hosts by domain name.

Remember that this applies equally to any *in-addr.arpa* zones you may run. Until their parent zones add delegation to your servers, name servers on the Internet won't be able to reverse map addresses on your networks.

To determine whether or not your zone's delegation has made it into your parent zone's name servers, query a parent name server for the NS records for your zone. If the parent name server has the data, any name server on the Internet can find it:

```
% nslookup
Default Server: terminator.movie.edu
Address: 192.249.249.3
```

```
> server a.root-servers.net.  —Query a root name server
Default Server:  a.root-servers.net
Address:  198.41.0.4

> set norecurse              —Instruct the server to answer out of its own data
> set type=ns                —and to look for NS records
> 249.249.192.in-addr.arpa.  —for 249.249.192.in-addr.arpa
Server:  a.root-servers.net
Address:  198.41.0.4

*** a.root-servers.net can't find 249.249.192.in-addr.arpa.: Non-existent domain
```

Here, the delegation clearly hasn't been added yet. You can either wait patiently or, if an unreasonable amount of time has passed since you requested delegation from your parent zone, contact your parent zone's administrator and ask what's up.

10. Incorrect Subdomain Delegation

Incorrect subdomain delegation is another familiar problem on the Internet. Keeping delegation up to date requires human intervention—informing your parent zone's administrator of changes to your set of authoritative name servers. Consequently, delegation information often becomes inaccurate as administrators make changes without letting their parents know. Far too many administrators believe that setting up delegation is a one-shot deal: they let their parents know which name servers are authoritative once when they set up their zone and then they never talk to them again. They don't even call on Mother's Day.

An administrator may add a new name server, decommission another, and change the IP address of a third, all without telling the parent zone's administrator. Gradually, the number of name servers correctly delegated to by the parent zone dwindles. In the best case, this leads to long resolution times as querying name servers struggle to find an authoritative name server for the zone. If the delegation information becomes badly out of date and the last authoritative name server is brought down for maintenance, the information within and below the zone will be inaccessible.

If you suspect bad delegation from your parent zone to your zone, from your zone to one of your children, or from a remote zone to one of its children, you can check with *nslookup*:

```
% nslookup
Default Server:  terminator.movie.edu
Address:  192.249.249.3

> server a.root-servers.net.    —Set server to the parent zone's name server that
                                —you suspect has bad delegation
Default Server:  a.root-servers.net
Address:  198.41.0.4
```

```
> set type=ns                    —Look for NS records
> hp.com.                        —for the zone in question
Server:  a.root-servers.net
Address:  198.41.0.4

Non-authoritative answer:
hp.com          nameserver = RELAY.HP.COM
hp.com          nameserver = HPLABS.HPL.HP.COM
hp.com          nameserver = NNSC.NSF.NET
hp.com          nameserver = HPSDLO.SDD.HP.COM

Authoritative answers can be found from:
hp.com          nameserver = RELAY.HP.COM
hp.com          nameserver = HPLABS.HPL.HP.COM
hp.com          nameserver = NNSC.NSF.NET
hp.com          nameserver = HPSDLO.SDD.HP.COM
RELAY.HP.COM         internet address = 15.255.152.2
HPLABS.HPL.HP.COM        internet address = 15.255.176.47
NNSC.NSF.NET        internet address = 128.89.1.178
HPSDLO.SDD.HP.COM        internet address = 15.255.160.64
HPSDLO.SDD.HP.COM        internet address = 15.26.112.11
```

Let's say you suspect that the delegation to *hpsdlo.sdd.hp.com* is incorrect. You now query *hpsdlo.sdd.hp.com* for data in the *hp.com* zone (e.g., the SOA record for *hp.com*) and check the answer:

```
> server hpsdlo.sdd.hp.com.
Default Server:  hpsdlo.sdd.hp.com
Addresses:  15.255.160.64, 15.26.112.11

> set norecurse
> set type=soa
> hp.com.
Server:  hpsdlo.sdd.hp.com
Addresses:  15.255.160.64, 15.26.112.11

Non-authoritative answer:
hp.com
        origin = relay.hp.com
        mail addr = hostmaster.hp.com
        serial = 1001462
        refresh = 21600 (6 hours)
        retry   = 3600 (1 hour)
        expire  = 604800 (7 days)
        minimum ttl = 86400 (1 day)

Authoritative answers can be found from:
hp.com          nameserver = RELAY.HP.COM
hp.com          nameserver = HPLABS.HPL.HP.COM
hp.com          nameserver = NNSC.NSF.NET
RELAY.HP.COM         internet address = 15.255.152.2
HPLABS.HPL.HP.COM        internet address = 15.255.176.47
NNSC.NSF.NET        internet address = 128.89.1.178
```

If *hpsdlo.sdd.hp.com* really were authoritative for *hp.com*, it would have responded with an authoritative answer. The administrator of the *hp.com* zone can tell you whether *hpsdlo.sdd.hp.com* should be an authoritative name server for *hp.com*, so that's who you should contact.

Another common symptom of this is a "lame server" error message:

```
Oct 1 04:43:38 terminator named[146]: Lame server on '40.234.23.210.in-addr.arpa'
(in '210.in-addr.arpa'?): [198.41.0.5].53 'RS0.INTERNIC.NET': learnt(A=198.41.0.
21,NS=128.63.2.53)
```

Here's how to read that: your name server was referred by the name server at 128.63.2.53 to the name server at 198.41.0.5 for a name in the domain *210.in-addr. arpa,* specifically *40.234.23.210.in-addr.arpa.* The response from the name server at 198.41.0.5 indicated that it wasn't, in fact, authoritative for *210.in-addr.arpa,* and therefore either the delegation that 128.63.2.53 gave you is wrong or the server at 198.41.0.5 is misconfigured.

11. Syntax Error in resolv.conf

Despite the *resolv.conf* file's simple syntax, people do occasionally make mistakes when editing it. And, unfortunately, lines with syntax errors in *resolv.conf* are silently ignored by the resolver. The result is usually that some part of your intended configuration doesn't take effect: either your local domain name or search list isn't set correctly, or the resolver won't query one of the name servers you configured it to query. Commands that rely on the search list won't work, your resolver won't query the right name server, or it won't query a name server at all.

The easiest way to check whether your *resolv.conf* file is having the intended effect is to run *nslookup. nslookup* will kindly report the local domain name and search list it derives from *resolv.conf,* plus the name server it's querying, when you type *set all,* as we showed you in Chapter 12, *nslookup and dig:*

```
% nslookup
Default Server:  terminator.movie.edu
Address:  192.249.249.3

> set all
Default Server:  terminator.movie.edu
Address:  192.249.249.3

Set options:
  nodebug       defname       search        recurse
  nod2          novc          noignoretc    port=53
  querytype=A   class=IN      timeout=5     retry=4
  root=ns.nic.ddn.mil.
  domain=movie.edu
  srchlist=movie.edu

>
```

Check that the output of *set all* is what you expect, given your *resolv.conf* file. For example, if you set *search fx.movie.edu movie.edu* in *resolv.conf*, you expect to see:

```
domain=fx.movie.edu
srchlist=fx.movie.edu/movie.edu
```

in the output. If you don't see what you're expecting, look carefully at *resolv.conf*. If there's nothing obvious, look for unprintable characters (with *vi*'s *set list* command, for example). Watch out for trailing spaces, especially; on older resolvers, a trailing space after the domain name will set the local domain name to include a space. No real top-level domain names actually end with spaces, of course, so all of your non-dot-terminated lookups will fail.

12. Local Domain Name Not Set

Failing to set your local domain name is another old standby gaffe. You can set it implicitly by setting your *hostname* to your host's fully qualified domain name or explicitly in *resolv.conf*. The characteristics of an unset local domain name are straightforward: folks who use single-label names (or abbreviated domain names) in commands get no joy:

```
% telnet br
br: No address associated with name
% telnet br.fx
br.fx: No address associated with name
% telnet br.fx.movie.edu
Trying...
Connected to bladerunner.fx.movie.edu.
Escape character is '^]'.

HP-UX bladerunner.fx.movie.edu A.08.07 A 9000/730 (ttys1)
login:
```

You can use *nslookup* to check this one, much as you do when you suspect a syntax error in *resolv.conf*:

```
% nslookup
Default Server:  terminator.movie.edu
Address:  192.249.249.3

> set all
Default Server:  terminator.movie.edu
Address:  192.249.249.3

Set options:
  nodebug         defname         search          recurse
  nod2            novc            noignoretc      port=53
  querytype=A     class=IN        timeout=5       retry=4
  root=ns.nic.ddn.mil.
  domain=
  srchlist=
```

Notice that neither the local domain name nor the search list is set. You can also track this down by enabling debugging on the name server. (This, of course, requires access to the name server, which may not be running on the host that the problem is affecting.) Here's how the debugging output from a BIND 9 name server might look after trying those *telnet* commands:

```
Sep 26 16:17:58.824 client 192.249.249.3#1032: query: br A
Sep 26 16:17:58.825 createfetch: br. A
Sep 26 16:18:09.996 client 192.249.249.3#1032: query: br.fx A
Sep 26 16:18:09.996 createfetch: br.fx. A
Sep 26 16:18:18.677 client 192.249.249.3#1032: query: br.fx.movie.edu A
```

On a BIND 8 name server, it would look something like this:

```
Debug turned ON, Level 1

datagram from [192.249.249.3].1057, fd 5, len 20
req: nlookup(br) id 27974 type=1 class=1
req: missed 'br' as '' (cname=0)
forw: forw -> [198.41.0.4].53 ds=7 nsid=61691 id=27974 0ms retry 4 sec

datagram from [198.41.0.4].53, fd 5, len 20
ncache: dname br, type 1, class 1
send_msg -> [192.249.249.3].1057 (UDP 5) id=27974

datagram from [192.249.249.3].1059, fd 5, len 23
req: nlookup(br.fx) id 27975 type=1 class=1
req: missed 'br.fx' as '' (cname=0)
forw: forw -> [128.9.0.107].53 ds=7 nsid=61692 id=27975 0ms retry 4 sec

datagram from [128.9.0.107].53, fd 5, len 23
ncache: dname br.fx, type 1, class 1
send_msg -> [192.249.249.3].1059 (UDP 5) id=27975

datagram from [192.249.249.3].1060, fd 5, len 33
req: nlookup(br.fx.movie.edu) id 27976 type=1 class=1
req: found 'br.fx.movie.edu' as 'br.fx.movie.edu' (cname=0)
req: nlookup(bladerunner.fx.movie.edu) id 27976 type=1 class=1
req: found 'bladerunner.fx.movie.edu' as 'bladerunner.fx.movie.edu'
    (cname=1)
ns_req: answer -> [192.249.249.3].1060 fd=5 id=27976 size=183 Local
Debug turned OFF
```

Contrast this with the debugging output produced by the application of the search list in Chapter 13. The only names looked up here are exactly what the user typed, with no domain names appended at all. Clearly, the search list isn't being applied.

13. Response from Unexpected Source

One problem we've seen increasingly often in the DNS newsgroups is the "response from unexpected source." This was once called a Martian response: it's a response that comes from an IP address other than the one your name server sent a query to. When a BIND name server sends a query to a remote server, BIND conscientiously makes sure that answers come only from the IP addresses on that server. This helps minimize the possibility of accepting spoofed responses. BIND is equally demanding of itself: a BIND server makes every effort to reply via the same network interface that it received a query on.

Here's the error message you'd see upon receiving a possibly unsolicited response:

```
Mar  8 17:21:04 terminator named[235]: Response from unexpected source ([205.199.
4.131].53)
```

This can mean one of two things: either someone is trying to spoof your name server, or—more likely—you sent a query to an older BIND server or a different make of name server that's not as assiduous about replying from the same interface it receives queries on.

Transition Problems

With the release of BIND 8, and now BIND 9, many Unix operating systems are updating their resolvers and name servers. Some features of the most recent versions of BIND, however, may seem like errors to you after you upgrade to a new version. We'll try to give you an idea of some changes you may notice in your name server and your name service after making the jump.

Resolver Behavior

The changes to the resolver's default search list described in Chapter 6 may seem like a problem to your users. Recall that with a local domain name set to *fx.movie. edu*, your default search list will no longer include *movie.edu*. Therefore, users accustomed to using commands like *telnet db.personnel* and having the partial domain name expanded to *db.personnel.movie.edu* will have their commands fail. To solve this problem, you can use the *search* directive to define an explicit search list that includes your local domain name's parent. Or, just tell your users to expect the new behavior.

Name Server Behavior

Before Version 4.9, a BIND name server would gladly load data in any zone from any zone data file that the name server read as a primary master. If you configured the name server as the primary master for *movie.edu* and told it that the *movie.edu* data was in *db.movie.edu*, you could stick data about *hp.com* in *db. movie.edu* and your name server would load the *hp.com* resource records into the cache. Some books even suggested putting the data for all your *in-addr.arpa* zones in one file. Ugh.

All BIND 4.9 and later name servers ignore any "out of zone" resource records in a zone data file. So if you cram PTR records for all your *in-addr.arpa* zones into one file and load it with a single *zone* statement or *primary* directive, the name server ignores all the records not in the named zone. And that, of course, means loads of missing PTR records and failed *gethostbyaddr( )* calls.

BIND does log that it's ignoring the records in *syslog*. The messages look like this in BIND 9:

```
Sep 26 13:48:19 terminator named[21960]: dns_master_load: db.movie.edu:16:
ignoring out-of-zone data
```

And like this in BIND 8:

```
Jan  7 13:58:01 terminator named[231]: db.movie.edu:16: data "hp.com" outside zone
    "movie.edu" (ignored)
Jan  7 13:58:01 terminator named[231]: db.movie.edu:17: data "hp.com" outside zone
    "movie.edu" (ignored)
```

The solution is to use one zone data file and one *zone* statement or *primary* directive per zone.

Interoperability and Version Problems

With the move to BIND 9 and the introduction of Microsoft DNS Server, more interoperability problems are cropping up between name servers. There are also a handful of problems unique to one version or another of BIND or the underlying operating system. Many of these are easy to spot and correct, and we would be remiss if we didn't cover them.

Zone Transfer Fails Because of Proprietary WINS Record

When a Microsoft DNS Server is configured to consult a WINS server for names it can't find in a given zone, it inserts a special record into the zone data file. The record looks like this:

```
@   IN   WINS   &IP address of WINS server
```

Unfortunately, WINS is not a standard record type in the IN class. Consequently, if there are BIND slaves that transfer this zone, they'll choke on the WINS record and refuse to load the zone:

```
May 23 15:58:43 terminator named-xfer[386]: "fx.movie.edu IN 65281" - unknown type
(65281)
```

The workaround for this is to configure the Microsoft DNS Server to filter out the proprietary record before transferring the zone. You do this by selecting the zone in the left-hand side of the DNS Manager screen, right-clicking on it, and selecting

Properties. Click on the *WINS Lookup* tab in the resulting *Zone Properties* window, shown in Figure 14-1.

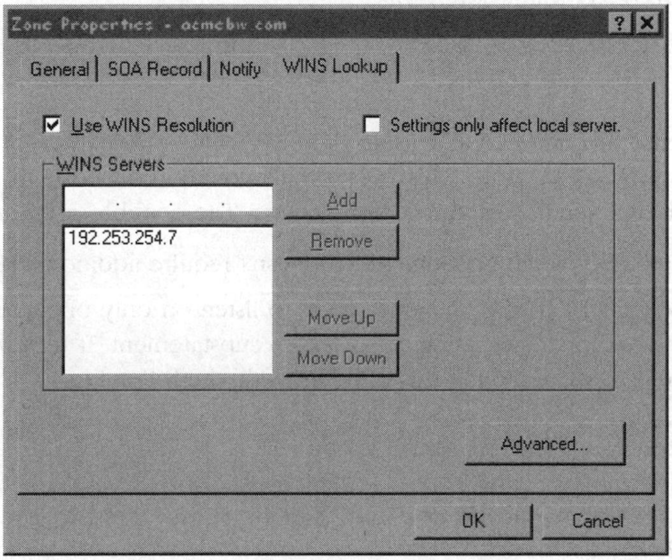

Figure 14-1. Zone Properties window

Checking *Settings only affect local server* will filter out the WINS record for that zone. However, if there are any Microsoft DNS Server slaves, they won't see the record either, even though they could use it.

Name Server Reports "No NS Record for SOA MNAME"

You'll see this error only on BIND 8.1 servers:

```
May 8 03:44:38 terminator named[11680]: no NS RR for SOA MNAME "movie.edu" in
    zone "movie.edu"
```

The 8.1 server was a real stickler about the first field in the SOA record. Remember that one? In Chapter 4, *Setting Up BIND*, we said that it was, by convention, the domain name of the primary master name server for the zone. BIND 8.1 assumes it is and checks for a corresponding NS record pointing the zone's domain name to the server in that field. If there's no such NS record, BIND emits that error message. It will also prevent NOTIFY messages from working correctly. The solution is either to change your MNAME field to the domain name of a name server listed in an NS record or to upgrade to a newer version of BIND 8. Upgrading is the better option since BIND 8.1 is so old. The check was removed at BIND 8.1.1.

Name Server Reports "Too Many Open Files"

On hosts with many IP addresses or a low limit on the maximum number of files a user can open, BIND will report:

```
Dec 12 11:52:06 terminator named[7770]: socket(SOCK_RAW): Too many open files
```

and die.

Since BIND tries to *bind()* to and listen on every network interface on the host, it may run out of file descriptors. This is especially common on hosts that use lots of virtual interfaces, often in support of web hosting. The possible solutions are:

- Use name-based virtual hosting, which doesn't require additional IP addresses.

- Configure your BIND 8 or 9 name server to listen on only one or a few of the host's network interfaces using the *listen-on* substatement. If *terminator.movie. edu* is the host we're having this problem with, the following:

  ```
  options {
      listen-on { 192.249.249.3; };
  };
  ```

  will tell *named* on *terminator.movie.edu* to *bind()* only to the IP address 192.249.249.3.

- Reconfigure your operating system to allow a process to open more file descriptors concurrently.

Resolver Reports "Looked for PTR, Found CNAME"

This is another problem related to BIND's strictness. On some lookups, the resolver logs:

```
Sep 24 10:40:11 terminator syslog: gethostby*.getanswer: asked for
    "37.103.74.204.in-addr.arpa IN PTR", got type "CNAME"
Sep 24 10:40:11 terminator syslog: gethostby*.getanswer: asked for
    "37.103.74.204.in-addr.arpa", got "37.32/27.103.74.204.in-addr.arpa"
```

What happened here is that the resolver asked the name server to reverse map the IP address 204.74.103.37 to a domain name. The server did, but in the process found that *37.103.74.204.in-addr.arpa* was actually an alias for *37.32/27.103.74. 204.in-addr.arpa*. That's almost certainly because the folks who run *103.74.204. in-addr.arpa* are using the scheme we described in Chapter 9, *Parenting*, to delegate part of their namespace. The BIND 4.9.3-BETA resolver, however, doesn't understand that and flags it as an error, thinking it didn't get the domain name or the type it was after. And, believe it or not, some operating systems ship with the BIND 4.9.3-BETA resolver as their system resolver.

The only solution to this problem is to upgrade to a newer version of the BIND resolver.

Name Server Startup Fails Because UDP Checksums Disabled

On some hosts running SunOS 4.1.x, you'll see this error:

```
Sep 24 10:40:11 terminator named[7770]: ns_udp checksums NOT turned on: exiting
```

named checked to make sure UDP checksumming was turned on on this system, and it wasn't, so *named* exited. *named* is insistent on UDP checksumming for good reason: it makes copious use of UDP and needs those UDP datagrams to arrive unmolested.

The solution to this problem is to enable UDP checksums on your system. The BIND distribution has documentation on that in *shrcs/sunos/INSTALL* and *shres/sunos/ISSUES* (in the BIND 4 distribution) or *src/port/sunos/shres/ISSUES* (in the BIND 8 distribution).

SunOS Resolver Is Configured, but Host Doesn't Use DNS

This problem is implementation-specific. Some administrators on SunOS 4 hosts configure their resolvers with *resolv.conf* and naively assume that *ping*, *telnet*, and their brethren should work right away. However, in Chapter 6 we discussed how SunOS 4 implements the resolver (in *ypserv*, you may recall). If the host isn't running NIS, configuring the resolver won't do it. The administrator will either have to set up at least an empty *hosts* map or replace the resolver routines. For details on both of these options, see the section "Sun's SunOS 4.x" in Chapter 6.

Other Name Servers Don't Cache Your Negative Answers

You'd need a keen eye to notice this problem, and, if you're running BIND 8, you'd also have to have turned off an important feature to have caused the problem. If you're running BIND 9, though, the feature is turned off by default. If you're running a BIND 8 or 9 name server and other resolvers and servers seem to ignore your server's cached negative responses, *auth-nxdomain* is probably off.

auth-nxdomain is an *options* substatement that tells a BIND 8 or 9 name server to flag cached negative responses as authoritative, even though they're not. That is, if your name server has cached the fact that *titanic.movie.edu* does not exist from the authoritative *movie.edu* name servers, *auth-nxdomain* tells your server to pass along that cached response to resolvers and servers that query it as though it were the authoritative name server for *movie.edu*.

The reason this feature is sometimes necessary is that some name servers check to make sure that negative responses (like an NXDOMAIN return code or no records with a NOERROR return code) are marked authoritative. In the days before negative caching, negative responses *had* to be authoritative, so this was a sensible sanity check. With the advent of negative caching, however, a negative response could come from the cache. To make sure that older servers don't ignore such answers, though, or consider them errors, BIND 8 and 9 let you falsely flag those responses as authoritative. In fact, that's the default behavior for a BIND 8 name server, so you shouldn't see remote queriers ignoring your BIND 8 server's negative responses unless you've explicitly turned off *auth-nxdomain*. BIND 9 name servers, on the other hand, have *auth-nxdomain* off by default, so queriers may ignore their responses even if you haven't touched the config file.

TTL Not Set

As we mentioned in Chapter 4, RFC 2308 was published just before BIND 8.2 was released. RFC 2308 changed the semantics of the last field in the SOA record to be the negative caching TTL and introduced a new control statement, $TTL, to set the default TTL for a zone data file.

If you upgrade to a BIND 8 name server newer than 8.2 without adding the necessary $TTL control statements to your zone data files, you'll see messages like this one in your name server's *syslog* output:

```
Sep 26 19:34:39 terminator named[22116]: Zone "movie.edu" (file db.movie.edu): No
default TTL ($TTL <value>) set, using SOA minimum instead
```

BIND 8 generously assumes that you just haven't read RFC 2308 yet and is content to use the last field of the SOA record as both the zone's default TTL and its negative caching TTL. BIND 9, however, isn't so forgiving:

```
Sep 26 19:35:54 terminator named[22124]: dns_master_load: db.movie.edu:7: no TTL
specified
Sep 26 19:35:54 terminator named[22124]: dns_zone_load: zone movie.edu/IN:
database db.movie.edu: dns_db_load failed: no ttl
Sep 26 19:35:54 terminator named[22124]: loading zones: no ttl
Sep 26 19:35:54 terminator named[22124]: exiting (due to fatal error)
```

So before upgrading to BIND 9, be sure that you add the necessary $TTL control statements.

TSIG Errors

As we said in Chapter 11, transaction signatures require time synchronization and key synchronization (the same key on either end of the transaction, plus the same key name) to work. Here are a couple of errors that may arise if you lose time synchronization or use different keys or key names.

First, here's an error you'd see on a BIND 8 name server if you had configured TSIG but had too much clock skew between your primary master name server and a slave:

```
Sep 27 10:47:49 wormhole named[22139]: Err/TO getting serial# for "movie.edu"
Sep 27 10:47:49 wormhole named-xfer[22584]: SOA TSIG verification from server
[192.249.249.3], zone movie.edu: message had BADTIME set (18)
```

Here, your name server tried to check the serial number of the *movie.edu* zone on *terminator.movie.edu* (192.249.249.3). The response from *terminator.movie.edu* didn't verify because *wormhole.movie.edu*'s clock showed a time more than 10 minutes different from the time the response was signed. The *Err/TO* message is just a byproduct of the failure of the TSIG-signed response to verify.

If you use a different key name on either end of the transaction, even if the data the key name refers to is the same, you'll see an error like this one from your BIND 8 name server:

```
Sep 27 12:02:44 wormhole named-xfer[22651]: SOA TSIG verification from server
[209.8.5.250], zone movie.edu: BADKEY(-17)
```

This time, the TSIG-signed response didn't check out because the verifier couldn't find a key with the name specified in the TSIG record. You'd see the same error if the key name matched but pointed to different data.

As always, BIND 9 is considerably more closed-mouthed about TSIG failure, reporting only:

```
Sep 27 13:35:42.804 client 192.249.249.1#1115: query: movie.edu SOA
Sep 27 13:35:42.804 client 192.249.249.1#1115: error
```

at debug level 3 for both of the previous scenarios.

Problem Symptoms

Some problems, unfortunately, aren't as easy to identify as the ones we listed. You'll experience some misbehavior but won't be able to attribute it directly to its cause, often because any of a number of problems can cause the symptoms you see. For cases like this, we'll suggest some of the common causes of these symptoms and ways to isolate them.

Local Name Can't Be Looked Up

The first thing to do when a program like *telnet* or *ftp* can't look up a local domain name is to use *nslookup* or *dig* to try to look up the same name. When we say "the same name," we mean *literally* the same name—don't add labels and a trailing dot if the user didn't type either one. Don't query a different name server than the user did.

As often as not, the user mistyped the name or doesn't understand how the search list works and just needs direction. Occasionally, you'll turn up real host configuration errors:

- Syntax errors in *resolv.conf* (problem 11 in the "Potential Problem List" earlier in this chapter)

- An unset local domain name (problem 12)

You can check for either of these using *nslookup*'s *set all* command.

If *nslookup* points to a problem with the name server rather than with the host configuration, check for the problems associated with the type of name server. If the name server is the primary master for the zone, but it isn't responding with data you think it should:

- Check that the zone data file contains the data in question and that the name server has loaded it (problem 2). A database dump can tell you for sure whether the data was loaded.

- Check the configuration file and the pertinent zone data file for syntax errors (problem 5). Check the name server's *syslog* output for indications of those errors.

- Ensure that the records have trailing dots, if they require them (problem 6).

If the name server is a slave server for the zone, you should first check whether or not its master has the correct data. If it does and the slave doesn't:

- Make sure you've incremented the serial number on the primary master (problem 1).

- Look for a problem on the slave in updating the zone (problem 3).

If the primary master *doesn't* have the correct data, of course, diagnose the problem on the primary.

If the problem server is a caching-only name server:

- Make sure it has its root hints (problem 7).

- Check that your parent zone's delegation to your zone exists and is correct (problems 9 and 10). Remember that to a caching-only server, your zone looks just like any other remote zone. Even though the host it runs on may be inside your zone, the caching-only name server must be able to locate an authoritative server for your zone from your parent zone's servers.

Remote Names Can't Be Looked Up

If your local lookups succeed but you can't look up domain names outside your local zones, there is a different set of problems to check:

- First, did you just set up your name servers? You might have omitted the root hints data (problem 7).

- Can you *ping* the remote zone's name servers? Maybe you can't reach the remote zone's servers because of connectivity loss (problem 8).

- Is the remote zone new? Maybe its delegation hasn't yet appeared (problem 9). Or the delegation information for the remote zone may be wrong or out of date due to neglect (problem 10).

- Does the domain name actually exist on the remote zone's servers (problem 2)? On all of them (problems 1 and 3)?

Wrong or Inconsistent Answer

If you get the wrong answer when looking up a local domain name, or an inconsistent answer depending on which name server you ask or when you ask, first check the synchronization between your name servers:

- Are they all holding the same serial number for the zone? Did you forget to increment the serial number on the primary master after you made a change (problem 1)? If you did, the name servers may all have the same serial number, but they will answer differently out of their authoritative data.

- Did you roll the serial number back to one (problem 1 again)? Then the primary master's serial number will appear much lower than the slaves' serial numbers.

- Did you forget to reload the primary master (problem 2)? Then the primary will return (via *nslookup* or *dig*, for example) a different serial number from the one in the zone data file.

- Are the slaves having trouble updating from their master(s) (problem 3)? If so, they should have *syslog*ged appropriate error messages.

- Is the name server's round robin feature rotating the addresses of the domain name you're looking up?

If you get these results when looking up a domain name in a remote zone, you should check whether the remote zone's name servers have lost synchronization. You can use tools like *nslookup* and *dig* to determine whether the remote zone's administrator forgot to increment the serial number, for example. If the name servers answer differently from their authoritative data but show the same serial number, the serial number probably wasn't incremented. If the primary master's serial number is much lower than the slaves', the primary's serial number was probably accidentally reset. We usually assume a zone's primary master name server is running on the host listed in the MNAME (first) field of the SOA record.

You probably can't determine conclusively that the primary master hasn't been reloaded, though. It's also difficult to pin down updating problems between remote name servers. In cases like this, if you've determined that the remote name servers are giving out incorrect data, contact the zone administrator and (gently) relay what you've found. This will help the administrator track down the problem on the remote end.

If you can determine that a parent name server—a remote zone's parent, your zone's parent, or even one in your zone—is giving out a bad answer, check whether this is coming from old delegation information. Sometimes this requires contacting both the administrator of the remote zone and the administrator of its parent to compare the delegation and the current, correct list of authoritative name servers.

If you can't induce the administrator to fix the data or if you can't track down the administrator, you can always use the *bogus* substatement or *bogusns* directive to instruct your name server not to query that particular server.

Lookups Take a Long Time

Slow name resolution is usually due to one of two problems:

- Connectivity loss (problem 8), which you can diagnose with name server debugging output and tools like *ping*

- Incorrect delegation information (problem 10) pointing to the wrong name servers or the wrong IP addresses

Usually, going over the debugging output and sending a few *ping*s will point to one or the other: either you can't reach the name servers at all, or you can reach the hosts but the name servers aren't responding.

Sometimes, though, the results are inconclusive. For example, the parent name servers delegate to a set of name servers that don't respond to *ping*s or queries, but connectivity to the remote network seems all right (a *traceroute*, for example, will get you to the remote network's "doorstep"—the last router between you and the host). Is the delegation information so badly out of date that the name servers have long since moved to other addresses? Are the hosts simply down? Or is there really a remote network problem? Usually, finding out requires a call or a message to the administrator of the remote zone. (Remember, *whois* gives you phone numbers!)

rlogin and rsh to Host Fails Access Check

This is a problem you expect to see right after you set up your name servers. Users unaware of the change from the host table to domain name service won't know to update their *.rhosts* files. (We covered what needs to be updated in Chapter 6.) Consequently, *rlogin*'s or *rsh*'s access check will fail and deny the user access.

Other causes of this problem are missing or incorrect *in-addr.arpa* delegation (problems 9 and 10) or forgetting to add a PTR record for the client host (problem 4). If you've recently upgraded to BIND Version 4.9 or newer and have PTR data for more than one *in-addr.arpa* zone in a single zone data file, your name server may be ignoring the out-of-zone data. Any of these situations will result in the same behavior:

```
% rlogin wormhole
Password:
```

In other words, the user is prompted for a password despite having set up password-less access with *.rhosts* or *hosts.equiv*. If you were to look at the *syslog* file on the destination host (*wormhole.movie.edu*, in this case), you'd probably see something like this:

```
May  4 18:06:22 wormhole inetd[22514]: login/tcp: Connection
      from unknown (192.249.249.213)
```

You can tell which problem it is by stepping through the resolution process with your favorite query tool. First query one of your *in-addr.arpa* zone's parent name servers for NS records for your *in-addr.arpa* zone. If these are correct, query the name servers listed for the PTR record corresponding to the IP address of the *rlogin* or *rsh* client. Make sure they all have the PTR record and that the record maps to the right domain name. If not all the name servers have the record, check for a loss of synchronization between the primary master and the slaves (problems 1 and 3).

Access to Services Denied

Sometimes *rlogin* and *rsh* aren't the only services to go. Occasionally you'll install BIND on your server and your diskless hosts won't boot, and hosts won't be able to mount disks from the server, either.

If this happens, make sure that the case of the domain names your name servers return agrees with the case your previous name service returned. For example, if you are running NIS and your NIS host maps contain only lowercase names, you should make sure your name servers also return lowercase domain names. Some programs are case-sensitive and won't recognize names in a different case in a data file, such as */etc/bootparams* or */etc/exports*.

Can't Get Rid of Old Data

Sometimes, after decommissioning a name server or changing a server's IP address, you'll find the old address record lingering around. An old record may show up in a name server's cache or in a zone data file weeks or even months later. The record clearly should have timed out of any caches by now. So why's it still there? Well, there are a few reasons this happens. We'll describe the simpler cases first.

Old delegation information

The first (and simplest) case occurs if a parent zone doesn't keep up with its children or if the children don't inform the parent of changes to the authoritative name servers for the zone. If the *edu* administrators have this old delegation information for *movie.edu*:

```
$ORIGIN movie.edu.
@          86400    IN    NS    terminator
           86400    IN    NS    wormhole
terminator 86400    IN    A     192.249.249.3
wormhole   86400    IN    A     192.249.249.254 ; wormhole's former
                                                ; IP address
```

then the *edu* name servers will give out the bogus old address for *wormhole. movie.edu*.

This is easily corrected once it's isolated to the parent zone's name servers: just contact the parent zone's administrator and ask to have the delegation information updated. If your parent zone is one of the gTLDs, you may be able to fix the problem by filling out a form on your registrar's web site to modify the information about the name server. If any of the child zone's name servers have cached the bad data, kill them (to clear out their caches), delete any backup zone data files that contain the bad data, then restart them.

Registration of a non-name server

This is a problem unique to the gTLD zones: *com*, *net*, and *org*. Sometimes, you'll find the gTLD name servers giving out stale address information about a host in one of your zones—and not even a name server! But why would the gTLD name servers have information about an arbitrary host in one of your zones?

Here's the answer: you can register hosts in the gTLD zones that aren't name servers at all, such as your web server. For example, you could register an address for *www.foo.com* through a *com* registrar, and the *com* name servers will give out that address. You shouldn't, though, because you'll lose a fair amount of control over the address. If you need to change the address, it could take a day or more to push the change through your registrar. If you run the *foo.com* primary master name server, you can make the change almost instantly.

What have I got?

How do you determine which of these problems is plaguing you? Pay attention to which name servers are distributing the old data and which zones the data relates to:

- Is the name server a gTLD name server? Check for a stale, registered address.

- Is the name server your parent name server but not a gTLD name server? Check the parent for old delegation information.

That's about all we can think to cover. It's certainly not a comprehensive list, but we hope it'll help you solve the more common problems you encounter with DNS and give you ideas about how to approach the rest. Boy, if we'd only had a troubleshooting guide when *we* started!

15

In this chapter:
- *Shell Script Programming with nslookup*
- *C Programming with the Resolver Library Routines*
- *Perl Programming with Net::DNS*

Programming with the Resolver and Name Server Library Routines

"I know what you're thinking about," said Tweedledum; "but it isn't so, nohow."

"Contrariwise," continued Tweedledee, "if it was so, it might be; and if it were so, it would be; but as it isn't, it ain't. That's logic."

I bet you think resolver programming is hard. Contrariwise! It isn't very hard, really. The format of DNS messages is quite straightforward—you don't have to deal with ASN.1* at all, as you do with SNMP. And you have nifty library routines to make parsing DNS messages easy. We've included portions of RFC 1035 in Appendix A, *DNS Message Format and Resource Records*. However, you might find it handy to have a copy of RFC 1035 to look at as we go through this chapter; at least have a copy of it nearby when you write your own DNS programs.

Shell Script Programming with nslookup

Before you go off and write a C program to do your DNS chore, you should write the program as a shell script using *nslookup* or *dig*. There are good reasons to start with a shell script:

- You can write the shell script much faster than you can write the C program.

- If you're not comfortable with DNS, you can work out the details of your program's logic with a quick shell script prototype. When you finally write the C

---

* ASN.1 stands for Abstract Syntax Notation. ASN.1 is a method of encoding object types, accepted as an international standard by the International Organization for Standardization.

program, you can focus on the additional control you have with C rather than spending your time reworking the basic functionality.

- You might find out that the shell script version does your task well enough so that you don't have to write the C program after all. And not only is it quicker to write shell scripts, but they're easier to maintain if you stick with them for the long run.

If you prefer Perl over plain old shell programming, you can use Perl instead. At the end of this chapter, we'll show you how to use the Perl Net::DNS module written by Michael Fuhr.

A Typical Problem

Before you write a program, you need a problem to solve. Let's suppose you want your network management system to watch over your primary master and slave name servers. You want it to notify you of several problems: a name server that isn't running (it might have died), a name server that is not authoritative for a zone it is supposed to be authoritative for (the config file or zone data file might have been messed up), or a name server that has fallen behind in updating its zone data (the primary master's serial number might have been decreased accidentally).

Each of these problems is easily detectable. If a name server is not running on a host, the host sends back an ICMP *port unreachable* message. You can find this out with either a query tool or the resolver routines. Checking whether a name server is authoritative for a zone is easy: ask it for the zone's SOA record. If the answer is nonauthoritative or the name server does not have the SOA record, there's a problem. You'll have to ask for the SOA record in a *nonrecursive* query so that the name server doesn't go off and look up the SOA record from another server. Once you have the SOA record, you can extract the serial number.

Solving This Problem with a Script

This problem requires a program that takes the domain name of a zone as an argument, looks up the name servers for that zone, and then queries each of those name servers for the SOA record for the zone. The response will show whether the name server is authoritative, and it will show the zone's serial number. If there is no response, the program needs to determine if there's even a name server running on the host. Once you write this program, you should run it on each zone you want to watch over. Since this program looks up the name servers (by looking up the NS records for the zone), we assume that you have listed all your name servers in NS records in your zone data. If that's not the case, you will have to change this program to read a list of name servers from the command line.

Let's write the basic program as a shell script that uses *nslookup*. First, we figure out what the output of *nslookup* looks like so that we can parse it with Unix tools.

We'll look up NS records to find out which name servers are supposed to be authoritative for the zone, both when the server is authoritative for the zone that contains the NS records and when it isn't:

```
% nslookup
Default Server:  relay.hp.com
Address:  15.255.152.2

> set type=ns
```

Find out what the response looks like when the name server is not authoritative for the NS records:

```
> mit.edu.
Server:  relay.hp.com
Address:  15.255.152.2

Non-authoritative answer:
mit.edu  nameserver = STRAWB.MIT.EDU
mit.edu  nameserver = W20NS.MIT.EDU
mit.edu  nameserver = BITSY.MIT.EDU

Authoritative answers can be found from:
MIT.EDU  nameserver = STRAWB.MIT.EDU
MIT.EDU  nameserver = W20NS.MIT.EDU
MIT.EDU  nameserver = BITSY.MIT.EDU
STRAWB.MIT.EDU  internet address = 18.71.0.151
W20NS.MIT.EDU   internet address = 18.70.0.160
BITSY.MIT.EDU   internet address = 18.72.0.3
```

Then find out what the response looks like when the name server *is* authoritative for the NS records:

```
> server strawb.mit.edu.
Default Server:  strawb.mit.edu
Address:  18.71.0.151

> mit.edu.
Server:  strawb.mit.edu
Address:  18.71.0.151

mit.edu  nameserver = BITSY.MIT.EDU
mit.edu  nameserver = STRAWB.MIT.EDU
mit.edu  nameserver = W20NS.MIT.EDU
BITSY.MIT.EDU   internet address = 18.72.0.3
STRAWB.MIT.EDU  internet address = 18.71.0.151
W20NS.MIT.EDU   internet address = 18.70.0.160
```

You can see from this output that we can grab the domain names of the name servers by looking for the lines that contain *nameserver* and saving the last field. When the name server wasn't authoritative for the NS records, it printed them twice, so we'll have to weed out duplicates.

Next, we look up the SOA record for the zone, both when the server is authoritative for the zone that contains the SOA record and when it isn't. We turn off *recurse* so the name server doesn't go off and query an authoritative name server for the SOA:

```
% nslookup
Default Server:  relay.hp.com
Address:  15.255.152.2

> set type=soa
> set norecurse
```

Find out what the response looks like when the name server is not authoritative and does not have the SOA record:

```
> mit.edu.
Server:  relay.hp.com
Address:  15.255.152.2

Authoritative answers can be found from:
MIT.EDU nameserver = STRAWB.MIT.EDU
MIT.EDU nameserver = W20NS.MIT.EDU
MIT.EDU nameserver = BITSY.MIT.EDU
STRAWB.MIT.EDU  internet address = 18.71.0.151
W20NS.MIT.EDU   internet address = 18.70.0.160
BITSY.MIT.EDU   internet address = 18.72.0.3
```

Then find out what the response looks like when the name server *is* authoritative for the zone:

```
> server strawb.mit.edu.
Default Server:  strawb.mit.edu
Address:  18.71.0.151

> mit.edu.
Server:  strawb.mit.edu
Address:  18.71.0.151

mit.edu
        origin = BITSY.MIT.EDU
        mail addr = NETWORK-REQUEST.BITSY.MIT.EDU
        serial = 1995
        refresh = 3600 (1H)
        retry   = 900 (15M)
        expire  = 3600000 (5w6d16h)
        minimum ttl = 21600 (6H)
```

When the name server was not authoritative for the zone, it returned references to other name servers. If the name server had previously looked up the SOA record and cached it, the name server would have returned the SOA record and said that it was nonauthoritative. We need to check for both cases. When the name server returns the SOA record and it is authoritative, we can grab the serial number from the line that contains *serial*.

Now we need to see what *nslookup* returns when no name server is running on a host. We'll change servers to a host that does not normally run a name server and look up an SOA record:

```
% nslookup
Default Server:  relay.hp.com
Address:  15.255.152.2

> server galt.cs.purdue.edu.
Default Server:  galt.cs.purdue.edu
Address:  128.10.2.39

> set type=soa
> mit.edu.
Server:  galt.cs.purdue.edu
Address:  128.10.2.39

*** galt.cs.purdue.edu can't find mit.edu.: No response from server
```

Last, we need to see what *nslookup* returns if a host is not responding. We can test this by switching name servers to an unused IP address on our LAN:

```
% nslookup
Default Server:  relay.hp.com
Address:  15.255.152.2

> server 15.255.152.100
Default Server:  [15.255.152.100]
Address:  15.255.152.100

> set type=soa
> mit.edu.
Server:  [15.255.152.100]
Address:  15.255.152.100

*** Request to [15.255.152.100] timed-out
```

In the last two cases, the error message was written to *stderr*.[*] We can make use of that fact when writing our shell script. Now we are ready to compose the shell script. We'll call it *check_soa*:

```
#!/bin/sh
if test "$1" = ""
then
    echo usage: $0 zone
    exit 1
fi
ZONE=$1
#
# Use nslookup to discover the name servers for this zone ($1).
# Use awk to grab the name server's domain names from the nameserver lines.
# (The names are always in the last field.)  Use sort -u to weed out
```

---

[*] Not all versions of *nslookup* print the last error message for a timeout. Be sure to check what yours prints.

```
# duplicates; we don't actually care about collation.
#
SERVERS=`nslookup -type=ns $ZONE |\
               awk '/nameserver/ {print $NF}' | sort -u`
if test "$SERVERS" = ""
then
    #
    # Didn't find any servers.  Just quit silently; nslookup will
    # have detected this error and printed a message.  That will
    # suffice.
    #
    exit 1
fi
#
# Check each server's SOA serial number.  The output from
# nslookup is saved in two temp files: nso.$$ (standard output)
# and nse.$$ (standard error).  These files are rewritten on
# every iteration.  Turn off defname and search since we
# should be dealing with fully qualified domain names.
#
# NOTE: this loop is rather long; don't be fooled.
#
for i in $SERVERS
do
    nslookup >/tmp/nso.$$ 2>/tmp/nse.$$ <<-EOF
      server $i
      set nosearch
      set nodefname
      set norecurse
      set q=soa
      $ZONE
EOF
    #
    # Does this response indicate that the current server ($i) is
    # authoritative?  The server is NOT authoritative if (a) the
    # response says so, or (b) the response tells you to find
    # authoritative info elsewhere.
    #
    if egrep "Non-authoritative|Authoritative answers can be" \
                                     /tmp/nso.$$ >/dev/null
    then
      echo $i is not authoritative for $ZONE
      continue
    fi
    #
    # We know the server is authoritative; extract the serial number.
    #
    SERIAL=`cat /tmp/nso.$$ | grep serial | sed -e "s/.*= //"`
    if test "$SERIAL" = ""
    then
        #
        # We get here if SERIAL is null.  In this case, there should
        # be an error message from nslookup; so cat the "standard
        # error" file.
        #
```

```
        cat /tmp/nse.$$
    else
        #
        # Report the server's domain name and its serial number.
        #
        echo $i has serial number $SERIAL
    fi
done  # end of the "for" loop
#
# Delete the temporary files.
#
rm -f /tmp/nso.$$ /tmp/nse.$$
```

Here is what the output looks like:

```
% check_soa mit.edu
BITSY.MIT.EDU has serial number 1995
STRAWB.MIT.EDU has serial number 1995
W20NS.MIT.EDU has serial number 1995
```

If you are pressed for time, this short tool will solve your problem, and you can go on to other work. If you find that you are checking lots of zones and that this tool is too slow, you'll want to convert it to a C program. Also, if you want more control over the error messages—rather than relying on *nslookup* for error messages— then you'll have to write a C program. We'll do just that later in this chapter.

C Programming with the Resolver Library Routines

Before writing any code, though, you need to be familiar with the DNS message format and the resolver library routines. In the shell script we just wrote, *nslookup* parsed the DNS message. In a C program, though, you have to do the parsing. Let's start this section on programming by looking at the DNS message format.

DNS Message Format

You've seen the DNS message format before, in Chapter 12, *nslookup and dig*. It looks like this:

- Header section
- Question section
- Answer section
- Authority section
- Additional section

The format of the header section is described in RFC 1035 on pages 26–28, and also in Appendix A of this book. It looks like this:

```
query identification number (2 octets)
query response (1 bit)
opcode (4 bits)
authoritative answer (1 bit)
truncation (1 bit)
recursion desired (1 bit)
recursion available (1 bit)
reserved (3 bits)
response code (4 bits)
question count (2 octets)
answer record count (2 octets)
name server record count (2 octets)
additional record count (2 octets)
```

You'll also find opcode, response code, type, and class values defined in *arpa/nameser.h* as well as routines to extract this information from a message. We'll discuss these routines, part of the name server library, shortly.

The question section is described on pages 28–29 of RFC 1035. It looks like this:

```
domain name (variable length)
query type (2 octets)
query class (2 octets)
```

The answer, authority, and additional sections are described on pages 29–30 of RFC 1035. These sections comprise some number of resource records that look like this:

```
domain name (variable length)
type (2 octets)
class (2 octets)
TTL (4 octets)
resource data length (2 octets)
resource data (variable length)
```

The header section contains a count of how many of these resource records are in each section.

Domain Name Storage

As you can see, the names stored in the DNS message are of variable length. Unlike C, DNS does not store the names as null-terminated strings. Domain names are stored as a series of length/value pairs ending with an octet of zero. Each label in a domain name is composed of a length octet and a label. A name like *venera.isi.edu* is stored as:

```
6 venera  3  isi  3 edu 0
```

You can imagine how much of a DNS message could be devoted to storing names. The developers of DNS recognized this and came up with a simple way to compress domain names.

Domain Name Compression

Often, an entire domain name or, at least, the trailing labels of a domain name match a name already stored in the message. Domain name compression eliminates the repetition of domain names by storing a pointer to the earlier occurrence of the name instead of inserting the name again. Here is how it works. Suppose a response message already contains the name *venera.isi.edu*. If the name *vaxa.isi.edu* is added to the response, the label *vaxa* is stored, and then a pointer to the earlier occurrence of *isi.edu* is added. So how are these pointers implemented?

The first two bits of the length octet indicate whether a length/label pair or a pointer to a length/label pair follows. If the first two bits are zero, then the length and label follow. As you may remember from way back in Chapter 2, *How Does DNS Work?*, a label is limited to 63 characters. That's because the length field has only the remaining six bits for the length of the label—enough to represent the lengths 0–63. If the first two bits of the length octet are ones, then what follows is not a length but a pointer. The pointer is the last six bits of the length octet *and* the next octet—14 bits in total. The pointer is an offset from the start of the DNS message. Now, when *vaxa.isi.edu* is compressed into a buffer containing only *venera.isi.edu*, this is what results:

```
byte offset: 0 123456 7 890 1 234 5 6 7890 1    2
             -------------+-------------+--------
pkt contents: 6 venera 3 isi 3 edu 0 4 vaxa 0xC0 7
```

The *0xC0* is a byte with the high two bits ones and the rest of the bits zeros. Since the high two bits are ones, this is a pointer instead of a length. The pointer value is seven—the last six bits of the first octet are zeros and the second octet is seven. At offset seven in this buffer, you find the rest of the domain name that begins with *vaxa*, which is *isi.edu*.

In this example, we only showed compressing two domain names in a buffer, not a whole DNS message. A DNS message would have had a header as well as other fields. This example is intended only to give you an idea of how the domain name compression works. Now the good news: you don't really need to care how names are compressed as long as the library routines do it properly. What you do need to know is how parsing a DNS response message can get messed up if you are off by one byte. For example, try to expand the name starting with byte two instead of byte one. You'll discover that "v" doesn't make a very good length octet or pointer.

The Resolver Library Routines

The resolver library contains the routines that you need to write your application. You'll use these routines to generate queries. You'll use the *name server library* routines, explained next, to parse the response.

In case you're wondering why we're not using the BIND 9 resolver routines in our code, well, they haven't been written yet. BIND 9 includes library routines to perform lots of powerful DNS functions, but they're oriented toward the BIND 9's name server's needs and are very complicated to use, we're told. The developers tell us that a simpler resolver library is coming and that in the meantime, we should use the BIND 8 resolver library. A program linked against the BIND 8 library routines will work just fine with a BIND 9 name server.

Here are the header files you must include:

```
#include <sys/types.h>
#include <netinet/in.h>
#include <arpa/nameser.h>
#include <resolv.h>
```

Now let's look at the resolver library routines.

---

res_search

```
int res_search(const char *dname,
               int class,
               int type,
               u_char *answer,
               int anslen)
```

res_search is the "highest level" resolver routine, and is called by *gethostbyname*. *res_search* applies the search algorithm to the domain name passed to it. That is, it takes the domain name it receives (*dname*), "completes" the name (if it's not fully qualified) by adding the various domain names from the resolver search list, and calls *res_query* until it receives a successful response, indicating that it found a valid, fully qualified domain name. In addition to implementing the search algorithm, *res_search* looks in the file referenced by your HOSTALIASES environment variable. (The HOSTALIASES variable was described in Chapter 6, *Configuring Hosts.*) So it also takes care of any "private" host aliases you might have. *res_search* returns the size of the response or fills in *h_errno* and returns −1 if there was an error or the answer count is zero. (*h_errno* is like *errno*, but for DNS lookups.)

Therefore, the only parameter that's really of interest to *res_search* is *dname*; the others are just passed through to *res_query* and the other resolver routines. The other arguments are:

class

The class of the data you're looking up. This is almost always the constant C_IN, the Internet class. The class constants are defined in *arpa/nameser.h*.

type

The type of data you're looking up. Again, this is a constant defined in *arpa/nameser.h*. A typical value would be T_NS to retrieve a name server record, or T_MX to retrieve an MX record.

answer

A buffer in which *res_search* will place the response message. Its size should be at least PACKETSZ (from *arpa/nameser.h*) bytes.

anslen

The size of the *answer* buffer (e.g., PACKETSZ).

res_search returns the size of the response or –1 if there was an error.

---

res_query

```
int res_query(const char *dname,
              int class,
              int type,
              u_char *answer,
              int anslen)
```

res_query is one of the "midlevel" resolver routines. It does all the real work in looking up the domain name: it makes a query message by calling *res_mkquery*, sends the query by calling *res_send*, and looks at enough of the response to determine whether your question was answered. In many cases, *res_query* is called by *res_search*, which just feeds it the different domain names to look up. As you'd expect, these two functions have the same arguments. *res_query* returns the size of the response, or it fills in *h_errno* and returns –1 if there was an error or the answer count was zero.

---

res_mkquery

```
int res_mkquery(int op,
                const char *dname,
                int class,
                int type,
                const u_char *data,
                int datalen,
                const u_char *newrr,
                u_char *buf,
                int buflen)
```

res_mkquery creates the query message. It fills in all the header fields, compresses the domain name into the question section, and fills in the other question fields.

The *dname*, *class*, and *type* arguments are the same as for *res_search* and *res_query*. The remaining arguments are:

op

> The "operation" to be performed. This is normally QUERY, but it can be IQUERY (inverse query). However, as we've explained before, IQUERY is seldom used. BIND Versions 4.9.4 and later, by default, do not even support IQUERY.

data

> A buffer containing the data for inverse queries. It is NULL when *op* is QUERY.

datalen

> The size of the *data* buffer. If *data* is NULL, then *datalen* is zero.

newrr

> A buffer used for the dynamic update code (covered in Chapter 10, *Advanced Features*). Unless you are playing with this feature, it is always NULL.

buf

> A buffer in which *res_mkquery* places the query message. It should be PACKETSZ or larger, like the answer buffer in *res_search* and *res_query*.

buflen

> The size of the *buf* buffer (e.g., PACKETSZ).

res_mkquery returns the size of the query message or −1 if there was an error.

---

res_send

```
int res_send(const u_char *msg,
             int msglen,
             u_char *answer,
             int anslen)
```

res_send implements the retry algorithm. It sends the query message, *msg*, in a UDP datagram, but it can also send it over a TCP stream. The response message is stored in *answer*. This routine, of all the resolver routines, is the only one to use black magic (unless you know all about connected datagram sockets). You've seen these arguments before in the other resolver routines:

msg

> The buffer containing the DNS query message.

msglen

> The size of the message.

answer

The buffer in which to store the DNS response message.

anslen

The size of the answer message.

res_send returns the size of the response or –1 if there was an error. If this routine returns –1 and *errno* is ECONNREFUSED, then there is no name server running on the target name server host.

You can look at *errno* to see if it is ECONNREFUSED after calling *res_search* or *res_query*. (*res_search* calls *res_query*, which calls *res_send*.) If you want to check *errno* after calling *res_query*, clear *errno* first. That way, you know the current call to *res_send* was the one that set *errno*. However, you don't have to clear *errno* before calling *res_search*. *res_search* clears *errno* itself before calling *res_query*.

---

res_init

```
int res_init(void)
```

res_init reads *resolv.conf* and initializes a data structure called *_res* (more about that later). All the previously discussed routines will call *res_init* if they detect that it hasn't been called previously. Or you can call it on your own; this is useful if you want to change some of the defaults before calling the first resolver library routine. If there are any lines in *resolv.conf* that *res_init* doesn't understand, it ignores them. *res_init* always returns zero, even if the manpage reserves the right to return –1.

---

herror and h_errno

```
extern int h_errno;
int herror(const char *s)
```

herror is a routine like *perror*, except that it prints out a string based on the value of the external variable *h_errno* instead of *errno*. The only argument is:

s   A string used to identify the error message. If a string *s* is supplied, it is printed first, followed by ":" and a string based on the value of *h_errno*.

Here are the possible values of *h_errno*:

HOST_NOT_FOUND

The domain name does not exist. The return code in the name server response was NXDOMAIN.

TRY_AGAIN

Either the name server is not running, or the name server returned SERVFAIL.

NO_RECOVERY

Either the domain name could not be compressed because it was an invalid domain name (e.g., a name missing a label—.*movie.edu*) or the name server returned FORMERR, NOTIMP, or REFUSED.

NO_DATA

The domain name exists, but there is no data of the requested type.

NETDB_INTERNAL

There was a library error unrelated to the network or name service. Instead, see *errno* for the problem description.

The _res Structure

Each of the resolver routines (i.e., each routine whose name starts with *res_*) makes use of a common data structure called *_res*. You can change the behavior of the resolver routines by changing *_res*. If you want to change the number of times *res_send* retries a query, you can change the value of the *retry* field. If you want to turn off the resolver search algorithm, you turn off the RES_DNSRCH bit from the *options* mask. You'll find the all-important *_res* structure in *resolv.h*:

```
struct __res_state {
    int      retrans;    /* retransmission time interval */
    int      retry;      /* number of times to retransmit */
    u_long   options;    /* option flags - see below. */
    int      nscount;    /* number of name servers */
    struct sockaddr_in
             nsaddr_list[MAXNS];  /* address of name server */
#define nsaddr nsaddr_list[0]     /* for backward compatibility */
    u_short  id;                  /* current packet id */
    char     *dnsrch[MAXDNSRCH+1]; /* components of domain to search */
    char     defdname[MAXDNAME];  /* default domain */
    u_long   pfcode;              /* RES_PRF_ flags - see below. */
    unsigned ndots:4;             /* threshold for initial abs. query */
    unsigned nsort:4;             /* number of elements in sort_list[] */
    char     unused[3];
    struct {
             struct in_addr  addr;  /* address to sort on */
             u_int32_t       mask;
    } sort_list[MAXRESOLVSORT];
};
```

The *options* field is a simple bit mask of the enabled options. To turn on a feature, turn on the corresponding bit in the options field. Bit masks for each of the options are defined in *resolv.h*; the options are:

RES_INIT

If this bit is on, then *res_init* has been called.

RES_DEBUG

This bit causes resolver debugging messages to be printed, if the resolver routines were compiled with DEBUG, that is. Off is the default.

RES_AAONLY

Requires the answer to be authoritative, not from a name server's cache. It's too bad this isn't implemented, as it would be a useful feature. Given the BIND resolver's design, this feature would have to be implemented in the name server, and it's not.

RES_PRIMARY

Query the primary master name server only—again, not implemented.

RES_USEVC

Turn this bit on if you'd like the resolver to make its queries over a virtual circuit (TCP) connection instead of with UDP datagrams. As you might guess, there is a performance penalty for setting up and tearing down a TCP connection. Off is the default.

RES_STAYOPEN

If you are making your queries over a TCP connection, turning this bit on causes the connection to be left open, so you can use it to query the same remote name server again. Otherwise, the connection is torn down after the query has been answered. Off is the default.

RES_IGNTC

If the name server response has the truncation bit set, then the default resolver behavior is to retry the query using TCP. If this bit is turned on, the truncation bit in the response message is ignored and the query is not retried using TCP. Off is the default.

RES_RECURSE

The default behavior for the BIND resolver is to send recursive queries. Turning this bit off turns off the "recursion desired" bit in the query message. On is the default.

RES_DEFNAMES

The default behavior for the BIND resolver is to append the local domain name to any domain name that does not have a dot in it. Turning this bit off turns off appending the local domain name. On is the default.

RES_DNSRCH

The default behavior for the BIND resolver is to append each element of the search list to a domain name that does not end in a dot. Turning this bit off turns off the search list function. On is the default.

RES_INSECURE1

The default behavior for a 4.9.3 or later BIND resolver is to ignore answers from name servers that were not queried. Turning this bit on disables this security check. Off (i.e., security check on) is the default.

RES_INSECURE2

The default behavior for a 4.9.3 or later BIND resolver is to ignore answers in which the question section of the response does not match the question section of the original query. Turning this bit on disables this security check. Off (i.e., security check on) is the default.

RES_NOALIASES

The default behavior for the BIND resolver is to use aliases defined in the file specified by the user's HOSTALIASES environment variable. Turning this bit on disables the HOSTALIASES feature for 4.9.3 and later BIND resolvers. Previous resolvers did not allow this feature to be disabled. Off is the default.

RES_USE_INET6

Tells the resolver to return IPv6 addresses (in addition to IPv4 addresses) to the *gethostbyname* function.

RES_ROTATE

Normally, a resolver that sends repeated queries always queries the first name server in *resolv.conf* first. With RES_ROTATE set, a BIND 8.2 or later resolver sends its first query to the first name server in *resolv.conf*, its second to the second name server, and so on. See the *options rotate* directive in Chapter 6 for details. The default is not to rotate name servers.

RES_NOCHECKNAME

Since BIND 4.9.4, resolvers have checked the domain names in responses to make sure they conform to the naming guidelines described in Chapter 4, *Setting Up BIND*. BIND 8.2 resolvers offer the option of turning the name checking mechanism off. Off (i.e., name check on) is the default.

RES_KEEPTSIG

This option tells a BIND 8.2 or later resolver not to strip the TSIG record from a signed DNS message. This way, the application that called the resolver can examine it.

RES_BLAST

"Blast" all recursive servers by sending queries to them simultaneously. Not implemented yet.

RES_DEFAULT

This isn't a single option, but rather a combination of the RES_RECURSE, RES_DEFNAMES, and RES_DNSRCH options, all of which are on by default. You normally won't need to set RES_DEFAULT explicitly; it's set for you when you call *res_init*.

The Name Server Library Routines

The name server library contains routines you need to parse response messages. Here are the header files you must include:

```
#include <sys/types.h>
#include <netinet/in.h>
#include <netdb.h>
#include <arpa/nameser.h>
#include <resolv.h>
```

Following are the name server library routines.

---

ns_initparse

```
int ns_initparse(const u_char *msg,
                 int msglen,
                 ns_msg *handle)
```

ns_initparse is the first routine you must call before you use the other name server library routines. *ns_initparse* fills in the data structure pointed to by *handle*, which is a parameter passed to other routines. The arguments are:

msg
　　A pointer to the beginning of the response message buffer.

msglen
　　The size of the message buffer.

handle
　　A pointer to a data structure filled in by *ns_initparse*.

ns_initparse returns zero on success and –1 if it fails to parse the message buffer.

---

ns_msg_base, ns_msg_end, and ns_msg_size

```
const u_char *ns_msg_base(ns_msg handle)
const u_char *ns_msg_end(ns_msg handle)
int ns_msg_size(ns_msg handle)
```

These routines return a pointer to the start of the message, a pointer to the end of the message, and the size of the message. They return the data you passed into *ns_initparse*. The only argument is:

handle
　　A data structure filled in by *ns_initparse*.

---

ns_msg_id

```
u_int16_t ns_msg_id(ns_msg handle)
```

ns_msg_id returns the identification from the header section (described earlier) of the response message. The only argument is:

handle
> A data structure filled in by *ns_initparse*.

---

ns_msg_get_flag

```
u_int16_t ns_msg_get_flag(ns_msg handle, ns_flag flag)
```

ns_msg_get_flag returns the "flag" fields from the header section of the response message. Its arguments are:

handle
> A data structure filled in by *ns_initparse*.

flag
> An enumerated type that can have the following values:

```
ns_f_qr     /* Question/Response */
ns_f_opcode /* Operation Code */
ns_f_aa     /* Authoritative Answer */
ns_f_tc     /* Truncation Occurred */
ns_f_rd     /* Recursion Desired */
ns_f_ra     /* Recursion Available */
ns_f_z      /* Must Be Zero */
ns_f_ad     /* Authentic Data (DNSSEC) */
ns_f_cd     /* Checking Disabled (DNSSEC) */
ns_f_rcode  /* Response Code */
ns_f_max
```

---

ns_msg_count

```
u_int16_t ns_msg_count(ns_msg handle, ns_sect section)
```

ns_msg_count returns a counter from the header section of the response message. Its arguments are:

handle
> A data structure filled in by *ns_initparse*.

section
> An enumerated type that can have the following values:

```
ns_s_qd /* Query: Question section */
ns_s_zn /* Update: Zone section */
ns_s_an /* Query: Answer section */
ns_s_pr /* Update: Prerequisite section */
ns_s_ns /* Query: Name Server section */
ns_s_ud /* Update: Update section */
ns_s_ar /* Query|Update: Additional records section */
```

ns_parserr

```
int ns_parserr(ns_msg *handle,
               ns_sect section,
               int rrnum,
               ns_rr *rr)
```

ns_parserr extracts information about a response record and stores it in *rr*, which is a parameter passed to other name server libarary routines. The arguments are:

handle

A pointer to a data structure filled in by *ns_initparse*.

section

The same parameter described in *ns_msg_count*.

rrnum

A resource record number for the resource records in this section. Resource records start numbering at zero. *ns_msg_count* tells you how many resource records are in this section.

rr A pointer to a data structure to be initialized.

ns_parserr returns zero on success and –1 if it fails to parse the response buffer.

ns_rr routines

```
char *ns_rr_name(ns_rr rr)
u_int16_t ns_rr_type(ns_rr rr)
u_int16_t ns_rr_class(ns_rr rr)
u_int32_t ns_rr_ttl(ns_rr rr)
u_int16_t ns_rr_rdlen(ns_rr rr)
const u_char *ns_rr_rdata(ns_rr rr)
```

These routines return individual fields from a response record. Their only argument is:

rr A data structure filled in by *ns_parserr*.

ns_name_compress

```
int ns_name_compress(const char *exp_dn,
                     u_char *comp_dn,
                     size_t length,
                     const u_char **dnptrs,
                     const u_char **lastdnptr)
```

ns_name_compress compresses a domain name. You won't normally call this routine yourself—you'll let *res_mkquery* do it for you. However, if you need to compress a name for some reason, this is the tool to do it. The arguments are:

exp_dn

The "expanded" domain name that you supply; i.e., a normal, null-terminated string containing a fully qualified domain name.

comp_dn

The place where *ns_name_compress* will store the compressed domain name.

length

The size of the *comp_dn* buffer.

dnptrs

An array of pointers to previously compressed domain names. *dnptrs[0]* points to the beginning of the message; the list ends with a NULL pointer. After you've initialized *dnptrs[0]* to the beginning of the message and *dnptrs[1]* to NULL, *dn_comp* updates the list each time you call it.

lastdnptr

A pointer to the end of the *dnptrs* array. *ns_name_compress* needs to know where the end of the array is so it doesn't overrun it.

If you want to use this routine, look at how it is used in the BIND source in *src/lib/resolv/res_mkquery.c* (BIND 8) or *res/res_mkquery.c* (BIND 4). It's often easier to see how to use a routine from an example than from an explanation. *ns_name_compress* returns the size of the compressed name or −1 if there was an error.

---

ns_name_uncompress

```
int ns_name_uncompress(const u_char *msg,
                       const u_char *eomorig,
                       const u_char *comp_dn,
                       char *exp_dn,
                       size_t length)
```

ns_name_uncompress expands a "compressed" domain name. You'll use this routine if you parse a name server response message, as we do in *check_soa*, the C program that follows. The arguments are:

msg

A pointer to the beginning of your response message.

eomorig

A pointer to the first byte after the message. It is used to make sure that *ns_name_uncompress* doesn't go past the end of the message.

comp_dn

A pointer to the compressed domain name within the message.

exp_dn
> The place where *ns_name_uncompress* will store the expanded name. You should always allocate an array of MAXDNAME characters for the expanded name.

length
> The size of the *exp_dn* buffer.

ns_name_uncompress returns the size of the compressed name or −1 if there was an error. You might wonder why *ns_name_uncompress* returns the size of the *compressed* name, not the size of the *expanded* name. It does this because when you call *ns_name_uncompress*, you are parsing a DNS message and need to know how much space the compressed name took in the message so that you can skip over it.

ns_name_skip

```
int ns_name_skip(const u_char **ptrptr, const u_char *eom)
```

ns_name_skip is like *ns_name_uncompress*, but instead of uncompressing the name, it just skips over it. The arguments are:

ptrptr
> A pointer to a pointer to the name to skip over. The original pointer is advanced past the name.

eom
> A pointer to the first byte after the message. It is used to make sure that *ns_name_skip* doesn't go past the end of the message.

ns_name_skip returns zero if successful. It returns −1 if it fails to uncompress the name.

ns_get16 and ns_put16

```
u_int ns_get16(const u_char *cp)
void  ns_put16(u_int s, u_char *cp)
```

The DNS messages have fields that are unsigned short integer (type, class, and data length, to name a few). *ns_get16* returns a 16-bit integer pointed to by *cp*, and *ns_put16* assigns the 16-bit value of *s* to the location pointed to by *cp*.

ns_get32 and ns_put32

```
u_long ns_get32(const u_char *cp)
void   ns_put32(u_long l, u_char *cp)
```

These routines are like their 16-bit counterparts except that they deal with a 32-bit integer instead of a 16-bit integer. The TTL (time to live) field of a resource record is a 32-bit integer.

Parsing DNS Responses

The easiest way to learn how to parse a DNS message is to look at code that already does it. Assuming that you have the BIND source code, the best file to look through is *src/lib/resolv/res_debug.c* (BIND 8) or *res/res_debug.c* (BIND 4). (If you're really determined to use BIND 9, you might have to read almost 3000 lines of *lib/dns/message.c*.) *res_debug.c* contains *fp_query* (or *res_pquery* in BIND 8.2 and later), the function that prints out the DNS messages in the name server debugging output. Our sample program traces its parentage to code from this file.

You won't always want to parse the DNS response manually. An "intermediate" way to parse the response is to call *p_query*, which calls *fp_query*, to print out the DNS message. Then use Perl or *awk* to grab what you need. Cricket has been known to wimp out this way.

A Sample Program: check_soa

Let's now look at a C program to solve the same problem for which we wrote a shell script earlier.

Here are the header files that are needed, the declarations for external variables, and the declarations of functions. Notice that we use both *h_errno* (for the resolver routines) and *errno*. We limit this program to checking 20 name servers. You'll rarely see a zone with more than 10 name servers, so an upper limit of 20 should suffice:

```
/*****************************************************************
 * check_soa -- Retrieve the SOA record from each name server    *
 *      for a given zone and print out the serial number.        *
 *                                                               *
 * usage: check_soa zone                                         *
 *                                                               *
 * The following errors are reported:                            *
 *      o There is no address for a server.                      *
 *      o There is no server running on this host.               *
 *      o There was no response from a server.                   *
 *      o The server is not authoritative for the zone.          *
 *      o The response had an error response code.               *
 *      o The response had more than one answer.                 *
 *      o The response answer did not contain an SOA record.     *
 *      o The expansion of a compressed domain name failed.      *
 *****************************************************************/

/* Various header files */
#include <sys/types.h>
#include <netinet/in.h>
#include <netdb.h>
#include <stdio.h>
#include <errno.h>
#include <arpa/nameser.h>
#include <resolv.h>
```

```
/* Error variables */
extern int h_errno;  /* for resolver errors */
extern int errno;    /* general system errors */

/* Our own routines; code included later in this chapter */
void nsError();             /* report resolver errors */
void findNameServers();     /* find a zone's name servers */
void addNameServers();      /* add name servers to our list */
void queryNameServers();    /* grab SOA records from servers */
void returnCodeError();     /* report response message errors */

/* Maximum number of name servers we will check */
#define MAX_NS 20
```

The main body of the program is small. We have an array of string pointers, *nsList*, to store the names of the name servers for the zone. We call the resolver function *res_init* to initialize the *_res* structure. It wasn't necessary for this program to call *res_init* explicitly since it would have been called by the first resolver routine that used the *_res* structure. However, if we had wanted to modify the value of any of the *_res* fields before calling the first resolver routine, we would have made the modifications right after calling *res_init*. Next, the program calls *findNameServers* to find all the name servers for the zone referenced in *argv[1]* and to store them in *nsList*. Last, the program calls *queryNameServers* to query each of the name servers in *nsList* for the SOA record for the zone:

```
main(argc, argv)
int argc;
char *argv[];
{
    char *nsList[MAX_NS];  /* list of name servers */
    int  nsNum = 0;        /* number of name servers in list */

    /* sanity check: one (and only one) argument? */
    if(argc != 2){
        (void) fprintf(stderr, "usage: %s zone\n", argv[0]);
        exit(1);
    }

    (void) res_init();

    /*
     * Find the name servers for the zone.
     * The name servers are written into nsList.
     */
    findNameServers(argv[1], nsList, &nsNum);

    /*
     * Query each name server for the zone's SOA record.
     * The name servers are read from nsList.
     */
    queryNameServers(argv[1], nsList, nsNum);

    exit(0);
}
```

The routine *findNameServers* follows. This routine queries the local name server for the NS records for the zone. It then calls *addNameServers* to parse the response message and store away all the name servers it finds. The header files, *arpa/nameser.h* and *resolv.h*, contain declarations we make extensive use of:

```c
/****************************************************************
 * findNameServers -- find all of the name servers for the    *
 *    given zone and store their names in nsList.  nsNum is    *
 *    the number of servers in the nsList array.               *
 ****************************************************************/
void
findNameServers(domain, nsList, nsNum)
char *domain;
char *nsList[];
int  *nsNum;
{
    union {
        HEADER hdr;            /* defined in resolv.h */
        u_char buf[NS_PACKETSZ]; /* defined in arpa/nameser.h */
    } response;               /* response buffers */
    int responseLen;          /* buffer length */

    ns_msg handle;  /* handle for response message */

    /*
     * Look up the NS records for the given domain name.
     * We expect the domain name to be a fully qualified, so
     * we use res_query().  If we'd wanted the resolver search
     * algorithm, we would have used res_search() instead.
     */
    if((responseLen =
            res_query(domain,       /* the zone we care about */
                    ns_c_in,        /* Internet class records */
                    ns_t_ns,        /* Look up name server records*/
                    (u_char *)&response,      /*response buffer*/
                    sizeof(response)))        /*buffer size    */
                            < 0){  /*If negative    */
        nsError(h_errno, domain); /* report the error       */
        exit(1);                  /* and quit               */
    }

    /*
     * Initialize a handle to this response.  The handle will
     * be used later to extract information from the response.
     */
    if (ns_initparse(response.buf, responseLen, &handle) < 0) {
        fprintf(stderr, "ns_initparse: %s\n", strerror(errno));
        return;
    }

    /*
     * Create a list of name servers from the response.
     * NS records may be in the answer section and/or in the
     * authority section depending on the DNS implementation.
     * Walk through both.  The name server addresses may be in
```

```
 *   the additional records section, but we will ignore them
 *   since it is much easier to call gethostbyname() later
 *   than to parse and store the addresses here.
 */

/*
 * Add the name servers from the answer section.
 */
addNameServers(nsList, nsNum, handle, ns_s_an);

/*
 * Add the name servers from the authority section.
 */
addNameServers(nsList, nsNum, handle, ns_s_ns);
}

/******************************************************************
 * addNameServers -- Look at the resource records from a          *
 *      section.  Save the names of all name servers.             *
 ******************************************************************/
void
addNameServers(nsList, nsNum, handle, section)
char *nsList[];
int  *nsNum;
ns_msg handle;
ns_sect section;
{
    int rrnum;   /* resource record number */
    ns_rr rr;    /* expanded resource record */

    int i, dup; /* misc variables */

    /*
     * Look at all the resource records in this section.
     */
    for(rrnum = 0; rrnum < ns_msg_count(handle, section); rrnum++)
    {
        /*
         * Expand the resource record number rrnum into rr.
         */
        if (ns_parserr(&handle, section, rrnum, &rr)) {
            fprintf(stderr, "ns_parserr: %s\n", strerror(errno));
        }

        /*
         * If the record type is NS, save the name of the
         * name server.
         */
        if (ns_rr_type(rr) == ns_t_ns) {

            /*
             * Allocate storage for the name.  Like any good
             * programmer should, we test malloc's return value,
             * and quit if it fails.
             */
```

```
        nsList[*nsNum] = (char *) malloc (MAXDNAME);
        if(nsList[*nsNum] == NULL){
            (void) fprintf(stderr, "malloc failed\n");
            exit(1);
        }

        /* Expand the name server's domain name */
        if (ns_name_uncompress(
                    ns_msg_base(handle),/* Start of the message   */
                    ns_msg_end(handle), /* End of the message      */
                    ns_rr_rdata(rr),    /* Position in the message */
                    nsList[*nsNum],     /* Result                  */
                    MAXDNAME)           /* Size of nsList buffer   */
                            < 0) {      /* Negative: error         */
            (void) fprintf(stderr, "ns_name_uncompress failed\n");
            exit(1);
        }


        /*
         * Check the domain name we've just unpacked and add it to
         * the list of name servers if it is not a duplicate.
         * If it is a duplicate, just ignore it.
         */
        for(i = 0, dup=0; (i < *nsNum) && !dup; i++)
            dup = !strcasecmp(nsList[i], nsList[*nsNum]);
        if(dup)
            free(nsList[*nsNum]);
        else
            (*nsNum)++;
        }
    }
}
```

Notice that we don't explicitly check for finding zero name server records. We don't need to check because *res_query* flags that case as an error; it returns −1 and sets *herrno* to *NO_DATA*. If *res_query* returns −1, we call our own routine, *nsError*, to print out an error string from *h_errno* instead of using *herror*. The *herror* routine isn't a good fit for our program because its messages assume you are looking up address data (e.g., if *h_ errno* is *NO_DATA*, the error message is "No address associated with name").

The next routine queries each name server that we've found for an SOA record. In this routine, we change the value of several of the *_res* structure fields. By changing the *nsaddr_list* field, we change which name server *res_send* queries. We disable the search list by turning off bits in the *options* field—all the domain names that this program handles are fully qualified:

```
/****************************************************************
 * queryNameServers -- Query each of the name servers in nsList *
 *      for the SOA record of the given zone.  Report any       *
 *      errors encountered (e.g., a name server not running or  *
 *      the response not being an authoritative response).  If  *
 *   there are no errors, print out the serial number for the zone. *
 ****************************************************************/
```

```
void
queryNameServers(domain, nsList, nsNum)
char *domain;
char *nsList[];
int nsNum;
{
    union {
        HEADER hdr;                  /* defined in resolv.h */
        u_char buf[NS_PACKETSZ];     /* defined in arpa/nameser.h */
    } query, response;               /* query and response buffers */
    int responseLen, queryLen;       /* buffer lengths */

    u_char      *cp;          /* character pointer to parse DNS message */

    struct in_addr saveNsAddr[MAXNS];  /* addrs saved from _res */
    int nsCount;                  /* count of addresses saved from _res */
    struct hostent *host;  /* structure for looking up ns addr */
    int i;                     /* counter variable */

    ns_msg handle;  /* handle for response message */
    ns_rr rr;       /* expanded resource record */

    /*
     * Save the _res name server list since
     * we will need to restore it later.
     */
    nsCount = _res.nscount;
    for(i = 0; i < nsCount; i++)
      saveNsAddr[i] = _res.nsaddr_list[i].sin_addr;

    /*
     * Turn off the search algorithm and turn off appending
     * the local domain name before we call gethostbyname();
     * the name server's domain names will be fully qualified.
     */
    _res.options &= ~(RES_DNSRCH | RES_DEFNAMES);

    /*
     * Query each name server for the zone's SOA record.
     */
    for(nsNum-- ; nsNum >= 0; nsNum--){

        /*
         * First, we have to get the IP address of every name server.
         * So far, all we have are domain names.  We use gethostbyname()
         * to get the addresses, rather than anything fancy.
         * But first, we have to restore certain values in _res
         * because _res affects gethostbyname().  (We altered
         * _res in the previous iteration through the loop.)
         *
         * We can't just call res_init() again to restore
         * these values since some of the _res fields are
         * initialized when the variable is declared, not when
         * res_init() is called.
         */
```

```
    _res.options |= RES_RECURSE;   /* recursion on (default) */
    _res.retry = 4;                /* 4 retries (default)    */
    _res.nscount = nsCount;        /* original name servers  */
    for(i = 0; i < nsCount; i++)
        _res.nsaddr_list[i].sin_addr = saveNsAddr[i];

    /* Look up the name server's address */
    host = gethostbyname(nsList[nsNum]);
    if (host == NULL) {
        (void) fprintf(stderr,"There is no address for %s\n",
                                        nsList[nsNum]);
        continue; /* nsNum for-loop */
    }

    /*
     * Now got ready for the real fun.  host contains IP
     * addresses for the name server we're testing.
     * Store the first address for host in the _res
     * structure.  Soon, we'll look up the SOA record...
     */
    (void) memcpy((void *)&_res.nsaddr_list[0].sin_addr,
        (void *)host->h_addr_list[0], (size_t)host->h_length);
    _res.nscount = 1;

    /*
     * Turn off recursion.  We don't want the name server
     * querying another server for the SOA record; this name
     * server ought to be authoritative for this data.
     */
    _res.options &= ~RES_RECURSE;

    /*
     * Reduce the number of retries.  We may be checking
     * several name servers, so we don't want to wait too
     * long for any one server.  With two retries and only
     * one address to query, we'll wait at most 15 seconds.
     */
    _res.retry = 2;

    /*
     * We want to see the response code in the next
     * response, so we must make the query message and
     * send it ourselves instead of having res_query()
     * do it for us.  If res_query() returned -1, there
     * might not be a response to look at.
     *
     * There is no need to check for res_mkquery()
     * returning -1.  If the compression was going to
     * fail, it would have failed when we called
     * res_query() earlier with this domain name.
     */
    queryLen = res_mkquery(
                ns_o_query,      /* regular query        */
                domain,          /* the zone to look up */
                ns_c_in,         /* Internet type        */
```

```
                ns_t_soa,        /* look up an SOA record */
                (u_char *)NULL,  /* always NULL        */
                0,               /* length of NULL     */
                (u_char *)NULL,  /* always NULL        */
                (u_char *)&query,/* buffer for the query */
                sizeof(query)); /* size of the buffer   */

    /*
     * Send the query message.  If there is no name server
     * running on the target host, res_send() returns -1
     * and errno is ECONNREFUSED.  First, clear out errno.
     */
    errno = 0;
    if((responseLen = res_send((u_char *)&query,/* the query  */
                        queryLen,         /* true length*/
                        (u_char *)&response,/*buffer   */
                        sizeof(response))) /*buf size*/
                            < 0){          /* error */
        if(errno == ECONNREFUSED) { /* no server on the host */
            (void) fprintf(stderr,
                "There is no name server running on %s\n",
                nsList[nsNum]);
        } else {                 /* anything else: no response */
            (void) fprintf(stderr,
                "There was no response from %s\n",
                nsList[nsNum]);
        }
        continue; /* nsNum for-loop */
    }

    /*
     * Initialize a handle to this response.  The handle will
     * be used later to extract information from the response.
     */
    if (ns_initparse(response.buf, responseLen, &handle) < 0) {
        fprintf(stderr, "ns_initparse: %s\n", strerror(errno));
        return;
    }

    /*
     * If the response reports an error, issue a message
     * and proceed to the next server in the list.
     */
    if(ns_msg_getflag(handle, ns_f_rcode) != ns_r_noerror){
        returnCodeError(ns_msg_getflag(handle, ns_f_rcode),
                                        nsList[nsNum]);
        continue; /* nsNum for-loop */
    }

    /*
     * Did we receive an authoritative response? Check the
     * authoritative answer bit.  If this name server isn't
     * authoritative, report it, and go on to the next server.
     */
    if(!ns_msg_getflag(handle, ns_f_aa)){
        (void) fprintf(stderr,
```

```
                          "%s is not authoritative for %s\n",
                       nsList[nsNum], domain);
                continue; /* nsNum for-loop */
        }

        /*
         * The response should only contain one answer; if more,
         * report the error, and proceed to the next server.
         */
        if(ns_msg_count(handle, ns_s_an) != 1){
            (void) fprintf(stderr,
                "%s: expected 1 answer, got %d\n",
                nsList[nsNum], ns_msg_count(handle, ns_s_an));
            continue; /* nsNum for-loop */
        }

        /*
         * Expand the answer section record number 0 into rr.
         */
        if (ns_parserr(&handle, ns_s_an, 0, &rr)) {
                if (errno != ENODEV){
                        fprintf(stderr, "ns_parserr: %s\n",
                                strerror(errno));
                }
        }

        /*
         * We asked for an SOA record; if we got something else,
         * report the error and proceed to the next server.
         */
        if (ns_rr_type(rr) != ns_t_soa) {
            (void) fprintf(stderr,
                "%s: expected answer type %d, got %d\n",
                nsList[nsNum], ns_t_soa, ns_rr_type(rr));
            continue; /* nsNum for-loop */
        }

        /*
         * Set cp to point the the SOA record.
         */
        cp = (u_char *)ns_rr_rdata(rr);

        /*
         * Skip the SOA origin and mail address, which we don't
         * care about.  Both are standard "compressed names."
         */
        ns_name_skip(&cp, ns_msg_end(handle));
        ns_name_skip(&cp, ns_msg_end(handle));

        /* cp now points to the serial number; print it. */
        (void) printf("%s has serial number %d\n",
            nsList[nsNum], ns_get32(cp));

    } /* end of nsNum for-loop */
}
```

Notice that we use recursive queries when we call *gethostbyname*, but non-recursive queries when we look up the SOA record. *gethostbyname* may need to query other name servers to find the host's address. But we don't want the name server querying another server when we ask it for the SOA record—it's *supposed* to be authoritative for this zone, after all. Allowing the name server to ask another server for the SOA record would defeat the error check.

The next two routines print out error messages:

```
/*****************************************************************
 * nsError -- Print an error message from h_errno for a failure *
 *       looking up NS records.  res_query() converts the DNS   *
 *       message return code to a smaller list of errors and    *
 *       places the error value in h_errno.  There is a routine *
 *       called herror() for printing out strings from h_errno  *
 *       like perror() does for errno.  Unfortunately, the      *
 *       herror() messages assume you are looking up address    *
 *       records for hosts.  In this program, we are looking up *
 *       NS records for zones, so we need our own list of error *
 *       strings.                                               *
 *****************************************************************/
void
nsError(error, domain)
int error;
char *domain;
{
    switch(error){
        case HOST_NOT_FOUND:
            (void) fprintf(stderr, "Unknown zone: %s\n", domain);
            break;
        case NO_DATA:
            (void) fprintf(stderr, "No NS records for %s\n", domain);
            break;
        case TRY_AGAIN:
            (void) fprintf(stderr, "No response for NS query\n");
            break;
        default:
            (void) fprintf(stderr, "Unexpected error\n");
            break;
    }
}


/*****************************************************************
 * returnCodeError -- print out an error message from a DNS     *
 *       response return code.                                  *
 *****************************************************************/
void
returnCodeError(rcode, nameserver)
ns_rcode rcode;
char *nameserver;
{
    (void) fprintf(stderr, "%s: ", nameserver);
    switch(rcode){
        case ns_r_formerr:
```

```
              (void) fprintf(stderr, "FORMERR response\n");
              break;
          case ns_r_servfail:
              (void) fprintf(stderr, "SERVFAIL response\n");
              break;
          case ns_r_nxdomain:
              (void) fprintf(stderr, "NXDOMAIN response\n");
              break;
          case ns_r_notimpl:
              (void) fprintf(stderr, "NOTIMP response\n");
              break;
          case ns_r_refused:
              (void) fprintf(stderr, "REFUSED response\n");
              break;
          default:
              (void) fprintf(stderr, "unexpected return code\n");
              break;
      }
  }
```

To compile this program using the resolver and name server routines in *libc*:

```
% cc -o check_soa check_soa.c
```

Or, if you've newly compiled the BIND code as we describe in Appendix C, *Compiling and Installing BIND on Linux*, and want to use the latest header files and resolver library:

```
% cc -o check_soa -I/usr/local/src/bind/src/include \
check_soa.c /usr/local/src/bind/src/lib/libbind.a
```

Here is what the output looks like:

```
% check_soa mit.edu
BITSY.MIT.EDU has serial number 1995
W20NS.MIT.EDU has serial number 1995
STRAWB.MIT.EDU has serial number 1995
```

If you look back at the shell script output, it looks the same, except that the shell script's output is sorted by the name server's name. What you can't see is that the C program ran much faster.

Perl Programming with Net::DNS

If using the shell to parse *nslookup*'s output seems too awkward and writing a C program seems too complicated, consider writing your program in Perl using the Net::DNS module written by Michael Fuhr. You'll find the package at *http://www. perl.com/CPAN-local/modules/by-module/Net/Net-DNS-0.12.tar.gz*.

Net::DNS treats resolvers, DNS messages, sections of DNS messages, and individual resource records as objects and provides methods for setting or querying each object's attributes. We'll examine each object type first, then give a Perl version of our *check_soa* program.

Resolver Objects

Before making any queries, you must first create a resolver object:

```
$res = new Net::DNS::Resolver;
```

Resolver objects are initialized from your *resolv.conf* file, but you can change the default settings by making calls to the object's methods. Many of the methods described in the Net::DNS::Resolver manual page correspond to fields and options in the *_res* structure described earlier in this chapter. For example, if you want to set the number of times the resolver tries each query before timing out, you can call the *$res->retry* method:

```
$res->retry(2);
```

To make a query, call one of the following methods:

```
$res->search
$res->query
$res->send
```

These methods behave like the *res_search*, *res_query*, and *res_send* library functions described in the C programming section, though they take fewer arguments. You must provide a domain name, and you can optionally provide a record type and class (the default behavior is to query for A records in the IN class). These methods return Net::DNS::Packet objects, which we'll describe next. Here are a few examples:

```
$packet = $res->search("terminator");
$packet = $res->query("movie.edu", "MX");
$packet = $res->send("version.bind", "TXT", "CH");
```

Packet Objects

Resolver queries return Net::DNS::Packet objects, whose methods you can use to access the header, question, answer, authority, and additional sections of a DNS message:

```
$header     = $packet->header;
@question   = $packet->question;
@answer     = $packet->answer;
@authority  = $packet->authority;
@additional = $packet->additional;
```

Header Objects

DNS message headers are returned as Net::DNS::Header objects. The methods described in the Net::DNS::Header manual page correspond to the header fields described in RFC 1035 and in the *HEADER* structure used in C programs. For example, if you want to find out if this is an authoritative answer, you would call the *$header->aa* method:

```
if ($header->aa) {
    print "answer is authoritative\n";
} else {
    print "answer is not authoritative\n";
}
```

Question Objects

The question section of a DNS message is returned as a list of Net::DNS::Question objects. You can find the name, type, and class of a question object with the following methods:

```
$question->qname
$question->qtype
$question->qclass
```

Resource Record Objects

The answer, authority, and additional sections of a DNS message are returned as lists of Net::DNS::RR objects. You can find the name, type, class, and TTL of an RR object with the following methods:

```
$rr->name
$rr->type
$rr->class
$rr->ttl
```

Each record type is a subclass of Net::DNS::RR and has its own type-specific methods. Here's an example that shows how to get the preference and mail exchanger out of an MX record:

```
$preference = $rr->preference;
$exchanger  = $rr->exchange;
```

A Perl Version of check_soa

Now that we've described the objects Net::DNS uses, let's look at how to use them in a complete program. We've rewritten *check_soa* in Perl:

```
#!/usr/local/bin/perl -w

use Net::DNS;

#----------------------------------------------------------------------
# Get the zone from the command line.
#----------------------------------------------------------------------

die "Usage:  check_soa zone\n" unless @ARGV == 1;
$domain = $ARGV[0];
```

```
#------------------------------------------------------------------------
# Find all the name servers for the zone.
#------------------------------------------------------------------------

$res = new Net::DNS::Resolver;

$res->defnames(0);
$res->retry(2);

$ns_req = $res->query($domain, "NS");
die "No name servers found for $domain: ", $res->errorstring, "\n"
    unless defined($ns_req) and ($ns_req->header->ancount > 0);

@nameservers = grep { $_->type eq "NS" } $ns_req->answer;

#------------------------------------------------------------------------
# Check the SOA record on each name server.
#------------------------------------------------------------------------

$| = 1;
$res->recurse(0);

foreach $nsrr (@nameservers) {

    #--------------------------------------------------------------------
    # Set the resolver to query this name server.
    #--------------------------------------------------------------------

    $ns = $nsrr->nsdname;
    print "$ns ";

    unless ($res->nameservers($ns)) {
        warn ": can't find address: ", $res->errorstring, "\n";
        next;
    }

    #--------------------------------------------------------------------
    # Get the SOA record.
    #--------------------------------------------------------------------

    $soa_req = $res->send($domain, "SOA");
    unless (defined($soa_req)) {
        warn ": ", $res->errorstring, "\n";
        next;
    }

    #--------------------------------------------------------------------
    # Is this name server authoritative for the zone?
    #--------------------------------------------------------------------

    unless ($soa_req->header->aa) {
        warn "is not authoritative for $domain\n";
        next;
    }
```

```
#----------------------------------------------------------------
# We should have received exactly one answer.
#----------------------------------------------------------------

unless ($soa_req->header->ancount == 1) {
    warn ": expected 1 answer, got ",
        $soa_req->header->ancount, "\n";
    next;
}

#----------------------------------------------------------------
# Did we receive an SOA record?
#----------------------------------------------------------------

 unless (($soa_req->answer)[0]->type eq "SOA") {
    warn ": expected SOA, got ",
        ($soa_req->answer)[0]->type, "\n";
    next;
}

#----------------------------------------------------------------
# Print the serial number.
#----------------------------------------------------------------

    print "has serial number ", ($soa_req->answer)[0]->serial, "\n";
}
```

Now that you've seen how to write a DNS program using a shell script, a Perl script, and C code, you should be able to write one on your own using the language that best fits your situation.

16

Miscellaneous

"The time has come," the Walrus said, "To talk of many things: Of shoes—and ships—and sealing-wax—Of cabbages—and kings—And why the sea is boiling hot—And whether pigs have wings."

It's time we tied up loose ends. We've already covered the mainstream of DNS and BIND, but there's a handful of interesting niches we haven't explored. Some of these may actually be useful to you, like instructions on how to accommodate Windows 2000 with BIND; others may just be interesting. We can't in good conscience send you out into the world without completing your education!

Using CNAME Records

We talked about CNAME resource records in Chapter 4, *Setting Up BIND*. We didn't tell you everything about CNAME records, though; we saved that for this chapter. When you set up your first name servers, you didn't care about the subtle nuances of the magical CNAME record. Maybe you didn't realize that there was more than we explained; maybe you didn't care. Some of this trivia is interesting, some is arcane. We'll let you decide which is which.

CNAMEs Attached to Interior Nodes

If you've ever renamed your zone because of a company reorganization, you may have considered creating a single CNAME record that pointed from the zone's old domain name to its new domain name. For instance, if the *fx.movie.edu* zone were renamed *magic.movie.edu*, we'd be tempted to create a single CNAME record to map all the old domain names to the new names:

```
fx.movie.edu.  IN  CNAME magic.movie.edu.
```

With this in place, you'd expect a lookup of *empire.fx.movie.edu* to result in a lookup of *empire.magic.movie.edu*. Unfortunately, this doesn't work—you *can't* have a CNAME record attached to an interior node like *fx.movie.edu* if it owns other records. Remember that *fx.movie.edu* has an SOA record and NS records, so attaching a CNAME record to it violates the rule that a domain name be either an alias or a canonical name, not both.

If you're running BIND 9, though, you can use the brand-spanking-new DNAME record (introduced in Chapter 10, *Advanced Features*) to create an alias from your zone's old domain name to its new one:

```
fx.movie.edu.  IN  DNAME  magic.movie.edu.
```

The DNAME record can coexist with other record types at *fx.movie.edu*—like the SOA record and NS records that are undoubtedly there—but you *can't* have any other domain names that end in *fx.movie.edu*. It'll "synthesize" CNAME records from domain names in *fx.movie.edu* to like domain names in *magic.movie.edu* when the names in *fx.movie.edu* are looked up.

If you don't have BIND 9, you'll have to create aliases the old-fashioned way—a CNAME record for each individual domain name within the zone:

```
empire.fx.movie.edu.       IN  CNAME  empire.magic.movie.edu.
bladerunner.fx.movie.edu.  IN  CNAME  bladerunner.magic.movie.edu.
```

If the subdomain isn't delegated, and consequently doesn't have an SOA record and NS records attached, you can also create an alias for *fx.movie.edu*. However, this will apply only to the domain name *fx.movie.edu* and not to other domain names in the *fx.movie.edu* zone.

Hopefully, the tool you use to manage your zone data files will handle creating CNAME records for you. (*h2n*, which was introduced in Chapter 4, does just that.)

CNAMEs Pointing to CNAMEs

You may have wondered whether it was possible to have an alias (CNAME record) pointing to another alias. This might be useful in situations where an alias points from a domain name outside your zone to a domain name inside your zone. You may not have any control over the alias outside your zone. What if you want to change the domain name it points to? Can you simply add another CNAME record?

The answer is yes: you can chain together CNAME records. The BIND implementation supports it, and the RFCs don't expressly forbid it. But while you *can* chain CNAME records, is it a wise thing to do? The RFCs recommend against it because of the possibility of creating a CNAME loop and because it slows resolution. You may be able to do it in a pinch, but you probably won't find much sympathy on the Net if something breaks. And all bets are off if a new (non-BIND-based) name server implementation emerges.[*]

CNAMEs in the Resource Record Data

For any other record besides a CNAME record, you must have the canonical domain name in the resource record data. Applications and name servers won't operate correctly otherwise. As we mentioned back in Chapter 5, *DNS and Electronic Mail*, for example, *sendmail* only recognizes the canonical name of the local host on the right side of an MX record. If *sendmail* doesn't recognize the local host's name, it won't strip the right MX records out when paring down the MX list, and may deliver mail to itself or to less-preferred hosts, causing mail to loop.

BIND 8 name servers log messages like these when they encounter aliases on the right side of a record:

```
Sep 27 07:43:48 terminator named[22139]: "digidesign.com IN NS" points to a CNAME
(ns1.digidesign.com)
Sep 27 07:43:49 terminator named[22139]: "moreland.k12.ca.us IN MX" points to a
CNAME (mail.moreland.k12.ca.us)
```

Multiple CNAME Records

One pathological configuration that honestly hadn't occurred to us—and many pathological configurations *have* occurred to us—is multiple CNAME records attached to the same domain name. Some administrators use this with round robin to rotate between RRsets. For example, the records:

```
fullmonty   IN   CNAME   fullmonty1
fullmonty   IN   CNAME   fullmonty2
fullmonty   IN   CNAME   fullmonty3
```

could be used to return all the addresses attached to *fullmonty1*, then all the addresses of *fullmonty2*, then all the addresses of *fullmonty3* on a name server that didn't recognize this as the abomination it is. (It violates the "CNAME and other data" rule, for one.)

BIND 4 doesn't recognize this as a misconfiguration; BIND 8 and 9.1.0 and later do. BIND 8 lets you permit it if you want to with:

```
options {
                multiple-cnames yes;
};
```

In BIND 9, there's no option to allow it. The default, naturally, is to disallow it.

---

[*] And one has (the Microsoft DNS Server, shipped with Windows NT and Windows 2000). It also permits CNAMEs that point to CNAMEs, though.

Looking Up CNAMEs

At times you may want to look up a CNAME record itself, not data for the canonical name. With *nslookup* or *dig*, this is easy to do. You can either set the query type to *cname*, or set the query type to *any* and then look up the name:

```
% nslookup
Default Server:  wormhole
Address:  0.0.0.0

> set query=cname
> bigt
Server:  wormhole
Address:  0.0.0.0

bigt.movie.edu  canonical name = terminator.movie.edu
> set query=any
> bigt
Server:  wormhole
Address:  0.0.0.0

bigt.movie.edu  canonical name = terminator.movie.edu
> exit

% dig bigt.movie.edu cname
; <<>> DiG 8.3 <<>> bigt.movie.edu cname
;; res options: init recurs defnam dnsrch
;; got answer:
;; ->>HEADER<<- opcode: QUERY, status: NOERROR, id: 4
;; flags: qr aa rd ra; QUERY: 1, ANSWER: 1, AUTHORITY: 3, ADDITIONAL: 4
;; QUERY SECTION:
;;      bigt.movie.edu, type = CNAME, class = IN

;; ANSWER SECTION:
bigt.movie.edu.          1D IN CNAME      terminator.movie.edu.
```

Finding Out a Host's Aliases

One thing you can't easily do with DNS is find out a host's aliases. With the host table, it's easy to find both the canonical name of a host and any aliases: no matter which you look up; they're all there, together, on the same line:

```
% grep terminator /etc/hosts
192.249.249.3  terminator.movie.edu terminator bigt
```

With DNS, however, if you look up the canonical name, all you get is the canonical name. There's no easy way for the name server or the application to know whether aliases exist for that canonical name:

```
% nslookup
Default Server:  wormhole
Address:  0.0.0.0
```

```
> terminator
Server:  wormhole
Address:  0.0.0.0

Name:    terminator.movie.edu
Address:  192.249.249.3
```

If you use *nslookup* or *dig* to look up an alias, you'll see that alias and the canonical name. *nslookup* and *dig* report both the alias and the canonical name in the message. But you won't see any other aliases that might point to that canonical name:

```
% nslookup
Default Server:  wormhole
Address:  0.0.0.0

> bigt
Server:  wormhole
Address:  0.0.0.0

Name:    terminator.movie.edu
Address:  192.249.249.3
Aliases:  bigt.movie.edu

> exit
% dig bigt.movie.edu
; <<>> DiG 8.3 <<>> bigt.movie.edu
;; res options: init recurs defnam dnsrch
;; got answer:
;; ->>HEADER<<- opcode: QUERY, status: NOERROR, id: 4
;; flags: qr aa rd ra; QUERY: 1, ANSWER: 2, AUTHORITY: 3, ADDITIONAL: 4
;; QUERY SECTION:
;;      bigt.movie.edu, type = A, class = IN

;; ANSWER SECTION:
bigt.movie.edu.          1D IN CNAME      terminator.movie.edu.
terminator.movie.edu.    1D IN A          192.249.249.3
```

About the only way to find out all the CNAMEs for a host is to transfer the whole zone and pick out the CNAME records in which that host is the canonical name:

```
% nslookup
Default Server:  wormhole
Address:  0.0.0.0

> ls -t cname movie.edu
 [wormhole.movie.edu]
$ORIGIN movie.edu.
bigt                     1D IN CNAME      terminator
wh                       1D IN CNAME      wormhole
dh                       1D IN CNAME      diehard
>
```

Even this method shows you the aliases only within that zone—there could be aliases in a different zone, pointing to canonical names in this zone.

Wildcards

Something else we haven't covered in detail yet is DNS *wildcards*. There are times when you want a single resource record to cover any possible name, rather than creating zillions of resource records that are all the same except for the domain name to which they apply. DNS reserves a special character, the asterisk (*), to use in zone data files as a wildcard name. It will match any number of labels in a name as long as there isn't an exact match with a name already in the name server's database.

Most often, you'd use wildcards to forward mail to non-Internet-connected networks. Suppose our site weren't connected to the Internet, but we had a host that relayed mail between the Internet and our network. We could add a wildcard MX record to the *movie.edu* zone for Internet consumption that points all our mail to the relay. Here is an example:

```
*.movie.edu.  IN  MX  10 movie-relay.nea.gov.
```

Since the wildcard matches one or more labels, this resource record would apply to names such as *terminator.movie.edu, empire.fx.movie.edu,* or *casablanca. bogart.classics.movie.edu.* The danger with wildcards is that they clash with search lists. This wildcard also matches *cujo.movie.edu.movie.edu,* making wildcards dangerous to use in our internal zone data. Remember that some versions of *sendmail* apply the search list when looking up MX records:

```
% nslookup
Default Server:  wormhole
Address:  0.0.0.0

> set type=mx                          —Look up MX records
> cujo.movie.edu                       —for cujo
Server:  wormhole
Address:  0.0.0.0

cujo.movie.edu.movie.edu      —This isn't a real host's name!
        preference = 10, mail exchanger = movie-relay.nea.gov
```

What are the limitations of wildcards? Wildcards do not match domain names for which there is already data. Suppose we *did* use wildcards within our zone data, as in these partial contents of *db.movie.edu*:

```
*    IN  MX  10 mail-hub.movie.edu.
et   IN  MX  10 et.movie.edu.
jaws IN  A   192.253.253.113
fx   IN  NS  bladerunner.fx.movie.edu.
fx   IN  NS  outland.fx.movie.edu.
```

Mail to *terminator.movie.edu* is sent to *mail-hub.movie.edu,* but mail to *et.movie. edu* is sent directly to *et.movie.edu.* An MX lookup of *jaws.movie.edu* would result in a response saying there was no MX data for that domain name. The wildcard doesn't apply because an A record exists. The wildcard also doesn't apply to domain names in *fx.movie.edu* because wildcards don't apply across delegation. Nor does the wildcard apply to the domain name *movie.edu,* because the wildcard amounts to zero or more labels *followed by a dot,* followed by *movie.edu.*

A Limitation of MX Records

While we are on the topic of MX records, let's talk about how they can result in mail taking a longer path than necessary. The MX records are a list of data returned when the domain name of a mail destination is looked up. The list isn't ordered according to which exchanger is closest to the sender. Here is an example of this problem. Your non-Internet-connected network has two hosts capable of relaying Internet mail to your network. One host is in the U.S., and one host is in France. Your network is in Greece. Most of your mail comes from the U.S., so you have someone maintain your zone and install two wildcard MX records—the highest preference to the U.S. relay and a lower preference to the relay in France. Since the U.S. relay is at a higher preference, *all* mail will go through that relay (as long as it is reachable). If someone in France sends you a letter, it will travel across the Atlantic to the U.S. and back because there is nothing in the MX list to indicate that the French relay is closer to that sender.

Dialup Connections

Another relatively recent development in networking that presents a challenge to DNS is the dialup Internet connection. When the Internet was young, and DNS was born, there was no such thing as a dialup connection. With the enormous explosion in the Internet's popularity and the propagation of Internet service providers who offer dialup Internet connectivity to the masses, a whole new breed of problems with name service has been introduced.

The basic goal when setting up DNS to work with dialup is to enable every host in your network to resolve the domain names of every host it needs to access. (Of course, when your connection to the Internet is down, your hosts probably don't need to resolve Internet domain names.) If you're using dial-on-demand, there's the additional goal of minimizing unnecessary dialouts: if you're looking up the domain name of a host on your local network, that shouldn't require your router to bring up a connection to the Internet.

We'll separate dialup connections into two categories: manual dialup, by which we mean a connection to the Internet that must be brought up by a user; and dial-on-demand, which implies the use of a device—often a router, but sometimes just a host running Linux or another server operating system—to connect to the Internet automatically whenever hosts generate traffic bound for the Internet. We'll also describe two scenarios for each category of dialup: one in which you have just one host dialing up a connection to the Internet, and one in which you have a small network of hosts dialing up a connection. Before we talk about these scenarios, though, let's discuss what causes dialouts and how to avoid them.

What Causes Dialouts

Many users, particularly in Europe, where ISDN is popular, connect to the Internet via dial-on-demand connections. Nearly all of these users want to minimize, if not completely prevent, unnecessary connections to the Internet. Connection setup is often more expensive than successive minutes, and always takes time.

BIND name servers, unfortunately, aren't terribly well suited to running behind dial-on-demand connections. They periodically send system queries to look up the current list of root name servers, even when the name server isn't resolving domain names. And the operation of the search list can cause the name server to query remote name servers. For example, say your local domain name is *tinyoffice.megacorp.com* and you have a local name server authoritative for that zone. Your default search list, on some resolvers, might include:

```
tinyoffice.megacorp.com
megacorp.com
```

Let's say you try to FTP to one of your local systems, *deadbeef.tinyoffice. megacorp.com*, but you misspell it *deadbeer*:

```
% ftp deadbeer
```

Because of your search list, your resolver would first look up *deadbeer.tinyoffice. megacorp.com*. Your local name server, authoritative for the *tinyoffice.megacorp. com* zone, can tell that domain name doesn't exist. But then your resolver appends the second domain name in the search list and looks up *deadbeer.megacorp.com*. To figure out whether that domain name exists, your name server needs to query a *megacorp.com* server, which will require bringing up the dial-on-demand link.

Avoiding Dialouts

There are several general techniques that will help you minimize unnecessary dialouts. The first, and probably simplest, is to run a version of BIND that supports negative caching (which means anything newer than BIND 4.9.5, but we certainly prefer BIND 8 and 9). That way, if you mistakenly put *deadbeer* into a configuration file, your name server looks up *deadbeer.megacorp.com* once, and then caches the fact that the domain name doesn't exist for the duration of *megacorp. com*'s negative caching TTL.

Another technique is to use a minimal search list. If your local domain name is *tinyoffice.megacorp.com*, you could make do with a search list of just *tinyoffice.megacorp.com*. That way, a typo won't cause a dialout.

Using a modern resolver is also important. The default search list for a post–BIND 4.9 resolver is just the local domain name, which qualifies as "minimal" in our book. And a modern resolver knows to try a domain name with dots as-is, even if it doesn't end in a dot.

Finally, you can use other naming services, such as */etc/hosts*, for local name resolution and configure your resolvers to use DNS only if a name cannot be found in */etc/hosts*. As long as you keep the names of all your local hosts in */etc/hosts*, you won't need to worry about needless connections to the Internet.

Now let's apply these techniques to our scenarios.

Manual Dialup with One Host

The easiest way to deal with the simple dialup scenario is to configure your host's resolver to use a name server provided by your Internet service provider (ISP). Most ISPs run name servers for their subscribers' use. If you're not sure whether your ISP provides name servers for your use, or if you don't know what their IP addresses are, check their web site, send them email, or give them a call.

Some operating systems, such as Windows 95, 98, and NT, let you define a set of name servers for use with a particular dialup provider. So, for example, you can configure one set of name servers to use when you dial up UUNet and another to use when you dial up your office. This is useful if you dial in to multiple ISPs.

This configuration is usually adequate for most casual dialup users. Name resolution will fail unless the dialup connection is up, but that's not likely to be a problem, since there's no use for Internet name service without Internet connectivity.

Some of you, however, may want to run a name server when your dialup connection is active. It could help your performance by caching domain names you look up frequently, for example. This is easy to set up with a Unix-like operating system such as Linux: you'll typically use a script like *ifup* to bring up your dialup connection and *ifdown* to bring it down. If that's the case, there are probably also scripts called *ifup-post* and *ifdown-post* that *ifup* and *ifdown* call, respectively, after they've done most of their work. You can start *named* as *named* or with *ndc start* in *ifup-post*, and shut it down with *ndc stop* or *rndc stop* in *ifdown-post*. About the only other thing you'd need to do is set your local domain name in *resolv.conf*. The default resolver behavior, querying a name server on the local host, should do fine both when the name server's running and when it's not.

Manual Dialup with Multiple Hosts

The simplest solution to use with the multiple host/manual dialup scenario is similar to the resolver-only configuration. You can configure your resolvers to use your ISP's name servers, but also configure the resolvers to check */etc/hosts* (or NIS, if you go for that sort of thing) *before* querying a name server. Then make sure your */etc/hosts* file contains the names of all the hosts on your local network.

If you'd like to run a name server locally, you only need to modify this configuration slightly: configure the resolvers to use your local name server instead of your ISP's. This will give you the benefits of local caching, but local name resolution will work (via */etc/hosts*) even when your connection to the Internet is down. You may as well start and stop the local name server from *ifup-post* and *ifdown-post*, as described earlier.

For those of you who really want to use DNS for *all* name resolution, you can forgo the */etc/hosts* file and create forward-mapping and reverse-mapping zones on your local name server for your hosts. You should trim your resolvers' search lists to the bare minimum, though, to minimize the chance that you'll induce your name server to look up some wacky remote domain name.

Dial-on-Demand with One Host

If you have a single host with a dial-on-demand connection to the Internet, your simplest solution is still a resolver-only configuration. Configure your resolver to use your ISP's name servers, and when the resolver needs to look up a domain name, it'll query one of those name servers and bring up the link. If there are some domain names that your host looks up routinely as part of "housekeeping," like *localhost* or *1.0.0.127.in-addr.arpa*, you can add those to */etc/hosts* and configure your resolver to check */etc/hosts* before querying a name server.

If you'd like to run a name server locally, make sure it is able to map *localhost* and *1.0.0.127.in-addr.arpa* to 127.0.0.1 and *localhost*, respectively, and trim your search list to the minimum.

If your name server brings up the link more than you think it should, try turning on query logging (with *options query-log* on a BIND 4.9 name server, *ndc querylog* on a BIND 4.9 or 8 name server, or *rndc querylog* on a BIND 9.1.0 name server) and look for the domain names that bring up the link. If many of them are in a single zone, you might consider configuring your local name server as a slave for that zone. At least that way, you'll bring up the link at most only once per refresh interval to resolve domain names in the zone.

Dial-on-Demand with Multiple Hosts

The simplest solution in this scenario is exactly the same as the first solution we described in the section "Manual Dialup with Multiple Hosts": a resolver-only configuration with the resolvers configured to check */etc/hosts* before querying a name server. As with all dial-on-demand configurations, you'll want to trim your search list down.

Alternatively, you could try one of the two variants: running a local name server and using it as a backup to */etc/hosts*, or creating forward- and reverse-mapping zones for the local hosts on the local name server.

Running Authoritative Name Servers over Dial-on-Demand

This may sound like a silly subject to some of you—who would run an authoritative name server behind a dial-on-demand connection?—but in some parts of the world, where bandwidth and Internet connectivity aren't easy to come by, this is a necessity. And, believe it or not, BIND provides a mechanism to accommodate such name servers.

If you run an authoritative name server behind a dial-on-demand link, you want to concentrate zone maintenance activities into as short a window as possible. If your name server is authoritative for 100 zones, you'd rather not have zone refresh timers popping every few minutes and the resulting SOA queries bringing up the dial-on-demand link over and over again.

With BIND 8.2 and newer name servers and BIND 9.1.0 and later name servers, you can configure a *heartbeat interval*. The heartbeat interval is how frequently you'd like your name server to bring up its dial-on-demand connection, in minutes:

```
options {
    heartbeat-interval 180;      // 3 hours
};
```

The default is 60 minutes, and you can disable zone maintenance by setting the interval to zero.

If you then mark one or more of your zones as dialup zones, the name server will try to concentrate all maintenance of that zone into a short period and to perform the maintenance no more often than the heartbeat interval. For a slave zone, that means inhibiting the normal refresh timer (even ignoring the refresh interval, if it's smaller than the heartbeat interval!) and querying the master for the zone's SOA record only at the heartbeat interval. For a master zone, that means sending out NOTIFY messages, which will presumably bring up the dial-on-demand link and trigger a refresh on the slaves.

To mark all of a name server's zones as dialup zones, use the *dialup* substatement in an *options* statement:

```
options {
    heartbeat-interval 60;
    dialup yes;
};
```

To mark a single zone as a dialup zone, use the *dialup* substatement to the *zone* statement:

```
zone "movie.edu" {
    type master;
    file "db.movie.edu";
    dialup yes;
};
```

Dialup zones are also useful in another, perhaps unintended way: on name servers that serve as slaves for thousands of zones. Some ISPs provide slave service on a large scale but get bitten by miscreants who set their zone's refresh intervals far too low. Their name servers end up swamped with sending out SOA queries for those zones. By configuring all the zones as dialup zones and setting the heartbeat interval to something reasonable, ISPs can prevent this.

Network Names and Numbers

The original DNS specifications didn't provide the ability to look up network names based on a network number—a feature that was provided by the original *HOSTS.TXT* file. Since then, RFC 1101 has defined a system for storing network names; this system also works for subnets and subnet masks, so it goes significantly beyond *HOSTS.TXT*. Moreover, it doesn't require any modification to the name server software at all; it's based entirely on the clever use of PTR and A records.

Remember that to map an IP address to a name in DNS, you reverse the IP address, append *in-addr.arpa*, and look up PTR records. This same technique is used to map a network number to a network name, for example, to map network 15/8 to "HP Internet." To look up the network number, include the network bits and pad them with trailing zeros to make four bytes, and look up PTR data just as you did with a host's IP address. For example, to find the network name for the old ARPAnet, network 10/8, look up PTR data for *0.0.0.10.in-addr.arpa*. You get back an answer like *ARPAnet.ARPA*.

If the ARPAnet were subnetted, you'd also find an address record at *0.0.0.10.in-addr.arpa*. The address would be the subnet mask, 255.255.0.0, for instance. If you were interested in the subnet name instead of the network name, you'd apply the mask to the IP address and look up the subnet number.

This technique allows you to map the network number to a name. To provide a complete solution, there must be a way to map a network name to its network number. This, again, is accomplished with PTR records. The network name has PTR data that points to the network number (reversed with *in-addr.arpa* appended).

Let's see what the data might look like in HP's zone data files (the HP Internet has network number 15/8) and step through mapping a network number to a network name.

Partial contents of the file *db.hp.com*:

```
;
; Map HP's network name to 15.0.0.0.
;
hp-net.hp.com.          IN  PTR 0.0.0.15.in-addr.arpa.
```

Partial contents of the file *db.corp.hp.com*:

```
;
; Map corp's subnet name to 15.1.0.0.
;
corp-subnet.corp.hp.com.  IN  PTR 0.0.1.15.in-addr.arpa.
```

Partial contents of the file *db.15*:

```
;
; Map 15.0.0.0 to hp-net.hp.com.
; HP's subnet mask is 255.255.248.0.
;
0.0.0.15.in-addr.arpa.    IN  PTR hp-net.hp.com.
                          IN  A   255.255.248.0
```

Partial contents of the file *db.15.1*:

```
;
; Map the 15.1.0.0 back to its subnet name.
;
0.0.1.15.in-addr.arpa.    IN  PTR corp-subnet.corp.hp.com.
```

Here's the procedure to look up the subnet name for the IP address 15.1.0.1:

1. Apply the default network mask for the address's class. Address 15.1.0.1 is a class A address, so the mask is 255.0.0.0. Applying the mask to the IP address makes the network number 15.

2. Send a query (*type=A* or *type=ANY*) for *0.0.0.15.in-addr.arpa*.

3. The query response contains address data. Since there is address data at *0.0.0. 15.in-addr.arpa* (the subnet mask, 255.255.248.0), apply the subnet mask to the IP address. This yields 15.1.0.0.

4. Send a query (*type=A* or *type=ANY*) for *0.0.1.15.in-addr.arpa*.

5. The query response does not contain address data, so 15.1.0.0 is not further subnetted.

6. Send a PTR query for *0.0.1.15.in-addr.arpa.*

7. The query response contains the network name for 15.1.0.1: *corp-subnet.corp. hp.com.*

In addition to mapping between network names and numbers, you can also list all the networks for your zone with PTR records:

```
movie.edu.  IN  PTR  0.249.249.192.in-addr.arpa.
            IN  PTR  0.253.253.192.in-addr.arpa.
```

Now for the bad news: despite the fact that RFC 1101 contains everything you need to know to set this up, there's very little software we know of that actually *uses* this type of network name encoding, and very few administrators go to the trouble of adding this information. Until software actually makes use of DNS-encoded network names, about the only reason for setting this up is to show off. But that's a good enough reason for many of us.

Additional Resource Records

There are a number of resource records that we haven't covered yet in this book. The first of these, HINFO, has been around since the beginning but hasn't been widely used. The others were defined in RFC 1183 and several successive RFCs. Most are experimental, but some are on the standards track and are coming into more prevalent use. We'll describe them here to give you a little head start in getting used to them.

Host Information

HINFO stands for Host INFOrmation. The record-specific data is a pair of strings identifying the host's hardware type and operating system. The strings are supposed to come from the MACHINE NAMES and OPERATING SYSTEM NAMES listed in the "Assigned Numbers" RFC (currently RFC 1700), but this requirement is not enforced; you can use your own abbreviations. The RFC isn't at all comprehensive, so it's quite possible you won't find your system in the list anyway. Originally, host information records were intended to let services like FTP determine how to interact with a remote system. This would have made it possible to negotiate datatype transformations automatically, for example. Unfortunately, this didn't happen—few sites supply accurate HINFO values for all their systems. Some network administrators use HINFO records to help them keep track of machine types instead of recording the machine types in a database or a notebook. Here are two examples of HINFO records; note that the hardware type and operating system fields must be surrounded with quotes if they include any whitespace:

```
;
; These machine names and system names did not come from RFC 1700
;
wormhole  IN  HINFO  ACME-HW ACME-GW
cujo      IN  HINFO  "Watch Dog Hardware"  "Rabid OS"
```

Before you go adding them to your zone—particularly a zone visible from the Internet—you should know that HINFO records can present a security risk. By providing easily accessible information about a system, you may be making it easier for a hacker to break into it.

AFSDB

AFSDB has a syntax like that of the MX record, and semantics a bit like that of the NS record. An AFSDB record gives either the location of an AFS cell database server or of a DCE cell's authenticated name server. The type of server the record points to and the name of the host running the server are contained in the record-specific data portion of the record.

So what's an AFS cell database server? Or AFS, for that matter? AFS originally stood for the Andrew File System, designed by the good folks at Carnegie-Mellon University as part of the Andrew Project. (It's now an IBM product.) AFS is a network filesystem, like NFS, but one that handles the latency of wide area networks much better than NFS does and provides local caching of files to enhance performance. An AFS cell database server runs the process responsible for tracking the location of filesets (groups of files) on various AFS fileservers within a cell (a logical group of hosts). So being able to find the AFS cell database server is the key to finding any file in the cell.

And what's an authenticated name server? It holds location information about all sorts of services available within a DCE cell. A DCE cell? That's a logical group of hosts that share services offered by The Open Group's Distributed Computing Environment (DCE).

And now, back to our story. To access another cell's AFS or DCE services across a network, you must first find out where that cell's cell database servers or authenticated name servers are. Hence the new record type. The domain name the record is attached to gives the name of the cell the server knows about. Cells often share names with DNS domains, so this usually doesn't look at all odd.

As we said, the AFSDB record's syntax is like the MX record's syntax. In place of the preference value, you specify the number 1 for an AFS cell database server or 2 for a DCE authenticated name server.

In place of the mail exchanger host, you specify the name of the host running the server. Simple!

Say an *fx.movie.edu* systems administrator sets up a DCE cell (which includes AFS services) because she wants to experiment with distributed processing to speed up graphics rendering. She runs both an AFS cell database server and a DCE name server on *bladerunner.fx.movie.edu,* another cell database server on *empire.fx. movie.edu,* and another DCE name server on *aliens.fx.movie.edu.* She should set up the AFSDB records as follows:

```
; Our DCE cell is called fx.movie.edu, same as the domain name of the zone
fx.movie.edu.   IN  AFSDB  1 bladerunner.fx.movie.edu.
                IN  AFSDB  2 bladerunner.fx.movie.edu.
                IN  AFSDB  1 empire.fx.movie.edu.
                IN  AFSDB  2 aliens.fx.movie.edu.
```

X25, ISDN, and RT

These three record types were created specifically in support of research on next-generation internets. Two of the records, X25 and ISDN, are simply address records specific to X.25 and ISDN networks, respectively. Both take record-specific data appropriate to the type of network. The X25 record type uses an X.121 address (X.121 is the ITU-T recommendation that specifies the format of addresses used in X.25 networks). The ISDN record type uses an ISDN address.

ISDN stands for Integrated Services Digital Network. Telephone companies around the world use ISDN protocols to allow their telephone networks to carry both voice and data, creating an integrated network. Although ISDN's availability is spotty throughout the U.S., it has been widely adopted in some international markets. Since ISDN uses the telephone companies' networks, an ISDN address is just a phone number, and in fact consists of a country code, followed by an area code or city code, then by a local phone number. Sometimes there are a few extra digits at the end that you wouldn't see in a phone number, called a subaddress. The subaddress is specified in a separate field in the record-specific data.

Examples of the X25 and ISDN record types are:

```
relay.pink.com.  IN  X25  31105060845

delay.hp.com.    IN  ISDN  141555514539488
hep.hp.com.      IN  ISDN  141555514539488 004
```

These records are intended for use in conjunction with the Route Through (RT) record type. RT is syntactically and semantically similar to the MX record type: it specifies an intermediate host that routes *packets* (instead of mail) to a destination host. So now, instead of being able to route only mail to a host that isn't directly connected to the Internet, you can route any kind of IP packet to that host by using another host as a forwarder. The packet could be part of a Telnet or FTP session, or perhaps even a DNS query!

Like MX, RT includes a preference value indicating how desirable delivery to a particular host is. For example, the records:

```
housesitter.movie.edu.   IN  RT  10 relay.pink.com.
                         IN  RT  20 delay.hp.com.
```

instruct hosts to route packets bound for *housesitter.movie.edu* through *relay.pink. com* (the first choice) or through *delay.hp.com* (the second choice).

The way RT works with X25 and ISDN (and even A) records is like this:

1. Internet host A wants to send a packet to host B, which is not connected to the Internet.

2. Host A looks up host B's RT records. This search also returns all address records (A, X25, and ISDN) for each intermediate host.

3. Host A sorts the list of intermediate hosts and looks for its own domain name. If it finds it, the host removes its name and all intermediate hosts at higher preference values. This is analogous to *sendmail*'s "paring down" a list of mail exchangers.

4. Host A examines the address record(s) for the most preferred intermediate host that remains. If host A is attached to a network that corresponds to the type of address record indicated, it uses that network to send the packet to the intermediate host. For example, if host A were trying to send a packet through *relay.pink.com*, it would need connectivity to an X.25 network.

5. If host A lacks appropriate connectivity, it tries the next intermediate host specified by the RT records. For example, if host A lacked X.25 connectivity, it might fall back to connecting via ISDN to *delay.hp.com*.

This process continues until the packet is routed to the most preferred intermediate host. The most preferred intermediate host may then deliver the packet directly to the destination host's address (which may be A, X25, or ISDN).

Location

RFC 1876 defines an experimental record type, LOC, that allows domain administrators to encode the locations of their computers, subnets, and networks. In this case, location means latitude, longitude, and altitude. Future applications could use this information to produce network maps, assess routing efficiency, and more.

In its basic form, the LOC record takes latitude, longitude, and altitude (in that order) as its record-specific data. Latitude and longitude are expressed in the format:

```
<degrees> [minutes [seconds.<fractional seconds>]] (N|S|E|W)
```

Altitude is expressed in meters.

If you're wondering how in the world you're going to get that data, check out "RFC 1876 Resources" at *http://www.ckdhr.com/dns-loc*. This site, created by Christopher Davis, one of the authors of RFC 1876, is an indispensable collection of information, useful links, and utilities for people creating LOC records.

If you don't have your own Global Positioning System receiver to carry around to all of your computers—and we *know* many of you do—two sites that may come in handy are Etak's Eagle Geocoder at *http://www.geocode.com/eagle.html-ssi*, which you can use to find the latitude and longitude of most addresses in the United States, and AirNav's Airport Information at *http://www.airnav.com/airports*, which lets you find the elevation of the closest airport to you. If you don't have a major airport near you, don't worry: the database even includes the helipad at my neighborhood hospital!

Here's a LOC record for one of our hosts:

```
huskymo.boulder.acmebw.com.   IN  LOC  40 2 0.373 N 105 17 23.528 W 1638m
```

Optional fields in the record-specific data allow you to specify how large the entity you're describing is, in meters (LOC records can describe networks, after all, which can be quite large), as well as the horizontal and vertical precision. The size defaults to one meter, which is perfect for a single host. Horizontal precision defaults to 10,000 meters, and vertical precision to 10 meters. These defaults represent the size of a typical ZIP or postal code, the idea being that you can fairly easily find a latitude and longitude given a ZIP code.

You can also attach LOC records to the names of subnets and networks. If you've taken the time to enter information about the names and addresses of your networks in the format described in RFC 1101 (covered earlier in this chapter), you can attach LOC records to the network names:

```
;
; Map HP's network name to 15.0.0.0.
;
hp-net.hp.com.   IN   PTR 0.0.0.15.in-addr.arpa.
                 IN   LOC 37 24 55.393 N 122 8 37 W 26m
```

SRV

Locating a service or a particular type of server within a zone is a difficult problem if you don't know which host it runs on. Some zone administrators have attempted to solve this problem by using service-specific aliases in their zones. For example, at Movie U. we created the alias *ftp.movie.edu* and pointed it to the domain name of the host that runs our FTP archive:

```
ftp.movie.edu.    IN    CNAME      plan9.fx.movie.edu.
```

This makes it easy for people to guess a domain name that will get them to our FTP archive, and separates the domain name people use to access the archive from the domain name of the host it runs on. If we were to move the archive to a different host, we could simply change the CNAME record.

The experimental SRV record, introduced in RFC 2052, is a general mechanism for locating services. SRV also provides powerful features that allow zone administrators to distribute load and provide backup services, similar to what the MX record provides.

A unique aspect of the SRV record is the format of the domain name it's attached to. Like service-specific aliases, the domain name to which an SRV record is attached gives the name of the service sought, as well as the protocol it runs over, concatenated with a domain name. The labels representing the service name and the protocol begin with an underscore to distinguish them from labels in the domain name of a host. So, for example:

```
_ftp._tcp.movie.edu
```

represents the SRV records someone FTPing to *movie.edu* should retrieve in order to find the *movie.edu* FTP servers, while:

```
_http._tcp.www.movie.edu
```

represents the SRV records someone accessing the URL *http://www.movie.edu* should look up in order to find the *www.movie.edu* web servers.

The names of the service and protocol should appear in the latest Assigned Numbers RFC (the most recent as of this writing is RFC 1700) or be unique names used only locally. Don't use the port or protocol *numbers*, just the names.

The SRV record has four resource record–specific fields: *priority, weight, port*, and *target*. Priority, weight, and port are unsigned 16-bit numbers (between 0 and 65535). Target is a domain name.

Priority works very similarly to the preference in an MX record: the lower the number in the priority field, the more desirable the associated target. When searching for hosts offering a given service, clients should try targets at the same priority before trying those at a higher priority value.

Weight allows zone administrators to distribute load to multiple targets. Clients should query targets that are at the same priority in proportion to their weight. For example, if one target has a priority of zero and a weight of one, and another target also has a priority of zero but a weight of two, the second target should receive twice as much load (in queries, connections, whatever) as the first. It's up to the service's clients to direct that load: they typically use a system call to choose a random number. If the number is, say, in the top one-third of the range, they try the first target, and if the number is in the bottom two-thirds of the range, they try the second target.

Port specifies the port on which the service being sought is running. This allows zone administrators to run servers on nonstandard ports. For example, an administrator could use SRV records to point web browsers at a web server running on port 8000 instead of the standard HTTP port (80).

Target, finally, specifies the domain name of a host on which the service is running (on the port specified in the port field). Target must be the canonical name of the host (not an alias), with address records attached to it.

So, for the *movie.edu* FTP server, we added these records to *db.movie.edu*:

```
_ftp._tcp.movie.edu.   IN  SRV  1  0  21  plan9.fx.movie.edu.
                       IN  SRV  2  0  21  thing.fx.movie.edu.
```

This instructs SRV-capable FTP clients to try the FTP server on *plan9.fx.movie.edu*'s port 21 first when accessing *movie.edu*'s FTP service, and then to try the FTP server on *thing.fx.movie.edu*'s port 21 if *plan9.fx.movie.edu*'s FTP server isn't available.

The records:

```
_http._tcp.www.movie.edu.   IN  SRV  0  2  80    www.movie.edu.
                            IN  SRV  0  1  80    www2.movie.edu.
                            IN  SRV  1  1  8000  postmanrings2x.movie.edu.
```

direct web queries for *www.movie.edu* (the web site) to port 80 on *www.movie.edu* (the host) and *www2.movie.edu*, with *www.movie.edu* getting twice the queries that *www2.movie.edu* does. If neither is available, the queries will go to *postmanrings2x.movie.edu* on port 8000.

To advertise that a particular service isn't available, use a dot in the target field:

```
_gopher._tcp.movie.edu.  IN  SRV  0  0  0  .
```

Unfortunately, support for the SRV record among clients is, to put it mildly, thin—with Windows 2000 being the glaring exception. (More about that later in this chapter.) That's really too bad, given how useful SRV could be. Since SRV isn't widely supported, don't use SRV records in lieu of address records. It's prudent to include at least one address record for the "base" domain name to which your SRV records are attached, and more if you'd like the load spread between addresses. If you only list a host as a backup in the SRV records, don't include its IP address. Also, if a host runs a service on a nonstandard port, don't include an address record for it since there's no way to redirect clients to a nonstandard port with an A record.

So, for *www.movie.edu*, we included all these records:

```
_http._tcp.www.movie.edu.   IN  SRV  0  2  80    www.movie.edu.
                            IN  SRV  0  1  80    www2.movie.edu.
                            IN  SRV  1  1  8000  postmanrings2x.movie.edu.
```

```
www.movie.edu.          IN  A   200.1.4.3 ; the address of www.movie.edu and
                        IN  A   200.1.4.4 ; the address of www2.movie.edu
                                          ; for the benefit of non-SRV aware
                                          ; clients
```

Browsers that can handle SRV records will send twice as many requests to *www. movie.edu* as to *www2.movie.edu*, and will use *postmanrings2x.movie.edu* only if both of the main web servers are unavailable. Browsers that don't use SRV records will have their requests round-robined between the addresses of *www.movie.edu* and *www2.movie.edu*.

DNS and WINS

In our first edition—oh, for those simpler days!—we mentioned the close alignment between NetBIOS names and domain names, but noted that, alas, there was no way for DNS to function as a NetBIOS name server. Basically, a name server would need to support dynamic updates to function as a NetBIOS name server.

Of course, BIND 8 and 9 support dynamic updates. Unfortunately, the DHCP server in Windows NT 4.0 doesn't send dynamic updates to name servers. It talks only to Microsoft's WINS servers. WINS servers handle their own peculiar, proprietary dynamic updates, though only for NetBIOS clients. In other words, a WINS server doesn't speak DNS.

However, Microsoft provides a name server in Windows NT 4.0, which in turn can talk to WINS servers. The Microsoft DNS Server has a nice graphical administration tool, as you would expect from Microsoft, and provides a handy hook into WINS: you can configure the server to query a WINS server for address data if it doesn't find the data in a DNS zone.

This is done by adding a new WINS record to the zone. The WINS record, like the SOA record, is attached to the zone's domain name. It acts as a flag to tell the Microsoft DNS Server to query a WINS server if it doesn't find an address for the name it's looking up. The record:

```
@       0    IN   WINS          192.249.249.39 192.253.253.39
```

tells the Microsoft DNS Server to query the WINS servers running at 192.249.249.39 and 192.253.253.39 (in that order) for the name. The zero TTL is a precaution against the record being looked up and cached.

There's also a companion WINS-R record that allows a Microsoft DNS Server to reverse map IP addresses using a NetBIOS NBSTAT request. If an *in-addr.arpa* zone contains a WINS-R record, like:

```
@       0    IN   WINS-R        movie.edu
```

and the IP address sought doesn't appear in the zone, the name server will attempt to send a NetBIOS NBSTAT request to the IP address being reverse mapped. This amounts to calling a phone number and asking the person on the other end, "What's your name?" The result has a dot and the domain name in the record-specific data appended, in this case ".movie.edu".

These records provide valuable glue between the two namespaces. Unfortunately, the integration isn't perfect. As they say, the devil is in the details.

The main problem, as we see it, is that only the Microsoft DNS Servers support the WINS and WINS-R records.* Therefore, if you want lookups in the *fx.movie.edu* zone to be relayed to the Special Effects Department's WINS server, then all *fx. movie.edu* name servers must be Microsoft DNS Servers. Why? Imagine that the name servers for *fx.movie.edu* were mixed, some Microsoft DNS Servers and some BIND. If a remote name server needed to look up a NetBIOS name in *fx.movie. edu*, it would choose which of the *fx.movie.edu* name servers to query according to roundtrip time. If the server it happened to choose were a Microsoft DNS Server, it would be able to resolve the name to a dynamically assigned address. But if it happened to choose a BIND server, it wouldn't be able to resolve the name.

The best DNS-WINS configuration we've heard of so far puts all WINS-mapped data in its own zone, say *wins.movie.edu*. All the name servers for *wins.movie.edu* are Microsoft DNS Servers, and the zone *wins.movie.edu* contains just an SOA record, NS records, and a WINS record pointing to the WINS servers for *wins. movie.edu*. This way, there's no chance of inconsistent answers between authoritative servers for the zone.

Reverse-mapping data, of course, can't easily be split into separate zones for BIND and Microsoft name servers to maintain. So if you want both traditional, PTR record–based reverse mapping and WINS-R-enhanced reverse mapping, you'll need to host your reverse-mapping zones solely on Microsoft DNS Servers.

Another problem is that WINS and WINS-R are proprietary. BIND name servers don't understand them, and in fact a BIND slave that transfers a WINS record from a Microsoft DNS Server primary master will fail to load the zone because WINS is an unknown type. (We discussed this, and how to work around it, in Chapter 14, *Troubleshooting DNS and BIND*.)

The answer to these problems is the DNS standard dynamic update functionality introduced in BIND 8, described in Chapter 10, and the support for it in Windows 2000. Dynamic update allows authorized addition and deletion of records in a

---

* And a few commercial products such as MetaInfo's Meta IP/DNS, which is a port of BIND 8 with WINS capabilities added on. Stock BIND, however, can't talk to WINS servers.

BIND name server, which in turn gives the folks at Microsoft the functionality they need to use DNS as a name service for NetBIOS. So without further ado . . .

DNS and Windows 2000

Windows 2000 can use standard dynamic updates to register hosts in DNS. For a Windows 2000 client, *registration* means adding a name-to-address mapping and an address-to-name mapping for that client, information Windows clients formerly registered with WINS servers. For a Windows 2000 server, registration involves adding records to a zone to tell clients which services it's running and where (on which host and port). For example, a Windows 2000 Domain Controller uses dynamic update to add an SRV record telling Windows 2000 clients where the Windows 2000 domain's Kerberos service is running.

How Windows 2000 Uses Dynamic Update

So what gets added when a client registers? Let's reboot a Windows 2000 client in the Special Effects Lab and see.

Our client is called *mummy.fx.movie.edu*. It has the fixed IP address 192.253.254.13 (it doesn't get its address from our DHCP server). At boot time, the dynamic update routines on the client go through the following steps:

1. Look up the SOA record for *mummy.fx.movie.edu* on the local name server. Though there isn't an SOA record for that domain name, the authority section of the response includes the SOA record of the zone that contains *mummy.fx. movie.edu*, which is *fx.movie.edu*.

2. Look up the address of the name server in the MNAME field of the SOA record, *bladerunner.fx.movie.edu*.

3. Send a dynamic update to *bladerunner.fx.movie.edu* with two prerequisites: that *mummy.fx.movie.edu* isn't an alias (i.e., doesn't own a CNAME record) and that it doesn't already have an address record pointing to 192.253.254.13. The dynamic update contains no update section; it's just a probe to see what's out there.

4. If *mummy.fx.movie.edu* already points to its address, stop. Otherwise, send another dynamic update to *bladerunner.fx.movie.edu* with the prerequisites that *mummy.fx.movie.edu* isn't an alias and doesn't have an address record already. If the prerequisites are satisfied, the update adds an address record pointing *mummy.fx.movie.edu* to 192.253.254.13. If *mummy.fx.movie.edu* already has an address record, the client sends an update to delete that address record and add its own.

5. Look up the SOA record for *254.253.192.in-addr.arpa.*

6. Look up the address of the name server in the MNAME field of the SOA record (though since the MNAME field contains *bladerunner.fx.movie.edu*, which we looked up recently, and Windows 2000 has a caching resolver, this shouldn't require another query).

7. Send a dynamic update to *bladerunner.fx.movie.edu* with the prerequisite that *13.254.253.192.in-addr.arpa* isn't an alias. If the prerequisite is satisfied, the update adds a PTR record mapping 192.253.254.13 back to *mummy.fx.movie.edu*. If *13.254.253.192.in-addr.arpa* is an alias, stop.

If we'd been using the Microsoft DHCP Server from Windows 2000, the DHCP server, by default, would have added the PTR record. There's also an option in the DHCP server's MMC-based management interface that allows the administrator to specify that the DHCP server add both the PTR record and the A record. If the DHCP server had added the A record, though, it wouldn't have set a prerequisite.

Servers, particularly Windows 2000 Domain Controllers, register lots of information in DNS using dynamic update, both when they're first set up and periodically thereafter. (The *netlogon* service, for example, registers its SRV records *hourly!*) This allows clients to locate services on whichever host and port they're running. Since we just set up a Windows 2000 domain called *fx.movie.edu*, let's take a look at the records that our Domain Controller, *matrix.fx.movie.edu*, added:

```
$ORIGIN fx.movie.edu.
@                            600        A      192.253.254.14
_kerberos._tcp.dc._msdcs     600        SRV    0 100 88   matrix.fx.movie.edu.
_ldap._tcp.dc._msdcs         600        SRV    0 100 389  matrix.fx.movie.edu.
_ldap._tcp.e437709a-1862-11d3-8eda-00400536c213.domains._msdcs 600  SRV  0 100 389
matrix.fx.movie.edu.
e4377099-1862-11d3-8eda-00400536c213._msdcs  600  CNAME  matrix.fx.movie.edu.
gc._msdcs                    600        A      192.253.253.14
_ldap._tcp.gc._msdcs         600        SRV    0 100 3268 matrix.fx.movie.edu.
_ldap._tcp.pdc._msdcs        600        SRV    0 100 389  matrix.fx.movie.edu.
_gc._tcp                     600        SRV    0 100 3268 matrix.fx.movie.edu.
_kerberos._tcp               600        SRV    0 100 88   matrix.fx.movie.edu.
_kpasswd._tcp                600        SRV    0 100 464  matrix.fx.movie.edu.
_ldap._tcp                   600        SRV    0 100 389  matrix.fx.movie.edu.
_kerberos._udp               600        SRV    0 100 88   matrix.fx.movie.edu.
_kpasswd._udp                600        SRV    0 100 464  matrix.fx.movie.edu.
```

Whoa! That's a lot of records!

These records tell Windows 2000 clients where the services offered by the Domain Controller, including Kerberos and LDAP, are running.[*] You can see from the SRV

---

[*] For an explanation of the function of each of these records, see Microsoft Knowledge Base article Q178169.

records that they're all running on *matrix.fx.movie.edu*, our only Domain Control-ler. If we had another Domain Controller, you'd see nearly twice as many SRV records.

The owner names of all the SRV records end in *fx.movie.edu*, the name of the Windows 2000 domain. If we'd called our Windows 2000 domain *effects.movie.edu*, the dynamic update routines would have updated the zone containing the domain name *effects.movie.edu*, *movie.edu*. Of course, that would really clutter up *movie.edu*, since it has other delegated subdomains running Windows 2000. Con-sequently, we made sure we named our Windows 2000 domain after our zone.

Problems with Windows 2000 and BIND

While Microsoft's decision to replace WINS with DNS was noble, the implementa-tion poses some problems for folks who run BIND name servers. First, Windows 2000 clients and DHCP servers have a nasty habit of deleting address records owned by the same domain name as the clients or servers. For example, if we let the users in the Special Effects Lab configure their own computers and choose their computers' names, and one user happened to use a name that was already taken, maybe by one of our rendering servers, his computer would try to delete the conflicting address record (that of the rendering server) and add its own. That's not very sociable.

Luckily, that behavior can be corrected on the client. The client does, in fact, check to see whether the domain name it's using already owns an address record by setting the prerequisite in step 4. (It just deletes it if it does exist, by default.) But you can follow the instructions in Microsoft Knowledge Base article Q246804 to tell the client not to delete conflicting records. The price? A client can't differen-tiate between an address being used by a different host with the same domain name and an address that formerly belonged to it, so if the client changes addresses, it can't automatically update the zone.

If you elect to have your DHCP server handle all registration, you don't have the option of leaving conflicting addresses alone. The DHCP server doesn't use pre-requisites to detect collisions; it just unceremoniously deletes conflicting address records.

Given the limitations of having the DHCP server handle all of the registering, why would anyone consider it? Because if you allow any client to register itself and you can only use primitive, IP address–based access lists to authorize dynamic updates, you are allowing *any client's address* to dynamically update your zones. Savvier users of those clients could easily fire off a few custom-made dynamic updates to change your zone's MX records or the address of your web server.

Secure Dynamic Update

Surely Microsoft doesn't just live with these problems, right? No, not with the Microsoft DNS Server. The Microsoft DNS Server supports GSS-TSIG, a dialect of TSIG (which we covered in Chapter 11, *Security*). A client that uses GSS-TSIG retrieves a TSIG key from a Kerberos server, then uses it to sign a dynamic update. The use of GSS, the Generic Security Service, to retrieve the key means that an administrator doesn't need to hardcode a key on each of his clients.

Since the name of the TSIG key the client uses to sign the update is just the domain name of the client, the name server can make sure that only the client that added an address can delete it later, simply by tracking the domain name of the TSIG key used to add a given record. Only an updater with the same TSIG key is allowed to delete that record.

Windows 2000 clients try GSS-TSIG-signed dynamic updates if their unsigned dynamic updates are refused. You can also configure them to send signed updates first by following the instructions in Knowledge Base article Q246804, mentioned earlier.

BIND and GSS-TSIG

Unfortunately, BIND name servers don't yet support GSS-TSIG, so you can't use Windows 2000's secure dynamic update with BIND. A forthcoming version of BIND 9, however, is scheduled to support GSS-TSIG. Once BIND does support GSS-TSIG, you'll be able to use all of the update policy rules described in Chapter 10 to control which keys can update which records. A simple set of rules that says:

```
zone "fx.movie.edu" {
    type master;
    file "db.fx.movie.edu";
    update-policy {
        grant *.fx.movie.edu. self *.fx.movie.edu. A;
        grant matrix.fx.movie.edu. self matrix.fx.movie.edu. ANY;
        grant matrix.fx.movie.edu. subdomain fx.movie.edu. SRV;
    };
};
```

may be enough to let Windows 2000 clients and servers register what they need in your zone.

What to Do?

In the meantime, how do you handle the proliferation of Windows 2000 on your network? Well, Microsoft would advise you to "upgrade" all of your name servers

to the Windows 2000 version of the Microsoft DNS Server. But if you like BIND—
and we do—you'd probably like some other options.

Handling Windows 2000 clients

The first (and probably most common) option for handling your Windows 2000 clients is to create a delegated subdomain for all of them to live in. We might call ours
win.fx.movie.edu. Within *win.fx.movie.edu*, anything goes: clients can stomp on
other clients' addresses and someone may send a bunch of hand-crafted dynamic
updates to add bogus records to the zone. The intent is to create a sandbox (or jail,
if you prefer) that the clients can't break out of and that they can trash if they want
to. If you have kids, you have an intuitive understanding of this concept.

By default, a Windows 2000 client will try to register itself in a forward-mapping
zone with the same name as its Windows 2000 domain. So we'll have to do some
extra configuration to tell our clients to register in *win.fx.movie.edu* instead of in
fx.movie.edu. In particular, we'll have to go to a window that resides at *My Com-
puter->Properties->Network Identification->Properties->More*, uncheck *Change primary DNS suffix when domain membership changes*, and type *win.fx.movie.edu* in
the field labeled *Primary DNS suffix of this computer*. On *all* our clients.

Another possibility is to leave your clients in your main production zone (for our
lab, that's *fx.movie.edu*) but to allow dynamic updates only from the address of
the DHCP server. Then you configure your DHCP server to assume responsibility
for maintaining both A records and PTR records. (You can add A and PTR records
for hosts that don't use DHCP manually.)

In this scenario, it's more difficult for the little imps to send their custom dynamic
updates to your name server, since it involves spoofing the address of the DHCP
server. It's still possible that someone will bring up a client with a domain name
that conflicts with an existing domain name in the zone, though.

Handling Windows 2000 servers

The main server you need to accommodate is the Domain Controller (or Controllers, if you have more than one). The DC wants to add the passel of SRV records
we showed earlier. If it can't add them at setup time, it'll write the records, in master file format, to a file called *System32\Config\netlogon.dns* under the system root.

First, you'll need to determine which zone you need to update. That's just a matter of finding the zone that would contain the Windows 2000 domain name. If
your Windows 2000 domain has the same name as an existing zone, of course,
that's the zone to update. Otherwise, just keep stripping off the leading labels of
your Windows 2000 domain until you get to the domain name of a zone.

Once you've got the zone that you need to update, you need to decide how to proceed. If you don't mind letting your Domain Controller dynamically update your zone, just add an appropriate *allow-update* substatement to the *zone* statement and you're done. If you'd rather not allow your DC complete control of the zone, you can leave dynamic updates disabled and let the DC create the *netlogon. dns* file. Then use an $INCLUDE control statement to read the contents of the file into your zone data file:

```
$INCLUDE netlogon.dns
```

If neither of these options appeals to you, because you want the DC to be able to change its SRV records but don't want it mangling your zone, you've still got a trick up your sleeve. You can take advantage of the funny format of the owner names in SRV records and create delegated subdomains called (in our case) *_udp. fx.movie.edu*, *_tcp.fx.movie.edu*, *_sites.fx.movie.edu*, and *_msdcs.fx.movie.edu*. We'll have to turn off name checking for *_msdcs.fx.movie.edu*, since the Domain Controller wants to add an address record to the zone in addition to a slew of SRV records. Then let the DC dynamically update these zones, but not your main zone:

```
acl dc { 192.253.254.13; };

zone "_udp.fx.movie.edu" {
    type master;
    file "db._udp.fx.movie.edu";
    allow-update { dc; };
};

zone "_tcp.fx.movie.edu" {
    type master;
    file "db._tcp.fx.movie.edu";
    allow-update { dc; };
};

zone "_sites.fx.movie.edu" {
    type master;
    file "db._sites.fx.movie.edu";
    allow-update { dc; };
};

zone "_msdcs.fx.movie.edu" {
    type master;
    file "db._msdcs.fx.movie.edu";
    allow-update { dc; };
    check-names ignore;
};
```

Now you've got the best of both worlds: dynamic registration of services with a safe production zone.

A

DNS Message Format and Resource Records

This appendix outlines the format of DNS messages and enumerates all the resource record types. The resource records are shown in their textual format, as you would specify them in a zone data file, and in their binary format, as they appear in DNS messages. You'll find a few resource records here that weren't covered in the book because they are experimental or obsolete.

We've included the portions of RFC 1035, written by Paul Mockapetris, that deal with the textual format of master files (what we called *zone data files* in the book) or with the DNS message format (for those of you who need to parse DNS packets).

Master File Format

(From RFC 1035, pages 33–35)

The format of these files is a sequence of entries. Entries are predominantly line-oriented, though parentheses can be used to continue a list of items across a line boundary, and text literals can contain CRLF within the text. Any combination of tabs and spaces acts as a delimiter between the separate items that make up an entry. The end of any line in the master file can end with a comment. The comment starts with a semicolon (;).

The following entries are defined:

```
blank[comment]

$ORIGIN domain-name [comment]

$INCLUDE file-name [domain-name] [comment]

domain-namerr [comment]

blankrr [comment]
```

Blank lines, with or without comments, are allowed anywhere in the file.

Two control entries are defined: $ORIGIN and $INCLUDE. $ORIGIN is followed by a domain name and resets the current origin for relative domain names to the stated name. $INCLUDE inserts the named file into the current file and may optionally specify a domain name that sets the relative domain name origin for the included file. $INCLUDE may also have a comment. Note that an $INCLUDE entry never changes the relative origin of the parent file, regardless of changes to the relative origin made within the included file.

The last two forms represent RRs. If an entry for an RR begins with a blank, then the RR is assumed to be owned by the last stated owner. If an RR entry begins with a *domain-name*, then the owner name is reset.

rr contents take one of the following forms:

```
[TTL] [class] type RDATA
[class] [TTL] type RDATA
```

The RR begins with optional TTL and class fields, followed by a type and RDATA field appropriate to the type and class. Class and type use the standard mnemonics; TTL is a decimal integer. Omitted class and TTL values default to the last explicitly stated values. Since type and class mnemonics are disjoint, the parse is unique.

domain-names make up a large share of the data in the master file. The labels in the domain name are expressed as character strings and separated by dots. Quoting conventions allow arbitrary characters to be stored in domain names. Domain names that end in a dot are called absolute, and are taken as complete. Domain names that do not end in a dot are called relative; the actual domain name is the concatenation of the relative part with an origin specified in an $ORIGIN, $INCLUDE, or argument to the master file-loading routine. A relative name is an error when no origin is available.

character-string is expressed in one of two ways: as a contiguous set of characters without interior spaces, or as a string beginning with " and ending with ". Inside a "-delimited string any character can occur, except for " itself, which must be quoted using a backslash (\).

Because these files are text files, several special encodings are necessary to allow arbitrary data to be loaded. In particular:

.   Of the root.

@   A free-standing @ is used to denote the current origin.

\X

> Where X is any character other than a digit (0–9), \ is used to quote that character so that its special meaning does not apply. For example, \. can be used to place a dot character in a label.*

\DDD

> Where each D is a digit in the octet corresponding to the decimal number described by DDD. The resulting octet is assumed to be text and is not checked for special meaning.†

( ) Parentheses are used to group data that crosses a line boundary. In effect, line terminations are not recognized within parentheses.‡

; A semicolon is used to start a comment; the remainder of the line is ignored.

Character Case

(From RFC 1035, page 9)

For all parts of the DNS that are part of the official protocol, all comparisons between character strings (e.g., labels, domain names, etc.) are done in a case-insensitive manner. At present, this rule is in force throughout the domain system without exception. However, future additions beyond current usage may need to use the full binary octet capabilities in names, so attempts to store domain names in 7-bit ASCII or use of special bytes to terminate labels, etc., should be avoided.

Types

Here is a complete list of resource record types. The textual representation is used in master files. The binary representation is used in DNS queries and responses. These resource records are described on pages 13–21 of RFC 1035.

A address

(From RFC 1035, page 20)

Textual Representation:

```
owner ttl class A address
```

Example:

```
localhost.movie.edu.   IN A 127.0.0.1
```

---

* Not implemented by BIND 4.8.3.

† Not implemented by BIND 4.8.3.

‡ BIND 4.8.3 allows parentheses only on SOA and WKS resource records.

Binary Representation:

```
Address type code: 1
    +--+--+--+--+--+--+--+--+--+--+--+--+--+--+--+--+
    |                    ADDRESS                    |
    +--+--+--+--+--+--+--+--+--+--+--+--+--+--+--+--+
where:
ADDRESS        A 32 bit Internet address.
```

CNAME canonical name

(From RFC 1035, page 14)

Textual Representation:

> *owner ttl class* CNAME *canonical-dname*

Example:

```
wh.movie.edu.   IN  CNAME  wormhole.movie.edu.
```

Binary Representation:

```
CNAME type code: 5
    +--+--+--+--+--+--+--+--+--+--+--+--+--+--+--+--+
    /                      CNAME                    /
    /                                               /
    +--+--+--+--+--+--+--+--+--+--+--+--+--+--+--+--+
where:
CNAME          A domain-name which specifies the canonical
               or primary name for the owner.  The owner name is
               an alias.
```

HINFO host information

(From RFC 1035, page 14)

Textual Representation:

> *owner ttl class* HINFO *cpu os*

Example:

```
grizzly.movie.edu.   IN  HINFO  VAX-11/780 UNIX
```

Binary Representation:

```
HINFO type code: 13
    +--+--+--+--+--+--+--+--+--+--+--+--+--+--+--+--+
    /                       CPU                     /
    +--+--+--+--+--+--+--+--+--+--+--+--+--+--+--+--+
    /                        OS                     /
    +--+--+--+--+--+--+--+--+--+--+--+--+--+--+--+--+
where:
CPU            A character-string which specifies the CPU type.
OS             A character-string which specifies the
               operating system type.
```

MB mailbox domain name (experimental)

(From RFC 1035, page 14)

Textual Representation:

owner ttl class MB *mbox-dname*

Example:

al.movie.edu.   IN   MB   robocop.movie.edu.

Binary Representation:

MB type code: 7
```
    +--+--+--+--+--+--+--+--+--+--+--+--+--+--+--+--+
    /                     MADNAME                   /
    /                                               /
    +--+--+--+--+--+--+--+--+--+--+--+--+--+--+--+--+
where:
MADNAME        A domain-name which specifies a host which has
               the specified mailbox.
```

MD mail destination (obsolete)

MD has been replaced with MX.

MF mail forwarder (obsolete)

MF has been replaced with MX.

MG mail group member (experimental)

(From RFC 1035, page 16)

Textual Representation:

owner ttl class MG *mgroup-dname*

Example:

admin.movie.edu.   IN   MG   al.movie.edu.
                   IN   MG   ed.movie.edu.
                   IN   MG   jc.movie.edu.

Binary Representation:

MG type code: 8
```
    +--+--+--+--+--+--+--+--+--+--+--+--+--+--+--+--+
    /                     MGMNAME                   /
    /                                               /
    +--+--+--+--+--+--+--+--+--+--+--+--+--+--+--+--+
```

where:

MGMNAME   A *domain-name* which specifies a mailbox which
                 is a member of the mail group specified by the
                 domain name.

MINFO mailbox or mail list information (experimental)

(From RFC 1035, page 16)

Textual Representation:

    owner ttl class MINFO *resp-mbox error-mbox*

Example:

    admin.movie.edu. IN MINFO al.movie.edu. al.movie.edu.

Binary Representation:

    MINFO type code: 14
        +--+--+--+--+--+--+--+--+--+--+--+--+--+--+--+--+
        /   RMAILBX   /
        +--+--+--+--+--+--+--+--+--+--+--+--+--+--+--+--+
        /   EMAILBX   /
        +--+--+--+--+--+--+--+--+--+--+--+--+--+--+--+--+
    where:
    RMAILBX   A *domain-name* which specifies a mailbox which
                     is responsible for the mailing list or mailbox.
                     If this domain name names the root, the owner of
                     the MINFO RR is responsible for itself. Note
                     that many existing mailing lists use a mailbox
                     X-request for the RMAILBX field of mailing list
                     X, e.g., Msgroup-request for Msgroup. This field
                     provides a more general mechanism.
    EMAILBX   A *domain-name* which specifies a mailbox which is
                     to receive error messages related to the mailing
                     list or mailbox specified by the owner of the
                     MINFO RR (similar to the ERRORS-TO: field which has
                     been proposed). If this domain name names the root,
                     errors should be returned to the sender of the
                     message.

MR mail rename (experimental)

(From RFC 1035, page 17)

Textual Representation:

    owner ttl class MR *new-mbox*

Example:

    eddie.movie.edu. IN MR eddie.bornagain.edu.

Binary Representation:

```
MR type code: 9
    +--+--+--+--+--+--+--+--+--+--+--+--+--+--+--+--+
    /                      NEWNAME                   /
    /                                                /
    +--+--+--+--+--+--+--+--+--+--+--+--+--+--+--+--+
where:
NEWNAME           A domain-name which specifies a mailbox which
                  is the proper rename of the specified mailbox.
```

MX mail exchanger

(From RFC 1035, page 17)

Textual Representation:

```
owner ttl class MX preference exchange-dname
```

Example:

```
ora.com.  IN  MX  0  ora.ora.com.
          IN  MX  10 ruby.ora.com.
          IN  MX  10 opal.ora.com.
```

Binary Representation:

```
MX type code: 15
    +--+--+--+--+--+--+--+--+--+--+--+--+--+--+--+--+
    |                     PREFERENCE                |
    +--+--+--+--+--+--+--+--+--+--+--+--+--+--+--+--+
    /                      EXCHANGE                  /
    /                                                /
    +--+--+--+--+--+--+--+--+--+--+--+--+--+--+--+--+
where:
PREFERENCE        A 16 bit integer which specifies the preference
                  given to this RR among others at the same owner.
                  Lower values are preferred.
EXCHANGE          A domain-name which specifies a host willing
                  to act as a mail exchange for the owner name.
```

NS name server

(From RFC 1035, page 18)

Textual Representation:

```
owner ttl class NS name-server-dname
```

Example:

```
movie.edu.  IN   NS  terminator.movie.edu
```

Binary Representation:

```
NS type code: 2
    +--+--+--+--+--+--+--+--+--+--+--+--+--+--+--+--+
    /                    NSDNAME                     /
    /                                               /
    +--+--+--+--+--+--+--+--+--+--+--+--+--+--+--+--+
```

where:

NSDNAME   A *domain-name* which specifies a host which
                     should be authoritative for the specified
                     class and domain.

NULL null (experimental)

(From RFC 1035, page 17)

Binary Representation:

```
NULL type code: 10
    +--+--+--+--+--+--+--+--+--+--+--+--+--+--+--+--+
    /                   anything                    /
    /                                               /
    +--+--+--+--+--+--+--+--+--+--+--+--+--+--+--+--+
```

Anything at all may be in the RDATA field so long as it is 65535
octets or less.

NULL is not implemented by BIND.

PTR pointer

(From RFC 1035, page 18)

Textual Representation:

   owner ttl class PTR *dname*

Example:

```
1.249.249.192.in-addr.arpa.   IN PTR wormhole.movie.edu.
```

Binary Representation:

```
PTR type code: 12
    +--+--+--+--+--+--+--+--+--+--+--+--+--+--+--+--+
    /                    PTRDNAME                    /
    +--+--+--+--+--+--+--+--+--+--+--+--+--+--+--+--+
```

where:

PTRDNAME   A *domain-name* which points to some location in
                     the domain name space.

SOA start of authority

(From RFC 1035, pages 19–20)

Textual Representation:

owner ttl class SOA *source-dname mbox (serial refresh retry expire minimum)*

Example:

```
movie.edu. IN SOA terminator.movie.edu. al.robocop.movie.edu. (
                    1        ; Serial
                    10800    ; Refresh after 3 hours
                    3600     ; Retry after 1 hour
                    604800   ; Expire after 1 week
                    86400 )  ; Minimum TTL of 1 day
```

Binary Representation:

```
SOA type code: 6
    +--+--+--+--+--+--+--+--+--+--+--+--+--+--+--+--+
    /                     MNAME                     /
    /                                               /
    +--+--+--+--+--+--+--+--+--+--+--+--+--+--+--+--+
    /                     RNAME                     /
    +--+--+--+--+--+--+--+--+--+--+--+--+--+--+--+--+
    |                     SERIAL                    |
    |                                               |
    +--+--+--+--+--+--+--+--+--+--+--+--+--+--+--+--+
    |                     REFRESH                   |
    |                                               |
    +--+--+--+--+--+--+--+--+--+--+--+--+--+--+--+--+
    |                      RETRY                    |
    |                                               |
    +--+--+--+--+--+--+--+--+--+--+--+--+--+--+--+--+
    |                     EXPIRE                    |
    |                                               |
    +--+--+--+--+--+--+--+--+--+--+--+--+--+--+--+--+
    |                     MINIMUM                   |
    |                                               |
    +--+--+--+--+--+--+--+--+--+--+--+--+--+--+--+--+
```

where:

MNAME	The *domain-name* of the name server that was the original or primary source of data for this zone.
RNAME	A *domain-name* which specifies the mailbox of the person responsible for this zone.
SERIAL	The unsigned 32 bit version number of the original copy of the zone. Zone transfers preserve this value. This value wraps and should be compared using sequence space arithmetic.
REFRESH	A 32 bit time interval before the zone should be refreshed.
RETRY	A 32 bit time interval that should elapse before a failed refresh should be retried.

EXPIRE   A 32 bit time value that specifies the upper limit
                on the time interval that can elapse before the
                zone is no longer authoritative.
MINIMUM   The unsigned 32 bit minimum TTL field that should
                be exported with any RR from this zone.

TXT text

(From RFC 1035, page 20)

Textual Representation:

    owner ttl class TXT *txt-strings*

Example:

    cujo.movie.edu. IN TXT "Location: machine room dog house"

Binary Representation:

TXT type code: 16

```
    +--+--+--+--+--+--+--+--+--+--+--+--+--+--+--+--+
    /                  TXT-DATA                    /
    +--+--+--+--+--+--+--+--+--+--+--+--+--+--+--+--+
```

where:
TXT-DATA   One or more *character-string*s.

WKS well-known services

(From RFC 1035, page 21)

Textual Representation:

    owner ttl class WKS *address protocol service-list*

Example:

    terminator.movie.edu. IN WKS 192.249.249.3 TCP (telnet smtp
                                                        ftp shell domain)

Binary Representation:

WKS type code: 11

```
    +--+--+--+--+--+--+--+--+--+--+--+--+--+--+--+--+
    |                   ADDRESS                    |
    +--+--+--+--+--+--+--+--+--+--+--+--+--+--+--+--+
    |     PROTOCOL     |                           |
    +--+--+--+--+--+--+--+                          |
    |                                              |
    /                   BIT MAP                    /
    /                                              /
    +--+--+--+--+--+--+--+--+--+--+--+--+--+--+--+--+
```

where:
ADDRESS   An 32 bit Internet address
PROTOCOL   An 8 bit IP protocol number
BIT MAP   A variable length bit map. The bit map must
                be a multiple of 8 bits long.

New Types from RFC 1183

AFSDB Andrew File System Data Base (experimental)

Textual Representation:

```
owner ttl class AFSDB subtype hostname
```

Example:

```
fx.movie.edu.   IN  AFSDB  1 bladerunner.fx.movie.edu.
                IN  AFSDB  2 bladerunner.fx.movie.edu.
                IN  AFSDB  1 empire.fx.movie.edu.
                IN  AFSDB  2 aliens.fx.movie.edu.
```

Binary Representation:

```
AFSDB type code: 18
    +--+--+--+--+--+--+--+--+--+--+--+--+--+--+--+--+
    |                  SUBTYPE                      |
    +--+--+--+--+--+--+--+--+--+--+--+--+--+--+--+--+
    /                  HOSTNAME                     /
    /                                               /
    +--+--+--+--+--+--+--+--+--+--+--+--+--+--+--+--+
where:
SUBTYPE        Subtype 1 is an AFS cell database server. Subtype 2
               is a DCE authenticated name server.
HOSTNAME       A domain-name which specifies a host that has a
               server for the cell named by the owner of the RR.
```

ISDN Integrated Services Digital Network address (experimental)

Textual Representation:

```
owner ttl class ISDN ISDN-address sa
```

Example:

```
delay.hp.com.   IN  ISDN  141555514539488
hep.hp.com.     IN  ISDN  141555514539488 004
```

Binary Representation:

```
ISDN type code: 20
    +--+--+--+--+--+--+--+--+--+--+--+--+--+--+--+--+
    /                ISDN ADDRESS                   /
    +--+--+--+--+--+--+--+--+--+--+--+--+--+--+--+--+
    /                SUBADDRESS                     /
    +--+--+--+--+--+--+--+--+--+--+--+--+--+--+--+--+
where:
ISDN ADDRESS   A character-string which identifies the ISDN number
               of owner and DDI (Direct Dial In) if any.
SUBADDRESS     An optional character-string specifying the
               subaddress.
```

RP Responsible Person (experimental)

Textual Representation:

```
owner ttl class RP mbox-dname txt-dname
```

Example:

```
; The current origin is fx.movie.edu
@            IN  RP  ajs.fx.movie.edu.     ajs.fx.movie.edu.
bladerunner  IN  RP  root.fx.movie.edu.    hotline.fx.movie.edu.
             IN  RP  richard.fx.movie.edu. rb.fx.movie.edu.
ajs          IN  TXT "Arty Segue, (415) 555-3610"
hotline      IN  TXT "Movie U. Network Hotline, (415) 555-4111"
rb           IN  TXT "Richard Boisclair, (415) 555-9612"
```

Binary Representation:

```
RP type code: 17
    +--+--+--+--+--+--+--+--+--+--+--+--+--+--+--+--+
    /                    MAILBOX                    /
    /                                               /
    +--+--+--+--+--+--+--+--+--+--+--+--+--+--+--+--+
    /                    TXTDNAME                   /
    /                                               /
    +--+--+--+--+--+--+--+--+--+--+--+--+--+--+--+--+
where:
MAILBOX        A domain-name that specifies the mailbox for
               the responsible person.
TXTDNAME       A domain-name for which TXT RR's exist.  A
               subsequent query can be performed to retrieve
               the associated TXT resource records at
               txt-dname
```

RT Route Through (experimental)

Textual Representation:

```
owner ttl class RT preference intermediate-host
```

Example:

```
sh.prime.com.  IN  RT  2   Relay.Prime.COM.
               IN  RT  10  NET.Prime.COM.
```

Binary Representation:

```
RT type code: 21
    +--+--+--+--+--+--+--+--+--+--+--+--+--+--+--+--+
    |                   PREFERENCE                  |
    +--+--+--+--+--+--+--+--+--+--+--+--+--+--+--+--+
    /                   INTERMEDIATE                /
    /                                               /
    +--+--+--+--+--+--+--+--+--+--+--+--+--+--+--+--+
```

```
where:
PREFERENCE          A 16 bit integer which specifies the preference
                    given to this RR among others at the same owner.
                    Lower values are preferred.
EXCHANGE            A domain-name which specifies a host which will
                    serve as an intermediate in reaching the host
                    specified by owner.
```

X25 X.25 address (experimental)

Textual Representation:

```
owner ttl class X25 PSDN-address
```

Example:

```
relay.pink.com.  IN  X25    31105060845
```

Binary Representation:

```
X25 type code: 19
    +--+--+--+--+--+--+--+--+--+--+--+--+--+--+--+--+
    /                   PSDN ADDRESS                /
    +--+--+--+--+--+--+--+--+--+--+--+--+--+--+--+--+
where:
PSDN ADDRESS        A character-string which identifies the PSDN
                    (Public Switched Data Network) address in the
                    X.121 numbering plan associated with owner.
```

New Types from RFC 1664

PX pointer to X.400/RFC 822 mapping information

Textual Representation:

```
owner ttl class PX preference RFC822 address X.400 address
```

Example:

```
ab.net2.it.  IN  PX  10    ab.net2.it.  O-ab.PRMD-net2.ADMDb.C-it.
```

Binary Representation:

```
PX type code: 26
    +--+--+--+--+--+--+--+--+--+--+--+--+--+--+--+--+
    |                    PREFERENCE                 |
    +--+--+--+--+--+--+--+--+--+--+--+--+--+--+--+--+
    /                      MAP822                   /
    /                                               /
    +--+--+--+--+--+--+--+--+--+--+--+--+--+--+--+--+
    /                     MAPX400                   /
    /                                               /
    +--+--+--+--+--+--+--+--+--+--+--+--+--+--+--+--+
```

```
where:
PREFERENCE    A 16 bit integer which specifies the preference given to
              this RR among others at the same owner.  Lower values
              are preferred.
MAP822        A domain-name element containing rfc822-domain, the
              RFC 822 part of the RFC 1327 mapping information.
MAPX400       A domain-name element containing the value of
              x400-in-domain-syntax derived from the X.400 part of
              the RFC 1327 mapping information.
```

Classes

(From RFC 1035, page 13)

CLASS fields appear in resource records. The following CLASS mnemonics and values are defined:

IN

> 1: the Internet

CS

> 2: the CSNET class (obsolete—used only for examples in some obsolete RFCs)

CH

> 3: the CHAOS class

HS

> 4: the Hesiod class

DNS Messages

In order to write programs that parse DNS messages, you need to understand the message format. DNS queries and responses are most often contained within UDP datagrams. Each message is fully contained within a UDP datagram. If the query and response are sent over TCP, they are prefixed with a two-byte value indicating the length of the query or response, excluding the two-byte length. The format and content of the DNS message are as follows.

Message Format

(From RFC 1035, page 25)

All communications inside the domain protocol are carried in a single format called a message. The top-level format of the message is divided into five sections (some may be empty in certain cases), shown here:

```
+---------------------+
|        Header       |
+---------------------+
|       Question      |  the question for the name server
+---------------------+
```

```
|      Answer      | RRs answering the question
+-----------------+
|     Authority    | RRs pointing toward an authority
+-----------------+
|    Additional    | RRs holding additional information
+-----------------+
```

The header section is always present. The header includes fields that specify which of the remaining sections are present, and also specifies whether the message is a query or a response, a standard query or some other opcode, etc.

The names of the sections after the header are derived from their use in standard queries. The question section contains fields that describe a question to a name server. These fields are a query type (QTYPE), a query class (QCLASS), and a query domain name (QNAME). The last three sections have the same format: a possibly empty list of concatenated resource records (RRs). The answer section contains RRs that answer the question; the authority section contains RRs that point toward an authoritative name server; and the additional records section contains RRs that relate to the query, but are not strictly answers for the question.

Header Section Format

(From RFC 1035, pages 26–28)

```
                                     1  1  1  1  1  1
     0  1  2  3  4  5  6  7  8  9  0  1  2  3  4  5
   +--+--+--+--+--+--+--+--+--+--+--+--+--+--+--+--+
   |                      ID                        |
   +--+--+--+--+--+--+--+--+--+--+--+--+--+--+--+--+
   |QR|   Opcode   |AA|TC|RD|RA|    Z    |  RCODE   |
   +--+--+--+--+--+--+--+--+--+--+--+--+--+--+--+--+
   |                    QDCOUNT                      |
   +--+--+--+--+--+--+--+--+--+--+--+--+--+--+--+--+
   |                    ANCOUNT                      |
   +--+--+--+--+--+--+--+--+--+--+--+--+--+--+--+--+
   |                    NSCOUNT                      |
   +--+--+--+--+--+--+--+--+--+--+--+--+--+--+--+--+
   |                    ARCOUNT                      |
   +--+--+--+--+--+--+--+--+--+--+--+--+--+--+--+--+
```

where:

ID	A 16 bit identifier assigned by the program that generates any kind of query. This identifier is copied the corresponding reply and can be used by the requester to match up replies to outstanding queries.
QR	A one bit field that specifies whether this message is a query (0), or a response (1).
OPCODE	A four bit field that specifies kind of query in this message. This value is set by the originator of a query and copied into the response. The values are:

0	a standard query (QUERY)
1	an inverse query (IQUERY)
2	a server status request (STATUS)
3-15	reserved for future use

AA   Authoritative Answer - this bit is valid in responses, and specifies that the responding name server is an authority for the domain name in question section. Note that the contents of the answer section may have multiple owner names because of aliases. The AA bit corresponds to the name which matches the query name, or the first owner name in the answer section.

TC   TrunCation - specifies that this message was truncated due to length greater than that permitted on the transmission channel.

RD   Recursion Desired - this bit may be set in a query and is copied into the response. If RD is set, it directs the name server to pursue the query recursively. Recursive query support is optional.

RA   Recursion Available - this bit is set or cleared in a response, and denotes whether recursive query support is available in the name server.

Z   Reserved for future use. Must be zero in all queries and responses.

RCODE   Response code - this 4 bit field is set as part of responses. The values have the following interpretation:

0	No error condition
1	Format error - The name server was unable to interpret the query.
2	Server failure - The name server was unable to process this query due to a problem with the name server.
3	Name Error - Meaningful only for responses from an authoritative name server, this code signifies that the domain name referenced in the query does not exist.
4	Not Implemented - The name server does not support the requested kind of query.
5	Refused - The name server refuses to perform the specified operation for policy reasons. For example, a name server may not wish to provide the information to the particular requester, or a name server may not wish to perform a particular operation (e.g., zone transfer) for particular data.
6-15	Reserved for future use.

QDCOUNT   an unsigned 16 bit integer specifying the number of entries in the question section.

ANCOUNT   an unsigned 16 bit integer specifying the number of resource records in the answer section.

NSCOUNT   an unsigned 16 bit integer specifying the number of name server resource records in the authority records section.

ARCOUNT   an unsigned 16 bit integer specifying the number of resource records in the additional records section.

Question Section Format

(From RFC 1035, pages 28–29)

The question section is used to carry the "question" in most queries, i.e., the parameters that define what is being asked. The section contains QDCOUNT (usually 1) entries, each of the following format:

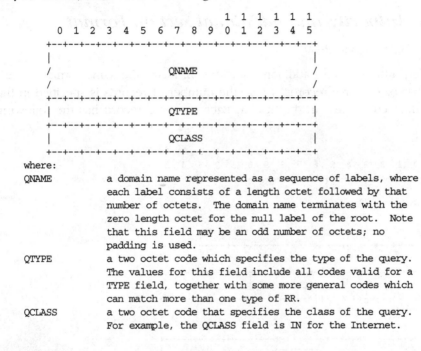

```
                                1 1 1 1 1 1
         0 1 2 3 4 5 6 7 8 9 0 1 2 3 4 5
        +--+--+--+--+--+--+--+--+--+--+--+--+--+--+--+--+
        |                                               |
        /                     QNAME                     /
        /                                               /
        +--+--+--+--+--+--+--+--+--+--+--+--+--+--+--+--+
        |                     QTYPE                     |
        +--+--+--+--+--+--+--+--+--+--+--+--+--+--+--+--+
        |                     QCLASS                    |
        +--+--+--+--+--+--+--+--+--+--+--+--+--+--+--+--+
```

where:

QNAME   a domain name represented as a sequence of labels, where each label consists of a length octet followed by that number of octets. The domain name terminates with the zero length octet for the null label of the root. Note that this field may be an odd number of octets; no padding is used.

QTYPE   a two octet code which specifies the type of the query. The values for this field include all codes valid for a TYPE field, together with some more general codes which can match more than one type of RR.

QCLASS   a two octet code that specifies the class of the query. For example, the QCLASS field is IN for the Internet.

QCLASS values

(From RFC 1035, page 13)

QCLASS fields appear in the question section of a query. QCLASS values are a superset of CLASS values; every CLASS is a valid QCLASS. In addition to CLASS values, the following QCLASS is defined:

*   255 Any class

QTYPE values

(From RFC 1035, pages 12–13)

QTYPE fields appear in the question part of a query. QTYPES are a superset of TYPEs, hence all TYPEs are valid QTYPEs. Also, the following QTYPEs are defined:

AXFR

     252 A request for a transfer of an entire zone

MAILB

253 A request for mailbox-related records (MB, MG, or MR)

MAILA

254 A request for mail agent RRs (obsolete—see MX)

* 255 A request for all records

Answer, Authority, and Additional Section Format

(From RFC 1035, pages 29–30)

The answer, authority, and additional sections all share the same format: a variable number of resource records, where the number of records is specified in the corresponding count field in the header. Each resource record has the following format:

```
                                  1 1 1 1 1 1
    0  1  2  3  4  5  6  7  8  9  0  1  2  3  4  5
  +--+--+--+--+--+--+--+--+--+--+--+--+--+--+--+--+
  |                                               |
  /                                               /
  /                     NAME                      /
  |                                               |
  +--+--+--+--+--+--+--+--+--+--+--+--+--+--+--+--+
  |                     TYPE                      |
  +--+--+--+--+--+--+--+--+--+--+--+--+--+--+--+--+
  |                     CLASS                     |
  +--+--+--+--+--+--+--+--+--+--+--+--+--+--+--+--+
  |                     TTL                       |
  |                                               |
  +--+--+--+--+--+--+--+--+--+--+--+--+--+--+--+--+
  |                   RDLENGTH                    |
  +--+--+--+--+--+--+--+--+--+--+--+--+--+--+--+--|
  /                     RDATA                     /
  /                                               /
  +--+--+--+--+--+--+--+--+--+--+--+--+--+--+--+--+
```

where:

NAME   a domain name to which this resource record pertains.

TYPE   two octets containing one of the RR type codes. This
                field specifies the meaning of the data in the RDATA
                field.

CLASS   two octets which specify the class of the data in the
                RDATA field.

TTL   a 32 bit unsigned integer that specifies the time
                interval (in seconds) that the resource record may be
                cached before it should be discarded. Zero values are
                interpreted to mean that the RR can only be used for the
                transaction in progress, and should not be cached.

RDLENGTH   an unsigned 16 bit integer that specifies the length in
                octets of the RDATA field.

```
RDATA           a variable length string of octets that describes the
                resource.  The format of this information varies
                according to the TYPE and CLASS of the resource record.
                For example, if the TYPE is A and the CLASS is IN,
                the RDATA field is a 4 octet ARPA Internet address.
```

Data Transmission Order

(From RFC 1035, pages 8–9)

The order of transmission of the header and data described in this document is resolved to the octet level. Whenever a diagram shows a group of octets, the order of transmission of those octets is the normal order in which they are read in English. For example, in the following diagram, the octets are transmitted in the order they are numbered.

```
    0                   1
    0 1 2 3 4 5 6 7 8 9 0 1 2 3 4 5
   +-+-+-+-+-+-+-+-+-+-+-+-+-+-+-+-+
   |       1       |       2       |
   +-+-+-+-+-+-+-+-+-+-+-+-+-+-+-+-+
   |       3       |       4       |
   +-+-+-+-+-+-+-+-+-+-+-+-+-+-+-+-+
   |       5       |       6       |
   +-+-+-+-+-+-+-+-+-+-+-+-+-+-+-+-+
```

Whenever an octet represents a numeric quantity, the leftmost bit in the diagram is the high order or most significant bit. That is, the bit labeled zero is the most significant bit. For example, the following diagram represents the value 170 (decimal).

```
    0 1 2 3 4 5 6 7
   +-+-+-+-+-+-+-+-+
   |1 0 1 0 1 0 1 0|
   +-+-+-+-+-+-+-+-+
```

Similarly, whenever a multi-octet field represents a numeric quantity, the leftmost bit of the whole field is the most significant bit. When a multi-octet quantity is transmitted, the most significant octet is transmitted first.

Resource Record Data

Data Format

In addition to two- and four-octet integer values, resource record data can contain *domain names* or *character strings*.

Domain name

(From RFC 1035, page 10)

Domain names in messages are expressed in terms of a sequence of labels. Each label is represented as a one-octet length field followed by that number of octets. Since every domain name ends with the null label of the root, a domain name is terminated by a length byte of zero. The high order two bits of every length octet must be zero, and the remaining six bits of the length field limit the label to 63 octets or less.

Message compression

(From RFC 1035, page 30)

In order to reduce the size of messages, the domain system utilizes a compression scheme that eliminates the repetition of domain names in a message. In this scheme, an entire domain name or a list of labels at the end of a domain name is replaced with a pointer to a prior occurrence of the same name.

The pointer takes the form of a two-octet sequence:

```
+--+--+--+--+--+--+--+--+--+--+--+--+--+--+--+--+
| 1  1|                OFFSET                   |
+--+--+--+--+--+--+--+--+--+--+--+--+--+--+--+--+
```

The first two bits are ones. This allows a pointer to be distinguished from a label, since the label must begin with two zero bits because labels are restricted to 63 octets or less. (The 10 and 01 combinations are reserved for future use.) The OFF-SET field specifies an offset from the start of the message (i.e., the first octet of the ID field in the domain header). A zero offset specifies the first byte of the ID field, etc.

Character string

(From RFC 1035, page 13)

Character string is a single length octet followed by that number of characters. *Character string* is treated as binary information, and can be up to 256 characters in length (including the length octet).

B

BIND Compatibility Matrix

Table B-1 shows you which versions of BIND support various features.

Table B-1. BIND Compatibility Matrix

Feature	BIND Version			
	4.9.7	8.1.2	8.2.3	9.1.0
Multiprocessor support				X
Dynamic update		X	X	X
TSIG-signed dynamic update			X	X
TSIG-based update policy				X
NOTIFY		X	X	X
Incremental zone transfer			X	X
Forwarding	X	X	X	X
Forward zones			X	X
Use of RTT for forwarders			X	
Views				X
Round robin	X	X	X	X
Configurable RRset order			X	
Configurable sort list	X		X	X
Disabling recursion	X	X	X	X
Recursion access list			X	X

Table B-1. BIND Compatibility Matrix (continued)

Feature	BIND Version			
	4.9.7	8.1.2	8.2.3	9.1.0
IPv6 features				
AAAA records	X	X	X	X
A6 records				X
DNAME records				X
Bitstring labels				X
Following DNAME and A6 chains				X
Query access lists	X[a]	X	X	X
Zone transfer access lists	X[b]	X	X	X
DNSSEC features				
Loading SIG, KEY and NXT RRs			X	X
Verify "chain of trust"				X
Dynamic updating secure zones				X

[a] Via secure_zone TXT RRs
[b] Via xfrnets

C

Compiling and Installing BIND on Linux

The versions of BIND shipped with most versions of Linux are fairly recent—usually BIND 8.2.2 for the most recent Linux releases. Still, BIND 8.2.3 is the most current BIND release, and the ISC recommends that you upgrade to BIND 9. For those of you who can't wait until your version of Linux updates to BIND 8.2.3 or 9.1.0, this appendix will show you how to do it yourself.

Instructions for BIND 8.2.3

Compiling and installing BIND 8.2.3 is easy. Here are detailed instructions to follow.

Get the Source Code

First, you've got to get the source code. There's a copy on *ftp.isc.org*, available for anonymous FTP:

```
% cd /tmp
% ftp ftp.isc.org.
Connected to isrv4.pa.vix.com.
220 ProFTPD 1.2.0 Server (ISC FTP Server) [ftp.isc.org]
Name (ftp.isc.org.:user): ftp
331 Anonymous login ok, send your complete e-mail address as password.
Password:
230 Anonymous access granted, restrictions apply.
Remote system type is UNIX.
Using binary mode to transfer files.
ftp>
```

Now you need to find the right file:

```
ftp > cd /isc/bind/src/cur/bind-8
250 CWD command successful.
ftp > binary
```

```
200 Type set to I.
ftp > get bind-src.tar.gz
local: bind-src.tar.gz remote: bind-src.tar.gz
200 PORT command successful.
150 Opening BINARY mode data connection for bind-src.tar.gz (1309147 bytes).
226 Transfer complete.
1309147 bytes received in 23 seconds (56 Kbytes/s)
ftp > quit
221 Goodbye.
```

Unpack the Source Code

Now you've got the compressed *tar* file that contains the BIND source. Just use the *tar* command to uncompress and un*tar* it:

```
% tar -zxvf bind-src.tar.gz
```

(This assumes you've got a version of *tar* that can handle compressed, gzipped files; if you don't, you can get a new copy of *tar* via anonymous FTP from *ftp.gnu. org* in */gnu/tar/tar-1.13.tar.*) This will create a *src* directory with several subdirectories, including *bin*, *include*, *lib*, and *port*. The contents of these subdirectories is as follows:

bin

> Source code for all BIND binaries, including *named*.

include

> Copies of include files referenced by the BIND code. You should use these to build your name server instead of using the ones shipped with your system, since they have been updated.

lib

> Source code for libraries used by BIND.

port

> Information BIND uses to customize compilation settings and compile-time options for various operating systems.

Use the Proper Compiler Settings

Before you can build everything, you'll need a C compiler. Nearly every version of Linux comes with *gcc*, the GNU C compiler, which works fine. If you need to get *gcc*, you can find information at *http://www.fsf.org/software/gcc/gcc.html.*

By default, BIND assumes that you're using the GNU C compiler and various other GNUish utilities, such as *flex* and *byacc*. These are a standard part of most Linux development environments. If your version of Linux uses different programs, though, you'll need to modify *port/linux/Makefile.set*. This file lets BIND know which programs to use.

Build Everything

Next, you compile everything from the top-level directory. First, run:

```
% make stdlinks
```

Then run:

```
% make clean
% make depend
```

This removes any old object files you might have sitting around from previous compilation attempts and updates the *Makefile* dependencies. Then, compile the source code by running:

```
% make all
```

The source code should compile without any errors. Next, install the new *named* and *named-xfer* programs into */usr/sbin*. You'll need to become root to do this. Use the command:

```
# make install
```

Instructions for BIND 9.1.0

Here's how to compile and install BIND 9.1.0 on your Linux host.

Get the Source Code

As with BIND 8.2.3, you've got to get the source code first. And again, this requires FTPing to *ftp.isc.org*:

```
% cd /tmp
% ftp ftp.isc.org.
Connected to isrv4.pa.vix.com.
220 ProFTPD 1.2.1 Server (ISC FTP Server) [ftp.isc.org]
Name (ftp.isc.org.:user): ftp
331 Anonymous login ok, send your complete email address as your password.
Password:
230 Anonymous access granted, restrictions apply.
Remote system type is UNIX.
Using binary mode to transfer files.
ftp>
```

Change to the right directory and get the file you need:

```
ftp> cd /isc/bind9/9.1.0/
250 CWD command successful.
ftp> get bind-9.1.0.tar.gz
local: bind-9.1.0.tar.gz remote: bind-9.1.0.tar.gz
200 PORT command successful.
150 Opening BINARY mode data connection for bind-9.1.0.tar.gz (3299471 bytes).
226 Transfer complete.
```

```
3299471 bytes received in 92.4 secs (35 Kbytes/sec)
ftp> quit
221 Goodbye.
```

Unpack the Source Code

Use the *tar* command to uncompress and un*tar* the compressed *tar* file:

```
% tar zxvf bind-9.1.0.tar.gz
```

Unlike the BIND 8.2.3 distribution, this will create a *bind-9.1.0* subdirectory of your working directory for all of the BIND source code. (BIND 8 distributions always unpacked everything into the working directory.) The *bind-9.1.0* subdirectory will have subdirectories called:

bin
> Source code for all BIND binaries, including *named*.

contrib
> Contributed tools.

doc
> Documentation for BIND, including the invaluable Administrator Resource Manual.

lib
> Source code for libraries used by BIND.

make
> Makefiles.

Run Configure and Build Everything

Also unlike BIND 8, BIND 9 uses the near-miraculous *configure* script to determine the appropriate includes and compiler settings. Read through the README file to determine whether you need any special settings. *configure* supports command-line options that allow you to build without threads, use a different installation directory, and much more. To run *configure*:

```
% ./configure
```

Or, if you need to disable threads, for example, run:

```
% ./configure disable-threads
```

To build BIND, type:

```
% make all
```

The source code should compile without errors. To install BIND, type this as root:

```
# make install
```

That's all there is!

Top-Level Domains

This table lists all the two-letter country codes and all the top-level domains that aren't countries. Not all of the countries are registered in the Internet's namespace at the time of this writing, but there aren't many missing.

Domain	Country or Organization	Domain	Country or Organization
AC	Ascension Island	BD	Bangladesh
AD	Andorra	BE	Belgium
AE	United Arab Emirates	BF	Burkina Faso
AF	Afghanistan	BG	Bulgaria
AG	Antigua and Barbuda	BH	Bahrain
AI	Anguilla	BI	Burundi
AL	Albania	BJ	Benin
AM	Armenia	BM	Bermuda
AN	Netherlands Antilles	BN	Brunei Darussalam
AO	Angola	BO	Bolivia
AQ	Antarctica	BR	Brazil
AR	Argentina	BS	Bahamas
ARPA	ARPA Internet	BT	Bhutan
AS	American Samoa	BV	Bouvet Island
AT	Austria	BW	Botswana
AU	Australia	BY	Belarus
AW	Aruba	BZ	Belize
AZ	Azerbaijan	CA	Canada
BA	Bosnia and Herzegovina	CC	Cocos (Keeling) Islands
BB	Barbados	CD	Congo, Democratic Republic of the

Domain	Country or Organization	Domain	Country or Organization
CF	Central African Republic	FX	France, metropolitan
CG	Congo	GA	Gabon
CH	Switzerland	GB	United Kingdom[a]
CI	Cote d'Ivoire	GD	Grenada
CK	Cook Islands	GE	Georgia
CL	Chile	GF	French Guiana
CM	Cameroon	GG	Guernsey, Alderney, and Sark (British Channel Islands)
CN	China	GH	Ghana
CO	Colombia	GI	Gibraltar
COM	Generic (formerly Commercial)	GL	Greenland
CR	Costa Rica	GM	Gambia
CU	Cuba	GN	Guinea
CV	Cape Verde	GOV	U.S. Federal Government
CX	Christmas Island	GP	Guadeloupe
CY	Cyprus	GQ	Equatorial Guinea
CZ	Czech Republic	GR	Greece
DE	Germany	GS	South Georgia and the South Sandwich Islands
DJ	Djibouti	GT	Guatemala
DK	Denmark	GU	Guam
DM	Dominica	GW	Guinea-Bissau
DO	Dominican Republic	GY	Guyana
DZ	Algeria	HK	Hong Kong
EC	Ecuador	HM	Heard and McDonald Islands
EDU	Education	HN	Honduras
EE	Estonia	HR	Croatia
EG	Egypt	HT	Haiti
EH	Western Sahara	HU	Hungary
ER	Eritrea	ID	Indonesia
ES	Spain	IE	Ireland
ET	Ethiopia	IL	Israel
FI	Finland	IM	Isle of Man
FJ	Fiji	IN	India
FK	Falkland Islands (Malvinas)	INT	International entities
FM	Micronesia, Federated States of	IO	British Indian Ocean Territory
FO	Faroe Islands	IQ	Iraq
FR	France	IR	Iran

[a] In practice, the United Kingdom uses "UK" for its top-level domain.

Domain	Country or Organization	Domain	Country or Organization
IS	Iceland	ML	Mali
IT	Italy	MM	Myanmar
JE	Jersey (British Channel Island)	MN	Mongolia
JM	Jamaica	MO	Macau
JO	Jordan	MP	Northern Mariana Islands
JP	Japan	MQ	Martinique
KE	Kenya	MR	Mauritania
KG	Kyrgyzstan	MS	Montserrat
KH	Cambodia	MT	Malta
KI	Kiribati	MU	Mauritius
KM	Comoros	MV	Maldives
KN	Saint Kitts and Nevis	MW	Malawi
KP	Korea, Democratic People's Republic of	MX	Mexico
KR	Korea, Republic of	MY	Malaysia
KW	Kuwait	MZ	Mozambique
KY	Cayman Islands	NA	Namibia
KZ	Kazakhstan	NATO	North Atlantic Treaty Organization
LA	Lao People's Democratic Republic	NC	New Caledonia
LB	Lebanon	NE	Niger
LC	Saint Lucia	NET	Generic (formerly Networking Organizations)
LI	Liechtenstein	NF	Norfolk Island
LK	Sri Lanka	NG	Nigeria
LR	Liberia	NI	Nicaragua
LS	Lesotho	NL	Netherlands
LT	Lithuania	NO	Norway
LU	Luxembourg	NP	Nepal
LV	Latvia	NR	Nauru
LY	Libyan Arab Jamahiriya	NU	Niue
MA	Morocco	NZ	New Zealand
MC	Monaco	OM	Oman
MD	Moldova, Republic of	ORG	Generic (formerly Organizations)
MG	Madagascar	PA	Panama
MH	Marshall Islands	PE	Peru
MIL	U.S. Military	PF	French Polynesia
MK	Macedonia, the Former Yugoslav Republic of	PG	Papua New Guinea

Domain	Country or Organization	Domain	Country or Organization
PH	Philippines	TF	French Southern Territories
PK	Pakistan	TG	Togo
PL	Poland	TH	Thailand
PM	St. Pierre and Miquelon	TJ	Tajikistan
PN	Pitcairn	TK	Tokelau
PR	Puerto Rico	TM	Turkmenistan
PS	Palestinian Authority	TN	Tunisia
PT	Portugal	TO	Tonga
PW	Palau	TP	East Timor
PY	Paraguay	TR	Turkey
QA	Qatar	TT	Trinidad and Tobago
RE	Reunion	TV	Tuvalu
RO	Romania	TW	Taiwan, Province of China
RU	Russian Federation	TZ	Tanzania, United Republic of
RW	Rwanda	UA	Ukraine
SA	Saudi Arabia	UG	Uganda
SB	Solomon Islands	UK	United Kingdom
SC	Seychelles	UM	United States Minor Outlying Islands
SD	Sudan	US	United States
SE	Sweden	UY	Uruguay
SG	Singapore	UZ	Uzbekistan
SH	St. Helena	VA	Holy See (Vatican City State)
SI	Slovenia	VC	Saint Vincent and The Grenadines
SJ	Svalbard and Jan Mayen Islands	VE	Venezuela
SK	Slovakia	VG	Virgin Islands (British)
SL	Sierra Leone	VI	Virgin Islands (U.S.)
SM	San Marino	VN	Vietnam
SN	Senegal	VU	Vanuatu
SO	Somalia	WF	Wallis and Futuna Islands
SR	Suriname	WS	Samoa
ST	Sao Tome and Principe	YE	Yemen
SU	Union of Soviet Socialist Republics	YT	Mayotte
SV	El Salvador	YU	Yugoslavia
SY	Syrian Arab Republic	ZA	South Africa
SZ	Swaziland	ZM	Zambia
TC	Turks and Caicos Islands	ZR	Republic of Zaire
TD	Chad	ZW	Zimbabwe

E

BIND Name Server and Resolver Configuration

BIND Name Server Boot File Directives and Configuration File Statements

Here's a handy list of all the boot file directives and configuration file statements for the BIND name server, as well as configuration directives for the BIND resolver. Some of the directives and statements exist only in later versions, so your name server may not support them yet. Newer directives or statements are labeled with the specific version of BIND in which they were introduced (e.g., 8.2+). If they've been around a long time, they aren't labeled.

BIND 4 Boot File Directives

directory

Function:

Sets the name server's working directory

Syntax:

```
directory new-directory
```

Example:

```
directory /var/named
```

See also:

8.x.x and 9.x.x *options* statement, *directory* substatement

Covered in Chapter 4, *Setting Up BIND*.

primary

Function:

Configures a name server as the primary master for a zone

Syntax:

```
primary domain-name-of-zone file
```

Example:

```
primary movie.edu   db.movie.edu
```

See also:

8.x.x and 9.x.x *zone* statement, type *master*

Covered in Chapter 4, *Setting Up BIND.*

secondary

Function:

Configures a name server as a slave for a zone

Syntax:

```
secondary domain-name-of-zone ip-address-list [backup-file]
```

Example:

```
secondary movie.edu   192.249.249.3 bak.movie.edu
```

See also:

8.x.x and 9.x.x *zone* statement, type *slave*

Covered in Chapter 4, *Setting Up BIND.*

cache

Function:

Sets the name of the file from which to load the root hints (the names and addresses of the root name servers)

Syntax:

```
cache   .     file
```

Example:

```
cache   .     db.cache
```

See also:

8.x.x and 9.x.x *zone* statement, type *hint*

Covered in Chapter 4, *Setting Up BIND.*

forwarders

Function:

Configures the name server(s) to send unresolved queries to

Syntax:

```
forwarders ip-address-list
```

Example:

```
forwarders 192.249.249.1 192.249.249.3
```

See also:

8.x.x and 9.x.x *options* statement, *forwarders* substatement

Covered in Chapter 10, *Advanced Features.*

sortlist

Function:

Specifies networks to prefer over others

Syntax:

```
sortlist network-list
```

Example:

```
sortlist 10.0.0.0
```

See also:

8.2+ and 9.1.0+ *options* statement, *sortlist* substatement

Covered in Chapter 10, *Advanced Features.*

slave

This directive is the same as the 4.9.x directive *options forward-only* and the 8.x.x and 9.x.x *options* substatement *forward.*

include (4.9+)

Function:

Includes the contents of another file in *named.boot*

Syntax:

```
include file
```

Example:

```
include  bootfile.primary
```

See also:

8.x.x and 9.x.x *include* statement

Covered in Chapter 7, *Maintaining BIND.*

stub (4.9+)

Function:

Specifies a child zone that your name server should periodically get delegation information for

Syntax:

```
stub domain-name-of-zone ip-address-list [backup-file]
```

Example:

```
stub movie.edu 192.249.249.3 stub.movie.edu
```

See also:

8.x.x and 9.x.x *zone* statement, type *stub*

Covered in Chapter 9, *Parenting*.

options (4.9+)

options forward-only

Function:

Prevents your name server from resolving domain names independently of a
forwarder

See also:

8.x.x and 9.x.x *option* statement, *forward* substatement

Covered in:

Chapter 10, *Advanced Features*

options no-recursion

Function:

Prevents your name server from performing recursive resolution of domain
names

See also:

8.x.x and 9.x.x *options* statement, *recursion* substatement

Covered in Chapter 10, *Advanced Features*, and Chapter 11, *Security*.

options no-fetch-glue

Function:

Prevents your name server from fetching missing glue when constructing a
response

See also:

8.x.x *options* statement, *fetch-glue* substatement

Covered in Chapter 10, *Advanced Features*, and Chapter 11, *Security*.

options query-log

Function:

Logs all queries received by your name server

See also:

8.x.x and 9.1.0+ *logging* statement, category *queries*

Covered in Chapter 7, *Maintaining BIND*, and Chapter 14, *Troubleshooting DNS and BIND*.

options fake-iquery

Function:

Tells your name server to respond to old-fashioned inverse queries with a made-up answer instead of an error

See also:

8.x.x *options* statement, *fake-iquery* substatement

Covered in Chapter 12, *nslookup and dig*.

limit (4.9+)

limit transfers-in

Function:

Restricts the total number of zone transfers your name server will attempt at any one time

See also:

8.x.x and 9.x.x *options* statement, *transfers-in* substatement

limit transfers-per-ns

Function:

Restricts the number of simultaneous zone transfers your name server will request from any one name server

See also:

8.x.x and 9.x.x *options* statement, *transfers-per-ns* substatement

limit datasize

Function:

Increases the size of the data segment *named* uses (works only on some operating systems)

See also:

8.x.x and 9.1.0+ *options* statement, *datasize* substatement

All covered in Chapter 10, *Advanced Features*.

xfrnets (4.9+)

Function:

Restricts zone transfers from your name server to a list of IP addresses or networks

Syntax:

```
xfrnets ip-address-or-network-list
```

Example:

```
xfrnets 15.0.0.0 128.32.0.0
```

See also:

8.x.x and 9.x.x *options* and *zone* statements, *allow-transfer* substatement

Covered in Chapter 11, *Security*.

bogusns (4.9+)

Function:

Tells your name server not to query a list of name servers known to give bad answers

Syntax:

```
bogusns ip-address-list
```

Example:

```
bogusns 15.255.152.4
```

See also:

8.x.x and 9.1.0+ *server* statement, *bogus* substatement

Covered in Chapter 10, *Advanced Features*.

check-names (4.9.4+)

Function:

Configures the name checking mechanism

Syntax:

```
check-names primary|secondary|response fail|warn|ignore
```

Example:

```
check-names primary ignore
```

See also:

8.x.x *options and zone* statements, *check-names* substatement

Covered in Chapter 4, *Setting Up BIND*.

BIND 8 Configuration File Statements

acl

Function:

Creates a named address match list

Syntax:
```
acl name {
    address_match_list;
};
```

Covered in Chapter 10, *Advanced Features*, and Chapter 11, *Security*.

controls (8.2+)

Function:

Configures a channel used by *ndc* to control the name server

Syntax:
```
controls {
    [ inet ( ip_addr | * ) port ip_port allow address_match_list; ]
    [ unix path_name perm number owner number group number; ]
};
```

Covered in Chapter 7, *Maintaining BIND*.

include

Function:

Inserts the specified file at the point that the *include* statement is encountered

Syntax:
```
include path_name;
```

Covered in Chapter 7, *Maintaining BIND*.

key (8.2+)

Function:

Defines a key ID that can be used in a *server* statement or an address match list to associate a TSIG key with a particular name server

Syntax:
```
key key_id {
    algorithm algorithm_id;
    secret secret_string;
};
```

Covered in Chapter 10, *Advanced Features*, and Chapter 11, *Security*.

logging

Function:

Configures the name server's logging behavior

Syntax:

```
logging {
  [ channel channel_name {
    ( file path_name
        [ versions ( number | unlimited ) ]
        [ size size_spec ]
      | syslog ( kern | user | mail | daemon | auth | syslog | lpr |
                 news | uucp | cron | authpriv | ftp |
                 local0 | local1 | local2 | local3 |
                 local4 | local5 | local6 | local7 )
      | null );

      [ severity ( critical | error | warning | notice |
                   info | debug [ level ] | dynamic ); ]
      [ print-category yes_or_no; ]
      [ print-severity yes_or_no; ]
      [ print-time yes_or_no; ]
  }; ]

  [ category category_name {
    channel_name; [ channel_name; ... ]
  }; ]
  ...
};
```

Covered in Chapter 7, *Maintaining BIND*.

options

Function:

Configures global options

Syntax:

```
options {
  [ allow-query { address_match_list }; ]
  [ allow-recursion { address_match_list }; ]
  [ allow-transfer { address_match_list }; ]
  [ also-notify { ip_addr; [ ip_addr; ... ] }; ]
  [ auth-nxdomain yes_or_no; ]
  [ blackhole { address_match_list }; ]
  [ check-names ( master | slave | response ) ( warn | fail | ignore ); ]
  [ cleaning-interval number; ]
  [ coresize size_spec; ]
  [ datasize size_spec; ]
  [ deallocate-on-exit yes_or_no; ]
  [ dialup yes_or_no; ]
  [ directory path_name; ]
  [ dump-file path_name; ]
```

```
     [ fake-iquery yes_or_no; ]
     [ fetch-glue yes_or_no; ]
     [ files size_spec; ]
     [ forward ( only | first ); ]
     [ forwarders { [ ip_addr ; [ ip_addr ; ... ] ] }; ]
     [ has-old-clients yes_or_no; ]
     [ heartbeat-interval number; ]
     [ host-statistics yes_or_no; ]
     [ interface-interval number; ]
     [ lame-ttl number; ]
     [ listen-on [ port ip_port ] { address_match_list }; ]
     [ maintain-ixfr-base yes_or_no; ]
     [ max-ixfr-log-size number; ]
     [ max-ncache-ttl number; ]
     [ max-transfer-time-in number; ]
     [ memstatistics-file path_name; ]
     [ min-roots number; ]
     [ multiple-cnames yes_or_no; ]
     [ named-xfer path_name; ]
     [ notify yes_or_no; ]
     [ pid-file path_name; ]
     [ query-source [ address ( ip_addr | * ) ] [ port ( ip_port | * ) ]; ]
     [ recursion yes_or_no; ]
     [ rfc2308-type1 yes_or_no; ]
     [ rrset-order { order_spec; [ order_spec; ... ] }; ]
     [ serial-queries number; ]
     [ sortlist { address_match_list }; ]
     [ stacksize size_spec; ]
     [ statistics-file path_name; ]
     [ statistics-interval number; ]
     [ topology { address_match_list }; ]
     [ transfer-format ( one-answer | many-answers ); ]
     [ transfer-source ( ip_addr | * ); ]
     [ transfers-in  number; ]
     [ transfers-per-ns number; ]
     [ treat-cr-as-space yes_or_no; ]
     [ use-id-pool yes_or_no; ]
     [ use-ixfr yes_or_no; ]
     [ version version_string; ]
  };
```

Covered in Chapter 4, *Setting Up BIND*, Chapter 10, *Advanced Features*, Chapter 11, *Security*, and Chapter 16, *Miscellaneous*.

server

Function:

Defines the characteristics to be associated with a remote name server

Syntax:

```
server ip_addr {
  [ bogus yes_or_no; ]
  [ keys { key_id [ key_id ... ] }; ]
```

```
    [ support-ixfr yes_or_no; ]
    [ transfer-format ( one-answer | many-answers ); ]
};
```

Covered in Chapter 10, *Advanced Features*, and Chapter 11, *Security*.

trusted-keys (8.2+)

Function:

Configures the public keys of security roots for use in DNSSEC

Syntax:

```
trusted-keys {
  domain-name flags protocol_id algorithm_id public_key_string;
  [ domain-name flags protocol_id algorithm_id public_key_string; [ ... ] ]
};
```

Covered in Chapter 11, *Security*.

zone

Function:

Configures the zones maintained by the name server

Syntax:

```
zone "domain_name" [ ( in | hs | hesiod | chaos ) ] {
  type master;
  file path_name;
  [ allow-query { address_match_list }; ]
  [ allow-transfer { address_match_list }; ]
  [ allow-update { address_match_list }; ]
  [ also-notify { ip_addr; [ ip_addr; ... ] ]
  [ check-names ( warn | fail | ignore ); ]
  [ dialup yes_or_no | notify; ]
  [ forward ( only | first ); ]
  [ forwarders { [ ip_addr; [ ip_addr; ... ] ] }; ]
  [ ixfr-base path_name; ]
  [ ixfr-tmp-file path_name; ]
  [ maintain-ixfr-base yes_or_no; ]
  [ notify yes_or_no; ]
  [ pubkey flags protocol_id algorithm_id public_key_string; ]
};

zone "domain_name" [ ( in | hs | hesiod | chaos ) ] {
  type slave;
  masters [ port ip_port ] { ip_addr; [ ip_addr; ... ] };
  [ allow-query { address_match_list }; ]
  [ allow-transfer { address_match_list }; ]
  [ allow-update { address_match_list }; ]
  [ also-notify { ip_addr; [ ip_addr; ... ] };
  [ check-names ( warn | fail | ignore ); ]
  [ dialup yes_or_no; ]
  [ file path_name; ]
```

```
    [ forward ( only | first ); ]
    [ forwarders { [ ip_addr; [ ip_addr; ... ] ] }; ]
    [ ixfr-base path_name; ]
    [ max-transfer-time-in number; ]
    [ notify yes_or_no; ]
    [ pubkey flags protocol_id algorithm_id public_key_string; ]
    [ transfer-source ip_addr; ]
};

zone "domain_name" [ ( in | hs | hesiod | chaos ) ] {
  type stub;
  masters [ port ip_port ] { ip_addr; [ ip_addr; ... ] };
  [ allow-query { address_match_list }; ]
  [ allow-transfer { address_match_list }; ]
  [ allow-update { address_match_list }; ]
  [ check-names ( warn | fail | ignore ); ]
  [ dialup yes_or_no; ]
  [ file path_name; ]
  [ forward ( only | first ); ]
  [ forwarders { [ ip_addr ; [ ip_addr ; ... ] ] }; ]
  [ max-transfer-time-in number; ]
  [ pubkey flags protocol_id algorithm_id public_key_string; ]
  [ transfer-source ip_addr; ]
};

zone "domain_name" [ ( in | hs | hesiod | chaos ) ] {
  type forward;
  [ forward ( only | first ); ]
  [ forwarders { [ ip_addr ; [ ip_addr ; ... ] ] }; ]
};

zone "." [ ( in | hs | hesiod | chaos ) ] {
  type hint;
  file path_name;
  [ check-names ( warn | fail | ignore ); ]
};
```

Covered in Chapter 4, *Setting Up BIND*, and Chapter 10, *Advanced Features*.

BIND 9 Configuration File Statements

acl

Function:

Creates a named address match list

Syntax:

```
acl name {
    address_match_list;
};
```

Covered in Chapter 10, *Advanced Features*, and Chapter 11, *Security*.

controls

Function:

Configures a channel used by *rndc* to control the name server

Syntax:
```
controls {
    [ inet ( ip_addr | * ) port ip_port allow address_match_list keys key_list; ]
    [ inet ... ; ]
};
```
Covered in Chapter 7, *Maintaining BIND*.

include

Function:

Inserts the specified file at the point that the *include* statement is encountered

Syntax:
```
include path_name;
```
Covered in Chapter 7, *Maintaining BIND*.

key

Function:

Defines a key ID that can be used in a *server* statement or an address match list to associate a TSIG key with a particular name server

Syntax:
```
key key_id {
    algorithm algorithm_id;
    secret secret_string;
};
```
Covered in Chapter 10, *Advanced Features*, and Chapter 11, *Security*.

logging

Function:

Configures the name server's logging behavior

Syntax:
```
logging {
    [ channel channel_name {
        ( file path_name
            [ versions ( number | unlimited ) ]
            [ size size_spec ]
        | syslog ( kern | user | mail | daemon | auth | syslog | lpr |
                    news | uucp | cron | authpriv | ftp |
                    local0 | local1 | local2 | local3 |
```

```
                local4 | local5 | local6 | local7 )
    | stderr
    | null );

  [ severity ( critical | error | warning | notice |
                info  | debug [ level ] | dynamic ); ]
  [ print-category yes_or_no; ]
  [ print-severity yes_or_no; ]
  [ print-time yes_or_no; ]
}; ]

[ category category_name {
  channel_name; [ channel_name; ... ]
}; ]
...
};
```

Covered in Chapter 7, *Maintaining BIND*.

options

Function:

   Configures global options

Syntax:

```
options {
  [ additional-from-auth yes_or_no; ]
  [ additional-from-cache yes_or_no; ]
  [ allow-notify { address_match_list }; ]
  [ allow-query { address_match_list }; ]
  [ allow-recursion { address_match_list }; ]
  [ allow-transfer { address_match_list }; ]
  [ also-notify { ip_addr [ port ip_port ] ; [ ip_addr [ port ip_port ] ; ... ] };
]
  [ auth-nxdomain yes_or_no; ]
  [ blackhole { address_match_list }; ]
  [ cleaning-interval number; ]
  [ coresize size_spec; ]
  [ datasize size_spec; ]
  [ dialup yes_or_no; ]
  [ directory path_name; ]
  [ dump-file path_name; ]
  [ files size_spec; ]
  [ forward ( only | first ); ]
  [ forwarders { [ ip_addr ; [ ip_addr ; ... ] ] }; ]
  [ heartbeat-interval number; ]
  [ interface-interval number; ]
  [ lame-ttl number; ]
  [ listen-on [ port ip_port ] { address_match_list }; ]
  [ listen-on-v6 [ port ip_port ] { address_match_list }; ]
  [ max-cache-ttl number; ]
  [ max-ncache-ttl number; ]
  [ max-refresh-time number; ]
```

```
    [ max-retry-time number; ]
    [ max-transfer-idle-in number; ]
    [ max-transfer-idle-out number; ]
    [ max-transfer-time-in number; ]
    [ max-transfer-time-out number; ]
    [ min-refresh-time number; ]
    [ min-retry-time number; ]
    [ notify yes_or_no | explicit; ]
    [ notify-source ( ip_addr | * ) [ port ip_port ]; ]
    [ notify-source-v6 ( ip6_addr | * ) [ port ip_port ]; ]
    [ pid-file path_name; ]
    [ port ip_port; ]
    [ query-source [ address ( ip_addr | * ) ] [ port ( ip_port | * ) ]; ]
    [ query-source-v6 [ address ( ip6_addr | * ) ] [ port ( ip_port | * ) ]; ]
    [ recursion yes_or_no; ]
    [ recursive-clients number; ]
    [ sig-validity-interval number; ]
    [ sortlist { address_match_list }; ]
    [ stacksize size_spec; ]
    [ statistics-file path_name; ]
    [ tcp-clients number; ]
    [ tkey-dhkey key_name key_tag; ]
    [ tkey-domain domain_name; ]
    [ transfer-format ( one-answer | many-answers ); ]
    [ transfer-source ( ip_addr | * ) [ port ip_port ]; ]
    [ transfer-source-v6 ( ip6_addr | * ) [ port ip_port ]; ]
    [ transfers-in  number; ]
    [ transfers-out number; ]
    [ transfers-per-ns number; ]
    [ version version_string; ]
    [ zone-statistics yes_or_no; ]
};
```

Covered in Chapter 4, *Setting Up BIND*, Chapter 10, *Advanced Features*, Chapter 11, *Security*, and Chapter 16, *Miscellaneous*.

server

Function:

Defines the characteristics to be associated with a remote name server

Syntax:

```
server ip_addr {
  [ bogus yes_or_no; ]
  [ keys { key_id [ key_id ... ] }; ]
  [ provide-ixfr yes_or_no; ]
  [ request-ixfr yes_or_no; ]
  [ transfers number; ]
  [ transfer-format ( one-answer | many-answers ); ]
};
```

Covered in Chapter 10, *Advanced Features*, and Chapter 11, *Security*.

trusted-keys

Function:

Configures the public keys of security roots for use in DNSSEC

Syntax:

```
trusted-keys {
  domain-name flags protocol_id algorithm_id public_key_string;
  [ domain-name flags protocol_id algorithm_id public_key_string; [ ... ] ]
};
```

Covered in Chapter 11, *Security*.

view

Function:

Creates and configures a view

Syntax:

```
view "view_name" [ ( in | hs | hesiod | chaos ) ] {
  match-clients { address_match_list };
  [ allow-notify { address_match_list }; ]
  [ allow-query { address_match_list }; ]
  [ allow-recursion { address_match_list }; ]
  [ allow-transfer { address_match_list }; ]
  [ also-notify { ip_addr; [ ip_addr; ... ] }; ]
  [ auth-nxdomain yes_or_no; ]
  [ cleaning-interval number; ]
  [ forward ( only | first ); ]
  [ forwarders { [ ip_addr; [ ip_addr; ... ] ] }; ]
  [ key ... ]
  [ lame-ttl number; ]
  [ min-refresh-time number; ]
  [ min-retry-time number; ]
  [ max-cache-ttl number; ]
  [ max-ncache-ttl number; ]
  [ max-transfer-idle-out number; ]
  [ max-transfer-time-out number; ]
  [ max-refresh-time number; ]
  [ max-retry-time number; ]
  [ notify yes_or_no | explicit; ]
  [ provide-ixfr yes_or_no; ]
  [ query-source [ address ( ip_addr | * ) ] [ port ( ip_port | * ) ]; ]
  [ query-source-v6 [ address ( ip6_addr | * ) ] [ port ( ip_port | * ) ]; ]
  [ recursion yes_or_no; ]
  [ request-ixfr yes_or_no; ]
  [ server ... ]
  [ sig-validity-interval number; ]
  [ sortlist { address_match_list }; ]
  [ transfer-format ( one-answer | many-answers ); ]
  [ transfer-source ( ip_addr | * ) [ port ip_port ]; ]
  [ transfer-source-v6 ( ip6_addr | * ) [ port ip_port ]; ]
```

```
    [ trusted-keys ... ]
    [ zone ... ]
};
```

Covered in Chapter 10, *Advanced Features*, and Chapter 11, *Security*.

zone

Function:

Configures the zones maintained by the name server

Syntax:

```
zone "domain_name" [ ( in | hs | hesiod | chaos ) ] {
  type master;
  file path_name;
  [ allow-notify { address_match_list }; ]
  [ allow-query { address_match_list }; ]
  [ allow-transfer { address_match_list }; ]
  [ allow-update { address_match_list }; ]
  [ allow-update-forwarding { address_match_list }; ]
  [ also-notify { ip_addr [ port ip_port ]; [ ip_addr [ port ip_port ]; ... ]
  [ database string; [ string; ... ] ]
  [ dialup yes_or_no | notify; ]
  [ forward ( only | first ); ]
  [ forwarders { [ ip_addr; [ ip_addr; ... ] ] }; ]
  [ max-refresh-time number; ]
  [ max-retry-time number; ]
  [ max-transfer-idle-out number; ]
  [ max-transfer-time-out number; ]
  [ min-refresh-time number; ]
  [ min-retry-time number; ]
  [ notify yes_or_no | explicit; ]
  [ sig-validity-interval number; ]
  [ update-policy { update_policy_rule; [ ... ] }; ]
};

zone "domain_name" [ ( in | hs | hesiod | chaos ) ] {
  type slave;
  masters [ port ip_port ] { ip_addr [ port ip_port ] [ key key_id ]; [ ip_addr [
port ip_port ] [ key key_id ]; ... ] };
  [ allow-query { address_match_list }; ]
  [ allow-transfer { address_match_list }; ]
  [ allow-update { address_match_list }; ]
  [ allow-update-forwarding { address_match_list }; ]
  [ also-notify { ip_addr [ port ip_port ]; [ ip_addr [ port ip_port ]; ... ]
};
  [ dialup yes_or_no | notify | notify-passive | refresh | passive; ]
  [ file path_name; ]
  [ forward ( only | first ); ]
  [ forwarders { [ ip_addr; [ ip_addr; ... ] ] }; ]
  [ max-refresh-time number ; ]
  [ max-retry-time number ; ]
```

```
     [ max-transfer-idle-in number; ]
     [ max-transfer-idle-out number; ]
     [ max-transfer-time-in number; ]
     [ max-transfer-time-out number; ]
     [ min-refresh-time number ; ]
     [ min-retry-time number ; ]
     [ notify yes_or_no | explicit; ]
     [ transfer-source ( ip_addr | * ) [ port ip_port ]; ]
     [ transfer-source-v6 ( ip6_addr | * ) [ port ip_port ]; ]
   };

   zone "domain_name" [ ( in | hs | hesiod | chaos ) ] {
     type stub;
     masters [ port ip_port ] { ip_addr [ [port ip_port ] [ key key_id ]; [ ip_addr
   [ port ip_port ] [ key key_id ]; ... ] };
     [ allow-query { address_match_list }; ]
     [ allow-transfer { address_match_list }; ]
     [ allow-update { address_match_list }; ]
     [ allow-update-forwarding { address_match_list }; ]
     [ dialup yes_or_no | passive | refresh; ]
     [ file path_name; ]
     [ forward ( only | first ); ]
     [ forwarders { [ ip_addr ; [ ip_addr ; ... ] ] }; ]
     [ max-refresh-time number ; ]
     [ max-retry-time number ; ]
     [ max-transfer-idle-in number; ]
     [ max-transfer-idle-out number; ]
     [ max-transfer-time-in number; ]
     [ max-transfer-time-out number; ]
     [ min-refresh-time number ; ]
     [ min-retry-time number ; ]
     [ transfer-source ( ip_addr | * ) [ port ip_port ]; ]
     [ transfer-source-v6 ( ip6_addr | * ) [ port ip_port ]; ]
   };

   zone "domain_name" [ ( in | hs | hesiod | chaos ) ] {
     type forward;
     [ forward ( only | first ); ]
     [ forwarders { [ ip_addr ; [ ip_addr ; ... ] ] }; ]
   };

   zone "." [ ( in | hs | hesiod | chaos ) ] {
     type hint;
     file path_name;
   };
```

Covered in Chapter 4, *Setting Up BIND*, and Chapter 10, *Advanced Features*.

BIND Resolver Statements

The following statements are for the resolver configuration file, */etc/resolv.conf*.

domain

Function:

Defines your resolver's local domain name

Syntax:

    domain domain-name

Example:

    domain corp.hp.com

Covered in Chapter 6, *Configuring Hosts.*

search

Function:

Defines your resolver's local domain name and search list

Syntax:

    search local-domain-name next-domain-name-in-search-list
    ... last-domain-name-in-search-list

Example:

    search corp.hp.com pa.itc.hp.com hp.com

Covered in Chapter 6, *Configuring Hosts.*

nameserver

Function:

Tells your resolver to query a particular name server

Syntax:

    nameserver IP-address

Example:

    nameserver 15.255.152.4

Covered in Chapter 6, *Configuring Hosts.*

; and # (4.9+)

Function:

Adds a comment to the resolver configuration file

Syntax:

    ; free-format-comment

    or

    # free-format-comment

Example:

```
# Added parent domain to search list for compatibility with 4.8.3
```

Covered in Chapter 6, *Configuring Hosts.*

sortlist (4.9+)

Function:

Specifies networks for your resolver to prefer

Syntax:

```
sortlist network-list
```

Example:

```
sortlist 128.32.4.0/255.255.255.0 15.0.0.0
```

Covered in Chapter 6, *Configuring Hosts.*

options ndots (4.9+)

Function:

Specifies the number of dots an argument must have in it so that the resolver
will look it up before applying the search list

Syntax:

```
options ndots:number-of-dots
```

Example:

```
options ndots:1
```

Covered in Chapter 6, *Configuring Hosts.*

options debug (4.9+)

Function:

Turns on debugging output in the resolver

Syntax:

```
options debug
```

Example:

```
options debug
```

Covered in Chapter 6, *Configuring Hosts.*

options no-check-names (8.2+)

Function:

Turns off name checking in the resolver

Syntax:

```
options no-check-names
```

Example:

```
options no-check-names
```

Covered in Chapter 6, *Configuring Hosts.*

options attempts (8.2+)

Function:

Specifies the number of times the resolver should query each name server

Syntax:

```
options attempts:number-of-attempts
```

Example:

```
options attempts:2
```

Covered in Chapter 6, *Configuring Hosts.*

options timeout (8.2+)

Function:

Specifies the resolver's per-name server timeout

Syntax:

```
options timeout:timeout-in-seconds
```

Example:

```
options timeout:1
```

Covered in Chapter 6, *Configuring Hosts.*

options rotate (8.2+)

Function:

Rotates the order in which the resolver queries name servers

Syntax:

```
options rotate
```

Example:

```
options rotate
```

Covered in Chapter 6, *Configuring Hosts.*

Index

We'd like to hear your suggestions for improving our indexes. Send email to *index@oreilly.com*.

577

About the Authors

Paul Albitz is a software engineer at Hewlett-Packard. Paul earned a Bachelor of Science degree from the University of Wisconsin, LaCrosse, and a Master of Science degree from Purdue University.

Paul worked on BIND for the HP-UX 7.0 and 8.0 releases. During this time he developed the tools used to run the *hp.com* domain. Since then Paul has worked on networking HP's DesignJet plotter and on the fax subsystem of HP's OfficeJet multifunction peripheral. Before joining HP, Paul was a system administrator in the CS Department of Purdue University. As system administrator, he ran versions of BIND before BIND's initial release with 4.3 BSD. Paul and his wife, Katherine, live in San Diego, CA.

Cricket Liu matriculated at the University of California's Berkeley campus, that great bastion of free speech, unencumbered Unix, and cheap pizza. He joined Hewlett-Packard after graduation and worked for HP for nine years.

Cricket began managing the *hp.com* zone after the Loma Prieta earthquake forcibly transferred the zone's management from HP Labs to HP's Corporate Offices (by cracking a sprinkler main and flooding Labs' computer room). Cricket was *hostmaster@hp.com* for over three years, and then joined HP's Professional Services Organization to found HP's Internet consulting program.

Cricket left HP in 1997 to form Acme Byte & Wire, a DNS consulting and training company, with his friend (and now co-author) Matt Larson. Network Solutions acquired Acme in June 2000, and later the same day merged with VeriSign. Cricket is now Director of DNS Product Management for VeriSign Global Registry Services.

Cricket, his wife, Paige, and their son, Walt, live in Colorado with two Siberian Huskies, Annie and Dakota. On warm weekend afternoons, you'll probably find them on the flying trapeze or wakeboarding behind Betty Blue.

Colophon

Our look is the result of reader comments, our own experimentation, and feedback from distribution channels. Distinctive covers complement our distinctive approach to technical topics, breathing personality and life into potentially dry subjects.

The insects featured on the cover of *DNS and BIND* are grasshoppers. Grasshoppers are found all over the globe. Of over 5000 species, 100 different grasshopper species are found in North America. Grasshoppers are greenish-brown, and range in length from a half inch to four inches, with wingspans of up to six inches. Their bodies are divided into three sections: the head, thorax, and abdomen, with three pairs of legs and two pairs of wings.

Male grasshoppers use their hind legs and forewings to produce a "chirping" sound. Their hind legs have a ridge of small pegs that are rubbed across a hardened vein in the forewing, causing an audible vibration much like a bow being drawn across a string.

Grasshoppers are major crop pests, particularly when they collect in swarms. A single grasshopper can consume 30mg of food a day. In collections of 50 or more grasshoppers per square yard—a density often reached during grasshopper outbreaks—grasshoppers consume as much as a cow would per acre. In addition to consuming foliage, grasshoppers damage plants by attacking them at vulnerable points and causing the stems to break off.

Emily Quill was the production editor and proofreader for *DNS & BIND, Fourth Edition*. Leanne Soylemez was the copyeditor, and also provided production assistance. Catherine Morris and Matt Hutchinson performed quality control reviews. Brenda Miller wrote the index. Production assistance was provided by Edith Shapiro and Sada Preisch.

Edie Freedman designed the cover of this book, using a 19th-century engraving from the Dover Pictorial Archive. Emma Colby and Erica Corwell produced the cover layout with QuarkXPress 4.1 using Adobe's ITC Garamond font.

David Futato and Melanie Wang designed the interior layout, based on a series design by Nancy Priest. Anne-Marie Vaduva converted the files from Microsoft Word to FrameMaker 5.5.6 using tools created by Mike Sierra. The text and heading fonts are ITC Garamond Light and Garamond Book; the code font is Constant Willison. The illustrations that appear in this book were produced by Robert Romano and Jessamyn Read using Macromedia Freehand 9 and Adobe Photoshop 6. This colophon was written by Clairemarie Fisher O'Leary.

Whenever possible, our books use a durable and flexible lay-flat binding. If the page count exceeds this binding's limit, perfect binding is used.

More Titles from O'Reilly

Network Administration

TCP/IP Network Administration, 3rd Edition

By Craig Hunt
3rd Edition April 2002
746 pages, ISBN 1-56592-322-7

This is a complete guide to setting up and running a TCP/IP network for administrators of networks of systems, as well as for lone home systems that access the Internet. It starts with the fundamentals: what the protocols do and how they work, how addresses and routing are used to move data through the network, and how to set up a network connection.

Managing NFS and NIS, 2nd Edition

By Hal Stern, Mike Eisler & Ricardo Labiaga
2nd Edition July 2001
510 pages, ISBN 1-56592-510-6

This long-awaited new edition of a classic, now updated for NFS Version 3 and based on Solaris 8, shows how to set up and manage a network filesystem installation. *Managing NFS and NIS* is the only practical book devoted entirely to NFS and the distributed database NIS; it's a "must-have" for anyone interested in Unix networking.

sendmail, 2nd Edition

By Bryan Costales & Eric Allman
2nd Edition January 1997
1050 pages, ISBN 1-56592-222-0

sendmail, 2nd Edition, covers sendmail Version 8.8 from Berkeley and the standard versions available on most systems. This cross-referenced edition offers an expanded tutorial and solution-oriented examples, plus topics such as the #error delivery agent, sendmail's exit values, MIME headers, and how to set up and use the user database, mailertable, and smrsh.

Internet Core Protocols: The Definitive Guide

By Eric Hall
1st Edition February 2000
472 pages, Includes CD-ROM
ISBN 1-56592-572-6

Internet Core Protocols: The Definitive Guide provides the nitty-gritty details of TCP, IP, and UDP. Many network problems can only be debugged by working at the lowest levels—looking at all the bits traveling back and forth on the wire. This guide explains what those bits are and how to interpret them. It's the only book on Internet protocols written with system and network administrators in mind.

Network Troubleshooting Tools

By Joseph D. Sloan
1st Edition August 2001
364 pages, ISBN 0-596-00186-X

Network Troubleshooting Tools helps you sort through the thousands of tools that have been developed for debugging TCP/IP networks and choose the ones that are best for your needs. It also shows you how to approach network troubleshooting using these tools, how to document your network so you know how it behaves under normal conditions, and how to think about problems when they arise so you can solve them more effectively.

O'REILLY®

TO ORDER: **800-998-9938** • **order@oreilly.com** • **www.oreilly.com**
ONLINE EDITIONS OF MOST O'REILLY TITLES ARE AVAILABLE BY SUBSCRIPTION AT **safari.oreilly.com**
ALSO AVAILABLE AT MOST RETAIL AND ONLINE BOOKSTORES

How to stay in touch with O'Reilly

1. Visit our award-winning web site

http://www.oreilly.com/

★ "Top 100 Sites on the Web"—PC Magazine
★ CIO Magazine's Web Business 50 Awards

Our web site contains a library of comprehensive product information (including book excerpts and tables of contents), downloadable software, background articles, interviews with technology leaders, links to relevant sites, book cover art, and more. File us in your bookmarks or favorites!

2. Join our email mailing lists

Sign up to get email announcements of new books and conferences, special offers, and O'Reilly Network technology newsletters at:

http://www.elists.oreilly.com

It's easy to customize your free elists subscription so you'll get exactly the O'Reilly news you want.

3. Get examples from our books

To find example files for a book, go to:

http://www.oreilly.com/catalog

select the book, and follow the "Examples" link.

4. Work with us

Check out our web site for current employment opportunites:

http://jobs.oreilly.com/

5. Register your book

Register your book at:

http://register.oreilly.com

6. Contact us

O'Reilly & Associates, Inc.
1005 Gravenstein Hwy North
Sebastopol, CA 95472 USA
TEL: 707-827-7000 or 800-998-9938
         (6am to 5pm PST)
FAX: 707-829-0104

order@oreilly.com
For answers to problems regarding your order or our products. To place a book order online visit:

http://www.oreilly.com/order_new/

catalog@oreilly.com
To request a copy of our latest catalog.

booktech@oreilly.com
For book content technical questions or corrections.

proposals@oreilly.com
To submit new book proposals to our editors and product managers.

international@oreilly.com
For information about our international distributors or translation queries. For a list of our distributors outside of North America check out:

http://international.oreilly.com/distributors.html

O'REILLY®

TO ORDER: **800-998-9938** • **order@oreilly.com** • **www.oreilly.com**
ONLINE EDITIONS OF MOST O'REILLY TITLES ARE AVAILABLE BY SUBSCRIPTION AT **safari.oreilly.com**
ALSO AVAILABLE AT MOST RETAIL AND ONLINE BOOKSTORES